PRACTICAL POSER 6

LIMITED WARRANTY AND DISCLAIMER OF LIABILITY

THE CD-ROM THAT ACCOMPANIES THIS BOOK MAY BE USED ON A SINGLE PC ONLY. THE LICENSE DOES NOT PERMIT THE USE ON A NETWORK (OF ANY KIND). YOU FURTHER AGREE THAT THIS LICENSE GRANTS PERMISSION TO USE THE PRODUCTS CONTAINED HEREIN, BUT DOES NOT GIVE YOU RIGHT OF OWNERSHIP TO ANY OF THE CONTENT OR PRODUCT CONTAINED ON THIS CD-ROM. USE OF THIRD-PARTY SOFTWARE CONTAINED ON THIS CD-ROM IS LIMITED TO AND SUBJECT TO LICENSING TERMS FOR THE RESPECTIVE PRODUCTS.

CHARLES RIVER MEDIA, INC. ("CRM") AND/OR ANYONE WHO HAS BEEN INVOLVED IN THE WRITING, CREATION, OR PRODUCTION OF THE ACCOMPANYING CODE ("THE SOFTWARE"), OR THE THIRD-PARTY PRODUCTS CONTAINED ON THIS CD-ROM, CANNOT AND DO NOT WARRANT THE PERFORMANCE OR RESULTS THAT MAY BE OBTAINED BY USING THE SOFTWARE. THE AUTHOR AND PUBLISHER HAVE USED THEIR BEST EFFORTS TO ENSURE THE ACCURACY AND FUNCTIONALITY OF THE TEXTUAL MATERIAL AND PROGRAMS CONTAINED HEREIN; WE, HOWEVER, MAKE NO WARRANTY OF THIS KIND, EXPRESS OR IMPLIED, REGARDING THE PERFORMANCE OF THESE PROGRAMS. THE SOFTWARE IS SOLD "AS IS" WITHOUT WARRANTY (EXCEPT FOR DEFECTIVE MATERIALS USED IN MANUFACTURING THE DISC OR DUE TO FAULTY WORKMANSHIP); THE SOLE REMEDY IN THE EVENT OF A DEFECT IS EXPRESSLY LIMITED TO REPLACEMENT OF THE DISC, AND ONLY AT THE DISCRETION OF CRM.

THE AUTHOR, THE PUBLISHER, DEVELOPERS OF THIRD-PARTY SOFTWARE, AND ANYONE INVOLVED IN THE PRODUCTION AND MANUFACTURING OF THIS WORK SHALL NOT BE LIABLE FOR DAMAGES OF ANY KIND ARISING OUT OF THE USE OF (OR THE INABILITY TO USE) THE PROGRAMS, SOURCE CODE, OR TEXTUAL MATERIAL CONTAINED IN THIS PUBLICATION. THIS INCLUDES, BUT IS NOT LIMITED TO, LOSS OF REVENUE OR PROFIT, OR OTHER INCIDENTAL OR CONSEQUENTIAL DAMAGES ARISING OUT OF THE USE OF THE PRODUCT.

THE SOLE REMEDY IN THE EVENT OF A CLAIM OF ANY KIND IS EXPRESSLY LIMITED TO REPLACEMENT OF THE BOOK AND/OR CD-ROM, AND ONLY AT THE DISCRETION OF CRM.

THE USE OF "IMPLIED WARRANTY" AND CERTAIN "EXCLUSIONS" VARY FROM STATE TO STATE, AND MAY NOT APPLY TO THE PURCHASER OF THIS PRODUCT.

PRACTICAL POSER 6

DENISE TYLER
AUDRE VYSNIAUSKAS

CHARLES RIVER MEDIA, INC.
Hingham, Massachusetts

Cover Design: Tyler Creative
Front Cover Image: Audre Vysniauskas
Back Cover Image: Philebus

CHARLES RIVER MEDIA, INC.
10 Downer Avenue
Hingham, Massachusetts 02043
781-740-0400
781-740-8816 (FAX)
info@charlesriver.com
www.charlesriver.com

This book is printed on acid-free paper.

Denise Tyler and Audre Vysniauskas. *Practical Poser 6*
ISBN: 1-58450-443-9

Library of Congress Cataloging-in-Publication Data

Tyler, Denise.
Practical Poser 6 / Denise Tyler and Audre Vysniauskas.— 1st ed.
p. cm.
Includes index.
ISBN 1-58450-443-9 (pbk. with cd : alk. paper)
1. Poser (Computer file) 2. Computer animation. 3. Computer graphics.
4. Human figure in art—Computer programs. I. Vysniauskas, Audre. II. Title.
TR897.7.T965 2005
006.6'93—dc22

2005033588

Printed in the United States of America
05 7 6 5 4 3 2 First Edition

CHARLES RIVER MEDIA titles are available for site license or bulk purchase by institutions, user groups, corporations, etc. For additional information, please contact the Special Sales Department at 781-740-0400.

Requests for replacement of a defective CD-ROM must be accompanied by the original disc, your mailing address, telephone number, date of purchase, and purchase price. Please state the nature of the problem, and send the information to CHARLES RIVER MEDIA, INC., 10 Downer Avenue, Hingham, Massachusetts 02043. CRM's sole obligation to the purchaser is to replace the disc, based on defective materials or faulty workmanship, but not on the operation or functionality of the product.

To "Doctor Geep," whose unending assistance to the members of the Poser community has helped many.

CONTENTS

ACKNOWLEDGMENTS

There are so many talented individuals that work behind the scenes to make a book happen. In the case of this book, there are so many that deserve mention. In particular, we would like to thank the following:

From Denise and Audre

Thank you to our publisher, Jenifer Niles, whose unflagging support, nerves of steel, and patience of a saint were appreciated more than she'll ever know . . . hope you liked the chocolate! Also, to Uli Klumpp and Daryl Wise of e-Frontier for opening so many doors, and keeping them open.

From Denise

I would like to thank Ed, my better half, for his never-ending support and friendship . . . you're my rock! To my mom, who survived a tough battle during the progress of this book. To my brother Paul, who does so much for so many. And to the members of the Poser community, who were constant inspiration for every word written in this book.

From Audre

I would like to thank my husband Ray for his continued support; and my parents, Albina and Jonas, for teaching me that it is okay to be different.

PREFACE

During the planning stages of this book, we asked the members of the online Poser community which questions were most frequently asked by members of the Poser community. The responses helped us formulate the topics that we should address in this book. Interestingly enough, the topics requested fell into beginning, intermediate, and advanced level skills.

This book assumes that you have reviewed the Poser 6 Reference Manual and Poser 6 Tutorial Manual that ship with Poser 6 before you attempt some of the tutorials in this book. We have tried to go light on theory and heavy on practical use of the most requested topics and procedures.

The book begins by gettiing you up to speed on beginner- to intermediate-level skills that you need to know in the Pose Room. You start with the basics of the Poser 6 interface, and learn in a logical manner how to build scenes. You'll also learn how to use lights and cameras, and how to create and save your own light and cameras sets to the Poser library.

We then move to intermediate-level topics, mainly covering the features that you'll find in the other Poser rooms. You'll learn how to prepare photographs so that you get the best results in the Face Room. You'll also learn how to create and save custom faces in the Face Room. You'll learn how to use the Hair Room to add hair to Poser clothing or props, and how to pick up hair colors from underlying textures. You'll also learn how to work with the various types of Poser clothing, and the differences between conforming clothing and dynamic clothing. Finally, you'll learn how to decipher materials in the advanced Material Room view.

Some of the most frequently asked questions involve creating and customizing Poser clothing. Though these are advanced-level skills that often require software other than Poser, it is a topic that is of great interest and need to Poser users, and we will address this need in the final chapters of the book. First, you'll learn how to use magnets to create morphs in Poser.

You'll also learn the steps involved to export and import morphs to and from an external morphing program. Through several chapters, you'll learn the procedures involved in modeling a simple piece of clothing, how to create UV maps for common clothing articles (shirts, skirts, and pants), how to assign materials in clothing, and how to group them correctly so that your models work correctly in Poser. You'll also learn how to save different types of Poser content into the Poser libraries so that they work properly.

Finally, in Section IV, you'll learn what makes the Poser rendering engine work, and how you can enhance your Poser renders so that they look their best. The techniques that you learn in this book will help you get up to speed very quickly with the questions that Poser users ask most. We are also open to suggestions and additional questions that can be covered in future editions of this book, and will watch the various forums in the online Poser communities for questions or comments from our readers.

CHAPTER

1

POSER 6 OVERVIEW

In This Chapter

- The Poser Workspace
- The Poser Libraries
- An Overview of the Other Poser Rooms
- Conclusion

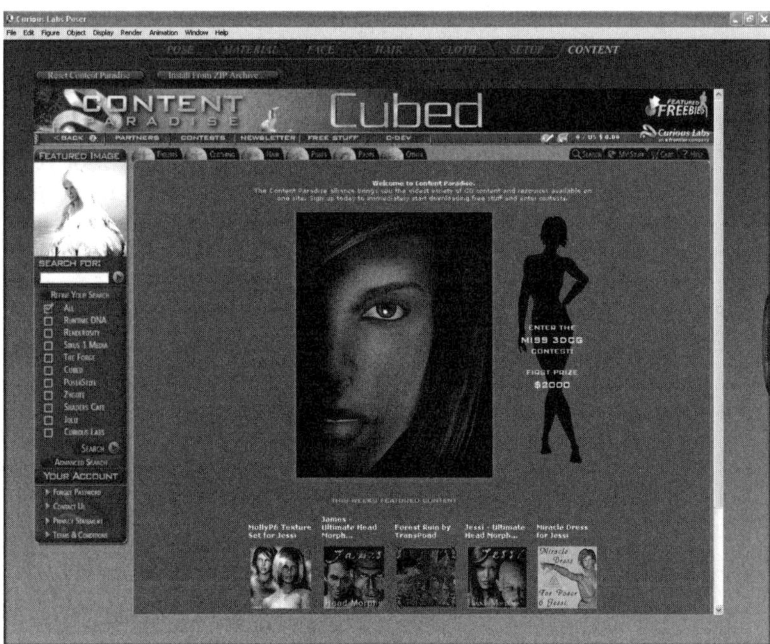

Poser® 6 is the latest release of a truly remarkable graphics application that is unique, addictive, and fun to use. From its humble beginnings as a figure reference tool for traditional artists, Poser has blossomed into a full-featured application that contains many of the capabilities you would expect to find in much more expensive software. With this software, hobbyists and professionals alike can create art or animation that ranges from cartoon to photorealistic, at a very affordable cost. Dollar for dollar, Poser provides the highest enjoyment-bang-for-the-buck ratio that you can find.

This book will help you hit the ground running by teaching you the tasks Poser artists want, and need, to learn to get up to speed quickly and achieve the best results. You'll learn how to create Poser scenes, how to add realism to your Poser characters, and even how to make your own Poser clothing. You'll learn practical, real-world tasks that will help you reach your goals—most important, you'll have fun while you're learning it. So, let's get started!

This chapter will help familiarize you with the Poser program as you learn your way around the various rooms and libraries. You'll get a brief overview of the main areas of the Poser interface and learn what you can do in each area. You'll also learn how to set up your preferences so that Poser starts with the configuration that you prefer. For those of you already using Poser, you'll get a quick update on what's new with Poser 6.

THE POSER WORKSPACE

When you first open Poser you see the screen shown in Figure 1.1. This is the *Pose Room*, where you'llspend most of your time building your scenes. It contains all of the controls necessary to pose, light, view, and animate the content in your scene.

The main areas in the Pose Room are as follows:

Menu Area: Gives you access to Poser's menu commands. There are nine menu groups: File, Edit, Figure, Object, Display, Render, Animation, Window, and Help. This book will show you how to put many of these commands to use in the real world. The *Poser 6 Reference Manual* (included with Poser 6) gives a command-by-command reference of each of the Poser menu dialogs.

Editing Tools: This area provides tools that help you pose and modify the content in your scene. The tools you see here depend on which of the Poser rooms you're working in.

Room Tabs: Allow you to switch to another of Poser's rooms to edit materials, create faces, work with dynamic hair or clothing, set up figures, or browse for additional Poser content on the Web.

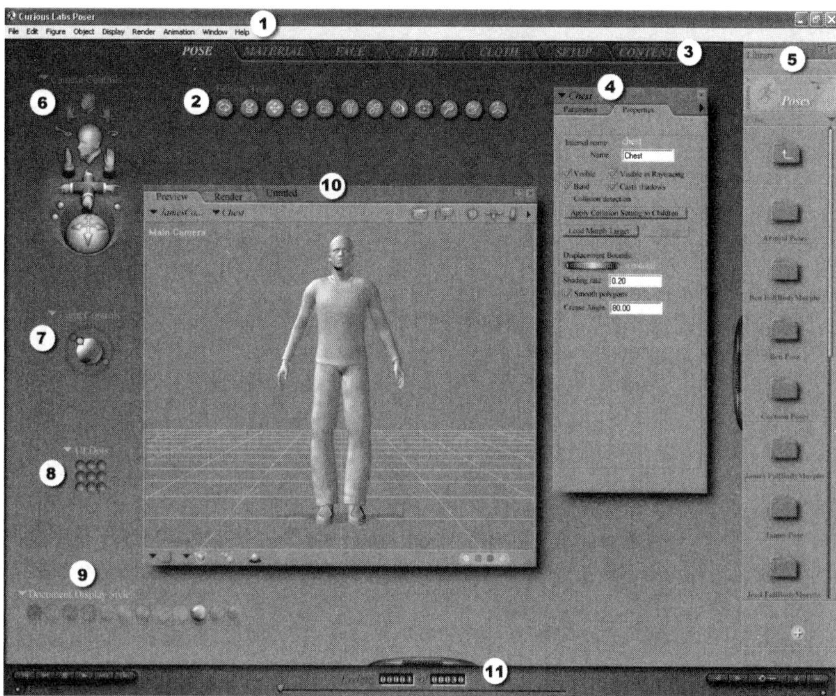

FIGURE 1.1 The Pose Room is the area you'll use while building your scenes and positioning your objects.

Parameters Window: Provides dials that pose and morph the selected figure and define its properties. The Parameters tab contains dials that allow you to taper, scale, pose, and position the selected body part or prop. In some cases, the parameter dials allow you to change the appearance of figures or clothing using *morphs*. The Properties tab allows you to set various properties of an object, such as its visibility, ability to cast shadows, or to detect object collisions.

Library: Stores all of your Poser content for quick access. You'll learn more about Libraries in this chapter, and where to install purchased and downloaded content in Chapter 2, "Using Third-Party Content."

Camera Controls: Allow you to select and adjust cameras. Chapter 4, "Using Cameras," will teach you how to use, create, and save cameras.

Light Controls: Allow you to create, adjust, and position lights for your scene. Poser 6 includes exciting new lighting features that create extremely realistic renders. You'll learn more about them in Chapter 5, "Mastering Lights and Shadows."

User Interface (UI), Pose, and Camera Dots: Allow you to save and retrieve up to nine versions of interface settings, poses, and camera positions. To select the type of dot you want to use—*Pose Dot, Camera Dot, or UI Dot*—click the arrow to the left of the label, and choose Pose Dots, Camera Dots, or UI Dots from the pull-down menu.

Document Display Styles: Allow you to choose how the objects in your scene are displayed. Display styles range from *wireframe* to *texture shaded*. You can set display styles for all content in the scene, for an entire figure, or any part (or element) of a figure or prop.

Document Window: The main work area in the Pose Room. This window shows the currently selected camera's view. The document window controls will be explained in Chapter 3, "Building Scenes."

Animation Controls: Allow you to move forward or backward in the animation timeline, add or remove animation keyframes, and insert or delete animation frames.

The Poser Libraries

One of the most impressive benefits of Poser is that it comes with a vast quantity of ready-to-use content that is arranged in several different library categories. The content includes realistic and cartoon figures, clothing, hair, preset lights, scenery, and more. There are literally hundreds of different library files included with Poser, allowing you to get up and running quickly. Figure 1.2 shows the Library Palette found in Poser 6. In order to understand where things go and why, you'll need to learn a little bit about Poser history along the way.

Undocking and Resizing the Library Palette

New to Poser 6 is the ability to resize and reposition the Library Palette. Above and to the right of the Library Palette tab in Figure 1.3, you'll see two icons. The first icon toggles the Library Palette window into two columns or contracts it back into its docked position. When undocked, one column shows the content of the current library and the other displays the library categories. When the Library Palette is undocked, you can resize it to display as many columns of content as you like. Figure 1.3 shows the Library Palette in its expanded view.

FIGURE 1.2 The Poser 6 Library Palette makes it convenient to access and organize content.

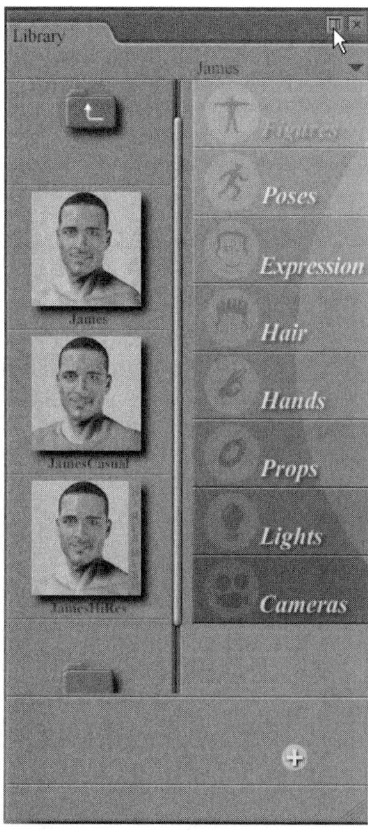

FIGURE 1.3 Click the maximize icon in the upper-right corner of the Library Palette window to undock and expand or resize the Library Palette window.

The Figures Library

Starting from the top of the Library Palette, the Figures Library is shown in Figure 1.4. This library typically stores *poseable* human and animal figures (*characters*). It also stores *conforming clothing*, a type of clothing that automatically assumes the pose of the figure that wears it, or assumes the pose of the figure it's set to conform to. You'll also find conforming hair and scenery characters that are poseable.

When content is poseable, it typically has multiple parts that are joined together by some sort of hierarchy—similar to a skeleton—and you can bend, twist, or turn parts of the character to pose them as you like. Keep in mind that characters, or poseable figures, can also be things like bicycles, clothing, or machinery that has moving parts and aren't limited to being only organic entities. You'll learn more about poseable and conforming figures in Chapter 3, "Building Scenes."

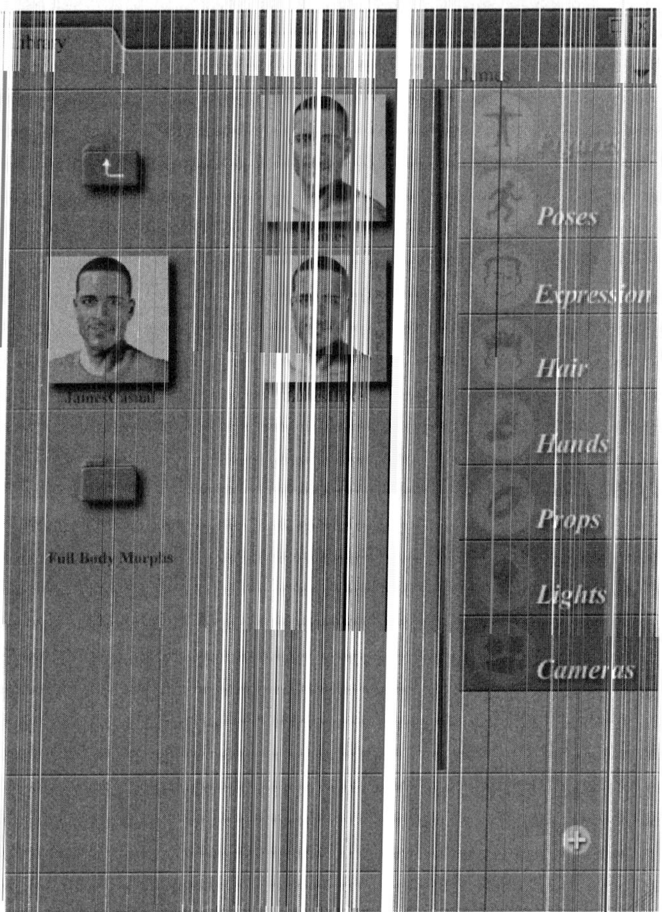

FIGURE 1.4 The Figures Library stores poseable characters like figures, hair, clothing, and props.

The Poses Library

The Poses Library, shown in Figure 1.5, stores a wide variety of poses that serve many different functions. The original intent of the Poses Library was to allow the user to save and store still or animated figure poses so they could easily be applied to another figure, or used in another project. For example, let's say you've posed your current figure to make it look like it's dancing. If you save the pose to the Poses Library, you can select another figure and apply the same pose to it. Now, both figures are doing the same dance.

Over time, third-party content developers and community members discovered new uses for pose files, so you have to pay attention to their descriptions. The Poses Library now stores many files that serve purposes other than posing your figure. The most commonly used alternatives are poses that change the material of an object (*MAT* poses), poses that apply morph settings to a figure (*MOR* poses), and poses that add (*inject*) or remove custom morphs to or from a figure (*INJ* or *REM* poses).

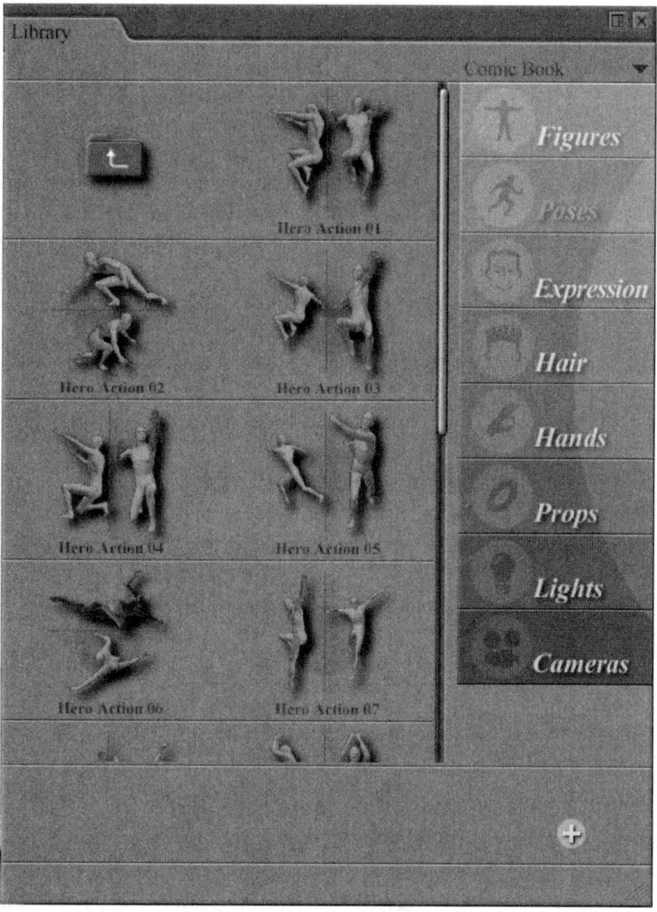

FIGURE 1.5 The Poses Library, originally intended for poses like you see here, also stores poses that change the texture or add morphs to an object or figure.

The Expression Library

The Expression Library, known as the Face Library in earlier Poser versions, stores facial expressions for your Poser characters. Figure 1.6 shows some of the facial expressions that are furnished for Jessi, the Poser 6 female. Because expressions are dependent upon the morphs included in a figure's face, they may or may not work on figures other than those for which they were created. You will get the best results if you use expressions on the figures for which they are intended.

FIGURE 1.6 The Expression Library holds facial expressions for your Poser characters.

The Hair Library

The Hair Library stores hair for your characters. Unlike previous versions of Poser, you can now store *all* hair types (*prop hair, conforming hair,* and *dynamic hair*) in the Hair Library. This is evident in Figure 1.7, where you see hair that is labeled "Strand" (for dynamic hair) and "Trans Map" (for hair that is usually conforming, as in the case of this example).

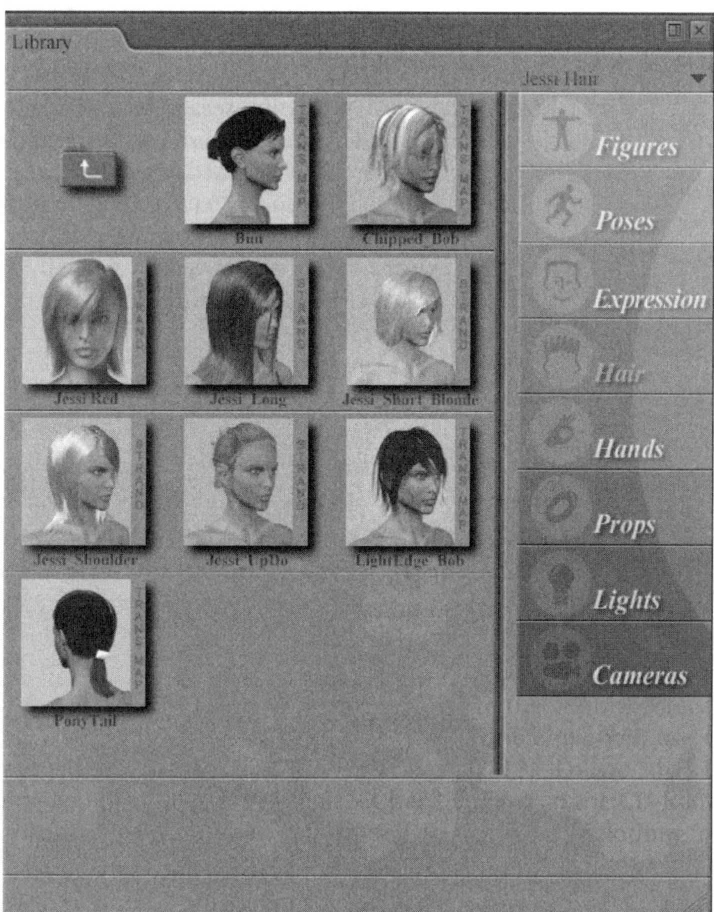

FIGURE 1.7 The Hair Library stores prop-based, conforming, and dynamic hair models.

In older versions of Poser, the Hair Library was strictly intended for hair that was modeled in a 3D application. This original hair type is a special type of prop that uses the *HR2* file extension, or *HRZ* for its compressed counterpart.

Some HR2 hair automatically attaches, or *smart props,* itself to the figure's head. Other HR2 hair requires that you attach it to the figure's head yourself with the Object > Change Parent command. The difference is whether or not the person who created the hair remembered to make the hair "smart." The biggest challenge with this type of hair, especially when it is long or contains many components, is that you need to *morph* it (bend, shape, scale, and so on) to look natural after you pose the head, neck, and shoulders.

Another type of commonly used hair is conforming hair, which conforms to a figure the same way conforming clothing does; when you bend or turn the head, the hair follows along. Conforming hair uses a CR2 extension (*CRZ* in its compressed form) because it is actually a figure that is also a character. You will find conforming hair in the Figures Library.

Poser 5 introduced *strand-based hair,* also known as dynamic hair. This type of hair is most effective in animations because it can react to wind forces, gravity, and position changes. Dynamic hair files use an HR2 or HRZ extension and are stored in the Hair Library.

You will still be able to install older conforming hair characters into the Figures Library, if you prefer to keep them in their originally installed locations. However, it's nice to have the ability to store all hair, regardless of type, in the Hair Library for easy access.

It's not hard to make conforming hair compatible with the Hair Library. Using your operating system's File Manager (or equivalent), make a copy of the CR2 (or CRZ, if compressed) and its associated PNG library thumbnail. Place the copied files into the same file folder (directory) that contains your existing Hair Library files and change the CR2 extension to HR2 (or the CRZ extension to HRZ). It can't be any simpler than that!

The Hands Library

The Hands Library stores hand poses for your Poser figures. You will achieve the best results if you use the hand poses that are designed for the figure you will apply them to. The reason for this is that the positions of the joints vary between characters; as a result, a pose made for one figure could make another figure's hand look deformed. Figure 1.8 shows hand poses that are made for Jessi. Several of the other figures supplied with Poser 6 come with hand poses as well.

The Props Library

The Props Library has also seen many changes over the years, and especially in this new release of Poser. The Props Library was originally intended for accessories such as furniture, scenery, hats, jewelry, and other props includ-

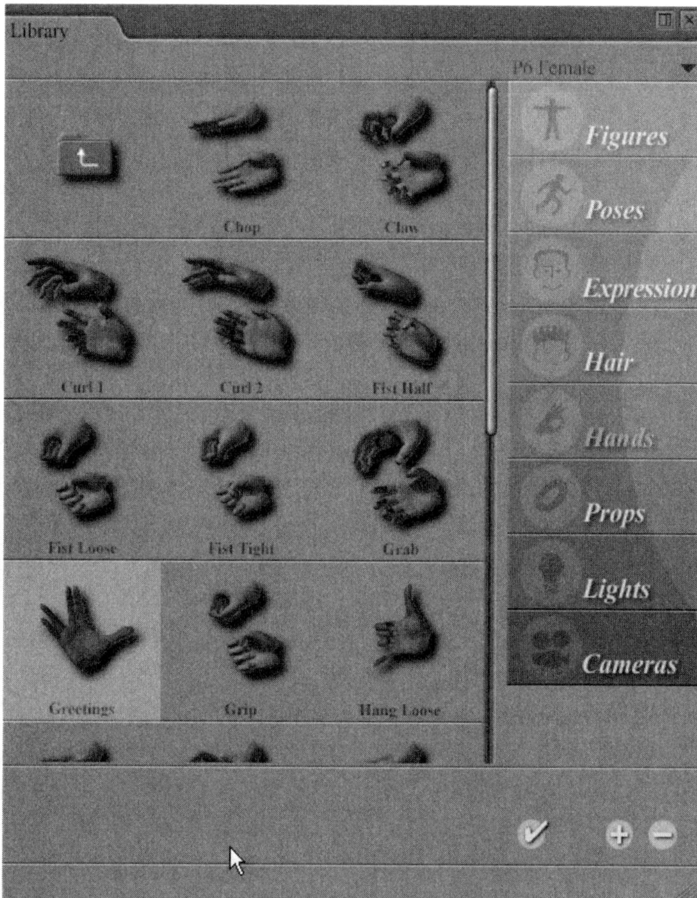

FIGURE 1.8 The Hands Library stores hand poses.

ing swords, guns, and other items that are not poseable. *Magnets,* a special type of prop that allows you to deform the shape of any Poser object, are also found in the Props Library. You'll learn more about magnets in Chapter 10, "Creating Custom Morphs."

In Poser 5, the Props Library was used to store dynamic clothing made to work with the Cloth Room. Since dynamic clothing is technically not "poseable" in the classic sense—because it doesn't have parts that join together in a hierarchy—the most logical place to store dynamic clothing was the Props Library, as opposed to the Figures Library, where conforming clothing was stored.

With Poser 6, you have the new option of keeping both dynamic and conforming clothing in the Props Library, as Figure 1.9 shows. However, you can still place conforming clothing in the Figures Library if you choose.

FIGURE 1.9 The Props Library can now store conforming *and* dynamic clothing in addition to other prop types.

To store conforming clothing in the Props Library, make a copy of the CR2 (or CRZ, if compressed) and its associated PNG library thumbnail using your operating system's File Manager program (or equivalent). Place the copied files into your existing file folder (directory) where your Props Library files are, and change the CR2 extension to PP2 (or the CRZ extension to PPZ). Developers might want to keep a backup copy of the CR2 file for further development of the clothing as a character file down the road.

The Lights Library

The Lights Library stores light sets that are composed of one or more lights. The lights found in the Light Sets category are older-style spotlight sets that have accompanied several Poser releases. Those familiar with earlier versions will be happy to see some new light sets that take advantage of the exciting new lighting features offered in Poser 6. For example, the light sets shown in Figure 1.10 take advantage of two new lighting features: *image-based lighting* and *ambient occlusion*, which will be explained in more detail in Chapter 5, "Mastering Lights and Shadows."

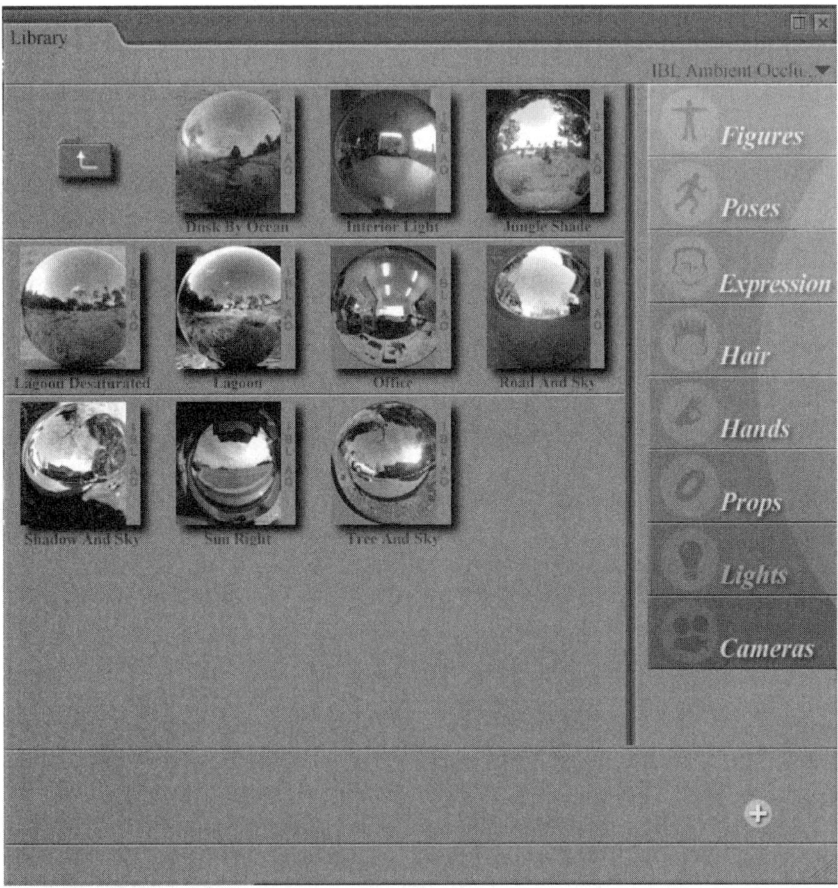

FIGURE 1.10 The Lights Library is a convenient place to store your favorite light sets so that you can quickly apply them to different projects.

The Cameras Library

The Cameras Library is shown in Figure 1.11. This library stores camera positions and settings that you might frequently use. For example, you might create a set of cameras that are zoomed into a figure's head from the front, back, left, and right so you can look for seams in a texture that you're creating, or fine-tune the shape of a face with morphs. Each time you find yourself setting up the same type of camera over and over again, stop and add it to your library. If you do this, you'll eventually have a collection of cameras that will save you time and effort because only minor adjustments will be required to fine-tune your existing project, rather than having to start from scratch every time.

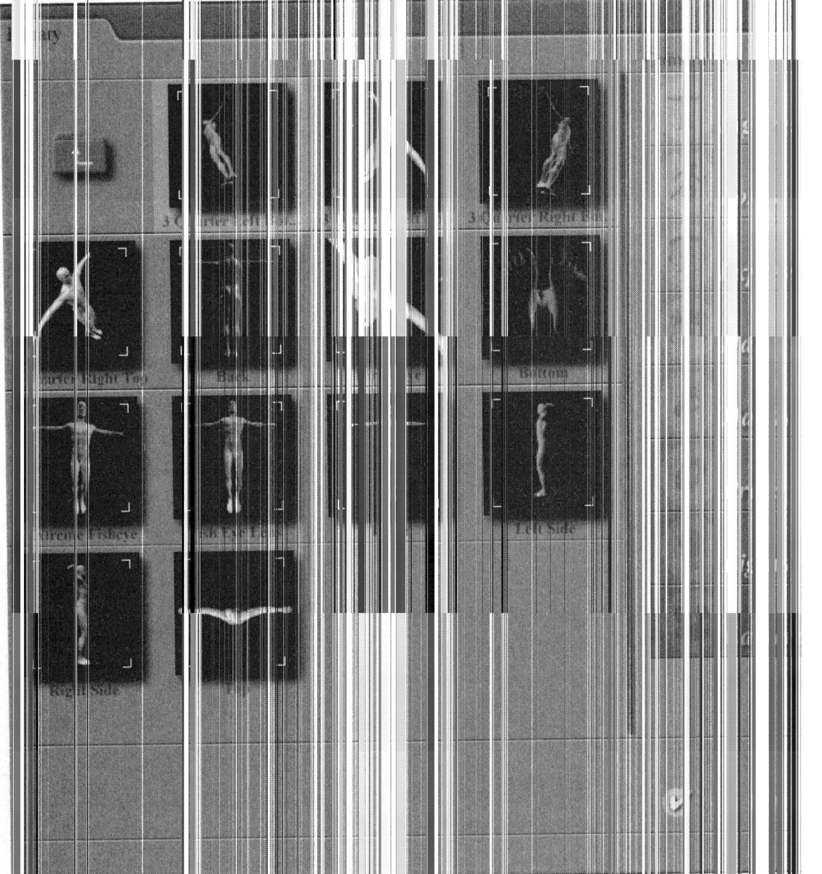

FIGURE 1.11 Store frequently used camera settings in the Camera Library.

The Materials Library

The last library in Poser is the Materials Library, which is visible only when you are in the Materials Room. Figure 1.12 shows some of the basic materials that are furnished with Poser 6, ranging from bricks to bubbles and from flame to frost. There are more than enough materials to pick apart, experiment with, and learn to make your own. Of course, you'll learn about materials in this book as well, in Chapter 9, "Assigning and Creating Materials."

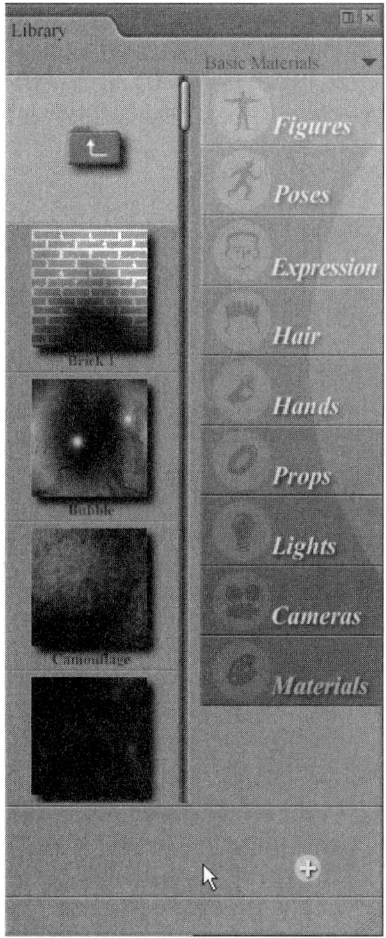

FIGURE 1.12 The Materials Library, visible only in the Materials Room, allows you to store and apply materials to your Poser objects.

TUTORIAL 1.1 ... OMIZING YOUR INTER... DOCUMENT WI...

u work in Poser you'll ... orkflow and find that you ...
y change settings or ... more often than others ...
ubtedly want to custo... orkspace at some point ...
own preferences. The ... e some of the things that ...
want to consider wh... ize your interface. You ...
to accomplish many of ... n Chapter 3, "Building Scenes,"
Chapter 5, "Mastering ... dows."

- ... hange the default fig... when you start Poser ...
  ew document. You'll ... that you tend to start with ...
  ame figure most of the ... eople start with ...
  hey can clothe it the w... e.
- ... hange your display st... t, scenes start in ...
  isplay style, which dis... untextured version of the Pose...
  ontent. If you prefer to vie... scenes with their actual ...
  howing, choose Displa... Style > Texture Shaded.
- ... urn off Inverse Kinema... e legs. IK is a feature th...
  ou to pose the limbs ... positioning the last ...
  hain of a limb. For exa... pose all parts ...
  moving the left foot. Alt... interfere with some ...
  e helpful for animation... yourself turning ...
  keeping it on, it's a goo... your default preferences.
- ... ero the pose of your ... you first load the default ...
  locument, the James ... s posed with his arms ...
  his sides and his legs ... hich is not a zero pose ...
  his joint and morph pa... set to numbers other th...
  You'll learn the quick... ero your figure in Chapter ...
  Building Scenes."
- ... urn genitals on or off, ... preferences. The Figure ...
  talia command toggles ... ff.
- ... Edit the existing lights ... default set of your own. ...
  and gray lights and pre... because they ...
  n the textures more ... e Chapter 5, "Mastering Lights
  and Shadows," for mor...
- ... Undock the Library Pale... ge it into as many ...
  find useful in order to ... that contain ...
- ... Move the Document ... second screen ...
  setup. This leaves lots ... nterface items ...
  wise be required to kee... onserve space.
- ... Start up with Room H... Help opens autom...
  you enter the Materia... Cloth, and Setup ...
  know how to use a roo... really need the ...
  tomatically. Choose W... Help to toggle ...

- Change the background color of the Poser interface. To change the background color, click the Paint Bucket icon in the Pose Room editing tools. Then click an empty space in the Poser interface window to open the Poser color palette. As you drag your mouse over the colors, the background color of the Poser interface changes. Light colors work best; darker colors can make the fonts hard to read, or even invisible. Once the mouse moves over a color you like, click to set it. Click the Paint Bucket icon again to exit color selection mode.

Once you get your interface and document settings set up the way you prefer, it's a simple procedure to set them as your default document and interface preferences:

1. Choose Edit > General Preferences. The General Preferences dialog shown in Figure 1.13 appears.

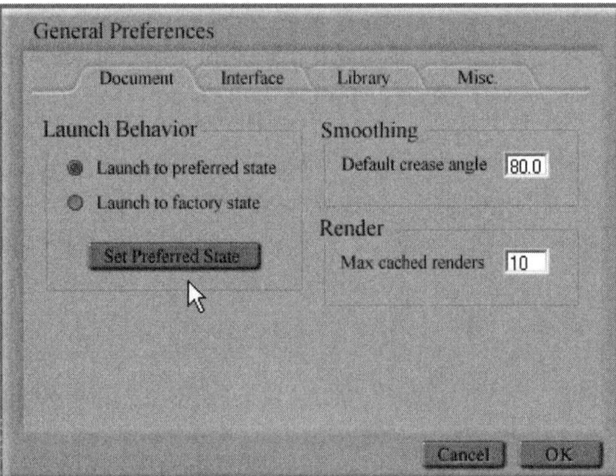

FIGURE 1.13 The General Preferences window allows you to configure the document window, interface, and other program settings to suit your preferences.

2. To configure Poser so that the document window starts up in its current state, first click the Set Preferred State button. Poser memorizes the status of your current document window, including its position and dimensions, and the figures, lighting, cameras, background color, and other settings as you have them set. Then select the Launch To Preferred State option in the Launch Behavior section. To launch the document window in the factory default state, choose Launch To Factory State.
3. The Default Crease Angle setting is adequate for most types of models, so until you have a reason to change it, you can leave this setting

as it is. Also, by default, Poser will store 10 renders in the render cache so that you can compare multiple versions of a render. Increase or decrease the Max Cached Renders number to suit your needs and computer resources.

4. The Interface tab, shown in Figure 1.14, relates to the launch behavior of your Poser interface. Things like window positions and visibility are set here. To configure Poser to launch the way that you last left your window layout, choose Launch To Previous State. To launch Poser with the default factory configuration, choose Launch To Factory State.
5. The default Poser display units are factory defaulted to feet (in English versions of Poser 6). Click the Display Units selector to choose Poser Native Units, Inches, Millimeters, Centimeters, or Meters.

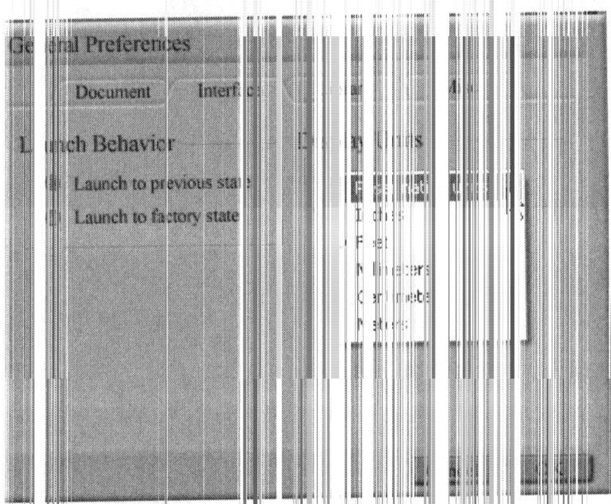

FIGURE 1.14 The Interface tab allows you to start up with previous interface settings or with factory defaults.

6. Click the Library tab to set your Library preferences, as shown in Figure 1.15. By default, when you double-click an item in the Figures Library, the figure is added to the scene. Choose Replace Existing if you want your double-click to replace the currently selected figure rather than add it to the scene.
7. In the Thumbnail Display section, choose Never Collapse Thumbnails to display all thumbnails in your library regardless of the number of items that are contained in it. To minimize scrolling when the number of thumbnails in one library exceeds a setting you specify, choose Display Text Only When Number Of Folder Items Exceeds, and then enter the desired number.

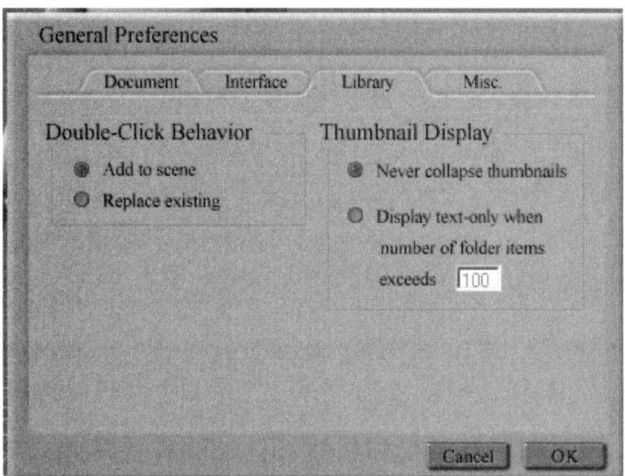

FIGURE 1.15 Use the Library tab to set the behavior and appearance of the thumbnails in your libraries.

8. The Misc tab, shown in Figure 1.16, contains settings that are of interest to developers and also allows you to check for updates to Poser 6. The Save Files area contains two options. The first, Use File Compression, is checked by default. This saves Poser files in a compressed format (file names ending in Z) that takes up less space on your hard drive. For the majority of users the default setting is fine. However, because the compressed files are in binary format, Poser content developers should uncheck this option so that the files remain editable using standard text-editing programs.

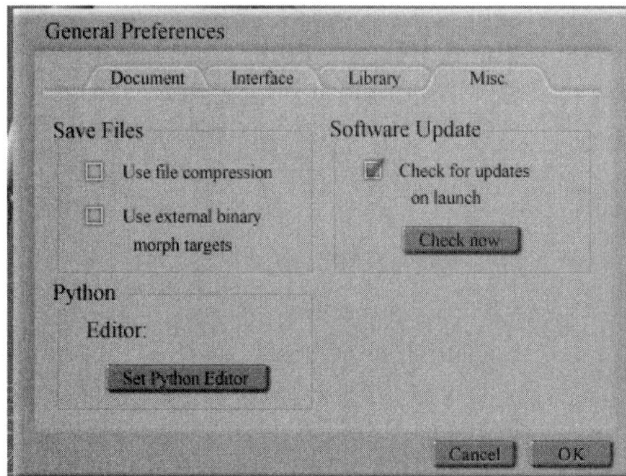

FIGURE 1.16 The Misc tab allows you to check for updates, save your files in either compressed or uncompressed formats, and use external binary morph targets.

9. The Use External Binary Morph Targets option is also enabled by default. Whenever you save a Poser file to your library, it will keep all of the object's morphs in an external file that is in a compressed format. The file uses a PMD extension and is referenced in the main Poser library file (CR2 for figures, *PP2* for props, and so on). If you create content that is also intended to be used with older versions of Poser, you should leave this option unchecked so that the morphs remain inside the Poser file.
10. The Python section contains a button that allows you to choose the editor that opens when you need to edit or create a Python script. Click the Set Python Editor button to locate the program that you want to use.
11. The Software Update section provides an option to enable or disable an update check when you start Poser. The default setting checks for updates when you start Poser. Uncheck the Check For Updates On Launch button to disable this feature. To perform a manual update check at any time, click the Check Now button.
12. After you are done setting your preferences, click OK. Your preferences will be saved in a *Poser.ini* file along with some additional *XML* files that will be located in the Poser 6 > Runtime > Prefs folder on your hard drive. You may want to back up a copy of these files and keep them in a safe place.

AN OVERVIEW OF THE OTHER POSER ROOMS

There are several other rooms in Poser, and each of them serves a specific purpose that enables you to customize, enhance, or configure new or existing characters and props. There are six additional rooms: The Material Room, the Face Room, the Hair Room, the Cloth Room, the Setup Room, and the Content Room (also known as Content Paradise). The following sections will explain each room briefly and tell you which chapter contains more information about them.

The Material Room

You can access the Material Room through the Material tab, or by choosing the Render > Materials command on the menu bar. You can use one of two methods to create materials: the Simple method, which allows you to quickly configure basic materials, including those that use texture, bump, transparency, and reflection maps. Or Poser 6 also features an advanced material setup interface (Figure 1.17) that includes procedural shaders. Procedural shaders are explained in more detail in Chapter 9, "Assigning and Creating Materials."

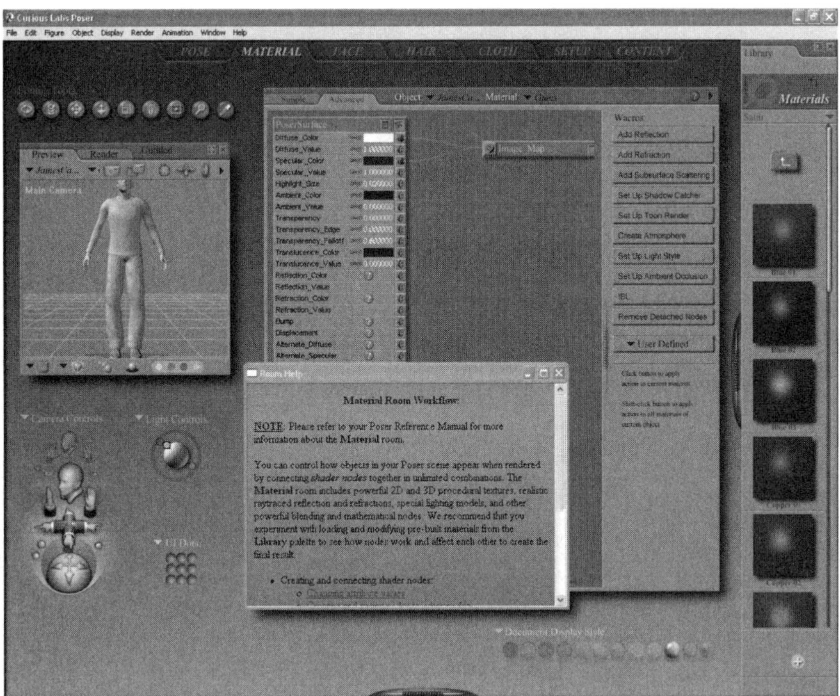

FIGURE 1.17 Create and assign materials for your Poser content in the Material Room. This is the advanced materials interface.

The Face Room

The Face Room, shown in Figure 1.18, allows you to create custom faces for the Poser 6 male and female (James and Jessi), and for the Poser 5 male and female (Don and Judy). The Photo Lineup area allows you to import a front and side photograph of a person's face and create a face texture from the imported photos. You can also create random faces based on morphs provided in the Face Room or use the Face Shaping Tool to create your own custom faces. Further information about the Face Room appears in Chapter 6, "Creating Custom Faces."

The Hair Room

The Hair Room is shown in Figure 1.19. This room allows you to create strand-based hair, also known as dynamic hair. One of the major advantages that dynamic hair has over geometry-based hair is that it moves in a very realistic manner during animation. Hair is grown in groups on a base called a *skull cap*. Each hair group has various growth properties,

FIGURE 1.18 The Face Room allows you to create face textures and custom faces for your Poser characters.

FIGURE 1.19 Create and animate dynamic hair styles in the Hair Room.

such as the length of the hair and how much it pulls down, back, or sideways. You can also specify the thickness and density of the hair, how kinky or curly it is, and how much or how little the hair bunches or clumps together. Further information about the Hair Room appears in Chapter 7, "Working with Poser Hair."

The Cloth Room

The Cloth Room, shown in Figure 1.20, allows you to add motion and gravity dynamics to your Poser clothing. After you "clothify" a piece of clothing (that is, after you turn it into cloth), you can assign several cloth-like properties to it. These properties include how resistant the cloth will be to folding, shearing, and stretching, and how lightweight or heavy the cloth is. You can also create various types of cloth in a single garment by specifying different dynamic groups. Chapter 8, "Working with Poser Clothing," shows you how to use the Cloth Room.

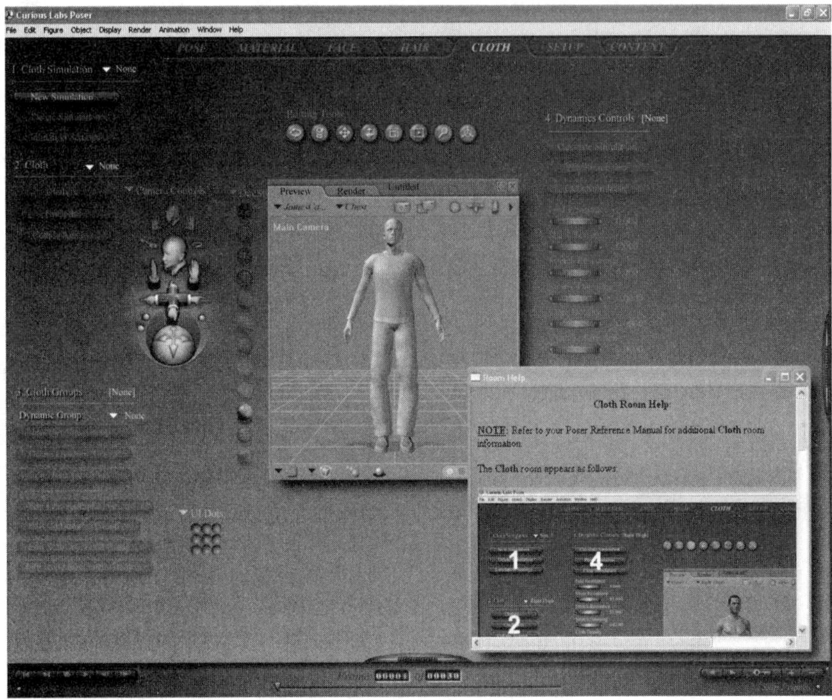

FIGURE 1.20 The Cloth Room allows you how to work with dynamic clothing that moves and drapes realistically.

The Setup Room

The more you learn about Poser, the more you will want to learn how to create your own clothing or poseable characters. The Setup Room, shown in Figure 1.21, will aid in the development of poseable characters or clothing. Here you can create bones that will control movement in the clothing or character, and dictate how they will respond when you bend, twist, or rotate the parts of the object. You will learn more about the Setup Room in Chapter 15, "From Modeler to Poser Library."

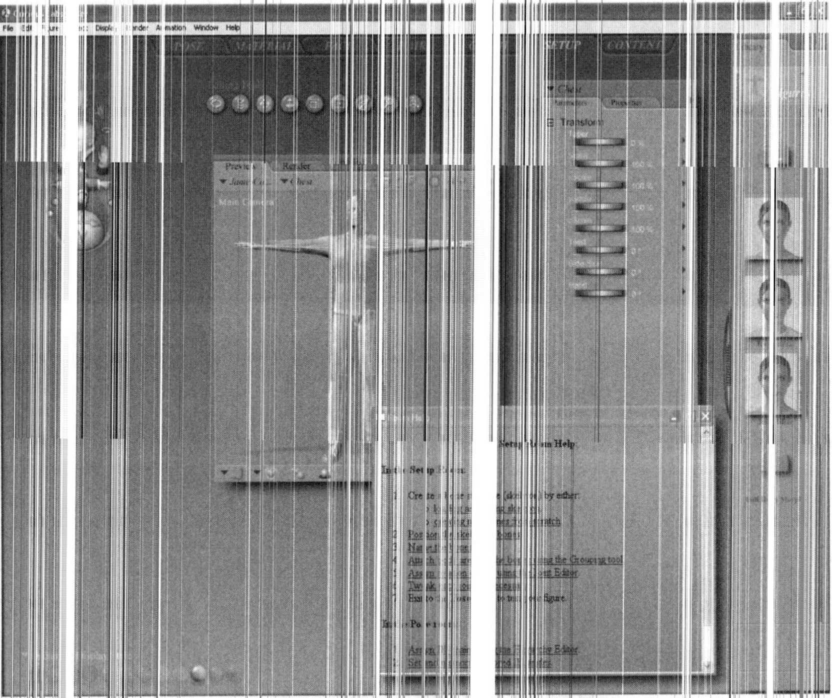

FIGURE 1.21 The Setup Room helps you define bones that determine how your Poser clothing and characters will move.

The Content Room (Content Paradise)

The final room in Poser is the Content Room, or Content Paradise, shown in Figure 1.22. This room features a built-in browser and catalog for many different types of Poser content that you can buy from various Poser development partners and community Web sites. You'll also find contest announcements, a Poser-related newsletter, and a content-developer support area. You'll learn more about third-party content in Chapter 2, "Using Third Party Content."

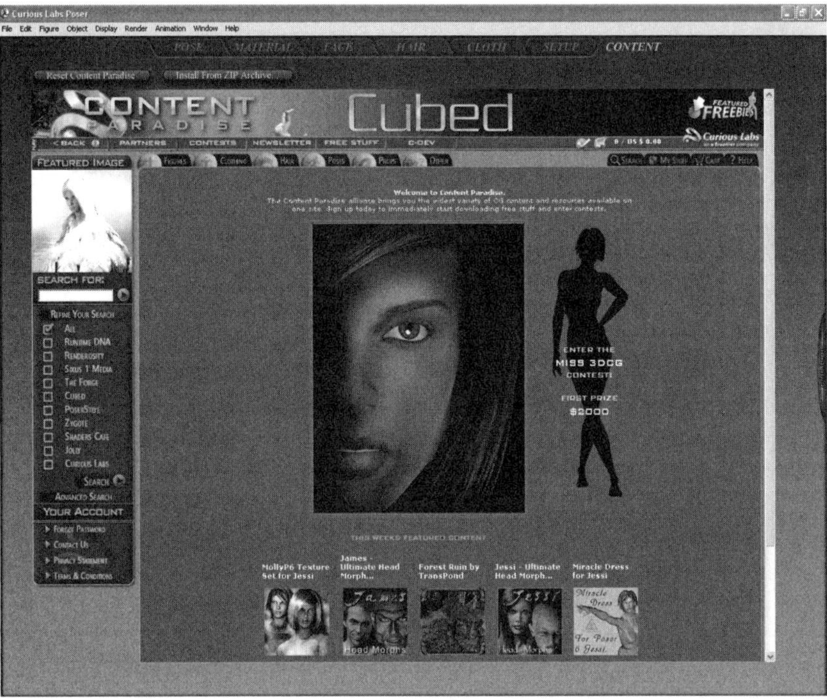

FIGURE 1.22 The Content Room (Content Paradise) provides access to a vast quantity of Poser content that you can use in your Poser scenes.

CONCLUSION

In this chapter you got a quick introduction to the Poser 6 interface and the various rooms that are at your disposal for creation, modification, or use of Poser content. You learned where to find content in the libraries and how to customize the Poser 6 default interface to suit your preferences. In the next chapter you'll learn more about obtaining and organizing third-party content for Poser.

CHAPTER

2

USING THIRD-PARTY CONTENT

In This Chapter

- Where You Can Find Content
- Maintaining Your Libraries
- Installing Poser Content from ZIP Files
- Conclusion

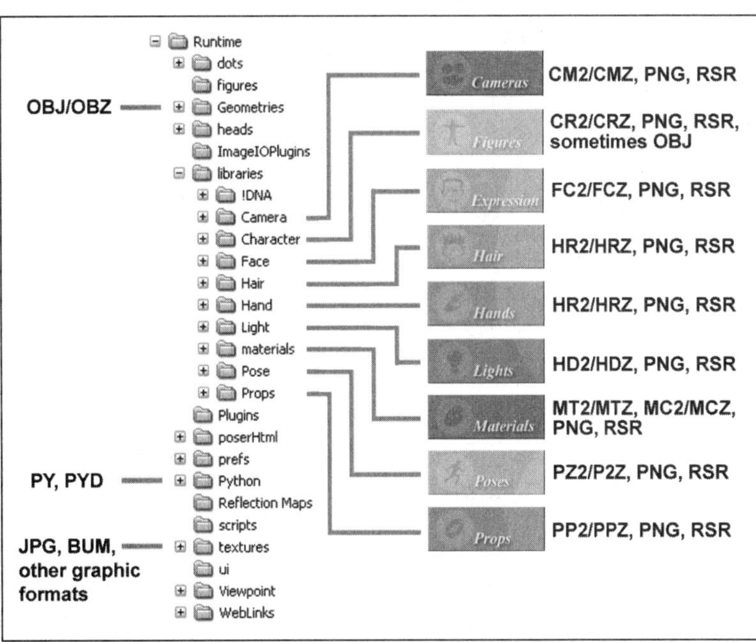

If you are new to Poser, you may be unaware that there are long-standing, very large groups of users who have been nurturing several online communities for quite some time. Through these various Poser communities, a substantial amount of ready-made content is available online for reasonable prices or even free. In this chapter, you'll learn about communities of Poser users, how to obtain content, and how you can organize and maintain your content in libraries.

Where to Find Content

There are two ways to obtain Poser content. The first way is to use Content Paradise, which is built into the Poser application and accessed through the Content tab of the user interface. The second way to find Poser content is to subscribe to one or more Poser communities where you can keep track of the latest and greatest creations in the Poser world. You will be amazed at the vast amount of content that is available to you, either free or at a very reasonable cost.

Content Paradise

When you click the Content tab in your Poser 6 workspace, you see Content Paradise, which is shown in Figure 2.1. You can also reach Content Paradise by pointing your browser to *http://www.contentparadise.com*.

Once there, you'll be able to browse through the selections that are available from many of the most popular Poser sites in one central location. The communities and artists that are linked to Content Paradise are listed in the left navigation bar. You can search through single, multiple, or all sites to locate your desired content. As you find content that you like, you can add it to your shopping cart, and in the end, make your purchase from several different sites all at once. You'll also receive an e-mail receipt from each site that you purchase content from, although your shopping cart will process your order in one transaction.

Other Poser Sites

There are quite a few Poser sites that sell Poser content or make it available for free download. Some feature user forums, while others provide a store or download section. With the number of Poser communities continually growing and changing, it's often very difficult to keep track of them all. However, the following sites are some of the hottest and most frequently mentioned as the Poser community's favorite sites to visit.

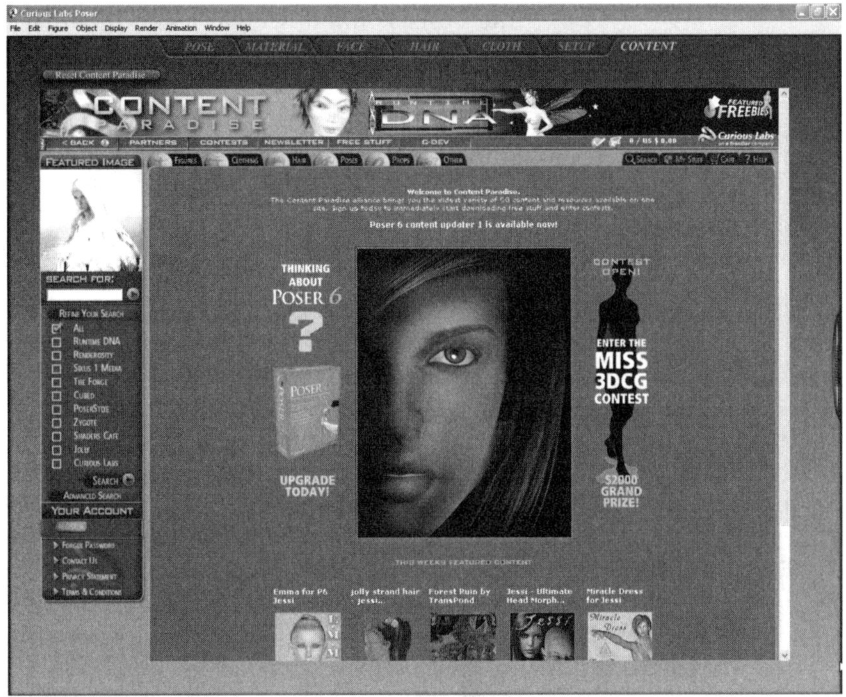

FIGURE 2.1 Content Paradise is available directly in the Poser workspace or by navigating to the Content Paradise Web site with your browser.

You may recognize some of these sites from Content Paradise, while others are very popular in their own right. These sites are featured in Figures 2.2 through 2.4:

Cubed (*http://www.cubed.ie* and Content Paradise) are the makers of Baby Dylan and Baby Jenny, perhaps the most realistic baby models available for Poser. These models are expressive and irresistible. New, photorealistic versions of the Poser animals and additional content are also planned for the future.

DAZ3D (*http://www.daz3d.com*), creators of the extremely popular Millennium Figures (Victoria, Michael, Stephanie, David, Young Teens, Preschool, and baby figures). Along with its high-quality human figures, DAZ3D also features excellent clothing, props, and accessories that are created by some of the top artists in the Poser community. Forums are also featured on the site.

Digital Babes (*http://www.digitalbabes2.com*), run by Kozaburo Yoshimura, who supplied many of the hair models that shipped with Poser 6. Arguably the most highly regarded hair creator in the Poser community, [illegible] makes his hair models available for free. You can download additional hair models from his site that are made to fit the [illegible] characters previously mentioned as well as the Poser 6 characters.

Jolly (*http://www.[illegible]*) and Content Paradise are relatively new to the Poser scene, but their content shows exciting quality and great promise. Jolly were the creators of the Jolly Troll, and were integral members of the content creation team for Poser 6. Their Jolly Troll is an amazing work of art, with incredibly realistic skin and morphs.

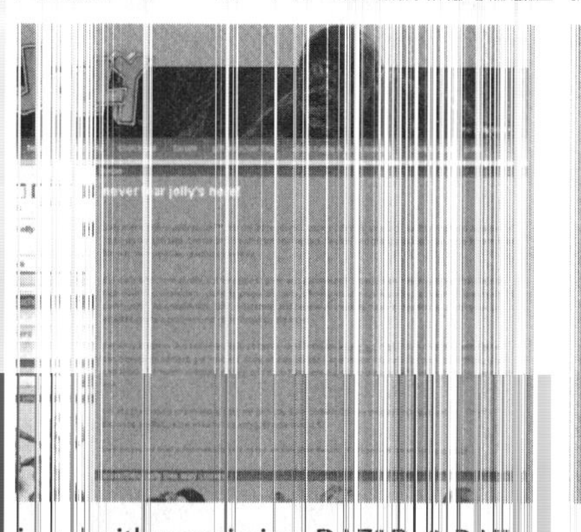

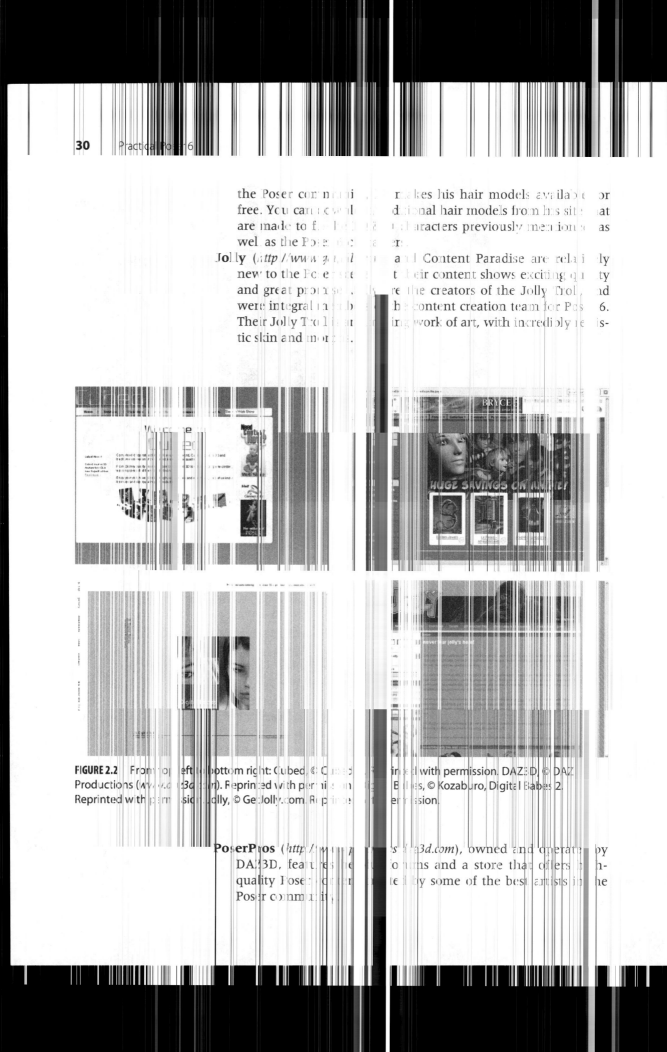

FIGURE 2.2 From top left to bottom right: Cubed, © Cubed [illegible]. Reprinted with permission. DAZ3D, © DAZ Productions (*www.daz3d.com*). Reprinted with permission. Digital Babes, © Kozaburo, Digital Babes 2. Reprinted with permission. Jolly, © GetJolly.com. Reprinted with permission.

PoserPros (*http://www.[illegible]s.daz3d.com*), owned and operated by DAZ3D, features the [illegible] forums and a store that offers high-quality Poser content created by some of the best artists in the Poser community.

PoserWorld (*http://www.poserworld.com*) offers an endless supply of clothing and textures for Poser and DAZ3D figures for a very reasonable monthly, annual, or lifetime subscription fee. Items are also available for individual purchase. This site is widely considered to be one of the best values in the Poser community.

Renderosity (*http://www.renderosity.com* and Content Paradise), one of the earliest and largest online art communities, features thousands of Poser items available for free and purchase. The site also hosts several forums and members galleries that focus on many of the most popular 2D and 3D graphics programs, the most active of which is its Poser forum.

Runtime DNA (*http://www.runtimedna.com* and Content Paradise), creators of LaRoo 2 LE, furnished with Poser 6, is home to a select group of Poser artists, many of whom were involved behind the scenes in the development of Poser 5 and Poser 6. The content developed by the Team DNA artists is always innovative and high quality, and their forums are very helpful and friendly.

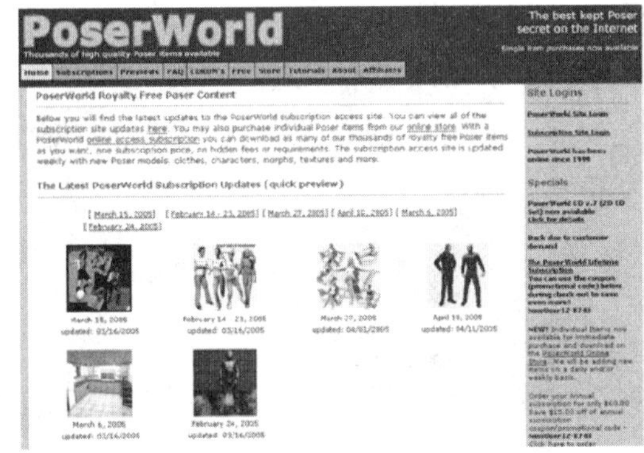

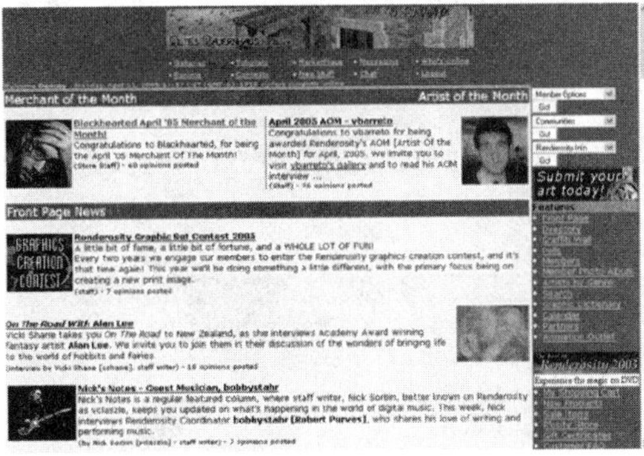

FIGURE 2.3 From top left to bottom right: PoserPros, © Daz Productions (poserpros.daz3d.com). Reprinted with permission. PoserWorld, © PoserWorld. Reprinted with permission. Renderosity, © Renderosity. Reprinted with permission. Runtime DNA, © Runtime DNA. Reprinted with permission.

- **Sixus1 Media** (*http://www.sixus1.com* and Content Paradise), creators of Alpha Man and Beta Boy and other figures for Poser 6, feature a store at their *http://poserproducts.com* URL. Here you can find unique and unusual characters from genres such as mythology, sci-fi, horror, fantasy, and more. Two additional URLs associated with Sixus1 Media where you can find forums and content are *http://www.poserforums.com* and *http://www.poserfreebies.com*.
- **The Forge** (*http://www.the-forge.ie* and Content Paradise) is the home of PoseAmation, which is a set of motion capture files that are compatible with Poser. Their product line includes animation packs that allow you to add walks, runs, battles, and other actions to your Poser animations.
- **Zygote** (*http://www.zygote.com* and Content Paradise) are makers of high-end, professional-quality 3D models for the commercial, broadcast, biomedical, multimedia, and games industries. You can find their high-quality biomedical models on their sister site, 3DSCI.com (*http://www.3dscience.com*) and at Content Paradise.

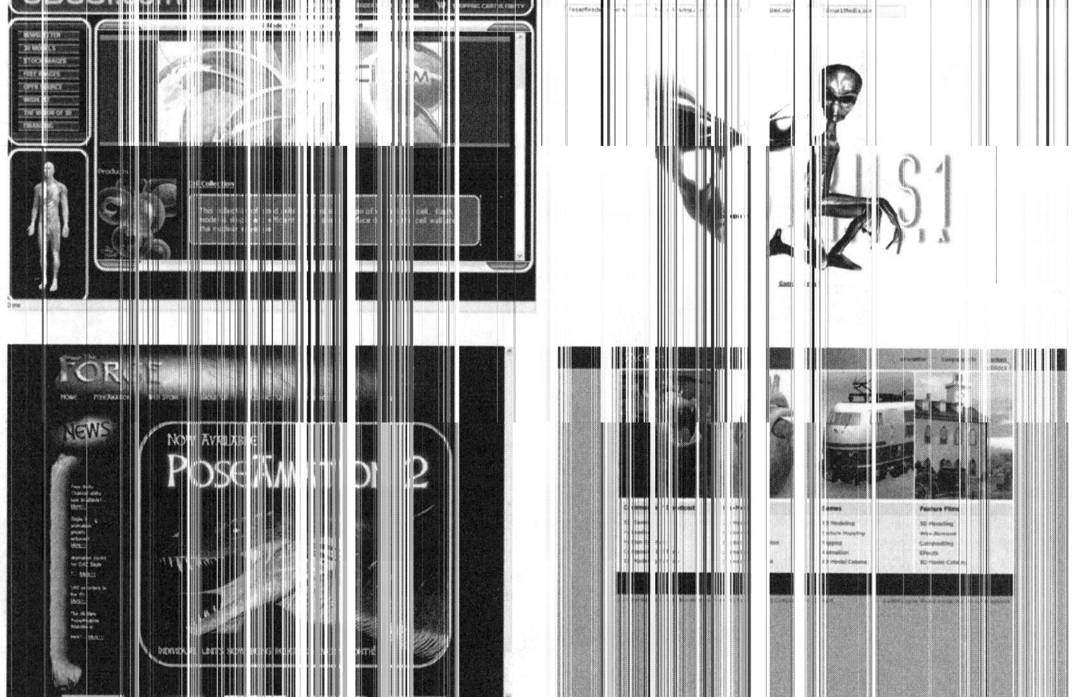

FIGURE 2.4 From top left to bottom right: 3DSCI.com © Zygote Media Group. Reprinted with permission. Sixus1 © Sixus1 Media, LLC. Reprinted with permission. The Forge, © The Forge.ie. Reprinted with permission. Zygote, © Zygote Media Group. Reprinted with permission.

Their models have been featured in the broadcast and motion picture industries. Their first Poser-related product is a full-featured set of male anatomy (including skin, skeleton, and internal organs) that is extremely realistic and perfect for medical and forensic illustration and animation. You will see rendered examples of this model in Chapter 17, "Postwork and Other Things to Consider."

Poser Library File Types and Where to Find Them

When you purchase third-party content, you receive it in one of two ways. The most common distribution method of Poser content is in a compressed *ZIP* or *SIT* file in which the content is already arranged in its correct Runtime folders. Other vendors, such as DAZ3D, place their content in an executable file that extracts it as needed into the Runtime path that you specify.

In most cases, the content should go into its correct location automatically. Once in a while, however, there is an error or omission that can prevent Poser from loading the files properly. Figure 2.5 shows the file extensions that are typically found in Poser content; which folders the files are installed into on your hard drive; and the corresponding Poser Library associated with each folder.

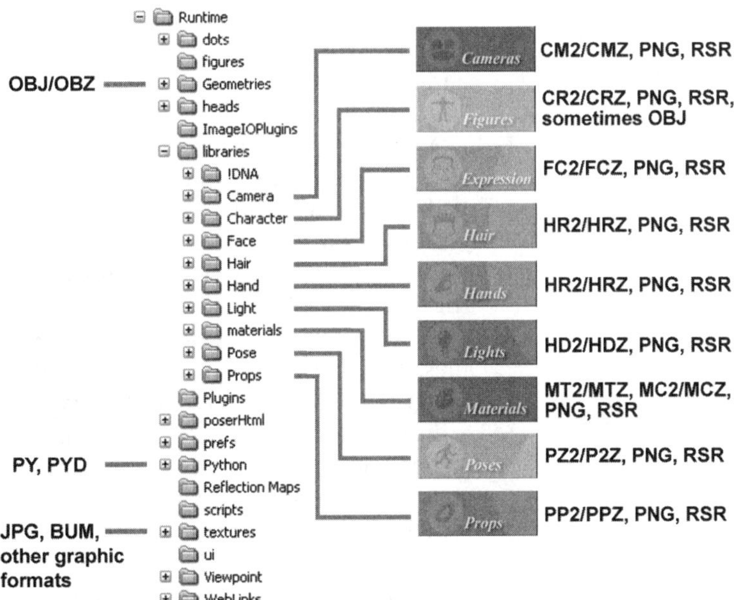

FIGURE 2.5 Poser content comes in various file formats. The files get installed within the Runtime folder structure that directly corresponds with the Poser libraries accessible through the Library Palette.

The following information briefly describes the types of files you are most likely to encounter when you purchase Poser content:

BUM files are bump map files (companion textures that give some content a bumpy appearance) that are required for older versions of Poser. Beginning with the Poser Pro Pack (released between Poser 4 and 5) you can use standard formats (typically JPG images) for bump maps. Bump maps are explained in more detail in Chapter 9, "Assigning and Creating Materials." They are typically located in the Runtime > Textures folder, in a subfolder that is named by the texture artist.

CM2 (CMZ when compressed) are camera files that are installed and saved into the Runtime > Libraries> Cameras folder and found in the Cameras Library.

CR2 (CRZ when compressed) are poseable or conforming figure files, which you will learn more about in the next chapter. The files are installed and saved into the Runtime > Libraries > Characters folder, and are found in the Figures Library.

FC2 (FCZ when compressed) are face poses, a special type of pose that manipulates the morphs associated with the head of a figure. The head of the figure must have the same morph targets that are controlled by the face pose to have any effect on the head morph. These files are installed and saved into the Runtime > Libraries > Face folder, and you will find them in the Expressions Library.

HD2 (HDZ when compressed) are hand poses. They are installed and saved into the Runtime > Libraries > Hand folder, and you will find them in the Hands Library.

HR2 (HRZ when compressed) are hair objects. They are installed and saved into the Runtime > Libraries > Hair folder, and you will find them in the Hair Library.

LT2 (LTZ when compressed) are light sets. They are installed and saved into the Runtime > Libraries> Light folder, and you find them in the Lights Library.

MC6 (MCZ when compressed) files are Poser 6 Material Collection files. They are installed and saved to the Runtime > Materials folder, and you find them in the Materials Library.

MT5 (MZ5 when compressed) is a single material file. They are installed and saved to the Runtime > Materials folder, and you find them in the Materials Library.

MTL files are material files that are generated when you export or save an *OBJ* file. These are not Poser-compatible files, but they are sometimes required to define material assignments in other 3D programs. You will sometimes see them saved with OBJ files.

OBJ (OBZ when compressed) is a Wavefront Object geometry file that is associated with a library item. Poser Pro Pack and earlier versions generate an accompanying *RSR* file the first time the object file is used. OBJ files are most commonly found in the Runtime > Geometries folder.

PMD files are external morph data files. When you save an object or project that contains morph data, Poser saves all of the morphs in a separate file, in the same directory as the saved file. Character files (such as CR2/CRZ files) make reference to these external morphs, so if you move them to a different location you will have to edit the referencing file.

Content developers should deselect the option to save external binary morphs in the General Preferences dialog to maintain compatibility with older Poser versions.

PP2 (**PPZ** when compressed) are prop files, which can serve a variety of functions. Prop files can be scenery, jewelry, figure add-ons, furniture, and other content that is not poseable. Dynamic clothing is also saved as a prop file. Beginning with Poser 6, you can also find conforming clothing with this extension. Prop files are installed into the Runtime > Libraries > Props folder and can be found in the Props Library.

PY files are Python scripts, usable with Poser Pro Pack and later versions of Poser. They are installed to the Runtime > Python folder.

PZ2 (**P2Z** when compressed) files are pose files, which can also serve a variety of purposes. Pose files began as files that when applied, posed an object in various positions. Later, they came to be used for poses that changed the materials applied to an object (MAT poses), or poses that set existing morphs to change the appearance of an object (MOR poses). Later, poses were used to add external morphs to a character or remove them from a character (INJ or REM poses). Pose files are installed into the Runtime > Libraries > Pose folder and can be found in the Poses Library.

RSR files, which you can find in any Poser library, are the thumbnail files used in the Library Palette for Poser 4 and earlier versions. Poser Pro Pack and later versions use PNG graphics for thumbnails. If no thumbnail graphic exists, you see the "shrugging man" icon.

MAINTAINING YOUR LIBRARIES

All physical Poser content files must reside within the master folder (file directory) named Runtime in order for Poser to be able to find it and properly display its associated library, which is accessed through the Library Palette. In earlier versions of Poser, the Runtime folder had to exist in the same folder that your Poser executable file was in. For example using the Windows default installation path for Poser 4, *all* Poser content had to reside within the C > Program Files > Curious Labs > Poser 4 > Runtime folder.

Starting with Poser 5, a new subfolder named Downloads was added to the Poser root folder, or directory. Within the Downloads directory is an additional Runtime folder that is intended to be a convenient and centrally located place for all of the content that you purchase or download. This also helps keep the content that you purchase or download separate from the content that is furnished with Poser, and makes it easier to back up your extra content.

Tutorial 2.1 Creating Runtime Folders on Your Hard Disk

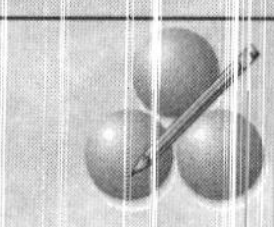

If you're like most Poser users, even a second folder isn't enough to manage all of your files. Eventually, several gigabytes of content gets too cumbersome to maintain in one or even two folders—and in the Poser world several gigabytes of content are not uncommon! With Poser 6's "Add New Runtime" library feature, you can create as many Runtime folders as you like. They can appear on any drive in your system, too.

With several gigabytes of content to manage, separating it into several smaller Runtime folders will enable you to locate it much more easily. For example, you might put all of Jessi's clothing in one Runtime folder; James' clothing in another; and designate one or more for DAZ3D Millennium figure clothing.

To create multiple Runtime folders on a secondary drive—your D drive, for example—follow these steps:

1. Using Microsoft (Internet Explorer, locate the drive onto which you want to store your extra Poser content. Using a Windows system for an example, let's assume your secondary hard drive is drive D.
2. Create a folder that will store your additional Runtime folders. For example, you can call the folder "Poser 6 Runtimes". It helps to indicate the version number in case you have Runtime content from previous versions of Poser.
3. Inside the new folder, create additional subfolders as needed. For example, if you want to create a folder that stores content for each of the third-party figures you use, you could create additional folders named James, Jessi, Victoria 3, Michael 3, Koshini, LaRoo, and so on. You might also want other folders for items that you can use for any character, such as Hair or Scenery. Eventually, you have a folder structure that looks similar to Figure 2.[illegible].

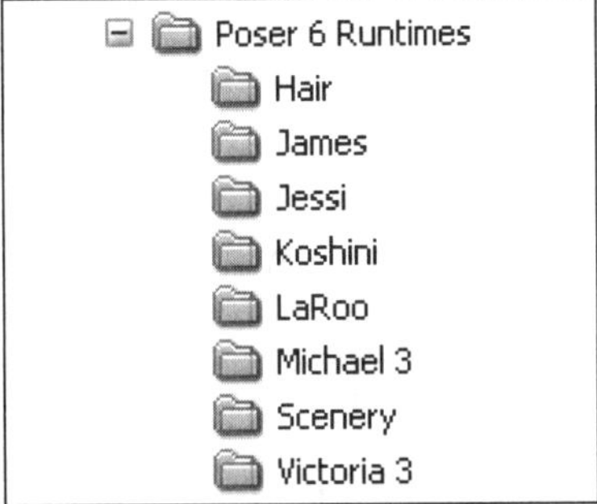

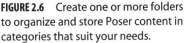

FIGURE 2.6 Create one or more folders to organize and store Poser content in categories that suit your needs.

TUTORIAL 2.2 ADDING A NEW RUNTIME FOLDER TO THE POSER LIBRARIES

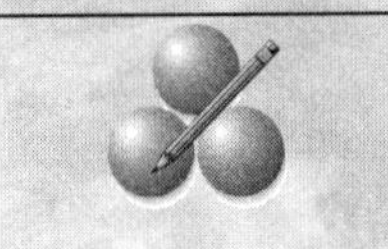

The second step in the process of creating additional Runtime folders is to make Poser 6 aware that they exist. Here is how you add new Runtime folders into the Poser Library Palette:

1. If the Poser Library Palette is hidden, click the bar at the right side of the interface to expand it.
2. If the Library Palette opens to display the library titles and not their contents, double-click any library category name (Figures, Cameras, and so on.) to display the contents within it.
3. The first folder in any library is usually a special folder, the "up folder," which has an arrow on it to indicate that clicking on this special folder will move you up to the next highest folder level. You can see an example of this special folder on the left side in Figure 2.7. To move to the very top, or root, of your currently selected library folder, continue clicking the "up folder" until you see a red dot next to the folder icon. The red dot tells you that you are at the top of your library structure, or the root. An example of the root-level library folder is shown on the right side of Figure 2.7. You can add new Runtime libraries while you are in the root folder.
4. Now that you are in the top-level folder, two icons will appear at the bottom of the Library Palette window: a check mark and a plus sign. When you hover your mouse over the plus sign icon you will see the words "Add Runtime". Click the plus-sign icon to open the Browse for Folder dialog.
5. Browse for the folder that you made earlier that contains your new Runtime folder, such as the Victoria 3 folder that is selected in Figure 2.8. (Remember, do not select the Runtime folder itself; rather, select

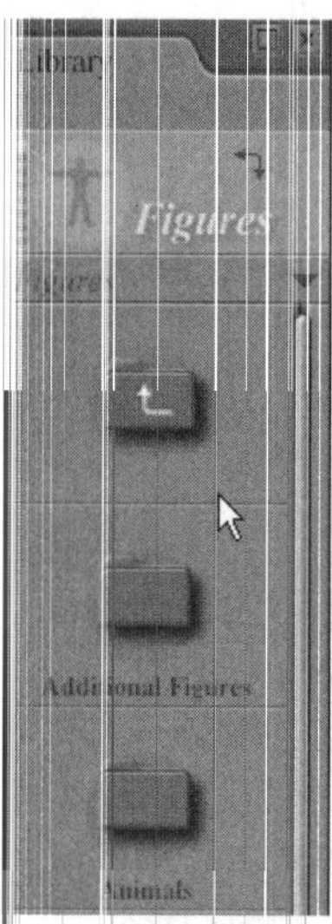

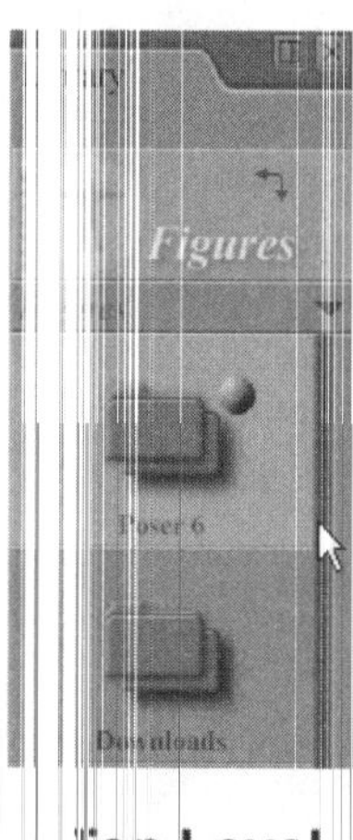

Top Level

Sub Level

FIGURE 2.7 To get to the top-level, or root library folder, click on the folder with the up arrow (left) until you see a red dot near the current Runtime folder you are using (right).

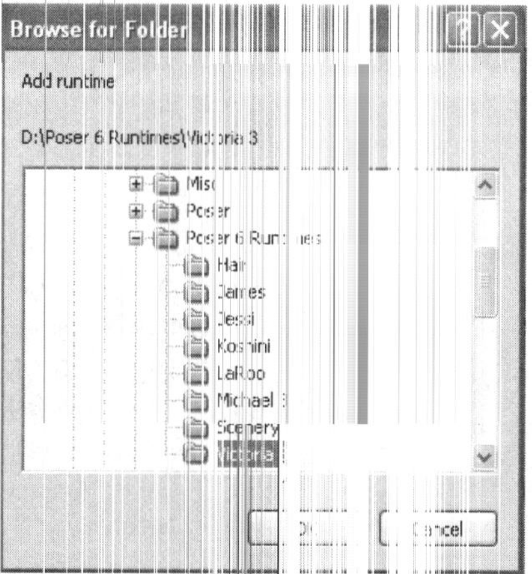

FIGURE 2.8 Use the Browse for Folder dialog to select the folder that will store your Runtime folder.

the folder that contains the Runtime folder—the one that is one level up from the Runtime folder.)

6. Click OK to return to the Library Palette window. You should now see a new library folder, the folder you selected in Step 5.

7. Repeat Steps 4 through 6 for each additional Runtime folder that you want to add to your library.

TUTORIAL 2.3 INSTALLING DAZ POSER CONTENT

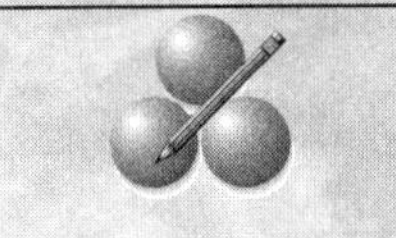

With your custom Runtime folders in place, and your purchased content in hand, you are now prepared to install your content.

Poser content is typically delivered in a ZIP or SIT compressed file format or in an executable program file, *EXE*. DAZ3D (makers of the Michael, Victoria, David, Stephanie, Aiko, Hiro, and other popular Poser figures) typically distribute their content in EXE files for Windows users, and in SIT files for Macintosh users. Other sites distribute content in ZIP files with the library folders properly nested within a Runtime folder.

The following is a typical sequence of events for installing DAZ3D's most recent products. Older versions of their installation program may vary slightly from these steps:

1. Open the EXE file that contains the product you purchased by double-clicking on it in your Windows Explorer or File Manager. Newer products will ask if you would like to include an uninstaller to remove all the files that go with this installation. Answer YES to include one, or NO to proceed without the uninstaller.
2. The first setup screen displays the name of the product that you are installing. Click NEXT to continue.
3. The Software License Agreement screen appears and prompts you to accept the terms of the license agreement. Please read the license agreement carefully to make sure you understand it and then click YES if you wish to continue, or NO to cancel the installation. You may also print the license agreement from this screen.
4. Once you agree to the license terms, a fourth screen will prompt you to choose a target application. If Poser 6 does not appear on the list of applications, choose "Poser (All Files)" and click NEXT to continue.
5. The Choose Destination Screen shown in Figure 2.9 appears. Click the Browse button to find and select the Runtime folder you want to install the content into. If you want to install the content in the Downloads Runtime library that is installed with Poser, select *C:\Program Files\Curious Labs\Poser 6\Downloads* as your installation path. If you want to install the content files to your custom Runtime folders, select one of the folders you created, such as *D:\Poser 6 Runtimes\Victoria 3* from the previous tutorial. After you successfully select your desired Runtime folder and return to the setup screen, click NEXT to continue.
6. Click NEXT again to install the content files. The setup program will display important notes regarding your product and where the files were installed so you can find them later on if necessary. Click NEXT

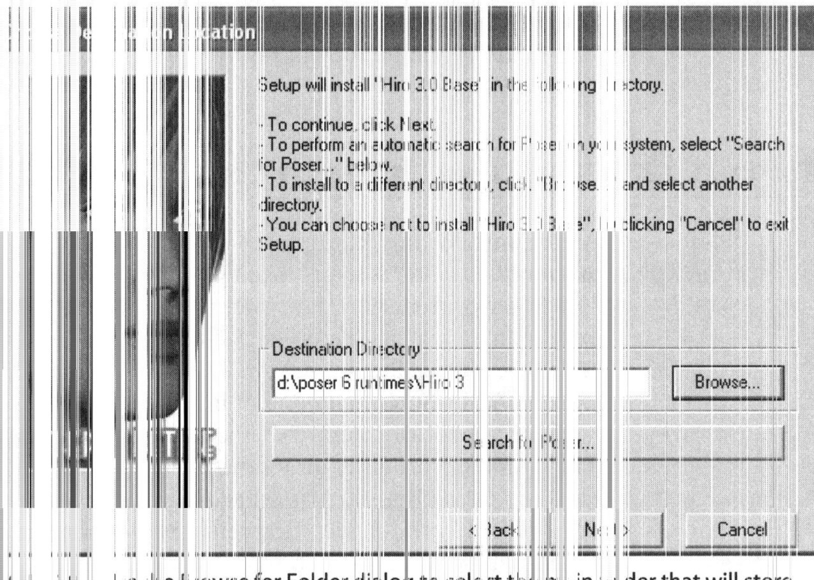

FIGURE [illegible] Use the Browse for Folder dialog to select the main folder that will store your new Runtime library folder.

5. Review the Readme file and close the setup program. Congratulations—your content has been successfully installed.

INSTALLING POSER CONTENT FROM ZIP FILES

If your product is distributed in a compressed format such as ZIP, you can use WinZip or a similar utility to extract the files to the desired library folder location. Before you extract the files, verify in WinZip that the installation paths begin with the Runtime folder. If they don't, the best option is to extract them to your desktop, and then manually move the contents of the Runtime subfolder into the desired location (such as *D:\Poser 6 Runtimes\Victoria 3*).

CONCLUSION

There are many places you can obtain ready-made content for your Poser scenes. The majority of this content is very reasonably priced and made by other Poser users. As you accumulate Poser content you may find it useful to rearrange it into one or more additional Runtime files, which you can link into separately from within the Poser Library Palette.

CHAPTER

3

BUILDING SCENES

In This Chapter

- Posing Controls and Parameter Dials
- Improving Poses
- Conclusion

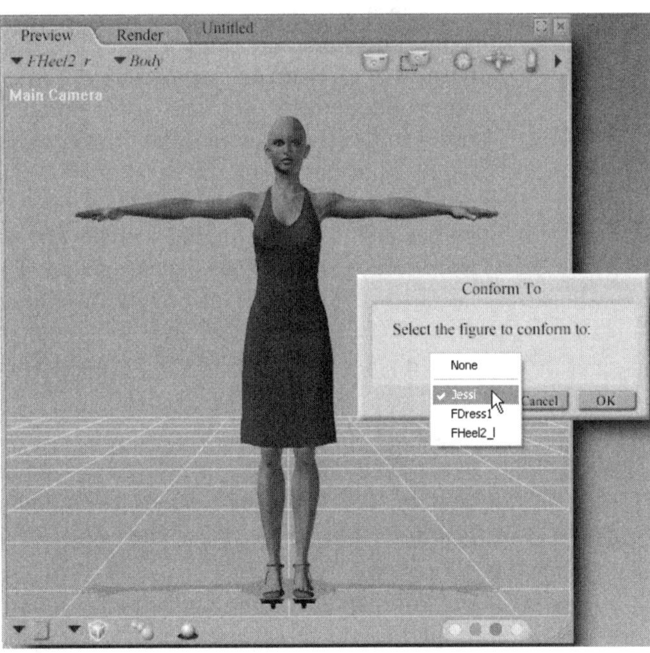

This chapter will go light on theory in order to concentrate on hands-on tasks and familiarize you with the things most commonly encountered when building a scene. There is a great deal to learn about posing a figure so that it is convincing and looks natural in the setting you create. In addition, those new to Poser will find answers to some of the most commonly asked questions regarding setting up scenes and posing figures so that they look exactly the way you want them to. To help you do this as naturally as possible, tutorials are presented in the order you would encounter them while working on a Poser scene. You'll work through some of the common questions, pitfalls, and puzzles that face new Poser users. You'll learn how to replace the default figure, how to add clothing and hair to your figure, and how to pose the figure the way you want.

TUTORIAL 3.1 REPLACING AND RENAMING FIGURES

When you first start Poser, it creates a new scene based upon the preferences defined in the General Preferences dialog. (See Chapter 1, "Poser Overview," for more information about the General Preferences dialog.) By default, Poser loads the James Casual figure in your scene when you open Poser or create a new Poser document.

There are two ways to replace a figure. One method is to delete the figure and then add a new one to the scene. Using this method, the new figure will appear in its default pose and you will lose whatever posing you applied to the original figure. An alternate method of replacing a figure is to use the Change Figure option in the Figures Library. The Change Figure option is the single check mark at the bottom of the Figures Library display of the Library Palette. First, select the figure you want replaced in your scene. Then in the Figures Library, locate and select the new figure. Now select the Change Figure option. The new figure from the Figures Library will take the place of the old figure and will also 'inherit' its pose. This way, you don't have to repose your new figure and can pick up right where you left off before the figure change.

When you replace a posed human figure, Poser applies the same pose to the new figure. However, any clothing you have conformed to the original figure will revert to its default pose and will no longer be conformed. You will need to reconform the clothing to the new figure.

Poser retains the names of all original figures in your scenes. For example, if you replace James Casual with Jessi, the name still appears as James Casual in your Poser scene. It's easier to keep track of the items in your scene if you rename them appropriately.

1. To start this example, choose File > New and create a new scene. By default, Poser will load James Casual into the scene unless you have changed the settings in the General Preferences dialog.
2. Click anywhere on the James Casual object mesh to make sure he is selected and is the current figure. Alternatively, you can choose James Casual from the pull-down menu that appears just beneath the Preview tab in the document window.
3. Open the Poser 6 Figures Library. For the purposes of this tutorial, browse to and choose the Jessi library and click either the Jessi or JessiHiRes library item to highlight it.
4. Click the Change Figure icon (the single check mark) at the bottom of the library window, as shown in Figure 3.1.

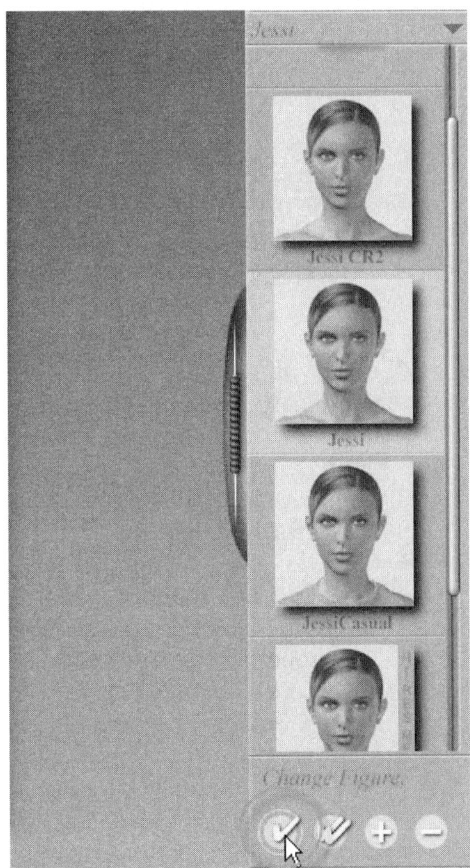

FIGURE 3.1 Click the Change Figure (single checkmark) icon to replace a figure.

5. Poser displays a dialog that asks if you want to keep any customized geometry that might appear in the figure. Unless you have made special modifications to the figure you are replacing, you don't need to check any options here. Answer OK to continue.

The options that appear in the Keep Customized Geometry dialog allow you to retain geometry changes that you have made to a figure so that you can reapply them to the new figure. For example, if you used the Object > Replace Body Part with Prop command to change your human character's head to an animal head; or you added special props such as eyes, teeth, or hair; or you wanted to reuse magnets that altered the appearance of your original figure. Check the applicable options to transfer the same changes to your new figure.

6. Next, Poser asks if you want to keep the figure's proportions through the figure change. This only applies if you made size changes to body parts using Scaling dials in the Parameters window. Click OK to continue with the figure change. Jessi appears in the scene.

The General Preferences dialog allows you to configure double-click behavior. By default, double-clicking a library item will add a new item to the scene. As an alternative, you can configure Poser to replace the currently selected item when you double-click. To locate this setting, choose Edit > General Preferences, and select the Library tab.

7. After you load Jessi, you will notice that Poser keeps the original figure name of James Casual. To rename her, click anywhere on Jessi to select her as the current figure, or choose James Casual from the figure selection menu at the top of the document window.
8. Choose Object > Properties. The Parameters/Properties window opens. If necessary, choose the Properties tab.
9. Click the down arrow to expand the selection menu in the top-left corner of the Properties window. Select Body from the list of items. The Name field should show the name of James Casual.
10. The properties for James Casual are shown in Figure 3.2. Click inside the Name field and edit the contents so that they are now Jessi. Press Enter to assign the new name. Now, when you click inside the document window to continue your scene, the name of the figure will reflect the changes you've just made.

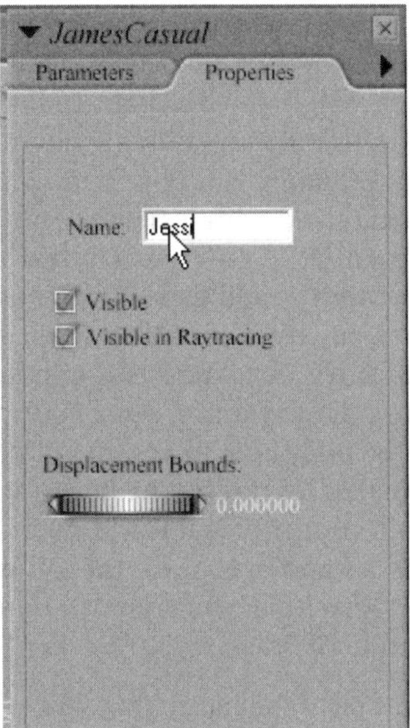

FIGURE 3.2 Use the Properties window to change the name of the body part on the currently selected figure to be something that is more meaningful and descriptive for your project.

TUTORIAL 3.2 TURNING INVERSE KINEMATICS (IK) OFF

Before we get into showing you how to turn Inverse Kinematics ON or OFF, it might be helpful if we explained what it is. And, in order to understand the concept of Inverse Kinematics it might help if we first introduce the concept of Kinematics. Kinematics is the study of the position, angle, velocity, and acceleration of connected objects and joints during motion. Let's say that you rotate your shoulder blade—you see that your elbow, wrist, and hand rotate and change position in response to the rotation of your shoulder. (In this example, your shoulder blade is the *first* element in the hierarchical chain, and your hand is the *last* element in the chain.) So, Kinematics is the science that will allow you to calculate how everything will rotate and move in response to the rotation of the shoulder.

Inverse Kinematics (IK) is the science of how the objects and joints in a hierarchical chain will respond when the *last* element of the chain is moved. With Inverse Kinematics turned ON, you can set the position of the *last* object in an IK chain (say, a figure's foot), and then move the *first* object in the IK chain (say, the hip), and the objects and joints between the two ends of the chain will bend and rotate to accommodate the change. When IK is OFF, you would be required to position and rotate each object in the chain individually, working your way downward starting from the hip and moving down to the foot.

While IK is a powerful feature that helps you achieve realistic poses quickly and with less effort, it does take some getting used to. When IK is turned ON, you'll quickly learn how to turn your figures into pretzels if you aren't used to it. It's important to remember that IK can, and often does, interfere with poses that you apply from the library as well. When you have IK turned ON, and you apply a pose from your Poses library, you might find that your figure's feet will stick to the floor while the rest of the body goes in another direction—and usually not in a good direction. It makes for interesting poses, at least. So, most of the time you'll probably want to turn IK OFF and use it on those occasions where you must position a hand or foot (or the tail-end object in a hierarchical chain).

Now that you understand what IK is, you'll need to know how to turn it OFF:

1. Select the figure that you want to affect. In this example, click Jessi to select her and make her the current figure.
2. Choose Figure > Use Inverse Kinematics, and then expand the selection menu as shown in Figure 3.3. If IK is ON for the individual legs, a check mark appears beside the part. If no check mark appears, IK is OFF for that part. Turn IK ON or OFF as needed. The poses that you choose from the Pose Library should work more predictably.

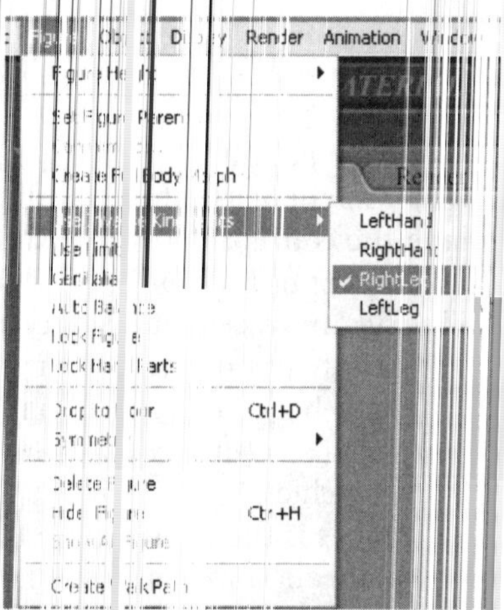

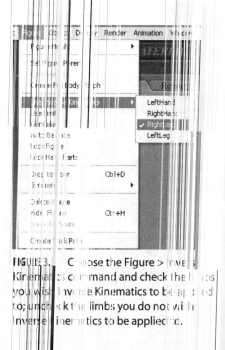

FIGURE 3.3 Choose the Figure > Inverse Kinematics command and check the limbs you wish Inverse Kinematics to be applied to; uncheck the limbs you do not wish Inverse Kinematics to be applied to.

TUTORIAL 3.3 USING PYTHON TO "ZERO" A FIGURE

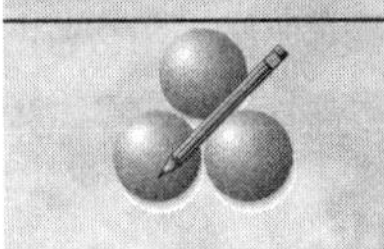

As you'll learn in Chapter 8, "Working with Poser Clothing," your Poser content may not fit a figure if you move, morph, or pose the figure before you add additional Poser content. What makes it even more confusing is that you may not have actually moved, morphed, or posed your figure, yet some of the clothing and accessories may still not conform properly! This problem with clothing and accessories occurs because the state that a figure or object comes into your Poser scene may not be the "zero pose" state of the figure or object. Most times, a figure is saved into the Poser library in a pose that its creator finds aesthetically pleasing, rather than the pose the figure started off with when its creator initially modeled it. As a result, it is often easier to add clothing and accessories to a figure after it has been restored to its zero pose.

Figures are most often modeled in a "T" pose; standing straight with legs together, arms horizontal and straight out to the side at shoulder height, and with their palms facing downward. This "T" pose that the figure exists in its original 3D object file is called the figure's zero pose. When you initially load a figure into your Poser scene, chances are the figure won't come into your scene in its zero pose. (For example, James Casual loads into a scene with his arms down at his side.) The problem with this is that when people create clothing and accessories for a Poser figure, they usually reference the default of the clothing to the zero pose of the figure.

Normally, getting a figure back into its zero pose requires going through every parameter dial associated with the figure and entering a zero into the parameter field. Fortunately, there is a very generous Python programming wizard known to the online Poser community as *ockham* (in the real world his name is David Drumright), who has written and made available to the community many invaluable PoserPython scripts that do some pretty amazing things. (You can visit his Web site at *http://ockhams-bungalow.com/Python.*) One of these scripts, ZeroAll, sets all joint rotations, translations and morphs in a figure to zero, in addition to setting all scaling to 100%, which effectively returns the figure to its original zero pose. You can download ZeroAll here:*http://ockhamsbungalow.com/Python/ZeroAll.zip.*

To obtain and use this wonderful script, follow these steps:

1. Download the ZeroAll script from *http://ockhamsbungalow.com/Python/ZeroAll.zip.*
2. Using WinZip or a similar utility, unzip the script to your Poser 6 > Runtime > Python > poserScripts file folder.
3. In Poser, select the figure that you want to "zero pose." For this example, choose Jessi, who should still be on your stage if you are following the tutorials from this chapter.

4. Choose File > Run Python Script. Locate the Poser 6 > Runtime > Python > poserScripts folder, and select ZeroAll.py to open it. You should see Jessi move into her zero position and pose, as shown in Figure 3.4.

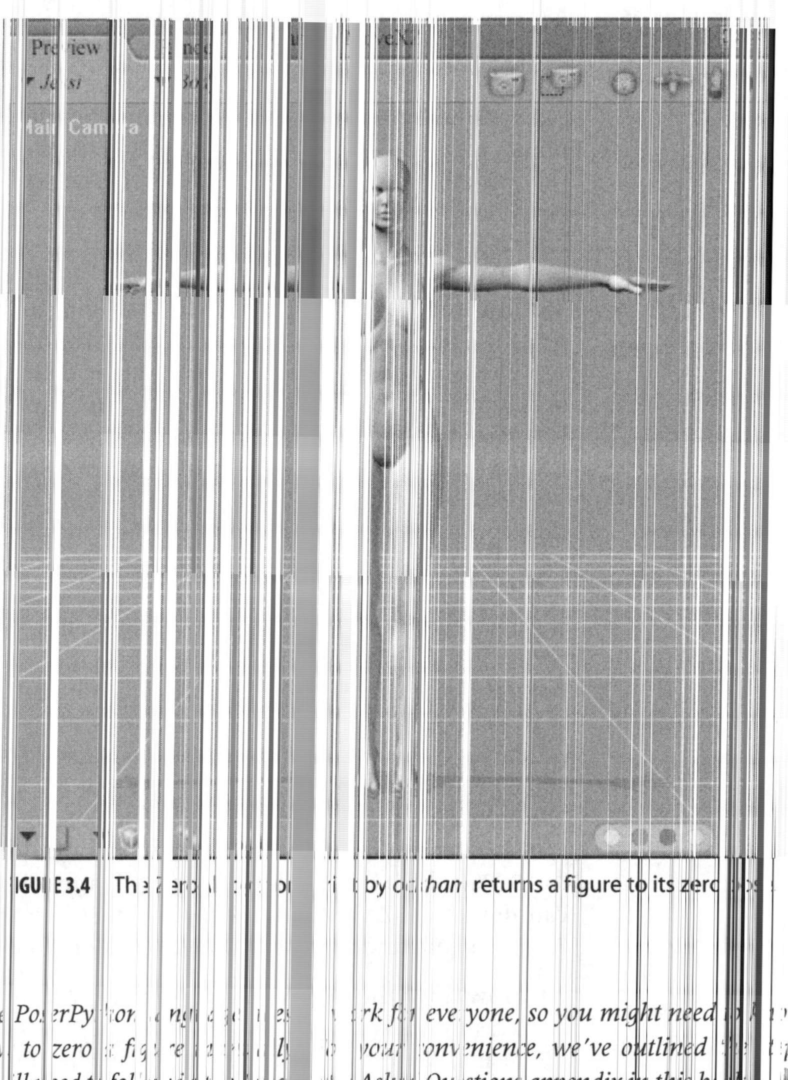

FIGURE 3.4 The ZeroAll.py script by [illegible] returns a figure to its zero position.

The PoserPython language does not work for everyone, so you might need to know how to zero a figure manually. For your convenience, we've outlined the steps you'll need to follow in the Frequently Asked Questions appendix in this book.

TUTORIAL 3.4 ADDING CONFORMING CLOTHING AND HAIR

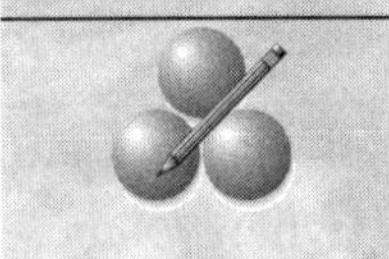

So far in this chapter you have added a figure, turned off Inverse Kinematics, changed the figure's name, and zeroed the pose. Perhaps it's time to add some clothing to your figure. But first, let's change to *Texture Shaded* mode so all the contents of your scene will be displayed using the textures that are currently applied to them. This will give your scene a more realistic appearance while you're viewing it in the document window.

Poser allows you to display the entire document window, a single figure, or a part (element) of a figure in one of 12 display styles. More information about these display styles, including examples of each, is found in the FAQ appendix in this book.

Conforming clothing is divided into body-part groups (such as chest, abdomen, hip, lShin, rShin, and so on). The body-part groups use the same names as those in the underlying figure. When you "conform" the clothing to the body, the groups in the conforming clothing mirror the settings of their corresponding counterparts in the figure. As a result, when you pose your base figure, the conforming clothing automatically follows the same pose.

The same applies to conforming hair, which works surprisingly well, even for hair that is long and needs to flow when you bend a figure's head. There are other types of hair as well. We'll discuss those in more detail in Chapter 7, "Working with Poser Hair."

Because conforming clothing is designed to fit and bend with a specific figure, it cannot be shared between figures without additional work, which can be quite involved. For example, Jessi (the Poser 6 female) cannot use clothing made for Judy (the Poser 5 female) because their body meshes and joint placement are quite different.

In this tutorial you will add some conforming clothing and hair to Jessi. With that in mind, let's look for some clothing for Jessi in the Poser 6 libraries and bring it into your scene. First, you'll set Poser up so that you can see the textures:

1. With Jessi in the zero pose position, choose Display > Document Style > Texture Shaded, or click the Texture Shaded icon in the Document Display Style controls. Jessi now appears with her default texture instead of in the gray shaded mode.
2. Within the Library Palette, Choose the Poser 6 > Props > Jessi Clothing library. Scroll down until you find Dress Gray. Click to highlight

the dress, and click the Apply Library Preset button (the single check mark icon) at the bottom of the library window. The dress appears in the scene.

3. The thumbnail in the library indicates that this dress is a conforming item. Conforming clothing adjusts itself automatically when you pose the figure it is conformed to; however, you have to manually attach, or conform it, to the figure first. To begin, look at the [illegible] menu just beneath the Preview [illegible] in the document window. Verify that FDress1 is shown as the currently selected figure (it should be if you have just added it to your scene). Alternatively, you can click anywhere on the dress [illegible] to select it as the current figure.
4. With the dress selected, choose Figure > Conform To. A dialog prompts you to select the figure that will wear the clothing. Click the down arrow to expand the list, and select Jessi (or whatever you named your figure). Then click OK to return to the document window.
5. In a similar manner, [illegible] Shoe Heels L and Shoe Heels R. Using the same procedure as the dress, add and conform each shoe, one at a time, to Jessi. You have just added three pieces of conforming clothing that will pose automatically when you apply a pose to Jessi. Your project should look as shown in Figure 3.5.

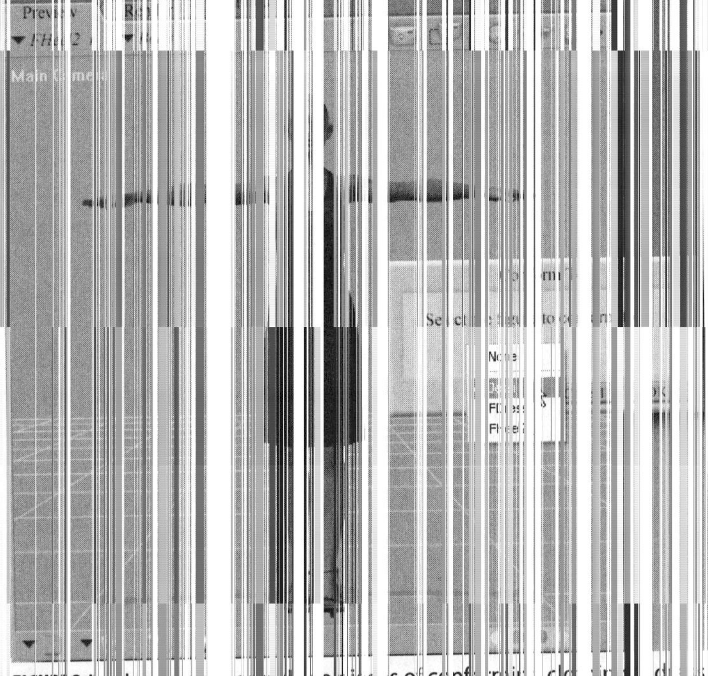

FIGURE 3.5 Jessi [illegible] wears three pieces of conforming clothing: a dress and a pair of shoes.

6. With your figure dressed and still in the zero pose, within the Library Palette choose the Poser 6 > Hair > Kozaburo > Jessi library.
7. Highlight the KyokoHairMK3_Jessi thumbnail. Check the Apply Library Preset icon at the bottom of the library to add the hair to your scene. The hair appears above Jessi's head.
8. As with the clothing in the previous steps, make sure the hair is the currently selected item. Then, choose Figure > Conform To, and choose to conform the hair to Jessi. Your project should look as shown in Figure 3.6.

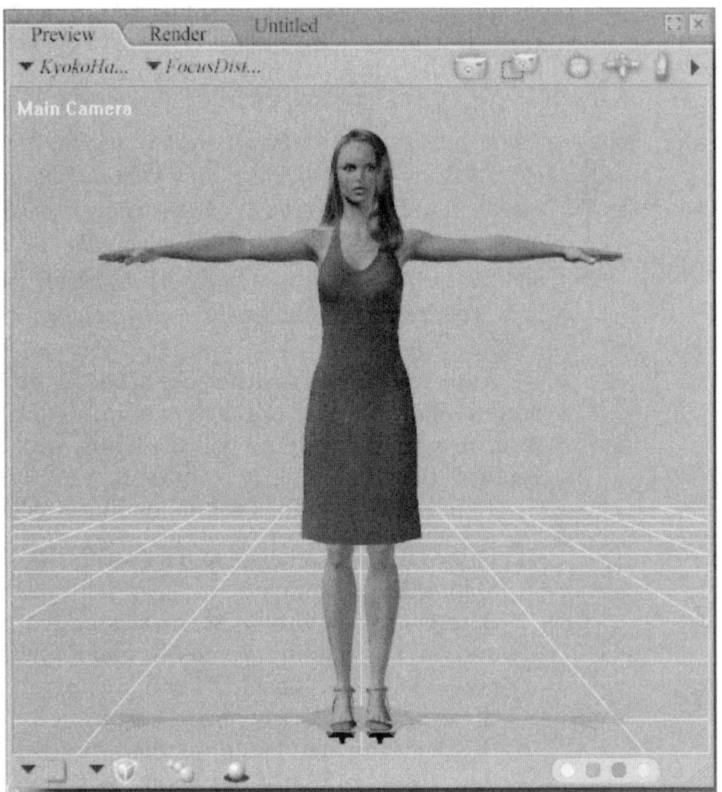

FIGURE 3.6 With clothing and hair on Jessi, she is now ready to pose.

9. At this point, it's probably not a bad idea to save your project. Choose File > Save from the menu. Browse to the folder in which you want to save your tutorial file and enter a filename. Press Enter to save the file onto your hard drive.

TUTORIAL 2.5 APPLYING AND BALANCING LIBRARY POSES

Poser 6 comes with many predefined poses for the Poser 6 figures. You can also obtain poses for many other popular Poser figures online. To find poses for Jessi, look in the Library Palette for Poser 6 > Poses > Jessi Poses libraries. By default, the poses are arranged into nine main categories: Action, Business, Conversation, Everyday, Lying Down, Running, Sitting, Standing, and Walking. Beneath those categories there may be additional subcategories.

With Jessi all dressed up, it seems appropriate that we put her in a stylish pose. We've purposely selected a pose for this tutorial that looks a bit off balance—like she's leaning against something or is about to fall over. To correct it, you'll use Poser's *Auto Balance* feature to help reposition her body to maintain her balance.

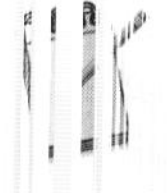

When you turn the Auto Balance feature on, you'll see spheres that [illegible] center of balance for the figure. Conforming clothing may also have [illegible] spheres as well. In most cases you don't have to reposition these spheres. However, if you change the body shape you can move the spheres to make the center of balance look more natural to the figure. If you do move the spheres, move them in small steps. You'll find that small increments go a long way.

Auto Balance adjusts the pose of the figure in response to any repositioning of a body part. In fact, even just clicking a body part will Auto Balance a pose. The figure will settle out with any changes [illegible] you turn the Auto Balance feature off.

To pose and balance Jessi, follow these steps:

1. In the Library Palette, go to the Poser 6 > Poses > Jessi Poses > Standing > Standing Poses library.
2. Before you apply the pose, make sure that Jessi is the current figure, and not her clothing. To do this you can either click one of her exposed body parts or select her name from the pull-down menu in the Preview tab to give her the focus.
3. Highlight the Stand 12 pose, then click the Apply Library Preset button at the bottom of the Library window. Your project should now look as shown in Figure [illegible].

If you accidentally apply a pose to Jessi's clothing instead of her body, there are two ways to correct it: From the menu, select the Edit > Undo command immediately after you apply the pose to the clothing. This reconforms the clothing to the figure. The other way to correct this mistake is to select the clothing that you applied the pose to and from the menu choose Figure > Conform To. Select the name of the figure that wears the clothing. The clothing should jump back into place or conform to the figure again.

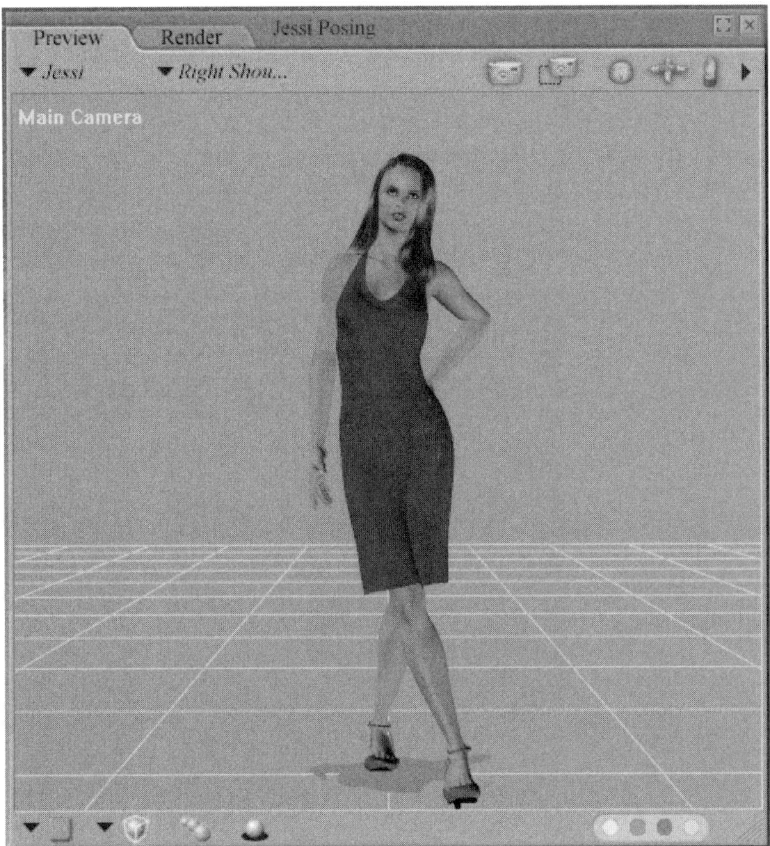

FIGURE 3.7 A standing pose from the Pose Library gives Jessi a much more relaxed and stylish posture.

4. If the Parameters window is not open, from the menu choose Window > Parameter Dials to display it.
5. For a simple demonstration of what auto-balancing is all about, choose Figure > Auto Balance to prepare for the next step.
6. Hover your mouse over the various body parts until you highlight Jessi's abdomen. (See the left side of Figure 3.8. The abdomen for the dress looks entirely different, so make sure you do not select the dress abdomen.) Once you highlight the abdomen, click it quickly without moving its position. After a brief calculation period, Poser auto-balances the figure based on the figure's current center of gravity. An example of an auto-balanced figure is shown in the right side of Figure 3.8. The upper body is now more in line with the lower body so that she isn't leaning over as much.

7. From the menu, choose Figure > Auto Balance again to turn the feature OFF.

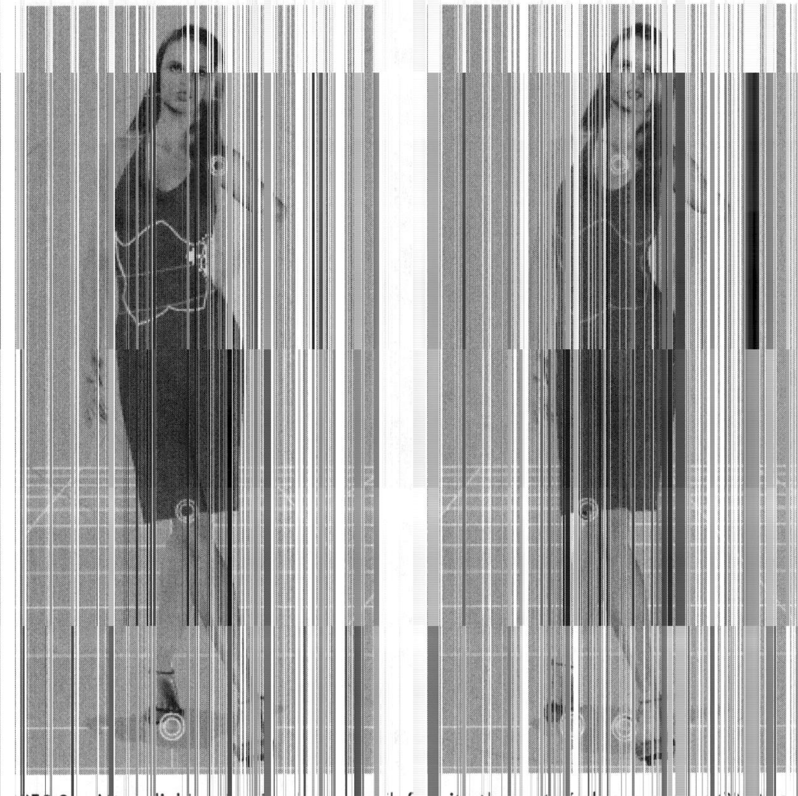

FIGURE 3.8 After clicking Jessi's ab [illegible] to her (left) with the Auto Balance option ON, the pose looks much more natural (right).

POSING CONTROLS AND PARAMETER DIALS

When you create or modify poses, there are a number of controls in Poser that help with the process. The Editing Tools palette, in the Pose Room as shown in Figure 3.9, helps you to position and rotate the objects in your scene.

The first seven controls in the Editing Tools serve the following purpose:

Rotate: Rotates a figure, body part, or prop.

Twist: Twists a figure, body part, or prop. This is the same as using the Twist dial in the Parameters window.

3. **Translate/Pull:** Moves a figure up, down, left, or right.
4. **Translate In/Out:** Moves a figure forward or backward.
5. **Scale:** Increases or decreases the size of a figure or body part.
6. **Taper:** Tapers a body part. To use, select the Taper tool, then drag your mouse over a body part to taper it. Drag to the left to increase the size of the outermost end of the chain or right to decrease the size.
7. **Chain Break:** Allows you to break the kinematic chain, which will prevent parts from moving when you pose other parts that are in the same chain. For example, if you don't want the shoulders to move when you pose the forearm and hands, you can apply a chain break to the shoulders. Once you have successfully applied a Chain Break, you will see a Chain Break icon on the figure. To remove the Chain Break from the figure, click the Chain Break tool to select it if it is not already selected, and then click the Chain Break icon on the figure where you want to relink the kinematic chain.

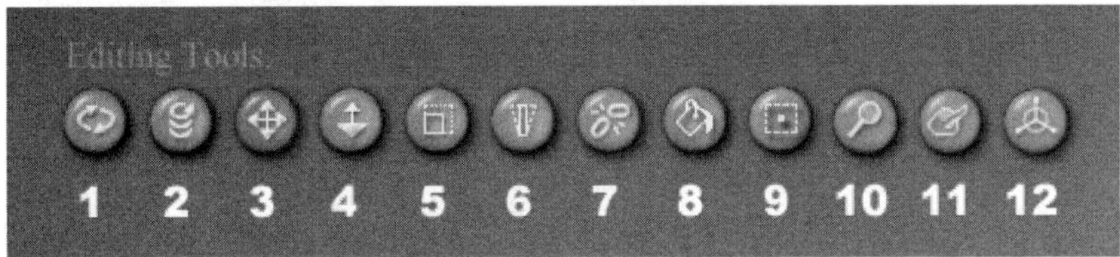

FIGURE 3.9 The first seven Editing Tools (numbered here for clarity) help with posing and positioning the items in your scene.

Most figures have parameters that you can modify using the dials on the Parameter palette that help you morph, or change the shape of a figure. For the moment, you're interested in the dials that relate to *posing* your figure, as shown in Figure 3.10. These dials are listed beneath the Transform heading of the Parameters palette. There are dials to taper, scale, rotate, and translate the selected body part. These dials also perform the same functions as the buttons on the Editing Tools palette (see Figure 3.9). For posing the body parts, the dials that are marked *Twist, Side-Side*, and *Bend* are the most-used.

Improving Poses

Good posing takes time and persistence. This is one of the reasons that third-party pose sets are popular. However, not all pose sets work as well as others. This is partly because of the skill of the posing artist and partly because poses work differently due to the differences in the joint definitions of different figures.

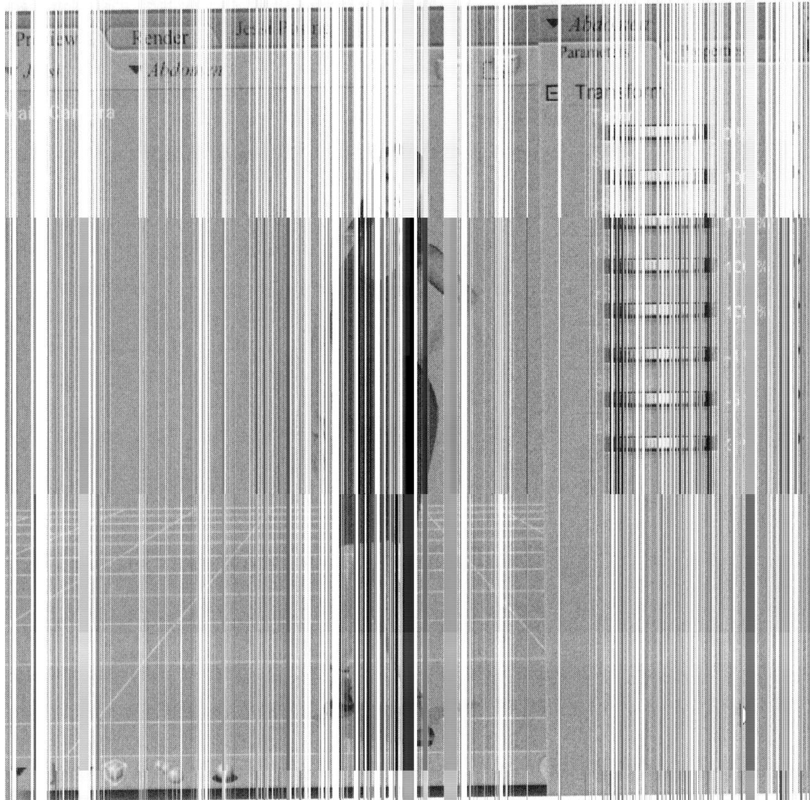

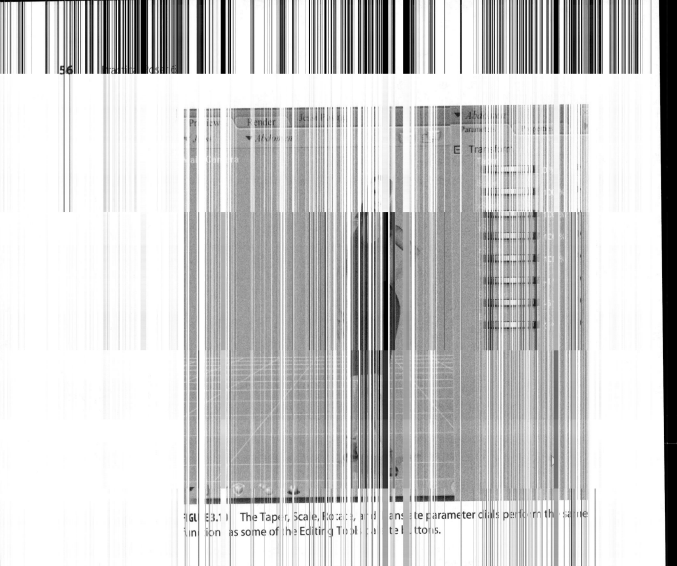

FIGURE 3.10 The Taper, Scale, Rotate, and Translate parameter dials perform the same functions as some of the Editing Tools palette buttons.

There are several artists in the community that take a great deal of care in the poses that they create. The most well-known pose expert in the community is a gentleman known as Schlabber, whose Web site can be found at http://www.schlabber.org. Other popular pose artists are (in alphabetical order) Bigt, Danie, Digiport Designs, Firebird, Ilona, IslandGirl, [illegible], and Val. You can find their poses at Renderosity (http://www.renderosity.com), Runtime DNA (http://www.runtimedna.com), DAZ 3D (http://www.daz3d.com), and PoserPros (http://poserpros.daz3d.com).

Figures are created with joint parameters that have limits defined. These limits keep motion within angles that are natural or desirable for the figure. However, on occasion you'll find poses that move body parts beyond natural or desirable limits that are appropriate for the figure. Common exaggerations include spines that bend too far; arms that twist and turn beyond natural movement ranges; fingers that splay beyond what would be possible under normal circumstances; and heads that turn without the corresponding movement in the attached neck. Figure 3.11 is a good example of an unnatural back pose.

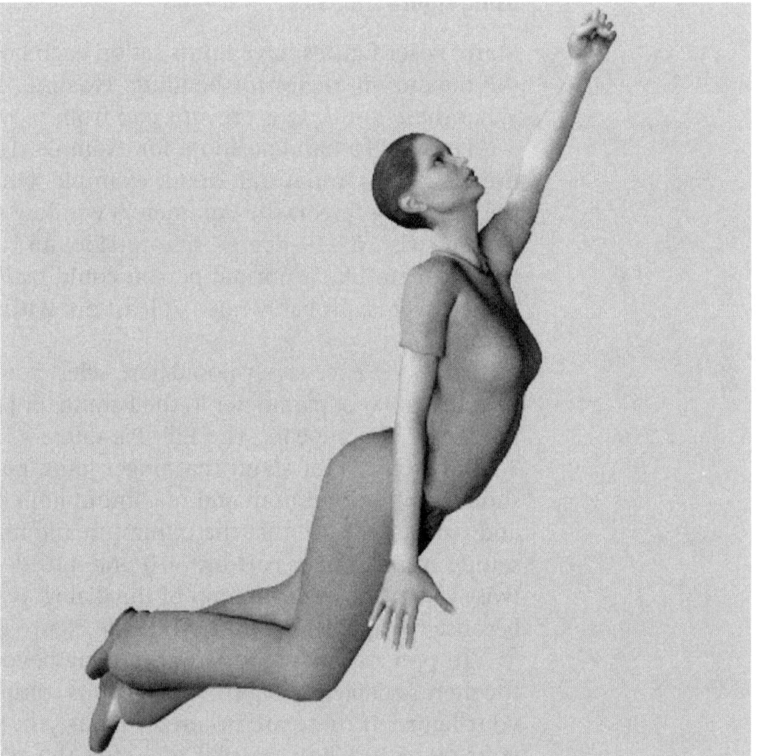

FIGURE 3.11 On occasion, you will encounter poses that exceed the range of motion (or range of comfort) that the figure would normally be in.

There really is no single answer as to how you can improve poses, so we'll address solutions in general terms rather than with specific tutorials. If a pose doesn't look natural there may be a couple of reasons why:

- The pose was created for a figure that has different body proportions and joint configuration than the figure you applied it to. An indication of this is when the end points of each limb don't fall in the same place, or fingers appear crooked. Finger positions seldom translate well from one model to another.
- One or more body parts are posed beyond their limits.

While it's not difficult to create and save poses, it can be time-consuming and meticulous work. However, Poser does offer some aids that will help your poses *and* your characters appear more realistic and natural.

Using Figure Limits

Many Poser figures have limits set on each body part. These limits define the maximum angles for bending, twisting, and turning the body part. What these limits do is prevent you from moving body parts in excess.

Let's take a hand position, for example. The hand pose shown in Figure 3.12 looks unnatural. In our example, when we click the first joint in the right ring finger, the Parameters window shows that it is set for a 2[illegible]-degree twist, a –19-degree side-to-side, and a –9-degree bend position. Does it seem like a normal person could *really* turn a finger that much? The answer is, probably not—at least not without having broken bones or joints.

To fix the excessively posed finger, select it and then click the right arrow next to the Twist parameter in the Parameter palette. Choose Settings from the menu that appears. The Edit Parameters Dial dialog, shown in Figure 3.12, tells you a lot about that finger joint. Each body part in your figure should have a minimum and maximum limit set for bending, side-to-side, and twisting. Notice that the minimum and maximum limits for the Twist setting of this finger part are [illegible] and [illegible]0 degrees, respectively. Yet, the twist value shown at the top of the dialog, is set to 21.[illegible]. This happened because we applied the pose while the Figure Limits were disabled.

To prevent body parts from moving beyond their preset limits, from the menu enable the Figure > Use Limits command *before* you start to pose your figure. If there are no preset limits you have the option of entering your own. Just be sure that you save the revised figure to your library after you set up your limits so you don't have to reenter the settings the next time you use the figure.

When posing or setting limits for a body part, think about how your own body moves that part. You really *can't* twist the lower part of your right ring finger plus or minus [illegible]0 degrees, unless you force it with your other hand, so sometimes even the preprogrammed limits might be excessive. Still, enabling figure limits does curb excessive poses.

Using Inverse Kinematics

Yes, earlier we did tell you to turn Inverse Kinematics off. But at times IK is very useful when you're creating your own poses, or completing animations—*if used in baby steps*. For example, let's say you have a character standing under a ball that's in the air, and you want to pose your character as if he has just caught the ball

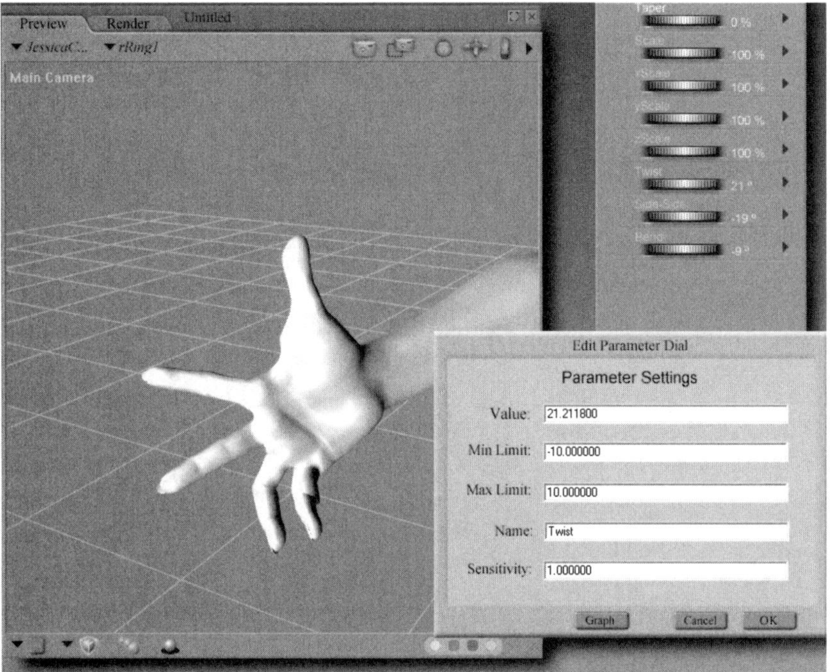

FIGURE 3.12 Each body part has a minimum and maximum angle limit set for Twist, Side-to-Side, and Bend. Set or edit these limits in the Edit Parameter Dial dialog.

Without IK on, you would have to start by bending the figure at the waist, and then twisting and tilting each body part all the way up through the hand in order to get it around the ball. Chances are you wouldn't get it right the first time so you'd have to keep tweaking each part until you get the hand in just the right spot.

To speed things up, choose the Figure > Use Inverse Kinematics option from the menu to turn IK ON for the applicable hand until your pose is complete. It also helps to have the Use Limits command ON before you move anything. Then you can 'grab' the hand with the Translate/Pull tool as shown in Figure 3.13. But be careful—if you drag too quickly you may still end up with your figure twisting like a pretzel. Move slowly and gently toward your target until you develop a feel for it. Remember: *baby steps!* You'll see the remaining body parts move accordingly. And, if you do this with Auto Balance turned on (see Tutorial 3.5, your figure will balance itself automatically. Turn IK OFF when you're done.

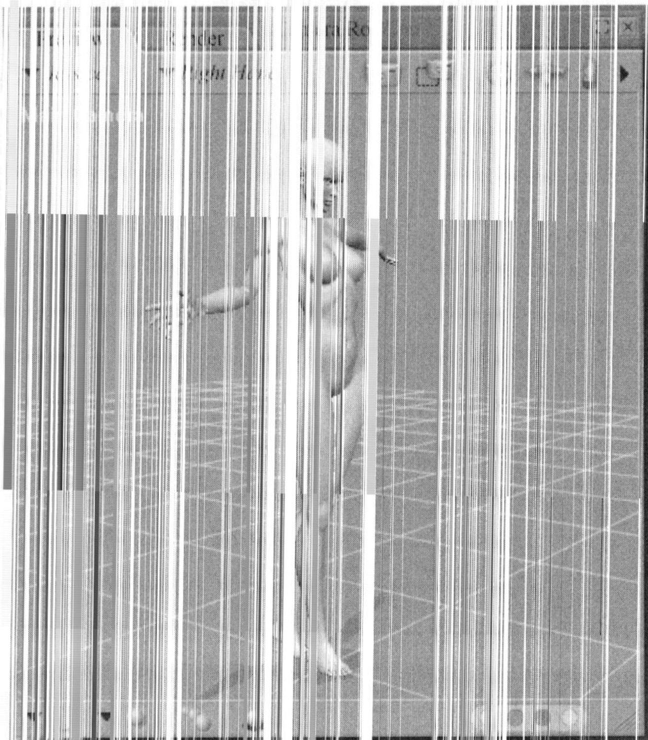

FIGURE 3.13 Turn Inverse Kinematics ON for posing hands and feet. With Auto Balance and Use Limits enabled you can move a hand into position. The other parts will follow and the figure will balance itself into a believable pose. Just remember to go slowly.

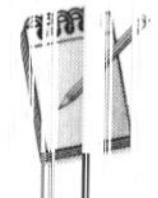

Normally, when you drag a figure's body part, Poser displays your scene in Fast Tracking Mode, which shows all objects as boxes while you move parts of your scene. This helps conserve on system resources. If your system resources allow, you can choose Display > Tracking > Full Tracking to view your objects in their geometric form while you move parts.

Preventing Accidental Changes

There will be times when you have some parts posed exactly as you want them, but other parts still need adjustment. You can prevent changes from occurring to body parts or props by locking them in place. There are a number of different ways to accomplish this. To lock one or more body parts and prevent changes to the pose, select the Object > Lock Actor command from the menu. The command must be applied to one body part or object at a time. Alternatively, you can use the Chain Break tool in the Editing Tools palette to lock part of a hierarchy chain in place.

To prevent changes to the pose of *any* part of the figure, choose the Figure > Lock Figure command from the menu. Make sure you select the figure that you want to lock and not any clothing that the figure might be wearing.

If you have meticulously posed the hands of your figure—around an object, for example—and they are exactly as you want them, you can use the Figure > Lock Hand Parts menu command to lock the fingers. This command prevents any changes to occur to the pose of the fingers in relation to the hand. You can still bend or twist the entire hand, but individual fingers will be prevented from moving.

Faces and Eyes are Poseable

One of the most common critiques of images created from people who are new to Poser is that images frequently show faces that have a "blank stare." The eyes are staring straight ahead and apparently not focusing on anything. One of the reasons for this may be because beginners aren't aware that *eyes are poseable*! Also, beginners may not be aware of the arsenal of expression morphs available in the Parameters palette for the Poser 6 figures (Figure 3.14). (You'll find them when you select the figure's head.) In addition, within the Expression > Ben, Kate, James, or Jessi library is a Random Face pose that will automatically generate random facial expressions for your Poser 6 figures. The Random Face pose parameter can yield some unique expressions!

To alleviate the 'blank stare syndrome' you'll need to become familiar with the mechanisms of getting your figure's eyes to look like they are focusing on the same thing. The most direct method is to pose one eye and then enter duplicate parameter settings for the remaining eye. To begin, either click the eye you want to pose or select it from the body parts list in the Parameters palette. You'll see two dials in the parameters window related to that eye: Up-Down (which makes the eye look upward or downward) and Side-Side (which makes the eye look toward the left or right). Get the first eye looking someplace that looks good for your scene, then select the other eye and manually enter the same Up-Down and Side-Side values. Now both eyes will be pointing toward the same place.

An alternative method for posing eyes and one that will make your figure look directly into the camera is to select the Object > Point At menu command. For example, if you want to use the Main camera to render your final image and want the figure to look directly into the camera, click each of the eyes and select the Object > Point At menu command. In both cases, when the Choose Actor dialog opens, select Main Camera from the list and click OK.

FIGURE 3.14 Faces and eyes are poseable and are a crucial part of any successful image.

For those cases where you want your figure to be focused on something within your scene—for example, their fist as they grasp an object—you can use the Object > Point At menu command. When the Choose Actor dialog opens, select the object that you want the eye to focus on from the list and click OK. Repeat for the other eye. The benefit of using this method to pose, or focus, the eyes of your figure is that you can then move an object or body part that the eyes are pointing at and they will automatically track the object.

Hands Can Be Expressive

Hands are often ignored during posing, which is a shame because a well-posed hand can do much to convey a mood or support the believability of your scene. Hand poses are a big part of body language; a clenched fist can convey anger while a relaxed hand pose can convey gentleness or serenity, for example. Figure 3.15 shows a 'before and after' example of a woman reaching upward, as if to grab something from over her head. Notice in the"before" (left) picture that her right arm and hand appear very stiff and unnatural, and that the left arm looks rigid. With a little bit of adjustment in the arms and hands, the "after" (right) image appears more natural and graceful.

It's a good idea to develop a standard procedure when posing a humanoid figure, and using your own body as a reference works remarkably well. Before you start, decide how closely your Poser figure will follow your own body standard; begin with the collar and consider how far forward and backward you can move *your* collarbone; become familiar with how much you can twist, bend, and rotate *your* shoulder comfortably; study your hands and wrist as *you* perform various grasping and expressive motions; and finally, pay attention to the differences of your joints, like your forearm, which doesn't rotate so much as bend and twist.

A good strategy for posing figures realistically is to think 'comfort' and what is practical for the mood and situation that you're trying to convey. In general, the more extreme you make your pose, the more work you'll need to do to make your audience believe it. For example, you might physically be able to bend your hand back at the wrist to about 85 degrees, but it's not natural looking or comfortable to do so—a 45-degree bend is much more natural and common. So, unless your figure is in an extreme situation, you might do best to stick with moderate poses that don't take push the limits of your parameters.

When posing hands, a good place to start is with the poses in the Hand libraries. You'll find standard poses for the Poser 6 male, Poser female, and the Poser 6 kids. Pick a hand position that comes close to your vision and work from there. To select one of the poses from the Hand Library, browse to locate the pose you want and click the Apply Library Preset button. A dialog asks if you want to apply the pose to your figure's right hand or left hand. Make your choice to apply the hand pose.

To fine-tune your hand pose, select the appropriate part in the Parameters palette (Right or Left Hand) and then work on the fingers individually or take advantage of the multi-finger pose controls like the Grasp, ThumbGrasp, and Spread. These parameter dials are shown in Figure 3.16.

Adding Scenery

In addition to clothing and posing your figure, you'll probably want to add more objects or figures to your scene. Adding additional figures makes it easier if you move your existing figure off of the default zero coordinate of your scene. To move your figure, select the hip or the entire body and use the X and Z Trans dials in the Parameters palette to move it sideways,

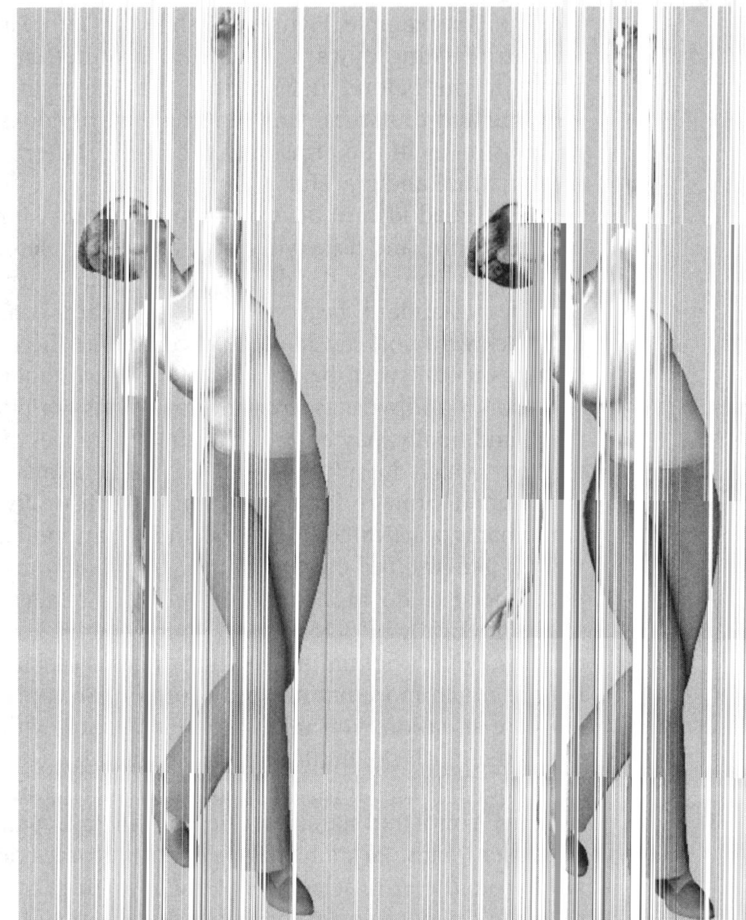

FIGURE [illegible].15 Hand poses are an important part of any figure pose. They affect the mood and presentation of your character and, if done well, make the entire image appear more natural and believable.

forward or backward. This will make room for the next figure you add, which will initially appear in the center of your scene.

There is a wealth of content furnished with Poser. You can find even more content online at numerous Poser communities. In addition to clothing for your figures, you'll find settings, scenery, accessories, props, textures, and much, much more.

Poser 6 comes with a wonderful scenery/set package, generously provided by Runtime DNA, which you'll find in the Figures > Runtime DNA > MicroCosm library accessible through the Library Palette. There are three parts to this figure: the MacroCosm (for a large scene); the Micro-

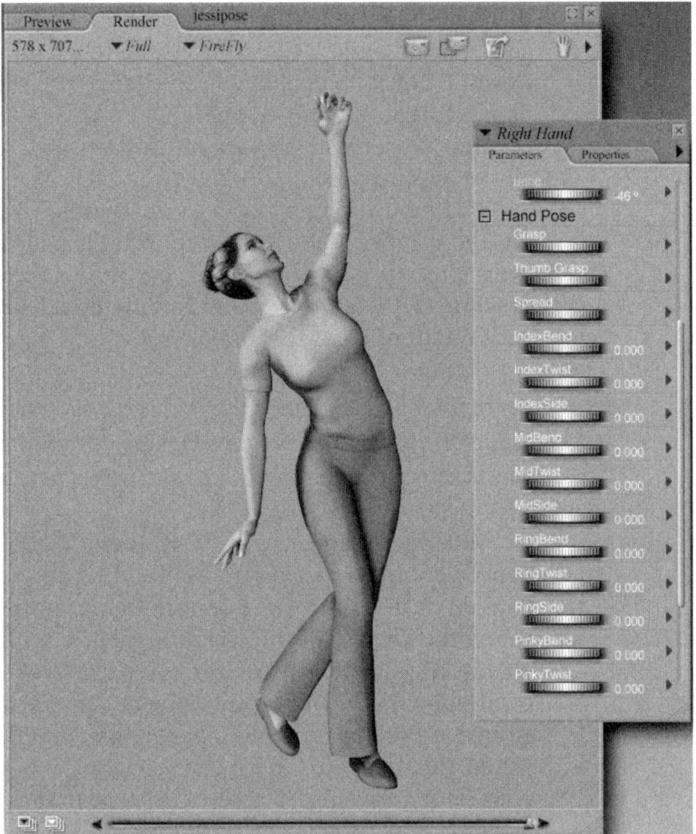

FIGURE 3.16 Standard poses for figure hands allow you to pose one or more fingers or finger parts at once.

Cosm (for a smaller scene); and a textured sky dome. Double-click the 'Macro Round 01 Tile' to add the large set to your scene. Then double-click the 'Sky Dome' to add it to your scene as well.

You can find complete instructions for using the MicroCosmLE set furnished with Poser 6 at Runtime DNA. The URL for the tutorial is http://www.rdna3d.com/Tutorials/MicroCosmLE.pdf. In addition, Runtime DNA has the full-featured version, MicroCosm, which has many add-ons and expansion sets available through its site (http://www.runtimedna.com), or through Content Paradise. (MicroCosm is a fully modular terrain-building system for Poser.)

After you add the MicroCosmLE item to your scene, select it. The set/scenery figure is named *Macro LgMap*, and it has one body part called *GPlane*. Open the Poses > Runtime DNA > MicroCosm library accessible through the Library Palette. You'll find the INJ Micros' pose, which will add morph targets and the associated parameter dials to the MicroCosmLE object to enable you to change the shape and appearance of the figure. Injection poses add parameter dials to an object, but they don't set the morphs for you, so you will still need to pose them, set either manually or apply a pose.

The mouse cursor turns to an hourglass during the process of injecting the morphs into the MacroCosmLE figure. After your morphs have been injected, new morphs appear in the Parameters window as shown in Figure 3.17. After the new parameter dials appear, you can experiment with different looks for the MacroCosmLE figure.

Depending on the speed and "horsepower" of your computer, the size of your object definition file, the number and complexity of the morph targets, and their associated parameters, injecting morphs can take quite a long [illegible].

When you render with your MacroCosmLE set, it may look like your figure got buried in a mound of sand, as shown in Figure 3.18. This may happen as a result of the terrain being morphed so that your figure is below the surface of the terrain, or *inside* a hill instead of on top of the terrain. If you morph the terrain excessively, you can actually have a condition where your figures, objects, support figures, and cameras are all inside the terrain while your lights remain above the terrain surface. When this happens, the terrain actually blocks the light from reaching your figure, causing your scene to render very dark or even completely black. The solution is to raise your figures, objects, and other props to the same level as, or higher than, the terrain.

While your initial impulse might be to use the menu command Figure > Drop to Floor to raise the position of your figure above the surface of the terrain, in this instance it will not fix your problem. This is because the Figure > Drop to Floor command only works effectively when the level of your ground terrain is at the default ground level for your scene. The Figure > Drop to Floor command actually resets the Y position, or vertical placement, of your object to zero. Since the current situation is one where the surface of our terrain is well above the scene's ground level, the Figure > Drop to Floor command won't fix our problem.

A great way to see the position of objects that may be obscured by others is to change the Document Style to Outline mode (Display > Document Style > Outline). Then choose one of the orthographic cameras (such as the right, left, front, and so on.) to view the scene, and you will be able to adjust your objects positions easily. For example, viewing through the left camera will allow you to adjust the position of the figure

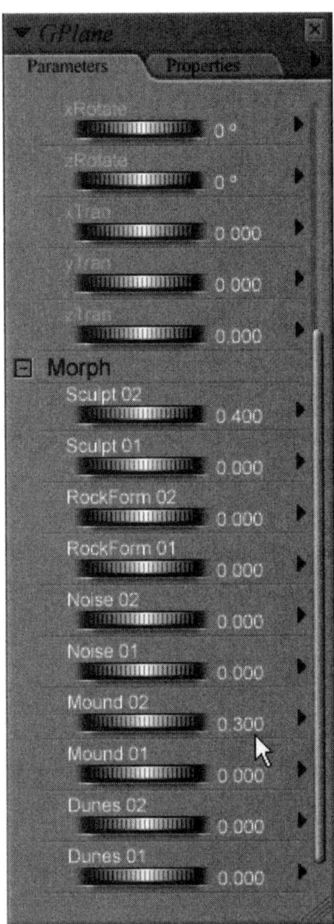

FIGURE 3.17 After you inject morphs into the MacroCosmLE object, you find new dials that help you shape the terrain.

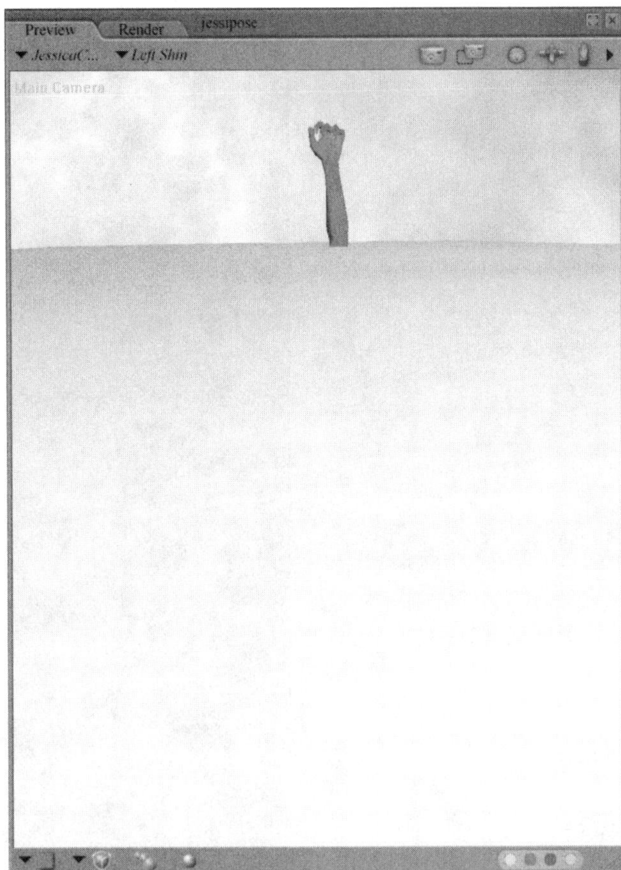

FIGURE 3.18 Where did Jessi go? She's under the surface of the terrain object, inside the hill. Select the hip or body, and adjust the Y Trans setting to raise her above the surface.

that is above the surface of the terrain. To adjust the position, Select the body or the hip of the figure you want to move (in this case, Jessica Casual), and increase the Y Trans setting until you see the feet match up with the height of the terrain. See Figure 3.19. for an example of Jessi's feet positioned above the terrain.

Once you're satisfied that your feet are touching the terrain properly, return your Main Camera view back to Texture Shaded display style. Because your figure is now in a different location you may find that your camera and lighting need to be adjusted. You'll learn more about those techniques in the following two chapters.

FIGURE 3.19 One way to simplify the positioning of objects in relation to each other is to take advantage of Poser's Outline style mode. If you adjust the YTran setting while viewing your scene in Outline style and use an orthographic camera, you can easily determine exactly where the feet touch the terrain.

After things are posed the way you like, you can go to the Material Room to apply one of the materials that comes with the MicroCosmLE figure. You'll find materials for it in the Materials > Runtime DNA > MicroCosm folder, accessed through the Library Palette. Use the Material Editor to select the Macro LgMap object and then its Ground surface. Double-click a material to apply it to the ground. The final result of our material selection is shown in Figure 3.20. Don't forget to use the File > Save menu command to save the project to your hard drive.

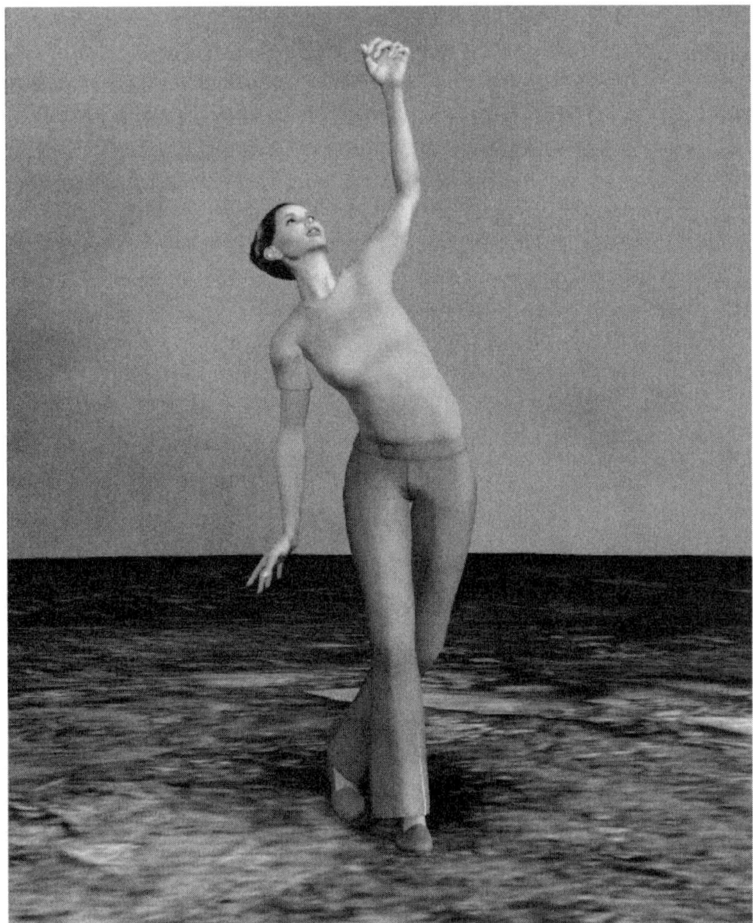

FIGURE 3.20 With everything in place and textured, Jessi now looks like she's really standing on surface of the terrain.

CONCLUSION

In this chapter you learned how to add a figure and apply conforming clothing to it. You also learned how to *zero pose* a figure, and use many of Poser's features to create and edit poses to make them more natural looking. You also learned how to add an environmental figure to your Poser scene and position your figure within that environment. The scene isn't yet complete—you still have cameras and lights to fine-tune to make your scene look its best. We'll tackle cameras in the next chapter.

Further reading about Building Scenes can be found in the Frequently Asked Questions appendix.

CHAPTER

4

USING CAMERAS

In This Chapter

- Camera Overview
- Using the Camera Controls
- Conclusion

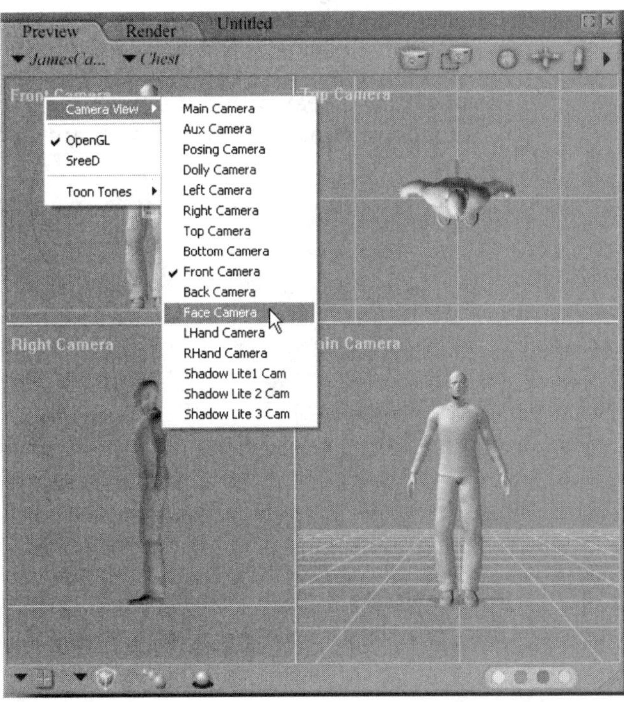

When you first create a new Poser scene, Poser displays the contents through the Main Camera. By default, this camera is set to view your scene through a 38-millimeter lens that is typically suitable for landscape renders and long-range scenes. There are several other cameras in Poser, and each of them has controls that are similar to real-world cameras. You can modify the camera properties and save them in several ways. In this chapter, you'll learn how to use Poser's cameras for different applications. You'll also learn how to save your own custom cameras, and how to point cameras and objects at each other.

CAMERA OVERVIEW

Poser comes with 15 different camera presets that can help you build and render scenes. Cameras can help you accomplish other tasks as well. For example, you can use the *Orthogonal Cameras* (From Right, From Left, From Top, From Bottom, From Front, and From Back) to help you customize and position characters and objects, position magnets, and set up joints for character development. You can use the *Left Hand Camera* and *Right Hand Camera* to help you pose a figure's hand to get the fingers just right.

Part of the versatility and power of Poser is the ease with which you can switch between the available cameras. The two most obvious ways to change your current camera view are with the interactive Camera Controls that appear within the Poser workspace, or with the Display > Camera menu options. Both methods are shown in Figure 4.1.

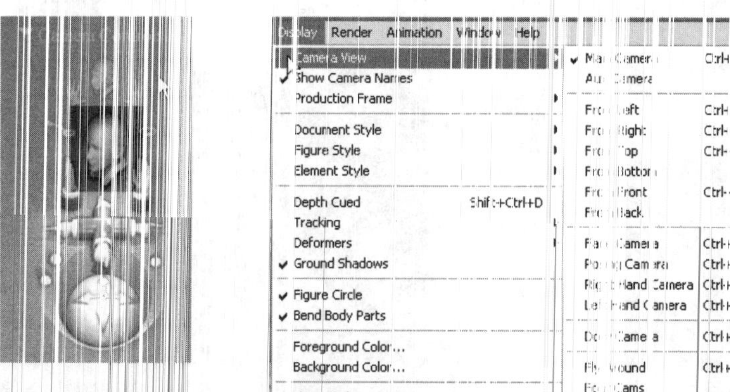

FIGURE 4.1 Use the Camera Selector in the interactive Camera Controls (left), or the Display > Camera menu command (right) to choose a camera view.

You can create final renders from any of the cameras in Poser.

Poser's cameras are intended to help you accomplish many diverse tasks and accommodate a variety of personal work styles and needs.

The *Main Camera, Auxiliary Camera,* and *Posing Camera* all work in a similar manner; they rotate about the center of your scene. (The focus of rotation can be changed, but by default, these cameras rotate around the center of the scene.) Most people happily stick with the Main Camera to compose *and* render their final scene; however, there are other cameras available: The Auxiliary Camera is an excellent tool to compose your scene from different viewpoints without having to change the position of your Main Camera, rather than using up several Pose Dots. The Posing Camera can be used to move around while posing the various body parts, props, and objects in your scene. Since there are two other cameras that operate in basically the same way, you might just move this camera around as a posing tool, without regard to where it ends up because it isn't used in any final renders.

The *Face Camera,* Left Hand Camera, and Right Hand Camera are specialized cameras that are specifically configured to assist you while you develop facial expressions or style hair or pose hands, for example. These cameras are, by default, centered on the body part for which they are named. They are invaluable tools that allow you to zoom around either the head of your figure or its hands, and view your work from many angles, easily and quickly.

The *Dolly Camera* is a unique camera in that it rotates about its own center, unlike the other perspective cameras that rotate around a point or object in your scene. The *Dolly Camera* is extremely useful for duplicating that traditional Hollywood-style camera movement in animations.

The Orthogonal Cameras (Right, Left, Front, Back, Top, and Bottom) are very useful when you are setting up joint parameters, positioning magnets, placing objects on top of other objects, resting things on the floor, and other instances where a perspective view makes it difficult to determine the exact position of objects. An orthogonal camera uses a technique called *orthogonal projection* that shows the view without any perspective distortions. To get an idea of how this is accomplished, imagine holding a huge sheet of X-Ray film in front of your camera, and then shooting parallel X-Rays from the very opposite side of your scene to expose an exact 'image shadow' of your objects onto the film. The key here is that the X-Rays are parallel. This means that objects are displayed at their actual sizes, regardless of how distant they are from the camera. Orthogonal cameras move along two of the three spatial axes, which vary depending on the camera view..

When you work with orthogonal cameras, you will probably find that having several up at once is a great help. You can divide your preview window into several camera views to allow you to view left, right, top, and bottom for quick and accurate placement of objects with respect to each other. Tutorial 4.1 shows you how to accomplish this.

TUTORIAL 4.1 USING AND SELECTING MULTIPLE CAMERA VIEWS

Poser 6 allows you to see more than one camera view at a time in your preview window. This is handy when you are trying to position content in your scene. You can select which camera to display in each of the views. To configure the preview window to display more than one camera, follow these steps:

1. From the menu, choose File > New to create a new scene in Poser. James Casual appears in the scene by default (unless you have made changes to your default settings).
2. Locate the Document Window Layout menu in the lower-left corner of the Document window. The Document Window Layout menu appears near the mouse pointer in Figure 4.2.
3. Click the down arrow to display the Document Window layout menu options. The Full Pane option displays one camera and is the default selection. Additional options divide the document window into two, three, or four camera views.

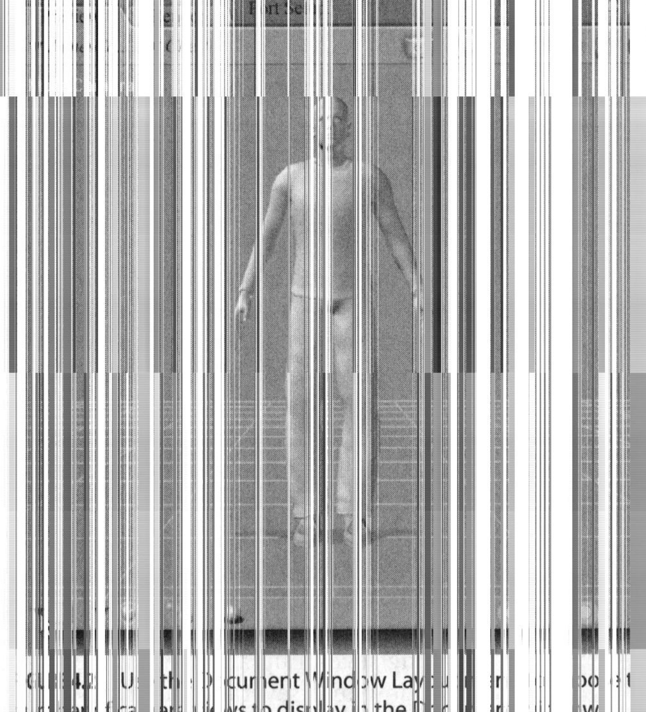

FIGURE 4.2 Use the Document Window Layout menu to choose the number of camera views to display in the Document window.

4. For this tutorial, choose "Four Ports". This divides the document window into four equal parts. By default, the views are Front Camera and Top Camera in the top row and Right Camera and Main Camera in the bottom row.

You can also choose the Display > Camera View > Four Cams menu command to display four camera views in the document window. To return to a single camera view document window, choose "Full Pane" from the Document Window Layout menu in the lower-left corner of the document window.

5. To change the camera that is displayed in one of the camera ports, right-click on the camera name. Choose "Camera View", and then drag right to open the menu shown in Figure 4.3. Then choose the camera that you want to display.

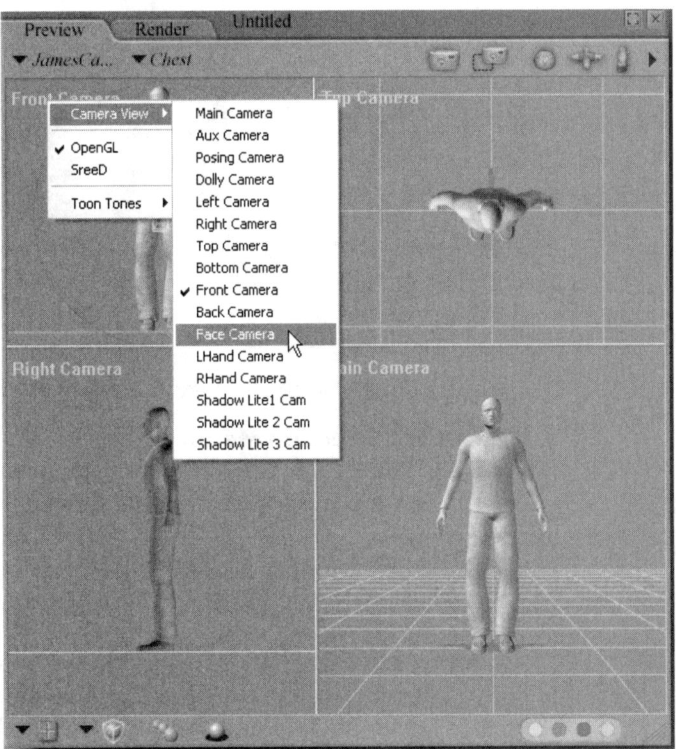

FIGURE 4.3 To change the camera that is displayed in a camera port, right-click the camera name to display the *Camera View* selection menu and select a camera from the list.

USING THE CAMERA CONTROLS

The Camera Controls, shown in Figure 4.4, allow you to interactively select and position cameras for various purposes. By default, the Main Camera is selected.

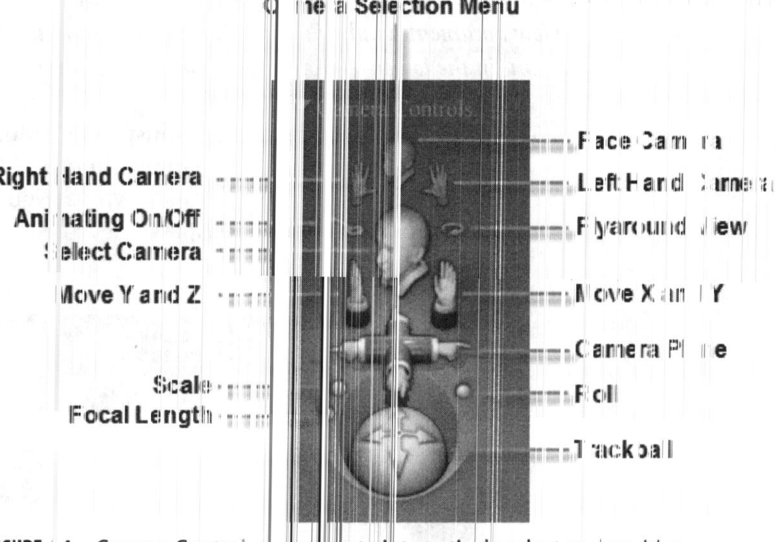

FIGURE 4.4 Camera Controls allow you to interactively select and position cameras.

The Camera Controls make the following functions available:

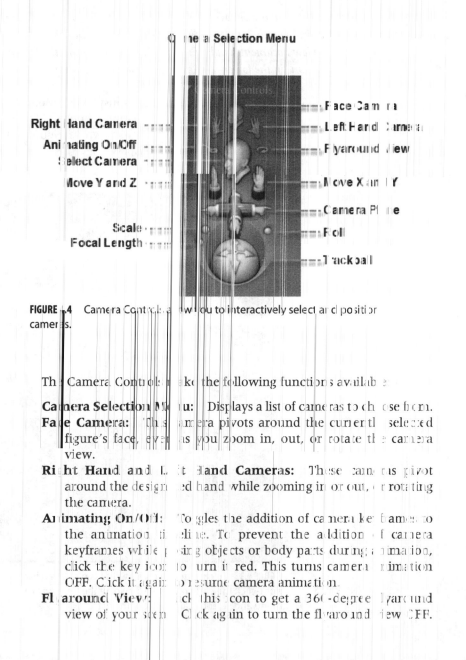

Camera Selection Menu: Displays a list of cameras to choose from.

Face Camera: This camera pivots around the currently selected figure's face, even as you zoom in, out, or rotate the camera view.

Right Hand and Left Hand Cameras: These cameras pivot around the designated hand while zooming in or out, or rotating the camera.

Animating On/Off: Toggles the addition of camera keyframes to the animation timeline. To prevent the addition of camera keyframes while posing objects or body parts during animation, click the key icon to turn it red. This turns camera animation OFF. Click it again to resume camera animation.

Flyaround View: Click this icon to get a 360-degree flyaround view of your scene. Click again to turn the flyaround view OFF.

Select Camera: Click to cycle through the various camera views: Main, Top, Front, Left, Right, Face, Posing, Left Hand, Right Hand, Dolly, Back, Bottom, and Auxiliary.

Move Y and Z: Click and drag left or right to move the camera along the Z (forward/backward) plane. Drag up or down to move the camera along the Y (up/down) plane.

Move X and Y: Click and drag left or right to move the camera along the X (left/right) plane. Click and drag up or down to move the camera along the Y (up/down) plane.

Camera Plane: Click and drag left or right to move the camera along the X (left/right) axis, or up or down to move the camera along the Z (forward or back) axis.

Scale: This zooms into or out from the scene without affecting focal or perspective settings.

Roll: Click and drag to roll the camera clockwise or counterclockwise.

Focal Length: Click and drag toward the left to decrease the camera's focal length; click and drag toward the right to increase the focal length.

Trackball: Drag the trackball to rotate the camera around its center; drag in the direction you want the camera to rotate.

TUTORIAL 4.2 ADJUSTING CAMERAS

The Parameters window contains dials that allow you to set camera parameters. Many of the parameters are the same as those in the interactive Camera Controls area. The Parameter window allows access to additional settings for the cameras. To view the parameters and properties of a camera as shown in Figure 4.5, select the camera from the menu at the top of the Parameters window.

The parameters are as follows:

Focal: Sets the camera's *focal length*. The default setting of the Main Camera is 38 millimeters, which is great for landscape renders because this focal length results in a fairly wide field of view. Smaller focal lengths produce a noticeable "fisheye" effect as more and more of the surrounding view is compressed into the camera's field of view.

Perspective: The perspective setting is usually calculated automatically by Poser and is the same as the focal setting. You can change the perspective of your current camera and zoom in or out without affecting the physical location of your camera. Changing this setting from the automatically calculated default

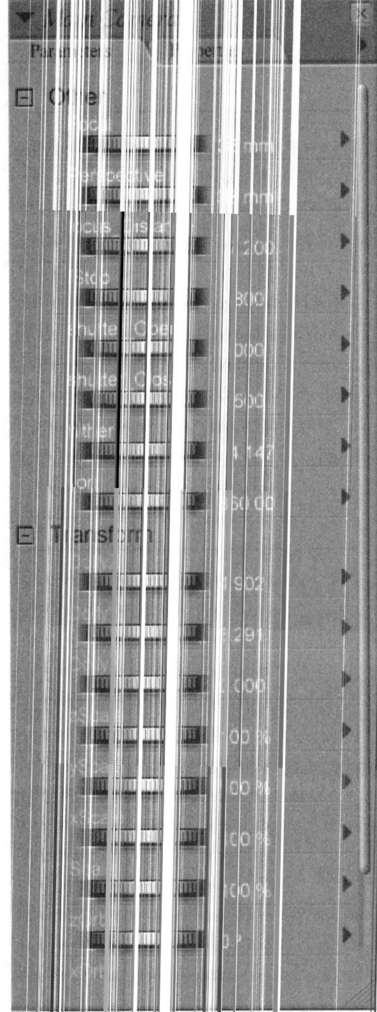

FIGURE 4.5 Poser camera parameters mimic settings found in real-world cameras.

can be confusing, so unless you have a reason, it's probably best to leave it at default.

Focus Distance: This setting allows you to specify the distance at which objects will be most in focus. A focus indicator moves backward or forward through the scene to indicate where focus will occur. Objects that are farther away from the focal plane will be blurred.

F-Stop: The F-Stop is a measure of the size of the lens aperture (the opening that allows light to come in to the camera during an exposure).

shutter_Open and **shutter_Close:** These two settings represent the point in an animation frame when the camera shutter opens and when the camera shutter closes. 0.0 represents the beginning of a frame, and 1.0 represents the end of a frame. The results of this setting are only visible when you activate 3D motion blur.

Hither: This setting controls the location of the *clipping plane*, which is a specified distance from the camera that defines what objects are visible. Anything between the camera and the clipping plane will not appear in the preview window. Once you get past the clipping plane you will see the objects in your scene. Figure 4.6 shows what happens if an object is too close to the Hither setting. If you see portions of your object disappear as if being dissected along the same plane, decrease the Hither setting until you can view the entire object.

Yon: This setting controls the far end of the clipping plane. Anything that lies beyond the Yon setting will not appear in your preview window. This parameter only applies with Open GL hardware rendering.

F-Stop settings determine the depth of field for your renders. The depth of field is a measure of how far in front of, and how far behind, your focus distance objects will remain in focus. A good rule of thumb about the relationship between F-Stop and depth of field is that the higher the F-Stop, the deeper (or longer), the field of focus. (For a quick explanation with examples explaining depth of field you can try the following online resources: http://www.dofmaster.com/dof_defined.html, and http://www.azuswebworks.com/photography/dof.html.)

A standard 'all purpose' camera lens in the real world is the 35 millimeter (35 mm), which you may recognize since most real-world, general-purpose cameras are referred to as '35mm Cameras.' The human eye sees the world using approximately a 60 mm lens. In the real world, 50 mm to roughly 70 mm lenses are recommended for portraiture. In fact, a 50 mm lens is called a 'portrait' lens by professional photographers and is considered a reasonably 'flat perspective' lens. Finally, a 135 mm lens is the start of the telephoto, or zoom lenses. A telephoto lens will make things appear closer to the camera and focus on a tighter region. An additional effect of using a telephoto-range lens is that your objects will appear very flat, or approach an orthogonal view. Poser does a great job mimicking real-world camera physics but you'll have to find your own comfort zones and preferences when working with various Focal settings and subjects.

FIGURE 4.6 If your object is too close to the Hither setting, parts of it may disappear. Decrease the Hither setting if portions of an object appear to be cut away by the camera plane.

When you create a new Poser scene, the Main Camera is set to 38 millimeters. The Face Camera is set to 50 millimeters. Renders can benefit from very simple adjustments to the cameras from their default values. It has been our experience that Poser cameras tend to *very slightly* exaggerate the lower focal length distortion, causing a bit more of a fisheye effect than real-world cameras might. This is partly because it's a common tendency when working with Poser to position the camera closer to subjects than would normally happen in the real world.

We suggest adding [illegible] millimeters to your cameras to get flatter and more compressed-looking objects. In fact, settings of both the Main Camera and the Face Camera can be doubled to ensure that your render does not look as though it is viewed through a fisheye lens. Many Poser users suggest camera settings of 80 to 120 millimeters for portrait work—this allows them to get a nice, full frame without having to worry about fisheye distortion.

In this tutorial, you'll make some simple adjustments to the Main and Face Cameras to reduce the fisheye effect in your renders:

1. From the menu choose File > New to create a new scene. James Casual appears in your document window (unless you have changed the default options).
2. Because document window size will affect camera settings in this tutorial, from the menu choose Window > Document Window Size, and enter dimensions of 500 width and 500 height. Click OK to resize the window.
3. Verify that the Document window displays the view from the Main Camera (the camera name appears in the upper-left corner of the window). Then use the selection menu in the Parameters window to choose Cameras > Main Camera. The Main Camera properties appear in the Parameters window.
4. Use the Camera Controls to interactively position and zoom the camera so that James' head and shoulders appear in the frame, similar to Figure 4.7. If you wish to position your camera exactly the same as what is in the figure, enter the following values in the Parameters window: DollyZ –6.880; DollyY 5.953; DollyX –0.090; zOrbit 0; xOrbit –4; and yOrbit 19.

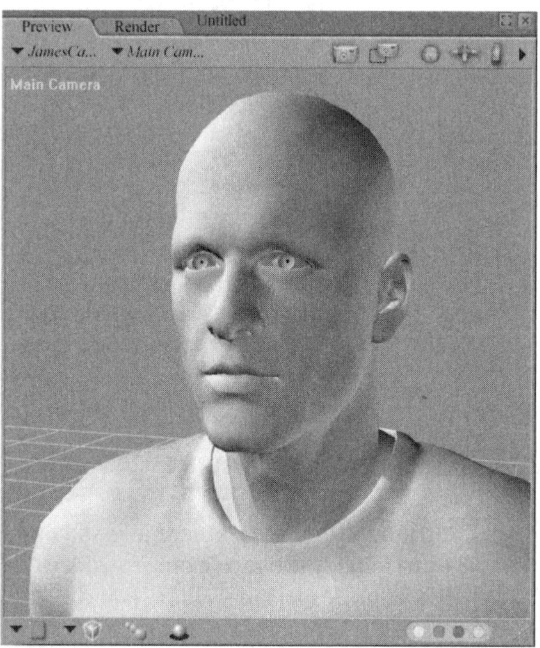

FIGURE 4.7 Zoom in so that James' head and shoulders fill the Main Camera view.

5. Notice that when the Main Camera is set for 38 millimeters, the head appears to be slightly distorted as if being viewed though a fisheye lens—the nose and chin seem quite large and out of proportion with the rest of the face. To remove some of this distortion, first change the millimeter setting on the camera. Increase the Focal setting to 80 millimeters.
6. After you adjust the focal setting, you'll notice that James moves closer toward the camera. Use the Camera Plane controls to move him away from the camera or adjust the DollyZ setting to −4.902. Now James' face should look similar to Figure 4.8. Continue from here making adjustments to the camera settings to suit your own preferences.

FIGURE 4.8 James looks more normal with a camera that has an 80-millimeter lens that is positioned slightly farther away.

TUTORIAL 4.3 CREATING AND SAVING CAMERAS

Although the Face Camera allows you to focus on the face, it is also helpful to look at the face from front, left, and right sides without perspective distortion, especially when you are trying to position magnets to create custom morphs for facial features and expressions. In this tutorial, you'll use some of the camera's Transform parameters to position and create useful head cameras.

The Transform parameters are very similar to those you see in any other object:

Dolly X, Y, and Z: The dolly settings move the camera left or right (X), up or down (Y), or forward and backward (Z).

x, y, and zScale: The x, y, and zScale settings scale the camera's width (X), height (Y), or depth (Z). In addition, the Scale setting increases or decreases the overall size of the camera.

x, y, and zOrbit: The x, y, and zOrbit settings rotate the cameras forward to backward (X), around (Y), or side to side (Z)

Roll, Pitch, and Yaw: These settings apply to the Dolly, Posing, Face, and Hand cameras and how they rotate around their own axes. Positive Roll settings turn the camera to its left (scene's right); positive Pitch settings make the camera pitch upward (scene appears to go downward); and positive Yaw settings tilt the camera to the left (scene appears to tilt right).

While the process to make these cameras is somewhat similar for all Poser figures, you'll create a set of cameras for James Casual here. These cameras will allow you to view his head from the front, back, left, and right when you add him to a Poser document from the library. To create and save the cameras, follow these steps:

1. Choose File > New from the menu to create a new scene. James Casual appears by default (unless you have changed the default settings).
2. From the menu, choose Display > Camera > From Front. This switches to the Front Camera view.
3. If the Parameters window is not open, select Window > Parameters from the menu to display it. Use the pull-down menu at the top of the Parameters window to display the parameters for the Front Camera as shown in Figure 4.9.
4. Adjust the Dolly Y setting and the Scale settings until you get a close-up of James' head. You'll find that you need settings of 44.000 for the Dolly Y parameter (which moves the camera up or down), and about 14% for the Scale parameter to be in the right ballpark.
5. To save this camera to the library, first open the Poser 6 Camera library in the Library Palette. At the top level of the Camera Library you should find a folder named Camera Sets.

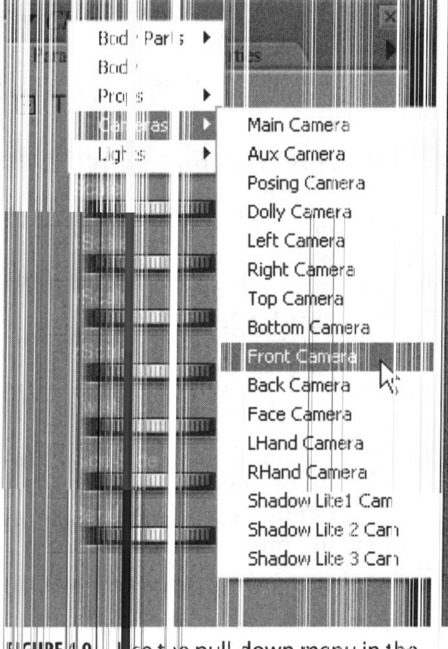

FIGURE 4.9 Use the pull-down menu in the Parameters window to select the Front Camera.

6. Expand the Camera Library menu as shown in Figure 4.10, and choose Add New Category. In the Library Name dialog, name the new library "James Head Cameras." Click OK to create the new library entry and folder on your hard drive.
7. Double-click the newly created library folder to open it. Then click the Add to Library button at the bottom of the Library Palette window. The New Set dialog appears.
8. Enter "James Head Front" for the camera set name. Then click the Select Subset button.
9. The Hierarchy Selection dialog displays all of the cameras you can choose from. In this case, you only need to select the Front Camera, which you used to create your current camera view. Check the Front Camera then choose OK to return to the New Set dialog.
10. Choose OK again to display the Save Frames dialog, which asks if you want to save a single-frame or multi-frame animation camera. Choose Single Frame and click OK. The new camera appears in the library.

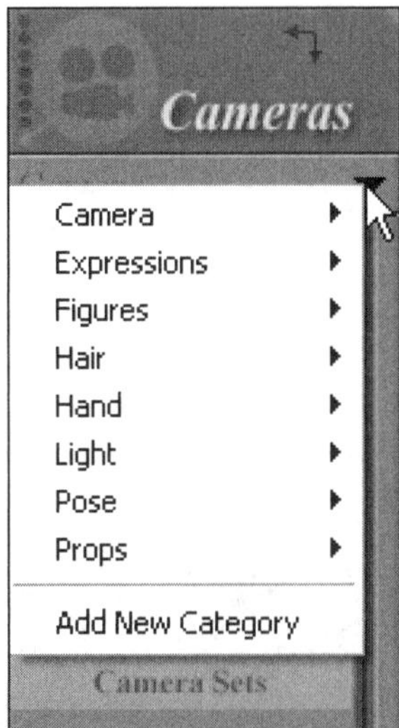

FIGURE 4.10 Expand the menu in the Camera library to create a new category.

11. For the Left Camera, select Display > Camera View > From Left from the menu. Then from the Parameters window select the Left Camera from the pull-down menu.
12. Set the Dolly Y parameter to 44. This will position it at the same height as the Front Camera. Then set the Scale to 14%.
13. Adjust the Dolly X setting until the head is centered in the document window (a setting of 1.000 works well).
14. Repeat Steps 7 through 10 to save the new camera as "James Head Left."
15. You can create Back and Right Head Cameras for James as well. When you're finished, your James Head Cameras library will look as shown in Figure 4.11. And you'll have a complete set of cameras that you can use while creating head morphs for James, or for checking out his head textures.

Refer to the Frequently Asked Questions appendix at the end of this book for information on how you can use camera dots to save cameras that you frequently use, or how to memorize and restore one camera that gets saved with your Poser project.

FIGURE 4.1 Four Head Cameras (Back, Front, Left, and Right) are created and saved for James.

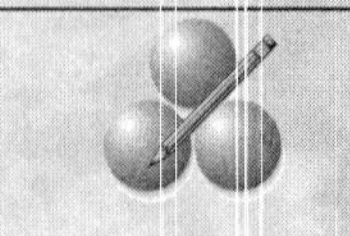

TUTORIAL 4.4 POINTING AND PARENTING CAMERAS AND OBJECTS

Poser cameras can track any object in your scene; conversely, any item in your scene can follow the position of a camera. For example, let's say you create an animation in which your figure walks around the scene in a circle. You can set up the project so that the camera always points at the head of this figure. As a result, the figure remains centered in the camera view while it walks around the scene.

In a similar manner, you can also point objects toward a camera. For example, you can point the eyes of a character so that it is always looking at a camera. Posing the eyes of your figure helps to get rid of the "blank stare syndrome" that the default eye position is famous for creating in renders. Posed eyes help give your character life and personality.

In addition to using the Point At feature to pose eyes, you can also use the Up-Down and Side-Side parameter dials.

To point eyes at a camera, follow these steps:

1. Pose your figure—get everything but the eyes exactly the way you want it.
2. Choose the camera that you would like to use for your final render. For this example, move the Main Camera closer to your figure's face for a portrait render. (The Face Camera is not available as a Point At option.)
3. Click one eye to select it. The object list beneath the Render tab displays *rightEye* or *leftEye* when either eye is selected.
4. Select *Object > Point At* from the menu. The Choose Actor dialog shown in Figure 4.12 appears. Notice that this dialog allows you to point the eye at anything in your scene. You can point it at an object the character is holding, for example; or another figure in the scene.
5. Choose the camera that you selected in Step 2 (in our case, the Main Camera). You can also choose "None" to remove a previous Point At choice. Then click OK to apply the setting.

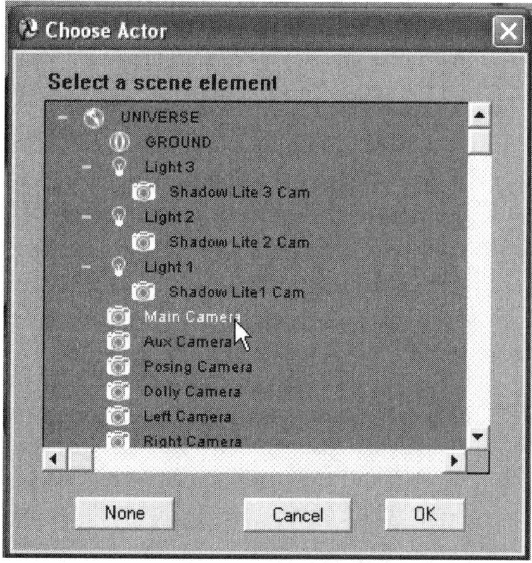

FIGURE 4.12 The Choose Actor dialog allows you to point an object toward any other figure, body part, object, light, or camera in your scene.

6. When you return to the Document window, one eye should be pointing at your camera. Select the other eye, and repeat Steps 4 and 5 to point it at the same camera. Figure 4.13 shows the eyes before and after they are posed. Notice the difference it can make to an image.

FIGURE 4.13 Before his eyes were posed, James had a blank stare (left). Once his eyes are pointed at the camera, James comes to life (right).

CONCLUSION

In this chapter you were introduced to several things you can do with the Poser cameras. The Camera Controls help you select and position cameras interactively. The Camera Parameters allow you to adjust settings and positions for a camera, one parameter at a time. You can point objects at the camera or point the camera at other objects.

Now that you've learned how to use cameras to improve the way your scene looks, you'll learn how to light your scene to improve your renders even more.

CHAPTER

5

MASTERING LIGHTS AND SHADOWS

In This Chapter

- An Overview of Lighting
- Poser 6 Light Types
- Poser 6 Shadow Types
- Lighting Controls
- Light Parameters and Properties
- Conclusion

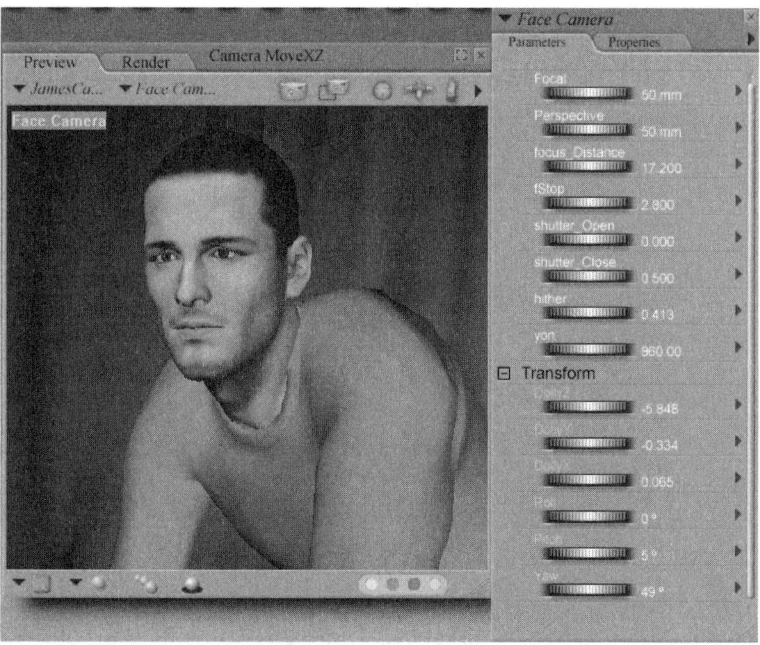

An Overview of Lighting

Ask any accomplished 3D artist and they will tell you that the *single most important thing* that can make or break a render is lighting!

Lighting adds realism and texture to a scene in ways that can't be accomplished with models or textures alone. Even detailed models and meticulously crafted textures will look mediocre if you don't pay attention to the way you light your scene. Poor lighting choices can make a render look dull and lifeless. Carefully planned lighting can make an image or scene come alive. With the new lighting and shadow features in Poser 6, what you can achieve is comparable what you would expect to see from software costing several times more.

In this chapter, you'll learn the basics of creating your own light setups. Starting from an unlit scene, you'll learn how to configure a standard three-point lighting system that will lay the groundwork for your understanding of how lights work. You'll also learn about the different types of lights and shadows and how to achieve the best results with them. You'll be able to create and modify light sets and make your renders look their best.

Poser 6 Light Types

There are four types of lights in Poser 6: *Infinite Lights, Spotlights, Point Lights*, and *Image-Based Lights*. Each of these light types shares similar properties such as color, angle, intensity, and a few other parameters. However, each type of light distributes light in a different way. Figure 5.1 shows a comparison of the four types of lights. All lights are configured to illuminate the figure's head.

- **Infinite Lights** shine light at the same angle throughout your scene. When you add an Infinite Light to your scene all of the content will be lit from the same angle and on the same side. For example, you can add a pale yellow Infinite Light to simulate sunlight or a pale blue Infinite Light to simulate moonlight in your scene. The light from an Infinite Light is parallel, resulting in orthogonal lighting.
- **Spotlights** shine light from a single point of origin and cast their light in a cone-shape. Spotlights are similar to lights used by photographers or in stage productions. You can control the angle and distance of the cone, allowing you to create lighting effects such as street lamps, candlelight, or the light from a crackling fire. Use the Angle End setting to adjust the size of the area that will be illuminated; higher values light larger areas while lower values light smaller areas.
- **Point Lights** are *omnidirectional* (meaning that they shine light in all directions from a central point). Point Lights are also called *global lights*. A soft Point Light in your scene can prevent total darkness in your render and give your scene a minimum threshold of ambient

light. Take care not to make point lights too bright, because they can wash out your scene and make it appear flat. Because point lights cast light in all directions throughout the scene it might take a long time to calculate depth map shadows. For that reason, these lights cast ray-traced shadows only.

- **Image-Based Lights** (IBLs) are new in Poser 6. They simulate many different colors in a single light. The colors and placement of the light in your scene are derived from an image or movie that you specify. The end result makes your render appear as if your character is actually a part of the original image or movie, making it a great choice for work that requires photorealism. Image-Based Lighting is *diffuse-only,* meaning that if you want specular highlights in your scene (such as eye glints or highlights in hair) you will need additional lighting that is not Image-Based lighting.

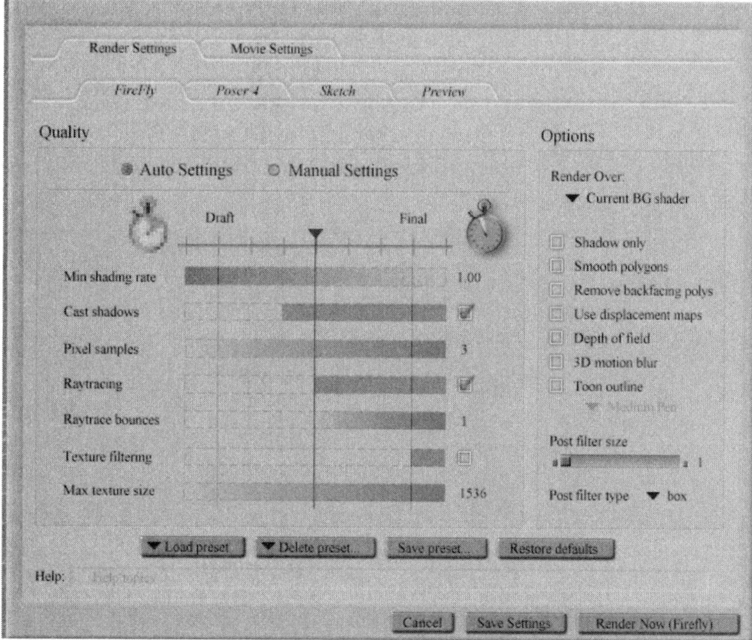

FIGURE 5.1 There are four types of lights in Poser 6: Infinite lights, Spotlights, Point Lights, and Image Based Lights.

POSER 6 SHADOW TYPES

You can choose which lights cast shadows in your scene. It is common practice to cast shadows from only one light in your scene, which results in reduced rendering times.

Lights in Poser 6 can cast several different types of shadows:

Depth Map Shadows: When you use Depth Map Shadows, Poser generates a shadow map for each light that uses them. By default, the shadow map for each light is 256 × 256 pixels. You can increase the shadow map size if the shadows look pixilated. Larger sizes produce more defined and accurate shadows, but also use more resources. (Remember that doubling your shadow map size will add four times the number of pixels that need to be calculated for the map.) You can also control the amount of blur on Depth Map Shadows with controls in the Properties window that is associated with the light. Depth Map Shadows are the best option for when you want shadows with softer edges and faster render times in general.

Raytrace Shadows: Raytrace Shadows are typically very sharp, and also very accurate with respect to the original shapes of the object meshes. They are calculated during the render, rather than before the render as is the case with Depth Map Shadows. Render times are significantly increased when using Raytrace Shadows. For the best results, use the Firefly render engine in Poser 6 with quality settings at least halfway, as shown in Figure 5.2. Raytrace shadows will not render when Firefly is set to draft render mode.

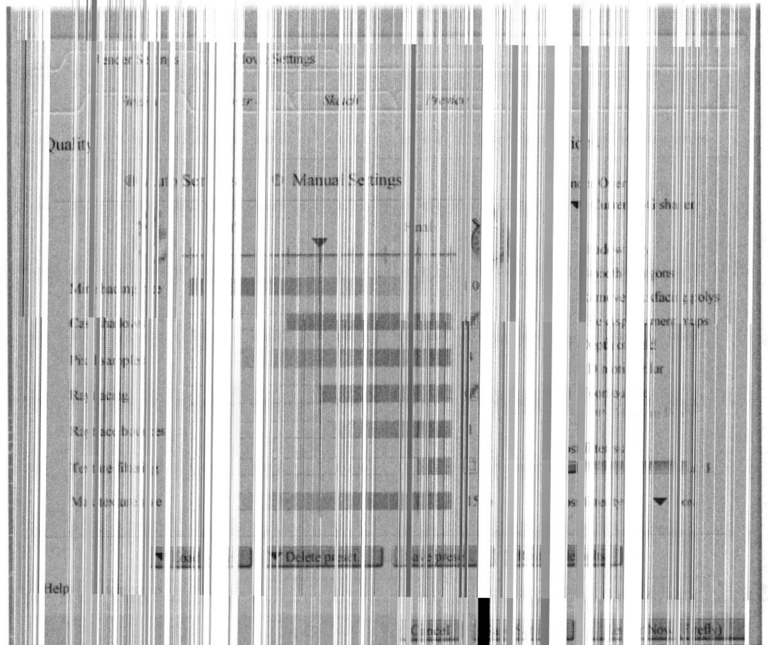

FIGURE 5.2 When using ray-traced lights, set the Firefly render quality settings to at least the halfway point if you want to also calculate Raytrace Shadows.

Ambient Occlusion: adds additional contrast to images by reducing the amount of ambient light in the shadows, making them appear darker. This option is typically used with Image-Based Lighting, but can also be used with the other light types.

LIGHTING CONTROLS

The Light Controls are shown in Figure 5.3. You can show or hide the light controls in the Pose Room, Material Room, Hair Room, or Cloth Room. To toggle the display of the light controls, choose Window > Light Controls.

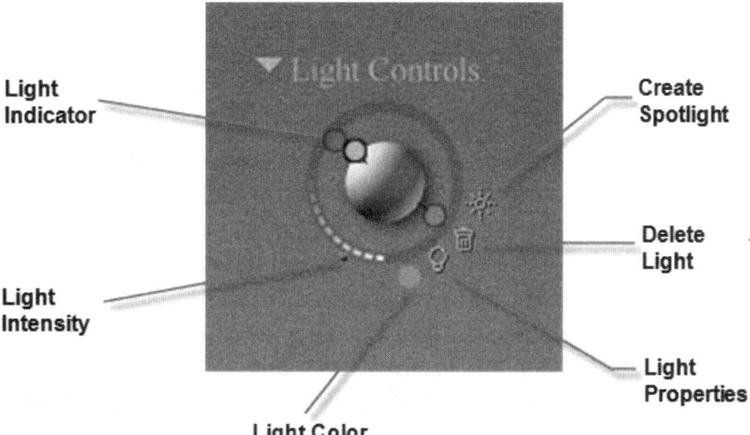

FIGURE 5.3 The Light Controls help you create, color, and position the lights in your scene.

A shadow map is basically a depth map of the scene as viewed from the light's point of view. The purpose of a shadow-depth map is to tell the render engine how far the effect of the light goes and which surfaces are in the front of others, from the light's perspective. At render time, the shadow map for each light is consulted to see if the spot on the currently calculating ray/object is receiving light from the light source or if it is in the shadow of another object or another part of itself.

What's the big deal about Ambient Occlusion? Diffuse reflection is a term that relates to the physics of light bouncing off of matte surfaces onto other surfaces. It is very expensive to take into account diffuse reflection accurately, so most render engines

have a tendency to create darker-than-real-world lighting because they only approximate real-world conditions and must make concessions to performance. In general, this means that when you want to create a more accurate-looking render, more light needs to be added to the mix; however, each light costs a great deal in terms of resources needed to render the scene. To approximate usable ambient lighting, you need to add dozens of lights at a minimum, so you can imagine the amount of computing power that can be consumed. The shortcut to ambient lighting is not to add dozens of discrete lights, but to add a global ambient lighting component. With global ambient lighting, no point on an object is totally in the dark. This is a great 'cheap' fix, but its downside is that basic ambient-lighting algorithms cause areas to look flat and they do not account for the cracks and shadows created by objects being close to each other. So, you had to choose between speedy renders that resulted in washed-out flat renders with global ambient light, or use dozens of lights and wait days for your render to finish. This is where ambient occlusion saves the day.

Ambient Occlusion is a measure of how much ambient light a point on the surface of an object surface is likely to receive. It works by simulating a huge dome light that surrounds the entire scene and then determining if a surface point is under or behind another object, for example, a spot behind your figure's ear. If it is, that point is marked as needing to be dark and it needs to end up much darker than the top-most object, say the top of your figure's head. This occlusion map is used at render time to darken the ambient levels where appropriate. This is a subtle and potent lighting effect that adds quite a bit of realism to renders without all of the expense of adding many diffuse lights to your scene. Ambient occlusion calculations still take up render time, but are not nearly as costly as brute-forcing the effect by using dozens of individually calculated light sources.

The light controls help you add, change, or remove lights from your scene as follows:

Create Spotlight: Click to create a new light, which is configured as a Spotlight by default. New lights generally appear above and to the right of the document window (left side facing you).

Delete Light: Deletes the currently selected light. Verify that you have selected the correct light before you delete it, as this action is not reversible.

Light Properties: Displays the properties of the currently selected light in the Properties window.

Light Colors: Click the Light Color icon to open a color picker, and select a new color for the light.

Light Intensity: Adjusts the brightness of the light from 0 to 100 percent.

Light Indicator: Click and drag a Light Indicator around the globe to position the light in your scene. The center of the globe represents the center of your camera view. As you rotate the camera, the positions of the lights move according to where they are with respect to your scene and the current camera view.

Light Parameters and Properties

After you create a light, you can select it in several different ways. In the Light Controls area, click one of the small circles around the globe to select the light you want to edit. You can also select a light from the parts list that appears at the top of the document window (just beneath the Render tab). You can also use the menu command, Window > Parameters, to open the Parameters window and select a light from the top pull-down menu. To view the properties for the light click the Properties tab. The parameters and properties for lights are shown in Figure 5.4.

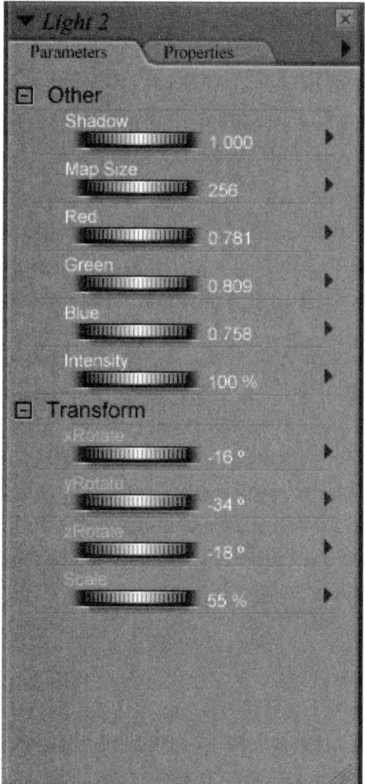

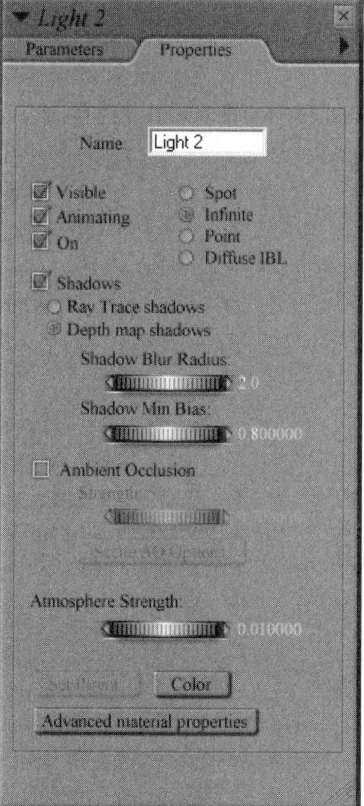

FIGURE 5.4 The Parameters and Properties of a light define the color, position, light type, shadow type, and much more.

You will find the following light settings in the Parameters window:

Shadow: Sets the strength of the shadow that is projected by the light. A value of 1 indicates 100% shadow strength. A value of 0 disables the shadow. Intermediate values make the shadow lighter or darker.

Map Size: Defines the size of the Depth Shadow Map for the associated light. The default is 256, which fits the shadow for the associated light into a 256 × 256-pixel square. Lower values can result in shadows with very rough, pixilated edges. Higher values create sharper shadows but also consume more system resources and rendering time.

Red, Green, and Blue: Defines the amount of Red, Green, and Blue that are mixed to create the light color. When all three values are set to 1, the resulting 'color' will be white (or a Red, Green, Blue value of 255, 255, 255). Color values are also automatically set when you choose a light color from the Light Controls color selector.

Intensity: Sets the strength of the light. The default intensity setting is 100%. Lower values create a dimmer light and higher values create a brighter light.

The selections in the Properties window provide the following functions:

Visible: Check to display the Light Indicator in the Document window. Uncheck this option to hide the Light Indicator.

Animating: On by default, this option creates a keyframe when you make changes to a light in any frame but the first frame. This allows you to animate light properties such as color, position, rotation, or intensity. Uncheck this option if you want your light to remain the same throughout an entire animation.

On: When unchecked, turns the light off so that it no longer shines light.

Shadows: Check this option if you want your light to cast shadows. It takes longer to render scenes in which multiple lights cast shadows. If you choose to cast shadows, choose one of the types of shadows (Ray Trace or Depth Map Shadows as introduced earlier).

TUTORIAL 5.1 DELETING LIGHTS

You may find that you have unnecessary lights in your scene. For example, when you create a new scene in Poser you get three infinite lights by default. (Light 1 is olive green in color and appears at the figure's right. Light 2 is gray and is the center light in the scene. Light 3 is a shade of orange and appears at the figure's left side.) Rather than editing each light individually, it might be easier to just start over. You may wish to delete these and create your own defaults. You may encounter situations when you purchase or download light sets that have so many extra lights turned OFF that it just makes sense to delete them. Or you might want to remove all of the lights in the scene and start from scratch.

There are two different ways to remove lights; in the first method you select and delete one light at a time; in the second method you delete all lights at once:

1. Use the menu command File > New to create a new scene for this tutorial. James Casual appears in the document window by default, with three lights.
2. Select one of the lights using any of the following methods, as shown in Figure 5.5:
   - Click one of the light indicators that appear around the globe in the Light Controls (1).
   - Choose a light from the Parts List beneath the Render tab in the Document window (2).
   - Choose a light from the Parts List in the Parameters window (3).

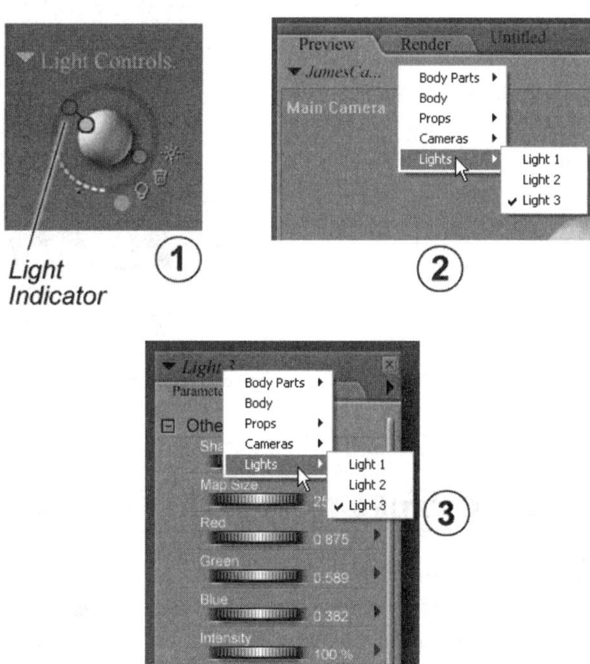

FIGURE 5.5 To select a light: click a light indicator (1), use the menu in the document window (2), or choose a light from the Parameters window (3).

3. To delete the selected light, click the Delete (trash can) icon in the Light Controls or use the Figure > Delete Figure menu command.
4. You can use a Python script to delete all lights in your scene. To begin, choose Window > Python Scripts from the menu. The Python Scripts window appears.
5. Click the Utility Funcs button. The Python Script menu shown in Figure 5.6 appears.
6. Click the Delete All Lights button. All lights in your scene are removed.

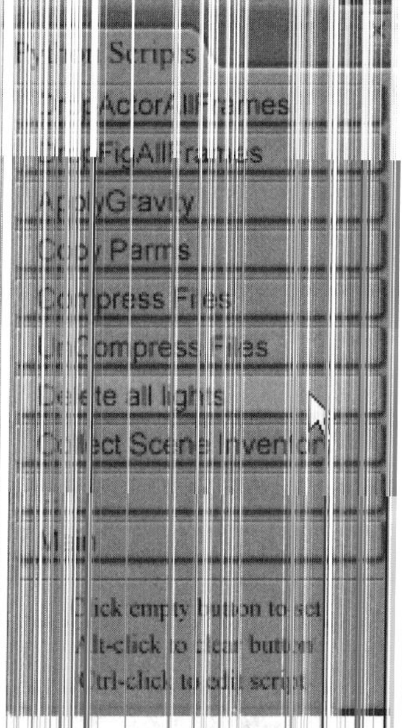

FIGURE 5.6 Use the Delete All Lights Python Script menu to delete all of the lights in your scene.

TUTORIAL 5.2 CREATING THREE-POINT STUDIO LIGHTING

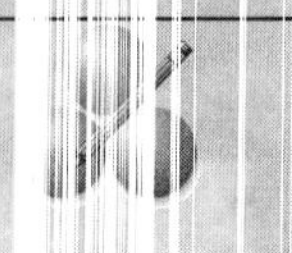

A versatile lighting setup for portrait or still-life photography is to use what is known as a *three-point lighting setup*. This lighting style typically uses three lights: a Key Light, a Fill Light, and a Back Light. In the following three-part tutorial, you'll learn more about the role each of these lights plays, and how to create them in Poser.

Before we get into the lighting part of our tutorial, we'll need to set up the scene.

1. Use the File > New menu command to create a new scene in Poser. James Casual appears in the scene.
2. Open the Poser 6 Poses Library in the Library Palette, and locate the James Pose > Sitting > On Chair library. Highlight the "On Chair 01" pose and apply it to James with the Apply Library Preset button.
3. Next we'll set up the Main Camera. For this tutorial, select the Face Camera. Position it as shown in Figure 5.7. Settings used here are default settings with the exception of the following: DollyZ -5.848012, DollyY -0.334330, and DollyX 0.064643, Pitch 5 degrees, and Yaw 49 degrees.

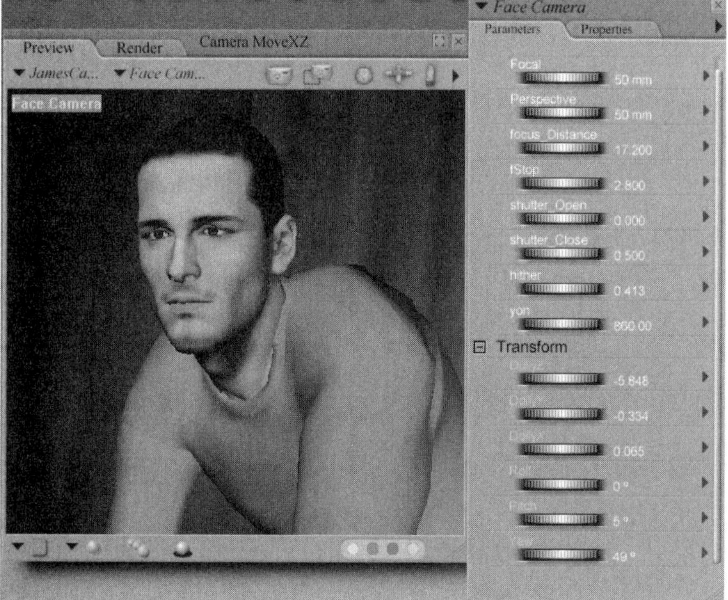

FIGURE 5.7 Position the Face Camera as shown here for your three-point lighting portrait render.

4. Use the Delete All Lights Python script (described in Tutorial 5.1) to delete the default lights. Your scene should now appear dark.

Creating the Key Light

The *Key Light* is the main light in the scene, and the one that defines the most visible lights and shadows. It typically appears anywhere between 15 and 45 degrees to the left or right of the camera, and 15 to 45 degrees higher than the camera. The lighting of a Key Light should appear similar to the lighting you want in your final scene, except that the shadows will be darker and have very harsh contrast. The most obvious choice for a Key Light is a spotlight that casts shadows.

5. When there are no lights in the scene, the Create Light icon is the only icon that appears in the Light Controls area. Click the icon to create a new light. The color of the light varies, but Poser usually places the light at about the 10 o'clock position near the Light Control globe. By default, Poser creates a spotlight, which is what we want to use for our Key Light.
6. We want to position our Key Light in front of the figure, and within 45 degrees of the Face Camera. When you see the light indicator in the exact center of the globe, it is in the same position as the current camera. To position the light appropriately for a Key Light, move the light indicator to the upper-left or upper-right area of the globe, as shown in Figure 5.3.

FIGURE 5.3 Position the light indicator above and to the left of the current camera position using the globe as reference.

7. With the Key Light in its proper position, the next step is to point it in the right direction. Select the camera and choose Object > Point At from the menu. Then, when the Choose Actor dialog appears, select James Casual's *head* as the object to point at.

8. White and gray lights are neutral color lights that don't modify the colors in the materials of the objects you are rendering. When the Red, Green, and Blue values are each set to 1, the light is pure white or gray, depending on the *Intensity* setting. Set the Red, Green, and Blue parameters to 1, and set the Intensity of the light to 100%. After you render, your image should look similar to Figure 5.9.

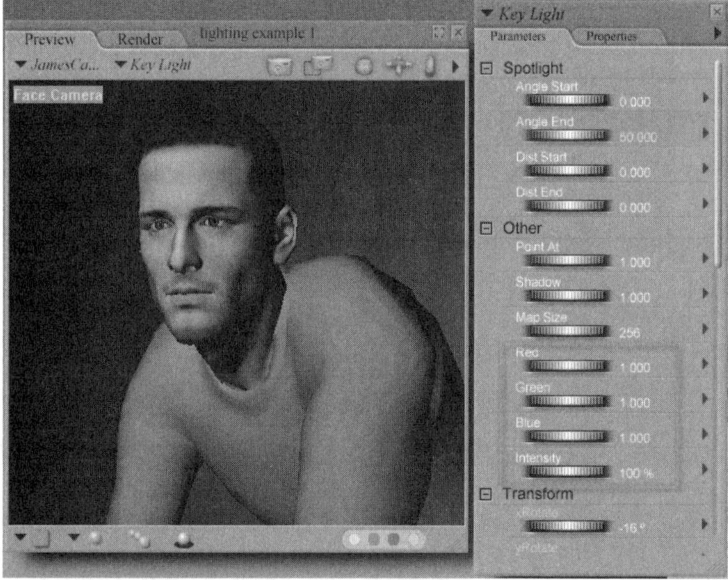

FIGURE 5.9 For pure white lighting, set the color parameters to 1; that is, Red, Green, and Blue all to a value of 1. Then set the intensity parameter to 100%.

9. If desired, adjust the Angle End setting of the light to light more or less of the area to your taste. For the example in this book, this value was left at the default of 70.
10. Go to the Parameters window, and click the Properties tab. Change the name of this light from "Light 1" to "Key Light". Press Enter to change the name.

Creating the Fill Light

The Fill Light softens the contrast of the Key Light, and makes more of the subject visible. The Fill Light usually comes from the opposite side of your Key Light (for example, if your Key Light is on the left, your Fill Light is on the right). Because they are typically used to add ambient color in your scene, Fill Lights are sometimes tinted to use a color that is predominant in the scene (such as blue for moonlight, or yellow for sunlight). Fills are usually about one-eighth to one-half as bright as the Key Light, depending upon how much shadow contrast you want in your final image. Spotlights can be used for Fill Lights, but Point Lights are more common. Shadows are optional. In addition, Fill Lights are sometimes created as diffuse-only lights, so that they do not add additional specular highlights to the scene in areas that are supposed to be shadowed.

To create the Fill Light, follow these steps:

1. Click the Create New Light icon again. A new light appears around the globe.
2. Move the Fill Light to the opposite side of the camera and toward the front. Asymmetric lighting tends to create a more dynamic and natural looking final result. Use your own judgment to place the camera so that the effect is pleasing to you. Figure 5.10 shows the new position for the Fill Light.

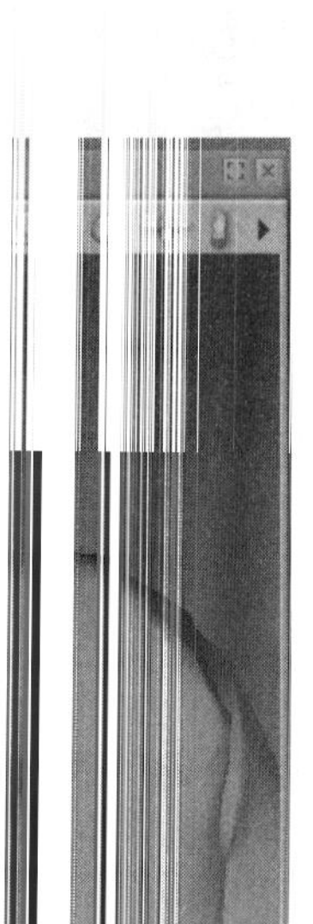

FIGURE 5.10 Position the Fill Light on the other side of the camera so that the effect is pleasing to you. Asymmetric lighting tends to create a more dynamic and natural looking final result.

3. If your scene has a backdrop or other scenery props, observe what the most predominant color is. If you don't want to use white as a fill, try to add a tint of that predominant color for ambience. For example, the curtain backdrop in this example is red, so a very pale shade of

red (somewhat pink) is selected for the Fill Light. (To change the color of the light, click the Light Color icon in the Light Controls.) The reason you do this is because in real life, light bounces off of all objects so that their colors interact with each other. By picking up a bit of the more predominant background color, you help simulate natural radiosity-type lighting effects and inter-object reflections.

4. When the color selector appears, select a color for your Fill Light, as shown in Figure 5.11. Try to select a less intense or pastel version of a color that is predominant in your scene. If, on the other hand, you would rather keep your Fill Lighting neutral, choose white or gray.

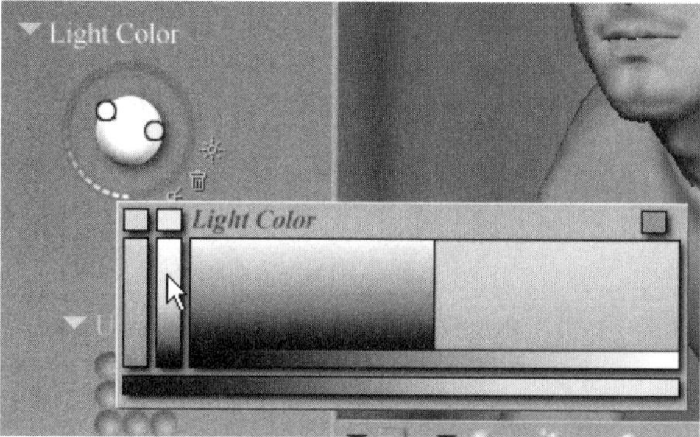

FIGURE 5.11 Try to select a less intense or pastel version of a color that is predominant in your scene for your Fill Lighting. If you would rather keep your Fill Lighting neutral, choose white or gray.

5. After you are satisfied with the color of your Fill Light, lower the intensity to somewhere between 20 and 80 percent (use 50 percent for this tutorial). Lower values will create more dramatic shadows. Higher values will create less contrast between lit and shadowed areas of your image.
6. Speaking of shadows, you might want to turn shadows off for the Fill Light. To do so, click the Properties tab (in the Parameters/Properties window). Uncheck the Shadows option. Try test renders with and without shadows to see which you prefer.
7. While you're in the Properties tab, change the name of the light to Fill Light. Then change the Fill Light to a Point Light as shown in Figure 5.12. This makes the Fill Light more closely match the Ambient Light, which fills the scene, rather than limiting it to the cone shape of a Spotlight.

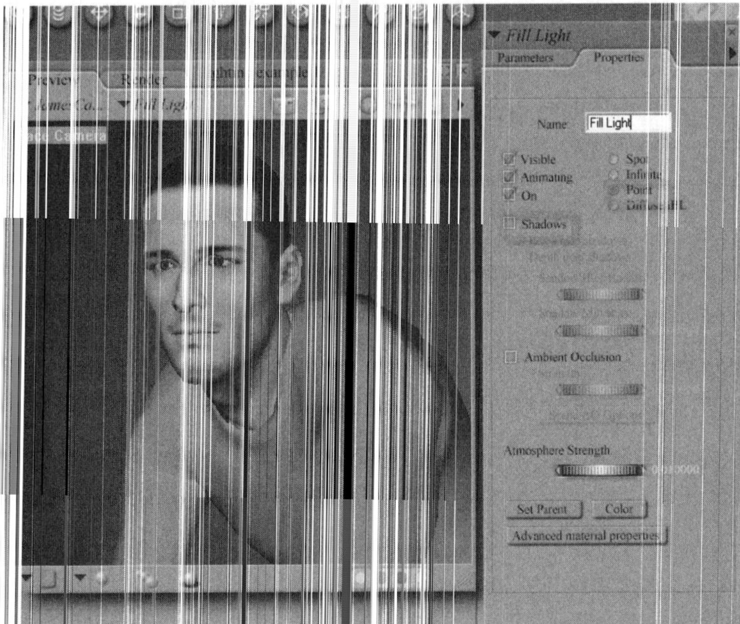

FIGURE 5.12 Optionally, turn off shadows for the Fill Light. Then change the light to a Point Light to make it behave more like Ambient Light, which fills the scene rather than limiting it to the cone shape of a Spotlight.

8. Now you can make the Fill Light diffuse-only, so that it will not add specular highlights that conflict with the main (key) light. First, click the Material tab to go into the Material Room.
9. The *Wacros* panel appears on the right-hand side of the material workspace. Click the Set Up Light Style button in the Wacros panel. (Wacros are scripts for the Poser 6 Material Room.)
10. A dialog prompts you to choose a light style for your current light. Verify that Fill Light (or the name of your Fill Light) is selected. Then choose Diffuse Only from the list of options in the dialog. Click OK to apply the new settings to the light.
11. Poser informs you that the light has been changed to diffuse-only. Click OK to exit the dialog.

Creating the Back Light

The Back Light appears above and behind the subject, and usually directly opposite the camera. The purpose of the Back Light is to separate the subject from the background by creating a rim of light around the top or side. A Spotlight or Point Light is good for a Back Light, and shadows are usually turned off since Back Lights are intended for highlights only, to pull the subject away from the background.

1. The easiest way to tell where the highlights will fall from the Back Light is to turn the other two lights off. Return to the Pose Room. Use the menu in the Properties window to select the Fill Light. Then uncheck the ON checkbox as shown in Figure 5.13. Repeat for the Key Light.

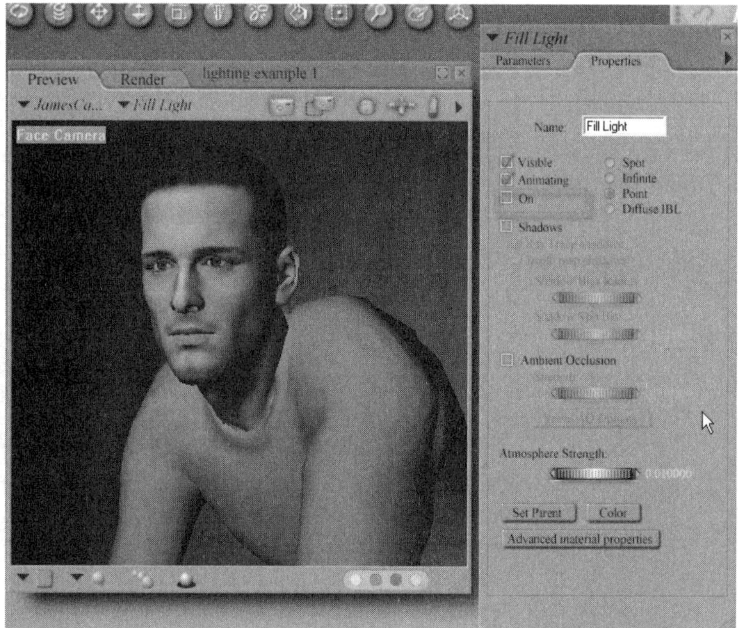

FIGURE 5.13 Turn the Key Light and Fill Light off so that you can see the highlights from the Back Light.

2. Click the Create Light icon for the third time. A new light appears around the globe.
3. In the Parameters window, change the color of the new light to white (Red, Green, and Blue values set to 1). Set the intensity to 115%. This will create a light that is slightly brighter than the others and will bring the highlights out when the light is behind the figure.

4. Verify that the light is still selected (if you changed the name of the other two lights, this new light should be named Light 1), and choose Object > Point At from the menu. Point the light at the figure's head.
5. In the Light Controls area, move the Light 1 indicator to the top and slightly behind the globe. Watch the document window until you get a backlighting effect that you are happy with. Figure 5.14 shows an example.

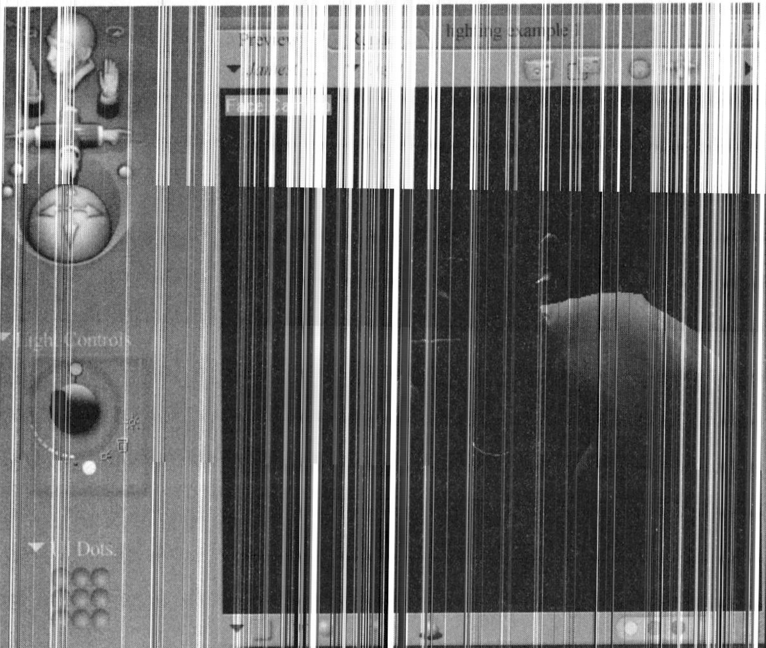

FIGURE 5.14 Adjust the position of the Back Light until you get a highlight that is acceptable.

6. Return to the Properties window and change the name of the current light to "Back Light". Uncheck the Shadows option.
7. While you're in the Properties window, choose the Key Light from the top menu in the Properties window. Turn it back on. Do the same for the Fill Light.
8. Render your result to check the final lighting. Make adjustments to your settings and tweak the light positions until you get the effect you want. Your scene should look similar to Figure 5.15.

FIGURE 5.15 A final rendered portrait using the three-point lighting technique.

Saving the Light Set

To save your final light set to the library, follow these steps:

1. In the Library Palette, select the Runtime folder in which you intend to save your light (for example, choose the Practical Poser 6 folder). Open the Lights Library within that Runtime.
2. Click the Add to Library button at the bottom of the library panel. The New Set dialog appears.
3. Enter a name for your new light set (such as James Portrait), and then click the Select Subset button. The Hierarchy Selection dialog appears and lists all lights in your scene.
4. Check the lights you want to include in the set. For example, if you want to include all three lights, check Key Light, Fill Light, and Back Light, as shown in Figure 5.16.
5. Click OK to return to the New Set dialog.
6. Click OK again to proceed. The Save Frames dialog appears. By default, the light settings will be saved from a single frame (which is the frame that currently appears in the document window). Accept the default, Single Frame, if you have not added keyframes to animate the lights. Then click OK to continue. The light set appears in your library, along with a thumbnail version of the scene as it was saved.

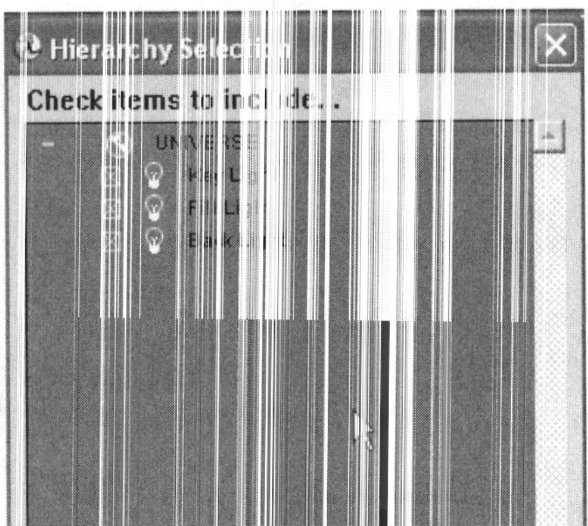

FIGURE 5.16 When saving a light set, make sure you choose the Select Subset button to check all lights in the Hierarchy Selection window.

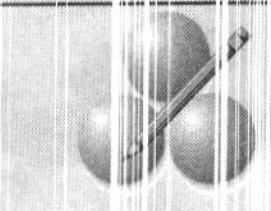

TUTORIAL 5.5 USING SHADOW LIGHT CAMERAS

Each light that you create in your scene has a camera associated with it. These cameras are called Shadow Light Cameras. They allow you to look into your scene as the light "sees" it, which is a great asset when you need position for lights and shadows to be accurate.

The following steps show you how to use Shadow Light cameras to refine the lighting that you created in Tutorial 5.2.

1. Using the scene that you created in the last tutorial, right-click on the camera name that appears in the document window. A selection menu appears.
2. Expand the Camera View submenu to display a list of cameras in your scene, as shown in Figure 5.17. At the bottom of the list you will see three Shadow Cam Lights. The numbers are assigned in the order in which you saved your cameras. Therefore, going by the previous tutorial, the lowest numbered light will be the Key Light; the next number will be the Fill Light; and the highest number will be the Back Light.

If you work with many lights in a scene it can become difficult keeping track of them all, especially when you try to remember which Shadow Cam Lites go with which light. Fortunately you can edit the names of the Shadow Cam Lites just like any other object in Poser—just open the Parameter window. The Name parameter is accessible under the Properties tab.

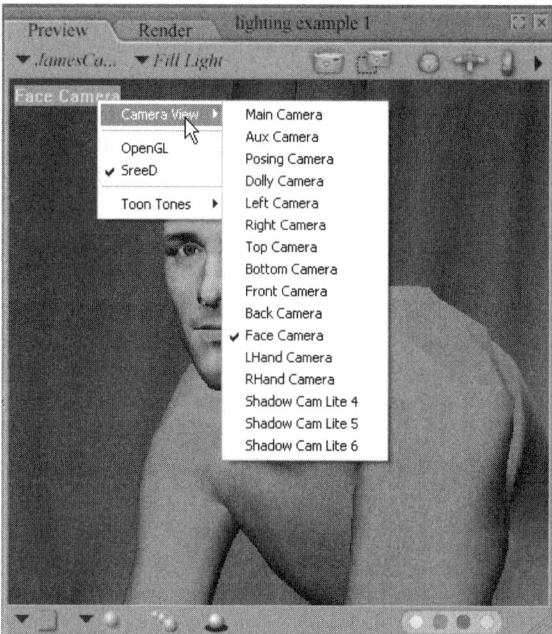

FIGURE 5.17 The shadow light cameras that appear in the Camera View menu are numbered in the order in which you created the lights.

3. Select the lowest-numbered Shadow Light camera. This should be the camera that looks through your Key Light. The Document window should update to look through the Shadow Light camera you've currently selected.
4. Open the Parameters window, and select the Key Light from its menu at the top.
5. Since the Key Light is now the current light, it will remain in the center of the Light Control globe no matter how you adjust the position of the light. For that reason, you'll find it much easier to use the Trans dials in the Parameters window to tweak the position of the Key Light while you observe the changes through the shadow camera:
   - Adjust the xTran dial to move the light left or right.
   - The yTran dial will move the light upward or downward.
   - The zTran dial will move the light forward or backward.

As you adjust the settings, think about where you want the shadows from the Key Light to fall. Remember that the shadows will fall in the direction from which you are viewing.

6. For Spotlights, make adjustments to the Angle Start and End settings as necessary. These settings control the starting and ending size of the light's cone, which increases or decreases the area that is covered by the light.
7. Spotlights and Point Lights also have Dist (Distance) Start and End settings. These settings control how near or far the light begins or ends from the point of origin. By default, light starts at the origin point (a setting of zero), and goes on infinitely (also a setting of 0). Adjust this setting to limit the range of your light. Figure 5.18 shows what happens after adjusting the Dist End setting of the Key Light. The left image is the default setting of 0. The right image shows a setting of about 13.5.
8. Adjust the strength of your shadow if necessary. If shadows are too dark, reduce the Shadow setting to a value below 1. A value of 0 turns the shadow off completely.
9. After your adjustments are made, choose the camera through which you want to render the image, and render your scene.

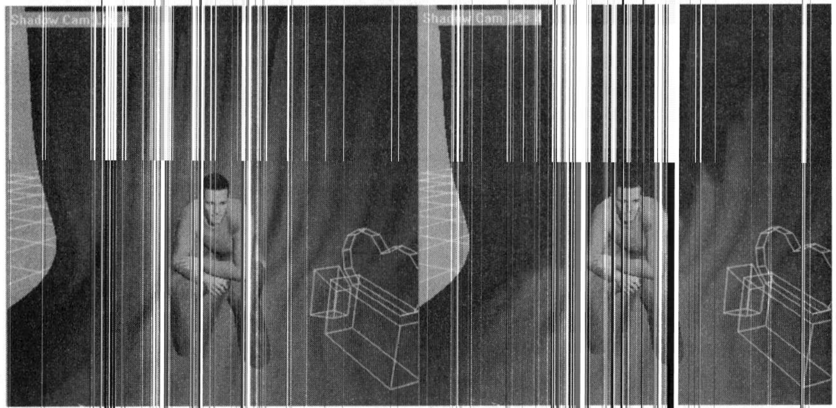

FIGURE 5.18 When you adjust the Dist End setting of a light, you control how near or far the light reaches from the point of origin.

TUTORIAL 5.4 USING PHOTOS AND IMAGE-BASED LIGHTING

One of the most exciting new features of Poser 6 is image based lighting (or IBL). Image-based lighting simulates the ambient colors in a photograph or movie, and lights your scene in a way that makes your Poser content appear as if it is part of the environment.

An Image-Based Light gets its light information from a *light probe*, which projects a photograph or movie onto a sphere to determine how the light will surround the content in your scene. In most cases, it makes sense to use the same image for your background and for the light probe. Figure 5.19 shows the comparison between a photograph and its associated light probe.

FIGURE 5.19 Light probes for Image-Based Lights use photographs or movies that are projected onto a sphere to determine the color and intensity of the light hitting the object in your scene.

While you can use a regular photograph as an image probe, you will get more accurate results with a spherical light probe. There are a couple of utilities that can help you make more accurate light probes. One such utility is HDR Shop, which at the time of this writing is free for non-commercial use and can be obtained from the Institute of Creative Technologies at http://www.ict.usc.edu/graphics/HDRShop/. An alternative is to use Flexify, which is reasonably-priced Photoshop-compatible plug-in available for purchase from Flaming Pear Software at http://www.flamingpear.com/flexify.html.

It is important to note that IBLs are diffuse-only. That is, they don't add highlights to an image. As a result, it's good practice to use other lights in addition to an IBL—for example, you can position a second light in approximately the same position as an IBL and use it for the specular highlights.

When using a standard three-point lighting arrangement with a photographic background, it seems a natural choice to use an IBL as a Fill Light so that you capture the ambient colors from the photograph or movie. If you use an IBL for your Fill Light, you might consider using the

Key Light to generate the predominant light in the scene (such as sunlight in an outdoor scene, or a streetlight or the moon in a night scene).

Poser 6 has also has a new feature that helps achieve more realism when using photos for a background. By default, the ground plane in Poser is set up as a *shadow catcher*. When set as a shadow catcher, the ground plane itself is invisible, but it captures the shadows as if the ground were solid. This allows you to apply realistic shadows to photographic backgrounds. If you align the default ground plane so that the perspective is the same as that in your photograph or movie, the ground plane will render a pretty decent low-cast shadow over the photographic background. It's a quick and simple solution.

To use the default ground plane as the floor in your scene, go to the Material Room and select the ground plane from the Object menu (Props > GROUND). Near the bottom of the Poser Surface window, uncheck the Shadow_Catch_Only option. This allows you to see the ground plane. To add a texture to the ground plane, click the Diffuse_Color node button and choose the node you wish to attach (such as a 2D Textures > Image Map node). You'll learn more about materials in Chapter 9, "Assigning and Creating Materials."

Adding a Photo Background

In this tutorial, we'll start with a default scene and load James Casual if he isn't already there. Then, add a photograph for the background image.

1. Choose File > New from the menu to create a new scene. James Casual appears in the Document window.
2. Choose File > Import > Background Picture from the menu. When the Open dialog appears, open the Content > RDNA > LindaWhite folder from the CD-ROM and select the FieryGizzard.JPG photo.

ON THE CD

3. Poser tells you that the width/height ratio of the background image is different than your document window. Answer YES to adjust the window to match the photograph.
4. This is a very large photo that may take up a lot of room on your screen. To reduce the size of the Document window while maintaining the aspect ratio, first move the Document window so that you can see its lower-right corner. Drag the corner upward and toward the left to resize the window to your preference.
5. If your Document window no longer displays the entire photo, select Window > Document Window Size from the menu. Then click the Match Background button and choose OK to complete the change.

6. To display the photograph in the background, select Display > Show Background Picture from the menu. You should now see the photograph fill the Document window, as shown in Figure 5.20.

FIGURE 5.20 The background image has been loaded into the document window.

If you go into the Material Room you will see other options that you can use as backgrounds for your Poser scenes. Choose "Background" from the Object menu. The Color channel of the Background palette will be attached to a BG Picture node. Alternatively, you can use a background color of your choice (specified in the BG Color node), solid black (Black node), or a background movie (BG Movie).

Matching the Render Dimensions to the Photo

When you work on lighting changes, you'll probably find that you need a lot of test renders. The usual process is tweak, render, tweak, render, tweak, and render again until you get it right. In order to render the entire photo in your scene, you'll have to set up the render dimensions so that they match the dimensions of your document window. Follow these steps:

1. Choose Render > Render Dimensions from the menu. The Render Dimensions dialog shown in Figure 5.21 appears.

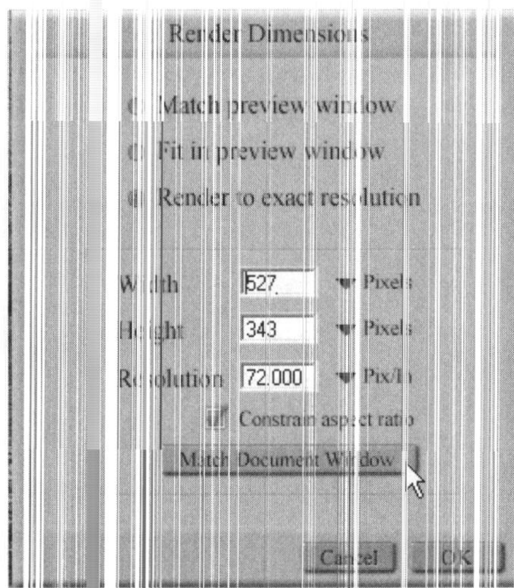

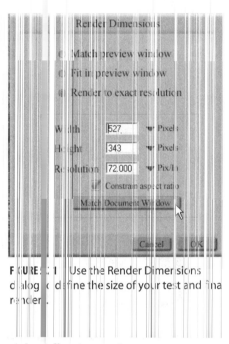

FIGURE 5.21 Use the Render Dimensions dialog to define the size of your test and final renders.

2. Choose one of the following options:
   - If you want your test renders to remain the same size as the preview window, choose the Match Preview Window option.
   - To render an image that is larger or smaller than the document window, first select the Render to Exact Resolution button. Make sure that the Constrain Aspect Ratio button is checked so that you maintain the required width-to-height ratio to display the photo properly. Then enter the desired width or height in either the Width or Height field. The other dimension should change accordingly to keep the photo in its proper aspect ratio.

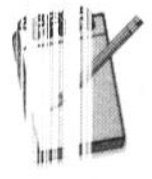

When rendering a scene that uses a background photo, it is recommended that you set the Firefly renderer to Final quality. You'll learn more about rendering in Chapter 16, "Rendering."

Positioning the Camera

Now you'll use poses in the Poser 6 Pose library to pose James so that it looks like he is walking over the rocks in the river. You'll also use the ground plane as a guide to get the correct perspective while you position James on the rocks.

To position James and the main camera, follow these steps:

1. In the Pose Room, open the Library Palette and browse to the Poser 6 > Poses > James Pose > Walking > Walking library.
2. Make sure that you have selected James Casual. Then highlight the Walk 10 pose and click the Apply Library Preset button.
3. If necessary, right-click the camera selection menu in the upper-left corner of the document window, and select the Main Camera (or, choose Display > Camera > Main Camera from the menu).
4. If you do not see the grid (for the default ground plane) superimposed over the photo, select Display > Guides > Ground Plane from the menu. It will also make it easier to see James' feet if you turn off the ground shadows (from the menu, choose Display > Ground Shadows to uncheck them).
5. Use the *camera plane* controls (the control with hands pointing in four directions) to move the figure back so that James appears in the horizontal and vertical center of the image.
6. Use the camera *trackball* control to turn the main camera so that James is walking toward the left-hand side of your screen, and so that the perspective of the ground plane matches the perspective in the photo. Figure 5.22 shows a good placement for the camera angle and position.

FIGURE 5.22 Position the camera so that James appears to be walking across the rocks, and so that the perspective of the ground plane matches that of the photograph.

Creating and Placing the Image-Based Light

Before we create the image-based light, we need to delete the default light set. Then we will add a light and use one of the wacros in the Material Room to create the image-based light.

To create the image-based light, follow these steps:

1. Choose Window > Python Scripts from the menu, and use the Utility Funcs > Delete All Lights script to delete the default light set from your scene.
2. Use the Create Light icon in the light controls to create a new spotlight. Change the color of the light to white.
3. Click the Material tab to enter the Material Room. In the Wacros panel at the right, click the IBL button. The Texture Manager dialog shown in Figure 5.23 appears.

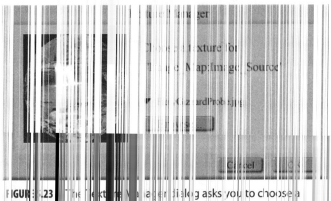

FIGURE 5.23 The Texture Manager dialog asks you to choose a texture for your light probe.

4. The Texture Manager dialog asks you to choose a texture for the image map. At this point, you will choose the image that you will use for the light probe. Click the Browse button and locate the Content > RDNA > Light Probe > FieryGizzardProbe.jpg image on the CD-ROM.
5. After you return to the Texture Manager dialog, click OK to exit. Poser asks if you want to create ambient occlusion for this light. This is a feature that prevents light from affecting recessed areas, making shadows appear darker. Choose YES to return to the Material Room.
6. Go back to the Pose Room and render the scene. In the case of an IBL, it won't matter where you position the light indicator around your scene. The light probe image determines how the scene is lit. Figure 5.24 shows an example of what your scene might look like at this point.

FIGURE 5.24 After rendering your image with the IBL, the scene looks pretty good! But, it can use a little more fine-tuning.

7. After you render the image you may decide that you want to add some highlights and shadows, because IBLs are diffuse-only. Click the Create Light button in the Light Controls to create a second light for the scene.
8. Observe the photograph and notice the direction that the sunlight is coming from. In this case, the sun is almost directly overhead. Judging by the strong shadows at the front of the rocks, the sun is directly overhead with a slight offset behind and to the left. Since the figure is almost in the center of the scene, it won't be difficult to place the light. In the Parameters window, set the x, y, and zTran and Rotate settings for the new light to zero. This puts the Spotlight on the floor in the very center of the scene, and pointing toward your right.
9. Choose Object > Point At from the menu and point the light at James' left shoulder.
10. Set the yTran setting to around 15. This raises the light well above the figure's head.
11. To move the light back slightly and toward your right, adjust the xTran (left-to-right) and zTran (front-to-back) settings to –1.
12. Render the scene again to check the shadows and highlights. Figure 5.25 shows the final result.

FIGURE 5.25 The second light has added depth to the highlights and shadows in the image.

CONCLUSION

What you learned in this chapter is only the beginning of your adventures with Poser lights. While it does take a fair amount of tweaking and experimentation to light a scene well, it is worth the time and effort. You should now have a good foundation that will enable you to experiment with lighting on your own. With a little experimenting, you should be able to develop lighting combinations and techniques that work best for your work style and preferences. Don't forget to read the Frequently Asked Questions appendix for additional tips and tricks on lighting.

CHAPTER

6 CREATING CUSTOM FACES

In This Chapter

- Face Room Overview
- Photo Lineup
- Conclusion

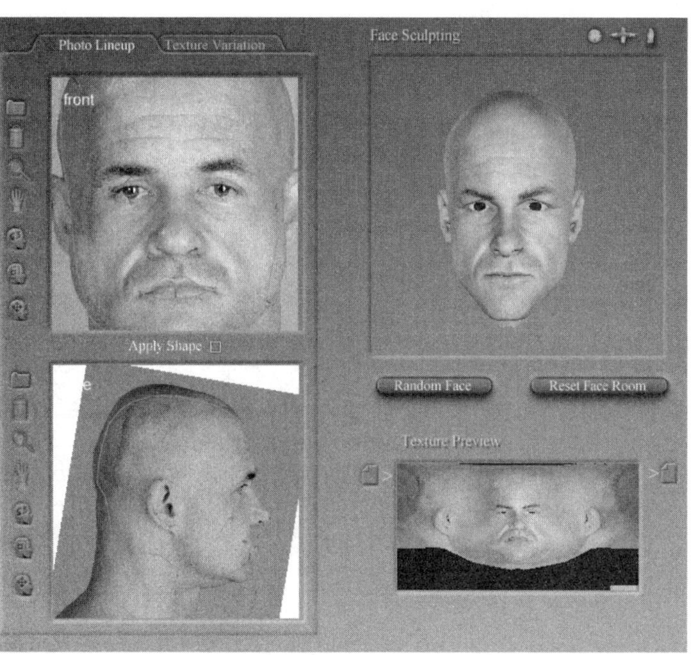

There are many ways to create custom faces in Poser. The most obvious method is to use the Face Room, which was introduced in Poser 5. This room allows you to customize the faces of the Poser 5 and 6 male and female characters. By importing front and side photos of a person, users can create a wide variety of characters. In fact, through the many facial morphs available in the Face Room the range of characters that you can create are limitless.

When Poser 6 was initially released, the Face Room only worked with the Poser 5 and Poser 6 males and females. Since that time, we have seen the release of Miki (an oriental female figure), and Koji (an oriental male figure that, at the time of this writing, is not yet supported by the Face Room). There is also word that Apollo Maximus 2005 will have Face Room support as well. A compact version of Apollo Maximus 2005 is furnished on the CD-ROM with this book.

Because there are also a wide variety of third-party figures available for use in Poser, you'll learn about a handy Poser 6 feature that works for any figure that contains morphs. With the *Randomize Morphs* Python script you can create unique faces for other Poser-compatible features.

Before you begin the tutorials in this chapter, it is recommended that you review the Face Room chapter in the Poser 6 Tutorial Manual that comes with Poser 6. From Poser, choose Help > Poser Tutorial Manual, and refer to Chapter 9, "The Face Room" for complete step-by-step tutorials. You'll also learn how to prepare photos for the best results.

This chapter gives a brief overview of the Face Room, and the various ways that you can apply Face Room heads to your Poser 6 figures. You'll also learn how to use the Randomize Morphs script on other figures to generate new character faces quickly and easily. And you'll learn the best way to match Face Room heads to your figure's body.

Face Room Overview

The main areas of the Face Room are shown in Figure 6.1. Each of these areas serves a specific purpose and helps you achieve a wide range of characters for your Poser scenes. The following sections give a brief overview of the Photo Lineup, Texture Variation, Face Sculpting, Texture Preview, Action Buttons, and Face Shaping Tool.

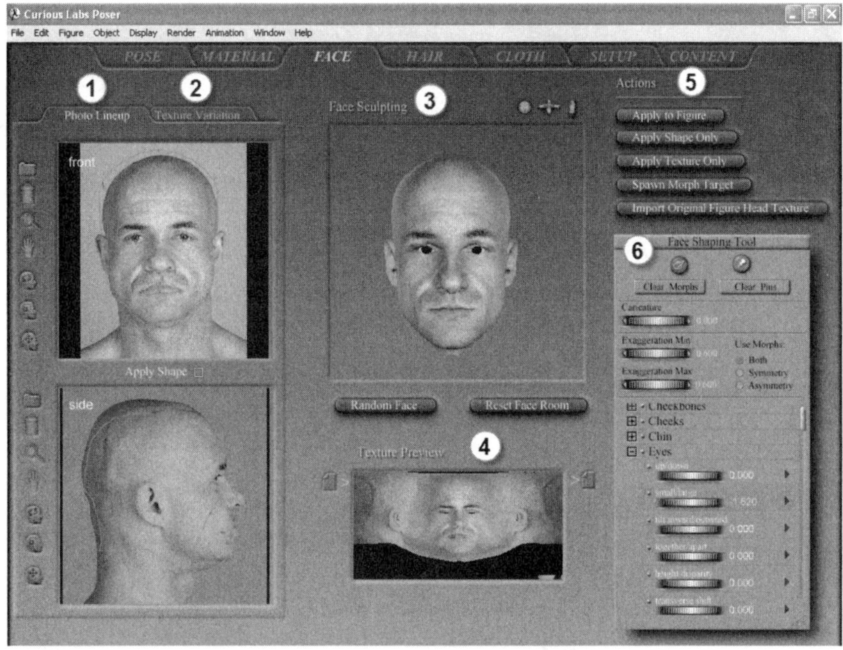

FIGURE 6.1 The Face Room Areas: Photo Lineup (1), Texture Variation (2), Face Sculpting (3), Texture Preview (4), Action Buttons (5), and Face Shaping Tool (6).

Photo Lineup

The Photo Lineup area, perhaps the most challenging part of the Face Room, is shown in Figure 6.2. Use this area to import front and side photos of the same person, and to create a face texture for your character. As you work with the facial outlines and feature points in the Face Room, you will get the best results in the Photo Lineup area if you take your time, save often, and make changes in baby steps.

Most people who are new to the Face Room try to use the Photo Lineup area to both morph and texture the Face Room head to look like the photos they are using. However, when you keep the Apply Shape option checked while you adjust the red outline and green feature points, you quickly end up with a severely distorted head and you need to start all over again. The best approach is to leave the Apply Shape option unchecked, and use the Photo Lineup area strictly for texture generation.

FIGURE 6.2 Use the Photo Lineup area to create a texture from front and side photos of a person.

And on that note, it's also good to prepare your figures so that you get the best results. The following tutorial shows some new discoveries since the *Poser 6 Tutorial Manual* was released with Poser 6.

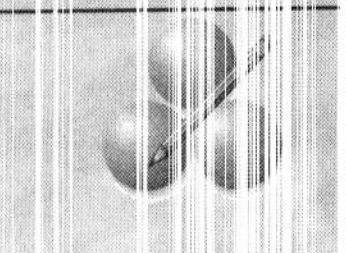

TUTORIAL 6.

PREPARING YOUR PHOTOS

The Poser 6 Tutorial Manual that comes with Poser 6 goes into great length about how to shoot and prepare photographs, as well as how to align the outlines and feature points. This tutorial shows you some new discoveries since that manual was written. You'll learn how to use some Face Room guides that have been prepared for James and Jessi (the Poser 6 adults) and Don and Judy (the Poser 5 adults). These guides will help you get the best texture results for these figures in the Face Room with the least amount of effort.

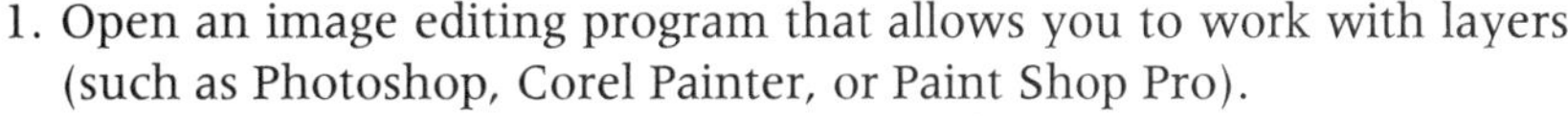

1. Open an image editing program that allows you to work with layers (such as Photoshop, Corel Painter, or Paint Shop Pro).

ON THE CD

2. Locate the Tutorials > Chap06 folder on the CD-ROM that accompanies this book. Open JamesFrontHead2048.png. This is an outline of James' head, eyes, nose, and mouth, which you should see on a transparent background.
3. Duplicate the outline on a new layer to create an overlay. (This step is for image editors that do not allow you to place anything beneath the base, or background, layer.)
4. Open the front view of the photo that you want to use in the Face Room (high-resolution photographs, such as those found at *http://www.3d.sk, Human Photo References for 3D Artists and Game Developers,* will give best results). Paste a copy of the photo into the first image you opened. Make sure that the red outline layer is *above* the photograph layer.
5. Scale the photograph so that the outline of the head stays slightly inside the photo. Figure 6.3 shows an example in Photoshop CS2 up to this point.

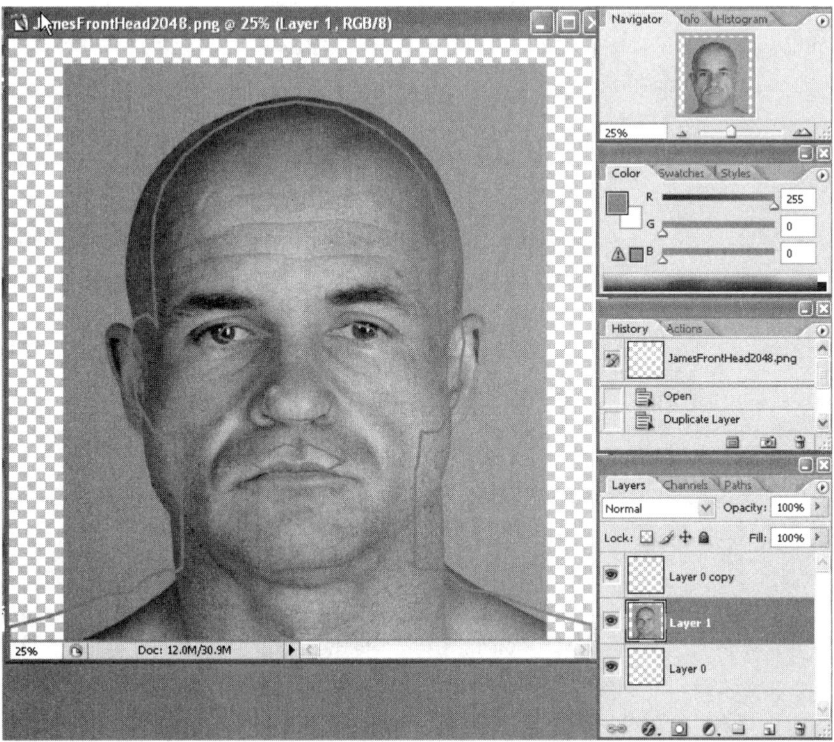

FIGURE 6.3 Load the front photo on a layer beneath the James head outline and scale the photo so that the outline is within the facial area.

6. Now, duplicate the photograph layer. If necessary, move the duplicate photo layer immediately above the first photo layer.
7. Make a selection that surrounds the eyebrows, eyes, nose, and mouth. Make sure that you have enough area around these features so that when you make the selection smaller, you will cover the features at their original size.
8. *Feather* or *soften* the edges of the selection. In this example we used 20-25 pixels; however, you might need to adjust this depending on how large your own photograph is.
9. Resize the facial features so that they match up as closely as possible to the features on the red outline. Figure 6.4 shows an example of what you are looking for.
10. If necessary, use the *rubber stamp* or *cloning* tool to blend areas where needed.

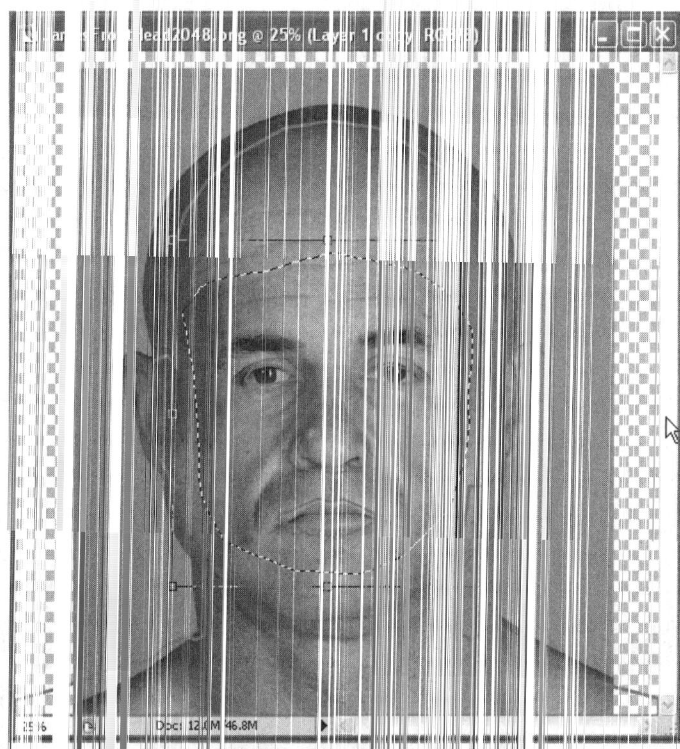

FIGURE 6.4 Scale the features on a copy of the photo layer so that they fit in the red feature outlines.

11. Now for the side view. This view is probably the most critical when it comes to avoiding distortion in the final texture. You may have already noticed that if you try to tilt the head outline using the tools in the Photo Preview area that the entire face and texture gets distorted. The way to prevent this is to tilt the side photo before you bring it in to the Face Room. The PNG outline for the side view helps you with this process. Open the JamesLeftHead2048.png file, which contains the outline for James' side view.
12. As you did with the front photo, scale the side view photo to size. The most important step is to *rotate* the head so that it matches the angle of the head outline. Figure 6.5 shows an example.

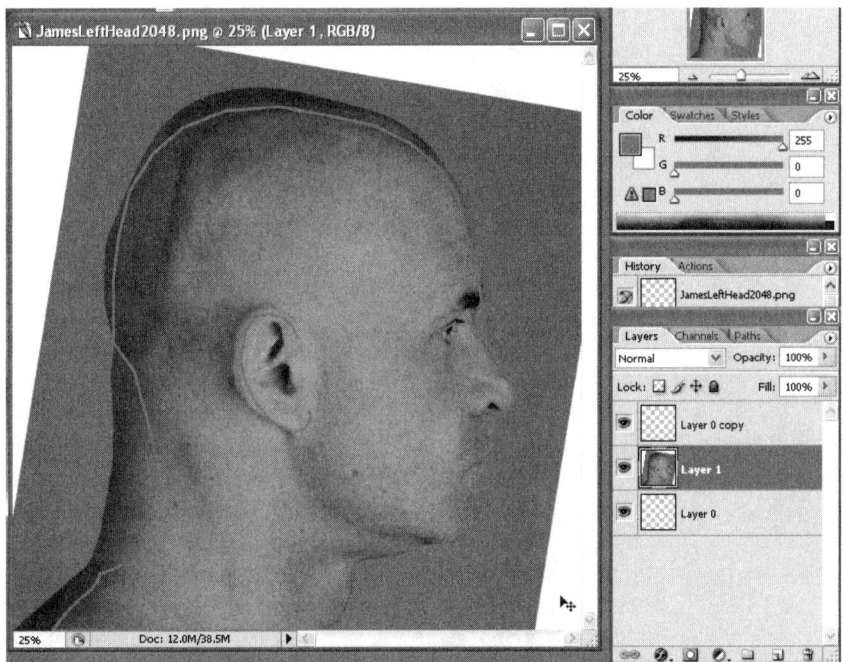

FIGURE 6.5 Scale and rotate the side view until it matches the angle of the head in the side view as close as possible.

13. Save the images as JamesFront and JamesLeft, preferably in a lossless format. The Face Room can accept images in JPG, PNG, BMP, TIF, GIF, and PCX formats. The JPG format is a lossy format, and GIF can only contain a maximum of 256 colors so you want to avoid those for this process. (See Chapter 11, "Creating Your Own Textures," for a discussion of lossy and lossless file compression.)

14. Import the revised photographs into the front and side views in the Photo Lineup area. You will probably see that the altered photographs make it much easier to create your new face texture with a minimal amount of resizing and moving the feature points. Only move the feature points when you need to refine the texture placement on the 3D model in the Face Sculpting window. Figure 6.6 shows an example of a finished texture after some points have been adjusted.

FIGURE 6.6 After you import the revised photos you will find it easier to create your head texture. Feature points will need minimal adjustment and fine tuning.

If you are using photographs to create a face texture, you have two options in matching head to body texture. When you save or try to apply the head texture to the figure in the Pose Room, Poser asks if you want to change the head texture to match the body texture. If you answer YES, Poser blends your head texture to the body texture by adding a graduated alpha (transparency) edge over the image. This

is a good option if you have a body texture that is close in color to the photographs you are using for your figure. If your new texture is too far off, you might have to create an original body texture, using photographs of the same person that you used in the Face Room, or bring both texture maps into your graphic editing program and make adjustments to the color of the body texture. Even if your texture is far off in color, having Poser blend the head texture down into the body texture may be a good way to get a baseline color and texture area to use when adjusting the rest of the body texture color.

Texture Variation

The Texture Variation area is shown in Figure 6.7. Use the controls in this area to apply color and shading changes that change the ethnicity, sex, or age of the face texture. You can also darken eyebrows or darken the lower face to create a beard.

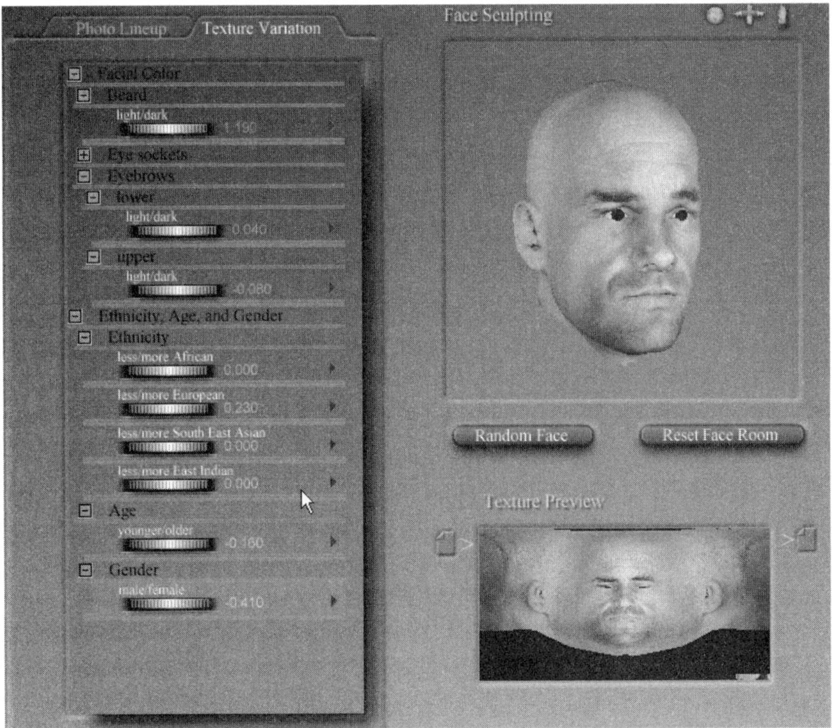

FIGURE 6.7 The Texture Variation area allows you to alter the texture for ethnicity, age, or gender differences.

In order to achieve consistent results between head and body textures when adding texture variation, you should start with head and body textures that match. The Face Room default texture is not the same as that used on James or Jessi. As a result, you will need to import James' or Jessi's head texture into the Face Room *before* you make your modifications. The following tutorial shows you how to do this.

If you have one or more light-skinned textures that you like but want to create darker-skinned ethnic characters, there are a number of approaches. One way to darken skin is to use the Material Room to adjust the procedural shaders for the skin. Try darkening the Diffuse Color for the face texture and body texture by the same amount. Try gray or a tinted gray color to keep from introducing additional colors to the skin tone. An alternative to the manual approach is to purchase the Poser 6 Realism Kit, by face_off (which is available at the marketplace at http://www.renderosity.com). This kit allows you to lighten or darken textures while adding other realistic features such as sheen, bump, and skin imperfections.

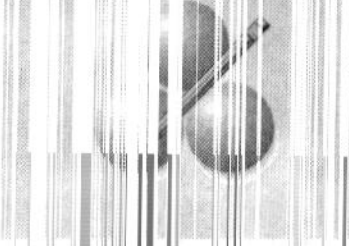

TUTORIAL 6.2 MATCHING ETHNIC TEXTURES TO THE BODY

In this tutorial you will load James into the scene and make ethnic changes to the figure. Then you will apply the altered head texture to James, and change the body texture to match.

To create an ethnic variation of a texture, follow these steps:

1. Create a new scene and replace James Casual with James or James Hi Res.
2. Switch to Texture Preview mode (Display > Document Style > Texture Shaded) and view the document with the Face camera.
3. Click the Face tab to enter the Face Room.
4. From the Actions section, click the button that reads Import Original Figure Head Texture. The Face Room imports the head texture that James is using in the Pose Room.
5. Click the Texture Variation tab to display the options in the Texture Variation area.
6. Expand the Ethnicity, Age, and Gender options and in turn expand the Ethnicity options. Set the Less/More African texture variation setting to 1.000
7. In the Face Shaping Tool (shown at the right side of the screen in Figure 6.8), expand the Ethnicity, Age, and Gender morph category, and in turn expand the Ethnicity morph category. Set the Less/More African morph to 0.600. Your character should now look as shown in Figure 6.8.

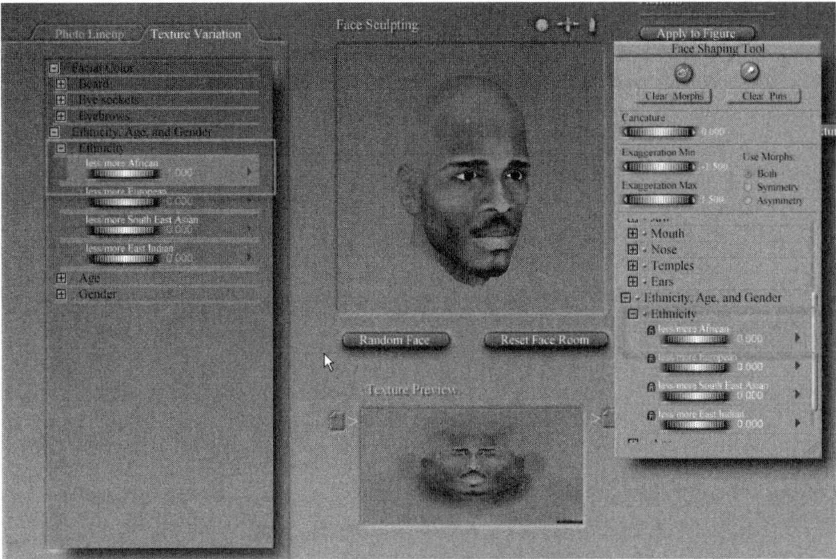

FIGURE 6.8 Changes in Texture Variation and the Face Shaping Tool sections create an African male.

8. In the Actions area, click the Apply Shape Only button to add the face morph to James. He should now have the facial features characteristic of an African male.

9 If you try to apply the head texture to James at this point, Poser automatically generates an alpha map that blends the head texture with the current body texture. Unfortunately, this won't look quite right with an ethnic texture. The way around it is to save the ethnic texture into a separate file and manually apply it to the head in the Material Room. To begin this process, click the Save icon that appears at the right of the Texture Preview area. Poser asks if you want to change the resolution of the texture. Answer YES to save the texture at 1024 × 1024. Choose the folder to which you want to save the texture, and name it "JamesEthnicHead." If you intend to add to or improve the texture in your image editor, save the texture to a lossless format such as TIF. If you will use this texture as the final version, you can save it as a JPG file with 100% quality.

10. Click the Material tab to enter the Material Room. Select James as the current figure and the Head as the current actor. You will see the material screen shown in Figure 6.9.

11. Notice the Image Map node that is attached to the Diffuse Color input. Click the name of the image map that appears in the Image Source

field. The Texture Manager opens and prompts you to locate an image. Locate and select the ethnic face texture that you saved earlier and click OK to apply the change.

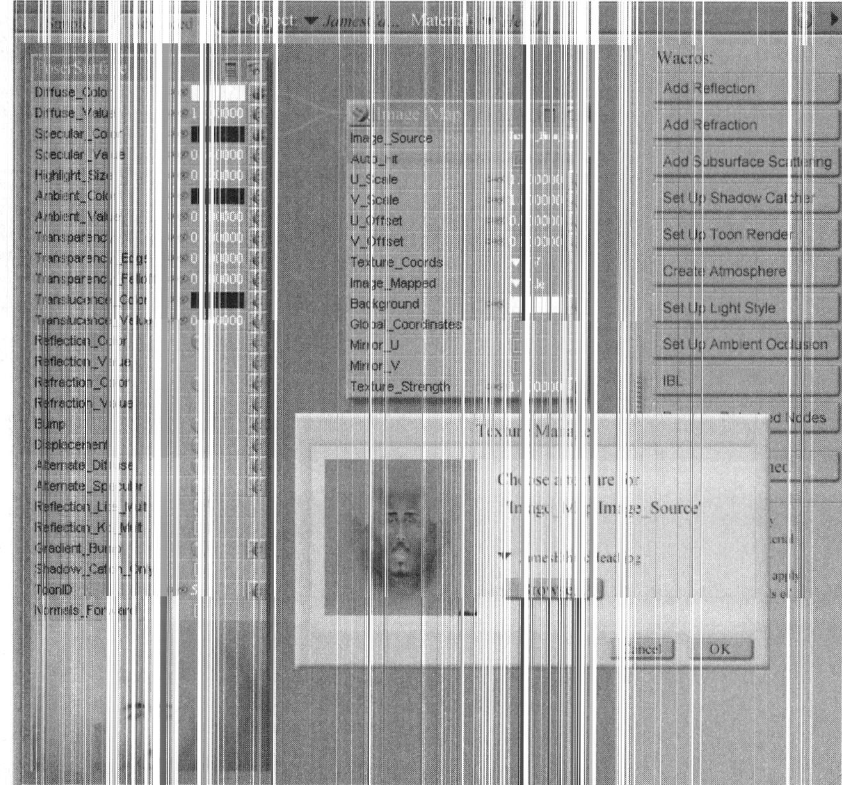

FIGURE 6.9 Change the texture map from the default James texture to the ethnic texture that you created in the Face Room.

12. Now select James' Body as the current material. Click the color square that represents the Diffuse Color.
13. After the Poser color selector window appears, click the tricolored square in the upper-right corner to open the RGB Color Picker. Set the RGB color values to 150, 150, and 150 to create a medium shade of gray as shown in Figure 6.10. The face and body colors should now match.

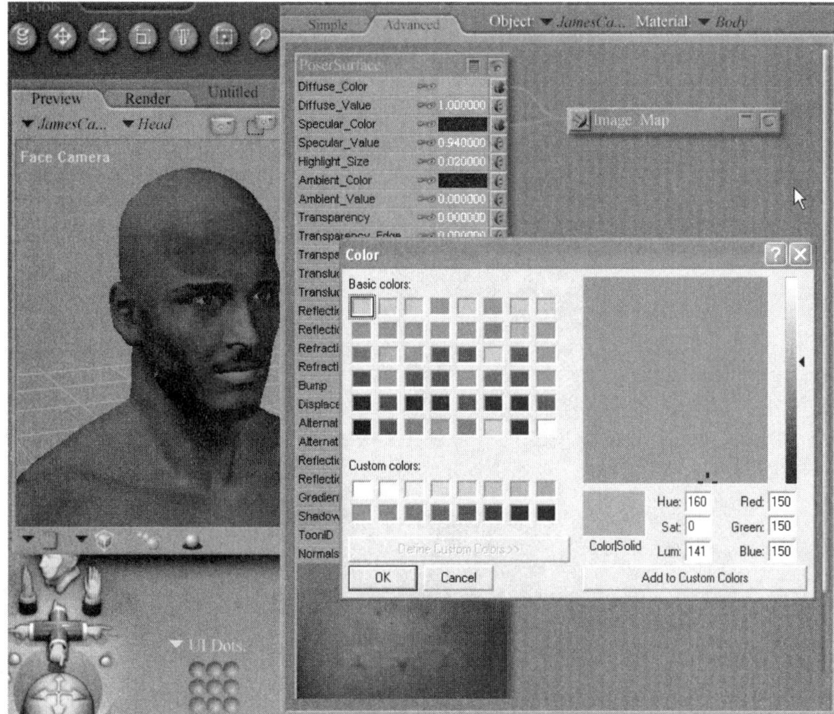

FIGURE 6.10 Change the diffuse color for the body to a medium shade of gray. Afterward it should match the ethnic head texture created in the Face Room.

Face Sculpting and Face Shaping Tool

Use the Face Sculpting area to view the changes in your face texture while you are moving feature points in the photo lineup area. You can use the mini camera controls in the Face Sculpting area to rotate the head around while you make changes to the texture.

The Face Sculpting area also allows you to visually sculpt, or create, morphs onto your Face Room head, as shown in Figure 6.11.

Click the Morph Putty icon (1) in the Face Shaping Tool, shown in Figure 6.11. Then click on the 3D preview in the Face Sculpting area in the area you want to morph (2). A green dot appears after you click an area that you can morph. Move the dot to reshape the morphs until you are satisfied.

Rather than sculpting the morphs by dragging with your mouse, you can dial-in a face using the many morph dials (3) available in the Face Shaping Tool. You can control the minimum and maximum range of all

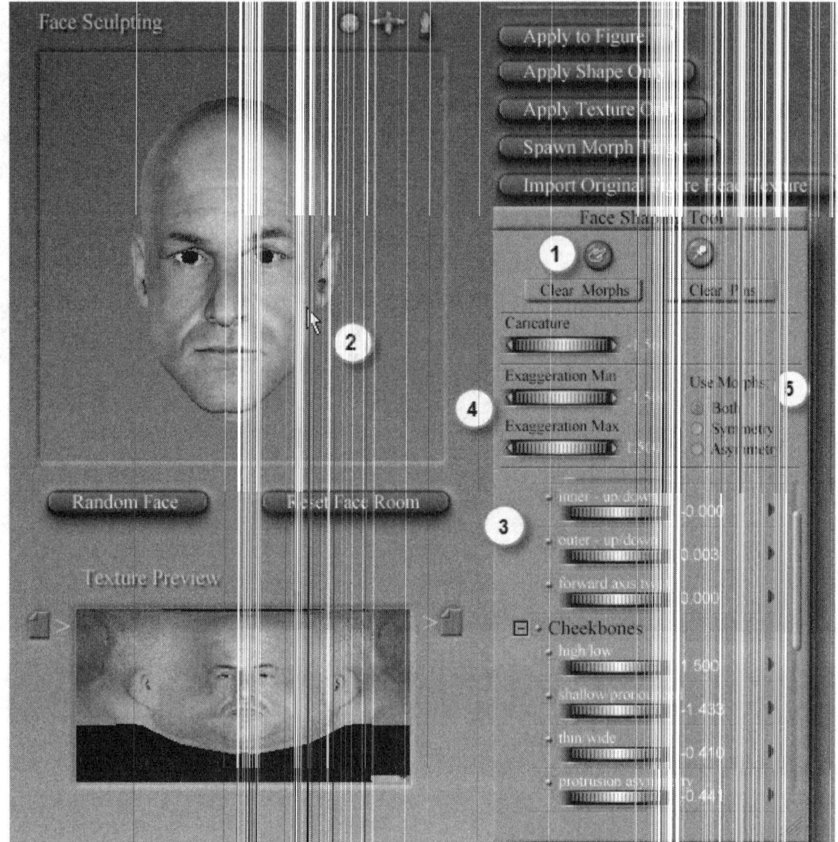

FIGURE 6.11 Preview your textures in the Face Sculpting area, and use the *morph putty* tool to visually sculpt your head shape.

dials by the values you enter in the Exaggeration Min and Exaggeration Max (4) settings in the Face Shaping Tool.

The Facial Morphs are arranged in the following categories. A value of zero means that the morph has no effect. Negative values morph the feature toward one end of the spectrum, while positive values morph the feature more toward the other end. The morphs listed below in italics add asymmetry to the face, which can make your character look more realistic and natural. The asymmetrical morphs are removed from use when you select the Symmetry option (5) in the Face Shaping Tool:

Bridge (subcategory of Nose): Shallow/Deep, Short/Long, *Transverse Shift*

Brow Ridge: High/Low, Inner-Up/Down, Outer-Up/Down, *Forward Axis Twist*

Cheekbones: High/Low, Shallow/Pronounced, Thin/Wide, *Protrusion Asymmetry*

Cheeks: Concave/Convex, Round/Gaunt

Chin: Forward/Backward, Pronounced/Recessed, Retracted/Jutting, Shallow/Deep, Small/Large, Short/Tall, Thin/Wide, *Chin Axis Twist, Forward Axis Twist, Transverse Shift*

Ears: Up/Down, Back/Front, Short/Long, Thin/Wide, *Vertical Shear, Forward Axis Shear*

Eyes: Up/Down, Small/Large, Tilt Inward/Outward, Together/Apart, *Height Disparity, Transverse Shift*

Face: Brow-Nose-Chin Ratio, Forehead-Sellion-Nose Ratio, Light/Heavy, Round/Gaunt, Thin/Wide, *Coronal Bend, Coronal Shear, Vertical Axis Twist*

Forehead: Small/Large, Short/Tall, Tilt Forward/Back, *Forward Axis Twist*

Jaw: Retracted/Jutting, Wide/Thin, Jaw-Neck Slope High/Low, Concave/Convex

Lips (subcategory of Mouth): Deflated/Inflated, Large/Small, Puckered/Retracted

Mouth: Drawn/Pursed, Happy/Sad, High/Low, Protruding/Relaxed, Tilt Up/Down, Underbite/Overbite, Mouth-Chin Distance Short/Long, *Corners Transverse Shift, Forward Axis Twist, Transverse Shift, Twist and Shift*

Nose: Up/Down, Flat/Pointed, Short/Long, Tilt Up/Down, *Frontal Axis Twist, Tip Transverse Shift, Transverse Shift, Vertical Axis Twist*

Nostrils (subcategory of Nose): Tilt Up/Down, Small/Large, Thin/Wide, *Frontal Axis Twist, Transverse Shift*

Sellion (subcategory of Nose): Up/Down, Shallow/Deep, Thin/Wide, *Transverse Shift*

Temples: Thin/Wide

There are also morphs in the Face Shaping Tool that vary ethnicity, age, and gender of your figure. They are as follows:

Age: Younger/Older

Ethnicity: Less/More African, Less/More European, Less/More South East Asian, Less/More East Indian

Gender: Male/Female

Texture Preview

The Texture Preview area, shown in Figure 6.12, provides a two-dimensional preview of the texture you are creating. The preview is a bit misleading, however, because the Face Room generates square texture maps with one exception: when you import textures for James or Jessi and then make texture variation modifications to them, the texture is exported at the same size as the original texture.

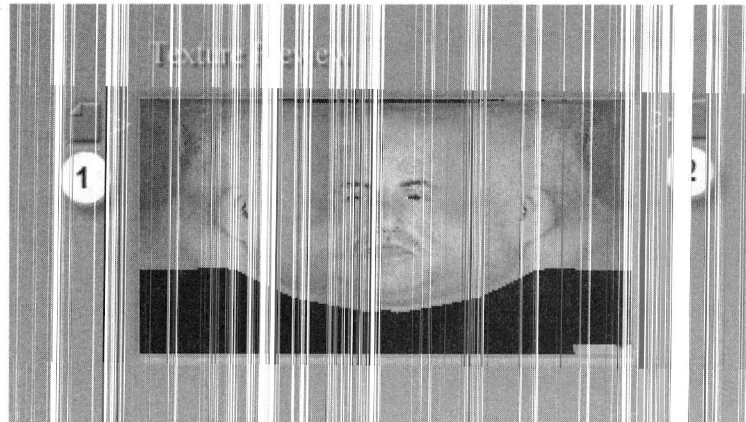

FIGURE 6.12 The Texture Preview area provides a small texture preview of the texture you are creating in the Face Room.

To use third-party textures

You may have third-party textures that you would like to use on James, Jessi, Don, or Judy. It can be helpful to use those face textures while you create a character morph in the Face Room. To import a third-party head texture into the Face Room, click the Import icon (1) that appears at the left of the Texture Preview area. Locate the face texture that you want to use, and click Open to return to the Face Room. Your third-party head texture should now appear on the head. You are now ready to create your character morph with the Face Shaping Tool.

To save Face Room textures

Because they are created on the fly, Face Room textures are not as perfect as those that are meticulously created by hand. They contain smudges, and may be slightly misaligned from the physical geometry of the features. For example, you might notice when you close the figure's eyes that there are unwanted smears on the eyelids. It's important to be aware that Face Room textures contain these undesirable artifacts; however, they still make a great starting point. You can always use the original photos to improve the Face Room texture in an image editing program afterward.

By default, Poser stores the Face Room textures in the Poser 6 > textures > faceroom folder, in PNG format. The filename is based on the date and time that you applied the texture to the figure. When you edit the faceroomSkin material in the Material Room, it points to the PNG file in this folder.

If you want to save the Face Room texture to a folder and filename that you choose, do the following: click the Export (2) icon in the Texture Preview area, locate the folder in which you want to save the texture, and use a filename and format of your own choosing. Use your custom texture in place of the faceroomSkin material in the Material Room (if you have already applied a Face Room texture).

Action Buttons

The Action Buttons are shown in Figure 6.13. Use these buttons to apply the shape of the head, the texture, or both to the currently selected figure in the Pose Room.

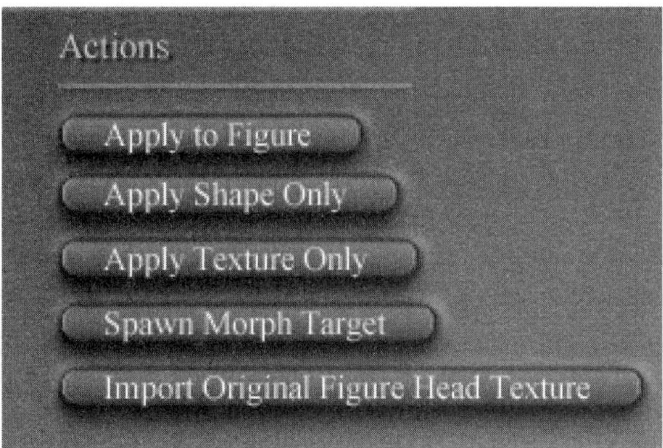

FIGURE 6.13 Action Buttons apply the head, texture, or both to the figure in the Pose Room.

If you only have one figure in the Pose Room, the changes will apply automatically. If you have multiple figures, make sure you have the correct figure selected as the current figure before you use these buttons.

Each button in the Action Buttons area serves the following purposes:

Apply to Figure: Click this button to apply the head shape and texture to the currently selected figure. This option replaces the default James head with the head you created in the Face Room.

If the new texture has sufficient resolution to be larger than 512 × 512, Poser asks if you want to change the texture resolution. Click NO to keep the texture at 512 × 512, or click YES to create a larger texture of the dimensions stated in the dialog. After Poser generates the texture, you may be informed that the face color is different than the figure color. Click NO to apply the face texture exactly as you see it in the Face Room (this will probably require that you create or alter the body texture yourself). If you click YES, Poser will create a blend between the Face Room texture and the body texture through the use of an alpha mask. Figure 6.14 shows a blended result.

Apply Shape Only: Applies the shape, but not the texture, to the figure that is currently selected in the Pose Room.

Apply Texture Only: Applies the texture, but not the face, to the figure that is currently selected in the Pose Room.

Spawn Morph Target: Adds morph dials for the head, left eye, and right eye to the figure that is currently selected in the Pose Room. When set to 1, the morph dials duplicate the face you created in the Face Room.

Import Original Figure Head Texture: Applies the head texture from the figure that is currently selected in the Pose Room onto the head in the Face Sculpting area.

FIGURE 6.14 If desired, Poser can blend the Face Room texture to the existing body texture to create a smooth transition.

TUTORIAL 6.3 SAVING MULTIPLE FACES IN ONE FIGURE

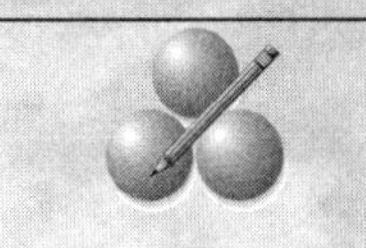

Many Poser users like to save one single figure that contains all of their characters. You can use the Face Room to generate a head morph and then apply it to your figure as a morph. Then save the figure to the library after you add the morph. When it's time to create another morph, start with this custom character.

To illustrate this process, we will generate some custom faces with the Random Face button that appears beneath the Face Sculpting area. We'll work with Jessi this time. Follow these steps:

1. Create a new scene, and replace James Casual with Jessi or JessiHiRes.
2. Turn off Inverse Kinematics, zero the figure, and turn on Texture Shaded mode. Refer to Chapter 3 for these steps if you need to refresh yourself with the procedures.
3. Change to the Face Camera, so that you can see Jessi's face as you create the new characters. Brighten the default lighting, if necessary, so that you can see the facial features more clearly.
4. Click the Face tab to enter the Face Room.
5. From the Action Buttons area, click the Import Original Figure Head Texture button. The default Jessi texture appears on the Face Room head.
6. With Jessi, it will help create more realistic faces if you set the Caricature value in the Face Shaping Tool to a negative number. For purposes of this tutorial, set the Caricature setting at –1.750. This will help create faces that are more realistic than those created with the setting at its default of zero. Leave the Exaggeration Min and Exaggeration Max settings at their defaults of –1.5 and 1.5 respectively.
7. Click the Random Face button until you get a face that you like. Figure 6.15 shows an example of a nice morph created in this manner.
8. Now, transfer the face to the figure in the Pose Room. Click the Spawn Morph Target button in the Actions area. Initially, it may not appear as though anything happened.
9. Go to the Pose Room. Select Jessi's head, and open the Parameters palette if necessary.
10. Scroll down to the bottom of the Parameters palette and you should see a new morph category named Morph, along with a new morph that is named "head," as shown in Figure 6.16. This is the head that you created in the Face Room. Click the arrow that appears at the right of the morph, and choose Settings to rename the dial to a character name that you recognize as your own (such as "Amy," for example).
11. The eyes also have a Face Room morph associated with them. Click the right eye to select it. In its Parameter window, you'll notice a new morph named "rightEye." This is the eye morph that is associated

FIGURE 6.15 Click the Random Face button until you get a face that you like.

FIGURE 6.16 Your Face Room morph appears in the head as a morph named head. Rename it to something that is more descriptive.

with your first Face Room morph. Rename this dial the same as you did the head. Repeat this step for the left eye.

If you dial the face, left eye, and right eye morphs to 1, the face should appear as it did in the Face Room. Don't forget to dial them back to zero when you want to use another morph or you may get unexpected results from the combination of the two morphs.

12. Repeat Steps 7 through 11 for additional characters, if desired.
13. When your morphs are all created and renamed, locate the Figures library to which you want to save your custom figures. Click the Add to Library icon (the 'plus' sign) at the bottom of the Library palette. The New Set dialog appears.
14. Enter a name for your multi-character figure, and click OK. A thumbnail appears in the library. Every time you want to add custom morphs, load this figure into the library, and resave it after you are finished.

TUTORIAL 6.4 RANDOMIZING FACES FOR THIRD-PARTY FIGURES

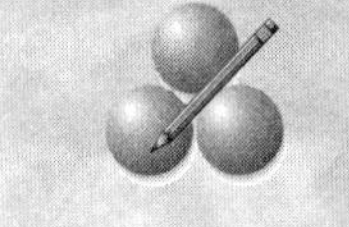

All is well for the adult figures that are furnished with Poser 6, and even for the Poser 5 adult figures. But not all third-party figures work in the Face Room, because their geometry isn't compatible.

Though Poser 6 doesn't offer a way to create textures from photos on third-party figures, it does offer a way to create random faces, based on the morphs included in a figure's face. It is the Randomize Morphs Python script, which you can access from the Python window. To use the Randomize Morphs script, follow these steps:

1. Create a new Poser document and add the figure that you want to morph. In the example in this tutorial, we are using Apollo Maximus, a figure that is available from RuntimeDNA (*http://www.runtimedna.com*) whose morphs work well with this feature.
2. The Randomize Morphs script randomizes all morphs that are present on the selected body part. So if you want to morph only specific regions, you'll have to delete morphs from figures that have them all built in, or inject specific morphs for figures that initially contain no morphs. For example, if you want to create some different noses, keep or add only the nose morphs. If you want to create some different mouths, keep or add only the mouth morphs. If you want to create different facial expressions, keep or add only the morphs that convey emotion.

Chapter 16, "Creating Custom Morphs," goes into more detail about morph creation and management.

3. Select the head of the figure whose face you want to change. Verify in the Parameters window that it contains all of the morphs you want to randomize.
4. Choose Window > Python Scripts. The Python Scripts window appears.
5. Click the Geom Mods button. You will see several buttons, along with the Randomize Morphs button shown in Figure 6.17.

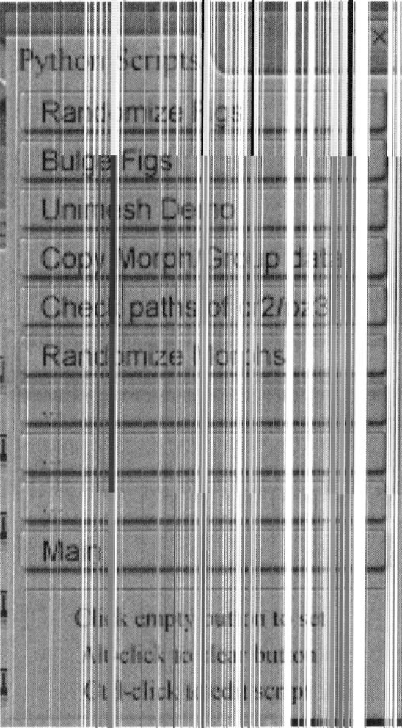

FIGURE 6.17 The Randomize Morphs Python script allows you to randomize morphs on any selected body part of any selected figure.

6. Click the Randomize Morphs button until you find a face you like.
7. To save the face, choose or create an Expressions library in which to save the face pose. Then click the Add to Library icon (the plus sign) at the bottom of the Library window. The New Set dialog appears. Click the Select Subset button to open the Hierarchy Selection window.
8. The Hierarchy selection window lists all morphs in the face, and they are all automatically selected. If you keep all of the morph settings checked, your face pose will always override the existing expression

when you apply it. If you check only some of the dials (for example, those pertaining to the mouth), the library pose will apply the mouth settings and leave the remaining areas untouched. After you make your selections, click OK to return to the New Set dialog

9. Click OK again to save the face expression to the library. The Save Frames dialog appears.
10. If this is a single-frame pose—that is, if you are not animating anything—leave the default selection as Single Frame. If you have created an animated facial pose, click the Multi frame animation option and designate the starting and ending frames to save.
11. Click OK to finalize the save operation. Your pose is added to the Expressions library.

CONCLUSION

Poser allows you to customize your Poser figures in a number of ways. Through the Face Room you can create several different characters of varying ethnicities that are based on the Poser 6 male and female (James and Jessi), or on the Poser 5 male and female (Judy and Don). If you have other third-party figures, Poser provides a way to create random expressions for them by using the Randomize Morphs Python script. You can also use built-in morphs on any character and manually dial in morphs that are built in to your figures.

In the following chapter, you'll learn how to use the Hair Room to add dynamic hair that moves while you animate your figures or add wind effects to your project. This exciting feature adds to the realism of your Poser renders and animations.

CHAPTER

7

WORKING WITH POSER HAIR

In This Chapter

- Types of Poser Hair
- Conforming Hair Revisited
- Styling Prop and Conforming Hair
- Basic Steps for Dynamic Hair
- Conclusion

In Chapter 3, "Building Scenes," you learned how to add conforming hair to a Poser figure. The hair used in that tutorial is actually one of three types of hair that you can use in Poser. The three types of hair are prop hair, conforming hair, and dynamic hair. In this chapter, you'll learn how to identify each of these hair types, the advantages that each has, and where to find them in your Poser libraries. You'll also learn how to use the Poser Hair Room to create dynamic hair and fur in Poser.

TYPES OF POSER HAIR

Over the years, Poser users have seen increasing realism in the hair objects that have been created for Poser figures. Today we have hair models that look real, along with strand-based dynamic hair that moves quite realistically when animated.

An example of each of the three hair types is shown, left to right, in Figure 7.1. Each of these hair types has strengths and weaknesses, and the following information will help you determine how to tell the difference between them, when to use them, and how to use them.

FIGURE 7.1 Poser 6 allows you to use three types of hair: prop hair, conforming hair, and strand-based dynamic hair.

TUTORIAL 7.1 USING PROP HAIR

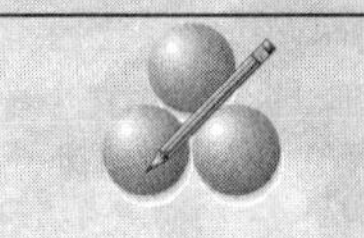

Hair props were first introduced in Poser 3, where they were found in the Hair Library that we still see in Poser 6. Prop hair uses the HR2 or HRZ extension when saved into the Hair Library. Because Poser 6 can include all three types of hair in the Hair Library, it can be difficult to tell at a glance from the library thumbnails which hair is prop hair and which is conforming hair. Even after you have used the hair in your scene, you may not be able to visually distinguish between the two types of hair. To determine if you are using prop hair, use the pull-down menus in the document window to display the contents in your scene. Prop hair appears beneath the Props submenu, as shown in Figure 7.2.

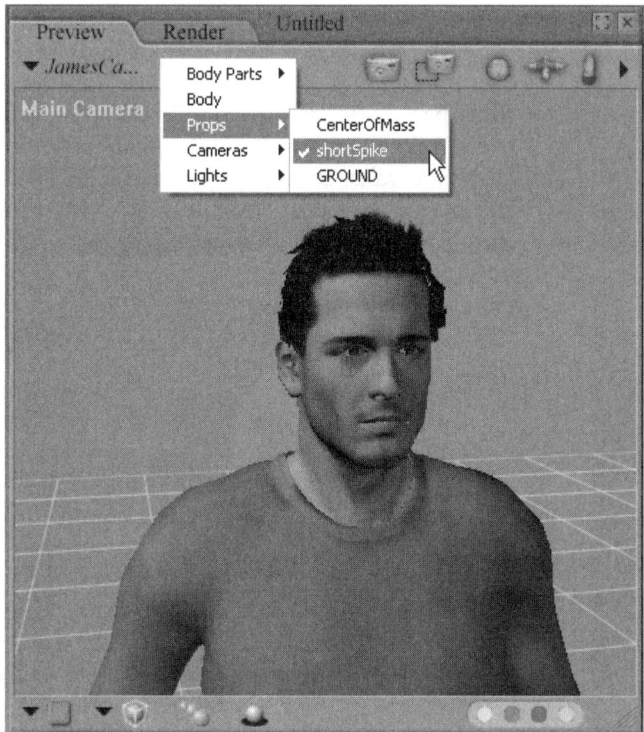

FIGURE 7.2 The menus in the document preview window list prop hair in the Props submenu.

Sometime after the release of Poser 4, hair props began to look more realistic, thanks to the pioneering efforts of Kozaburo, a prominent member of the Japanese Poser community. He created hair textures for the hair props that were furnished with Poser 4 and made them look much more realistic. But Poser enthusiasts really took notice when he added transparency maps and morphs to his own hair models. Transparency-mapped hair had realistic and irregular edges instead of straight, blunt edges. The included morphs allowed the hair props to be styled, lengthened, or shortened.

You will find hair models made by Kozaburo in the Poser 6 > Hair > Kozaburo Hair Library. These hair sets are preconfigured to fit the Poser 6 figures. Additional hair models are made to fit other popular Poser figures and are available for free download from his Web site at http://digitalbabes2.com/.

Of all hair types, prop hair is perhaps the easiest to use. Most prop hair models find and attach themselves to a figure's head, although some third-party hair props do not. In addition, prop hair is relatively easy to fit to figures other than those for which they are designed. Simply use the xTrans, yTrans, and zTrans dials to position the hair on the head, and use the xScale, yScale, and zScale dials to scale the hair to fit the alternate figure. You want to do this before you make any changes to the pose of your figure; otherwise getting the angles of the head and hair matched up can be quite time consuming.

In the following tutorial, you'll add James to the scene, and add prop hair to his head. Follow these steps:

1. Choose File > New to create a new Poser scene. Poser loads James Casual into the scene. Change the display mode to Textured (Display > Document Style > Texture Shaded).
2. Locate the Poser 6 > Figures > James > James hair library, and click the Change Figure icon at the bottom of the library window to replace James Casual with the Low-resolution James figure.
3. Switch to the Face Camera to get a closer view of James' head.
4. Open the Poser 6 > Hair > James Hair Library. Highlight the Parted Side hair thumbnail. Note that the thumbnail shows this hair as "transmap" hair, but does not identify if it is prop hair or conforming hair.
5. Click the Apply Library Preset button at the bottom of the library window. The hair should appear in your scene.
6. If your figure has been posed, the hair should appear on the figure's head as shown in Figure 7.3.

Some older prop hair created by third-party vendors may not automatically attach itself to the figure's head. After you add a prop hair model that you have never tried before, move the head slightly to determine that the hair moves with it. If the hair does not move with the head, reselect the hair as the current object. Then choose Object > Change Parent. When the Choose Parent window appears, select the figure's head as the parent. Choose OK to close the dialog. Your hair should now follow the figure's head.

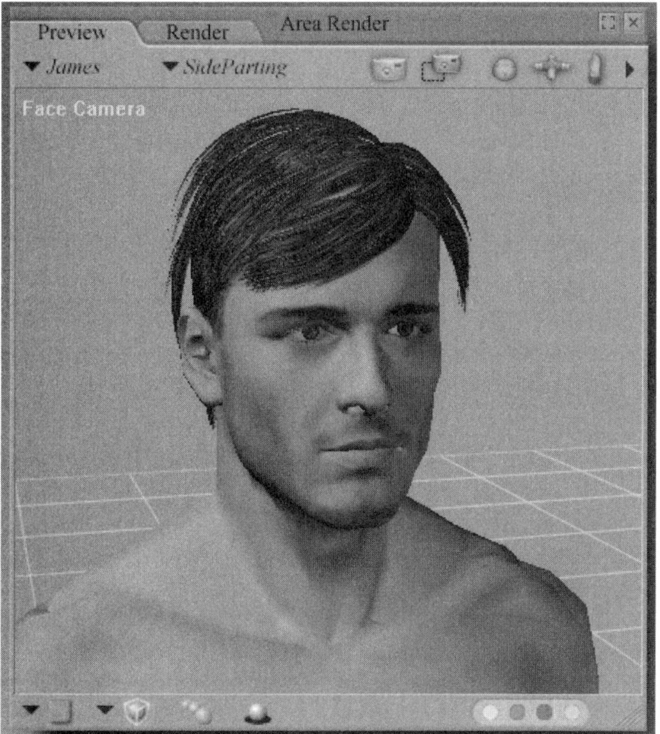

FIGURE 7.3 Prop hair should automatically find and attach itself to the figure's head.

Conforming Hair Revisited

Conforming hair, which you became familiar with in Chapter 3, "Building Scenes," is slightly different from the prop hair discussed earlier in this chapter. Conforming hair was first introduced in Poser 4, with the Conforming Curls hair model. As you learned in Chapter 3, you attach conforming hair to your figure with the Figure > Conform To command.

If necessary, please refer back to Tutorial 1.4, "Adding Conforming Clothing and Hair," to review the entire process of adding conforming hair to a figure.

Conforming hair contains body part groups much like conforming clothing does. The body part groups are named identically to those contained in the figure for which the conforming hair was made. For example, long hair that reaches to halfway down a figure's waist will probably contain groups named head, neck, chest, lCollar, and rCollar. When the figure bends or turns its head and neck, the hair automatically follows.

As mentioned earlier, Poser 6 allows you to store conforming hair in the Hair Library. However, most Poser content creators prefer to maintain compatibility with earlier versions of Poser. As a result, you'll most often find conforming hair in the Figures Library, where library items have a CR2 or CRZ extension. When you load conforming hair from the Poser 6 library, it will appear in the Figures list in the Document Preview window, as shown in Figure 7.4.

FIGURE 7.4 Conforming hair, most often found in the Figures library, is listed in the Figures list in the Document window.

One limitation of conforming hair is that it will not automatically work on figures other than those for which it was created. For example, a conforming hair object that is created for Poser 6's Jessi character will not work on DAZ's Victoria 3 figure right out of the box. To make conforming hair work properly for another figure, you'll need to resize and reposition the hair object, and create a new CR2 file that loads the proper joint configurations onto the repositioned hair object. Chapter 15, "From Modeler to Poser Library," discusses the process of creating conforming clothing and hair.

STYLING PROP AND CONFORMING HAIR

Many Poser hair artists add morphs that will lengthen, shorten, or style the hair object. Without morphs, you cannot easily modify the appearance of prop hair or conforming hair.

You'll learn more about morphs, including how to create your own, in Chapter 10, "Creating Custom Morphs."

When hair props have morphs, the morphs appear in the Parameters window when you select the hair prop. For example, Figure 7.5 shows Paradise Hair, a very popular hair prop by 3Dream, a vendor at Renderosity (*http://www.renderosity.com*). Though this hair prop was not originally created for Jessi, it only took a simple adjustment to place it on her head (yTran was set at –.146, and zTran set at .034). By changing some of the styling morph values to 1, you can make the pigtails longer than their default shoulder length, and move them to the front of her body so that they fall naturally.

It's not always easy to find styling morphs on conforming hair. The most obvious place to look is on the *head* body part of the conforming hair, because most would consider the head group to be the main part of the hair. Sometimes, though, you may find all of the morphs under the *body* part. In addition, extra parts may appear in the hair. An example of extra parts is found in the Aiko 3 Ponytail (available at *http://www.daz3d.com*) shown in Figure 7.6. Here, there are posing controls in the part named "Tail01" that control the bending, shaping, and twisting of the entire ponytail. When styling conforming hair, it is always good to check the Readme document that comes with the hair object. If there isn't one, check through all parts of the hair to see what the morphs do in each body part.

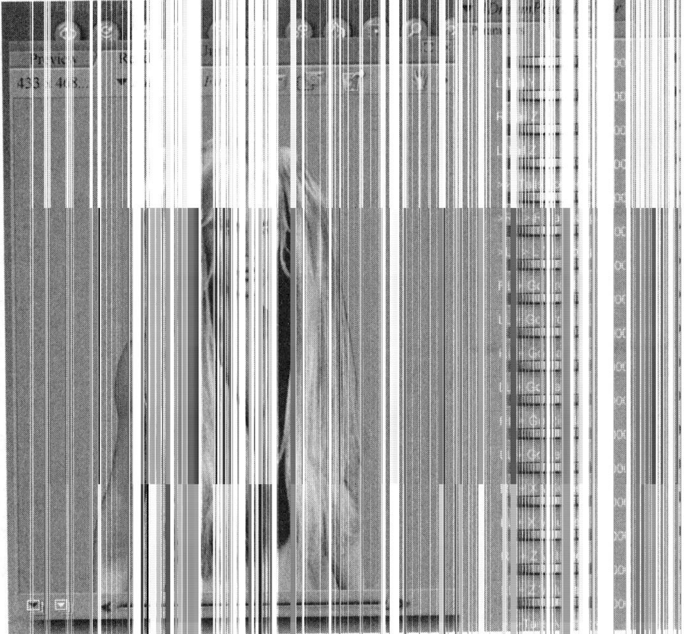

FIGURE 7.5 Many hair props contain styling morphs that let you easily change the appearance of the hair.

FIGURE 7.6 Conforming hair can contain extra body parts that have their own styling morphs.

Dynamic Hair

Dynamic hair, the third type of Poser hair, was introduced in Poser 5. Unlike the other two types of hair, which are based on polygons and geometry, dynamic hair is strand-based. What this means is that dynamic hair is actually made up of hair strands that "grow" from a prop called a skull cap. Though you can grow hair directly on a figure's head, skull caps are necessary in order to create hair that you can use more than once, or to create hair that you can share with others.

Dynamic hair has advantages and disadvantages over the geometry-based hair that you have already become familiar with. The key advantage is that dynamic hair can respond to changes in position, movement, and wind forces. Instead of creating morphs that make the hair move, you use controls in the Hair Room to calculate how the hair responds to those forces. You can also 'style' (bend and shape) individual guide hairs to create complex hair styles for your figure without ever having to adjust polygons in a 3D-modeling application.

The main disadvantage of dynamic hair is that all of the calculations and rendering consume a lot of resources. If your computer is barely above minimum recommended system specs, you may prefer prop or conforming hair because it requires fewer resources.

You'll find very detailed Hair Room tutorials in Chapter 11 of the Poser 6 Tutorial Manual, including information on how to create and group skull caps. You can access this manual through Poser 6 by choosing Help > Poser Tutorial Manual, or by opening the Poser 6 Tutorial Manual.pdf file located in your Poser 6 > Tutorials folder on your hard drive.

Basic Steps for Dynamic Hair

Because the Hair Room tutorials are quite thorough in the *Poser 6 Tutorial Manual*, we'll give only a brief explanation in this chapter so that we can move on to some hands-on tutorials that go a bit beyond the manual.

To create dynamic hair, you place a skull cap on the figure's head. This gives you a base from which you can grow hair. The skull cap can contain one or more hair growth groups, depending on the style of hair you want to create.

Skull caps are also called follicle sets in Poser 6. You can find skull caps for all of the Poser 6 figures in the Hair > Follicle Sets folder. You apply them to your figure in the same way that you apply a hair prop.

After you load [illegible] click [illegible] into your figure, click the Hair tab at the top [illegible] the [illegible] face to enter the [illegible] shown in Figure 7.[illegible]. This [illegible] main areas: [illegible] Groups, Growth Controls, S[illegible] and [illegible] Controls.

FIGURE 7[illegible] The Hair R[illegible] areas: Hair Gro[illegible] Controls, Styling Co[illegible] controls.

In [illegible] Face Room [illegible] the following functions [illegible] detail in the [illegible] *M[illegible]*:

Area 1 Hair Growth [illegible]

Before you can [illegible] object, you hav[illegible] *growth groups* [illegible] the [illegible] will [illegible] also sure you have selected [illegible] to [illegible] the New Growth Group bu[illegible] growth group [illegible] you want to affect. [illegible] the group [illegible] Growth Group button and [illegible] to se[illegible] Continue in this manner [illegible] finished creating [illegible] growth groups.

Area 2: Growth Controls

Select the group that you want to grow hair on from the Current Group menu in section 1. Then click the Grow Guide Hairs button to grow a starting group of hair. Use the dials or number settings in the Growth Controls area to specify the length and length variance (or "shagginess") of the hair. The Pull Back, Pull Down, and Pull Side controls are not intended for styling. Instead, they define the "base properties" of the hair. For example, hair on the sides of a male head normally pulls back. A buzz cut doesn't pull down at all; it goes straight up, so the Pull Down setting is a negative value. Long hair has more weight in real life, so it should be set to pull down.

Area 3: Styling Controls

The Styling Controls offer tools that help you select, deselect, move, twist, and curl hair. This is where the real styling takes place. Click the Style Hairs button to open the Hair Style Tool window, shown in Figure 7.8. Use the Select Hairs tool to select a group of hairs for styling. Once hairs are selected, the other tools are activated. You can translate, curl, scale, or twist hairs. Deselect some or all hairs with the Deselect Hairs tool, or click the Clear Selection button to deselect them all.

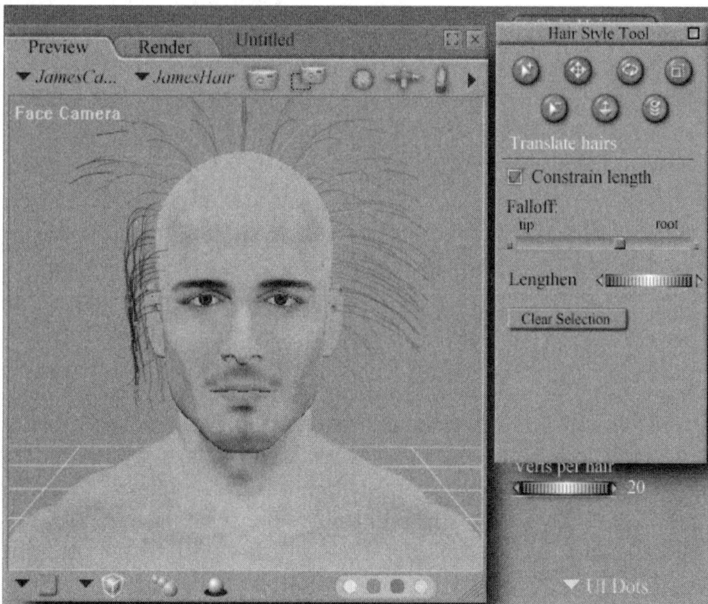

FIGURE 7.8 Use the controls in the Hair Style Tool to translate, curl, scale, or twist hairs.

When you uncheck the Constrain Length option, hairs will lengthen when you drag them; otherwise, use the Lengthen dial to lengthen or shorten the selected strands. The Falloff slider controls the amount of hair that is affected by your changes. To affect only the ends of the hair, move the slider more toward "tip." To affect the entire hair, move the slider more toward "root."

Area 4: Dynamics Controls

The Dynamics Controls, shown in Figure 7.9, contain settings that define how hair moves during animation, when objects collide against it, or how wind forces affect the hair. These settings are most important when you are using dynamic hair in an animation. However, they are also useful when you want to render a still image of hair while it is in motion, such as when a long-haired woman turns her head quickly.

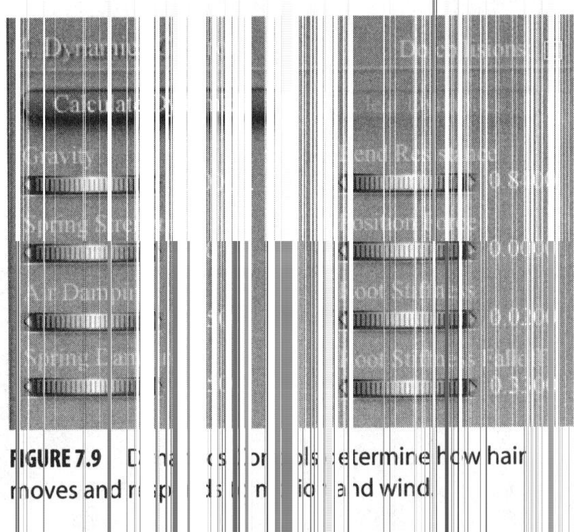

FIGURE 7.9 Dynamics Controls determine how hair moves and responds to motion and wind.

There are eight dynamics controls:

Gravity controls how much or how little the hair is affected by gravity. Higher values weigh hair down more, and negative values cause the hair to "float" (which is great for underwater or space scenes).

Spring Strength defines how much hair bounces when in motion (higher values are more bouncy).

Spring Damping settings define how stretchy it is (lower values allow the hair to bounce longer).

Air Damping settings define how much or how little the hair reacts to wind (higher values blow more easily).

Bend Resistance setting controls how much or how little the hair is allowed to fold or bend.

Position Force setting controls how much or how little the hair reacts to dynamic forces. Higher values cause the hair to remain stiffer and more resistant to movement, collision, and wind.

Root Stiffness setting controls the stiffness of the root of the hair (the hair closest to the head).

Root Stiffness Falloff setting controls how near or far from the head the stiffness range extends.

The Dynamic Controls area also includes a *Do Collisions* checkbox. When this option is checked, dynamic calculations will take longer, but they will also prevent the hair from intersecting with body parts or other objects that have collision detection enabled. To enable collision detection on a body part or object, select the part you want to configure.

TUTORIAL 7.2 CREATING A FUR COAT

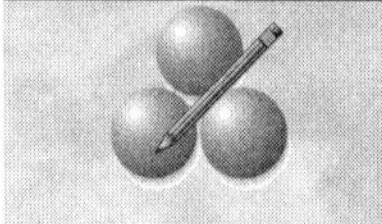

While the obvious use for the Hair Room is to create human hair, it can also serve many other purposes. For example, you can also use the Hair Room to create fur on animals or clothing.

When you create hair for Poser figures, you usually grow the hair on one body part: the head. When you add hair to conforming clothing, each body part (such as the hip, abdomen, or chest) will require its own hair group. As you select each body part, the Group Editor allows you to choose which polygons in that body part should grow hair.

You are able to grow hair directly on a figure's head, or on an animal, piece of clothing, or other object. However, when you save the hair object to the library, it will include references to the original vertices of the object. Because this referenced geometry is copyrighted information and contained within your hair object, you can only use the object and hair for your own personal use. In order to distribute a hair product (either free or for sale), the geometry on which it is based must be your own original creation or based on geometry that you specifically have distribution rights to.

Creating the Hair Groups

In the following tutorial, you'll generate the hair groups for each body part in the coat. There are eight body parts in all, each of which will have its own hair group that includes all of the polygons in the body part.

[illegible] create the f[illegible]r coat, [illegible] [illegible]ps:

[illegible] Tutorials [illegible] Chap0[illegible] [illegible]ROM that accompanies this bo[illegible] [illegible] Runtime fil[illegible]s to the [illegible] beneath your Poser 6 installat[illegible] [illegible] Runtime l[illegible]brary of [illegible] [illegible]s Runtime file contains the com[illegible] [illegible]terials that you will us[illegible] [illegible] tutorials in this chapter.

1. [illegible]hoose File > New to [illegible] Poser scene. Delete the defa[illegible] [illegible]e so that the scene [illegible] [illegible]itch to Texture Shaded disp[illegible] [illegible] (Display > Docu[illegible] > [illegible]ture Shaded).
2. [illegible] the default Pose[illegible] [illegible] Jessi Clothing library, and [illegible] [illegible]t Long" to the sce[illegible] [illegible] [illegible]nforming coat for Jess[illegible]. It [illegible] in the Select Figu[illegible] [illegible] as "FOverCoat."
3. [illegible] the Material tab [illegible] [illegible]aterial Room. Open the libr[illegible] [illegible] contains the Pract[illegible] [illegible] 6 [illegible]aterials mentioned just bef[illegible] [illegible] tutorial.
4. [illegible] sure that the FO[illegible] [illegible]ted as the current object in [illegible] [illegible]ct menu in the Ma[illegible] [illegible] highlight the FurCoat [illegible] [illegible], and click the Ap[illegible] [illegible]et button at the bottom of [illegible] [illegible]ry window. Poser [illegible] [illegible]terial to the fur coat texture[illegible]
5. [illegible] the Hair tab to [illegible] [illegible]oom. The coat appears in [illegible] [illegible]ment window [illegible] [illegible]ou just applied.
6. [illegible] the bottom sectio[illegible] [illegible] select the hip. Then clic[illegible] [illegible] Growth Group [illegible] [illegible] of the Hair Room. Wh[illegible] [illegible]mpted for a name [illegible] [illegible] group, name the group "Co[illegible] [illegible] Click OK to conti[illegible]
7. [illegible]eat Step 6 for the [illegible] [illegible] of the coat (abdomen, ch[illegible] [illegible]ar, lShldr, lForeA[illegible] [illegible] and rForeArm). Name [illegible]propriate sections "[illegible] [illegible] "Coat-Chest," "Coat-LColl[illegible] [illegible]t-LShoulder," "Co[illegible] [illegible] "Coat-RCollar," "Coat-RShl[illegible] [illegible] and "Coat-RFore[illegible] [illegible] are finished, all of the [illegible] [illegible] groups should [illegible] [illegible] Current Actor pull-do[illegible] [illegible]u, as shown in Fig[illegible]
8. [illegible] you create all of [illegible] [illegible] click the hip of the coat. Ve[illegible] [illegible] the Current Group [illegible] [illegible] of the Hair Room reads "Co[illegible]
9. [illegible] the Edit Growth [illegible] [illegible] Group Editor opens.
10. [illegible]ssign all of the pol[illegible] [illegible] click the Add All button in [illegible] [illegible]p Editor. All of th[illegible] [illegible] turn red.
11. [illegible]inue through all [illegible] [illegible] coat in a similar manner. [illegible] click each body pa[illegible] [illegible]ent window, its associated [illegible] [illegible]th group becomes [illegible] [illegible] Group Editor. Click a body p[illegible] [illegible] the document wind[illegible] [illegible] the Add All button in the Gr[illegible]

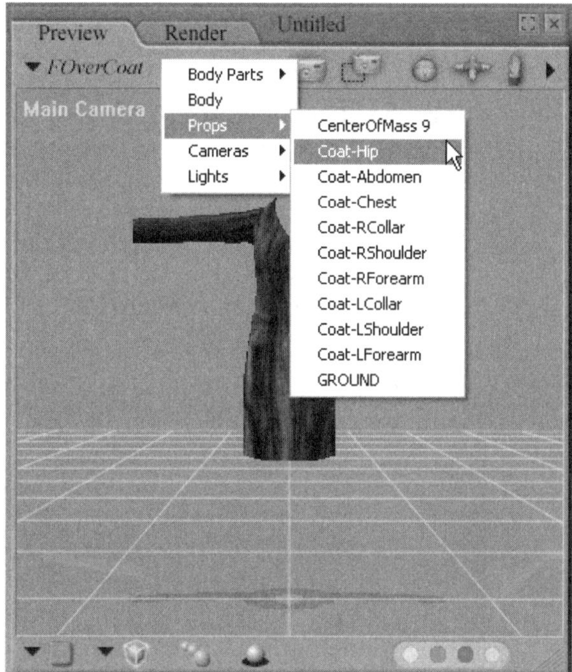

FIGURE 7.10 Create a new hair group for each body part in the coat. The hair groups appear as props in the Current Actor pull-down menu.

Editor. Continue in this manner until you work through each body-part group and add all of the polygons. Close the Group Editor after all polygons have been assigned.

Adding the Hair

After you create all of the hair growth groups and assign the polygons, you can grow the hair on each part. Start again with the hip, and work your way up as you add hair to each section until they are all complete. Proceed as follows:

1. Click the hip of the coat and verify that Coat-Hip is the currently selected hair growth group.
2. In the Growth Controls section, click the Grow Guide Hairs button. Hair appears on the hip section of the coat. Initially, it is rather long and sticks almost straight out.

3. Set the Hair Length to 0.2500 and the Pull Down at 0.00050. This decreases the length of the default hair strands and pulls them downward.
4. In the Styling Controls section, set the Hair Density to 50[illegible] ([illegible] hairs) to make the hair on the coat more full. Then reduce the Verts per Hair setting from the default of 20 down to 4. This will consume fewer resources and make the hair render more quickly. Also, to make the hair a little thicker than the default, increase the Tip Width setting to 0.60000 and the Root Width setting to 1.50000. Your coat should look similar to Figure 7.11.

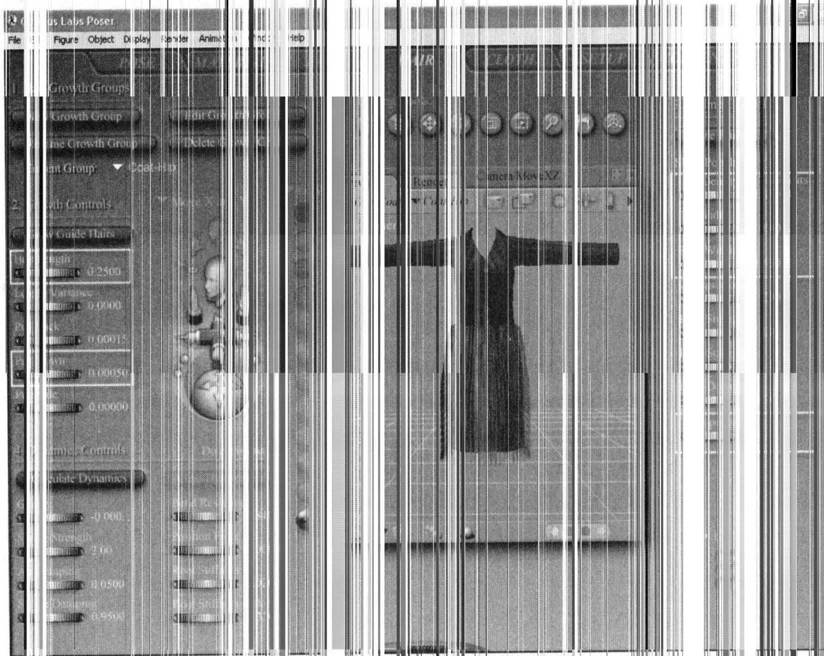

FIGURE 7.11 Fur is added to the hip section first.

5. Repeat Steps 2 through 4 for the abdomen, chest, right collar and left collar (settings for the sleeves follow next).
6. Click the right shoulder to select it in the document window. Set hair length to .2500 (the same length as all of the others) but instead of setting Pull Down to .0005, set Pull Side to .0005.
7. In the Styling Controls section, set the Hair Density to 50[illegible], reduce the Verts per Hair setting to 4, increase the Tip Width setting to 0.60000 and the Root Width setting to 1.50000.

8. Repeat the settings listed in Steps 6 and 7 for the right forearm.
9. Click the left shoulder to select it in the document window. Again, set hair length to .2500. Set the Pull Side to -.0005 (note the negative number).
10. In the Styling Controls section, set the Hair Density to 2500, reduce the Verts per Hair setting to 4, increase the Tip Width setting to 0.60000 and the Root Width setting to 1.50000.
11. Repeat the settings listed in Steps 9 and 10 for the left forearm. When you are finished, your coat should look as shown in Figure 7.12.

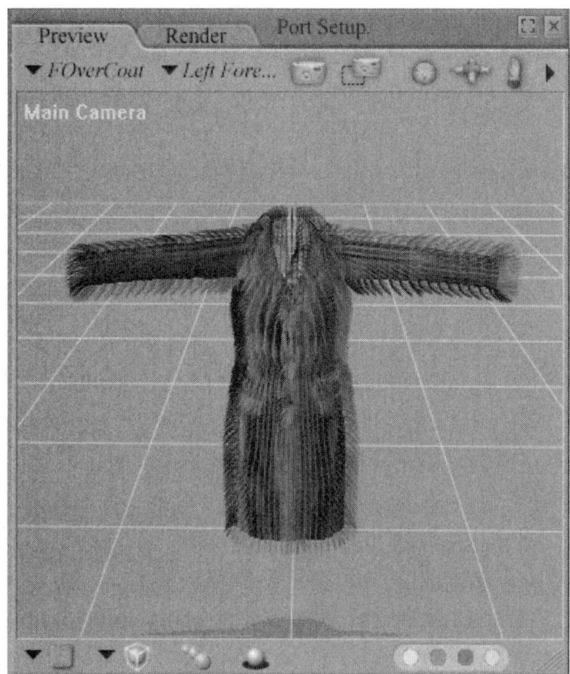

FIGURE 7.12 Using similar settings in all parts of the coat, the fur is now complete.

Changing the Hair Material

If you try to render the fur coat at this point, you'll notice that all of the fur uses the default light-blonde hair color. The Practical Poser 6 materials that you added to your Runtime contains a hair material that picks up the colors from the underlying texture that you applied at the beginning of this tutorial. To add this material to your hair sections, follow these steps:

1. Click the Material tab to open the Material Room.
2. Navigate to the Runtime library that contains the Practical Poser 6 materials that you installed for this tutorial.
3. Locate the Materials > Practical Poser 6 Library. You will find two materials for the fur coat. Highlight the material named "FurCoatHair."
4. From the Object menu in the Material Room, select Props > Coat-Hip, as shown in Figure 7.13.

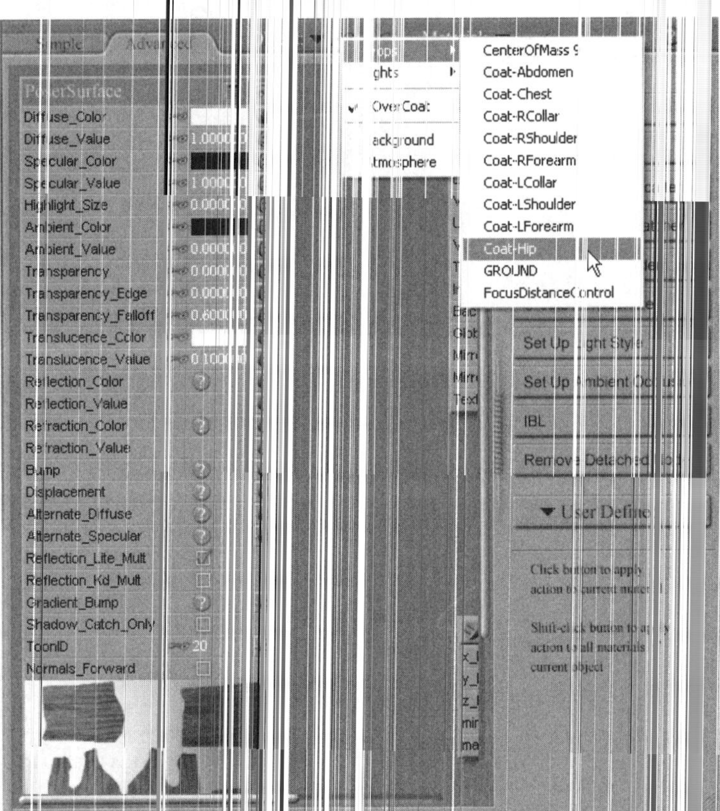

FIGURE 7.13 To assign hair materials to the coat, select the hair growth groups from the Props list.

5. Double-click the FurCoatHair material in the library to change the Coat-Hip material. The material will change to a hair node that uses the fur coat texture map to determine the coloring in the fur.
6. Select each hair growth group (shown earlier in Figure 7.13) one at a time, and change the hair materials until they are all complete.

7. Conforming clothing should be saved in the Figures Library. Choose or create a Figures Library folder in which to save the fur coat. Click the Add to Library button to save the conforming fur coat to the library. The New Set dialog prompts you for a name. Enter "Fur Coat"and click OK. The coat is saved to the library.

TUTORIAL 7.3 CREATING A FEATHERED QUILL PEN

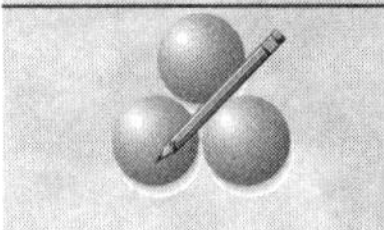

You don't have to limit the Hair Room to creating hair and fur—in fact, it's a great solution for grass, plants, and other natural objects such as feathers. In the following tutorial you will use the Hair Room to complete the feather of a quill pen.

To create the quill pen, follow these steps:

1. From the Practical Poser 6 library files that you installed for this chapter, locate the Props > Practical Poser 6 library. Add the QuillPen prop to an empty scene.
2. Click the Hair tab to open the Hair Room.
3. Click the New Growth Group button in section 1 of the Hair Room. Name the new growth group "Feathers 1."
4. Click the Edit Growth Group button. The Group Editor opens.
5. It is much easier to assign polygons by predefined materials than to select polygons in the Group Editor. The quill pen contains three material zones named *quill, feather1,* and *feather2*. The quill material is for the part of the pen that will not have hair. The feather1 material is for the feathers that will grow out in one direction, and feather2 will grow hair in the other direction. To pick one of the feather materials, click the Add Material button in the Group Editor. Then select feather1 from the dialog shown in Figure 7.14.
6. To create the second feather growth group, click the New Growth Group button in section 1 again. Name the new group "Feathers 2." Feathers 2 automatically becomes the current growth group in the Group Editor.
7. Click the Add Material button, and choose feather2 from the Add Material dialog.
8. Close the Group Editor after you create the second growth group.
9. Select Feathers_1 as the current growth group from the menu in section 1, as shown in Figure 7.15.
10. Click the Grow Guide Hairs button in section 2 of the Hair Room. Guide hairs grow out from the top and right side of the pen.
11. In the Growth Controls section, change the Hair Length to .2000. Set the Pull Down setting to –.00015 so that the hairs grow upward a little bit.

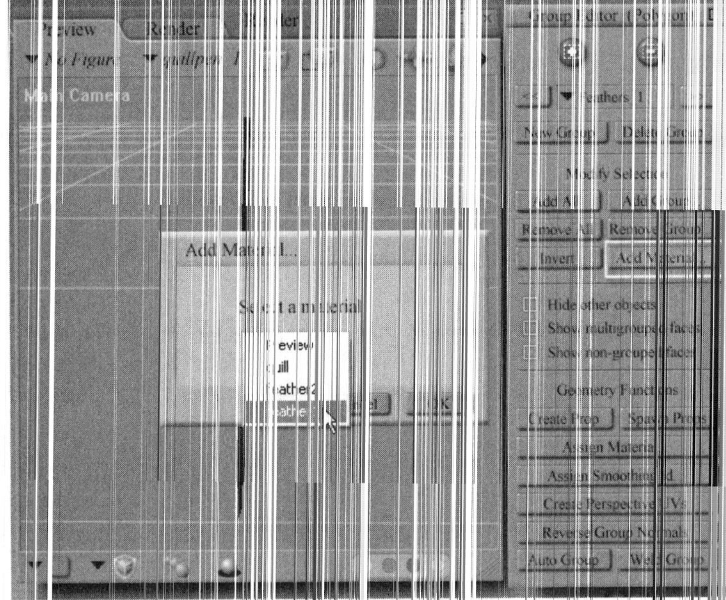

FIGURE 7.14 Select the feather1 material for the first row of feathers.

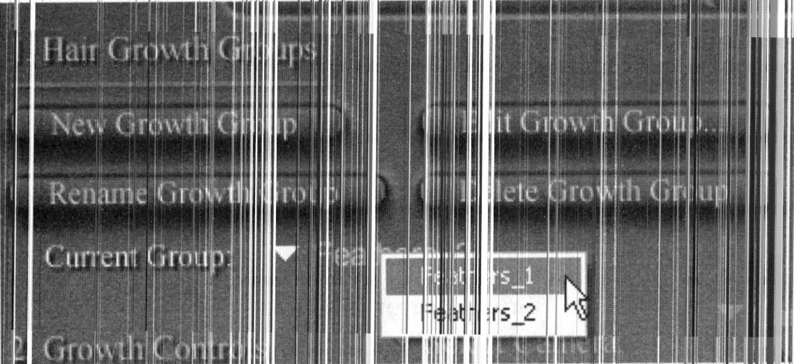

FIGURE 7.15 Select Feathers_1 to grow the first feather section.

12. Now, to create the feathers on the quill. In the Styling Controls section, set the hair density to 30000 (12[illegible] hairs). Increase Tip Width to 1, and Root Width to 2. Reduce the Verts per Hair setting to [illegible]. Render to see the results. Your feather should look similar to Figure 7.16.

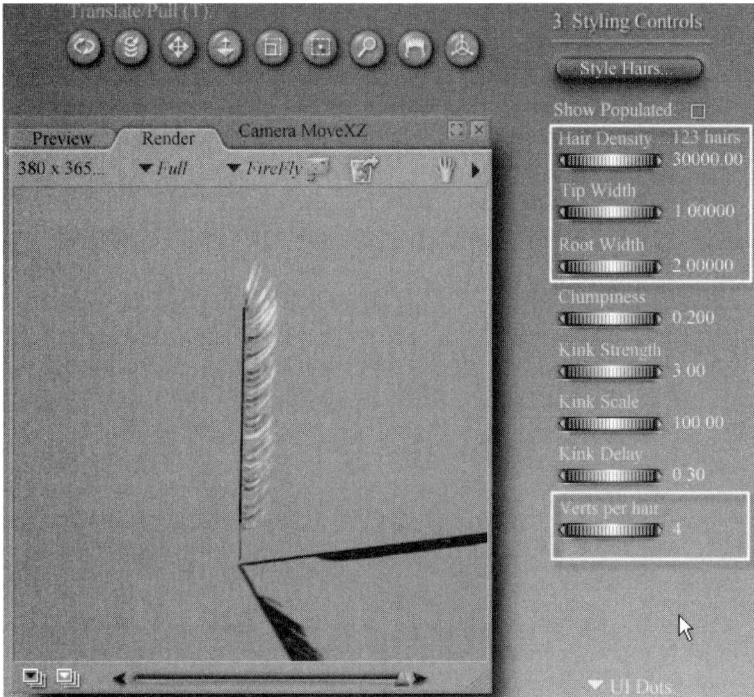

FIGURE 7.16 The first side of the feathers have been added.

13. Select Feathers_2 as the current growth group from the menu in section 1.
14. Click the Grow Guide Hairs button in section 2 of the Hair Room. Guide hairs grow out from the top and right side of the pen.
15. In the Growth Controls section, change the Hair Length to .2000. Set the Pull Down setting to –.00015 so that the hairs grow upward a little bit.
16. In the Styling Controls section, set the hair density for the second feather group to 30000 (129 hairs). Increase Tip Width to 1, and Root Width to 2. Reduce the Verts per Hair setting to 4. Render to see the results. Your feather should now look similar to Figure 7.17.
17. Click the Style Hairs button in the Styling Controls section to refine the feathering if desired. For example, the ends of the feathering branch out into two rows of vertices. You can select both rows of vertices and use to bring the ends closer together. You can curl or twist

FIGURE 7.17 The quill pen now contains feathering on the right and left sides.

the feathers to make the pen fancier, or you can shorten or lengthen specific hairs as desired.

18. When you are done with the quill pen, go back to the Practical Poser 6 Props Library. Click the Add to Library button (the 'plus' sign) at the bottom of the library window. Poser informs you that you should save the hair along with its parent prop. Click OK to continue.
19. In the New Set dialog, enter Feathered Pen for a name. Then click the Select Subset button to open the Hierarchy Selection dialog shown in Figure 7.18.
20. Check quillpen_1, Feathers_1, and Feathers_2 in the Hierarchy Selection dialog. Then click OK to return to the New Set dialog. Click OK again to save the pen to the library.

FIGURE 7.18 Hair groups (Feathers_1 and Feathers_2) should be saved to the library with the underlying prop (quillpen_1).

CONCLUSION

The Hair Room not only helps you create hair and fur for humans and animals, but with some creative thinking you can use it for other natural elements such as grass, sea anemones, flowers, pine trees, and feathers. In this chapter you learned some creative uses for the Hair Room and how to save your furry conforming clothing and props to the libraries. With imagination and patience, you can continue to use the Hair Room for more than hair and fur—the rest is up to you!

CHAPTER

8

WORKING WITH POSER CLOTHING

In This Chapter

- Types of Poser Clothing
- Common Clothing Problems
- Cloth Room Overview
- Creating and Saving Dynamic Clothing
- Conclusion

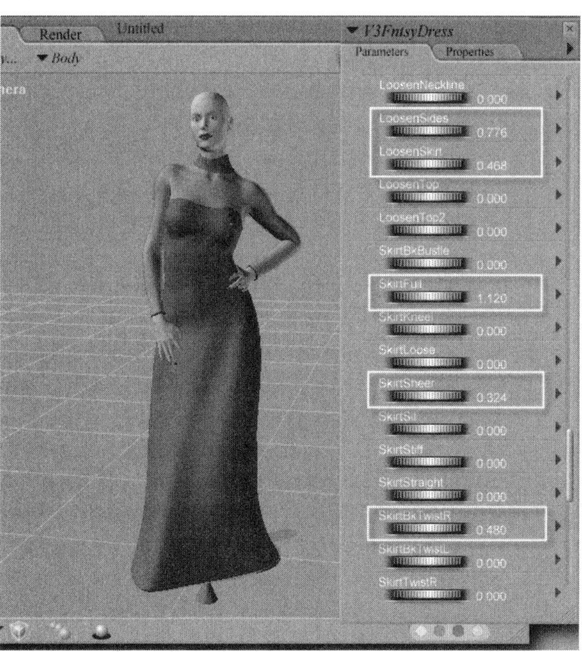

Types of Poser Clothing

Poser 6 allows you [illegible] with several types of clothing and props. Conforming clothing, wh[illegible] ou learned about in Chapte[illegible] "Building Scenes," is only o[illegible] ty[illegible] clothing that Poser figures can wear. You can also use dynamic c[illegible] Poser's Cloth Room. The Clo[illegible] allows you to turn clothi[illegible] garments that respond to [illegible] and wind in animation[illegible] over the figure in a more re[illegible] manner. You'll also learn a[illegible] ways that you can use props [illegible] thing.

Conforming Clothing

Conforming clothing [illegible] appears in the Figures [illegible] where it uses a CR2 or CRZ [illegible]. Poser 6 also allows conforming clothing in the Props Library [illegible] 2 or PPZ extension. When it [illegible] the Poser 6 Props library, [illegible] thumbnail designates it [illegible] clothing. As you le[illegible] Chapter 8, "Building Scenes," [illegible] the Figure > Conform [illegible] to "attach" conforming clothing to your figure. After [illegible] the clothing automatically [illegible] with the figure.

When you add [illegible] clothing to your scene, it [illegible] in the Select Figure men[illegible] the Preview tab in the D[illegible] window. If it does not [illegible] name assigned to it, it [illegible] as "Figure n", wh[illegible] lowest available number [illegible] the figure to your [illegible] rename the clothing to something more recognizable, select [illegible] object, choose its body part [illegible] actor, and rename [illegible] Properties window as shown in Figure [illegible].

Conforming clothing [illegible] some challenges, especially when it comes to posing [illegible]. We'll discuss some of these issues later in this chapter, in [illegible] "Common Clothing Problems."

Dynamic Clothing

Dynamic clothing, [illegible] is a prop. You will always find it in the Props Library, where [illegible] PP2 or PPZ extension. [illegible] dynamic clothing to [illegible] the Figure > Set Figure Parent [illegible] Change Parent co[illegible] Figure 8.2 shows an example [illegible] dynamic dress, which is bei[illegible] by DAZ 3D Stephanie Petite.

Aside from so[illegible] guidelines, there isn't [illegible] *technical* difference bet[illegible] dynamic clothing and the other types of accessories and props th[illegible] in Poser—that is, unti[illegible] it in the Cloth Ro[illegible] you need to *clothify* the pr[illegible] "cloth"), and perfo[illegible] calculations that make the clothing move with the figure in a [illegible] manner. One thing that [illegible] is that you have to [illegible] animation to use dynamic clothing in [illegible]

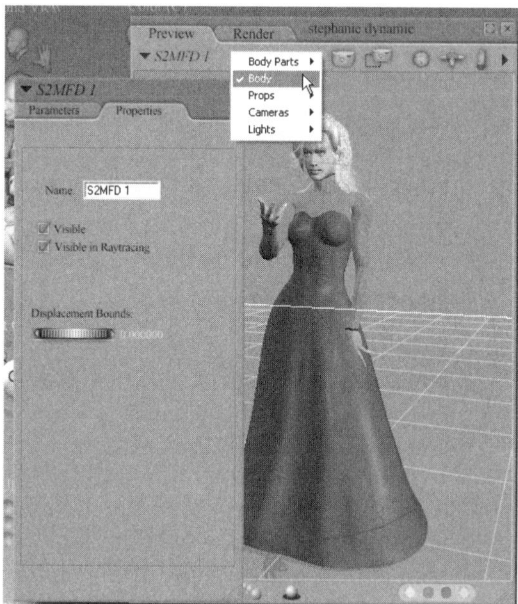

FIGURE 8.1 Conforming clothing appears in the Select Figure menu. Select the body and rename the clothing in the Properties window.

FIGURE 8.2 Dynamic clothing makes use of the Cloth Room to create realistic draping and folding.

[illegible]age. The purpose of th[illegible] [illegible]ation is to allow [illegible] [illegible], [illegible] information, how the cloth [illegible] [illegible] drape and f[illegible] [illegible] the figure. This allows Poser to gradually pose the [illegible] [illegible] steps, so that the [illegible] and [illegible] can follow the natural [illegible] [illegible] the figure. For a [illegible] [illegible] of the process, refer to [illegible] [illegible] of the *Poser [illegible] Manual* [illegible] Poser Tutorial Manual) [illegible] completing the [illegible] [illegible] in this chapter.

Props and Smart Props

You will, on occasion, find [illegible] [illegible] that don't fit [illegible] the [illegible] previously mentioned categ[illegible] [illegible] are considered [illegible]. Accessories, such as hats, glasses, and jew[illegible] are most often found in the Props library and have a PP2 or [illegible]Z ext[illegible]

Props can beh[illegible] [illegible], depending on [illegible] [illegible] standard props or smart props. [illegible] difference between [illegible] isn't really [illegible] [illegible], until you know what [illegible] looks for. Standard [illegible] and [illegible] props both appear in the Props [illegible] and both appear as props in the [illegible] Actor menu of the Document window.

Where you can notice the difference is after [illegible] add th[illegible] scene:

Standard props [illegible] appear in your [illegible] in their [illegible] modeled position. [illegible] generally, this [illegible] exact center of the stage. If [illegible] [illegible] other corner [illegible] the stage [illegible] you [illegible] prop was properly [illegible] into your scene.

It is [illegible] to attach a prop to a [illegible] which [illegible] figure is in its zero [illegible] pose (hence the reason [illegible] how to zero a figure [illegible] Chapter 3). [illegible] prop or [illegible] figure [illegible] already posed [illegible] late and rotate [illegible] position [illegible]. You [illegible] manually position [illegible] prop [illegible] the Trans[illegible] [illegible] the Parameters [illegible] you'll need to [illegible] the prop to the figure [illegible] and choosing [illegible] Change Parent. Make sure [illegible] prop to the appropriate body part ([illegible] head [illegible] earrings, or the [illegible] or a [illegible] you move the [illegible] body part, the prop [illegible] move a[illegible]

Smart props already [illegible] what they are supposed to be [illegible] or *parent*[illegible] to. [illegible] smart prop [illegible] was saved to the [illegible] it was attached to the [illegible] body part. When [illegible] [illegible] that, for example, it finds the head and positions it [illegible] the correct [illegible] angle based on the [illegible] of the figure's [illegible]. Figure [illegible] shows some examples of smart props that are included in the Jessi Clothing Props Library. The hat, glasses, and earrings all find their way to the correct places when you add them to Jessi. If the hat is made for a different figure, however, you may need to adjust the scale or position with the Parameter dials.

To "unattach" a prop from a figure, choose Object > Change Parent, and select "Universe" as the new parent of the prop.

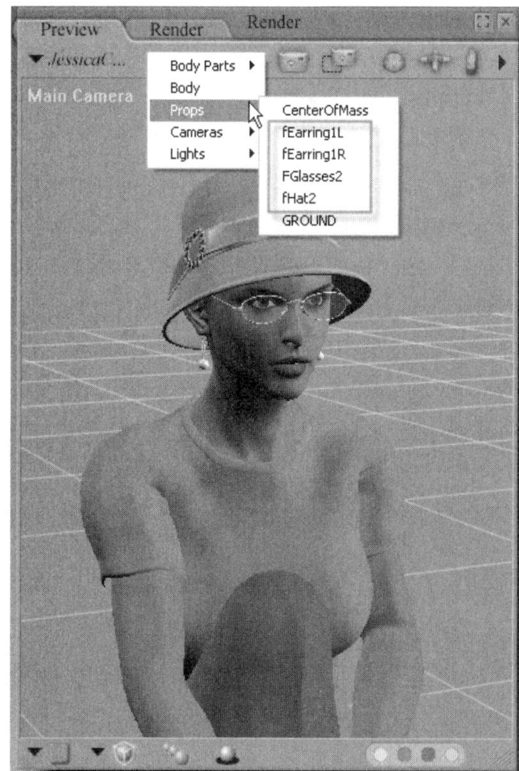

FIGURE 8.3 Smart props appear in the Current Actor menu, and automatically find and attach themselves to the proper body part.

Common Clothing Problems

Let's say you've added clothing to your figures, and something doesn't seem right. Body parts stick out. The clothing doesn't pose correctly, or it doesn't pose at all. Sometimes you add items from the library and you don't see clothing at all! What's going on, and how do you fix it? The following sections anticipate some of the more common problems that Poser users face and explain how to prevent them from occurring.

Clothing Doesn't Conform Correctly

Basically, in order for conforming clothing to work properly, you have to use clothing that was built for the figure that wears it. The main reason for this is because each figure has its own body shape, along with unique *joint parameters* that tell Poser how to bend and blend the body parts when you pose them.

If clothing is made for a different figure than the one you're working with, it's not enough to rescale the clothing so that it fits around the figure correctly. To work properly, conforming clothing must also use joint parameters that are extremely close, if not identical, to the figure that wears it.

It isn't always easy to determine if you have the right clothing. There are several Poser figures that have been released in multiple versions. For example, DAZ3D Victoria 1 and 2 have the same basic body shape and joint parameters, but Victoria 3 is built a bit differently. As a result, clothing made for Victoria 3 will not fit properly when placed on Victoria 1. Figure 8.4 shows an example of this. Because the joints on the two figures are different, *poke-through* is most evident in extreme poses.

FIGURE 8.4 Clothing for Victoria 3 is applied to Victoria 1 (left) and Victoria 3 (right). The differences in joints are most evident in extreme poses.

If your clothing doesn't seem to conform properly, here are some things that you can check:

Use clothing that is made for the figures you are using. Pay attention to the figures that you are using, and select clothing made for those figures. At the same time, be aware that there may be other "generations" of a figure that use different clothing parameters.

You accidentally posed the clothing and not the figure. You're not alone with this mistake. When you work with conforming clothing, it's all too easy to apply a pose to clothing instead of to the original figure. If you catch it right away, you can undo the operation with the Edit > Undo command. You can also reconform the clothing to the character with the Figure > Conform To command. A third option is to open the Joint Editor (Window > Joint Editor), select the clothing that is not posed correctly, and click the Zero Figure button in the Joint Editor to get the clothing back to its default state. Then apply the pose to the human figure.

The arms and legs bend when conformed. You're certain you are using the right clothing, but when you conform it to the figure the arms and legs bend. This is a common symptom when clothing is saved in a non-zero pose. Select the clothing and zero the pose with the Joint Editor as mentioned in the previous paragraph. Then choose Edit > Memorize > Figure. Resave the new memorized version to your Figures Library under a new name, and use your fixed version in place of the original.

Fixing Poke-throughs

Even when you put the right clothing on the right character, there will be times when you see skin poking through the clothing. In fact, you probably noticed it earlier in Figure 8.4, when you compared Victoria 1 and Victoria 3 posed in a tight-fitting catsuit.

If you frequent the Poser communities, you'll probably notice that tight-fitting clothing is quite common. While it's obvious that one of the reasons is because people like to create images of beautiful women in sexy clothing (a *mild* understatement in Poserdom), another reason is because tight-fitting clothing is easier to create and use than looser-fitting clothing, which requires adjustments in the joint parameters (not an easy task!).

One solution is to fix problem areas after you render, using an image editor to blend or clone surrounding areas over the skin that shows through the clothing. However, you can address them before you render you ...ce ne... ere ...re some ways that you can fix poke-throughs in Poser before you ...der:

- ...elect the bo...y part that is poking through the clothing. Open the Propert...s panel, and uncheck the Visible option to hide the offending bod... part as shown in Figure 8.5. Repeat this for each body part that is p...ing through the clothing.

FIGURE ... Select a part and uncheck the Visible option in the Properties window to hide a body part that pokes through clothing.

- Sometimes a body part is only partially covered by clothing, so you won't have the option of hiding it. In cases like these, select one of the problem sections in the clothing or the body of the clothing. Check the Parameters window for morphs that loosen the clothing in the offending body part, and use them to adjust the clothing.

- Another option to address partially covered body parts is to do two renders, one with the body part visible, another with the body part visible and then composite the two images in your favorite graphics editor. If you decide to use this method, you can also take advantage of Poser 6's Area Render feature and only re-render that small section of your scene as needed.
- For clothing that does not have sizing or adjusting morphs, use the xScale, yScale, or zScale dials in the Parameters window to scale the body part down, scale the clothing part up, or a combination of both.
- Use magnets to alter the shape of the clothing so that it fits better. Magnets allow you to shape and morph any object in Poser. You'll learn more about creating morphs in Chapter 10, "Creating Custom Morphs."

When Body Shapes are Different

Many Poser figures offer morphs that change the overall body shape. Busty, buxom women and muscular heroic men pervade the Poser art galleries, but when you try to create and dress one of your own, the figure bursts out of his or her clothing like the Incredible Hulk going through his metamorphosis. The morphed figure of James shown in Figure 8.6 shows you an example of this.

Having the ability to create your own characters is part of the fun of Poser. But what fun is it if they don't fit into their clothing? Certainly there must be a solution. Actually, there are several. For example:

- If you are using DAZ3Dfigures (Michael, Victoria, Stephanie Petite, David, Aiko, and others), many DAZ original conforming clothing products include most, if not all, of the morphs that the figures include. Other merchants that make clothing for DAZ3D figures include morphs that are compatible with only the most popular body morphs. When body morphs are included, a complete morph list usually appears on the DAZ3D product information pages. Use the same morph settings in the clothing as you did when you created your character.
- When conforming clothing does not contain body shaping morphs, you can use utilities such as The Tailor (available at *http://www.daz3d.com*) or Wardrobe Wizard (available at *http://www.philc.net*) to help create them. The Tailor allows you to alter clothing made for a particular figure so that it fits a morphed version of the same figure. Wardrobe Wizard is a Python script that converts clothing from one Poser figure to fit another. This utility supports clothing conversion between many of the popular Poser figures and boasts excellent support and frequent updates.

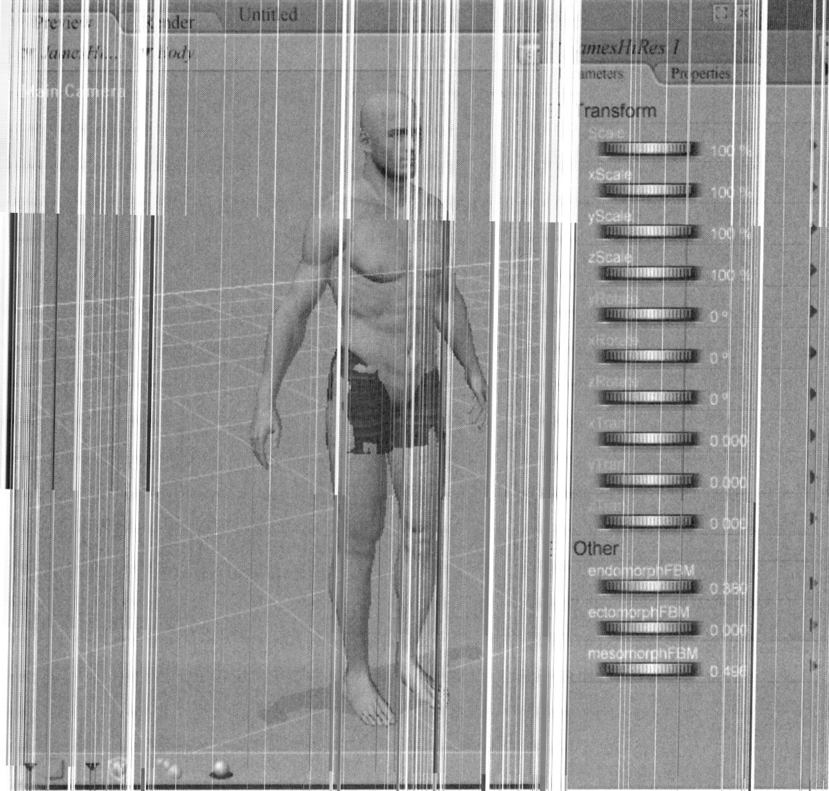

FIGURE 8.6 When you morph figures into custom characters, you also have to morph clothing to fit.

At the time of this writing, The Tailor requires the use of CR2s that are manually edited to remove all references to the Center of Mass props used for Auto Balancing in Poser 6. These extra parts result in errors when you try to open CR2 files that have been saved in Poser 6 libraries. The Tailor version 1.6 (or later) resolves this incompatibility.

- If you're a do-it-yourself type of person, you can use Poser's magnets or an external 3D modeling program to morph conforming clothing so that it fits your custom figure.
- Use dynamic clothing, and the power of the Cloth Room, to morph the clothing for you. Dynamic clothing is very easy to morph so that it fits custom figures. A full explanation of the process is included in the Poser 6 Tutorial Manual.

Posing Skirts

Before dynamic clothing was introduced in Poser 5, one of the "holy grails" of Poser was the development of skirts and long robes that moved and posed realistically. While dynamic clothing fills that void quite admirably, the quest for the ultimate conforming skirts still exists. In fact, of all the types of conforming clothing that you can use in Poser, the most difficult to develop and use are dresses, skirts, and robes.

The reasons for their difficulties are due, in part, to the technicalities involved in making Poser objects. When dividing the human character into body part groups, the right and left legs are separated by the hip. In order to pose automatically with a figure, the clothing must be divided in the same manner. That means that skirts, dresses, and other long robe-like garments have to be divided in a similar manner.

For dresses and similar clothing, you will often find right and left thighs serving as the legs of the skirt, and a full-length hip section separates the two sides. Because of this, the skirt has no shins, so it doesn't bend at the knees. Additionally, the center hip section remains fairly rigid and serves as the blending zone between the two legs. As Figure 8.7 shows, this design makes it difficult to achieve sitting poses in all but very short skirts. The middle hip section of the dress has a tendency to stretch and distort the texture when legs are moved sideways, forward, or backward.

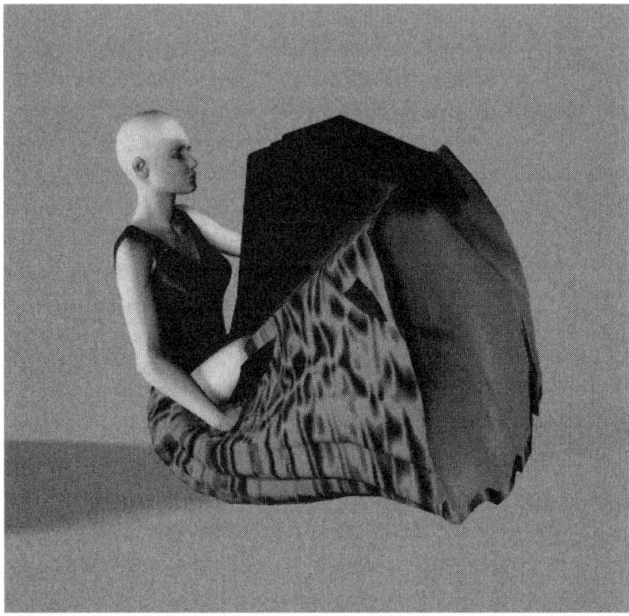

FIGURE 8.7 Long conforming skirts present problems in sitting positions.

As a result of these limitations, long dresses and skirts usually look their best with standing poses, and even then, mostly in poses where legs are not spread too far from their original straight position. To remedy some of these problems, *body handles* began to appear in Poser clothing and accessories.

Using Body Handles

As early as 2000, even before the release of Poser 5 and dynamic clothing, there was discussion in the Poser community about different ways to approach the morphing and posing of figures and clothing. Developers on the Poser technical boards began discussing the possibility of using *phantom* or *ghost body parts* (parts that are not actually visible on the body or clothing, but exist in the underlying hierarchy structure) to pose and otherwise manipulate clothing and figures. The challenge was developing them in such a way that the "average Joe" would be able to use them without too much difficulty.

As a result of the discussion regarding ghost parts, body handles as we know them today were introduced by Anton Kisiel and released at DAZ3D during the first quarter of 2002. This ingenious method of posing figures adds extra ghost parts to the figure's standard hierarchy. For example, in addition to the upper body parts, the abdomen, and the hip, a dress might have another extra part named "skirt." In order to pose the skirt, you drag a little piece of geometry called a body handle, which is typically shaped like a cone or a sphere. These body handles allow the user the freedom to work with clothing that poses in part with the character and in part by manual interaction.

While body handles can be used in long hair, beards, and extra clothing parts, you see them used most often in long dresses, robes, and other flowing clothing. The solution for dresses is to make the skirt as one group—the hip, or a different group named skirt (or something similar). The body handle appears centered beneath the figure, generally below ground level.

Figure 8.8 shows the DAZ Morphing Fantasy Dress for Victoria 3. Notice the cone-shaped body handle beneath the clothing. When you pose the figure, you can drag the body handle to position the skirt appropriately for the figure's pose.

After you pose the clothing with the body handles, you will typically find morphs that will improve the flow of the clothing. For example, in the DAZ3D Morphing Fantasy Dress, there are several morphs that appear in the Body that widen, loosen, flare, twist, and otherwise style the pose of the dress. Figure 8.9 shows an example of some of the morphs in use.

FIGURE 8.8 Drag the body handle, shown here as a cone, to position the clothing appropriately for the pose.

Posing Shoes

Shoes come in all shapes and sizes, ranging from sandals to thigh-high boots. For the most part, shoes conform to the feet in much the same way as other conforming clothing. As long as shoes are relatively flat, there isn't a lot of extra work involved to pose them.

The exception to this is shoes that have high heels. Because clothing is typically modeled around figures that are in their default pose, high heels look extremely strange when you first put them on your figure. The position of the shoes on the feet makes it look like your character has just stepped on a banana peel and is about to slip and fall. The heels are usually below ground level and appear to be poking through the floor. Figure 8.10 shows an example of high-heeled shoes that are added to a foot that is in its default pose.

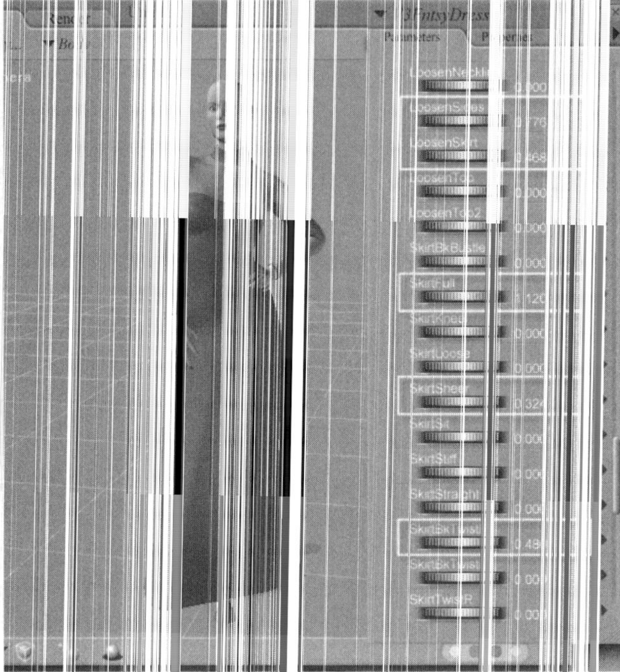

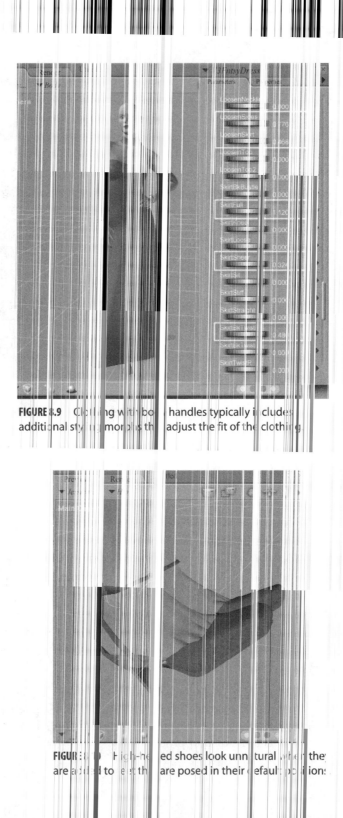

FIGURE 8.9 Clothing with body handles typically includes additional styling morphs that adjust the fit of the clothing.

FIGURE 8.10 High-heeled shoes look unnatural when they are added to feet that are posed in their default positions.

The solution to the posing of the feet is pretty obvious. You'll need to angle the front of the foot downward and possibly (but not all the time) angle the toes upward. While doing so, you also have to make sure that the shoes are landing properly on your floor or on the ground.

Let's use Jessi's Shoe Heel R and Shoe Heel L as examples. These are the same shoes that you added in the tutorials in Chapter 3, "Building Scenes." In order for these shoes to land properly on the floor, you have to bend each foot 35 degrees. After that, you'll need to raise or lower Jessi's hip or body so that the feet rest properly on your floor. The easiest way to do that is to use an Orthogonal Camera (left, right, front, or back) to view your scene without perspective. Zoom in on one of the feet, and make sure you see the plane of the floor or surface as well. Select the hip or body of the figure, and move the yTrans dial up or down as necessary to place the foot on the surface as shown in Figure 8.11.

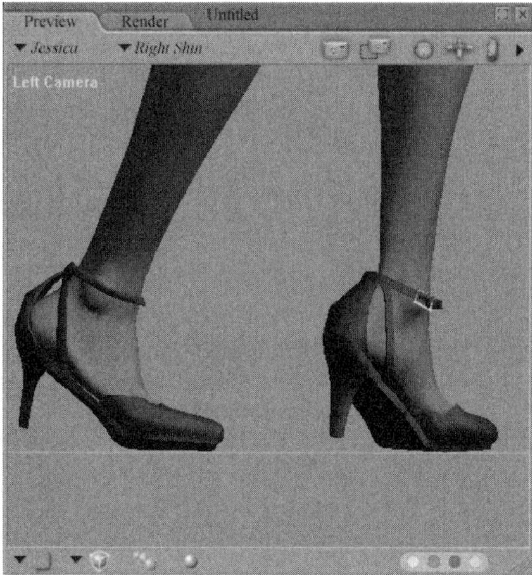

FIGURE 8.11 Make sure that your feet touch the ground after you reposition the foot.

Clothing Doesn't Load from the Library

There may be times when you add conforming or dynamic clothing to your scene and don't see it appear on your figure. If this happens, verify that you have selected your clothing from the Figures or Props library, instead of the Pose library, as shown in Figure 8.12.

FIGURE 8.12 Load figures, characters, or clothing from the Figures (left) or Props (center) libraries. The Poses Library (right) contains pose files that change the materials on the clothing in your scene.

The Pose library often contains library items that show clothing in the thumbnails, so it is very easy to get confused by them. The clothing thumbnails that you see in the Pose library apply textures or material settings to clothing that you have already added to your scene. These poses are more commonly known in the Poser community as MAT Poses (*MAT* being an abbreviation for *material*). Their sole purpose is to make it easier for users to apply different textures to their clothing.

MAT Poses Don't Load Textures Properly

As long as we're on the subject of MAT poses, we should probably mention one more problem that can occur when you use them. MAT poses only work properly on the figures or clothing for which the textures were created. Though objects can have materials that are named the same, the texture maps that are used from those materials must also be the same. For example, the Poser 5 female (Judy) and the Poser 6 female (Jessi) both have materials named Head, Body, Gums, and so on. However, the two figures have different UV map configurations, so any image-based textures are very different. To see an illustration of this point, look at Figure 8.13, which shows a comparison between the body texture for Judy and the body texture for Jessi.

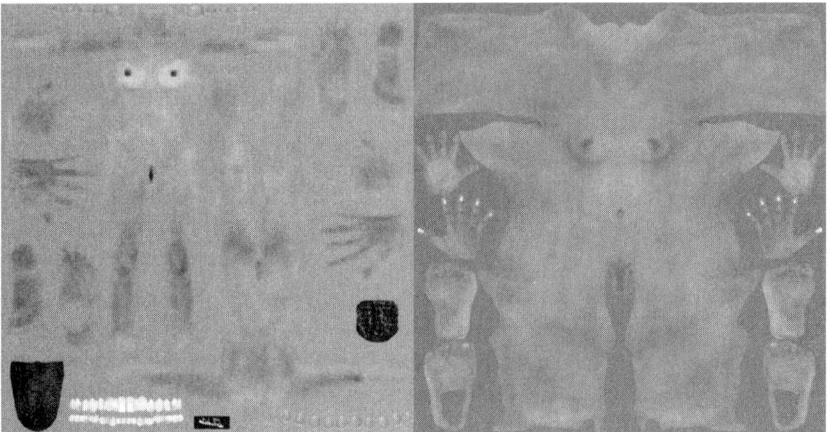

FIGURE 8.13 The body textures for Judy (left) and Jessi (right) are quite different, even though many of the materials in each figure have the same names.

Because the texture maps for Judy and Jessi are arranged differently, the body texture for Judy won't line up properly if you apply it to Jessi. Figure 8.14 shows the result when Judy's body texture is applied to Jessi. As you can see, portions of the teeth and tongue texture appear on Jessi's legs and feet.

Before you apply a MAT pose from the Pose Library, make sure that you have selected the correct object in your scene first. Then apply the MAT pose, and you should see the object change color or texture.

FIGURE [illegible] Textures do not line up properly when they are used on the wrong object.

CLOTH ROOM OVERVIEW

Now that we've covered some of the common problems that can occur when using conforming clothing, you'll learn a bit more about dynamic clothing and the Cloth Room. Dynamic clothing works a bit differently than conforming clothing. The main differences between conforming clothing and dynamic clothing appear in Table 8.1.

TABLE 8.1 Conforming Clothing versus Dynamic Clothing

CONFORMING CLOTHING	DYNAMIC CLOTHING
Able to handle complex geometry, such as multilayered clothing or overlapping faces more easily than dynamic clothing.	More particular about clothing construction. Avoid overlapping or self-intersecting geometry, or hems that fold underneath clothing.
Clothing geometry is divided into body part groups that are named the same as the figure for which they are created. The body part groups should match those of the underlying figure as closely as possible.	Clothing geometry contains only one group and is not divided into body part groups. However, you can use the Group Editor in the Cloth Room to create cloth groups that give areas of the clothing different dynamic properties that simulate different types of cloth.

→

To attach the clothing to the figure, select the clothing item and choose Figure > Conform To. Select the name of the character as the object to conform to.	To attach the clothing to the figure, select the clothing item and choose Object > Change Parent. Select the character's hip or body as the parent.
After conforming the object, the clothing poses automatically when you pose the character.	After assigning the parent, you must create a simulation in the Cloth Room to pose the clothing.
Morphs may be necessary to make the clothing move more realistically in an animation.	Cloth simulations make the clothing move realistically in an animation.

The Cloth Room is shown in Figure 8.15. This is where you change static clothing prop into clothing that can move and animate with more realism than conforming clothing. You accomplish this by working through the four main areas of the Cloth Room: the Cloth Simulation area (1), the Cloth area (2), the Cloth Groups area (3), and the Dynamics Controls area (4).

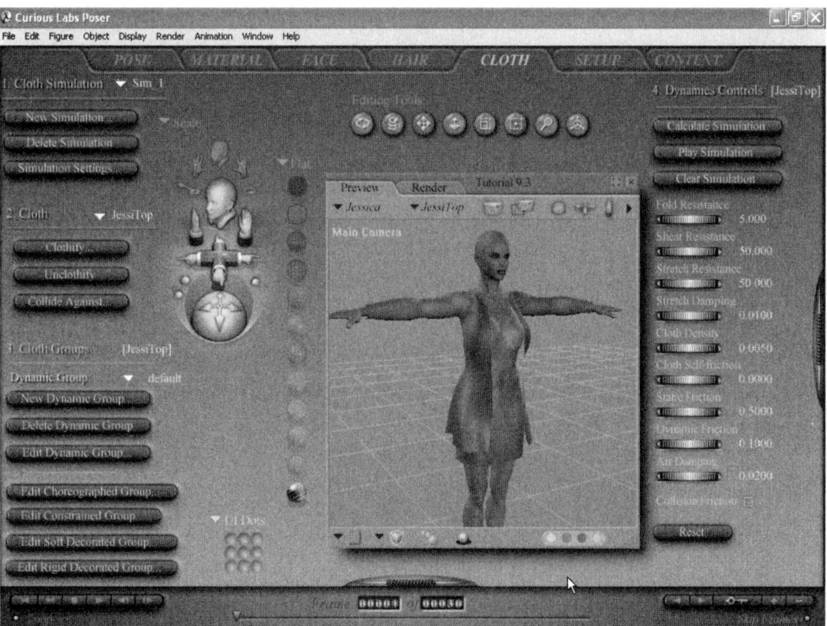

FIGURE 8.15 The Cloth Room contains features that help you create clothing that moves and animates realistically.

Each area of the Cloth Room serves specific purposes. For example, in the Cloth Simulation area, you assign a name and additional parameters for your cloth simulation. You specify parameters such as the range of frame numbers through which the simulation takes place, whether or not you want to drape the cloth before calculations start, and additional cloth collision options.

Use the Cloth Area to choose the item to turn into cloth and to specify the objects that will cause the clothing to react when the cloth collides against them. You can choose any body part on your figure, other clothing objects, or other props in your scene. Remember, however, that you should keep the number of collision objects as low as possible to conserve resources. The more items you select, the longer calculations will take, and the more resources will be used.

The Cloth Groups area contains several buttons that help you divide your clothing object into several types of cloth groups:

Dynamic groups give you the ability to create more than one type of clothing in your object. By default, all polygons in your clothing are assigned to one cloth group and they all behave the same. If you create additional dynamic groups, you can assign different properties to the vertices that are included in the new dynamic group.

Choreographed groups respond to keyframed animation.

Constrained groups help keep vertices in place in relation to your figure (for example, they will keep the strap of a dress in place on your figure's shoulder).

Soft Decorated groups are used for items such as pockets or other flexible decorations that are not attached to the main clothing mesh. This prevents the pockets from falling off the clothing.

Rigid Decorated groups are used for items such as buttons, cufflinks, jewelry, or other rigid objects that are a part of the clothing but not attached to the geometry.

Finally, the Dynamics Controls area contains several different parameters that help you define the behavior of the cloth.

Chapter 10 of the Poser 6 Tutorial Manual covers each area of the Cloth Room in great detail. Chapter 29 of the Poser 6 Reference Manual explains the Cloth Room controls and cloth simulations. We recommend that you review and become familiar with the material in both manuals before you proceed with the material in this chapter.

CREATING AND SAVING DYNAMIC CLOTHING

Though the Cloth Room is relatively easy to use, it is very resource-intensive. Chances are you may have a need to use more than one article of dynamic clothing in a scene. If resources are scarce, make sure you pay attention to the polygon counts in your dynamic clothing, especially if you are going to use more than one piece of dynamic clothing in each scene. Remember that each piece of clothing will require a separate simulation. You can either calculate all simulations at the same time or calculate each simulation individually.

It is also easier to use clothing that was designed to work together. For example, if you have a shirt, pants, vest, and coat that were purchased in the same set, chances are very good that they were designed in layers. In other words, if you put the shirt on, it tucks under the pants, the vest goes over the pants and shirt, and the coat goes over all other clothing without poking through the previous layers.

If you randomly pick clothing that was not designed to work together, you may need to adjust the scale of each layer of clothing or use magnets to reshape the clothing so that the underlying layers do not poke through the layer or layers that are above them.

If you do not address the poke-through issues in your dynamic clothing before you calculate the simulations, you may get error messages that the simulations have failed. This is because Poser expects the cloth to remain outside of the figure, so when clothing intersects the geometry of the figure calculations can go out of bounds.

TUTORIAL 8.1 LOADING THE CONTENT

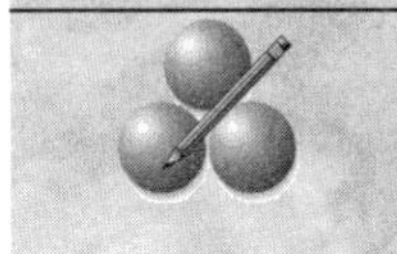

The clothing that you'll use in this tutorial was designed to work together. You'll add a top, skirt, and jacket to Jessi before you create the simulations. You'll begin this tutorial by importing each clothing article. Proceed as follows:

1. Before you open Poser, locate the JessiTop.obj, JessiSkirt.obj, and JessiJacket.obj files in the Tutorials > Chap08 folder on the CD-ROM that accompanies this book. Create a folder named PracticalPoser6 beneath the Poser 6 > Downloads > Runtime > Geometries folder, and copy the objects to that location.

2. Locate the JessiTop.jpg, JessiSkirt.jpg, and JessiJacket.jpg files in the Tutorials > Chap08 folder on the CD-ROM. Create a folder named "PracticalPoser6 beneath the Poser 6 > Downloads > Runtime > Textures folder, and copy the images to that location.

3. Load Jessi or Jessi Hi Res into a blank Poser scene.
4. Use the Figure > Use Inverse Kinematics command to turn IK off on each leg, and use the Joint Editor to zero the pose of Jessi. Then choose Display > Document Style > Texture Shaded to view Jessi in Texture Shaded mode.
5. Click the Cloth tab to enter the Cloth Room. If the HTML Room Help page appears, close it so that you have room to view the contents of the room.
6. Choose File > Import > Wavefront OBJ. The Import Wavefront OBJ dialog appears.
7. Navigate to the Downloads > Runtime > Geometries > Practical-Poser6 folder, and select JessiTop.obj. Click Open to display the Prop Import Options dialog shown in Figure 8.16.

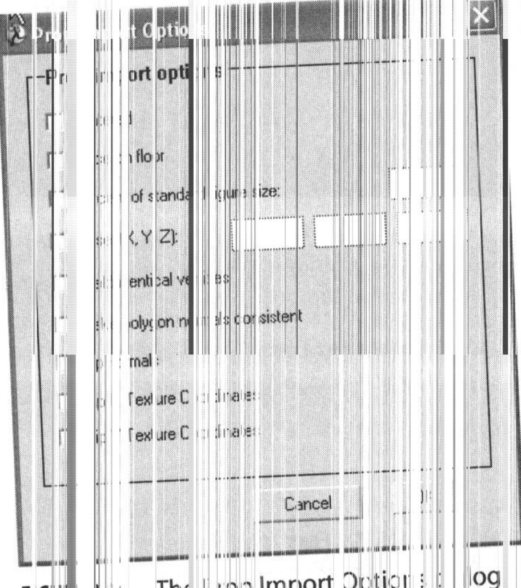

FIGURE 8.16 The Prop Import Options dialog appears when you import a 3D object into Poser.

8. The top will appear in the correct position when you import it into the scene. Therefore, you won't have to check any options when you import the top. Verify that all options in the Prop Import Options dialog are not checked, and click OK to continue. A progress bar appears while the object loads, and then the top appears in the scene.
9. With the top selected, choose Object > Change Parent. The Choose Parent dialog appears.
10. Select Jessi's hip as the parent for the top, as shown in Figure 8.17. Choose OK to continue.

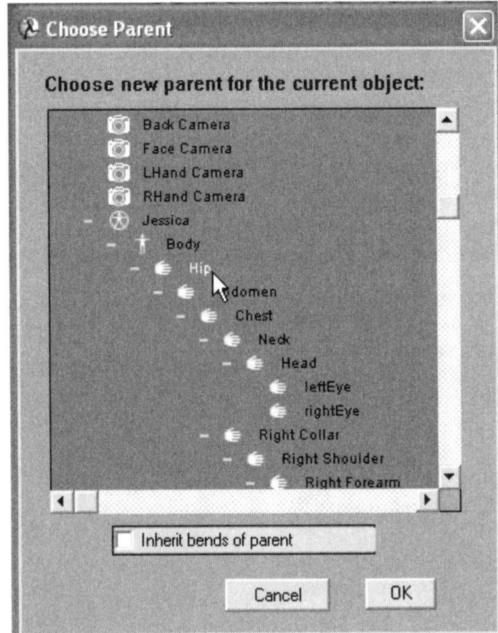

FIGURE 8.17 Select Jessi's hip as the parent to the clothing item.

11. Repeat Steps 6 through 10 to import JessiSkirt.obj from the same location as the top. Again select Jessi's hip as the parent to the skirt.
12. Repeat Steps 6 through 10 to import JessiJacket.obj from the same location as the top. Once more, Jessi's hip will be the parent to the jacket.

TUTORIAL 8.2 ADDING THE MATERIALS

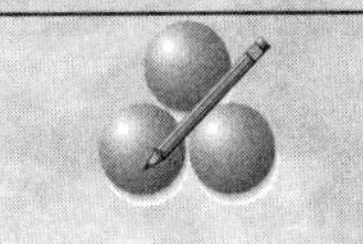

The next step in the process of creating dynamic clothing is to add the materials. We'll use the Simple view in the Material Room to assign the textures to each article of clothing. It's very easy to assign texture maps using the Simple view.

You'll learn much more about creating and assigning materials in the next chapter, but this tutorial will step you through the basics of creating some very simple materials for your dynamic clothing. Follow these steps:

1. Click the Material tab to enter the Material Room. If necessary, click the Simple tab to display the Simple material view.

2. Select JessTop from the Objects > Props menu in the Material Room as shown in Figure 8.18. The Collar material will be selected by default.

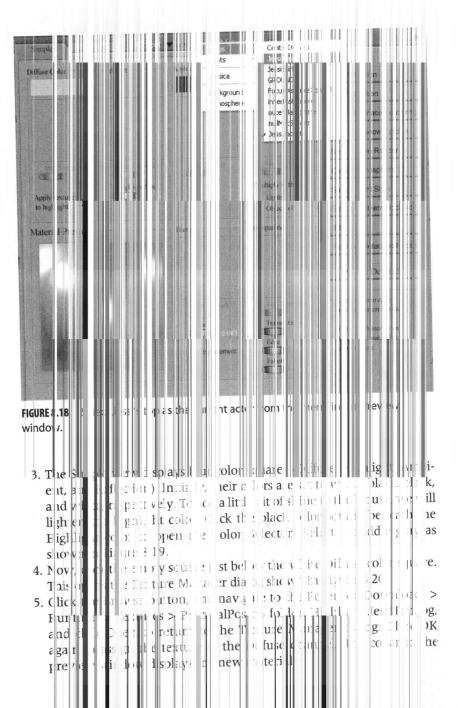

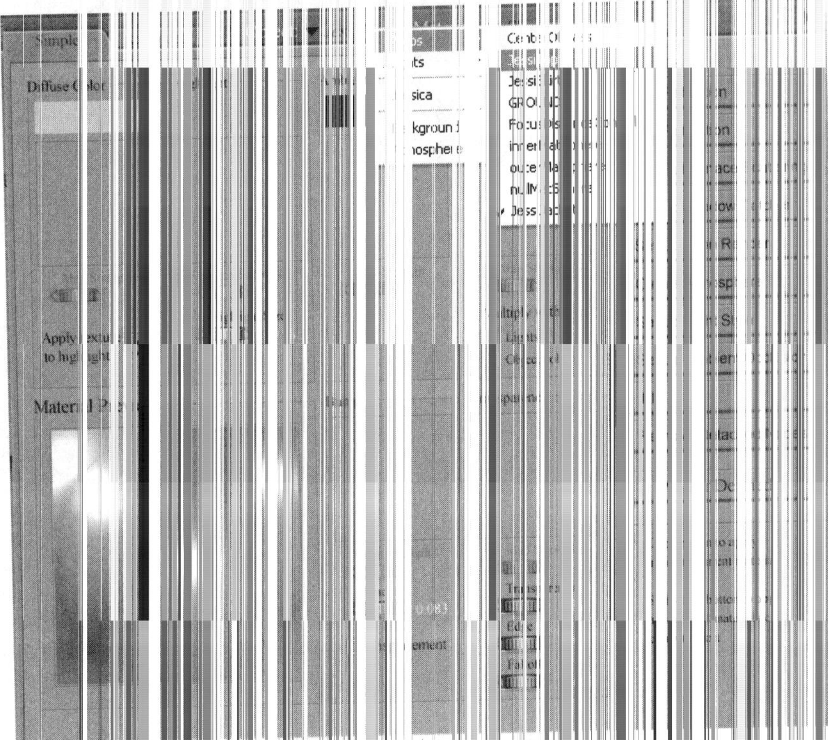

FIGURE 8.18 Select JessTop as the current actor from the menu in the Preview window.

3. The Simple view displays four color squares (Diffuse, Highlight, Ambient, and Reflection). Initially, their colors are set to white, black, black, and white, respectively. To add a little bit of shine to the blouse, we will lighten the Highlight color. Click the black color square beneath the Highlight color to open the Color Selector. Select a middle gray as shown in Figure 8.19.
4. Now, click the empty square just below the white Diffuse color square. This opens the Texture Manager dialog shown in Figure 8.20.
5. Click the Browse button, and navigate to the [illegible] > Downloads > Runtime > Textures > PracticalPoser6 folder. Highlight JessTop.jpg, and click Open to return to the Texture Manager dialog. Click OK again to assign the texture to the Diffuse channel. [illegible] color and the preview window displays the new material.

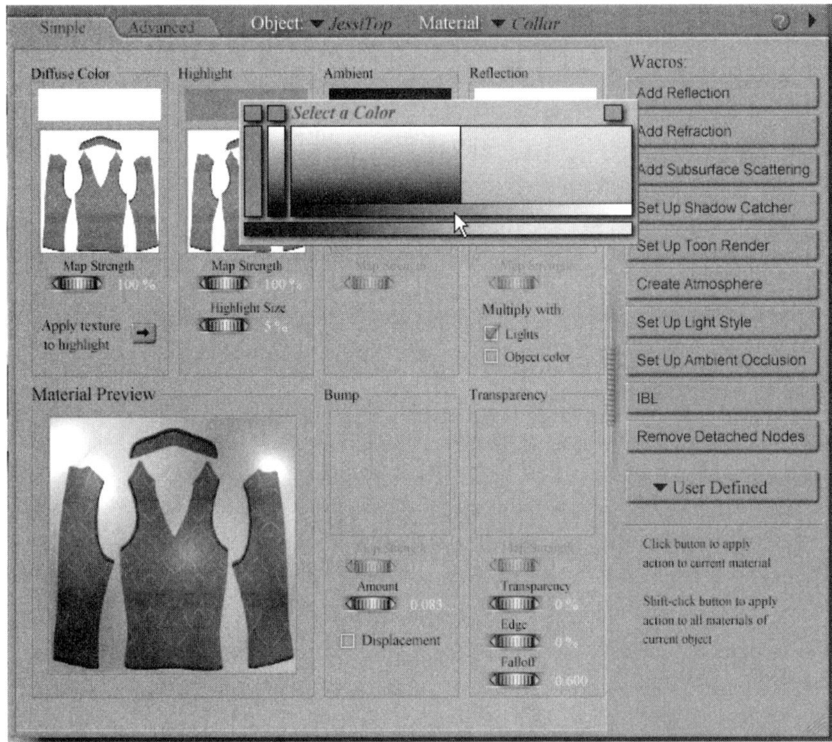

FIGURE 8.19 Select a middle gray for a highlight color. This will add some sheen to the shirt.

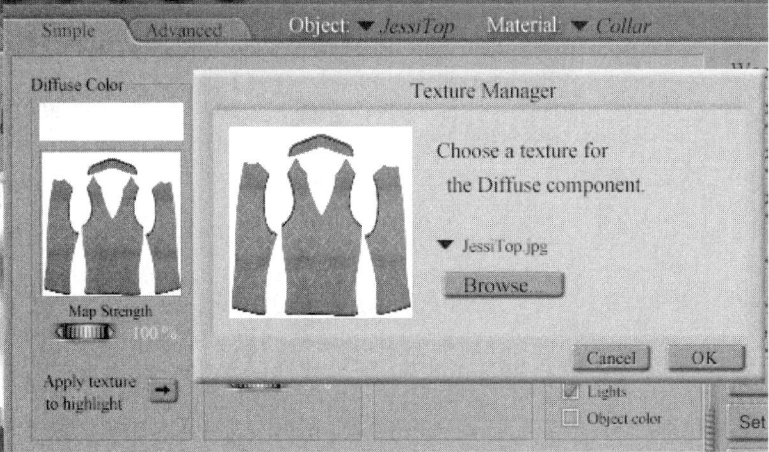

FIGURE 8.20 The Texture Manager dialog prompts you to select a texture for the Diffuse component.

6. You can also use the Diffuse texture to affect the highlights. To do so, click the Apply Texture To Highlight button as shown in Figure 8.21. The texture map then appears as an input to the Highlight channel. Reduce the Highlight size setting to 5% so that the shine doesn't overpower the top.

FIGURE 8.21 The Diffuse texture is copied to the Highlight channel, and the highlight size is reduced to 5%.

7. Poser 6 offers an easy way to apply the same material settings to any or all materials in the same object. Notice the right arrow that appears in the upper-right corner of the Simple material view. Click the right arrow to display the menu shown in Figure 8.22. Select Apply Material to All to copy the material settings from the collar to the other materials in the top. You will see the Preview window update the textures for JessiTop.
8. In a similar manner, repeat Steps 2 through 7 to apply the JessiSkirt.jpg texture to the skirt (which only has one material named "skin") and the JessJacket.jpg texture to the jacket (which has two materials

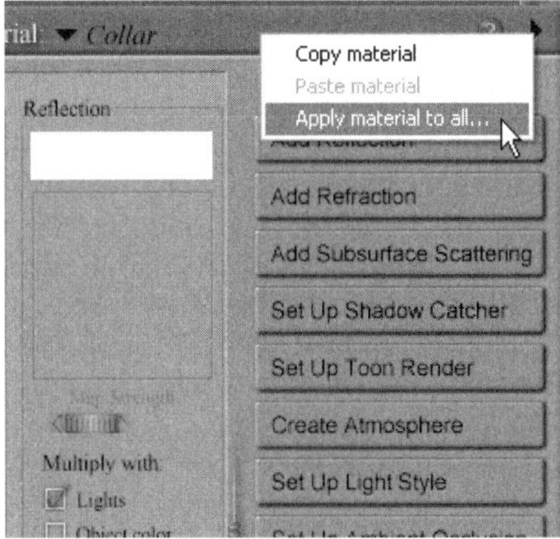

FIGURE 8.22 Use the Apply Textures to All command to apply the same material settings to all materials in the object.

named "sleeves" and "jacket"). Both textures can be found in the Poser 6 > Downloads > Runtime > Textures > PracticalPoser6 folder that you selected the top texture from. When all textures are assigned, your outfit will look as shown in Figure 8.23.

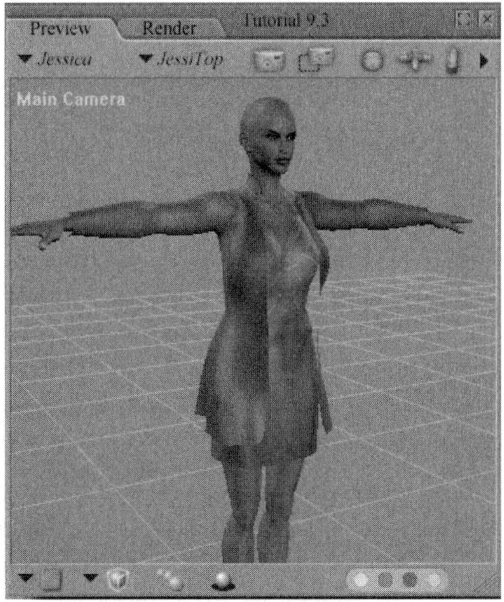

FIGURE 8.23 All materials are assigned to the top, skirt, and jacket.

TUTORIAL [illegible]3 CREATING MULTIPLE SIMULATIONS

When you have more than one layer of dynamic clothing on a figure, you should always create simulations for the underlying layers first and follow with [illegible] layers until you reach the top [illegible]. Think of the way that you dress and the order in which you put on your clothing. You put your shirt on before your pants or your [illegible]t, and you put the jacket on [illegible]h.

The same is true of dynamic clothing in Poser. In the case of the clothing that we [illegible] Jessi, we will create the simulation for the [illegible] first, and set it [illegible] with Jessi's torso. Then, we will create the simulation for the [illegible], and set it to collide with Jessi's lower body and the shirt. Finally, we will [illegible] the simulation for the jacket, [illegible] collide with some [illegible] Jessi's body parts as well as the top and the skirt. If you don't choose the [illegible] layers of clothing as collision objects, the layers above them [illegible] if the underlying layers aren't [illegible] and chances are, [illegible] the layers below.

Starting first with the [illegible] create the simulations as follows:

Click the Cloth [illegible] to [illegible] the Cloth Room if necessary.

Create animation keyframes for your figure, or place your figure in its final pose in a frame other than the first frame. These [illegible] are outlined in Chapter [illegible]0 of the *Poser 6 Tutorial Manual*.

Click the New Simulation button in area 1 of the Cloth Room. The Simulation Settings dialog shown in Figure 8.24 appears.

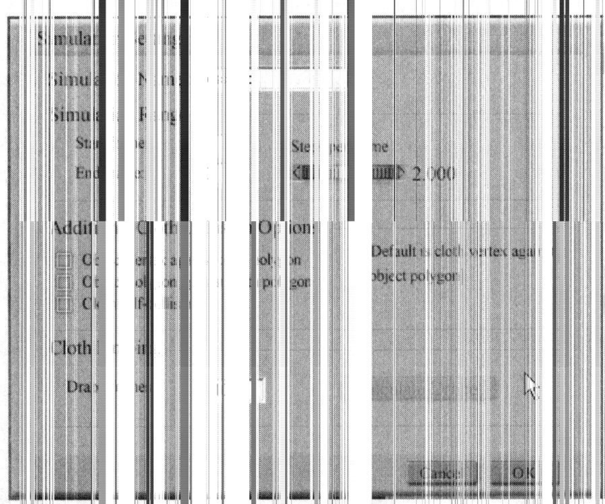

FIGURE 8.2[illegible] Simulation settings [illegible] create a new simulation for a dyn[illegible] clo[illegible] prop.

4. Enter "JessiTop" in the Simulation Name field.
5. The default settings create a simulation that starts at frame 1 and ends at frame 30 (the default length of a Poser animation). Leave these settings at their default.
6. Set the Cloth Draping value to 10 frames. This allows the top to settle on the figure's body before the dynamic control calculations begin. Then click OK to exit the Simulation Settings dialog.
7. Next, click the Clothify button in section 2 of the Cloth Room. The Clothify dialog shown in Figure 8.25 appears.

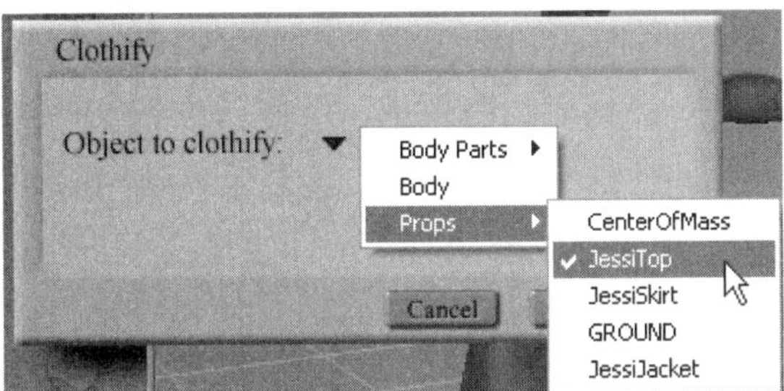

FIGURE 8.25 You must Clothify a dynamic clothing prop to turn it into dynamic cloth.

8. If necessary, select JessiTop from the Object to Clothify drop-down list, and then click the Clothify button. After you turn the object into cloth, the buttons in section 3 are enabled. These buttons are explained in detail in Chapter 10 of the Poser Tutorial Manual.
9. Before you leave the Cloth section, you have to tell Poser which objects the top is supposed to collide against. If you do not choose any collision objects, the clothing will fall to the ground. Generally, you want the clothing to collide with the smallest number of body parts possible, because it will save on system resources by reducing the number of calculations that have to take place. Click the Collide Against button to open the Cloth Collision Objects dialog shown in Figure 8.26.
10. To select collision objects, click the Add/Remove button in the Cloth Collision Objects dialog. The Hierarchy Selection dialog opens.
11. Select any body parts, clothing, or other objects that you expect will come into contact with Jessi's top. Select the hip, abdomen, chest, neck, right collar, and left collar. Figure 8.27 shows a portion of the selected parts.

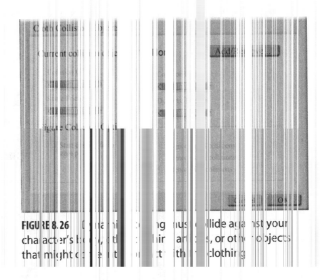

FIGURE 8.26 [illegible] must collide against your character's b[illegible], or other objects that might c[illegible] clothing.

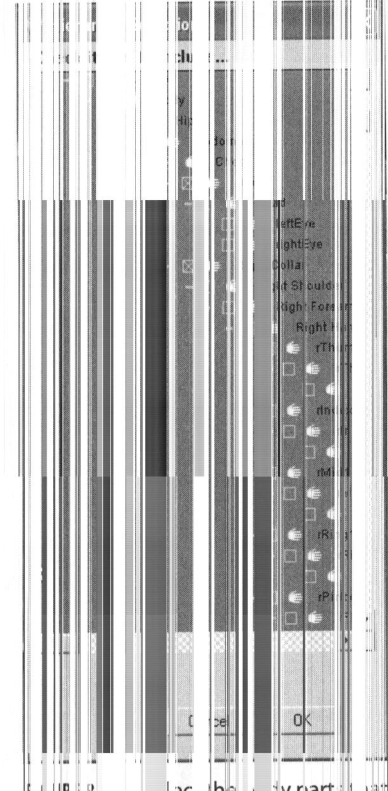

[illegible] the [illegible] part [illegible] the top.

12. Click OK to return to the Cloth Collision Objects dialog, and click OK again to assign the collision objects and return to the Cloth Room.
13. The next layer above the top is the skirt. This piece of clothing must be set to collide against some of Jessi's body parts, but must also collide with the top. To begin, click the New Simulation button in section 1 of the Cloth Room. Name the simulation JessiSkirt, and set the Drape Frames to 10, as shown in Figure 8.28.

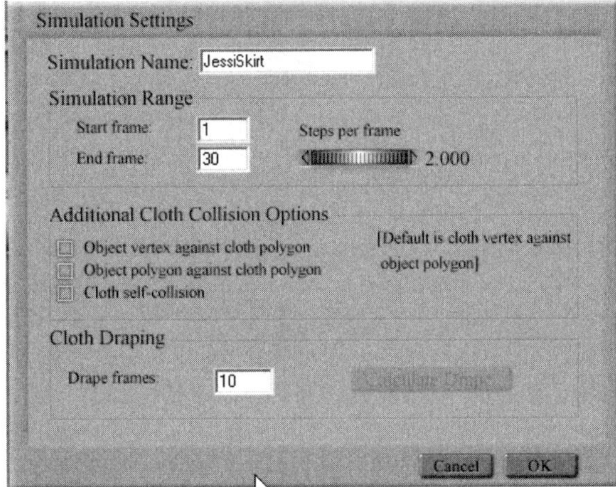

FIGURE 8.28 Create a new simulation for the skirt.

14. Click the Clothify button in section 2 of the Cloth Room. Select JessiSkirt as the object to clothify, and then click the Clothify button.
15. Click the Collide Against button in section 2 of the Cloth Room. When the Cloth Collision Objects dialog opens, click the Add/Remove button to open the Hierarchy Selection list.
16. Select Jessi's hip, abdomen, right thigh, right shin, left thigh, and left shin. Then scroll down to the bottom of the Hierarchy Selection list and check JessiTop, as shown in Figure 8.29. Click OK to return to the Cloth Collision objects dialog, and click OK again to return to the Cloth Room.
17. The final layer is the jacket, which must be set to collide against Jessi's arms, along with the top and the skirt. Once again, click the New Simulation button in section 1 of the Cloth Room. Name the simulation "JessiJacket," and set the Drape Frames to 10.
18. Click the Clothify button in section 2 of the Cloth Room. Select JessiJacket as the object to clothify, and then click the Clothify button.

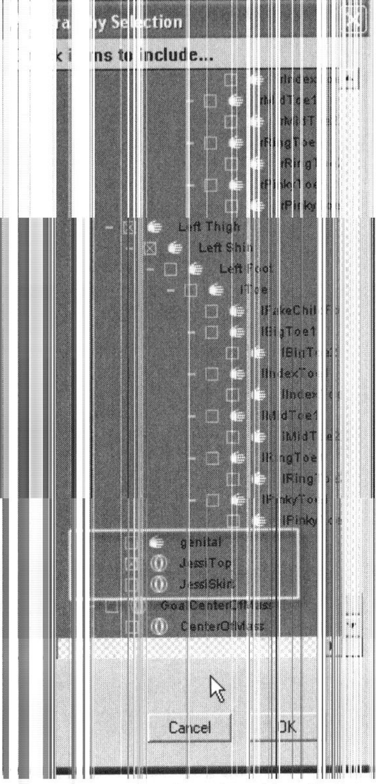

FIGURE 8.9 The skirt should collide against Jessi's top (listed as JessiTop) in addition to some of her body parts.

19. Click the Collide Against button in section 2 of the Cloth Room. When the Cloth Collision Objects dialog opens, click the Add/Remove button to open the Hierarchy Selection list.
20. Select Jessi's hip, neck, right collar, right shoulder, right forearm, left collar, left shoulder, and left forearm. Then, scroll down to the bottom of the Hierarchy Selection list and check JessiTop and Jessi Skirt as shown in Figure 8.9. Click OK to return to the Cloth Collision objects dialog, and click OK again to return to the Cloth Room.

TUTORIAL 8.4 CALCULATING MULTIPLE SIMULATIONS

The next step is to configure the dynamic properties of each item of clothing, and then calculate the simulations. Dynamic properties are explained

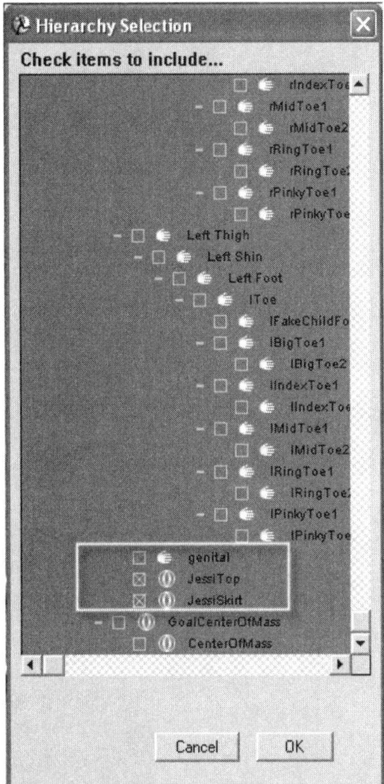

FIGURE 8.30 The jacket should collide against Jessi's top and skirt in addition to some of her body parts.

in Chapter 10 of the *Poser 6 Tutorial Manual* and will not be addressed here. The main purpose for this tutorial is to show you how to perform dynamic calculations when there are multiple simulations in one scene.

There are three different ways that you can approach multiple simulations, each of which is covered in the following mini-tutorials.

The following tutorials assume that all simulations have been set up properly for still images or animations (as described in the preceding tutorials or in the Poser 6 Tutorial Manual), and all dynamic properties have been set to the required settings for your simulations.

To calculate each simulation individually, follow these steps:

1. Select the cloth simulation that you want to calculate from the drop-down menu in the Cloth Simulation area, as shown in Figure 8.31. The simulations are listed in the order in which you created them.

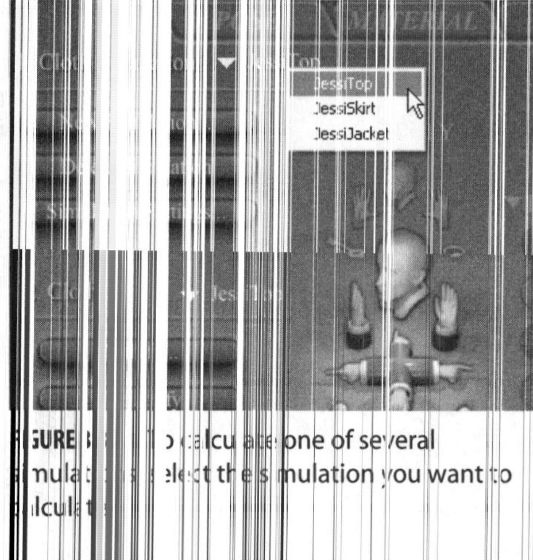

FIGURE 8.31 To calculate one of several simulations, select the simulation you want to calculate.

2. Click the Calculate Simulation button shown in Figure 8.32. The calculations are completed for the current simulation.

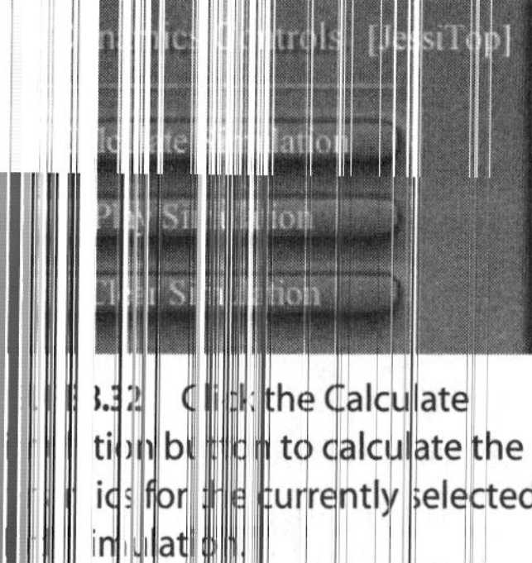

FIGURE 8.32 Click the Calculate Simulation button to calculate the dynamics for the currently selected simulation.

3. Repeat Steps 1 and 2 for additional simulations as required. If you created the clothing simulations in the correct order (as described in Tutorial 8.4), complete the calculations in the same order.

If you make changes to your poses, or you add or delete any frames in your animation, you will have to recalculate all simulations in your project. To calculate all of the simulations in the order in which you created them, choose Animation > Recalculate Dynamics, and select one of the options shown in Figure 8.33, as follows:

- Choose *All Cloth* to calculate all cloth simulations in the order in which they were created.

- Choose *All Hair* to calculate all dynamic hair simulations in the order in which they were created.
- Choose *All Cloth and Hair* to calculate all dynamic cloth and hair simulations in the order in which they were created. Cloth simulations are calculated before hair simulations.

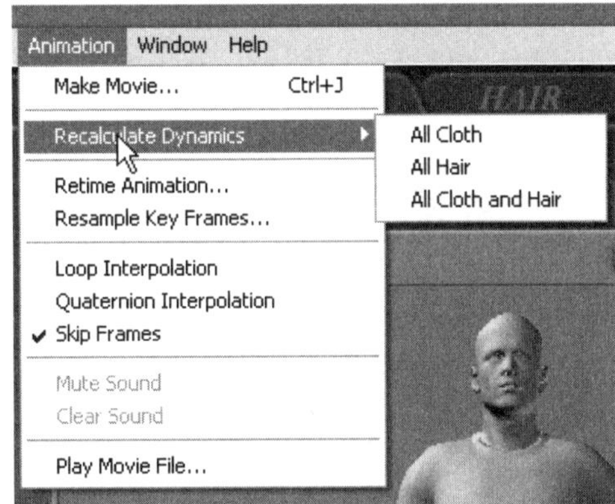

FIGURE 8.33 The Animation > Recalculate Dynamics commands allow you to calculate all cloth and/or hair simulations with one click.

CONCLUSION

In this chapter, you've learned about some of the most common issues that you'll have to think about when you work with Poser clothing. You've learned about some of the solutions that you can implement when clothing doesn't conform or fit correctly, how to use body handles for long skirts, and how to pose high-heeled shoes. You've also learned to pay attention to the libraries from which you load clothing, so that you don't accidentally use pose files that are meant to change the textures of an item that is already in your scene. You also got a brief overview of the Cloth Room and learned how to set up and configure multiple cloth simulations in your scene.

In the next chapter, you'll continue with some of the basic material knowledge that you learned in this chapter, and you'll learn how to use the Simple and Advanced material views to create and modify textures in your Poser scenes.

CHAPTER

9

ASSIGNING AND CREATING MATERIALS

In This Chapter

- Material Room Views
- Customizing Materials
- Conclusion

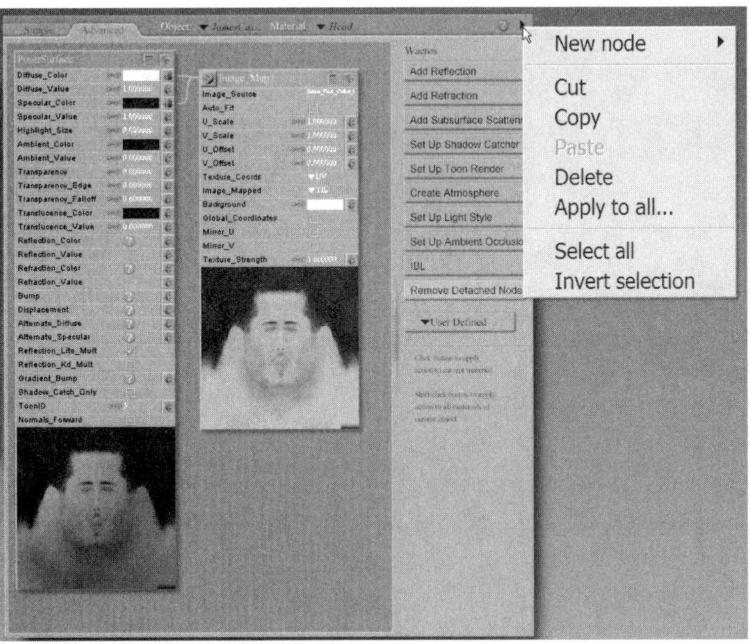

In this chapter, you'll learn to use the Poser Material Room. You'll learn about the Simple and Advanced views, [illegible] mapping (and why it's so important), and you'll be introduced to procedural shaders and nodes. In the tutorial section, you'll have an opportunity to transform James Casual and do amazing things with his materials—all without breaking out your graphics editing program or having to edit underlying image maps.

Before we talk about the specifics of material application and manipulation, let's get acquainted with the Material Room. Poser's Material Room enables you to quickly and easily create and edit complex materials. You see the results of your efforts immediately, and you don't need to be a programmer to create amazing materials. At the same time, there is no substitute for really understanding your tools. Your efforts will be well rewarded in this area if you are willing to invest several hours studying the Material Room and the properties of the various nodes.

Click the Material tab that appears at the top of the screen to open it. When you enter the Material Room, you'll see two tabs: Simple and Advanced. The Simple tab provides a streamlined interface that allows you to apply and modify basic materials that are based on simple color or image maps. When you need more control or a more complex material, use the *procedural shader nodes* in the Advanced view.

Poser's Material Room contains the following items (see Figure 9.1 for the Advanced Material Room components): Editing Tools Palette (1); Preview Window (2); Camera Controls (3); Lighting Controls (4); UI Dots (5); Document Display Style Toolbar (6); Help Window (7); Material

FIGURE 9.1 The main areas of the Material Room.

Room Interface Mode tabs (8); Object List menu (9); Material Group List menu (10); Wacros Drawer (11); Node Options pop-up menu (12); Library Palette (13); and Animation Drawer (14).

Editing Tools Palette (1): These are the same editing tools you find in the Pose Room, with the addition of the Eyedropper tool. The Eyedropper is found on the far right of the Editing Toolbar. Select this tool and click any object or any part of an object to load its material. Some complex objects may actually be divided into several different material groups; for example, the James Casual figure is divided into the following material groups: Gums, Tongue, TeethBottom, TeethTop, TopEyelashes, BottomEyelashes, Head, EyeTrans, Pupil, Iris, Eyeball, pants, Tshirt3, SkinBody, FingerNails, SoleShoe, Sole, laces, bow, Preview, ToeNails, Eyesocket.

Preview Window (2), Camera Control (3), Lighting Control (4), UI Dots (5), and the Document Display Style Toolbar (6): These serve the same functions as they do in the Pose Room.

Help (7): By default, Room Help will be visible when you first enter the Material Room. To close the help window, click on the Close icon (the "X" that appears on the top right of the window). If you close the Help windows in one or more rooms before you save your preferences, Poser remembers your choices.

Material Room Interface Mode tabs (8): These tabs allow you to switch between the Simple and Advanced material editing view formats.

Object List menu (9): The Object List menu allows you to select an object in the current scene. You can also select the Background, Atmosphere, and Lights.

Material Group List menu (10): The Material Group List menu allows you to select any of the materials that are associated with the current object. The current object appears in the Object List menu. See Figure 9.2 for an example of what you might find on the Material Group List menu.

The Poser 6 Tutorial Manual has a wonderful explanation of Material Groups, also known as Multi- and Sub-Object Materials. You can find this tutorial manual in the Tutorials folder of your main Poser 6 installation directory. For example, if you loaded Poser 6 into its default location on a Windows hard drive, the path to this Tutorial Manual would be: C > Program Files > Curious Labs > Poser 6 > Tutorials > Poser 6 Tutorial Manual.pdf. You can also choose Help > Poser Tutorial Manual to view the manual.

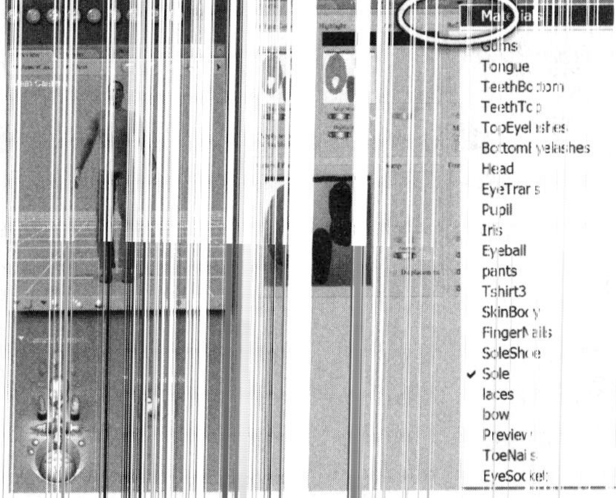

FIGURE 9.2 The Material Group List for the default James Casual figure as selected in the Simple view.

Wacros Drawer (11): Wacros are Python scripts created to work specifically with Materials. By default, there are ten predefined wacros that cover the most common Material Room tasks. You can create your own wacros scripts and make them available in the User Defined pop-up menu by placing them in the Poser 6 > Runtime > Python > poserScripts > Wacros > User Defined folder within your Poser 6 installation. This area of your screen is a *drawer,* which means that you can "close" the drawer to hide its contents by clicking on the drawer handle. Click the handle again to toggle the drawer open.

Python scripts should be installed in the default Poser runtime folder. If you install them in the Downloads folder or in another external runtime folder they may generate errors.

Node Options pop-up menu (12): This menu only appears in the Advanced material editing view. The Node Options pop-up menu is available only in the Advanced view by clicking on the Node Options menu icon, by right-clicking anywhere within the Advanced view window, or by right-clicking anywhere within a node. The Node Options menu allows you to cut, copy, paste, delete, apply to all, select all and invert select nodes. Some options on the menu act upon the currently selected node. Figure 9.3 shows the Node Options pop-up menu.

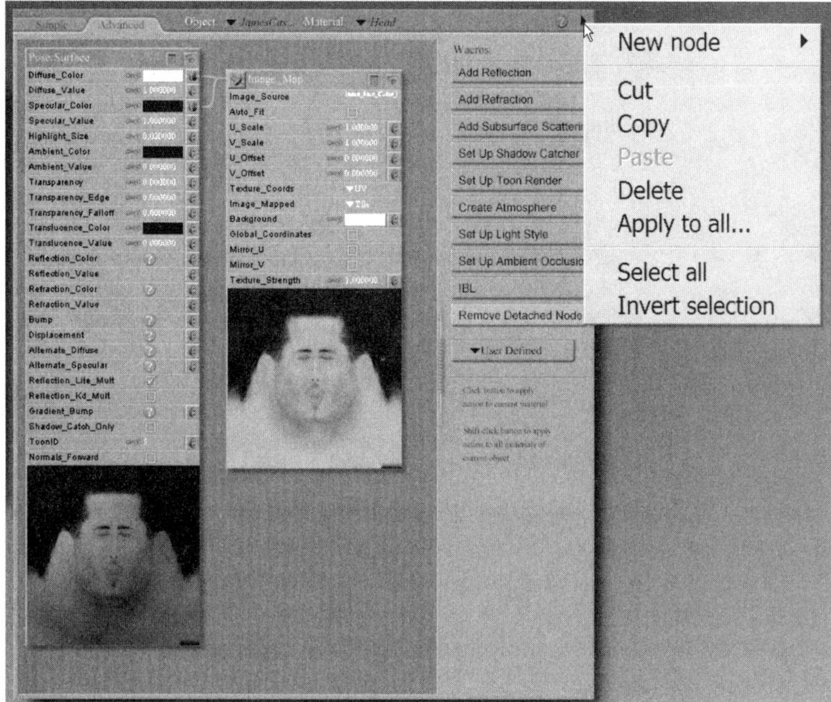

FIGURE 9.3 The Node Options menu is available only in the Advanced Material Room view.

Library Palette (13) and the Animation Drawer (14): These serve the same functions as they do in the Pose Room.

Material Room Views

Let's talk about the two options for viewing and editing materials—the Simple and Advanced views. Which one you ultimately end up using most will depend upon how complex your materials need to be. Keep in mind that Poser's Firefly rendering engine supports the use of procedural shaders, which you build, control, and manage in the Advanced view of the Material Room. If you are put off by the seemingly complex look of the Advanced view, you may be surprised to discover that it isn't as difficult, or confusing, as you might at first think.

The Simple Material View

The whole idea behind the Simple view is, well, to keep it simple. This view exposes the most commonly used properties of the most common types of materials used in Poser. It is much easier to create and assign textures to your materials in the Simple view, which is shown in Figure 9.4. Those who are familiar with Poser Pro Pack and earlier versions of Poser will find the Simple material view to be somewhat easier to use than the Advanced view. Here, you can assign texture maps and pertinent settings to Diffuse, Highlight, Ambient, Reflection, Bump, and Transparency maps and view a preview of the texture as you make your changes.

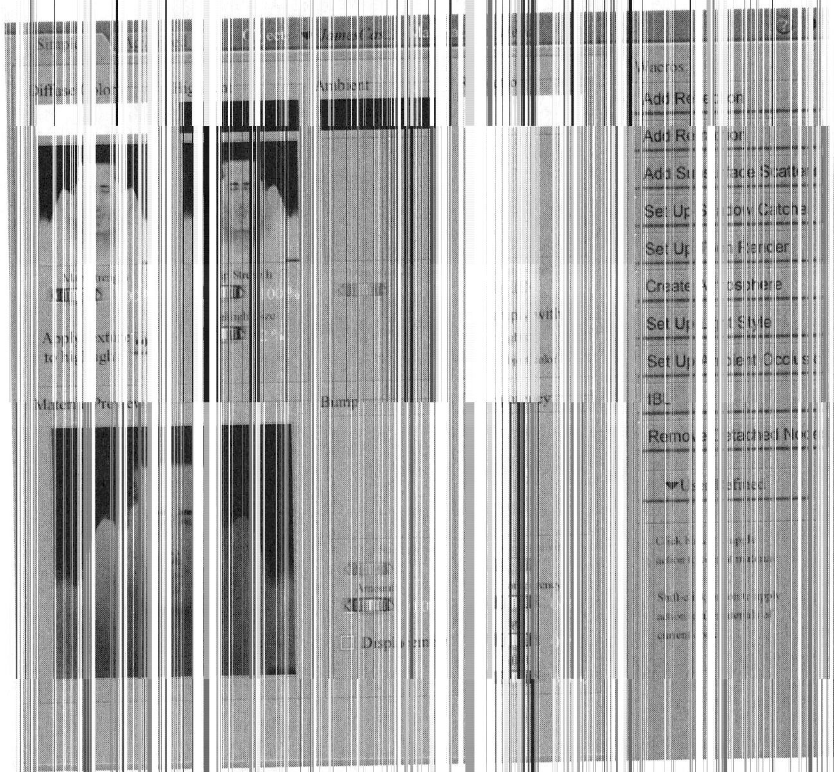

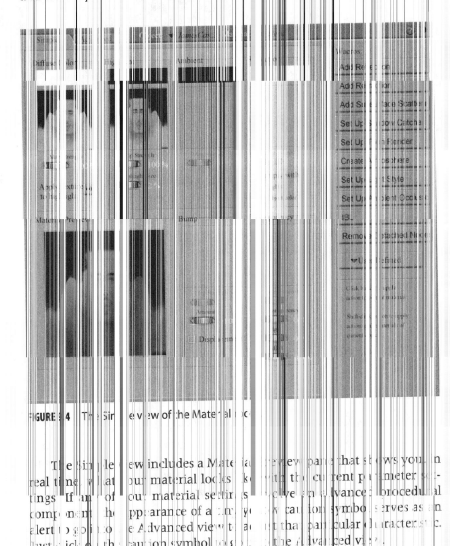

FIGURE 9.4 The Simple view of the Material Room.

The Simple view includes a Material Preview pane that shows you in real time what your material looks like with the current parameter settings. If any of your material settings involve an advanced procedural component, the appearance of a small yellow caution symbol serves as an alert to go into the Advanced view to adjust that particular characteristic. Just click on the caution symbol to go to the Advanced view.

While in the Simple view you can click the square texture preview area to assign an image map to any of the material components. This opens the Texture Manager dialog, shown in Figure 9.5, which provides a convenient method to browse for new image files or to select from a list of previously used image files.

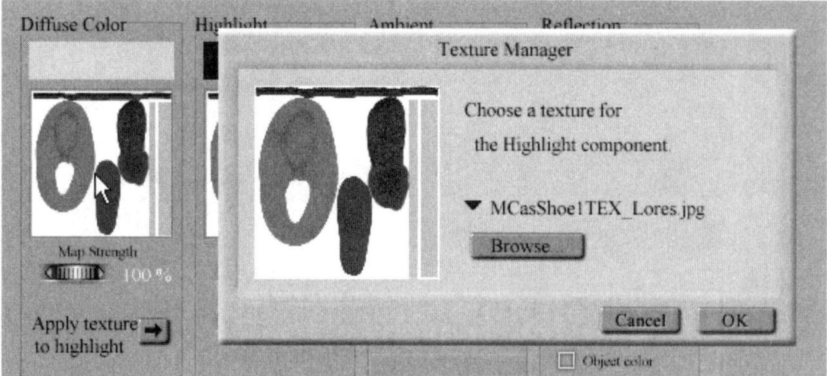

FIGURE 9.5 Click the texture preview window to quickly access the Texture Manager dialog.

The Simple view makes it easy to use images and movies as image maps. In the Advanced view, it takes a bit more effort, as static images and movies are applied using separate nodes.

Now let's examine the areas of the Simple view.

Diffuse Color

The Diffuse Color area of the Simple view is shown in Figure 9.6. Typically, an object's Diffuse Color is the primary color before any procedures or modifiers are added to the mix. An object's Diffuse Color can be a single, uniform color; it can be based on an image that is mapped onto the surface of the object (a texture map); or it can be based on a procedural calculation.

You can also have a color tint and an image texture, in which case your entire image map will be shifted into the direction of the applied Diffuse Color tint. If you do not want to tint your image map, leave the Diffuse Color set to white. It is easy to change the Diffuse Color. Just click on the color slot and pick your desired color.

FIGURE 9.6 The Diffuse component of a shader defines the main color of the object.

If you don't like Poser's Color Picker, click the rainbow icon at the top-right corner of Poser's Color Picker to open the system's RGB picker. Figure 9.7 shows the Poser Color Picker on the left and the RGB Color Picker on the right.

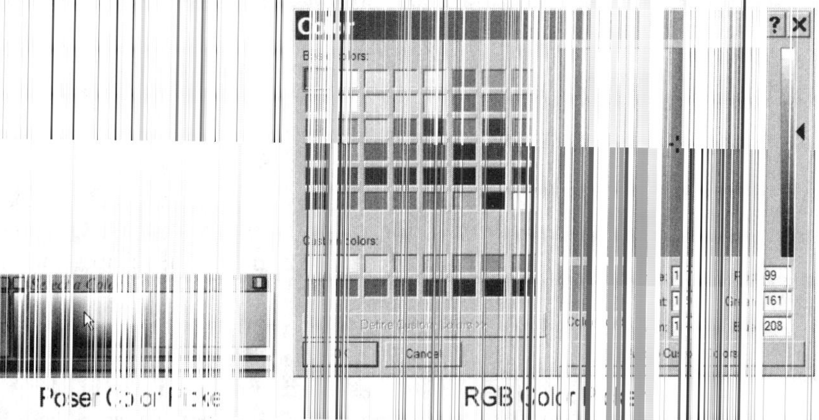

FIGURE 9.7 Two color pickers are available in Poser: Poser Color Picker and RGB Color Picker.

Highlights

The most common, and the quickest, method of creating believable Highlights on a material is to use the same map (or procedure) for both the base of the material (the Diffusion Color) and the Highlights. The Simple view makes this super-easy with a special button in the Diffuse Color section, "Apply texture to highlight." When you click this button, Poser copies the texture map from the Diffuse Color component to the Highlight component and saves you from having to manually browse for the file. The Highlight component of the Simple view translates into the *Specular root node* in the Advanced view, both of which are shown in Figure 9.8.

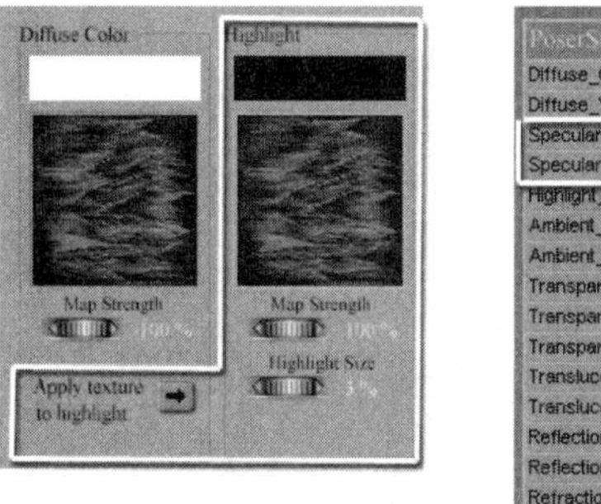

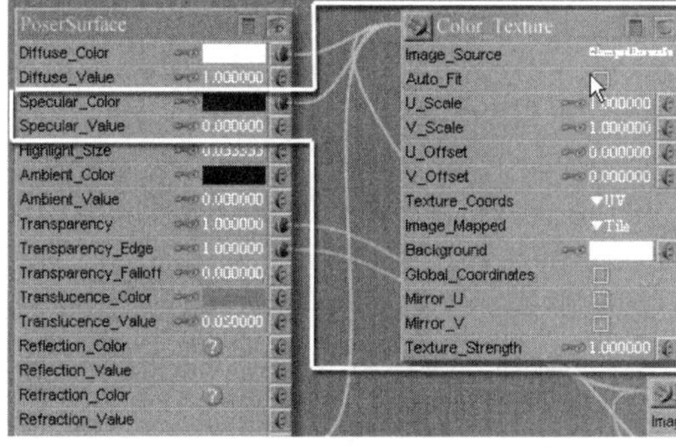

FIGURE 9.8 The Highlight section of the Simple view (left) translates to the Specular node in the Advanced view (right).

Highlights are the areas of your material where the majority of the light's frequencies reflect straight into the camera. They are particularly important for adding realism to eyes, glass, and other shiny materials. Highlights are usually white, but you can tie them into an image map or a procedural material if you prefer to create more complicated Highlight effects.

Some very interesting materials are created by varying the color of the Highlights. The type of Highlight you create will give visual clues to your audience about the properties of your material: smooth surfaces have sharp "high-key" or white Highlights, while rough surfaces have soft Highlights that pick up some of the color of the material they reflect from. Changing the Highlight size, large or small, and the color can greatly affect how your material is perceived.

Ambient

The Ambient section of the Simple view is shown in Figure 9.9. Ambient color simulates the general lighting condition in the environment. Because of this, the ambient color property is a bit different than the others, because it isn't affected by the other color properties. In fact, ambient color is essentially *emitted* from an object. Even if you delete all of the lights, an ambient color other than black will cause the object to appear self-illuminating. On the other hand, if you set the ambient color too bright, you will lose all the shadowed areas of the object and create an overall flattening effect on the materials applied.

FIGURE 9.9 Ambient color simulates the overall lighting condition of your environment.

Reflection

The Reflection section of the Simple view is shown in Figure 9.10. There are two ways to configure your material's Reflection component. The Simple view allows you to use a Reflection map, while the Advanced view allows you to use Raytraced reflections. A reflection map renders very quickly, while raytracing usually takes much longer to render.

FIGURE 9.10 Reflection maps are assigned in Simple view.

You can change the tint of your reflection by selecting a color or image (or procedural calculation) in addition to your main reflective element. You also have the option to "Multiply with Lights," which means that the Reflection effect will be darker where there is no light; in addition to "Multiply with Object color," which tints the Reflection effect with the current Diffuse Color.

Bump map

The Bump channel in the Simple view is shown in Figure 9.11. You can attach an image map to the bump property of your object. The map determines how bumpy your surface appears at each point. Light areas in the map correspond with the highest bump on the surface. Bump maps do not actually modify the underlying mesh; instead, they simulate a non-even surface texture and act upon those areas that are facing the camera. This means that the outlines of your object will not be changed, regardless of how high you make your bump values.

Within the Bump component's window in the Simple view you will find the Displacement check box. The Displacement option allows you to use the Bump map to actually alter the geometry of the surface of your object at render time. This means that your entire object will be affected by the amount of displacement that is applied by the map, including the

FIGURE 9.11 Bump maps add bumpiness to your object. A displacement option appears in the Simple view as well.

outline. With Displacement mapping, the surface will in fact be displaced from the original geometry by the amount defined in the Displacement parameter. If you use Displacement mapping, make sure you remember to set your *Min Displacement Bound* to a value high enough to accommodate the displacement of your materials.

Transparency

Transparency (shown in Figure 9.12 for Simple view) can be determined by a transparency map that is usually grayscale. Each point on an object's surface is determined by the amount of lightness or darkness on the transparency map, with darker values being more transparent. The Transparency value affects the material that faces the camera, predominantly near the center of the object with respect to the camera. Higher Transparency values make the camera-facing material more transparent.

The Edge parameter dictates how transparent the edge of the object will be. As you would expect, a high Edge value makes the edges of the object more transparent. The Falloff property sets the rate at which the transparency becomes more opaque as you approach the edges of an object. A smaller value produces a sharper edge, while larger values create a

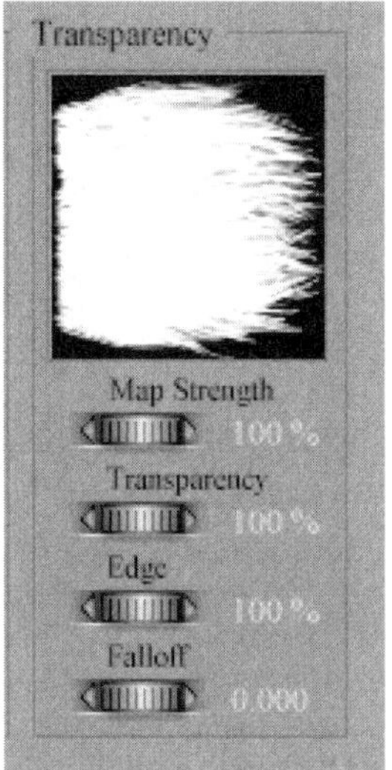

FIGURE 9.12 The light and dark areas of a transparency map determine which areas of a material are opaque and which are transparent.

more gradual transition and more of a cloudy-edge effect. If you set the Edge and Transparency to the same values there will be no Falloff (because there would be no difference between the two values, and therefore no transition).

The Advanced Material View

The Advanced view is really where you take advantage of the power of Poser's material capabilities, many of which work in conjunction with the Firefly rendering engine. When you open the Advanced view, you'll immediately notice that there are more parameters jammed into a smaller space. The left side of your Advanced view window displays the *root node.* Depending on what object you have selected in the Advanced view, the root node may have other nodes attached to it. For example, Figure 9.13 shows a material root node with connections to an Image Map node in the Advanced view.

So, what is a node? A node is a discrete building block used in the creation of a material. Nodes have specific types of input, internal parameters, formulas, and output, depending upon what type of node they are.

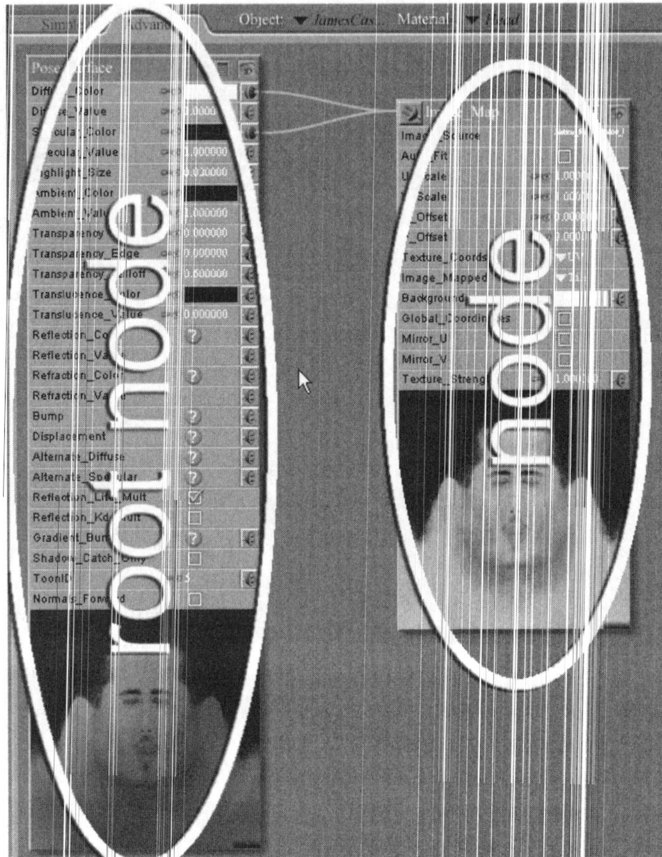

FIGURE 9.13 A material root node with connections to an Image Map node in the Advanced view.

The root node mixes together all of the material modifiers that are "plugged in" to it. A material modifier can be a static value, an image, a color, an algorithm, another node, or any combination of these things. There are four different types of root nodes that accommodate the various types of items that can use shaders. The most common node is a Material root node, but you'll also find three additional nodes that include specific properties for Backgrounds, Hair, and Lights.

The Advanced view of the Material Room is like a huge collection of pipes and control points that can be connected in an infinite number of ways to create the material you want. That's exactly what makes the Material Room seem overwhelming at first.

Here's an analogy for you: think of the Advanced view as a cookie factory. Raw ingredients (the various types of nodes) are brought into the system and mixed via several input pipes (the inputs and outputs of the nodes). Spices and chemicals are added to change the flavor (the parameters within the nodes, and the operations they perform). Finally, it all comes together to be baked in the oven (the root node, which combines everything). The final result is your wonderful-tasting cookie (the resulting material as shown in the root node preview pane).

The various nodes, when joined together, create a material that is also known as a procedural shader (also interchangeably referred to as a material shader or more simply as a shader.) All shaders start with a root node.

Nodes are versatile "black boxes" that act upon the input fed into them and output something else as a result of their unique actions. To connect a node to the root node, you click on the little 'plug' icon on the right side of the root node window. From there, choose New Node, and expand the menu to display the submenu shown in Figure 9.14.

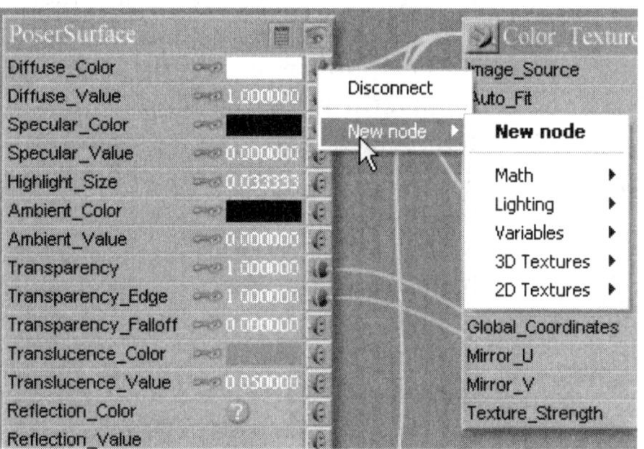

FIGURE 9.14 To attach a node, click the small "plug" icon and choose a node type from the New Node menu that appears.

There are five major types of nodes: Math, Lighting, Variables, 3D Textures, and 2D Textures. Within each major node category are several different nodes that behave in different ways.

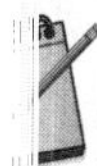

Chapter 35 of the Poser 6 Reference Manual, "Material Room Nodes," goes into great detail and does a wonderful job introducing each of the nodes available in the Material Room. This is where you'll get a brief description of what each of the parameters, inputs, and outputs of all the nodes do.

1. **Math** nodes perform mathematical calculations and transformations based on the values of their inputs. The Math node choices are Blender, Edge Blend, Component, Math Functions, Color Math, User Defined, Simple Color, Color Ramp, and HSV.
2. **Lighting** nodes work with lighting properties. Each of the five categories (Specular, Diffuse, Special, Ray Trace, and Environment Map) have a submenu of additional choices. Some interesting lighting nodes gather light from environmental inputs, like the *probelight* (in the Diffuse subcategory) and *gather* (in the Ray Trace subcategory) nodes.
3. **Variable** nodes return values based on the current point on an object being rendered. These nodes have very cryptic variable names such as N, P, frame_number, u, v, Du, Dv, dPdv, dPdu, dNdv, and dNdu. Their purpose is to look at various values that are being returned at any given point in time. For example, the N node returns the value of the normal at the current point on an object, the frame_number node returns the current frame number, and the V node returns the coordinate in space of the current point on the current object.
4. **3D Texture** nodes are math-based, (often fractal-based) and create output that is calculated for all three spatial dimensions (X, Y, and Z). Many of these nodes can be used to simulate natural materials. Nodes included in this category are Fractal Sum, fBm, Turbulence, Noise, Cellular, Clouds, Spots, Marble, Granite, Wood, and Wave3d.
5. **2D Texture** nodes produce output based on two-dimensional transformations (X and Y). You can use these nodes to create two-dimensional patterns such as Wave2D, Brick, Tile, and Weave. Two additional 2D textures, Image Map and Movie, allow you to choose image maps or animated AVI or MOV files as textures.

The Anatomy of Nodes

The variety and complexity of nodes can be overwhelming when you are trying to select the right node to develop a certain type of material, but after a little bit of practice you'll get the hang of which groups of nodes work best for your tasks.

A node's output (which appears in the upper-left corner of the node's "black box") can be used as input for any number of other nodes. Wherever you see a "plug" icon on the right side of a root node or a regular node, that indicates that you can plug the output of another node in to affect that parameter. For example, you can feed two images into a Subtract node (a subcategory of the Math nodes) and use the resulting output image to create the Diffuse_Color of your material. You can also use the same output to affect a gather node that affects the ambient input of your root node. It is common practice to use the same output to drive several parameters, and often helps make the materials and environments more believable. In real life, we often find that many properties of materials affect and are dependant upon each other.

The basic anatomy of nodes is shown in Figure 9.15, where you see the various components that can make up a node. Here you see the root node (1); Output (2); Parameter View Toggle (3); Output Preview Toggle (4); Input(s) (5); Output Preview Pane (6); Animation Toggle (7); Material Preview Pane (8). Each of these items serves the following purposes:

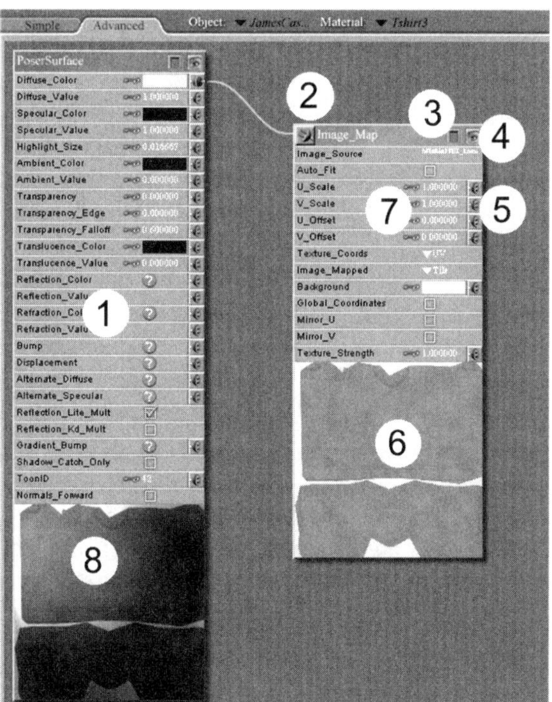

FIGURE 9.15 The basic anatomy of nodes.

Root node (1): The root node is the central gathering point for each shader. It accepts input from various components (colors, settings, and other nodes) to define and create the current material. A root node has no node outputs to connect to other nodes; instead, its "output" is the material shader itself. The root node shows a preview of the material in the Material Preview Pane (8) in real time—a handy feature when editing nodes and making changes to parameter values.

Output (2): Each node (except the root node) has at least one output connector. The output value is based on the functionality of the node, the input(s) fed into it, and the values of the parameters used in its calculations. Outputs are depicted by the male half of a two-pronged electrical plug.

Parameter View Toggle (3): This toggles the display of the node's parameter value area.

Output Preview Toggle (4): Toggles the display of the node's Output Preview Pane (6).

Input(s) (5): All nodes have at least one input connection, although not all nodes require external inputs to function. Inputs are depicted by the female half of a two-pronged electrical plug.

Output Preview Pane (6): Displays a preview of the node's current output.

Animation Toggle (7): Toggles animation ON and OFF for the selected parameter. The animation toggle icon is a small key.

Material Preview Pane (8): This pane, on the root node, shows a real-time display of the material with the current node and parameter configuration.

Using Nodes

Now that you know a bit about the anatomy of a node, let's examine how you actually go about handling them.

Parameter Values: Nodes typically accept several parameter types. The most common are numbers, colors, image files, and outputs from other nodes. To edit parameter values, click on the number you want to edit and either type the new value in the number field or use the dial to change the current value.

In the cases where the parameter is an image file (such as in the Image Map node), click the name of the image source and use the pull-down menu to browse your hard drive for the image file you need, or select an image that you have already used from the history list.

When the parameter is a color, click the color block to open up the Poser Color Picker. If you would rather use the RGB Color Picker, just click on the rainbow icon at the top right of the Poser Color Picker (refer to Figure 9.7, referenced earlier in this chapter, for the location of the Poser Color Picker).

Selecting Nodes Click any blank area within the node you want to select. You can select multiple nodes by pressing and holding the Shift key while selecting, or by using the Node Options pop-up menu to Select All nodes or to Invert selection.

Arranging Nodes The position of a node in your view window will have no effect on its operation. In fact, your material may become so complex that your nodes will "disappear" underneath your Wacros drawer. If this happens, just use the Advanced view scrollbar along the bottom to scroll to those hidden nodes. You may find that you need to rearrange the nodes to get a better idea of how they are interconnected. To move a node, select it and drag it to where you want it while holding down your left mouse button.

Creating New Nodes To create a node, use the Options menu and progress through the submenus to find the specific type of node you wish to create. Clicking on a node's input (or output) icon will also open the Options menu, except in this case the only available menu choice will be to make a New node. An alternate way to access the Options menu is to click a node's input (or output) icon and drag to create a wire. When you release the mouse, the Options menu will open up with the option to create a New node. These methods will only work when clicking on empty input and output icons. Just adding a new node won't do any good until you link it up to something.

Deleting Nodes To delete a node select and press the DEL key. Alternately you can right-click on the node and use the Options menu to Delete the node.

Linking Nodes You can click the output icon of one node and drag it over to the input icon of the node you wish to connect it to. Conversely, you can start with the input icon and drag to an output of another node to connect those two nodes. Once your nodes are connected successfully you will see "wires" going from one node to the other.

Moving Links To move a link to another node, just grab the end you want to move with your mouse, drag it to where you want it to go, and then release it. If you want to leave that end unconnected just drop it anywhere on the Advanced view window pane.

Many to Many Links Remember, you can connect the input and output of a node to as many other inputs and outputs of other nodes as you need! However, an o[illegible]put can only go to another node's input.

Deleting Links To delete a link, just click on the end you want to disconnect and drag it to anywhere on the Advanced window pane. You can also click on the [illegible] of the link you wish to delete and use the Options menu to Di[illegible] the [illegible] end of the link.

Animating Node Parameters To toggle animation ON or OFF, click the Animation Toggle icon [illegible] key for the parameter you wish to animate.

Node "Window Shades" When you start working with many nodes in your materials, you may want to minimize the nodes you are not currently focusing on. You can roll up a node into a smaller display a few different ways. You can toggle the display of the Output Preview by clicking on the Output Preview Toggle icon, the "eye" in the upper right of the node. You can also toggle the display of the node Parameters by clicking on the "window" icon just to the left of the "eye" icon. Figure 9.[illegible] shows the nodes in their various minimized and maximized configurations.

FIGURE 9.[illegible]6 Nodes can be minimized in several ways: (A) Full View, (B) Parameters hidden, (C) Output Preview hidden, (D) Parameters and Output View hidden.

CUSTOMIZING MATERIALS

A preliminary project file is included on the CD-ROM, so that you can begin this tutorial with some preset lights and background. The preliminary project file uses default textures, specifically those that come with your Poser 6 software. You have two ways to prepare for the following tutorial:

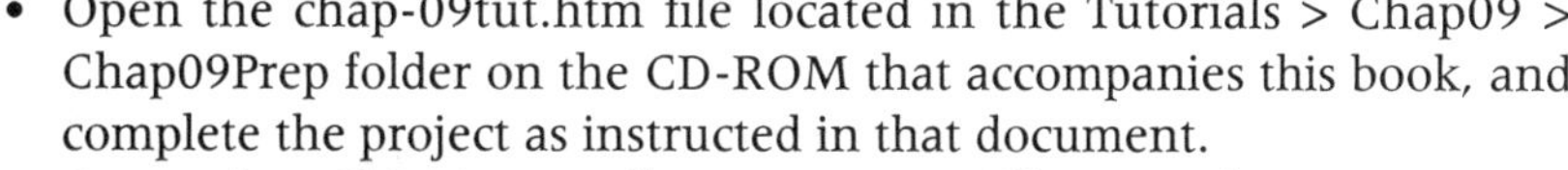

- Open the chap-09tut.htm file located in the Tutorials > Chap09 > Chap09Prep folder on the CD-ROM that accompanies this book, and complete the project as instructed in that document.

- Open the Ch09StarterFile.pz3 project file (or the compressed Ch09StarterFile.pzz version) located on the CD-ROM. This file provides a starting point for the tutorial that follows. (Note: If your current video resolution is smaller than that used when we created this starter file, the Preview Window will be too large for the screen. If this happens to you, just choose Window > Document Window Size, and enter smaller values for the width and the height. A good place to start is 375 for width and 400 for height. This should fit the image on your screen even if your current resolution is quite low.)

After using either of these methods to prepare for the tutorials, render the project so that you get a baseline render to start from. You may not be able to discern the details we're talking about from Figure 9.17, which is the rendered image created from the Ch09StarterFile.pz3 (or .pzz) project file. This is why you should render the image for yourself and examine it on your computer monitor or using your favorite graphics image editor. The render settings are already set up in the project, so all you'll need to do is use the Render > Render command. After you evaluate your baseline render you'll see that James Casual's hair has specular highlights that are too bright for the front-on lighting arrangement. The angle of the Main Camera, in this case, catches too many specular highlights in his hair.

Open your baseline render file in your favorite graphics program (such as Photoshop or Paint Shop Pro). Observe some of the problem areas in the materials in your render:

- You'll probably see white speckles that give the appearance of snow sprinkled on the top of his hair.
- His eyes are too luminous, showing too many specular highlights, that are also too large.
- His teeth glow like they are radioactive!
- His skin looks rather flat, plastic, and dull gray.
- His T-shirt can use some texture, such as a bump map.

[illegible]inally, [illegible]e wall behind him sh[illegible]ul[illegible] be spru[illegible]ed up to give the who[illegible] scene a [illegible]ore cohesive fe[illegible] and [illegible] up [illegible] of "place" wh[illegible]e thi[illegible] scene m[illegible]ht occur.

FIGURE 9.17 Th[illegible] base [illegible] using the Ch09 Starter File.

In the [illegible]llowing tutorial you'll [illegible] h[illegible] use the Advanced Ma[illegible] Room [illegible]ew to fix these [illegible]roble[illegible] [illegible] learn how to add [illegible] [illegible] and hook the[illegible] up t[illegible] parameters on the [illegible] [illegible] We'[illegible] give you a list of all [illegible] [illegible]des [illegible] need to create and whi[illegible] [illegible] node parameter to connect [illegible]des [illegible].

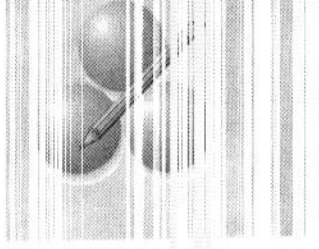

TUTORIAL 9.1 [illegible]W TO "READ" THE H[illegible]R S[illegible]R [illegible] REDUC[illegible] COMPLEXIT[illegible]

[illegible]is fir[illegible] tutorial is a lesso[illegible] in [illegible] apart, and reduce [illegible] [illegible] of a shader, to help [illegible] some of the logic [illegible] [illegible] them. We'll sta[illegible] wit[illegible] [illegible]aterial. We will examine [illegible] material *very* closely, [illegible] what makes a sha[illegible] [illegible]ck."

[illegible] open the hair material, cli[illegible] tab to enter the Mate[illegible] [illegible] if necessary. Next, click th[illegible] in the Material Room [illegible] [illegible] the Advanced view of the [illegible] Room. Hover the mouse [illegible] the preview window to see the cursor change into an Eyedropper. Click with the Eyedropper to select James Casual's hair. Alternately, from the Object List menu you can select Props > SideParting and then from the Material Group List menu select ClumpedHair. Either of these procedures should open the hair material in the Advanced view. Verify that ClumpedHair is selected in the Material Group List menu.

All of the nodes you see for the hair in the Advanced view aren't as confusing as they initially appear. The trick is to look at what is going on from *right to left*, instead of from *left to right*. Once you wrap your head around that little trick, a light might suddenly come on! We'll step you through each connection in the sections that follow.

Reviewing the Diffuse Color

Notice the Color_Textures node on the right side of the Advanced view. Click the filename that appears in the Image_Source setting (the first setting in the Color_Texture node). The Texture Manager appears, showing you a texture named ClumpedBrownSwatch1.jpg as the image source.

Exit the Texture Manager and return to the Advanced view. Four yellow lines come from the output of the Color Texture node, meaning that it is used for four different purposes in the hair material. If you follow the top yellow line from this texture source back to the root node, you'll see that it is attached to the Diffuse Color, giving the hair its color. The Diffuse Color inside the root node is set to white, so there is no additional tint added to the image map.

Reviewing the Bump Channel

Follow the third yellow line from the Color Texture to the Bump input on the root node. By plugging the hair texture in as a bump map, the light and dark values of the hair texture add some additional texture to the hair. Light values in the image "raise" the hair, and dark values "lower" it. The amount of texture is controlled by the Bump setting, which is set at .01. The higher this value is set, the more "bumpy" the hair appears.

Reviewing the Transparency Channel

A Transparency Map node also appears on the right side of the Advanced view. A transparency map named ClumpedTransSwatch1.jpg is the image source used for the transparency map.

Three green lines come from the output of the Color Texture node. Two of these lines are used for Transparency purposes. One ties into the Transparency input, and the other to the Transparency Edge input. For both of these inputs [illegible] thing that sees black from the transparency map is turned off or [illegible]. Anything that sees 100% white from the transparency map [illegible] as opaque as the Transparency and Transparency Edge settings allow them to be). Because the Transparency and Transparency Edge settings are both set to 1 in the root node, they allow the maximum [illegible] from the transparency map.

Reviewing the Specular and Alternate Specular Channels

We've saved the Specular and Alternate Specular channels for last, because they are the [illegible] complex to explain. There is a little bit more going on here than just plugging in a texture. So, we will take it step by step.

First, notice [illegible] Color Texture is plugged in to the Specular Color input of the root node. This occurs automatically if you click the Apply Texture to Highlight button in the Simple view. But look again—the Specular Color is set to black, and the Specular Value is set to 0. This basically turns the "normal" specular channel off—it works exactly the same as if there was nothing connected there at all. In fact, if you want to disconnect the input [illegible] the Specular Color channel, just click on the plug that appears at the right side of the Specular Color input (the plug that the Color Channel connects to). Then choose Disconnect from the menu that appears.

Now, look down near the bottom of the root node, where you see an Alternate Specular channel. If you follow the input backward, you see a number of things [illegible] look really confusing! So, let's follow it right to left . . . [illegible] right.

Follow the [illegible] from the Color Texture down to a Color Math node. Notice that [illegible] line also connects from the Color Math node back to the transparency map. Two inputs are required for the Color Math node, which is set to Multiply the two inputs. As a result, the Color Math node outputs [illegible] wherever black occurs in the transparency map. It [illegible] the color of the hair texture wherever white occurs in the transparency map. To see exactly what the Color Math node is outputting, click [illegible] the upper-right corner of the node to display the preview. [illegible] again to close the eye and turn it off.

Next, the Color Math node goes to an *HSV* (Hue, Saturation, Value) node. To see the settings in this node, click the Settings icon that appears to the left of the [illegible] upper right corner. Notice that Hue and Value are set to 1, [illegible] affected. However, notice that the Saturation setting [illegible] desaturates the hair color so that it is close to [illegible] but not [illegible]. (Again, you can click the Eye icon to see what happens [illegible] node.)

So the "almost grayscale" hair color goes into the Specular Color input for an Anisotropic node, which creates irregularly shaped highlights on an object. The amount of highlight is determined by the "almost grayscale" hair texture being used as the input—and remember that Multiply node? The "zero values" that are sent from the Multiply node to the rest of the path to the root node prevents the highlights from occurring in the transparent areas of the hair object, or where there isn't any hair. The remainder of the Alternate Specular input of the root node sees irregular highlights of varying brightness.

Reducing Complexity

Now that you've examined what makes the various nodes in the hair material tick, we're going to work on significantly reducing the complexity of the hair material. In this instance, we've decided to completely eliminate any anisotropic highlights and stick to the most basic hair configuration because sometimes, *simple* will work just fine. This is an example of reducing material complexity to speed up render times. We will be really focusing on James Casual's skin, where we'll be using more complex shaders that take more time to render. By reducing the complexity of as many materials as possible, we're improving our render time, and when you are waiting for your render to finish, every bit helps!

1. First, delete those nodes we no longer want to use. You will be deleting the anisotropic, hsv, and the Color_Math nodes. To delete the anisotropic node click the node to make it the current selection. Then right-click and choose Delete from the menu that appears. Repeat this process for the hsv node, and the Color_Math node.
2. Now, all you need to do is reset some of the root node's parameters. First, fix the Specular_Color parameter by changing the color to White (R=255, G=255, B=255). To change the color, just click anywhere in the black color square and then you can select white from the Default Color Picker. If you prefer to use the System Color picker, just click on the little rainbow on the upper-right side of the Default Color Picker's window and you can enter the Red, Green, and Blue values manually to make sure you get the exact color you want.
3. Next, adjust the Specular_Value to be 0.4.
4. Finally, adjust the Bump parameter value to be 0.31. When you are done, your new hair material should look like the material shown on the right side of Figure 9.18. The left side shows the original, default material for James Casual's hair.

Finished versions of all of the altered materials are located on the CD-ROM that accompanies this book. You can find them in the Tutorials > Chap09 > Runtime > Libraries > Materials > PracticalPoser6 > Chap09 folder.

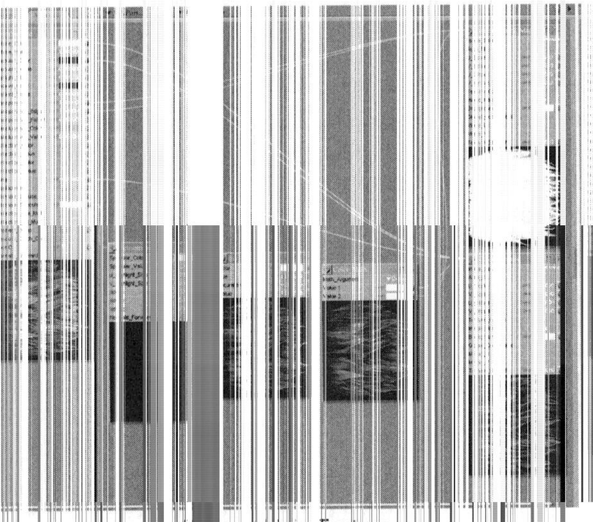

Default Hair Texture

New Reduced Node Hair Texture

FIGURE 9.18 James Casual's default hair material (left) is simplified to reduce the complexity of the material. The new version is shown on the right.

TUTORIAL 9.[illegible] REDUCING THE EYE HIGHLIGHTS

Now let's reduce the highlights that appear in JamesCasual's eyes and make the corners of his eye whites darker and warmer. Use the Eye Dropper tool to select one of his eyes by clicking the white portion of his eye. Make sure that EyeTrans is selected in the Material Group List menu. Alternately, use the Object List menu to select James Casual, and then use the Material Group List menu to select EyeTrans.

If you are serious about creating realistic-looking humans, you will need to study the color and shading qualities of the various parts of the human anatomy. A common mistake is to make eye-whites too bright and too white. The eyes are wet spheres with a rich supply of blood vessels [illegible] this space. They are encased in a fatty [illegible] deep recess in our skulls. Most times our eyeballs are receiving some type of shadow—from the upper eyelid and from the upper brow and forehead, and from the cheekbones. Our eyeball [illegible] is not perfectly smooth, but [illegible] covered by a network of tiny veins.

For our modified EyeTrans material, we are going to adjust some of the node settings, and make some adjustments that will soften the highlights and add ray-traced reflections and eye transparency. To begin, follow these steps:

1. In the root node, change the Specular Value setting from 5 to 0. You should immediately see the size of the highlights get smaller in the root node material preview.
2. In the Anisotropic Node, make adjustments to the following settings. The end result will be that the shapes of the reflections will change slightly.

SETTING	CHANGE FROM	CHANGE TO
Specular Value	.5	.62
U_Highlight Size	.07	.11
V_Highlight Size	.09	no change
XDir_X	0	.11
XDir_Y	0	.51
XDir_Z	1	.46

3. We're going to make some changes to the Reflection Color input on the root node. To begin, click the Reflection Color plug input and drag outward to display the New Node menu. Choose New Node > Lighting > Ray Trace > Reflect. This adds ray-traced reflections to the eyes. Leave the Reflect node at the default settings (Background is black, Quality is .2, Softness is 0, and RayBias is .025).
4. Adjust the Reflection Value setting in the root node from .75 to .95. When you are finished, your revised EyeTrans material shader should look as shown in Figure 9.19.
5. Next we'll tweak the whites of James Casual's eyeballs. We're going to add a bit more dusky-rose contrast to the outer edges of the whites of his eyes. This will help keep them from looking like they are radioactive, and also breathe some life into them by warming up the shadow of the eyeball with a supply of blood. We'll keep the shader nodes "as is" and adjust one color. To begin, select Eyeball from the Material Group List menu.
6. The values we change are both the Edge_Blend node's Inner_Color and Outer_Color properties. To start, click the white Inner_Color rectangle to open the Poser Color Picker. Then click the Rainbow icon in the upper-right corner of the Color Picker to open the standard System Color Picker. Using Red, Green, and Blue values, change the color to R=222, G=199, B=198. Now click the grey Outer_Color rectangle to open the Poser Color Picker. Then click the Rainbow icon in the upper right corner of the Color Picker to open the standard System Color Picker. Using Red, Green, and Blue values, change the color to R=184, G=133, B=107. The eyeballs should now appear warmer and more natural.

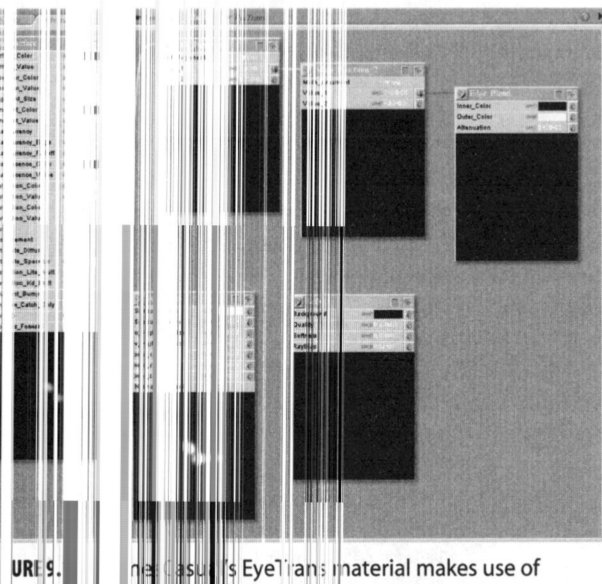

FIGURE 9.[illegible] [illegible] Casual's EyeTrans material makes use of Anisotropic properties to create noncircular specular highlights, and also [illegible] ray-traced reflections.

TUTORIAL [illegible].3 IMPRO[illegible]ING THE [illegible] MATERIALS

Now we'll add [illegible] Casual's skin to see if we can make it look more alive. We'll take [illegible] the skin node, which does a remarkable job simulating the [illegible] of human skin.

If you [illegible] some [illegible] how human skin looks under various lighting conditions, you'll [illegible] that the outermost layer isn't totally opaque. Our skin absorbs [illegible] refracts [illegible] also reflects it. Usually it has an excellent supply of blood close to the [illegible] skin also has surface imperfections that give it a distinctive texture—[illegible] scars, pimples, fatty deposits, wrinkles, and sags. By controlling the[illegible] you can give signals to your audience about the age and vitality of your [illegible].

We are aiming to make James Casual a younger man who is in good shape. He's rugged and has worked outdoors, so his face is going to show some imperfections and the pores of someone who been exposed to harsher climates.

1. Use the Eyedropper to select the skin on his head. Alternately you can use the Object List menu to select JamesCasual, and then select Head from the Material Group List menu.
2. Click the input plug to the Diffuse Color, and choose New Node > Lighting > Special > Skin. This adds a Skin node to the Diffuse Color channel and removes the connection to the previous texture. Set the Diffuse Value to 0.
3. Set values of the Skin node as follows: Ka = 0.6; Kd = 1; Ks = 1; Thickness = 4; eta = 2.
4. Drag a connection from the output of the Skin Node to the input of the Alternate Diffuse channel on the root node.
5. Connect the output of the Image Map to both the SkinColor and SheenColor inputs of the Skin node. This causes the Skin node to receive the skin and sheen colors from the texture map.
6. In the Skin node, set SkinColor and SheenColor to almost white (R=240, G=232, B=230).
7. In the root node, set the Specular_Value setting to 0.6. This reduces the amount of shine on the skin. Set the Highlight Size to .05 to reduce the size of the shiny areas.
8. Now we'll add a bump map to the root node. Click the Bump input plug, and drag to select New Node > 2D Textures > Image Map.
9. Use the Texture Manager to select the Poser 6 > Runtime > Textures > Poser 6 Textures > James > James_Face_Bump.jpg image for your bump map.
10. Set the Bump Value in the root node to .005.
11. Drag a connection from the bump map Image Map 2 output to the Displacement input on the root node. Set the Displacement setting to .001.
12. Compare your new skin texture to the example shown in Figure 9.20. If all settings are correct, do a test render to see the difference in the skin. The skin node adds depth and realism to skin textures by simulating a surface that has an upper layer that is translucent. You must also enable displacement render settings, using the Firefly render engine so that Poser can add surface irregularities to James Casual's head during render time.

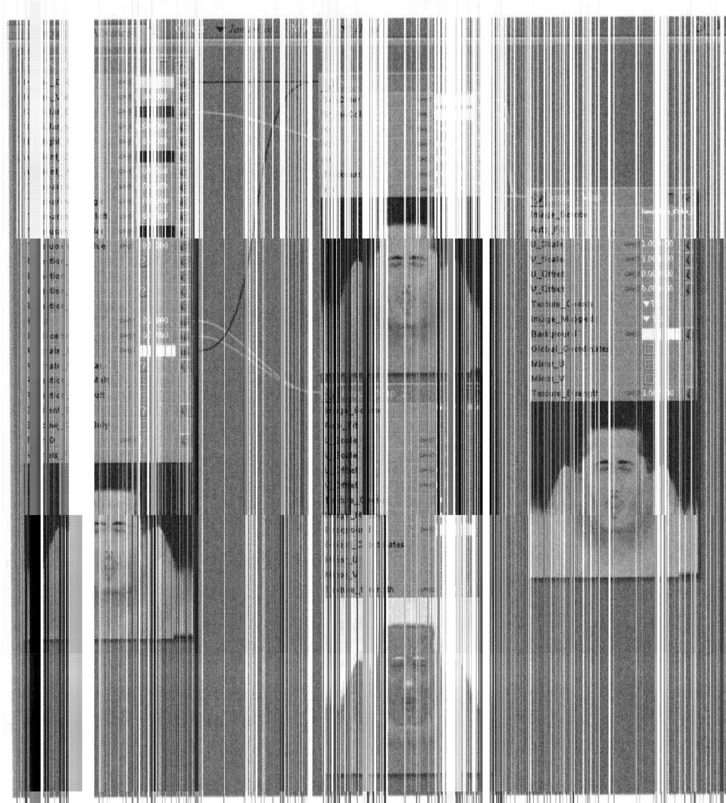

FIGURE 9.20 James Casual now takes advantage of the skin shader node.

TUTORIAL 9.4 MATCHING THE BODY MATERIALS

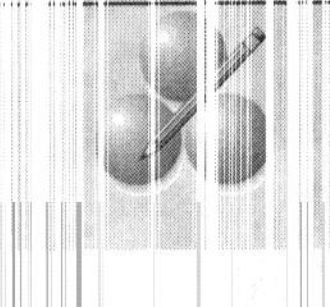

Now it's time to copy these Head material parameters from James Casual's Head material group to his SkinBody material group.

1. While you still have the Head material group selected, right-click anywhere in the Advanced view window. Choose *Select all* from the menu that appears to select all the Head material nodes.
2. Right-click in the Advanced view window again and choose the Copy command. This copies all the Head material nodes into your copy buffer.
3. Select SkinBody from the Material Group list menu (or use the Eyedropper to select an area on his lower neck) and make sure that you've got the SkinBody material group selected.
4. Right-click again in the Advanced view window and select the *Paste* command. You should see the Head material nodes appear in the window.

5. You should also notice that the Image_Map node that was connected to the SkinBody root node is now an orphan. To delete this original Image_Map node that isn't connected to anything, click the orphan map to make it the current selection. Then right-click and choose Delete from the menu that appears.
6. The only thing left to do is to switch out the maps that are being used in the Image_Map nodes. Select Image_Map_2, and replace the head image with the James_Body_Lores.jpg image map. You should be able to locate this in the image map history since it was used in the original SkinBody texture. Select the Image_Map_3 node and replace the Image_Source with the James_Body_Bump.jpg image file. Again, this file should already be in your history. The skin on JamesCasual's neck should now match, exactly, the skin on his Head. Figure 9.21 shows the shader nodes that make up JamesCasual's new SkinBody material.

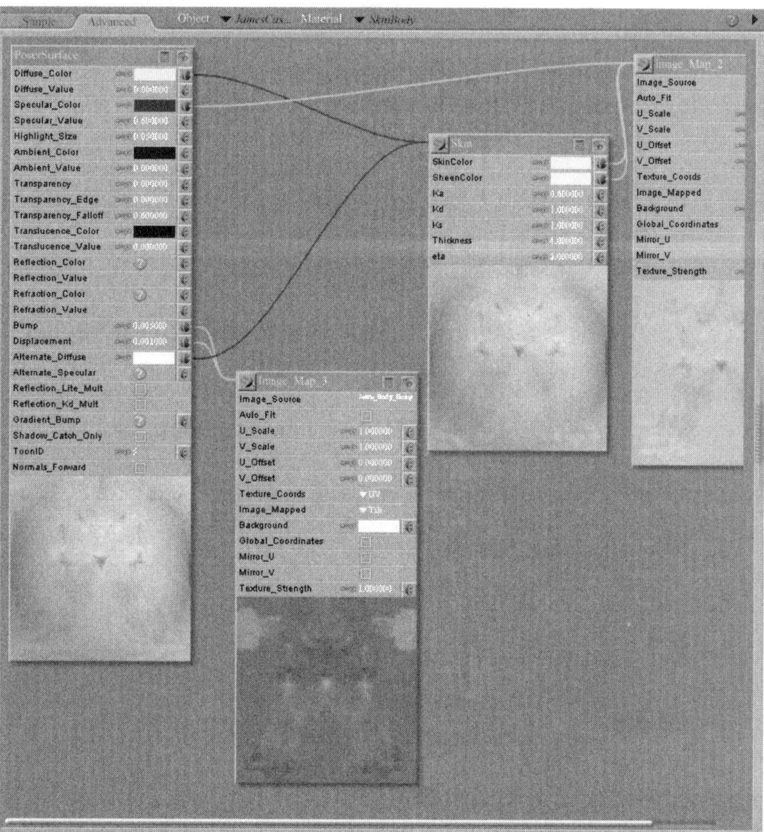

FIGURE 9.21 JamesCasual's new SkinBody material is now similar to his new Head material with the exception of the images.

TUTORIAL [illegible].5 CREATING NICE TEETH

The materials used for James Casual's teeth are white by default. Real teeth are rarely pure white, though they do have white specular highlights. We're going to set the materials for James Casual's upper (TeethTop) and lower teeth (TeethBottom) separately. The bottom teeth are going to be a bit darker than the top.

To modify the teeth textures, follow these steps:

1. Select the TeethTop material from the Material menu in the Advanced material view.
2. Adjust the Diffuse Color in the root node to R198, G19[illegible], B186 (a very light-gray color). Reduce the Diffuse Value to .7.
3. Click the input plug for the Diffuse Color and select the New Node > 3D Textures > Wood node. Apply the following settings to the Wood node:

SETTING	VALUE
Light Wood	R219, G226, B226
Dark Wood	R235, G226, B226
Scale	0.4
Turbulence	1
GlobalCoordinates	Unchecked
Noise Type	Improved

4. Set the Specular Value to 0 and the Highlight Size to 0.
5. Click the input node from the Alternate Diffuse channel in the root node, and drag out to select New Node > Lighting > Specular > Glossy. The Alternate Specular colors in the root node should be set to R=240, G=240, B=240, and the Glossy node should be set to White. Adjust the Glossy node settings as follows:

SETTING	VALUE
Ks	0.39
Roughness	0.1
Sharpness	.017
Normals Forward	Unchecked

6. Select the TeethBottom material from the Material menu in the Advanced material view. We will make these teeth slightly darker than the upper teeth.

7. Adjust the Diffuse Color in the root node to R158, G158, B124 (a slightly darker and yellowish-gray color than the upper teeth). Reduce the Diffuse Value to 0.7.
8. Click the input plug for the Diffuse Color, and select the New Node > 3D Textures > Wood node. Apply the following settings to the Wood node:

SETTING	VALUE
Light Wood	R214, G211, B181
Dark Wood	R235, G226, B226
Scale	0.4
Turbulence	1
GlobalCoordinates	Unchecked
Noise Type	Improved

9. Adjust the Specular Color in the root node to R237, G242, B239. Leave the Specular Value set at 1 and the Highlight Size at .02.

When you are finished with the above steps, your TeethTop and TeethBottom material nodes should look as shown in Figure 9.22.

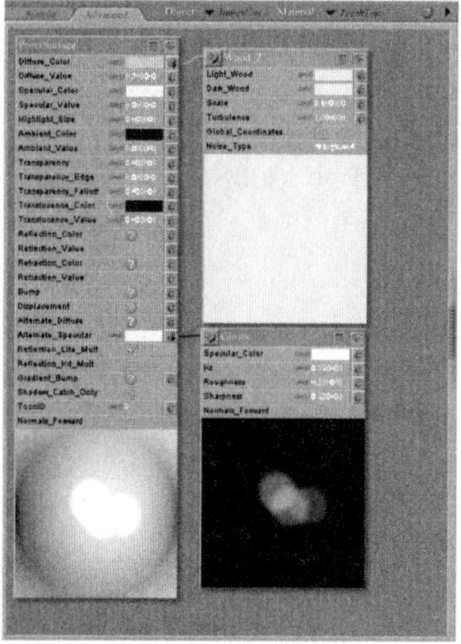

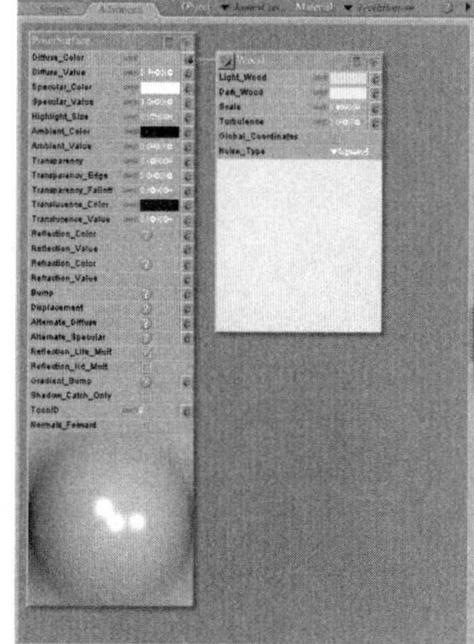

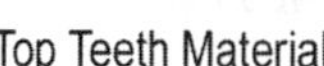

Top Teeth Material

Bottom Teeth Material

FIGURE 9.22 Comparison of the TeethTop and the TeethBottom material nodes and their parameter settings.

TUTORIAL 9.6 FIXING THE SHIRT

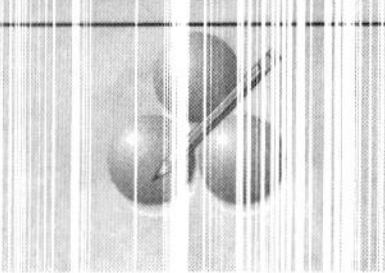

James Casual's shirt is rather plain, and uses a texture map with no bump map or surface enhancements. We'll change this drab T-shirt into a nice velour-type material that works specifically for this camera and light combination. We're going to use both the Bump and Displacement channels for texture enhancement.

1. Select the TShirt3 material from the Material menu in the Advanced material view.
2. Click the Diffuse Color rectangle in the root node. Change the Diffuse Color to R115, G117, B124.
3. Click the Background color rectangle in the Image_Map node. Change the Background Color to R82, G98, B13[illegible].
4. Drag a connection from the output of the Image_Map node to the input of the Specular Color channel in the root node. Set the Specular Color in the root node to R246, G246, B246 (a color that is very near white). Reduce the Specular Value to .5, and leave the Highlight Size at .016667.
5. Drag another connection from the output of the Image_Map node to the input of the Bump channel of the root node. Set the Bump parameter value in the root node to .0833.
6. Now we'll add a Displacement map to give the shirt even more texture. Click the Displacement input plug in the root node and drag out to select New Node > 2D Textures > Image Map. Click the Image Source name to open the Texture Manager, and navigate to and select the Poser 6 > Runtime > Textures > P6ClothingTextures > Male > WaveBumpbig4P6.jpg image. The Displacement parameter value in the root node should be .0008.
7. In the new Bump Map image node, change the U_Scale and V_Scale settings to .02.

After you complete the above changes, your shirt material should look as shown in Figure 9.23. The shirt is now complete.

If you decide to use the shirt material with different lights you may need to tweak the parameters. Also, if you want to transfer it to a different object, you'll need to replace the MTshirt3Text_Lores.jpg image map with one appropriate for the mesh you are using. You might even get away with replacing it with a seamless tile with similar properties, which would make the velour work for any object shape.

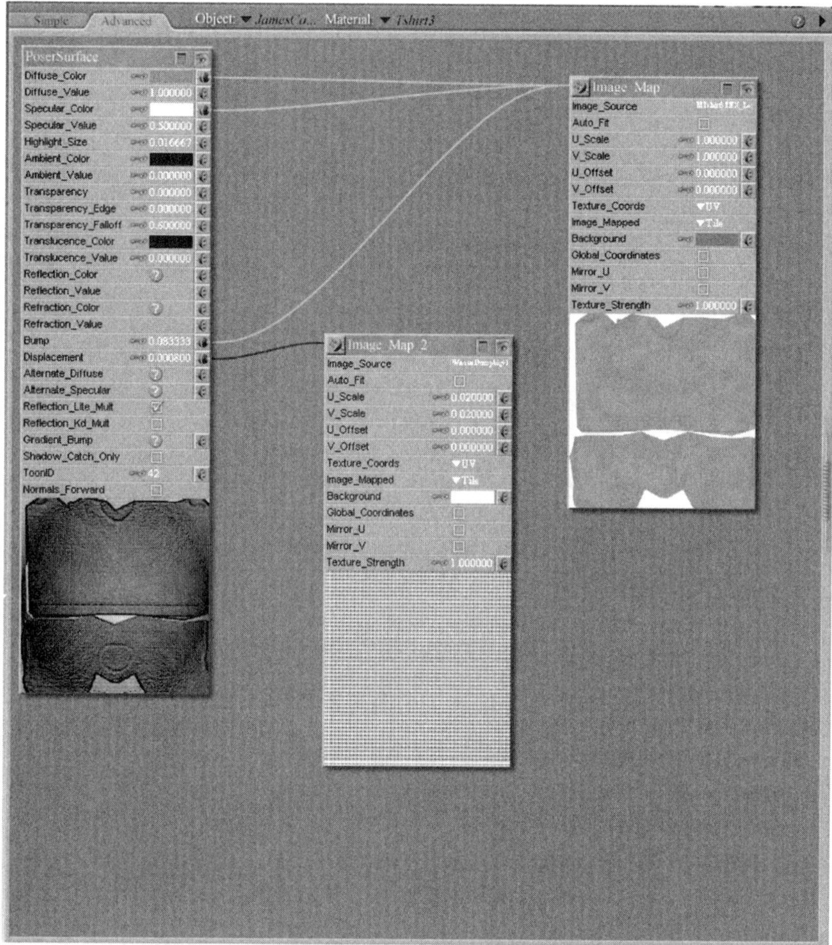

FIGURE 9.23 James Casual's shirt material resembles a dark velour.

TUTORIAL 9.7 IMPROVING THE BACKGROUND TEXTURE

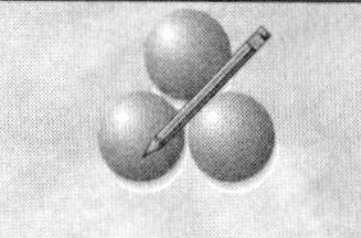

We're almost done! The last thing we need is to spruce up the back wall. (If you would rather apply the *box* material presets for this step, just browse to the Runtime > Libraries > Materials > PracticalPoser6 > Chap09 library and apply the Ch09BackWall material to the box prop's Preview material group.)

For this we'll use one of the images of weathered wood that comes with Poser 6.

1. Select the box with the Eyedropper, or use the Object List menu to select the box from the Props list.
2. Select the Preview material from the Material Group list menu.
3. For the Diffuse Color, click the color square and select a light shade of gray (R=196, G=196, B=196). The Diffuse_Value should be set to 1.
4. Click the Diffuse Color input plug at the root node and drag out to select New Node > 2D Textures > Image_Map. Use the Texture Manager to browse to and select the Poser 6 > Runtime > Libraries > Materials > Wood > OldWeatheredPlanks.bmp texture in your Poser 6 installation. Choose OK to return to the Material Room. In the Image_Map node, make sure that the Texture_Coords setting is set to UV and the Image_Mapped setting is None.
5. In the root node, set the Specular Color to black. Change both the Specular Value and Highlight Size settings to 0.
6. Click the Bump input plug in the root node. Drag out to select New Node > Math > HSV. Connect the output of the Image_Map node to the Color input of the HSV node. Then set the Saturation value to 0. This desaturates the colors of the texture input map to make the input to the Bump parameter grayscale. Set the Bump value in the root node to .016667.
7. Drag a connection from the output of the Math node to the input of the Displacement node. Set the Displacement value in the root node to .058333.
8. When you are finished with the background material, it will look as shown in Figure 9.24. Now your back wall should look like weathered wood.

Congratulations—you've just completed all the hard parts! Go ahead and render the scene to see what it looks like. You'll have to use the FireFly renderer because we are making use of Displacement maps and some specialized shader nodes. Try the Auto Settings > Final render quality. Make sure you also have Smooth polygons, Remove backfacing polys, and Use displacement maps selected. Reference Figure 9.25 to see what our finished render came out like, compared to our original default-everything baseline render.

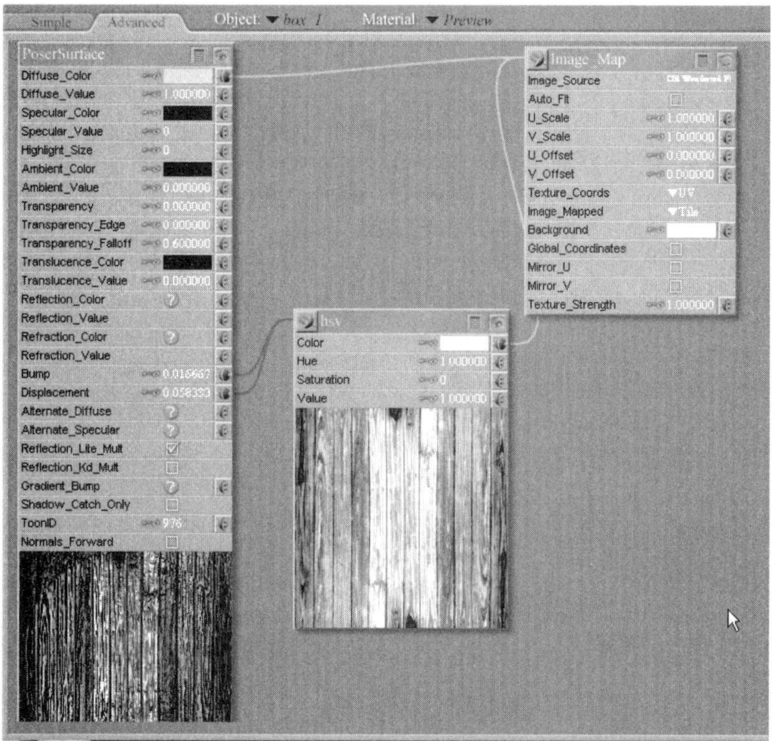

FIGURE 9.24 The weathered wood material that is applied to the box to form the back wall for our portrait makes use of both the Bump and Displacement parameters of the root node.

FIGURE 9.25 These renders compare the materials for JamesCasual after we have improved on them. The render on the right shows JamesCasual using default materials

CONCLUSION

Now that you have first-hand experience creating complex materials, you can see for yourself how powerful the Poser 6 material shaders are. You can tackle any material if you just study it and break it down into its components. You've learned that procedural shaders go a long way in making even low-resolution image maps look great.

With the knowledge you've acquired in this chapter, you don't ever have to be satisfied with flat and lifeless default materials again.

CHAPTER

10

CREATING CUSTOM MORPHS

In This Chapter

- What are Morphs?
- The Anatomy of a Morph
- Creating Morphs in Poser
- Creating Full Body Morphs with ZBrush
- Distributing Morphs
- Avoiding Problems
- Conclusion

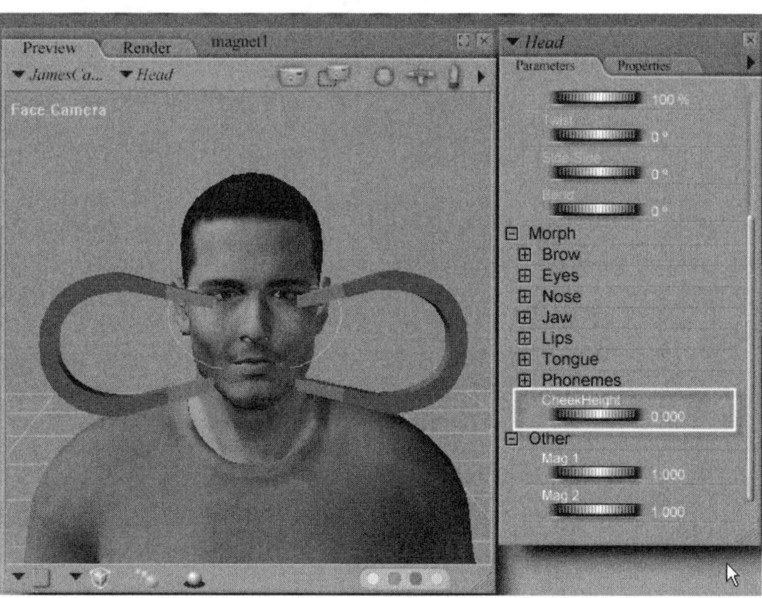

You've seen morphs mentioned in various places throughout this book. In this chapter, you'll learn what morphs are, how to create them, and how to manage the morphs you have. You'll also learn about *external binary morphs*, which is a feature that is new to Poser 6. We begin with an explanation of what morphs are and what they do.

What Are Morphs?

Morphs are used in Poser to alter the shape of a Poser object. For example, if you want to open a character's mouth or close the character's eyes or change the character's shape, you turn a dial to make that happen. For example, if you purchase DAZ3D's Victoria 3 along with her face and body morph packs, you get a wealth of morph targets that change her appearance and body shape. Figure 10.1 shows a portion of the face morphs that are available for Victoria 3.

FIGURE 10.1 DAZ3D figures such as Victoria 3 come with accessory morph packs that help you change their faces and body shapes.

When you move a body part with a bone, it always bends, twists, or turns around the same center point. The basic shape of the body part doesn't change much, except around that center point. Morphs, on the other hand, can affect one or all of the vertices in an object. For example, if you want to make your figure smile, or puff up his or her cheeks, or raise his or her eyebrows, or even gain or lose weight, you use one or more morphs to do it.

To make a morph work, you adjust dials in the Parameters window, or in the Face Shaping Tool in the Face Room. Simply adjust the dial to the left to decrease the value, or to the right to increase the value of the morph. You can also enter values in the number fields.

THE ANATOMY OF A MORPH

When you create a morph in Poser, or import a morph target that was created in an external program, Poser compares the starting shape (or the source shape) to the ending shape (or the target shape). When you save the morphed character to the library, the library file includes the *delta information* for each morph. That is, the library file stores information that describes how far each vertex in the morph moved, and from where and to where it moved.

Let's say, for example, that you see a dial that changes the size of the eyeballs on a character. When you increase the setting on the morph dial, the entire eye gets larger, as shown on the left eye in Figure 10.2. When you decrease the setting on the morph dial, the entire eye gets smaller. If each eye contains 200 vertices, the morph information adds 200 extra lines of information to your library file for each eye, because you are changing the position of every vertex in the eyeball.

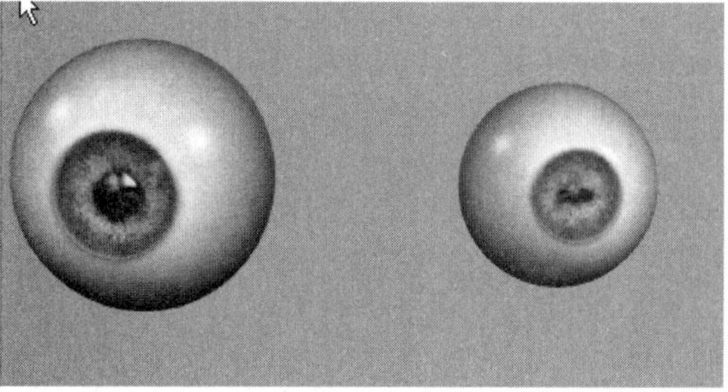

FIGURE 10.2 Morphs can affect all vertices in an object (left), or some of the vertices such as only those for the pupil of an eye (right).

On the other hand, let's say that there is another dial that only affects the vertices in the pupil of the eye. In this case, let's say that the dial only moves 20 of those 200 vertices. Poser doesn't store the morph information for all 200 of the vertices for that morph. Instead, it only stores the information for the 20 vertices that change the size of the pupil.

CREATING MORPHS IN POSER

If the figure or clothing doesn't have a morph that will accomplish what you want your Poser content to do, you have to create the morph yourself. There are several different programs that you can use to create morphs for Poser content. One method is to use Poser magnets, which help you deform the polygons in an object by pushing, pulling, twisting, moving, translating, or rotating them.

Once you wrap your head around the three basic parts of a magnet, it's not too difficult to create morphs with them. In fact, some very popular Poser morph artists create their morphs strictly with Poser magnets. One such artist is Capsces, whose character morph packs enhance many popular third-party Poser figures with entirely new levels of caricature and realism.

A magnet has three parts: the *magnet base*, the *magnet zone*, and the *magnet*. These parts are shown in Figure 10.3.

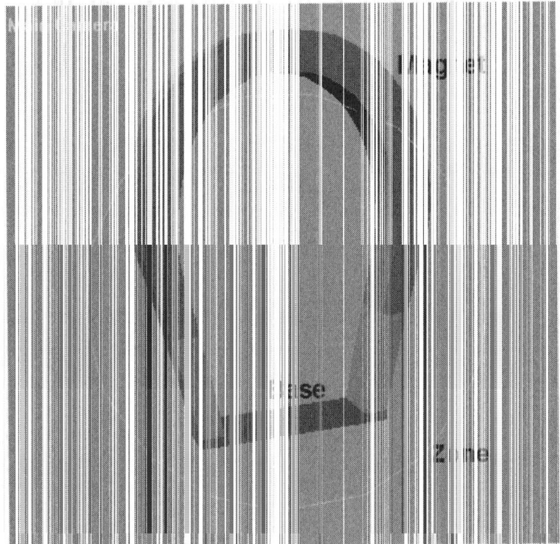

FIGURE 10.3 A magnet has three parts: the *magnet base*, the *magnet zone*, and the *magnet*.

- The magnet base is the bar-shaped rectangle that appears at the base of the magnet. This bar indicates where the force of the magnet has the most effect. Dials in the Parameters window allow you to scale the base, which changes the overall size of the magnet prop without affecting the geometry. If the magnet is too large or too small to work with, you can change the scale of the base to change the size of the magnet. Parameter dials also allow you to rotate and translate the position of the magnet base.
- The magnet zone is the spherical outline that indicates the area where the magnet will affect the object. The magnet will have the most effect in the center of the falloff zone (which initially appears as the outline of a sphere). The effect of the magnet gradually falls off as it reaches the outer edge of the zone. You adjust the shape of the magnet zone by increasing or decreasing the xScale, yScale, or zScale values of the magnet zone. When you enlarge the size of the magnet zone, you affect more polygons in the object you want to morph. Reduce the size of the magnet zone to affect fewer polygons. You can also translate or rotate the magnet zone on the x (left/right), y (up/down) or z (forward/backward) axis to position the magnet base away from the center point of the magnet zone.
- The magnet is the element that actually moves the polygons in the object. The polygons that move are determined by the position of the magnet base and the area defined by the magnet zone. You translate, rotate, or scale the magnet to move the polygons in the object. After you move the magnet, you can make changes to the placement of the magnet zone or magnet base until you achieve the desired shape of your morph.

TUTORIAL 10.1 CREATING MORPHS WITH POSER MAGNETS

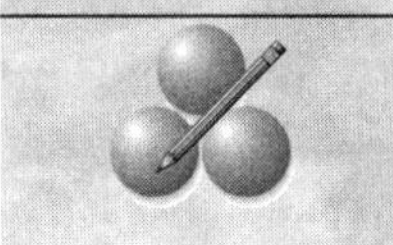

It will be easier to understand the function of each of the magnet parts if you use them yourself. In this tutorial, you'll create a morph for James Casual's face. The morph will change the shape of his cheeks. Actually, you'll use two magnets to create the morph: one on each side of the face.

To create the face morph for James Casual, follow these steps:

1. Create a new Poser scene, and load James Casual if necessary. Turn off Inverse Kinematics, and use the Joint Editor or the Zero All Python script to zero his pose.
2. Select the Face Camera, using the icon in the Camera Controls, or by choosing Display > Cameras > Camera View > Face Camera. Change the display to Texture Shaded mode.

3. Click James Casual's head to select it as the current actor. Then choose Object > Create Magnet. Your scene should look similar to Figure 10.4.

FIGURE 10.4 A magnet is created for James Casual's head.

4. The first thing you notice is that the magnet zone automatically encloses and is centered around the selected body part, and the magnet base appears near the base of the head. We want to affect one of the cheeks with this magnet. So let's start by moving the magnet right and upward toward the right cheek. Click the yellow magnet base to make it the current object. Adjust the xTran dial to -0.141, the yTran dial to 5.85[illegible] and the zTran dial to [illegible]351.
5. Since part of the magnet is buried inside his head, we can also rotate the magnet base so that you can see the magnet better. We'll also make the magnet a little smaller. Scale the magnet base to 7%, and adjust the zRotate value to 90 degrees. Your magnet should now look as shown in Figure 10.5.

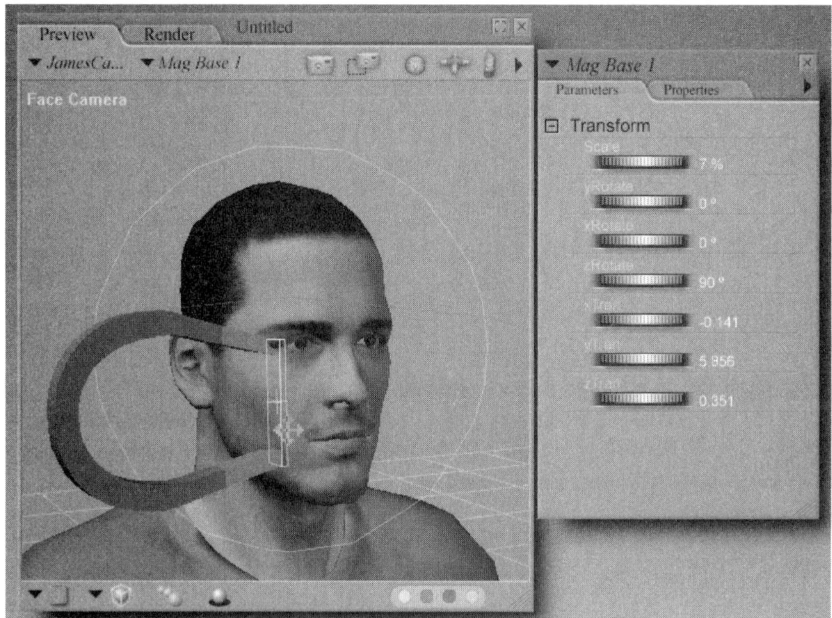

FIGURE 10.5 The magnet base is repositioned, scaled, and rotated.

Notice in Step 5 that instead of scaling and rotating the magnet (which would move the polygons in James Casual's face), we scaled and rotated the magnet base to change the size and rotation of the magnet. Always change the magnet base when you need to reposition or scale the magnets without affecting the geometry.

6. If you move the magnet at this point to morph the cheeks, the magnet will change the polygons in the entire head. This is because the magnet zone currently *surrounds* the entire head. We need to move the magnet zone forward, toward the front of the face, and decrease its size so that it only affects the right cheek. To begin, click the magnet zone (the white outline around the head) to make it the current object.
7. Adjust the camera so that you see James Casual's head toward the side (or use the head cameras that you created in Chapter 4, "Using Cameras.")
8. We're going to change all scale settings; zRotation values; and x, y, and zTran values for the magnet zone. We want to create an elliptical magnet zone that will enhance and raise James' right cheekbone. To modify the magnet zone, use the following settings:

Scale	[illegible]%
xScale	57%
yScale	47%
zScale	81%
zRotate	-40 degrees
xTran	-0.162
yTran	5.8[illegible]
zTran	0.870

9. Now that you have changed the shape of the magnet zone, we can move the magnet to examine how it affects the right cheek. We will scale the cheekbone so that it is a little bit larger, and also pull the faces forward (zTran) and to the right (xTran). After you set the Magnet values in the Parameters window as follows, your cheek magnet should look as shown in Figure 10.6.

Scale	107%
xTran	-0.378
zTran	0.[illegible]36

FIGURE 10.6 The new magnet makes the right cheekbone more pronounced.

TUTORIAL 10.2 SAVING A MAGNET

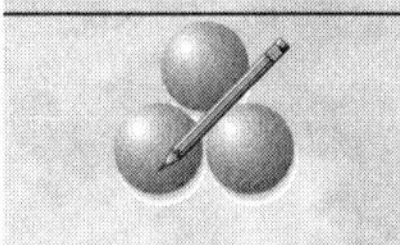

You have two options to create the magnet for the other side. The first option is to start from scratch with a new magnet. The second option is to save the first magnet to the library, and then mirror some of the settings to flip the magnet to the other side of the face. This tutorial will show you the latter approach.

1. You'll need to create a library category in the Props library of your choice, so that you can save your new magnet. Navigate to the Props library in the Runtime of your choosing. Click the down arrow at the top of the Props library and choose Add New Category from the menu shown in Figure 10.7.

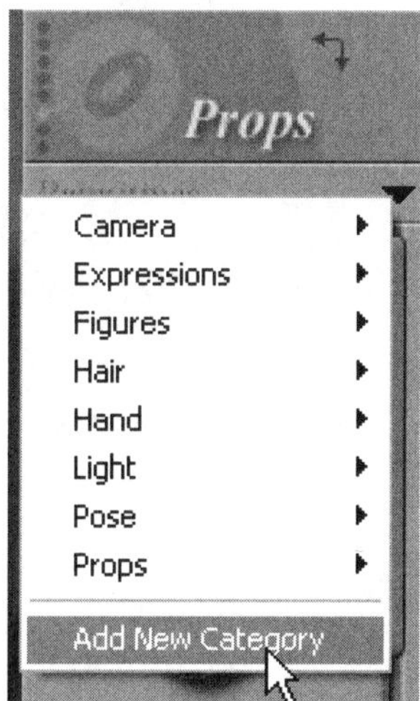

FIGURE 10.7 We add a new Props library category for our magnets.

2. The Library Name dialog prompts you for a new library name. James-Assign a name to the new Props library, such as "James Magnets." Click OK to continue.
3. Double-click your new library folder to select it as the current library.
4. Click the Magnet in your preview window, and then click the Add to Library icon at the bottom of the library window. The New Set dialog appears.
5. Click the Select Subset button to open the Hierarchy Selection dialog. Check Mag Base 1, Mag 1, and Mag Zone 1 as shown in Figure 10.8.

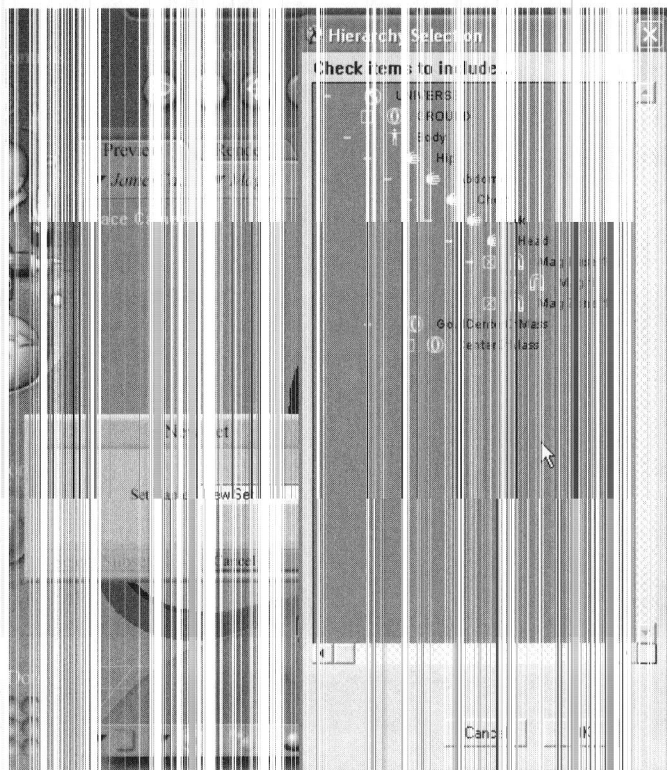

FIGURE 10.[illegible] When saving a magnet to your library, remember to select all three magnet components.

6. Click OK to return to the New Set dialog. Assign a name to the magnet, such as "JamesRightCheek." Click OK to save the magnet to the library.

TUTORIAL 10.3 MIRRORING A MAGNET

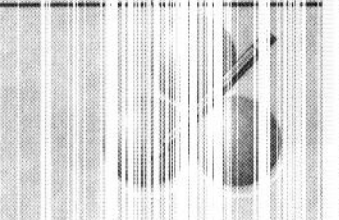

Now that you've created the magnet for one cheek, you need to create a magnet that does exactly the same thing on the other cheek. It's actually pretty easy to accomplish. Since you've saved the right cheek magnet to the library, you can modify the magnet that is already in your scene. You'll only have to make some minor adjustments to the settings that are already there.

To modify the existing magnet, follow these steps:

1. Save the existing magnet as described in Tutorial 10.2 if you have not already done so.

2. Click the magnet base. Change the xTran setting from –0.141 to 0.141 (in other words, change it from a negative number to the equal positive number). This places the base on the opposite side, in the same relative position.
3. Adjust the zRotate value from 90 degrees to –90 degrees. This flips the magnet in the other direction. Your magnet should now look as shown in Figure 10.9.

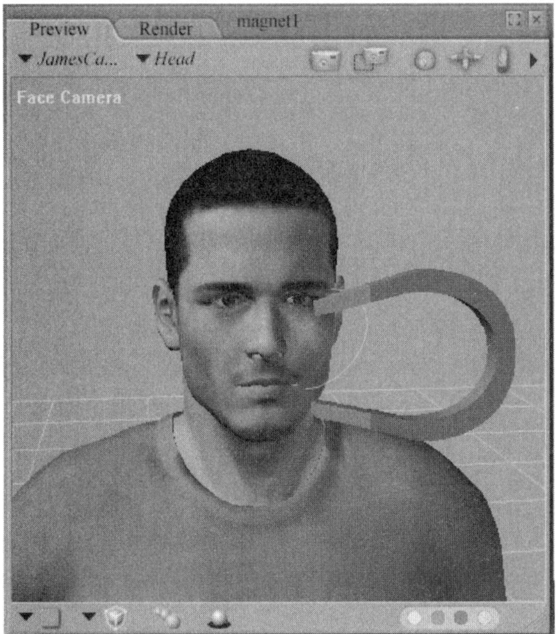

FIGURE 10.9 The magnet base is adjusted to position the magnet on the opposite cheek.

4. Now we have to change the magnet zone so that it flips the other way. Click the magnet zone to select it as the current object.
5. To rotate the magnet in the opposite direction, change the zRotate value from –40 to 40 degrees (change the negative value to a positive value). The ellipse rotates in the opposite direction.
6. Change the xTran value from –0.162 to .162 (changing the negative number to a positive number).
7. Now click the magnet. Change the xTran value from –.378 to .378 (changing the negative value to a positive value. Your magnet should now be a mirror opposite of the one you created for the right cheek.
8. Using the steps as described in Tutorial 10.2, save the magnet to the library as *JamesLeftCheek*.

Tutorial 10.4 Spawning a Single Morph Target

After you change the shape of a body part with a magnet, you have to "spawn" a morph target. Basically, spawning is a process that takes the shape of the magnetized part and turns it into a morph dial. Afterward, you can delete the magnet or magnets and set the morph dial to 1 to achieve the same shape as created by the magnets. Make sure to save the magnets to the library before you delete them so that you don't have to recreate them later.

Before we create the face morph, we'll add the right cheek magnet from the library so that both cheeks are symmetrical. Then we'll create a facial morph that moves both cheeks at the same time. Follow these steps:

1. Double-click the JamesRightCheek magnet in the library to add it back into the scene. Both cheeks should now be symmetrical.
2. Click James' head to select it as the current object. Both magnets appear next to the face.
3. Choose Object > Spawn Morph Target. The Morph Name dialog appears.
4. Enter a name for the morph dial (such as CheekHeight). Click OK to save the morph to the Parameters window. You should see the morph dial in the Morph section of your Parameters window as shown in Figure 10.10.

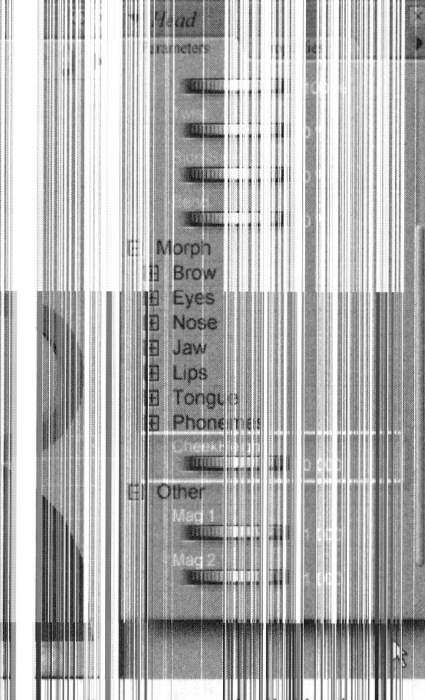

FIGURE 10.10 After you spawn the morph, you will see a morph dial in the Parameters Window.

5. Click one of the magnets, and press the Delete key to delete it. Answer OK to confirm that you want to delete the magnet.
6. Click the head to make the second magnet visible, then click the second magnet to select it. Press the Delete key, and then choose OK to confirm that you want to delete the magnet.
7. Click the head to select it as the current object. Then set the dial for your new morph target to 1. You should see the head morph as shown in Figure 10.11. You have now used magnets to create your first morph!

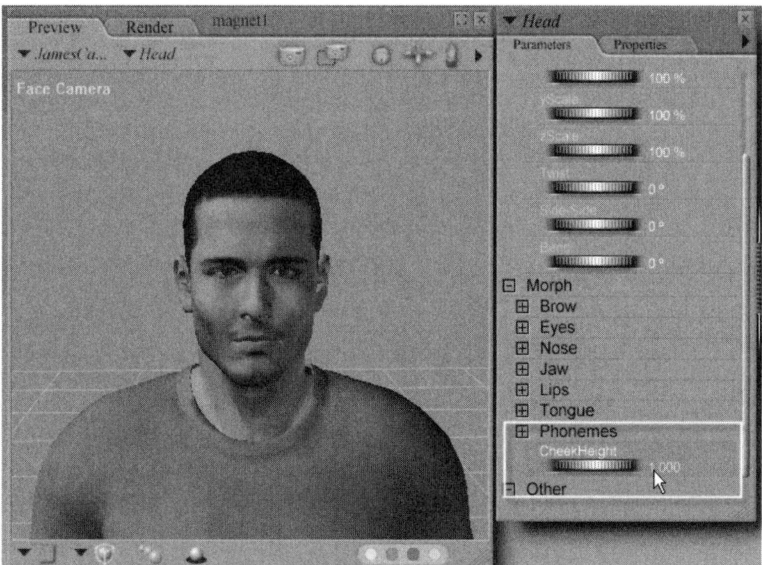

FIGURE 10.11 Remove the magnets and dial the morph dial to 1 to create the same effect as the magnets.

TUTORIAL 10.5 ONE MAGNET AFFECTS MULTIPLE BODY PARTS

You've learned how to affect one body part with more than one magnet, and now you'll learn the reverse—how to affect multiple body parts with one magnet. For this exercise, we'll continue with the scene that you have been working with in this chapter. This time, we'll add a magnet that will give James Casual a "pot belly." You will start by creating a magnet for the abdomen, and then add the additional body parts to the list that the magnet will affect.

To create a magnet that affects more than one body part, follow these steps:

1. Choose Display > Camera View > Main Camera to switch to the main camera view if necessary.
2. Click James Casual's abdomen to select it as the current actor.
3. Choose Object > Create Magnet. Note that the magnet initially appears inside James Casual, so that you cannot see it. You should, however, see Mag 1 displayed in the Parameters window, and you'll also see a small magnet zone that surrounds the abdomen, as shown in Figure 10.12.

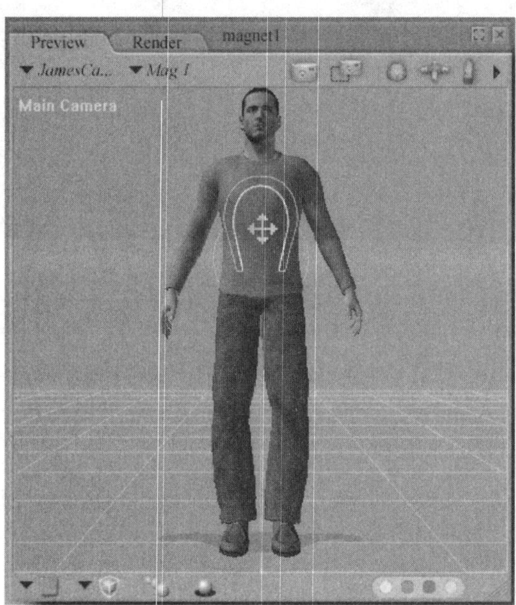

FIGURE 10.12 The magnet for the abdomen is placed inside James Casual's body.

4. Click the magnet base to select it, or choose Mag Base 1 from the menu in the Parameters window. Adjust the zTran value to .6 to bring the magnet outside of the abdomen.
5. Set the xRotate value for the magnet base to 90 degrees to rotate the magnet.
6. Right now, the magnet will only affect James Casual's abdomen. To add a second part, click the magnet to select it as the current object. Then click the Properties window, and click the button labeled Add

Element to Deform. The Choose Actor window shown in Figure 10.13 appears.

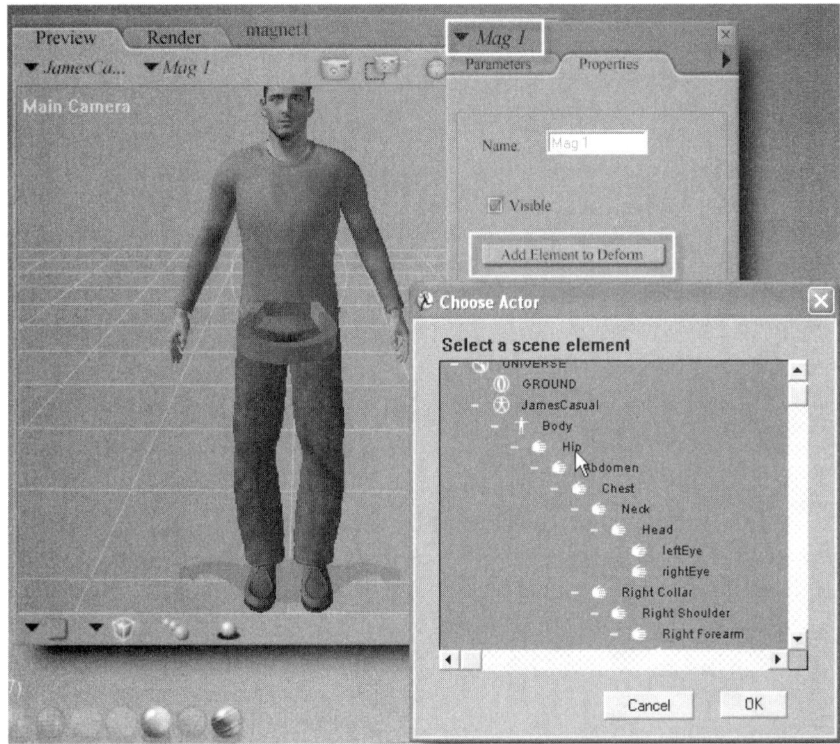

FIGURE 10.13 The Choose Actor window allows you to control more than one body part with a single magnet.

7. Select the hip from the Choose Actor window and click OK. You return to the Poser document.
8. Repeat Steps 6 and 7 to add the right thigh, left thigh, and chest to the magnet. Your magnet will now control five body parts.
9. Now click the magnet zone, and select the Properties window. Check the Group option, and then select each part in the list that does not have a checkmark beside it, until all of the body parts you added in Steps 6 through 8 are added to the magnet zone. Figure 10.14 shows all of the parts you should have.

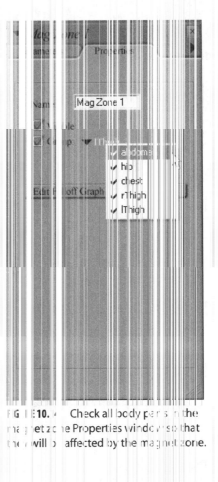

FIGURE 10.4 Check all body parts in the magnet zone Properties window so that they will be affected by the magnet zone.

10. Click the Parameters window, and make the following changes to the magnet zone. These changes will make the magnet zone narrower and move it forward on the z Axis, so that it only affects James' front area.

Scale	14%
zScale	60%
yTran	3.983
zTran	0.568

11. Now, click the magnet to select it. We will now see how it affects James Casual's belly. Change the following parameters on the magnet to make his belly wider and make it stick out more. Also, note

that because you rotated the magnet, the yTran moves the magnet forward and backward, instead of up and down as it normally would. When you're done, James should have a big belly as shown in Figure 10.15.

xScale	115%
yTran	2.915

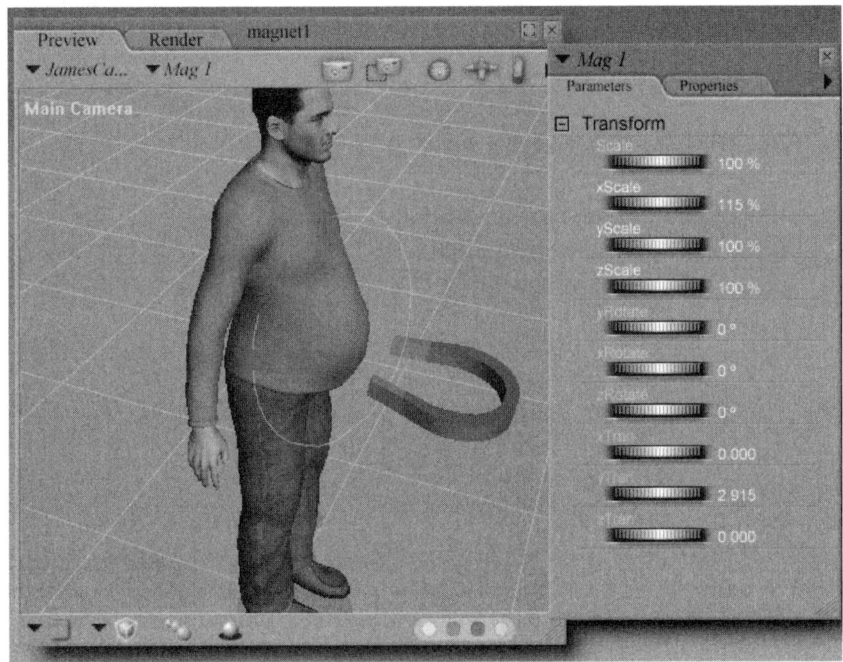

FIGURE 10.15 The magnet affects multiple body parts and creates a big belly on James.

12. Before you delete the magnet, you have to spawn morphs for each of the body parts affected by the magnet. For each of the affected body parts (chest, abdomen, hip, right thigh, or left thigh), select one of them. Choose Object > Spawn Morph Target. Name the morph target for each of the body parts as "PBMBigBelly" as shown in Figure 10.16. The prefix PBM reminds you that it is one of several *partial body morphs (PBMs)* that are to be combined into a final shape.
13. Save your magnet to the library, if desired, as described in Tutorial 10.2. Then delete the magnet. Your morphs are complete.

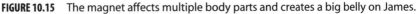

FIGURE 10.16 Spawn a morph target for each of the affected body parts, naming them all "PBMBigBelly."

TUTORIAL 10.6 CREATING FULL BODY MORPHS

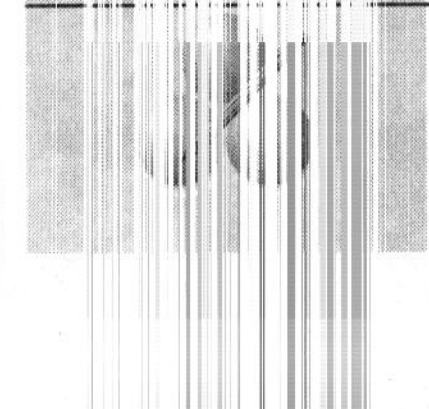

As you learned in the previous tutorial, you have to spawn each body part individually if a magnet affects more than one body part. You also learned that it is common to precede the name of each individual body part morph with "PBM." This gives you an indication that this morph dial should only be used in combination with other morphs of the same name.

So now we have several PBM morphs that, when combined, create a potbelly on James Casual. To make the dials work together, you set all of the PBMBigBelly dials to 1 to achieve your pot-bellied James figure. Then you create a Full Body Morph so that you can make your figure look pregnant with one dial, instead of several individual ones.

To create the full body morph, follow these steps:

1. Continuing from the previous tutorial, click James Casual's chest, and set the PBMBigBelly morph dial setting to 1.
2. Repeat Step 1 for the abdomen, hip, left thigh, and right thigh. James should now look as shown in Figure 10.17. All of the partial body morphs that make up the big belly morph have been dialed to 1.
3. Choose Figure > Create Full Body Morph. The Morph Name dialog appears.
4. Enter *BigBelly* for the morph name and choose OK.
5. Now go through each of the individual body parts to set all five PBMBigBelly morphs to zero (0). James Casual should return to his default shape.
6. Now with James Casual selected, choose Body from the current actor selection menu in the Parameters window, as shown in Figure 10.18. You should see your BigBelly full body morph in the section named Other. When you dial this morph to 1, you'll see all of the individual body parts morph together at the same time to create your big belly, as shown in Figure 10.19. Your full body morph is now complete.

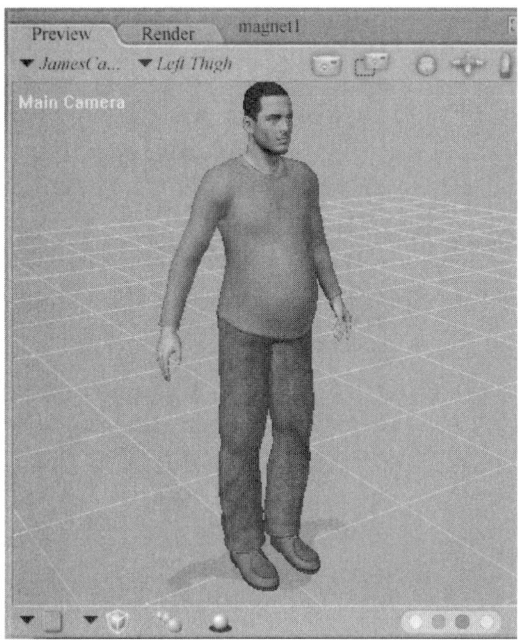

FIGURE 10.17 With all PBMBigBelly morphs dialed to 1, James Casual has a big belly.

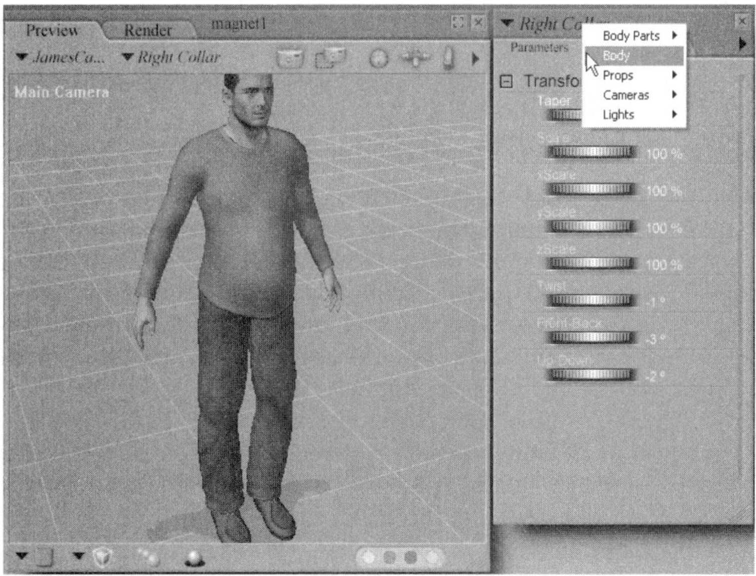

FIGURE 10.18 With James Casual selected, choose Body from the current actor menu.

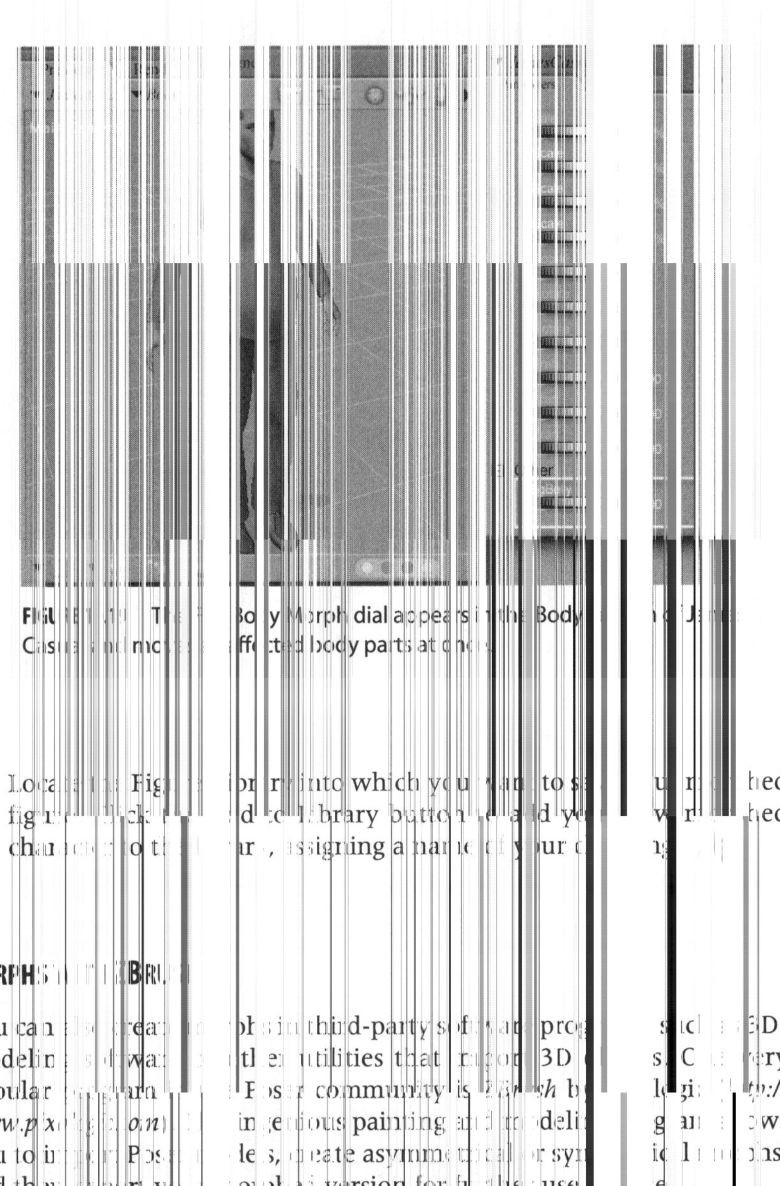

FIGURE 11.10 The [illegible] Body Morph dial appears in the Body [illegible] of James Casual and moves [illegible] affected body parts at once.

8. Locate the Fig[illegible] into which you [illegible] to s[illegible]hed figure. Click [illegible] Library button [illegible] y[illegible]hed character to the [illegible], assigning a name of your c[illegible]

C[illegible] BODY MORPHS [illegible] BRU[illegible]

You can also create [illegible] in third-party software prog[illegible] such as 3D-modeling software [illegible] utilities that [illegible] 3D [illegible]. [illegible] very popular program [illegible] Poser community is [illegible] by [illegible] (*http://www.pixologic.com*) [illegible] ingenious painting and modeling [illegible] allows you to import Poser models, create asymmetrical or sym[illegible] morphs, and then export your morphed version for further use [illegible].

The tutorial that follows is meant to give you the st[illegible] to get your object to and from Poser to ZBrush. For additional [illegible] relating to [illegible] with ZBrush, refer [illegible] the [illegible] Materials page on [illegible] Web site (*http://pixologic[illegible].html*), or [illegible] the [illegible] at ZBrush Central (*http://www.[illegible].com*).

TUTORIAL 10.7 IMPORTING INTO ZBRUSH

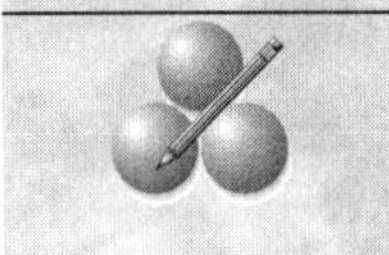

When you create morphs for Poser figures, it is always the safest option to start with the original OBJ file. This ensures that your morphs will reference the default positions of the vertices in the original object.

Most Poser content creators place the geometry files in the Runtime > Geometries subfolders. For example, you'll typically find geometry for DAZ3D Victoria 3, Michael 3, David 3, and Stephanie Petite in the Runtime > Geometries > DAZPeople folders. On the other hand, you'll find the geometry for the Poser 6 figures in the Runtime > Libraries > Character subfolders.

Once you determine the location of the original OBJ file, you can import the file into ZBrush and morph the figure as follows:

1. In ZBrush, choose Tool > Import, as shown in Figure 10.20.

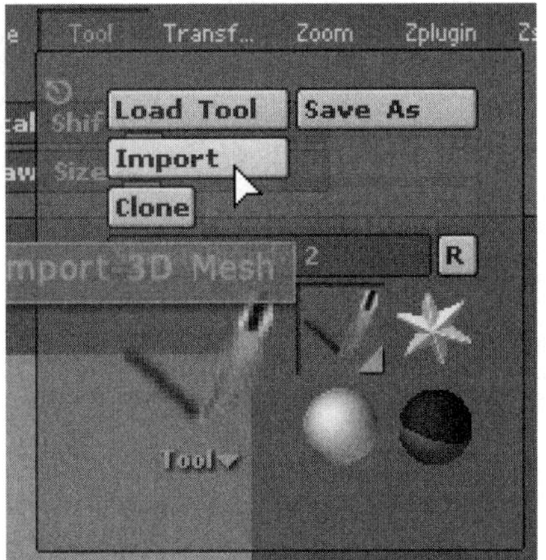

FIGURE 10.20 Use the Tool > Import command in ZBrush to import a Wavefront OBJ file.

2. Use the Import 3D Mesh dialog to navigate to the folder that contains the original OBJ file for the character you are going to morph. In this example, we decompressed the Jessi.OBZ file and saved it in the same folder as Jessi.OBJ. She is found in the Poser 6 > Runtime > Libraries > Character > Jessi folder in your Poser 6 installation. Highlight the OBJ file and click Open.

3. Starting from the center of the window, drag upward to size Jessi so that she fills the screen. She will initially appear backward as shown in Figure 10.21.

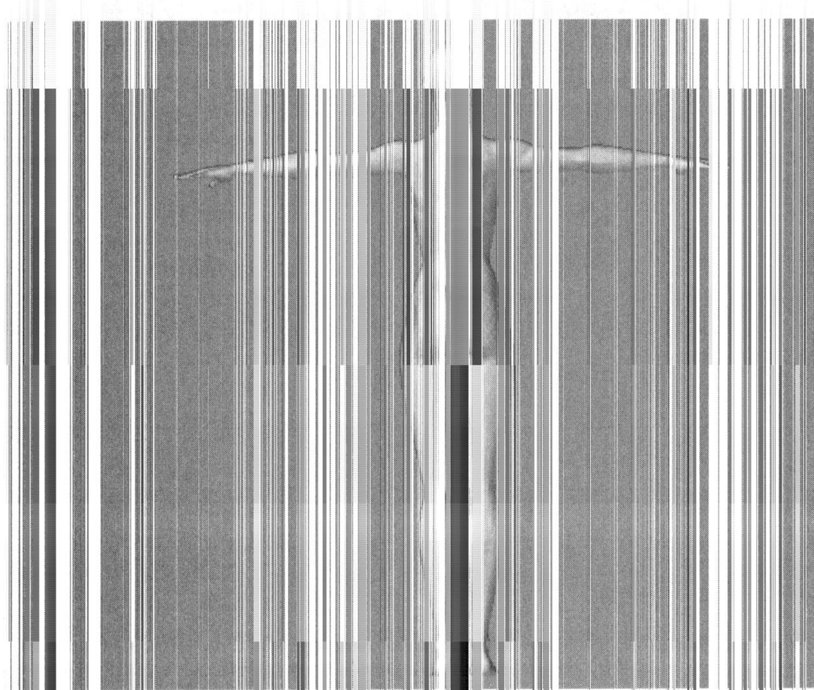

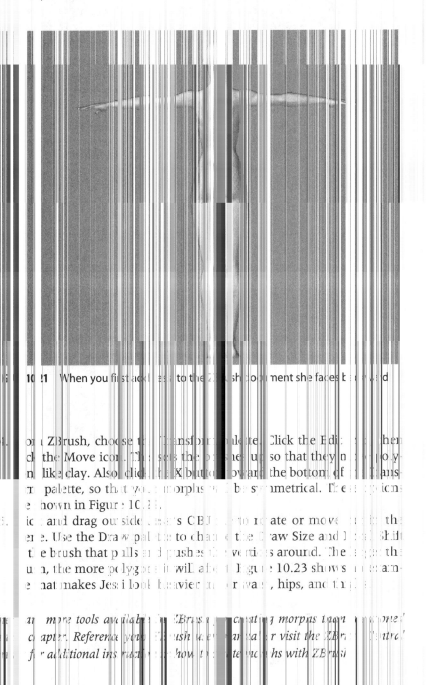

FIGURE 10.21 When you first add Jessi to the ZBrush document she faces backward.

4. In ZBrush, choose the Transform palette. Click the Edit button, then click the Move icon. This sets the brushes up so that they move polygons like clay. Also click the X button toward the bottom of the Transform palette, so that your morphs will be symmetrical. These options are shown in Figure 10.22.
5. Click and drag outside Jessi's OBJ file to rotate or move it in the scene. Use the Draw palette to change the Draw Size and Focal Shift of the brush that pulls and pushes the vertices around. The larger the brush, the more polygons it will affect. Figure 10.23 shows an example that makes Jessi look heavier in her waist, hips, and thighs.

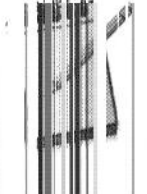

There are more tools available in ZBrush for creating morphs than mentioned in this chapter. Reference your ZBrush user manual or visit the ZBrush Central forum for additional instruction on how to create morphs with ZBrush.

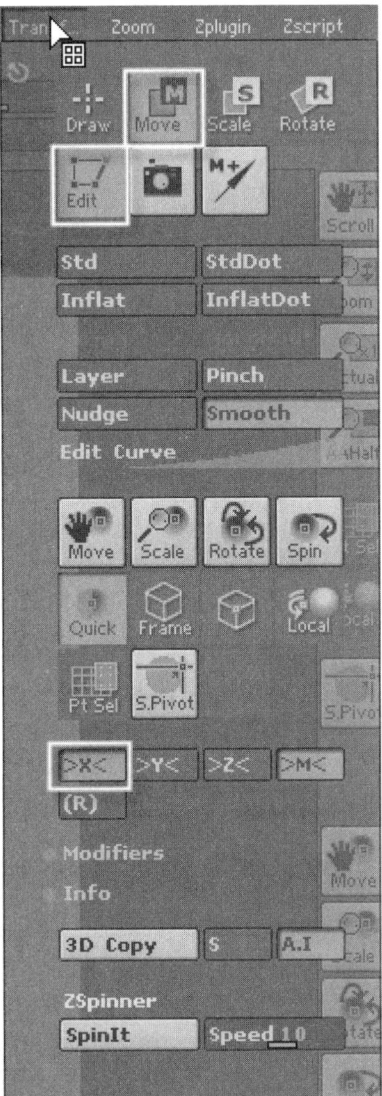

FIGURE 10.22 Choose Transform > Edit, and Transform > Move. Also, enable the X option to make your morphs symmetrical.

6. After you complete the morph to your liking, choose Tool > Export, as shown in Figure 10.24. Locate the morphed OBJ file in a folder that is separate from the original location. Name the morphed body something that will remind you what you changed, such as JessiBiggerTorso.OBJ.

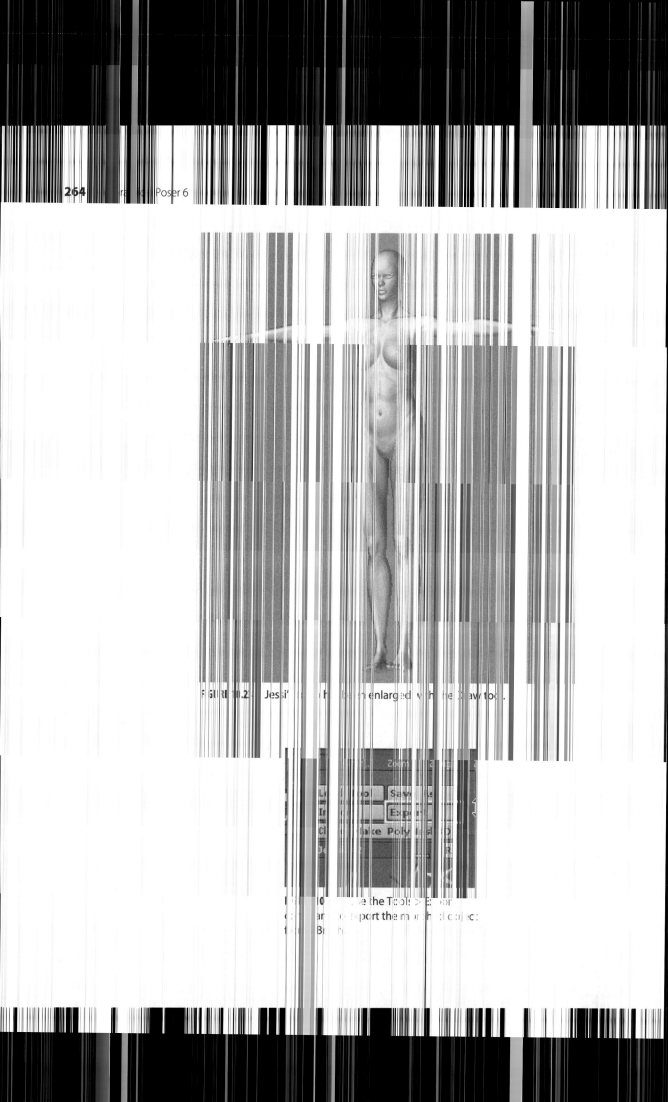

FIGURE 10.23 Jessi's [illegible] has been enlarged with the Draw tool.

FIGURE 10.24 Use the Tools > Export command to export the morphed object from ZBrush.

TUTORIAL 10.8 IMPORTING A MORPHED FIGURE INTO POSER

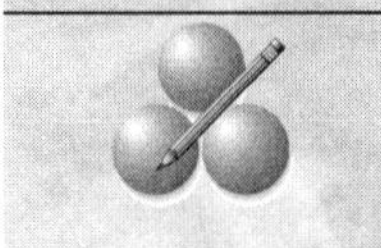

After you export your morphed OBJ file from ZBrush (or any other third-party morphing program), you have to reimport it into Poser so that you can split it apart into the various body groups.

To import the morphed figure into Poser, follow these steps:

1. Create a new scene in Poser and remove all objects from the scene.
2. Choose File > Import > Wavefront OBJ. The Import Wavefront OBJ dialog appears.
3. Navigate to the folder that contains your morphed object. Highlight the OBJ, and click Open to continue.
4. When the Prop Import Options dialog appears, uncheck all options. Click OK to continue. The morphed OBJ appears in the scene.

Before the morphed object file appears in the scene, Poser tells you it cannot locate a BMP bitmap file and asks if you want to look for it. ZBrush automatically saves a BMP file with the object file it exports. You won't need this BMP file for purposes of the morph, so you can choose not to open the file.

TUTORIAL 10.9 SPAWNING MULTIPLE MORPH TARGETS

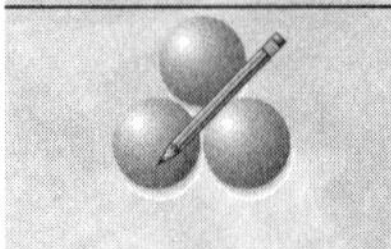

After you import the morphed object, you have to split the object apart into its individual body part groups. You use the Group Editor to do this. To create individual body parts from the imported model, follow these steps:

1. Click the Grouping Tool icon in the Editing Tools area. The icon is shown beneath the cursor in Figure 10.25.

FIGURE 10.25 Click the Grouping Tool icon to open the Group Editor.

2. If your morphed figure is not selected as the current object, choose it from the Current Actor menu in the document window. It will appear as a prop, as shown in Figure 10.26.

FIGURE 10.26 Select the morphed object file from the Props list in the document window.

3. Click the Spawn Props button located in the Geometry Functions section of the Group Editor window. After you spawn the props, you'll see one prop for each body part in the morphed object, as shown in Figure 10.27.

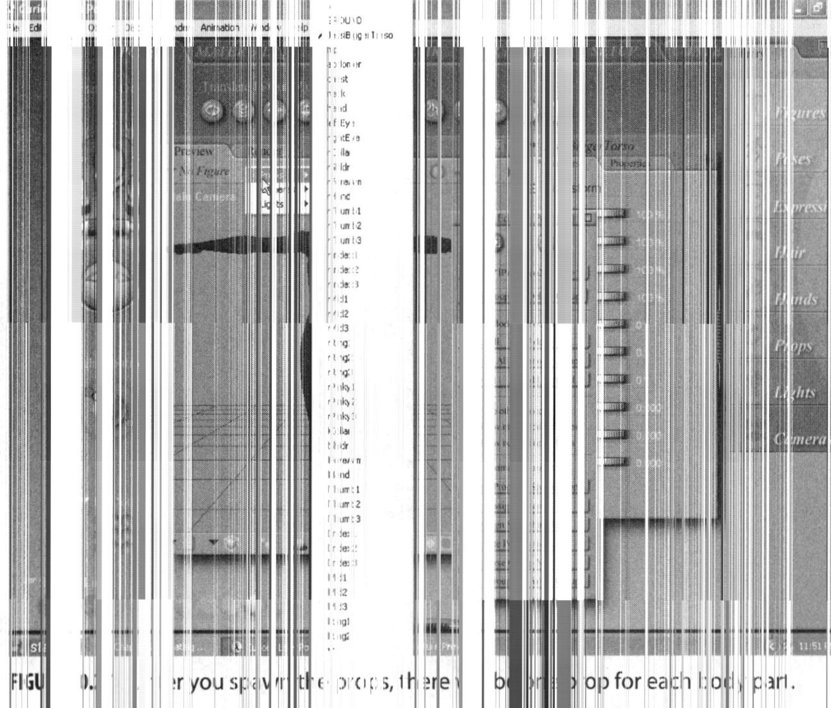

FIGURE 10.27 After you spawn the props, there will be one prop for each body part.

TUTORIAL 10.10 EXPORTING BODY PARTS

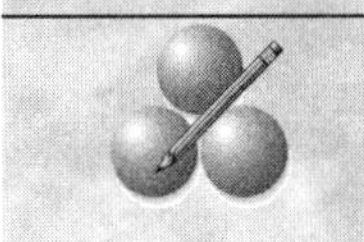

After you spawn all of the body parts, the next step is to export the parts that have changed, so that you can later import them back into Poser as morph targets. The morph that we created for Jessi affects her chest, abdomen, hip, left thigh, and right thigh. You don't have to export the parts that aren't affected by the morph you made in ZBrush.

To export each body part that has been morphed, follow these steps:

1. The whole object (that is, the version of the object before you broke it into pieces) still remains in the scene as a prop, and this may interfere with your ability to select the individual body parts. To delete the whole body prop, click the Current Actor menu to select it by name. In this example, the whole object is named "JessiBiggerTorso," as shown in Figure 10.28. Select the object and press the Delete key to delete it from the scene. Answer OK when Poser asks if you are sure you want to delete the object.

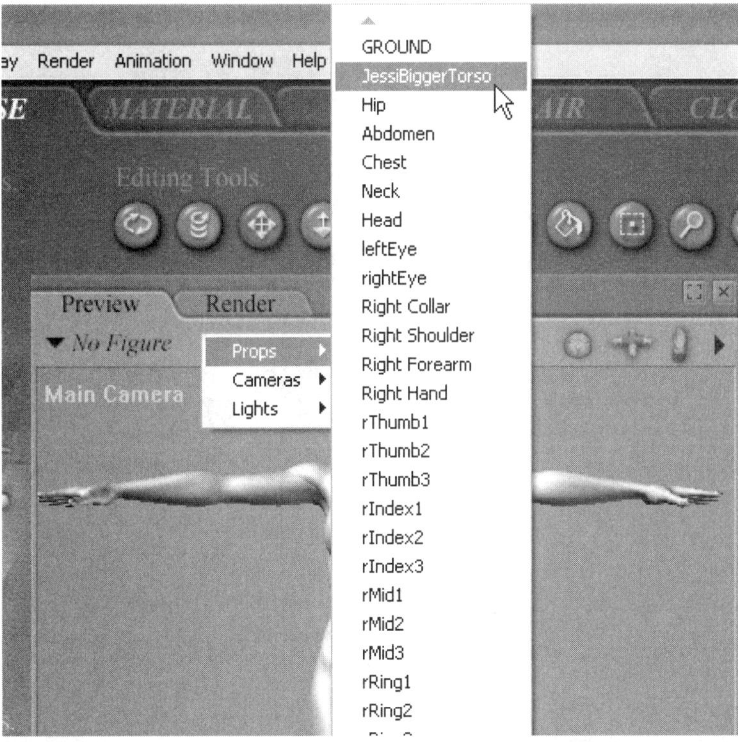

FIGURE 10.28 Delete the whole object from the scene so that it does not interfere with the selection of individual body parts.

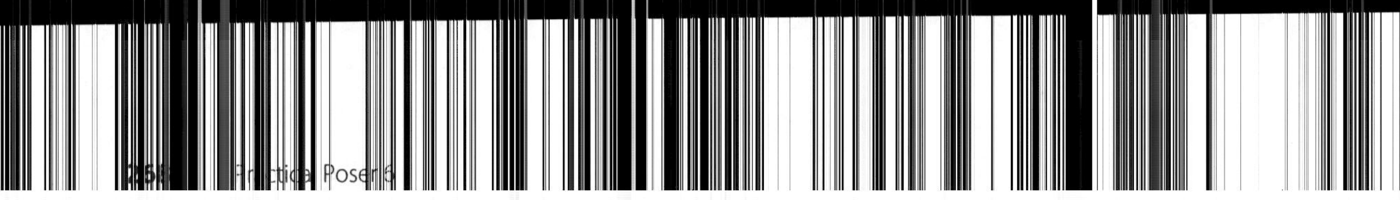

2. As mentioned earlier, you now want to export each body part that was affected by the morph you created in your third-party program. In this case, we have to export five parts, one at a time. To export the first object, choose File > Export > Wavefront OBJ. The Export Range dialog appears.
3. Since you only need to export one frame of the model (because it is not animated), leave the default selection of Single Frame. Press OK to continue.
4. The Hierarchy Selection window appears. Initially, all items are checked. To uncheck all of them, click the checkmark beside UNIVERSE. Then check the Chest part, as shown in Figure 10.29. Then click OK to continue.

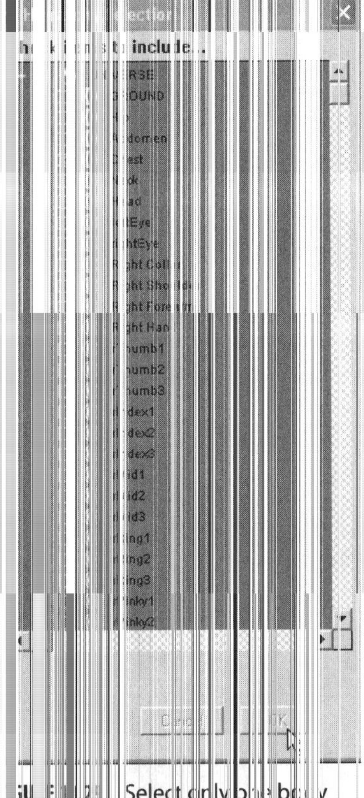

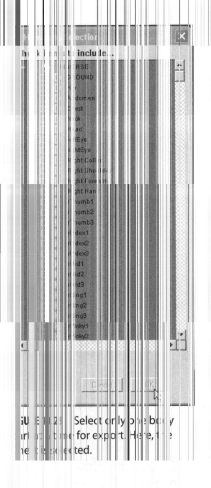

FIGURE 10.29 Select only one body part at a time for export. Here, the Chest is selected.

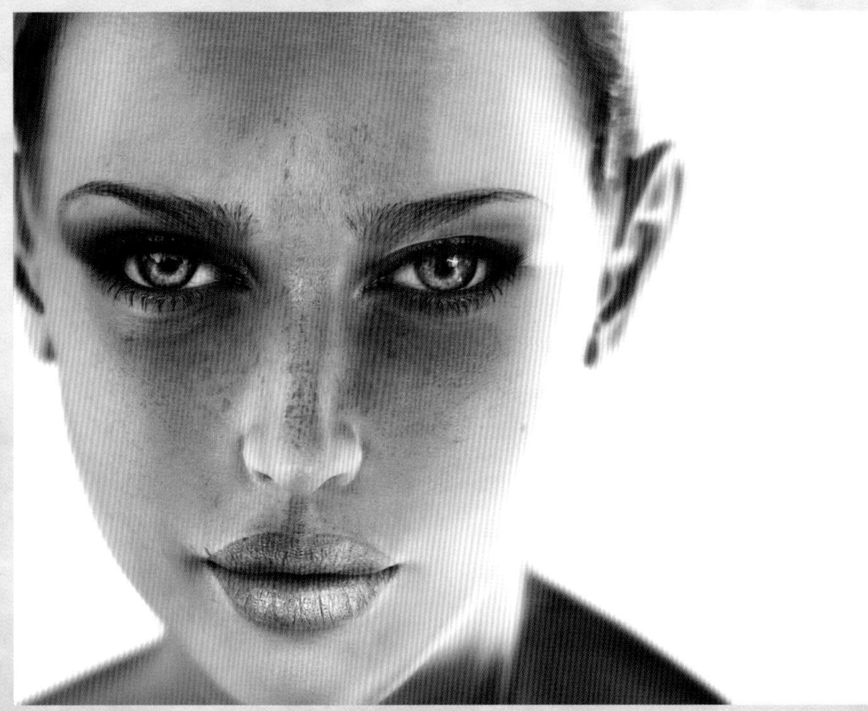

COLOR PATE 1 Blue Eyes. Courtesy of Mike J. Campau.

COLOR PATE 2 Snob. Courtesy of Scott Thigpen—*www.sthig.com*

COLOR PLATE 3 VIKING GIRL. Courtesy of Capstone Studios Inc., *www.Capstonestudios.com*. Artist John Taylor Dismukes, *www.dismukes.com*.

COLOR PLATE 4 Darkstar. Courtesy of Laura Haskell—*www.bluemoonnews.com*.

COLOR PATE 5 Geisha. Courtesy of Carina Dumais, Vlissingen, The Netherlands. Artist and Illustrator.

COLOR PATE 6 Get Out of My Cave. Image created by JAKC | PUBLITIA.

COLOR PLATE 7 Dance Club. Courtesy of Scott [illegible] *[illegible]ig.com.*

COLOR PLATE 8 [illegible]eshini. Courtesy of The Final Dream Charact[illegible] by M[illegible] *www.[illegible]heF[illegible] Dre[illegible].com.*

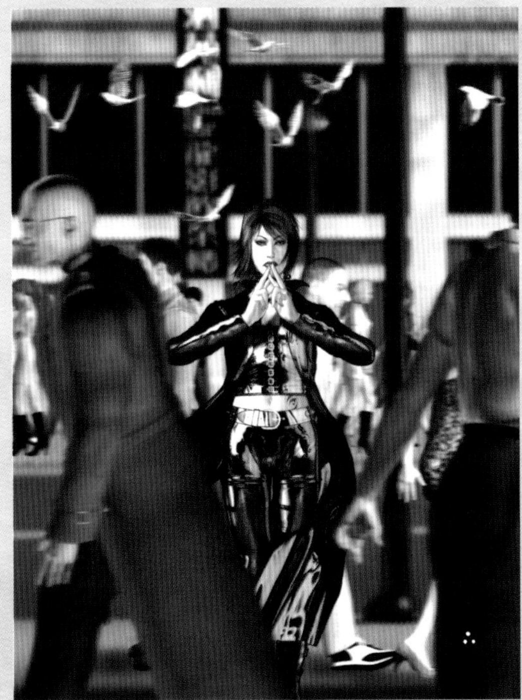

COLOR PATE 9 Meditation. Courtesy of Brian Jon Haberlin.

COLOR PATE 10 Tatoo Face. Courtesy of Carina Dumais, Vlissingen, The Netherlands. Artist and Illustrator.

COLOR PLATE 11 RocknRoll. Courtesy of Anne Marie Tobias, Transluminal Studios.

COLOR PLATE 12 Smiler. Courtesy of Brian Jon Haberlin.

COLOR PATE 13 The Blue Eyed Redhead. Courtesy of Adriana Vasilache.

COLOR PATE 14 The Man. Courtesy of Steve Harms.

COLOR PATE 15 TV Talk Show 10th Moon. Courtesy of Audre Vyshniauskas *www.audre.org*.

COLOR PATE 16 Umbrello. Courtesy of Philebus.

5. Use the Export as Wavefront OBJ dialog to locate the folder that will store the morph target geometry. Assign a name that starts with the morph name (JessiBiggerTorso), and follow it with the body part that you are exporting (Chest), as shown in Figure 10.30. Click Save to continue.

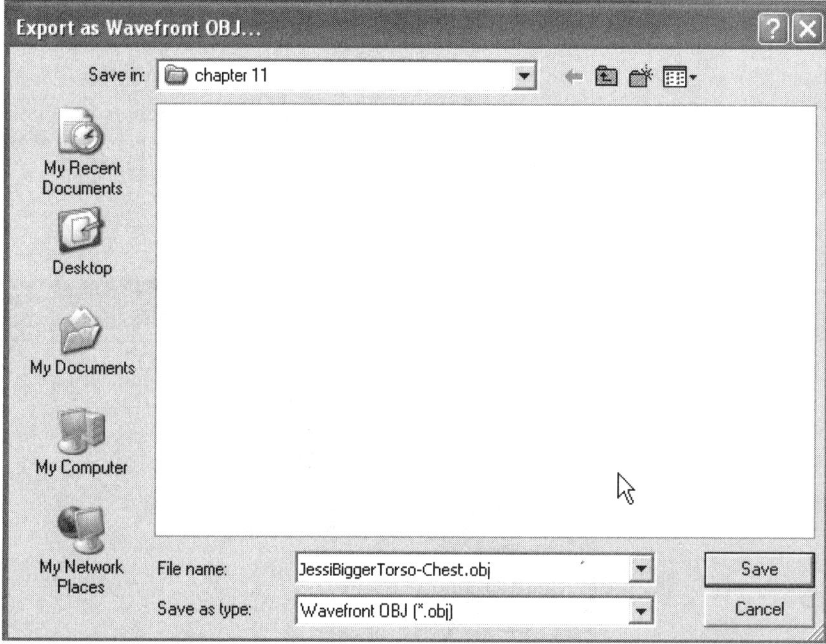

FIGURE 10.30 Name the morph target with the name of the morph, followed by the body part that you are exporting.

6. A list of options for exporting appears. The only item that should be checked is the last option "As Morph Target (No World Transformations)" as shown in Figure 10.31. This ensures that the morph will not move the body part from its default position when you use the morph. Click OK to export the first morph target.
7. After you export the Chest body part, click the Chest in the scene and press the Delete key. This serves as a reminder that you have already saved that part so that you don't save it twice.
8. Repeat Steps 2 through 7 for the remaining body parts that were affected by the morph you created. When you are finished, you should have a list of morphs that look similar to those shown in Figure 10.32.

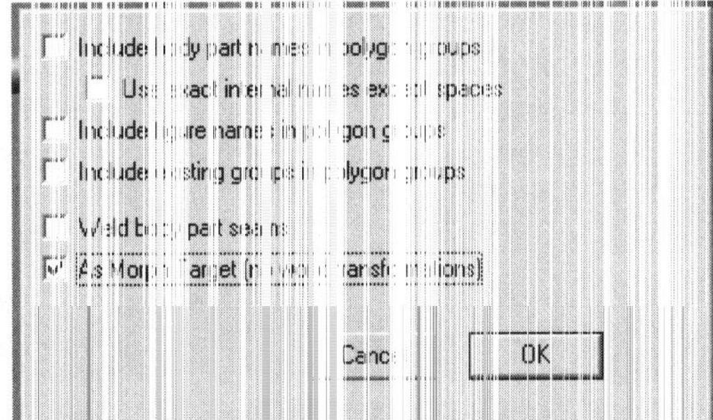

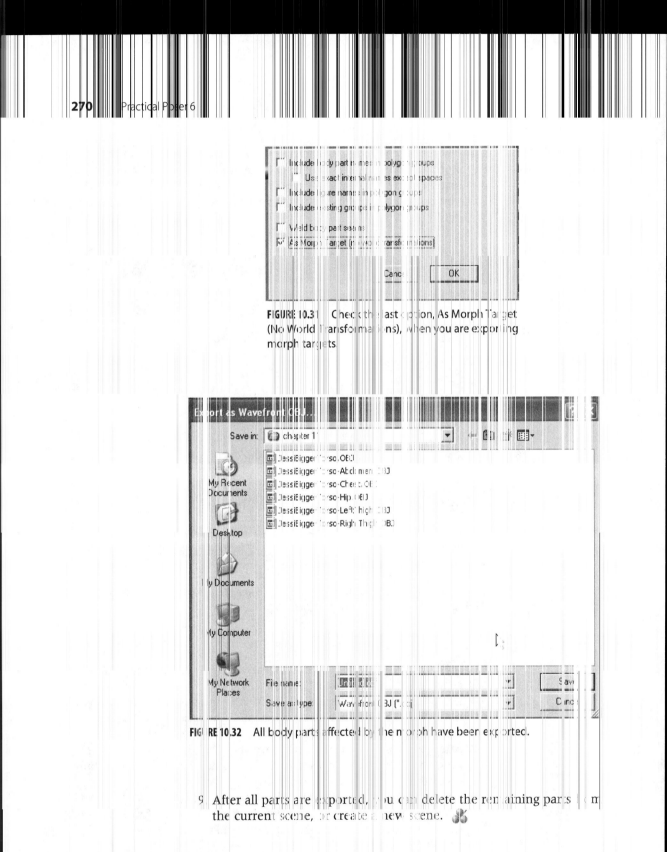

FIGURE 10.31 Check the last option, As Morph Target (No World Transformations), when you are exporting morph targets.

FIGURE 10.32 All body parts affected by the morph have been exported.

9. After all parts are exported, you can delete the remaining parts from the current scene, or create a new scene.

TUTORIAL 10.11 IMPORTING MORPHS TO YOUR FIGURE

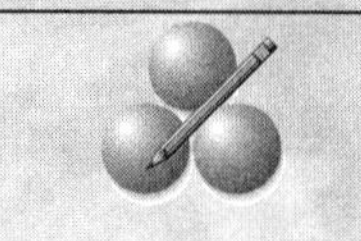

You're almost finished! The last step is to apply the morph targets to your figure. After you export each morphed body part, you use the Object > Load Morph Target command to import each of the morph targets to the appropriate body part.

When you import morph targets that have been created from other sources, you must remember two things. First, make sure you add the correct figure to your scene. For example, if you created the morphs for Jessi.OBJ, make sure that you add Jessi to your scene and not Jessi Hi-Res.

Secondly, make sure that you import the same body part that you currently have selected. For example, if you have selected the Chest as the body part to add the morph, make sure that you import the morphed Chest, and not the abdomen. If either of these steps is not taken, you will receive a message that says "Target Geometry has Wrong Number of Vertices." In order for morph targets to work, they must be applied to the geometry for which they were created. The geometry must have the exact same number of vertices, and they also must be listed in exactly the same order.

To import a morph target, follow these steps:

1. Load Jessi into an empty scene. Turn off Inverse Kinematics and zero her pose.
2. Click Jessi's chest to make it the current object.
3. Choose Object > Load Morph Target. The Load Morph Target dialog in Figure 10.33 appears.

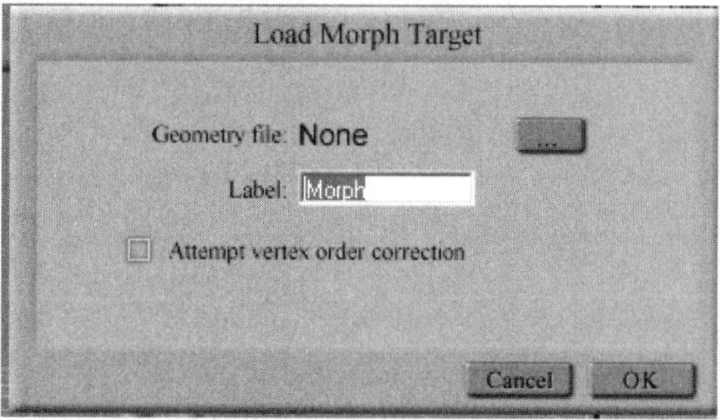

FIGURE 10.33 The Load Morph Target dialog adds morph targets that you have created in other applications.

4. Click the button at the right side of the Geometry File area to browse to the folder in which you stored your morph targets. Highlight the morph that you created for the chest (named JessiBiggerTorso-Chest in this example) and click Open. You return to the Load Morph Target dialog.

5. Add a name for the morph target. Because this is one of several body-part morphs that are used to create a single morph, name the morph "PBMBiggerTorso" as shown in Figure 10.34. Then click OK to continue.

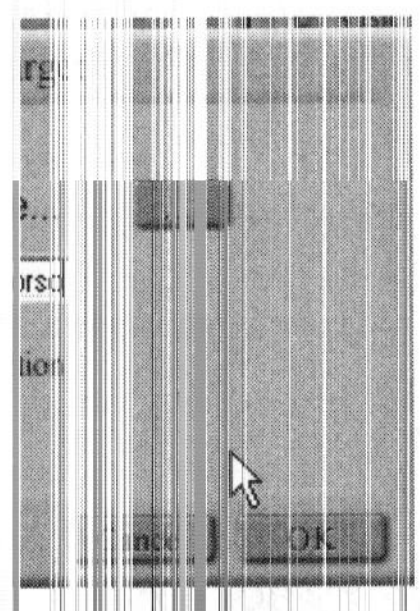

FIGURE 10.34 Assign a name to the new morph target.

6. Go to the Parameters window for the chest, where you will see your new morph in the Morph section of the dials. Set the dial to 1 to see if your morph dials in correctly.
7. Repeat Steps 3 through 5 for the remaining body parts (abdomen, hip, left thigh, and right thigh).
8. After you dial all of the morphs to 1, you can then create a full body morph as described in Tutorial 10.[illegible] Your morphed figure will look as shown in Figure 10.35.

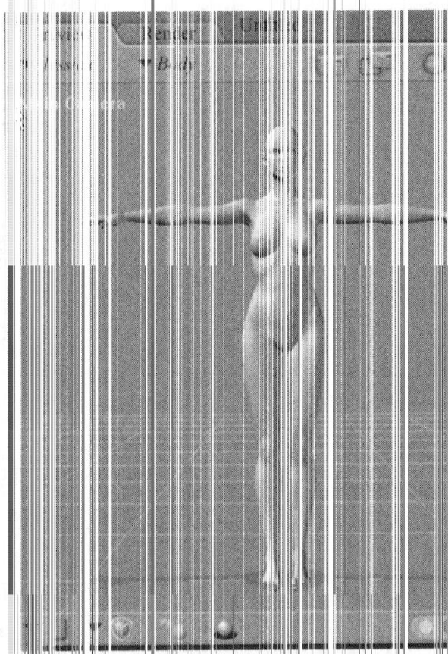
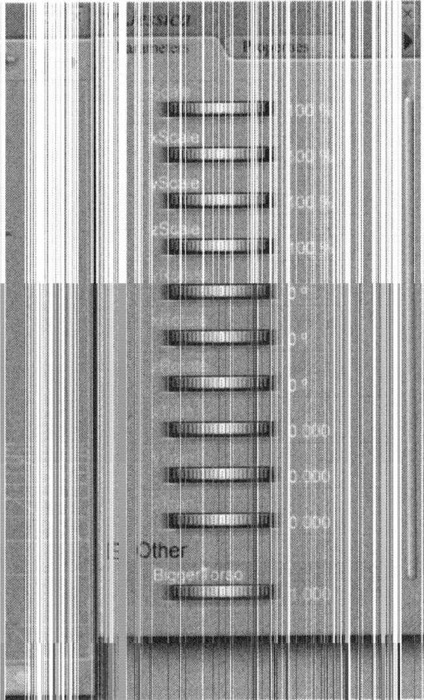

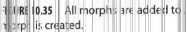

FIGURE 10.35 All morphs are added to Jessi's body and a new full body morph is created.

DISTRIBUTING MORPHS

There are a number of different ways that morphs can be distributed, and the method you use depends upon the user's license of the figure that you created the morphs for. Before you distribute any of your own custom morphs, be sure to verify which of the following methods is the correct way to distribute morphs for your figure:

- By default, Poser saves morph data for objects as external binary morph files. These files have a PMD extension, and are saved in the same library as the original character file. The only drawback to this option is that PMD files are compatible only with Poser 6. If you want to create morphs that are compatible with earlier versions of Poser you should disable this feature so that Poser saves the morph data within the CR2 file. To do so, choose Edit > General Preferences, and click the Misc tab. Uncheck the Use External Binary Morph Targets option as shown in Figure 10.36.

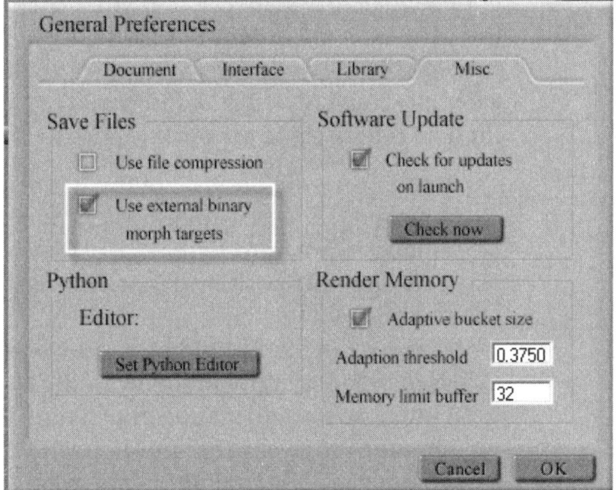

FIGURE 10.36 Uncheck the Use External Binary Morph Targets option to create morphs for earlier Poser versions.

- If you want to distribute morphs with your own original clothing, you can save the morph data within the CR2 library file. To do this, make sure you have the Use External Binary Morph Targets option unchecked, and also that you do not use file compression when saving your files to the library. Your morphs will be saved along with the clothing, in an editable CR2 file when saved in this manner.

- Many characters (most notably the DAZ3D Unimesh figures such as Victoria 3, Michael 3, David 3, and Stephanie Petite) are furnished with separate face and body morphs. The base character file has morph channels within it that are ready to accept "injected" morphs. The morph data is furnished separately, and library files are included in the Pose Library to inject or remove the morph data from the model. Utilities such as Injection Magic and Injection Pose Builder are available at DAZ3D to help you prepare injection morphs such as these. There are also some tutorials available at DAZ3D's Tutorial Arcana (*http://www.daz3d.com/support/tutorial/index.php?cat=6*) regarding creating injection morphs by hand or with the previously mentioned utilities.

AVOIDING PROBLEMS

There are a number of things that can go wrong when you create morphs. For example, the software that you use to create the morphs might place the vertices in a different order when you save the geometry. Or, you can accidentally move the geometry and when you apply it to your figure the geometry might fly off in a different direction than you intended. To avoid these problems, here are a few things to keep in mind:

- Don't move the position of the figure after you import the figure into your modeling program. For example, if the figure comes into your modeling program with its feet above or below ground level, don't translate the position. It will affect the ending position of your morphs.
- Many modeling programs cannot handle the extremely small scale used in Poser and you'll need utilities to scale the figures up for morphing, and then scaling the figure back down by the equivalent amount for importing into Poser. Because procedures vary from 3D program to 3D program, it's a good idea to touch base with others who use the same modeling software that you use. Chances are, they have figured out the best approaches for your software and can help you through the process.
- When using an external program for morphing, don't make any changes to the *construction* of the geometry. That is, don't weld vertices, don't add or remove vertices, don't subdivide any vertices. Doing so will make your morphs incompatible with the original figure.
- When you try to import a morph target into Poser, you might get a message that says "Target geometry has wrong number of vertices." Check first to make sure that you have selected the right body part to add the morph to. Then check to make sure that the morph target

you are importing was created for that body part. If the body parts are the same, that means you may have inadvertently added or removed vertices during the process of creating the morph. One way to verify this is to open the morphed version in UV Mapper Professional and compare the number of vertices in the original and in the morphed part.

- Sometimes the morph target appears to apply itself correctly. But when you dial the morph in, the body part looks all wrinkled and jumbled. This is because your morphing software reordered the vertices. If this happens, delete the morph from the Parameters window. Then when you reimport the morph as instructed in Tutorial 10.11, check the Attempt Vertex Order Correction option in the Load Morph Target dialog. This may resolve the problem. If it does not, UV Mapper Professional also has the capability to reorder vertices and you may be able to fix the morph that way.

CONCLUSION

Morphs help a character or clothing become more versatile. You can also use morphs to help fit clothing to a character more easily. Whether you decide to create morphs with Poser magnets, or with a third-party modeling program, you can add value to your own creations by providing a good selection of morphs that alter the appearance or function of your original creations. With the knowledge you've learned in this chapter, you'll be able to add versatility and functionality to your original Poser objects.

CHAPTER

11

CREATING YOUR OWN IMAGE-BASED TEXTURES

In This Chapter

- Maps in General
- File Types
- Copyrights
- Conclusion

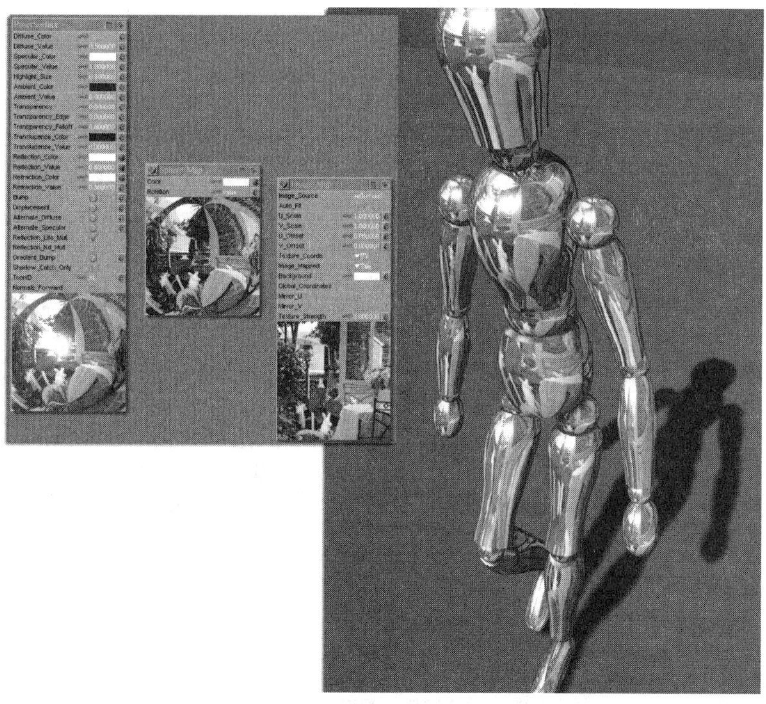

One of the most rewarding things about Poser is that it's really fun to make your own textures. Making your own textures expands the versatility of your Poser content, too. By applying different materials to your figures, you can set the scene for an alien invasion, or an 18th-century joust! In this chapter we'll discuss some of the fundamental concepts behind making textures. We'll explain what maps are, discuss some of the things to consider when creating photorealistic textures, and even show you a quick way to make your own seamless tiles.

MAPS IN GENERAL

If you've ever read anything about creating your own textures, you've probably heard the terms *texture map* and *image map*. At times, people use these terms interchangeably, and other times they mean different, if related, things. The confusion occurs because the terms texture map *and* image map are used when referring to *any* of the many types of maps used in 3D. For the sake of clarity, we've tried to stick to the most common uses of both terms and use the following to determine which "map" we are referring to:

- An *image map* is any image file that is mapped onto an object for the purpose of determining one of the properties of the object's material. It is the most generic reference.
- A *texture map* is one type of image map, used most often to determine an object's primary (diffuse) color.

So far, so good, right? Well, now it will get a little sticky. You see, the same image file that you use for the diffuse color of the object can also be used for any of the other material properties (such as bump, specularity, or displacement properties). The term "texture map" is commonly used for the *diffuse* channel of your material—that is, the channel that gives the image its primary color or colors. When a texture map is used for other purposes in addition to the diffuse channel, those purposes are secondary.

After a little practice you'll recognize the type of map by the context in which it's presented. In the end, regardless of what you call them, the ability to use maps of all types is the foundation of what makes Poser so powerful. They play an integral part of what goes into the creation of a material.

Texture Mapping

The most common use, and perhaps the primary application, of an image map in 3D is in *texture mapping*, where one or more images are mapped (or wrapped) onto the surface of an object, much like a coat of paint or a label on a can.

In the most obvious application, the texture map determines the color of the object's surface, but it can also be used to determine other attributes such as transparency, shine, and even the ambient color. When applied to multiple properties (channels) of an object's material shader, a texture map goes a long way toward giving the illusion of surface complexity. For example, a speedy way to enhance your material without any additional work is to drive the diffusion and displacement channels with the same texture map. This quickly and neatly defines the color of your object's surface, and also creates bumps in the object where the surface is lighter (whiter) and indentations where the texture is darker (blacker).

Texture mapping saves resources by creating complex-looking objects without having to build complex geometry. The effectiveness of texture mapping in 3D has led to a variety of ingenious applications for maps, and has even led to the creation of *non-image-based (procedural) maps*. Procedural maps are calculated at render time and use mathematical equations, (such as *fractals*) or maps that are created by tiling images repeatedly over the surface of the object. Once you understand the concept of using maps—either in the form of an image, some type of formula, or pattern that can be tiled—to encode the values of the properties of every point on the object's surface, you will be creating materials that take your work to a new level.

Image Map Templates

Related to maps are UVs, a term that refers to the coordinates that allow precise locations on the surface of a three-dimensional object to be referenced so that two-dimensional maps can be applied on the model with accuracy. More information about UVs and UV maps can be found in Chapter 13, "UV Mapping."

Once you generate the UV coordinates for your object, making them as even and distortion-free as possible, you can create an *image map template*. This template, which shows your three-dimensional object as a *flattened grid* or wireframe, serves as a guide that helps you create your image-based texture map. Image map templates show the boundaries of each material group as defined on your object, and also show where each polygon of your object is so you can create your image texture accordingly.

Figure 11.1 shows an example of a texture template generated from the UV coordinates of an object. Beside the template is the corresponding image texture map. Notice that the facial features on the painted texture are created in the same locations as those on the template.

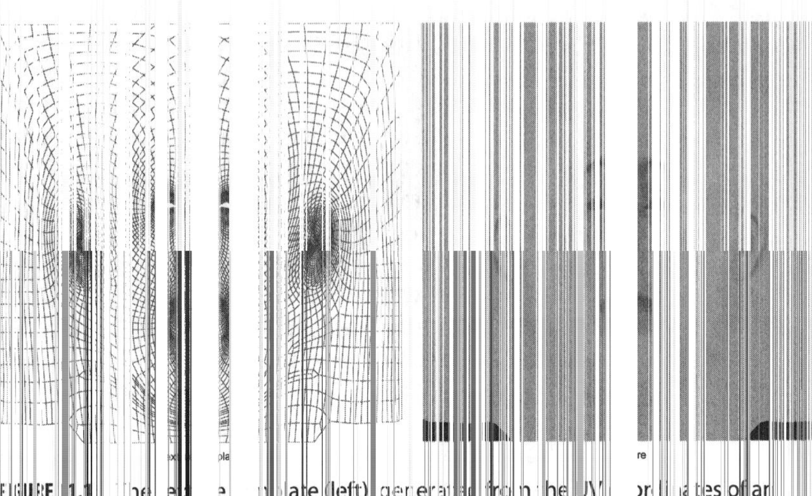

FIGURE 11.1 The texture template (left), generated from the UV coordinates of an object, serves as a guide to create an image texture map (right).

Texture Maps

Texture maps typically define the color of an object (*diffuse property*) at every point on its surface. For example, you can create a wood-grained texture map for a door or use photographs of a person to create a texture map for a human-like Poser character, as referenced earlier in Figure 11.1. In both cases, the texture map defines the primary color of your object at every point on its surface.

Bump Maps

Bump maps add the *illusion* of three-dimensional details to an otherwise smooth mesh surface. During rendering, lights and shadows that correspond with the varying brightness of the bump map create the impression of an irregular surface.

The bump calculations use only the brightness values of an image. As a result, bump maps are *usually* grayscale images. Light (white) values create areas that appear more bumped out from the original surface of the mesh, and dark (black) areas appear more indented or recessed from the surface. This effect is most apparent where the surface of the object is perpendicular to the camera and falls off as you get to the edges of the object. For this reason, bump maps are great for objects that are farther away or for objects whose edges are not prominent or are hidden behind other objects. Bump maps are not an appropriate solution when the edges of objects are visible, because they only affect surface areas that face the camera and the edges of your object remain smooth with respect to the camera, even if you apply a very rough bump map. See Figure 11.2 for an example of an object with and without a bump map applied to its bump channel. The sphere on the left uses a procedural texture tied into its diffuse channel, with no bump map. The sphere on the right uses the same procedural texture in the diffuse *and* bump channels of the root material node. Notice that the edges of the sphere remain smooth in both cases even though the center area of the right-most sphere appears to have irregularities in its surface.

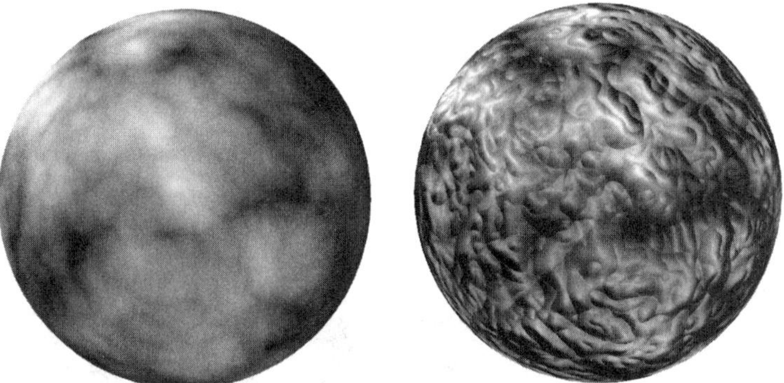

FIGURE 11.2 An object without a bump map (left), and with a bump map (right).

The technical explanation for how bump maps work to create the illusion of "bumpiness" is that they act on an object's normals only, and not on the actual object geometry. In Chapter 3 of the Poser 6 Tutorial Manual, "More 3D Elements," you'll find a very good explanation and diagram illustrating what normals are.

Displacement Map

Displacement maps are similar to bump maps in that they are used to add irregularities to the surface of your object. The amount of displacement varies based on the brightness values of the map. Color components of the map are ignored. Light (white) values result in more displacement while dark (black) values result in less displacement, with absolute black resulting in no displacement from the original mesh geometry at all. Unlike bump maps, displacement maps affect the edges of your object with respect to the perspective of your camera, making them appear rough and uneven at render time. Because displacement maps work without [illegible] ly [illegible] ging th[illegible] un[illegible]rlying mesh, the[illegible] an[illegible] to cre- [illegible] jo[illegible] look [illegible] ry [illegible]mplicated, even [illegible]ugh th[illegible] metry is [illegible] 1[illegible] u[illegible]ates how bump [illegible] displace[illegible] s affect [illegible] The left-most sphere uses a pr[illegible] texture [illegible] Turb[illegible] n[illegible] mapped into [illegible] middle [illegible] s the sa[illegible] e [illegible]ocedural texture [illegible]pped in[illegible] and [illegible] ames. [illegible] ght-most sphere [illegible] the [illegible] pr[illegible] re[illegible] mapped to the [illegible] displace- [illegible] Noti[illegible] th[illegible] only the sphere on the right [illegible] e poly- [illegible] is[illegible] ment a[illegible] its edges. You [illegible] use the [illegible] [illegible] placeme[illegible] e[illegible]bled in order to [illegible] polygon [illegible] der tim[illegible]

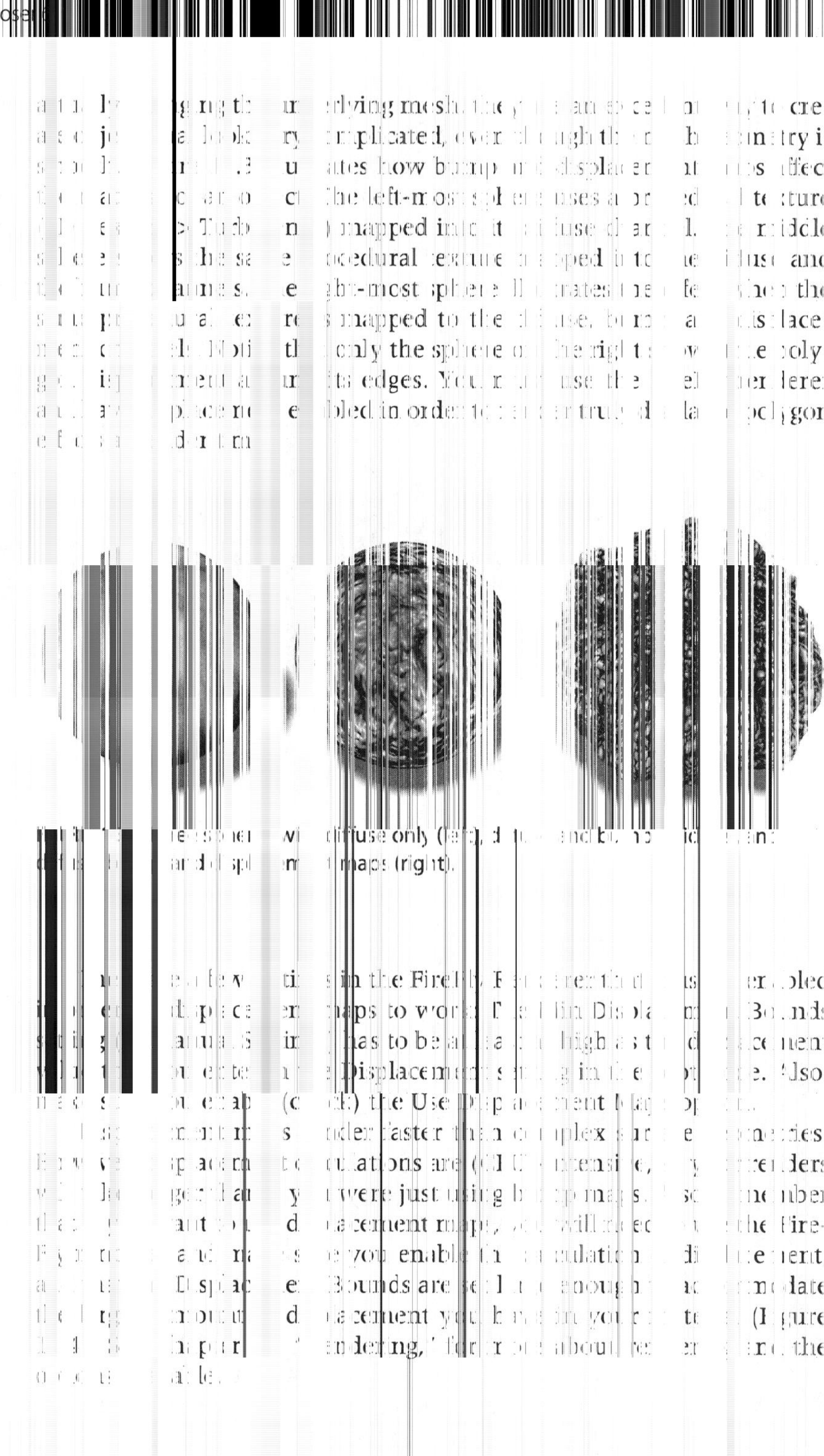

[illegible] re[illegible] sphere[illegible] wi[illegible] diffuse only (left), d[illegible] and bu[illegible] and [illegible] and displ[illegible] m[illegible] maps (right).

[illegible] e a few [illegible] ti[illegible] in the FireFly [illegible] enabled [illegible] displace[illegible] maps to work. [illegible] Bounds setting [illegible] manual. S[illegible] has to be a[illegible] high as [illegible] placement [illegible] Displacement s[illegible] in the [illegible]. Also, [illegible] enab[illegible] (c[illegible]) the Use Displacement Ma[illegible].

[illegible] ment m[illegible] s [illegible]nder faster than complex [illegible] metries. [illegible] displacement [illegible]lations are (CPU-)intensive, [illegible] renders [illegible] longer than [illegible] y[illegible] were just using b[illegible] maps. [illegible] member that [illegible] ant to [illegible] d[illegible]acement maps, [illegible] the Fire- Fly [illegible] ma[illegible] you enable th[illegible] ment, [illegible] Displac[illegible] Bounds are set [illegible] enough [illegible] modate the l[illegible] d[illegible]acement you [illegible] in your [illegible] (Figure [illegible] hapter [illegible]ndering," for [illegible] about [illegible] the [illegible] able.

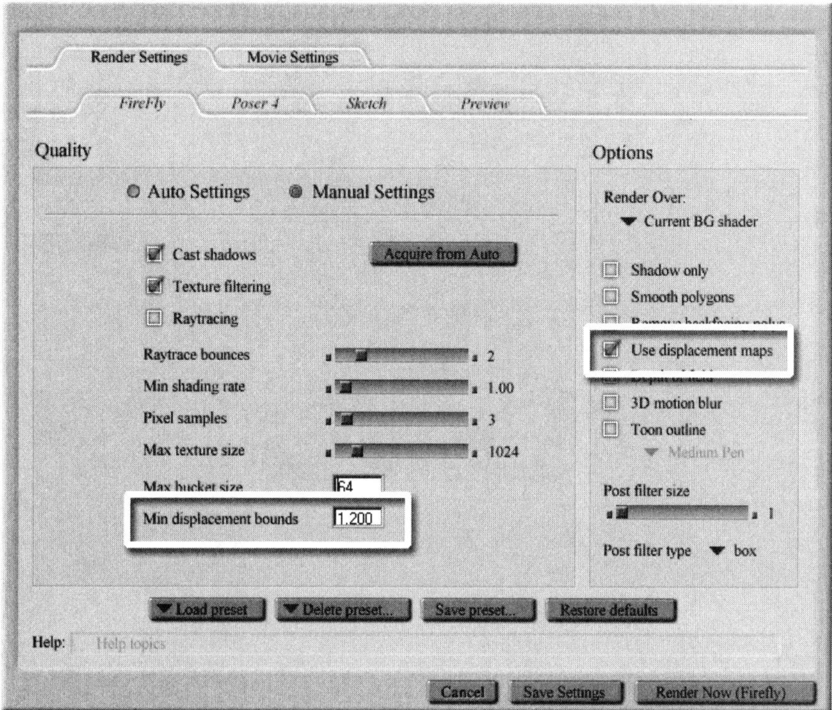

FIGURE 11.4 If you use displacement maps, make sure you use the FireFly renderer and configure displacement map settings properly.

Reflection Map

Reflection Maps are used to simulate the effects of a reflective surface. To accomplish this, reflection map image data is applied to a virtual sphere that surrounds your entire scene, which in turn reflects onto the surface of the object. Reflection maps interact with an object's other material properties; for example, in areas where the object material is darker, the resulting reflection will also be darker. Reflection maps are excellent for applications where true reflections of other objects are not required. They consume less of your resources and create believable reflections in appropriate situations, such as when you don't need accurate reflections of the object's surroundings. Figure 11.5 shows how a simple photograph can be used as a reflection map that gives the impression of a reflective surface. In this case, a photograph is tied into the reflection channels through a Sphere_Map node (select New Node > Lighting > Environment Map > Sphere_Map). The photograph makes the surface of the mannequin appear chrome-like.

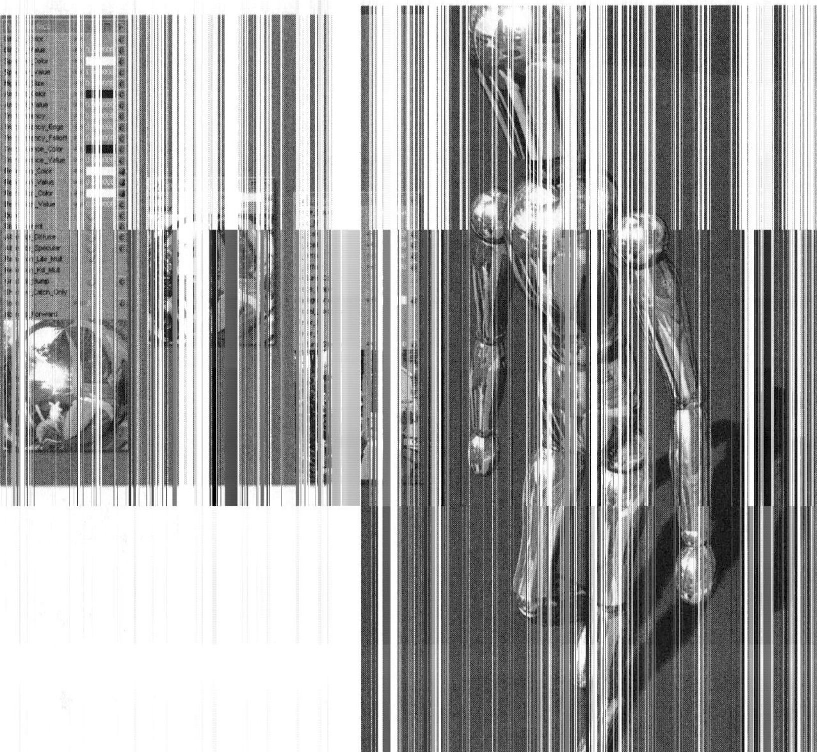

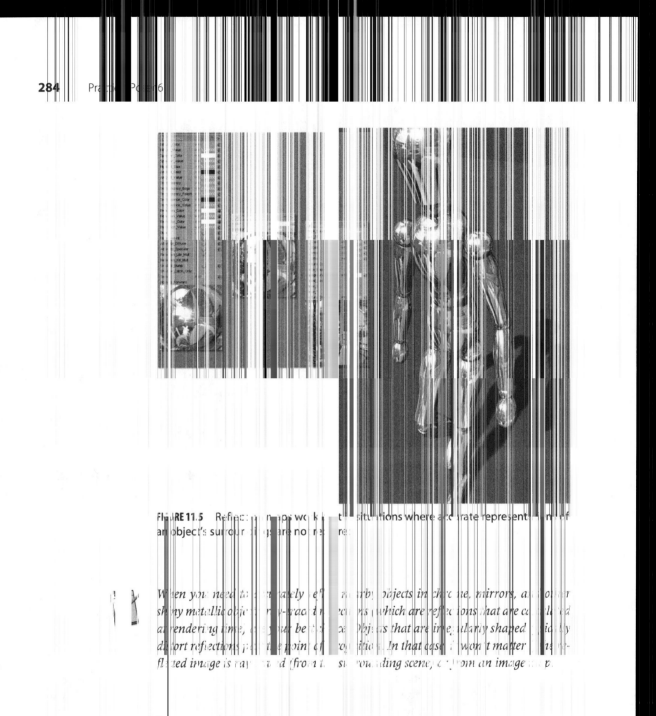

FIGURE 11.5 Reflection maps work best in situations where accurate representations of an object's surroundings are not required.

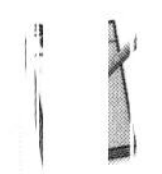

When you need to accurately reflect nearby objects in chrome, mirrors, and other shiny metallic objects, ray-traced reflections (which are reflections that are calculated at rendering time) are your best choice. Objects that are irregularly shaped typically distort reflections past the point of recognition. In that case, it won't matter if the reflected image is ray-traced (from the surrounding scene) or from an image map.

Transparency Maps

Transparency is a measure of how much light passes through an object. Transparency maps determine which portions of an object's surface are transparent and which are opaque. Because transparency maps only use the brightness values of an image and ignore the color data, they are usually grayscale images. Darker (black) values are rendered with more transparency, with absolute black representing full transparency and absolute white representing full opacity. Higher transparency effects allow more light to travel through the object; as a result, the area behind the object can be seen through the object more clearly.

The amount of transparency at each point is directly proportional to the value of the transparency map at that point. You typically use transparency maps in cases where you want holes to appear in your geometry but don't want to edit the underlying mesh, or when you want to soften and feather the ends of mesh-based hair that is normally blunt.

The root node in the Material Room includes two other settings that relate to transparency maps: Transparency Falloff and Transparency Edge. To configure the transparency properties of your material, make sure you confirm that the Falloff and Edge settings are correct for the effect you are trying to achieve. If you want something to be completely invisible, make sure that do not have any specularity (or shininess) on the portion that is transparent. The specular highlights will show the contour of the object that is transparent. See Chapter 9, "Assigning and Creating Materials," for more information on editing the transparency properties of your materials.

Figure 11.6 shows the Poser 6 mannequin with a simple transparency map applied in portions of the head and torso. Notice how the background shows through those areas as if there was no geometry in those locations.

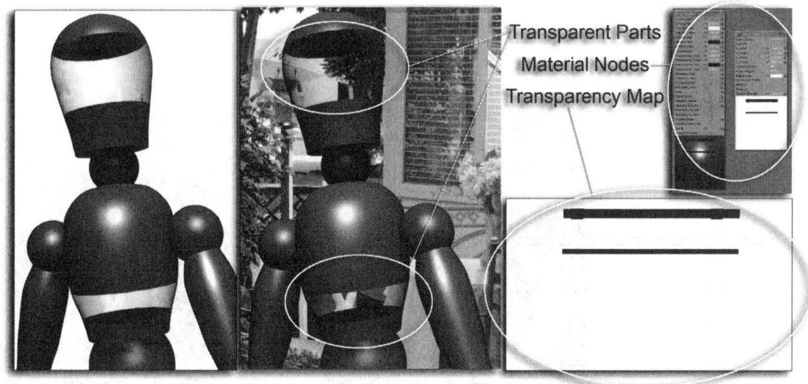

FIGURE 11.6 Poser 6 mannequin with a simple transparency map applied.

Creating Your Own Maps

You can use your favorite image editing program to make your own texture, bump, displacement, specular, or transparency maps. Image maps can also be used as inputs for procedural shaders to add diffuse, bump, transparency, displacement, or specular properties. We like to use Photoshop to work with image files. However, any good image-editing program should allow you to accomplish the things we discuss in this chapter.

Texture maps are created in one of two ways. Some maps cover an entire object, such as those for the human face or body. In those cases, the map must align exactly with certain features on the mesh. Other maps are tiled repeatedly to cover the surface of an object, like those that are used on buildings to create a brick-like surface. These types of image maps are typically *seamless*; that is, they are created in such a manner that when you line them up side to side they match up at the left and right seams, and when you line them up top to bottom they match up at those seams.

You can create seamless textures with a 2D image editor, although it takes a bit of work to get the seams to line up exactly. If you *really* get into the process of creating textures for your 3D objects or want to find an easier way to create flawless textures whose seams line up perfectly, you might consider investing in a program like Deep Paint 3D (shown in Figure 11.7) or Body Paint 3D. These are both extremely powerful (and pricey) software packages that enable you to interactively paint materials right onto your objects in 3D. They allow you to paint color, detail, specularity, and other parameters in real time. If you go this route, be prepared to spend some time with the software to harness the full potential of editing textures in 3D. Specialized software such as 3D material-creation software often requires a serious financial investment; however, for the truly serious texture artist, these tools are something to seriously consider.

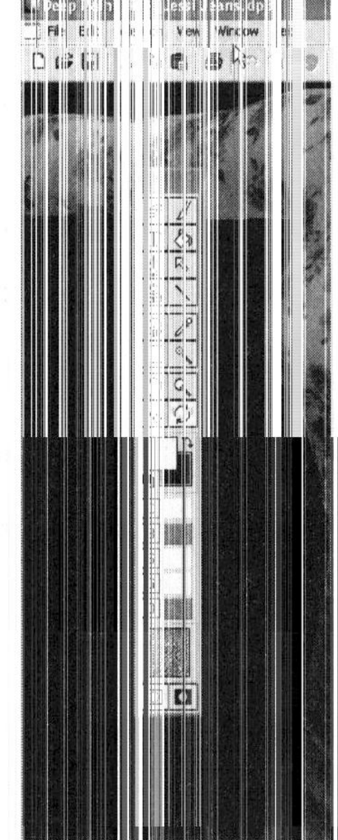
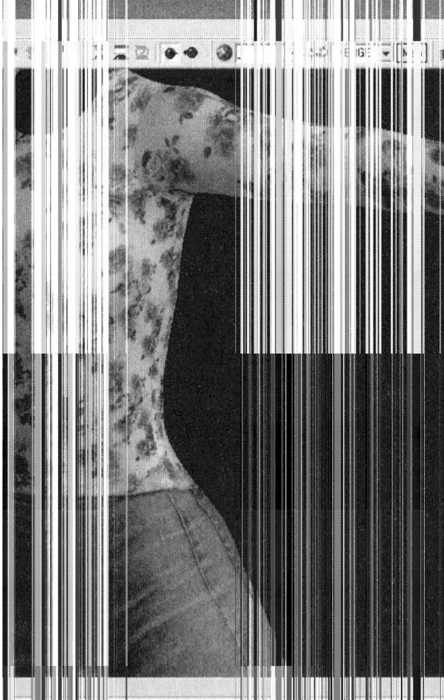
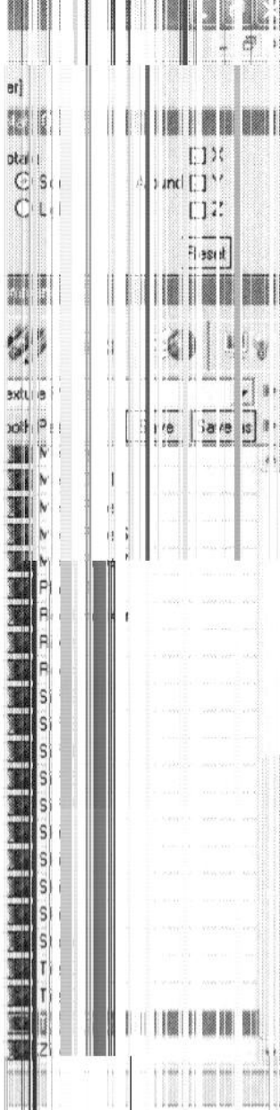

FIGURE 11.7 If you're serious about texturing, invest in a program that allows you to paint directly on your model. Deep Paint 3D is one such program.

In most cases when you create a texture for your figures, you use a texture template as a guide while you create your texture. If you can't locate the texture template for your mesh, you can always generate your own. See Chapter 13, "UV Mapping," for more information on how to make your own texture template based on the UV map of your object. For these examples, we used the free version of UV Mapper Classic to generate a texture template for the head material group of Ben, the Poser 6 young boy character. Reference Figure 11.8 to see Ben's head material texture template.

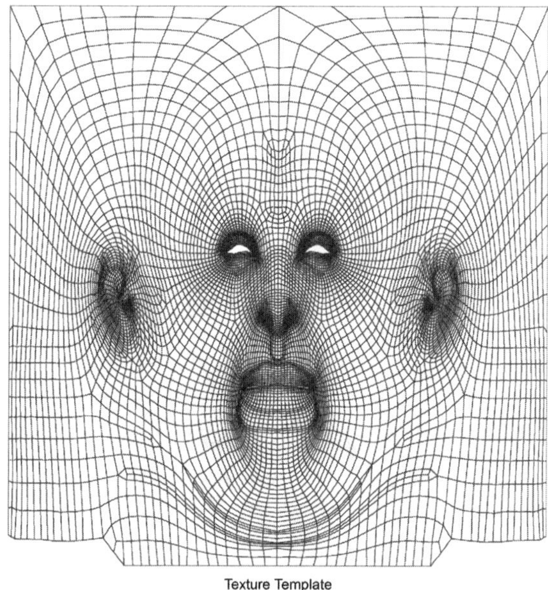

FIGURE 11.8 UV texture template for the head material group of Ben, the Poser 6 boy.

If you plan on making your image map by hand, it helps to have a high-resolution version of your texture template, ideally the same dimensions as the texture you plan on making. For example, if you want to create a texture that is 3000 pixels by 2000 pixels, you start with a texture template that is 3000 by 2000 pixels. This ensures that the lines and details in the template remain smooth and clean and you have an accurate account of polygon placement. Once you have your texture template file you can identify key areas that you need to pay special attention to. The Poser 6 family figures use a separate head and body image map, so you'll need to make templates for both the head and body material groups.

It's easier to visualize the location of the seams on your object if you color the edge polygons of your texture template with bright colors and then use the colored texture templates as material maps on your figure. The colored portions show you where the material group seams are, and the grid shows the polygons in various areas. This will also give you an idea of where distortions are likely to occur in your textures.

Figure 11.9 shows the UV texture template for a model [illegible]. The template is colored to identify the material seams and used on the figure to see where those seams appear at render time. Typically, when you use the texture template as the texture map for your object, you will see where each of the polygons is. Ben is rendered using the head material group's UV texture template at right to show the areas of the texture map that will need special care to ensure that the seams line up.

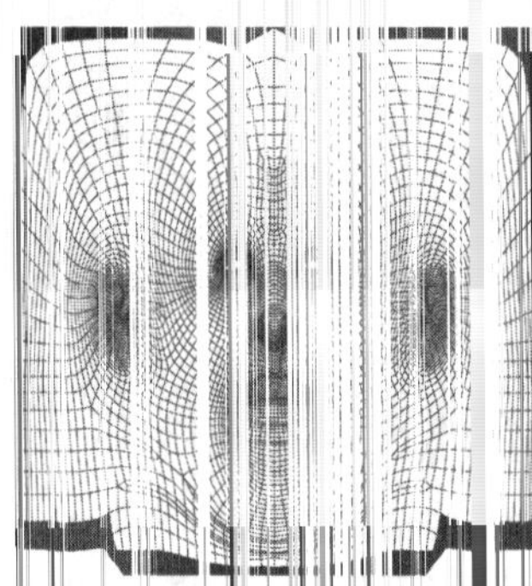

FIGURE 11.9 Ben's head material UV texture template colored to identify the material seams (left).

With Poser 6, you can also see the polygon arrangement of your mesh by viewing your scene in Smooth Shaded Lined display mode (Display > Document Style > Smooth Shaded Lined). You can change the width of your display lines in the Render options dialog in the Preview tab. See Figure 11.10 for an example of Ben viewed in Smooth Lined display mode with a Wireframe edge setting of 2.0. In this example, with an edge setting of 2.0, you get a great reference for where the various polygons in this mesh are.

Once you have a good template, what you do next will depend on whether you want to paint your texture using your favorite graphics editing program, or try to make a photorealistic texture from photographs of real people.

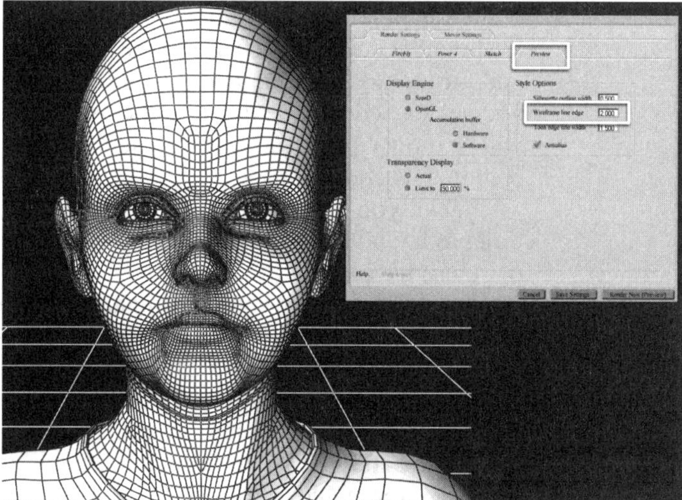

FIGURE 11.10 Ben viewed in Smooth Lined display mode with a Wirefame Line.

Image-Based or Photorealistic Textures

Photorealistic textures take a lot of work and practice, especially at the seams. These types of textures will test your abilities with both your graphics and your 3D software. However, photorealistic textures can be very rewarding and give you some fabulous results in your projects.

The best way to start is to have a willing subject who will let you get up close to capture the imperfections of real skin, hair follicles, and details of the various surfaces on the body. Lighting is important when you are obtaining the raw photos for your image-based textures. The best lighting is bright, but indirect, with no visible shadows. Shooting your photos outside is great for indirect lighting conditions especially if you can do so during an overcast day without cloud cover that is too thick. You should also plan on using reflectors to distribute the available light evenly on the surface of your model, to insure that areas on downward-sloping surfaces are lit the same as those above. An easy way to make a reflector is with metallic wrapping paper or aluminum foil wrapped around a piece of cardboard.

If you must shoot in artificial lighting, try using a sheer white fabric as a diffuser on your light to prevent blown-out highlights and prominent shadows. Also, if you need artificial lighting, the type of light you use will change the overall color tone of your images: camera flashes are considered white; sodium lights are yellow-orange; fluorescent are green-blue; quartz are bright yellow; halogen are yellow; photo floods are bright white-yellow; and incandescent are orange. It's easier to color-correct your texture after you get it assembled. Trying to color-correct before you create your texture will be more cumbersome, since you'd have to apply exactly the same correction to each raw image.

When you create human skin textures, it helps to use reference material as a guide. Place a mirror next to your computer, or obtain a series of reference photos that have been taken with good lighting and soft shadows. This allows you to compare the references to the texture that you are creating.

You can also find suitable reference images through online resources. If you want to use photos that you have downloaded from the Internet, make sure to ask permission from the original creator so that you do not violate any copyrights. You can avoid copyright infringement nightmares if you use reputable resources. Remember—unless it is *explicitly stated* that material is copyright free, royalty free, or in the public domain, you will not be able to use downloaded content in your project unless you obtain legitimate permission from the copyright holder. *When there is any doubt, check it out before you use it!*

Figure 11.11 shows an example of front and side head photos that were obtained from *http://www.3d.sk*, perhaps the most popular reference photo site available online for texture artists.

FIGURE 11.11 An example of front and side head photos obtained from *www.3d.sk*.
© Peter Levius, *www.3d.sk*. Reprinted with permission.

We highly recommend Peter Levius' figure reference Web site. This very reasonably-priced subscription site offers thousands of reference photographs that have been taken with the 3D artist in mind. Available from this site are complete sets of human, animal, and clothing photographs taken from several different angles so that you can create accurate texture maps for your projects. Navigate to http://www.3d.sk, where you can download some preview images before subscribing. A sister site, www.environment-textures.com, provides photographs of construction materials, doors, metals, and more. All photographs are royalty free, and can be used in personal or commercial texture projects.

Before you start placing your raw photos into your texture template, you may want to select a neutral skin color (or a prominent color from your photos) and use it to fill your base texture as a starting point. You can usually obtain a consistent skin tone from an area of a photograph of a person's back or stomach. Use a sample (as large and evenly toned as you can obtain) as a base to create a seamless tile, and then fill the template area with the skin tone. If you start with a base color that is similar to the overall color of your skin photos, your eye won't be shocked by large variations of color when you place your reference photos and it will be easier to envision your desired result without distraction. Place this skin layer in a layer directly above the template as shown in Figure 11.12.

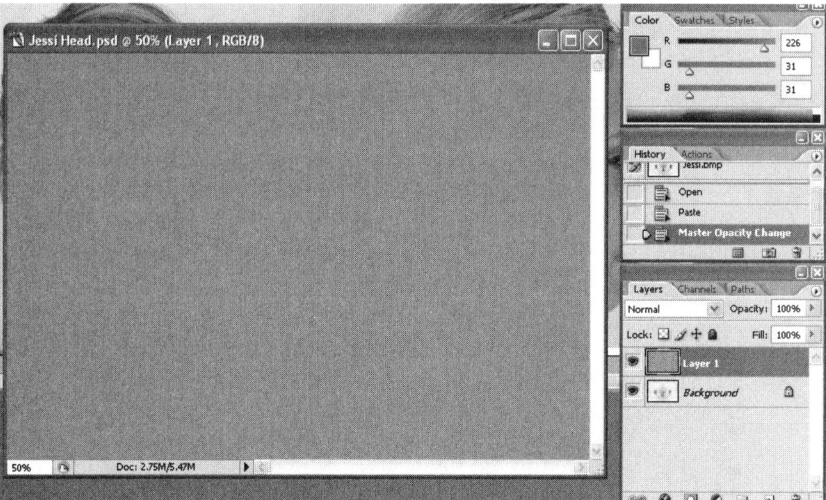

FIGURE 11.12 Place a solid layer of skin tone above your template layer.

Either turn off the skin layer temporarily or reduce its transparency so that you can see the template layer beneath it. Then begin to place the pieces of the photograph in their appropriate places. For example, you can create a feathered selection around one of the eyes in the photograph and paste the eye in a layer above the skin layer in your project. Size the eye selection so that it fits appropriately above the eye area in the template, as shown in Figure 11.13.

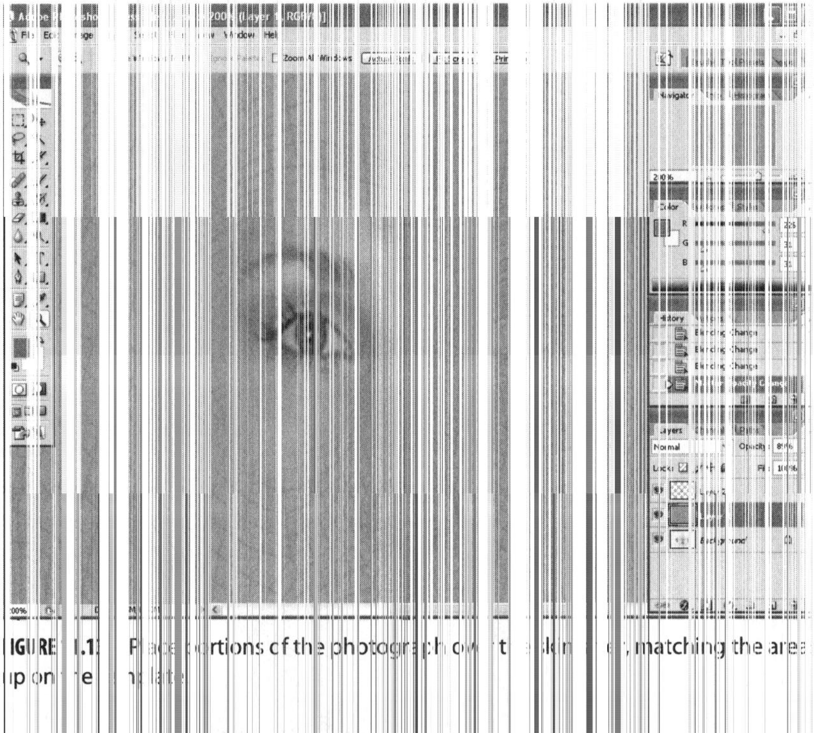

FIGURE 11.13 Place portions of the photograph over the skin layer, matching the areas up on the template.

Continue to place portions of the photograph in the appropriate places using as many layers as it takes. By placing the photographic segments on different layers, you can nudge them into place and make fine adjustments in size and rotation until they fit in the right place over the template. Also, most software that has layers also has capabilities such as blend layer functions that allow you to more easily fine-tune your texture. For example, with layers you can add a scar to your skin texture by placing a photo of a scar (the photo need not be from your original model) and use layer functions such as "luminosity" to maintain your existing skin tone and color while applying the luminosity from the layer that has the photo of the scar. This way you can mix and match source photos from different lighting conditions more easily, which expands your supply of source material.

Also, when you place your photos into your texture, use soft feathered edges. Avoid straight-line selections or sharp changes in texture. If your software has a clone tool (rubber stamp tool), that's a great way to get lots of area covered quickly and get a nice texture baseline established.

For creature, human, and animal textures, you can usually start a good base texture by working on one side first (either left or right half), and then mirror it for the other half. After you mirror your texture, make some changes to the skin features in the center, and in small and different areas on each side to make your texture less symmetrical (Figure 11.14).

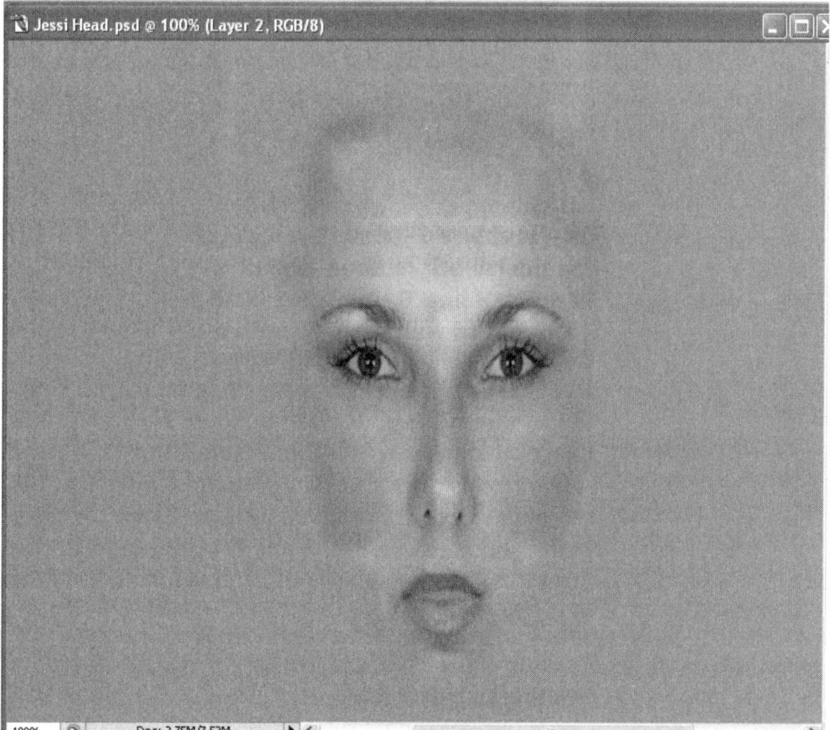

FIGURE 11.14 Try not to make your texture symmetrical. It will look more realistic with some assymetry.

If you're working on human skin, your texture should be uniform in overall brightness. As for shadows and highlights, try to avoid them at this stage. Many people add shadows and highlights in areas of their textures to add contour to the texture. This usually adds distracting dark and light streaks to your texture. To add subtle contour to your figure, creating a separate grayscale contour map in a separate file, and tie it to the displacement channel. With this technique, you can add features such as skin blemishes, scars, veins, and other slight rises and depressions in the overall mesh.

You will need to focus on areas where seams occur. Also, pay attention to areas where the texture may be distorted, such as areas around the mouth, eyes, and breasts. In general, areas that bend or have morphs applied will need special care to ensure that the texture can accommodate even the largest mesh deformation when the figure is distorted in some extreme poses or excessive body morphs are applied to a body.

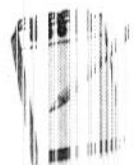

While working on your texture you will need to bring it into Poser often to render so you can see what it looks like. When you do this, make sure that your lights are neutral. Using colored lights at this stage can create textures that look horrible under any other lighting conditions. Neutral lights have equal red, blue, and green values.

After you get your base texture created, you will need to decide how realistic you wish your texture to be. If you want to go all the way, follow up with the creation of a displacement map, which will need to correspond with the features of your texture map. A great place to start is by using your finished texture map as the base for your displacement map. Convert your texture map image to grayscale, and in your graphics program maximize the contrast between the lightest pixel and the darkest for the largest range of displacement. In Photoshop CS, you do this with the Image > Adjustments > Auto Contrast menu command; however, most software these days has auto-contrast filters. In the case of the displacement map, remember that darker tones are for "divots" for hair follicles or indentations like wrinkles and creases, and lighter values will create features like scar tissue, pimples, and veins, which protrude from the surface of the mesh.

Painting Your Own Textures

The rules that you learned for photo-real textures also apply to painted textures. There is a slight difference: instead of placing photographs into various layers, you'll be using your favorite graphics application to paint in the various features of your texture maps. This does not mean that painted textures cannot utilize photographic elements to help create realism.

We'll show you the steps we took to create the basic texture you see in Figure 11.15. The White Rabbit texture is a perfect application to highlight the major steps in creating a hand-painted texture, because photo-realism is not the desired effect. Also, this texture shows that you can also be creative with the type of texture you paint. We've broken a single object into several parts (rabbit, top coat, ruffle shirt, pants, and booties) to create something that appears much more complex than it really is.

FIGURE 11.15 The White Rabbit texture is a perfect application for a hand-painted texture where photorealism is not the desired effect.

Start with the texture template, and place it into the top layer of our working texture map file. Select the white areas in the template and remove them, so that only the lines are visible and you can see the layers underneath are visible. See Figure 11.16 to see how we set up our file to begin creating our own painted template. At this point, our "working layer," the one below the texture template, is still completely white.

Once you set up your layers, it's relatively easy to fill in large areas of the texture. It is similar to coloring in a coloring book, except that you extend the texture slightly outside the bounds of the texture template. This ensures that seams match up during rendering, and that there are no discontinuities or discrepancies between your texture template and the actual rendered mapping.

Figure 11.17 shows our sample texture map (1) with the texture template visible on top of the actual texture. Compare this with just the texture itself (2 and 3). For the most part, you don't have to worry about "bumpiness" or anything else other than color of the objects. We use the geometry along with bump and/or displacement maps to create the appropriate shadows and highlights at render time. There are a few exceptions to this rule. For example, we can add shadows and highlights to

FIGURE 11.16 Initial working texture map file setup showing the top layer, which is the UV texture template, and the bottom layer, which will become the material texture map.

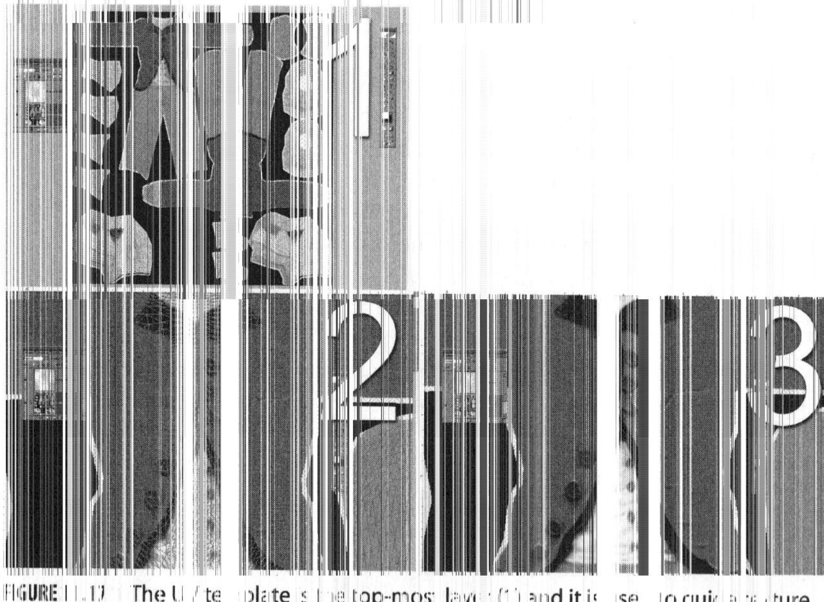

FIGURE 11.17 The UV template is the top-most layer (1) and it is used to guide texture creation. As you work, you can see the underlying texture in the layer below the texture template (2). The bottom layer (3) is the actual texture image.

create the illusion of buttons, or try to get more emphasis on the watch fob to make it look less flat.

After you create the texture map, use the same process to create the displacement map. In this case, the same file is used to create all of the various maps for our costume object. Copy the texture map layer to create a new layer, and convert the new layer to grayscale.

Then select various portions (for example, the coat and the pants) and fill them with an image that can give them some texture. For example, you can scan a sweater and use the knit texture as the basis from which to build the fabric portions of the material. You can also use a photograph of some fake fur as small, seamless tile fills for areas such as the head, feet, and tail. Scan the wrist portion of a knit jacket to create the recognizable knit that we see on the wrists of clothing.

To make seams that look sewn, accent the edges with black "dabs" that mimic the indentations and puckers that occur when knit material is sewn together. Figure 11.18 shows the final displacement map.

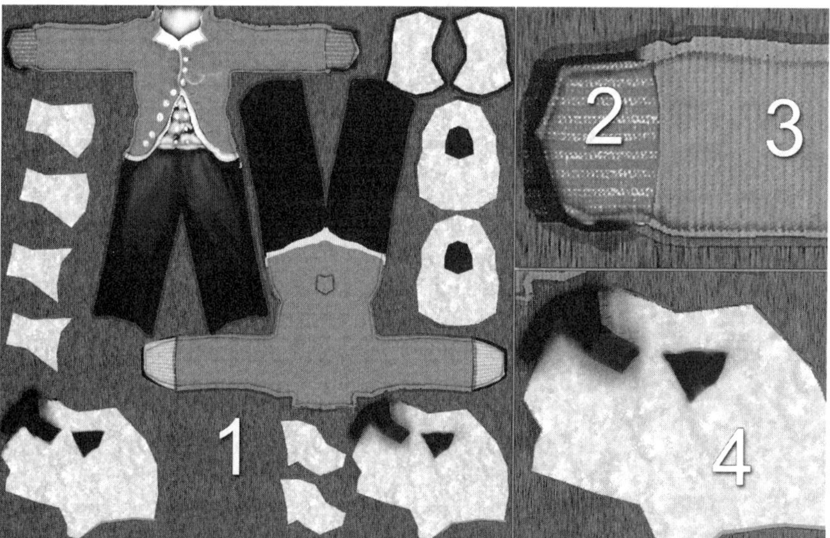

FIGURE 11.18 The completed displacement map in its entirety (1), with the sweater's wrist area (2), overall knit area (3), and fur texture (4).

For some complex textures, like human skin, it is common to have separate maps for diffusion, reflection, specularity, and transparency. They go a long way toward making the material believable. If you want to create additional maps, however, you should create them within the main working texture file.

The process of painting your own texture isn't necessarily difficult, as much as it is exacting. It requires many, many test renders and refinements before the entire texture and its associated bump, displacement, reflection, and transparency maps come together. As with any project you undertake on the computer it is always a good idea to save often. You should save a version of the working texture creation file at the end of every major step. This allows you to recover in the event of file loss. You can also create variations of a texture more easily as we can start with any one of the saved versions and branch off from there.

Scanning

Your scanner is an excellent tool for creating your own textures. You can put just about anything onto the bed of your scanner and get some interesting textures and patterns. While it might seem like a good idea to scan fabrics and wallpaper, you should be aware that patterns are often copyrighted and cannot be used to create derivative works without permission from the copyright holder. Be sure of the copyrights before you use something. On the other hand, material textures such as cotton, silk, burlap, and canvas make great royalty-free sources for scanned textures.

Seamless Tiles as Material Textures

One type of image, the seamless tile, provides a clever way to make materials for very large objects, or very detailed objects, without having to use a large image map file. By making copies of the image and tiling it as needed, the rendering engine reuses the same texture file over and over again. This method works exceptionally well for things like floors, walls, and other types of materials that have repeated patterns. Fabric-like materials, Scottish tartan fabrics (commonly used for kilts), parquet flooring, mosaic tile patterns, and even the entire faces of large buildings in a city scene where features like windows and bricks are common uses for seamless tiles.

You can make your own seamless tile image maps without too much effort, even if you only have the most basic image editor.

For this example we'll stick to making an interesting pattern that starts off with a random selection. As you get more comfortable with the process, you'll be able to select what will, and won't, make a good seamless tile for the application you have in mind. Also, we'll be using Photoshop CS as our graphics application. We'll stick to explaining the concept behind what we're doing so you should be able to duplicate each step in the graphics program of your choice, as long as you are somewhat familiar with its basic operations. Here's all you need to do:

1. First, open a likely image that you think will have some interesting areas that you can utilize in your seamless tile.
2. With your selection tool, select an area of interest. At this point, you'll need to be aware that the number of pixels you select will be one quarter (1/4) of the total size of our finished seamless tile.
3. Copy your selection into a new image document. (In Photoshop, copy the selection first and then open a new file. Your new file should default to the right size based on what's in your copy buffer. Then paste your copied selection into the new file.)
4. At this point, we'll mention something that you may or may not be required to address in your graphics program. In Photoshop when we paste a selection into a new document, the pasted selection appears on its own layer. (In older graphics applications, the pasted graphic may be blended with the background layer.) This is important because in most applications, the background layer has properties that are more difficult to deal with. If your application pastes your selection into the background layer, go ahead and make a new layer and copy your selection into it at this time. You can then delete your background layer.
5. Next you'll make the image canvas twice as wide and twice as tall. In Photoshop CS, you can make your canvas larger without resizing any of the content of your image. A quick way to resize is to use the percentage option (use 200%), rather than having to enter the exact number of pixels. Also, make sure that you select the upper-left quadrant as your "base" for the canvas so that your originally pasted selection appears in the upper-left section of your enlarged canvas. If your application does not allow you to independently resize your working canvas, you will need to manually calculate how many pixels your new canvas (image) size should be and then repaste your selection and drag it into the upper-left side of your image. You should end up with something that resembles Figure 11.19.
6. Next, make a copy of the layer that contains your selection.
7. Now, you'll do two things: first, flip the top-most layer horizontally—that is, flip it so that what was the left side becomes the right. Don't flip the whole document, just the top layer. Then you'll slide the top layer that has been flipped to the upper-right side of your working canvas. What you should see at that time is that in the center of your canvas, where the edges of the two selections meet, the pattern will line up. The right side mirrors the left. Figure 11.20 shows what ours looks like at this step.
8. It's time to merge the two layers into a single layer.
9. After you merge the layers, you will need to make a copy of the newly merged layer.
10. Once you have your copy, flip the top layer's contents top-for-bottom. In Photoshop CS, we use the Flip Vertical command.
11. Next, drag the top layer down into the bottom half of the canvas.

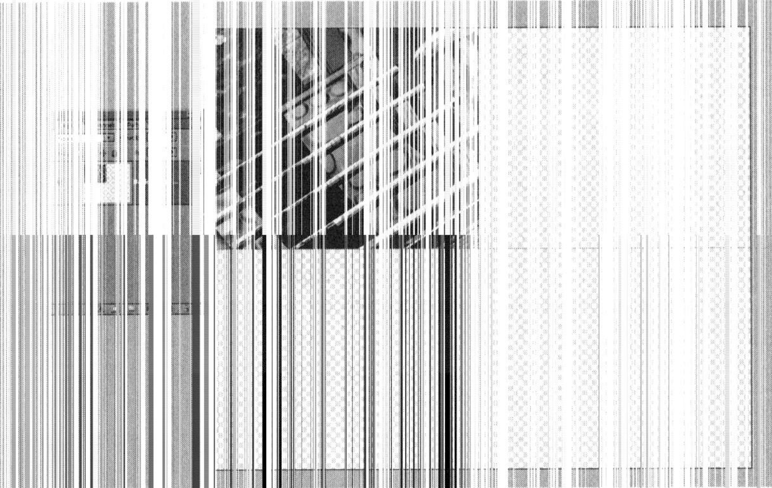

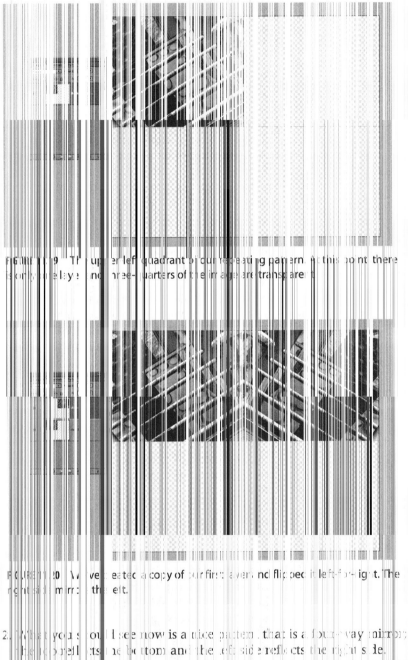

FIGURE 11.19 The upper left quadrant of our repeating pattern. At this point there is only one layer and three-quarters of the image are transparent.

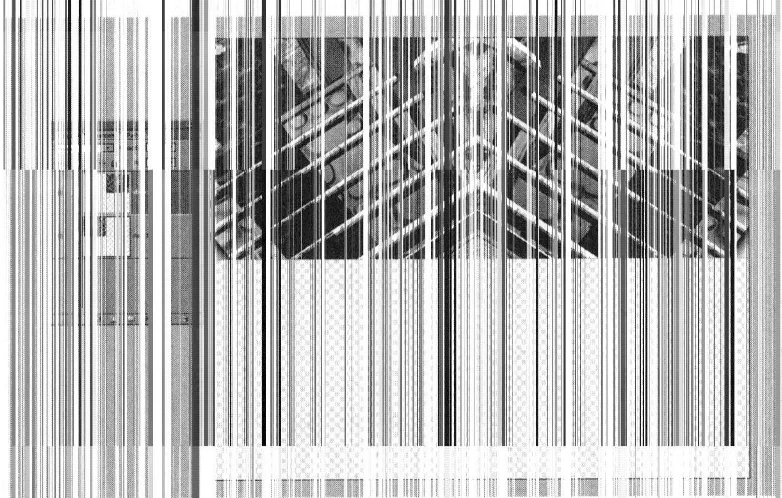

FIGURE 11.20 We've created a copy of our first layer and flipped it left-for-right. The right side mirrors the left.

12. What you should see now is a nice pattern that is a four-way mirror; the top reflects the bottom and the left side reflects the right side.
13. Now for the last step, to merge the two layers into a single one. In Photoshop CS you can merge two layers by accessing the layer palette menu and selecting Merge Layers. Figure 11.21 shows what we've ended up with.

FIGURE 11.21 Our final product is now a single layer image that is symmetric from top to bottom and left to right.

Congratulations—you've just made a repeating, tileable, image map! Because the image is symmetric both horizontally and vertically, Poser can repeat the image as many times as it needs to completely cover your object and there won't be any seams or discontinuities in the texture! See Figure 11.22 for an illustration showing our seamless tile image map in action. We've tied the seamless tile into the diffuse, bump, and displacement channels of the root node to get the effect of a richly patterned shirt.

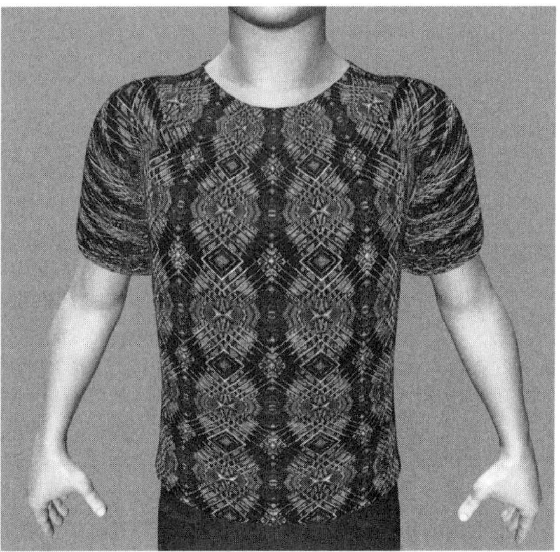

FIGURE 11.22 Our seamless tile has been used to transform Ben's plain white T-shirt into a richly patterned shirt.

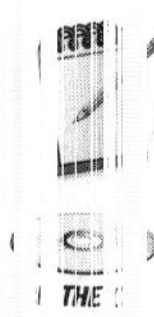

We've included about a thousand low-resolution textures on the CD-ROM that accompanies this book. Most of them are seamless tiles for you to experiment with and enjoy. You'll find them in the Content > Andre folder on the CD-ROM.

You aren't limited to image-based seamlessly tiled materials. Poser's sophisticated materials can come with procedural or math-based nodes that use math to create repeating patterns. These procedural shaders can be used to make bricks, floor tiles, and even wooden parquet tiles, with a bit of tweaking.

FILE TYPES

Poser and many of the image-editing tools used to create textures and maps use bitmapped image file formats. If you plan on making your own maps or modifying the ones you have, it is important to understand which file formats can suffer the most data degradation from processing and compression. Image file formats can be categorized into *lossless* formats and *lossy* formats:

- *Lossless* file formats are those that never jeopardize or modify the image data itself to achieve file size reduction, and those that don't offer any file size compression at all. Some popular lossless file formats include: BMP, TIF, TGA, and PSD.
- *Lossy* file formats are those that, in an effort to compact the file into its smallest possible space, take liberties with the image data and perform operations that usually degrade the quality of the image. The most popular lossy file format is JPG.

Lossless File Formats

Lossless file formats are wonderful. Being able to edit your image as many times as you want and never having to worry that what you save will be exactly what you see the next time you open your file for editing is great. Retaining details and color accuracy is important for those image files used for close-ups and those that contain a lot of detail to begin with. However, great-looking, large, crisp images will cost you larger amounts of disk space to store. In an effort to reduce storage space requirements, programmers came up with the idea of compressing graphics files at the time they are saved to your hard drive.

The most straightforward lossless compression algorithm is to use shorthand to represent more than 3 pixels in a row using the same color. Let's say your data looks like this: "10000111110110." The compressed version would be "14.0110," and would be read as follows: four all down, then four 0's, then four 1's, 0, 1, 1, and then a 0. The compressed version of the data takes up more increments of space, while the uncompressed version takes up 13. You can see that while you do manage to shave off some space, you really don't reduce the size of your file too much unless you have large, contiguous areas of a single color, in which case your compression ratio would go up dramatically.

LZW Compression

Fortunately, a more complex type of lossless compression was introduced in 1977. LZW compression, named after Lempel Ziv, looks at strings of data and replaces those strings with a more simple "code." It keeps a list of these codes in a table, and as it reads through the data it replaces known stings with its shorthand code. As it finds strings of data that it hasn't replaced, it creates another shorthand code for the new string and replaces it. The process is repeated as many times as necessary until several generations of data have been replaced with its shorthand, some of which can represent strings of its own shorthand generated from previous "runs." It works remarkably well and can give surprising compression ratios without losing any data! You might even recognize a commercial program that applies this compression to *any* file—it's called a PKZIP.

There are versions of the TIF file format that will allow you to compress image data without loss by applying LZW compression when saving your file. GIF, by its very nature is very lossy if you consider that it can only represent 256 colors in the first place, but if you have an image that started with that many colors or less, it is lossless from then on. GIF also does well with images that use large areas of a single color because it does do some simple compression. PSD files are also lossless. PNG, Portable Network Graphics, are intended to replace GIF files and can actually handle images using up to 48 bits per color. The standard color depth is 8 bits per color.

The GIF file format is capable of displaying 256 colors (or 256 shades of gray). How is it possible that a GIF only displays 256 colors, but it's really not too horrible at displaying photographs? A sneaky way that GIF images appear to display more than 256 colors is a method called dithering. Dithering is when you take two colors that are next to each other in solid blocks and create a transition between them that "checkerboards" the two colors together more gradually. Figure 11.29 shows a dithered GIF image.

Whenever you need to keep your image data pristine, or if plan on modifying an image anytime in the future, it is important that you store it in a lossless format. This decision may cost you a bit more disk space, but it won't cost you image quality. If the image has less than 256 colors, GIF is good. If it's continuous-tone then try TIF or TGA, PNG, or PSD. TIF, PSD, and PNG file formats do have file compression to varying degrees.

Lossy File Formats

Now, let's say that you don't really care if the image gets degraded as long as you can save hard drive space, or download time, as long as the image looks reasonably close to what you started with when viewing it on your monitor. In this case, you would be wise to consider the *lossy* image file formats. For online applications and quick downloading purposes there is one format that is ubiquitous: JPG. (The JPG file extension is a derivative of the original extension for this type of file, JPEG, which is short for the Joint Photographic Experts Group. This group is a committee created specifically to tackle the process of developing continuous-tone, photographic-type graphic image standards.)

The JPG format is really an excellent format as long as you understand its limitations. It allows for a variable compression setting so you can choose how much space you need to save by sacrificing image quality. Even at extremely high compression rates it does a marvelous job with continuous-tone images in certain situations. One of the critical things to understand about JPG is that it is intended to take advantage of known limitations of the human eye, particularly that it is more sensitive to the changes in brightness than to changes in color. JPG images are intended for viewing by humans (as opposed to optical computing applications or other applications where precision is critical), so color accuracy is sacrificed to reduce file size.

How does JPG work? The JPG algorithm divides an image into small blocks. Each block is summarized. The quality of the resulting compressed JPG is directly related to how large the block sample is—the larger the sample, the more compressed the resulting data becomes and the more the image quality is degraded. To put it another way, the compression algorithm runs through your image and looks at blocks of pixels. It decides what the "average" color of each block is and then replaces the entire block with a single color. The result of this block averaging is that all pixels in a block have the same color. JPG sampling can be very fine or very coarse, and it directly affects the quality of the final image. One of the effects of an image that has had extreme JPG compression applied is the appearance of "artifacts" or *jaggies* in the image.

What does all this mean to you as a Poser artist? It means that every time you *save* an image in the JPG format, you are *losing data*. The image you save is not the image you are looking at, even if you use the *best* JPG sampling rate! This is because the act of *saving* a JPG will invoke the compression algorithm that will resample your image. In fact, if you open and resave a JPG numerous times you will be continuously degrading, or "averaging" the pixel data of your graphic. See Figure 11.23 for an example of an image that was resaved as JPG several times and consequently underwent noticeable image degradation.

Figures 11.24 through 11.29 are images saved in various formats and various compression ratios. You can compare for yourself how compression ratio affects the quality of the image data and resulting file size.

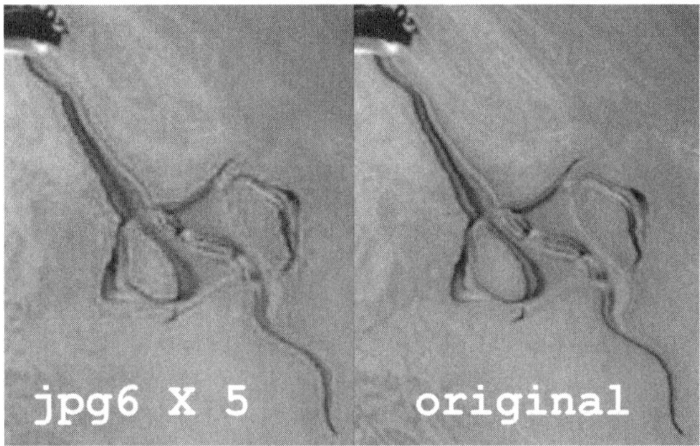

FIGURE 11.23 Extreme close-up showing the degradation of an image after it was saved as JPG using medium compression quality (6/12 in Photoshop), reopened, and resaved again, until it was resaved a total of five times.

FIGURE 11.24 Original file specifications: 1500x1500 pixels, RGB color space, PSD format, file size 5,174 kb.

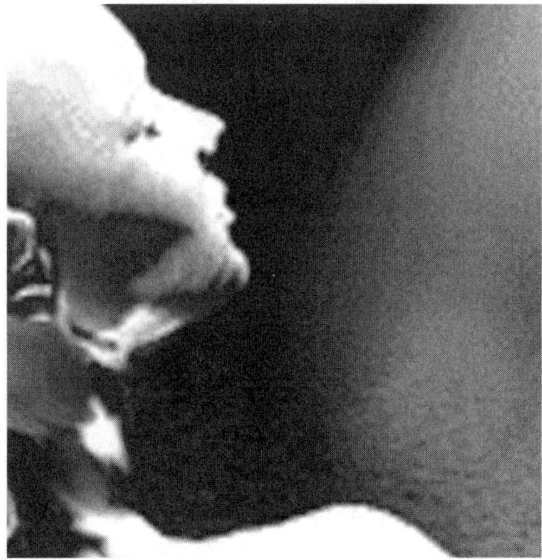

FIGURE 11.25 Converted to GIF, Indexed color, Local palette (Adaptive), 255 colors, none forced, diffusion dither 75%, no transparency, file size 880 kb.

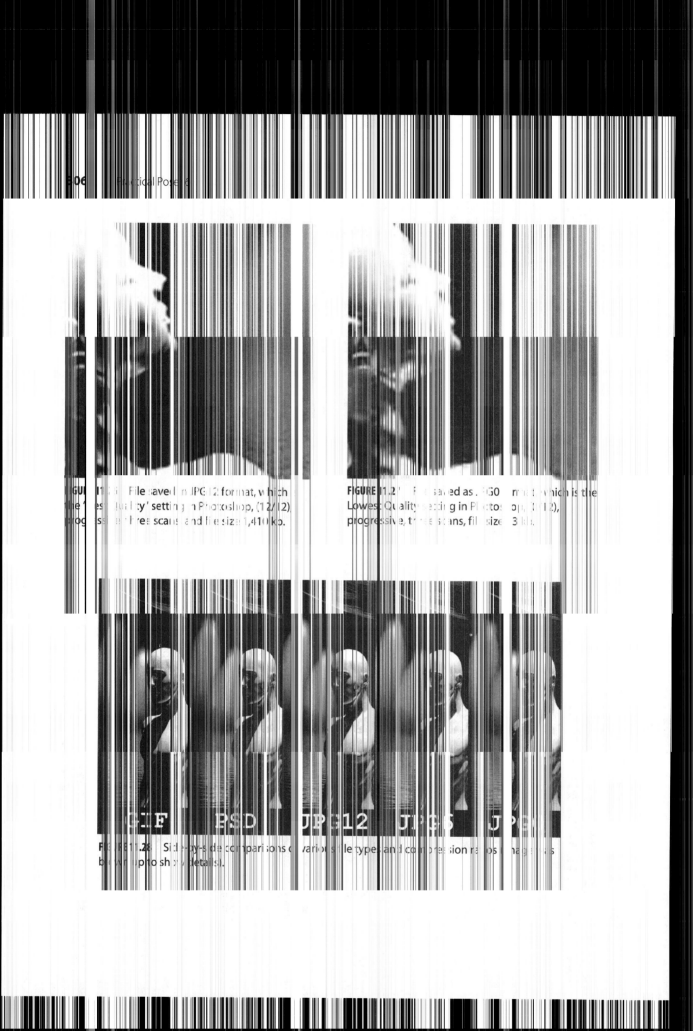

FIGURE 11.26 File saved in JPG12 format, which is the 'Best Quality' setting in Photoshop, (12/12), progressive, three scans and file size 1,410 kb.

FIGURE 11.27 File saved as JPG0 format, which is the Lowest Quality setting in Photoshop, (0/12), progressive, three scans, file size [illegible]3 kb.

FIGURE 11.28 Side-by-side comparisons of various file types and compression ratios (images are blown up to show details).

FIGURE 11.29 File saved as GIF; notice the dithering effects that are used to reduce the total number of colors in this image to 256.

If you are interested in learning more about file formats, lossy and lossless compression, and other fundamental concepts, you should check out the various computer graphic newsgroups and look for Web sites that provide technical specifications and examples. Also, a wonderful link that provides definitions of the most common graphics formats can be found at http://audre.org/GraphicFAQ.

Do your own experiments. Save your images using the various settings available to you and compare your images. Take a very good-quality TIF and save it using some of the different formats your image-editing software offers. Then compare the file sizes and most importantly, examine several areas of the image under very high magnification to see what has happened to your image. Study the results and make your own choices as to what formats best suit the way you work.

COPYRIGHTS

With regard to copyrights, the safest and best rule of thumb is: *if you didn't make it yourself, don't use it. Period.* The Internet has made it very easy to browse through thousands of Web sites and access images, information, and resources never before imaginable. It is very easy and tempting to download and use content for which you do not own the copyrights.

Copyrights are, quite literally, the right to copy something. If you are not the creator of something, and haven't specifically gotten permission from the person who owns it (either through purchase or transfer of copyrights, or through some documented means where copyright or reproductive right was transferred to you), then you do not have the right to copy it. Copying includes redistributing.

You do have the right to *view* copyrighted material, provided you do this as the copyright owner intended. With respect to Web pages and their content, this means that aside from viewing it on the owner's Web page (in the context and manner the owner has determined is acceptable), you really don't have the legal right to do anything else with the content. The exception to this is if they have made it obvious that the contents of their Web pages are free from copyright restrictions and are public domain.

Fair Use

"But what about Fair Use," you ask? Good question. The U.S. Copyright Office has this to say about Fair Use: "Section 107 contains a list of the various purposes for which the reproduction of a particular work may be considered 'fair,' such as criticism, comment, news reporting, teaching, scholarship, and research." (You can read Section 107 yourself here: *http://www.copyright.gov/title17/92chap1.html#107.*) Examples of fair use might include the following scenarios:

1. If you are an art critic and you write a column about something that is copyrighted, for example, a book, music, a play, or a piece of art, you can, in the context and for the sole purpose of your criticism, reproduce portions of the copyrighted material to illustrate your points. Comedic parody falls under this category.
2. If you're a student and you are presenting an academic paper or research, it is acceptable for you to include portions of copyrighted content that specifically relate to your subject.
3. If you are a teacher, you may reproduce copyrighted material for inclusion in your curriculum.

Not-For-Profit and Personal Use

People often confuse Fair Use with not-for-profit, or "personal" uses. The fact is, just because you choose not to make money with the material you have—for all intents and purposes, stolen—doesn't mean you're off the hook. Not-for-profit use might seem acceptable, but it still constitutes the copying, redistribution, and use of material that you do not have the rights to. In a court of law, a judge *may* take into account that your theft did not involve the direct gain of income for you. But the court will also realize that there probably was some other benefit that you derived—otherwise, why go through the effort of copying in the first place? (If you liked something enough that you went through the trouble of copying it, then you should have made an effort to purchase it.) The nature of your benefit will be assessed and a determination will be made as to whether or not the copyright holder is entitled to be compensated in any way by your use of the material.

In addition, if your use of the copyrighted material is construed as defamatory, destructive, or in any way damaging to the copyrighted material, the artist, or the artist's ability to gainfully employ themselves (that is, either finding work or selling the copyrighted material at a later time), you may be held accountable for lifetime damages. An example might be when you go to an artist's Web site and you download one of the files containing an image onto the hard drive of your computer. You then decide that you like it so much you will email that file to all of your friends. Each of them shares with other friends and within a month, everyone who has ever gotten email has gotten a copy of the image file.

Let's say that this artist has been trying to sell limited edition prints of this image. Ignoring, for the moment, that you have already broken the law by redistributing content to which you have no rights, what you may have inadvertently done is ruin their resale market for that image. It is not outside the realm of possibility that collectors might decide that the art is no longer as valuable due to its mass circulation via Internet communication. To calculate the amount of damage the artist might have incurred from this devaluation of their work, add up how many different ways the artist might have sold that work of their lifetime. (The lifetime value of a reasonably popular piece of art selling for only $30 per reprint can accumulate to tens of thousands of dollars!) If you want to share something you found on the Internet, it is safest to send a link to the original content, rather than downloading and sending the actual content in your email.

Finally, there is the issue of the copyright holder's right to choose and control the manner in which the material is accessed. When you copy, redistribute, or modify something copyrighted, you are infringing on the owner's right to determine when and where the property will be accessed, and in what context. Again, when you do this you take on the responsibility of the impact your actions might have on artists' ability to feed themselves.

What this means to you, the creator of Poser content, is that you need to be careful not to create your content (maps, textures, materials, and geometries) with sources that you can't account for. The best bet when searching for content for your own use, either commercial or personal, is to stick with reputable Web sites that specifically state, in clear language, that they have the right to distribute the content from their Web site. In addition, there should be a clear explanation of what is considered acceptable use. In some cases, people restrict the use of their content to only noncommercial applications, so be sure to read and understand the rules before you load something into your Poser library. *If in doubt, assume it is copyrighted!*

Derivative Works

Another point of confusion is in the case of Derivative Works. Most people believe that if they modify something enough (say, 80% of new work has been modified in some way), the original copyright can no longer affect their new work. This is simply not true. In order for a derivative work to be legal (and copyrightable) the copyright holder of the original work must have given copyright reproduction rights to the maker of the derivative work. The following excerpt from the *http://www.copyright.gov/circs/circ14.html* Web site explains it thus: "Only the owner of copyright in a work has the right to prepare, or to authorize someone else to create, a new version of that work. The owner is generally the author or someone who has obtained rights from the author."

What Copyrights Mean to You

When creating content for your Poser projects you should be aware of any copyrights or restrictions that may be in effect for each individual item that goes into everything you use. This means that you cannot copy the head of one model onto another, edit the underlying mesh or geometry of a model or take someone's texture map file and change some colors on it and then redistribute any of it without explicit permission from each of the original copyright holders.

For further study in regards to copyrights, we recommend the following Web resources:

- *http://www.copyright.gov/*
- *http://www.chillingeffects.org/*
- *http://darkwing.uoregon.edu/~csundt/copyweb#Useful*

CONCLUSION

In this chapter you've been introduced to some of the ways you can make your own textures. You've seen how you can make it easier to build textures if you start with the UV template and use layers, if you can. You've also seen a finished render using the hand-drawn texture for the White Rabbit. This should give you an idea of how to go about building your own texture maps for the various channels of your root node. You know how to make a seamless tile, too. We've also provided some things to consider if you want to make your own photo-real texture. You should also know which types of file formats to use for the various projects you have, and be familiar with the basics of when it's okay to copy and use things from the Internet or other sources. You are now ready to begin making your very own textures!

CHAPTER

12

MODELING YOUR OWN CONTENT

In This Chapter

- Popular Modeling Software
- Modeling Clothing in LightWave
- Conclusion

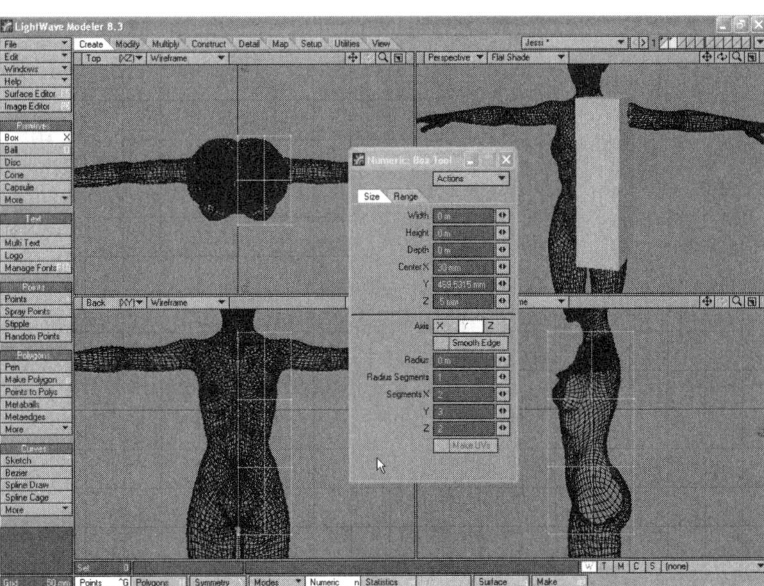

As you become more familiar with Poser, you might find yourself becoming very interested in creating your own Poser clothing and props. In fact, one of the questions that Poser users frequently ask is "How do I create my own clothing?"

As you'll learn in the next few chapters, making your own Poser clothing is quite involved. The first thing you'll need in order to create content for Poser is a 3D-modeling program. There are several popular packages, and their prices and features vary widely. Some 3D programs are free, while others will require a significant monetary investment.

In this chapter we'll give you some basic knowledge on the steps involved to create a simple dress in a modeling program. Though we are showing you the steps required to build a model in LightWave, the techniques you learn here may be similar to those you will find in other software packages that have similar features.

Popular Modeling Software

There are as many different ways to model clothing as there are different types of modeling programs. Some modeling programs work with *polygons*, and others have you design your geometry with *splines* that you later convert to polygons. It is hard to say which method is best, because it will depend upon your own preferences.

Because there are so many choices available in 3D software, you should shop around and try to demo versions of the software before you make your final decision. In addition to learning about the capabilities of each program, you should also research the costs involved to purchase and maintain your software licenses. Other factors to consider are features, ease of use, and technical support considerations.

Most of the software programs we mention in this chapter are used by members of the Poser community. You will find support forums for many of these modeling programs at the major Poser community Web sites (Renderosity, DAZ3D, Poser Pros, and RuntimeDNA).

For those of you who are looking into modeling software for the purpose of building your own Poser content, the following programs are widely used by members of the Poser community, and you'll find support forums for many of them at the major Poser community Web sites (Renderosity, RuntimeDNA, PoserPros, and DAZ3D).

- *Shade 8*, distributed by e-Frontier (the makers of Poser) was released in the fall of 2006. This tool is very popular in Japan and is gaining popularity in the Poser community. It offers the advantage of direct support of Poser files through its Poser Fusion utility. Shade is a spline-based modeling program that now features polygonal modeling tools in its new release. Shade 8 is available in two versions: Standard and

Professional. For additional information about Shade 8, visit *http://www.e-frontier.com/article/articleview/1535/1/652?sbss=652*. Tutorials are available on e-Frontier's Web site or at Shader's Café (*http://shaderscafe.com*).

- *Rhinoceros* (Rhino, for short) is another spline-based modeling program that is popular with several members of the Poser community. You can find information about Rhinoceros at *http://rhino3d.com*.
- *3DS Max*, by Autodesk (*http://usa.autodesk.com/*) is a longtime favorite professional-level modeling program that offers a broad range of features, though its price may place it out of reach of the casual or hobbiest user. Now in its eighth release, 3D Studio Max offers several different modeling approaches, including polygonal modeling and nurbs modeling. For further information about Max, visit *http://usa.autodesk.com/adsk/servlet/index?siteID=123112&id=5659451*.
- *LightWave 8*, by Newtek (*http://newtek.com*) is another modeling package that offers a lot of bang for the buck and also provides several different modeling methods. Its subdivision modeling tools make organic modeling very simple and easy, as demonstrated later in this chapter. For more information about LightWave 8 and the soon-to-be released LightWave 9, visit *http://www.newtek.com/lightwave*.
- If you want to learn 3D modeling for free, you will find that many Poser users highly recommend Wings 3D, a free subdivision modeler that was inspired by Nendo and Mirai from Izware. For additional information about this very popular modeling program, and to obtain it for free, visit *http://www.wings3d.com*.

TUTORIAL 12.1 DECOMPRESSING YOUR FIGURE'S OBJ FILE

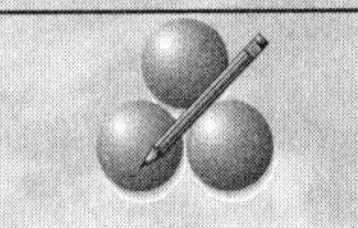

In order to create clothing that works correctly in Poser, you model your clothing around a figure as close to the original OBJ shape as possible—no morphs, no scaling, and no changes from the original position. The natural instinct is to load a figure in from the Library and that will be that. But with that approach comes potential problems: the library figure could have morphs set to change body shape or scaling that adjusts body proportions. The safest approach is to use the raw OBJ file and bring that directly into Shade, or to import it into Poser and save it as a PZ3 or PZZ file that you can import through PoserFusion.

But there is a slight catch on the Poser side. By default, Poser stores the OBJ files for the Poser 6 figures in compressed format, using an OBZ extension. That means that Shade (or any other 3D modeler) won't be able to read it. You'll have to convert the file from its OBZ zipped counterpart back to OBJ. If you prefer to compress your Poser files each time you save, you can use a Python script in Poser to selectively uncompress OBJ files. Here's how you use it:

1. Choose Window > Python Scripts to open the Python Scripts window. It opens to the main screen.
2. Click the Utility Functions button (the third from the top). You should see the selections shown in Figure 12.1.

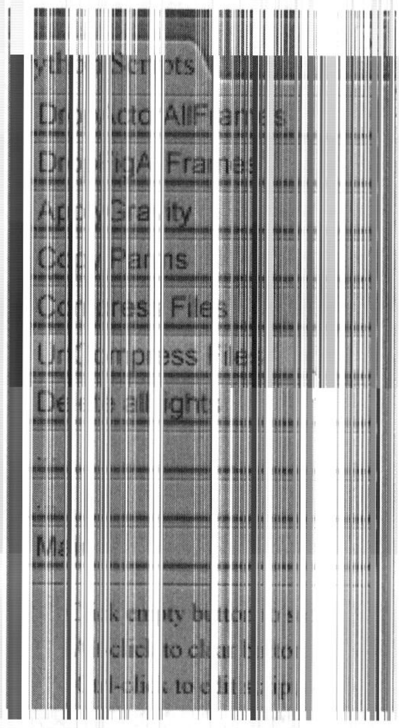

FIGURE 12.1 The Python Scripts window offers several utilities for geometry.

3. Click the UnCompress Files button. The dialog shown in Figure 12.2 appears. Click the Path button to locate the folder that contains Jessi's OBZ file (you will find it in the Poser 6 > Runtime > Libraries > Character > Jessi folder). Then check the UnCompress geometry files (.obj) option, as shown in Figure 12.2.
4. Click OK. A dialog runs through all of the files contained in the folder. Close the dialog when you see the last line read Uncompression complete. You should now see OBJ files in the same folder as the original OBZ files.

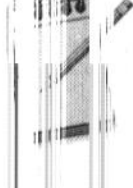

If you are unable to run Python scripts, you can open the OBZ file with a utility that "unzips" ZIP files. Simply start the software, and use its File > Open command to open the OBZ file. You should then be able to extract the OBJ file using that method.

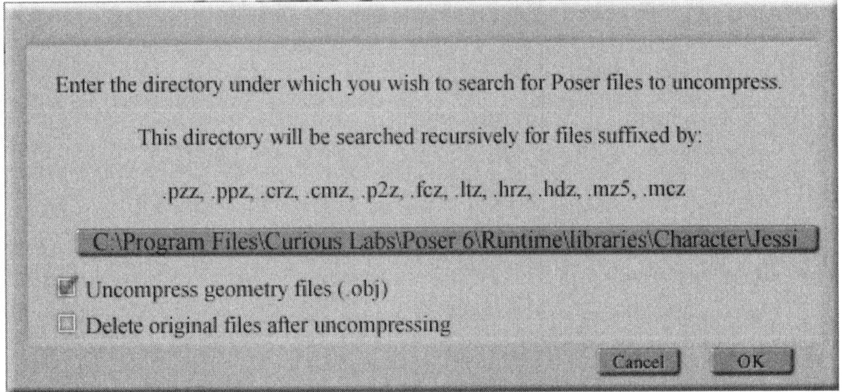
Enter the directory under which you wish to search for Poser files to uncompress.
This directory will be searched recursively for files suffixed by:
.pzz, .ppz, .crz, .cmz, .p2z, .fcz, .ltz, .hrz, .hdz, .mz5, .mcz
C:\Program Files\Curious Labs\Poser 6\Runtime\libraries\Character\Jessi
Uncompress geometry files (.obj)
Delete original files after uncompressing
Cancel
OK

FIGURE 12.2 Select the path to the Jessi OBZ file and choose the option that uncompresses the OBJ files.

MODELING CLOTHING IN LIGHTWAVE

LightWave 8 (by Newtek) is a popular 3D-modeling and -rendering program that is used by more than a few members of the Poser community. Its wealth of features and many available plug-ins make it a program that is well worth your money.

LightWave allows you to import WaveFront OBJ files directly, and it also handles Poser's small objects quite well. The easiest way to learn how to model clothing is to begin with primitives (such as a box) and use LightWave's subdivision modeling features to make organic shapes very easily. The next few sections give you an overview of the modeling process, by having you work through the steps of creating a very basic dress.

Importing the Figure

In the example that follows, we'll be creating an outfit for Jessi, so before you begin, make sure that you have decompressed the Jessi.OBZ file into a decompressed version (Jessi.OBJ). LightWave 8 can open OBJ files directly, and there is no need to rescale the object for LightWave.

To import Jessi into LightWave, choose File > Load Object. When the Load Object dialog appears, choose All Files from the Files Of Type drop-down list. This allows you to view the OBJ files in your folders. Navigate to the Poser 6 > Runtime > Libraries > Character > Jessi folder, and choose the uncompressed Jessi.OBJ file as shown in Figure 12.3. Click Open to import the file.

FIGURE 12.3 Choose the uncompressed OBJ file for Jessi.

After Jessi appears in the scene, press the A key to enlarge Jessi in all views. This zooms the view so that the figure fills each viewport.

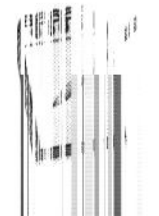

Notice that the top-right corner of each viewport contains several icons. From left to right, the crosshair icon pans the view. The curved arrows icon rotates the view. The magnifying glass icon zooms in or out. The last icon maximizes the selected viewport or returns it to its normal view.

Starting the Clothing

You can display Jessi in the first layer while you create clothing in additional layers. The layer controls in the upper-right corner of the Light Wave interface allow you to select which layers you see, and which layers are active. To activate a layer, click the upper triangle in the layer controls. To display a layer without making it active, click to highlight the bottom triangle in the layer indicator. Figure 12.4 shows Jessi displayed in the first layer, while the second layer is active so that you can start your clothing.

To begin the clothing, click the bottom triangle in the first layer of the layer controls to make Jessi visible, but not active. Then, click the top triangle in the second layer to make the second layer active.

Press 'N' to open the Numeric panel. This panel allows you to enter numeric values for your objects. Choose the Create tab, and click Box (or use the shortcut Shift+X). The Numeric panel turns into the Numeric: Box Tool panel.

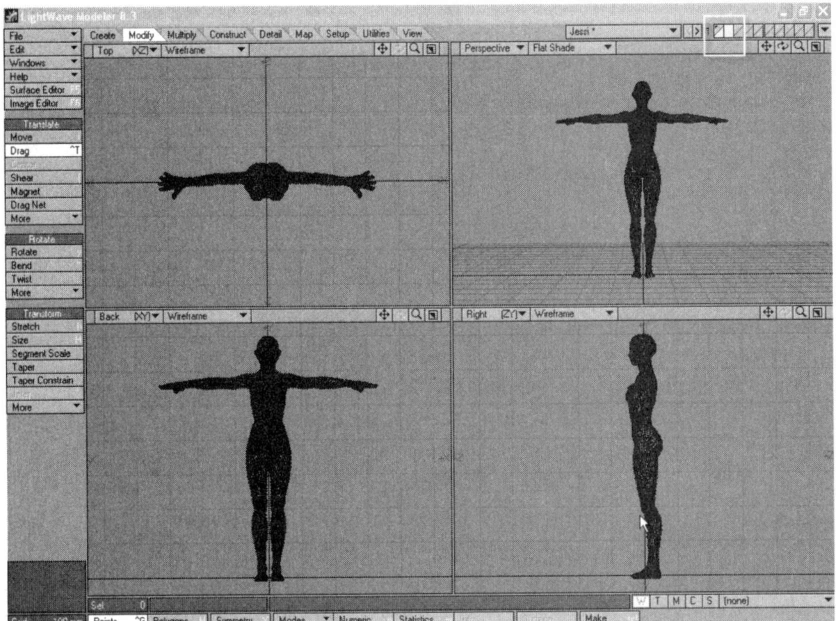

FIGURE 12.4 Layer controls appear in the upper-right corner of the LightWave interface. A colored rectangle indicates an active layer. A colored triangle indicates a visible but not active layer.

Start in the top view, and draw a box that starts from the middle of the scene. Position the box so that it starts at shoulder height and ends at the bottom of the hip. Use the Back and Right views to size the box so that it encloses Jessi's torso. In the Numeric panel, enter the following values, after which your scene should look similar to Figure 12.5.

Segments X	2
Segments Y	3
Segments Z	2

Click the Minimize icon in the upper-right corner of the numeric panel, and choose Create > Box (or use the shortcut Shift+X) to exit the Box tool. While in Point selection mode (Ctrl+G), draw a selection around the points at chest level. Then use the Modify > Drag tool (Ctrl+T) to position the points as shown in Figure 12.6. Deselect the Drag tool (Ctrl+T), and click in the bar above the Top viewport (at the location of the cursor in Figure 12.6) to deselect the vertices.

In a similar manner, adjust the vertices at shoulder level and hip level until your clothing object looks similar to that shown in Figure 12.7.

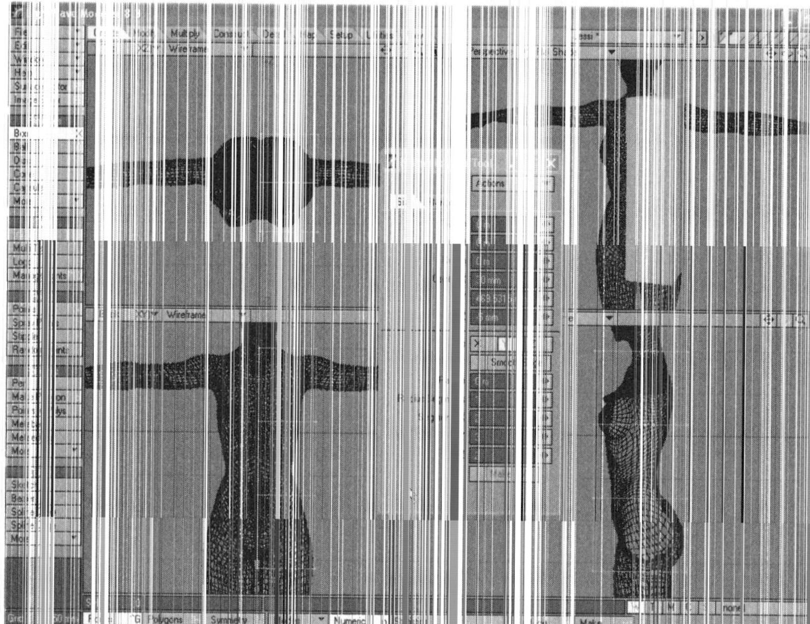

FIGURE 12.5 Start your clothing with a box that is divided into several segments.

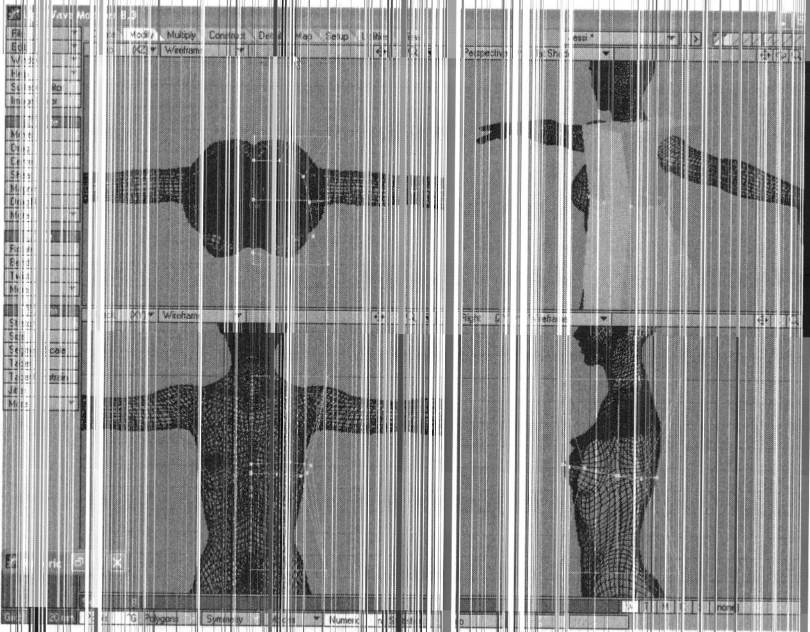

FIGURE 12.6 The vertices are moved around the chest.

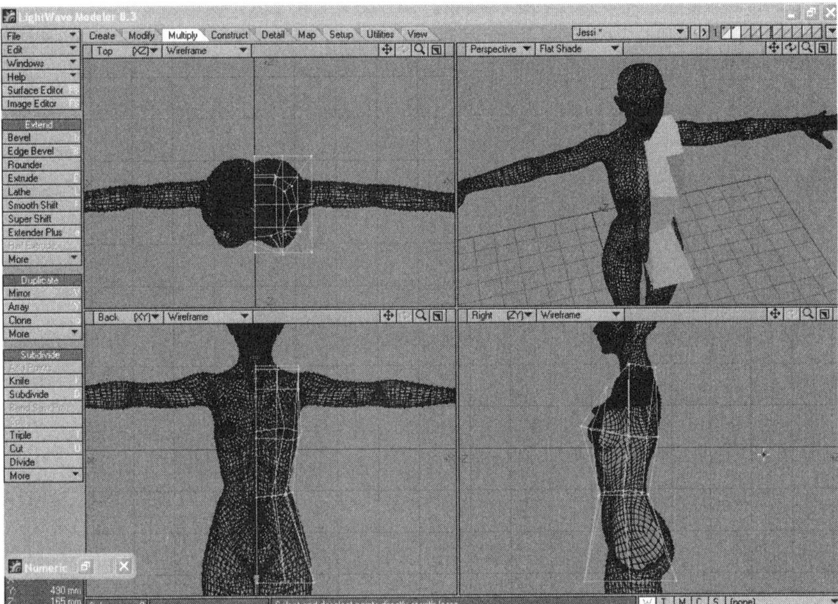

FIGURE 12.7 Vertices at shoulder level and hip level are adjusted so that they are more in line with the figure.

From the Multiply tab, select the Knife tool (Shift+K). Cut a line straight across the model just beneath chest level. Right-click to set the first cut, and then move both ends of the Knife tool to hip level as shown in Figure 12.8. Right-click to set the second cut. Then select the Knife tool (Shift+K) again to deactivate it.

Now, press the Tab key to change your clothing object into Subdivided surfaces. Notice how the surfaces of the model are smoother while you model in Subdivision mode. You'll probably need to use the Move and Drag tools in the Modify tab to make further adjustments to the vertices in the clothing model, so that it covers more of the body.

The amount of subdivision is controlled by the Patch Divisions setting in the General Options dialog. Choose Edit > General Options, and enter "3" for the Patch Divisions setting. This divides each side of the polygon into three sides when you subdivide your model. As a result, it will create nine smaller polygons from the original polygon. Be careful not to set this value too high, or your clothing will have far more polygons than it actually needs. As a rule of thumb, the polygons of the clothing model should be roughly the same size as those in the original character. Values between two and four are usually adequate, depending on your geometry.

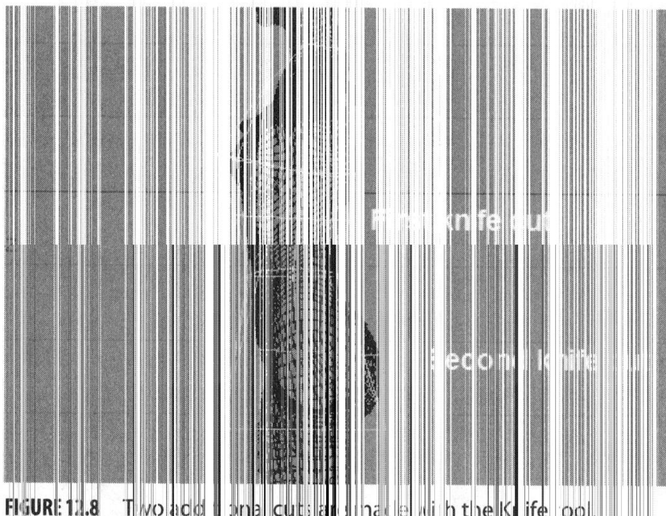

FIGURE 12.8 Two additional cuts are made with the Knife tool.

Switch to Polygon mode (Ctrl+H), and select the polygons in the middle of the clothing and also at the bottom of the clothing as shown in Figure 12.9. Press the Delete key to delete the selected polygons.

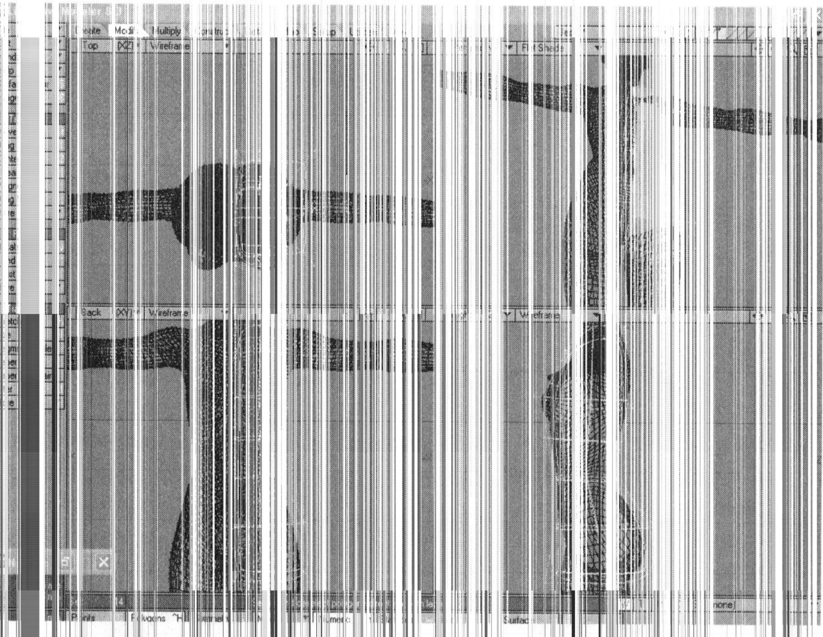

FIGURE 12.9 Delete the polygons in the middle and at the bottom of the clothing object.

Select the four polygons that cover Jessi's left breast. Click the Multiply tab, and select Super Shift (in the Extend command list). This creates four new polygons within the original four. Click the Super Shift command again to deactivate the command. Then use the Modify > Stretch and Modify > Move commands to size the breast polygons appropriately. Figure 12.10 shows the result.

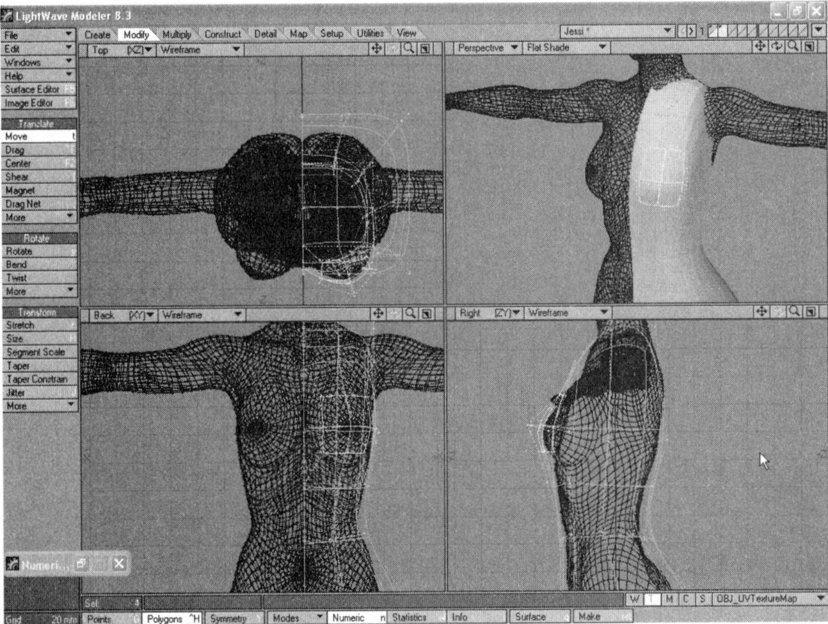

FIGURE 12.10 Use the Super Shift command (in the Multiply tab) to add some polygons to the breast area.

Select the two polygons that cover the area where the armhole would be. Again, choose the Super Shift command from the Multiply tab. Then use the Move, Stretch, and Rotate commands as necessary to position the new polygons over the armhole area as shown in Figure 12.11.

With the polygons from the armhole still selected, choose Super Shift once more to drag out some polygons to make up the sleeve. Then press the Delete key to delete the selected polygons at the end of the sleeve, so that you create the sleeve opening as shown in Figure 12.12.

Use the Knife tool to add three cuts—one just before the elbow, one in the middle of the elbow, and one just after the elbow. Then select the two polygons that overlap the neck area and delete them. Your clothing should now look similar to Figure 12.13.

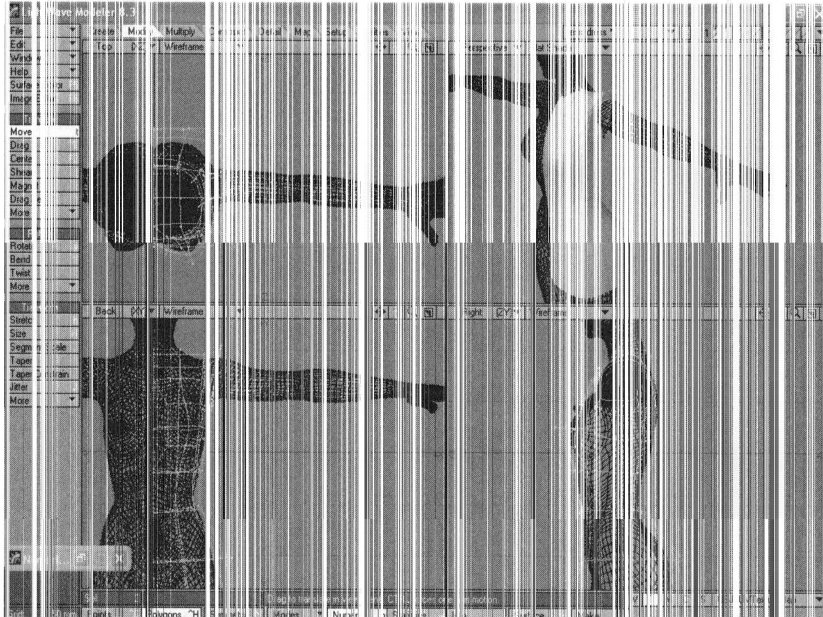

FIGURE 12.11 Use the Super Shift command (in the Multiply tab) to add some polygons to the armhole area.

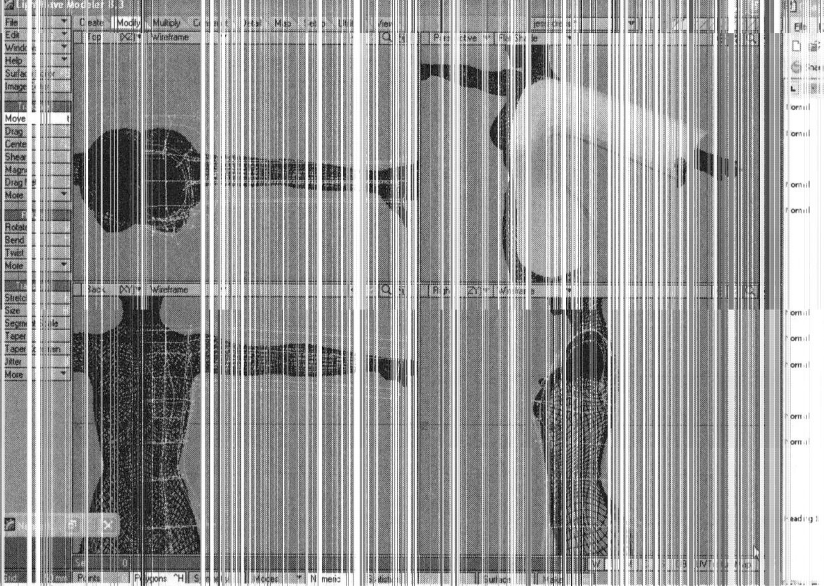

FIGURE 12.12 Use the Super Shift command (in the Multiply tab) to extend the arm out, and delete the polygons at the end to create the sleeve opening.

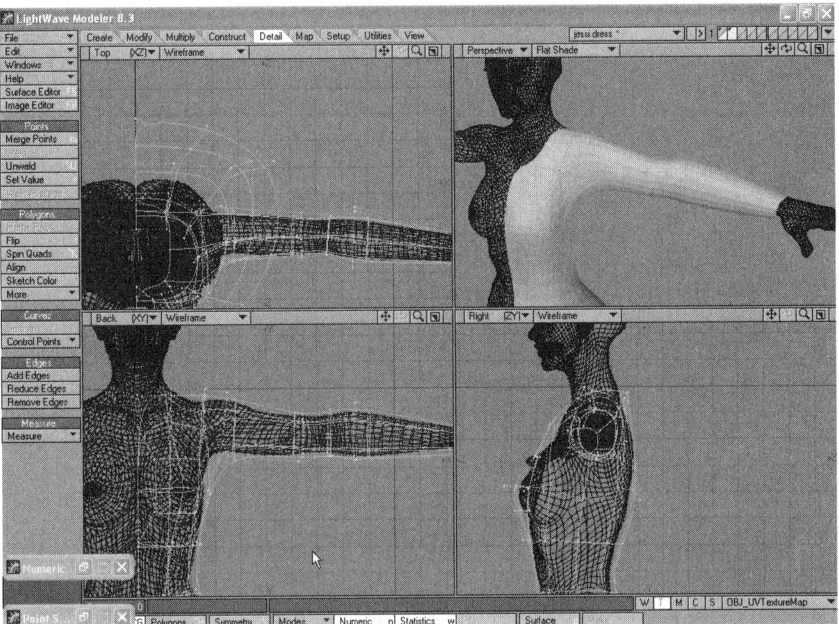

FIGURE 12.13 The fit of the sleeves is improved slightly, and polygons that overlap the neck are deleted.

Switch back to Point selection mode (Ctrl+G). Select the points around the hem, and then choose the Multiply > Extender Plus command to add some additional length. Continue to change the position of your points around with the Move (T) or Drag (Ctrl+T) tools to improve the fit and shape of the clothing.

Once you have the shape set to your liking, select all of the vertices that run along the center of the dress, as shown in Figure 12.14. Choose the Detail tab, and select the Set Value command. Make sure that the axis is set to X and the value is set to 0 m. This will move all of the center vertices to the exact center point.

Click the Multiply tab, and choose the Mirror command. Click in the top view, over the line that will be the center of the clothing. A mirrored image of the clothing appears. Verify in the Numeric panel that the X axis is selected, that the Center X, Y, and Z points are all at 0, and that the Merge Points option is checked as shown in Figure 12.15. Then deselect the Mirror command to finalize the operation. All points in the center should merge automatically, because you set all of their values to zero.

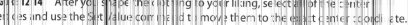

FIGURE 12.14 After you shape the clothing to your liking, select all of the center vertices and use the Set Value command to move them to the exact center coordinate.

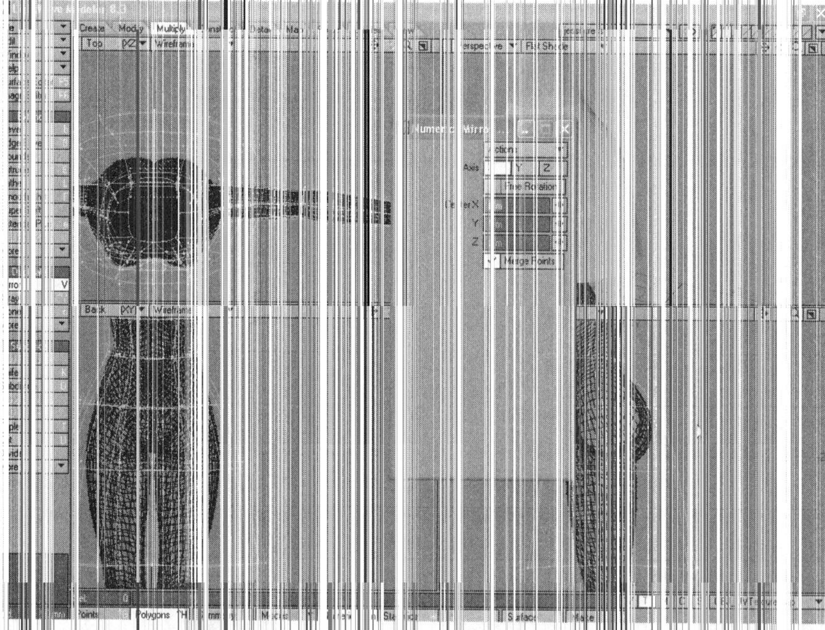

FIGURE 12.15 Use the Multiply > Mirror command to create the other side of the dress.

Now, click the Symmetry button at the bottom of the LightWave window (or use the shortcut Shift+Y). Now any changes you make to the right side of the clothing will mirror to the left. Adjust any vertices that you feel will give better shape to the dress.

Switch to Polygon selection mode (Ctrl+H), and copy the dress to the clipboard (Ctrl+C). Place a copy of the dress into the next available layer using Ctrl+V to paste it in. Choose File > Save Object, and save the file as Jessi Dress.lwo.

Finally, click the Construct tab, and choose Freeze from the Convert commands (or use the shortcut Ctrl+D). The number of polygons increases, and the dress is no longer in Subdivision mode. Your dress should look similar to Figure 12.16. After you freeze the dress, you can export the dress as a Wavefront OBJ file.

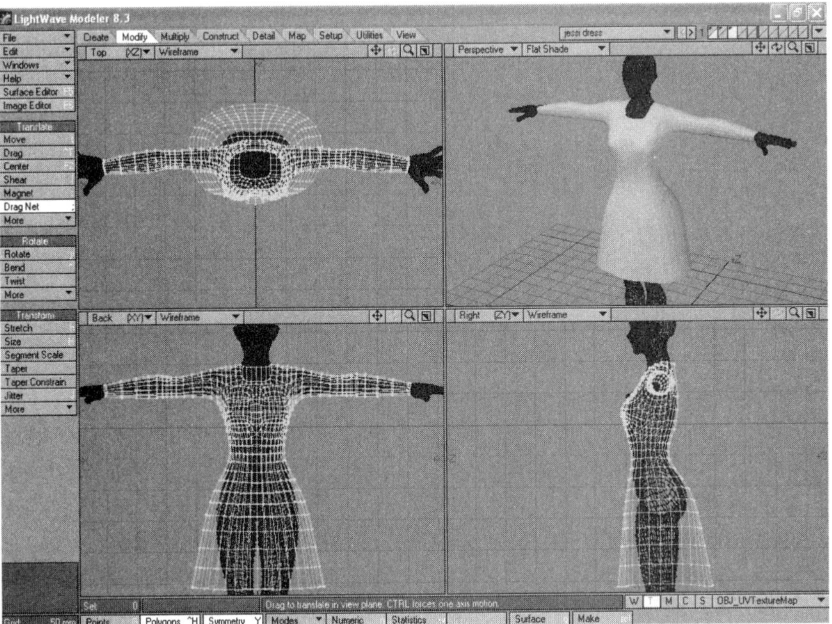

FIGURE 12.16 After you freeze the dress, it contains more polygons and is ready for exporting to Wavefront OBJ format.

To export the OBJ file, choose File > Export > Export OBJ. Locate the file in the folder of your choice, naming the file JessiShortDress.OBJ. In the next chapter you will learn how to use UV Mapper Professional to assign UV coordinates to a shirt, pants, and a skirt, and you can apply similar techniques to this dress.

Conclusion

Now that you have a taste of modeling your own clothing, hopefully you will continue to learn more on your own. In the chapters to come, you will learn how to assign UV coordinates, how to divide your clothing into groups and materials, and how to create your own textures. The journey has only just begun!

CHAPTER

13

UV MAPPING

In This Chapter

- Why You Need UV Maps
- Types of UV Maps
- Using UV Mapper Professional
- Making Templates
- Conclusion

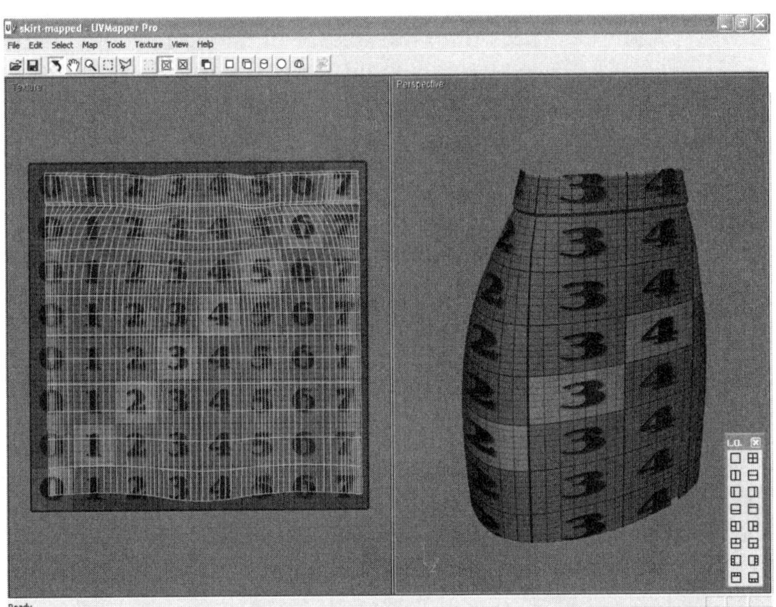

When you create an object in a 3D-modeling program, you need a way to tell the software how the surface of the object looks at each point. The material properties—like color, specularity, bumpiness, and so on—need to be assigned to each portion of the surface. In the 3D world, this information is contained in something called a *UV map*. A UV map is more or less a flattened representation of the surface of a 3D object. Without some way of mapping textures and other properties on the surface of an object, the entire surface of the object could only be one color or one material.

If poorly mapped, the UV map can make textures appear distorted. In this chapter you'll learn about various types of UV maps that you can generate, and how to break an object down into its basic shapes so that distortion and stretching are minimized when you map textures onto it.

Why You Need UV Maps

Basically, a UV map "flattens" the surface of a 3D object so that you can create a texture for it in a 2D paint program, such as Photoshop. To explain UV maps in simple terms, imagine peeling an orange and then smashing the peel flat onto the surface of the table. The peel of the orange would need to be cut in several places to accommodate being flattened out. The important thing is that, if we wanted to, we could pin the peel back onto the surface of the orange and all the seams would line up perfectly—we could wrap our orange back up in its peel. Another way to think of it is to imagine taking a map of the world and wrapping it around a sphere. If you have a map that is flat and rectangular, the poles appear to be as wide as the equator. But the Earth is truly a sphere, and the equator is wider than the poles, so in order to wrap a flat world map around a sphere, you would have to reduce the width of the texture toward the top and bottom of each side to make it fit without wrinkling.

UV maps work on the same principle. When you create a UV map, you are "unfolding" your three-dimensional object onto a flat plane. Along with telling the software what shape your object is, you are also determining which axis to orient the texture map to—in other words, whether you are looking at the object from the top, side, or front.

That is what a UV map does. It basically tells your 3D software that the pixels in one portion of a flat two-dimensional texture are applied to one or more specified polygons in the 3D model. So, in order to wrap the Earth texture around the sphere properly, you have to create a UV map that says, "Wrap a rectangular texture around this object in a spherical fashion and place the top-left corner of the image at this point of the 3D model."

Types of UV Maps

Most modeling or UV-mapping software allows you to create at least four common types of UV maps:

Spherical: Best for globes and other objects that are shaped like a sphere.

Planar: Best for flat objects, such as a door, a table top, or a mirror. A playing card is also a good example of planar mapping. If you flipped the card over, you'd see a mirror image of the map that is projected on the front.

Box: A natural for box-shaped objects that require a different texture or orientation on each side.

Cylindrical: Good for cans, sleeves, and many types of clothing. Cylindrical mapping can also include mapping for solid ends (also known as *end caps*) when needed.

If you take the time to use the right type of mapping on each object, or each portion of an object, you can avoid stretching and distortion. Sometimes the right mapping isn't obvious, especially with organic shapes. So you have to experiment with what works best. With careful study, you can break any object into one or more of these different shapes.

Before we get on with the tutorials, it will help you to see how the different types of mapping look on different shapes. It is important to note that the results of the various types of mapping also vary depending on which axis you orient the mapping to. With that in mind, the examples shown in Figures 13.1 through 13.3 show objects oriented as they would normally appear: top up, bottom down, and with front facing toward the viewer at a slight angle.

Figure 13.1 shows how a sphere looks when mapped with each of the different mapping types. In this example, both spherical (top left) and cylindrical (bottom right) mapping do an adequate job of mapping the sphere with minimal distortion. On the other hand, planar mapping (top right) creates distortion on the sides, and box mapping (bottom left) creates too many seams.

In Figure 13.2, you see a cube that is mapped with the various mapping types. The most natural choice for a cube is box mapping, shown at the bottom left. Spherical mapping (top left) distorts the map on all sides, and cylindrical mapping (bottom right) distorts the top and bottom. Planar mapping would map opposite sides perfectly, though the back side would be mirrored when it faced the camera, and the remaining four sides would be distorted. You *can* map each individual side of a box with planar mapping, but you would have to change the orientation of the planar map for each side. Box mapping does this for you automatically.

FIGURE 13.1 A sphere is usually mapped with spherical UVs (top left); remaining shots show planar (top right), box (bottom left), and cylindrical mapping (bottom right) on the sphere.

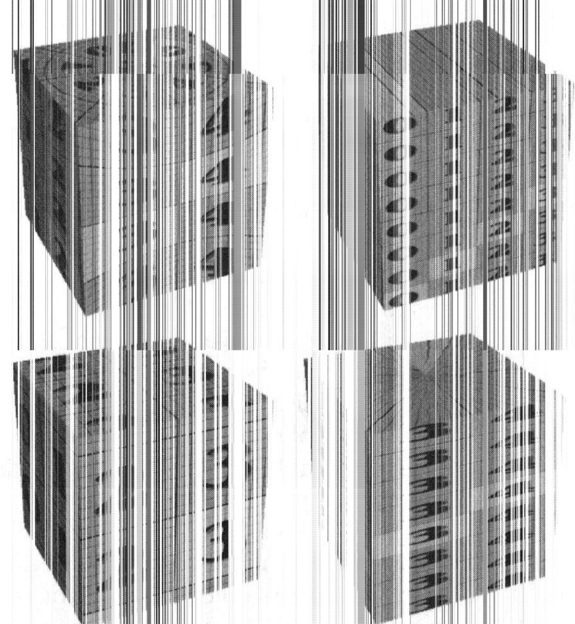

FIGURE 13.2 A box is usually mapped with six-sided box UVs (bottom left); remaining shots show the effects of spherical (top left), planar (top right), and cylindrical mapping (bottom right).

Figure 13.3 shows how the various types of mapping affect something that is cylindrical in shape. The natural choice is cylindrical (bottom right) if the object is open at either end. If closed at both ends, as a can of soup would be before you opened it, some UV-mapping programs give you the option to include the end caps in the UV map. In that case, the end caps would be mapped in flat, or planar, mode.

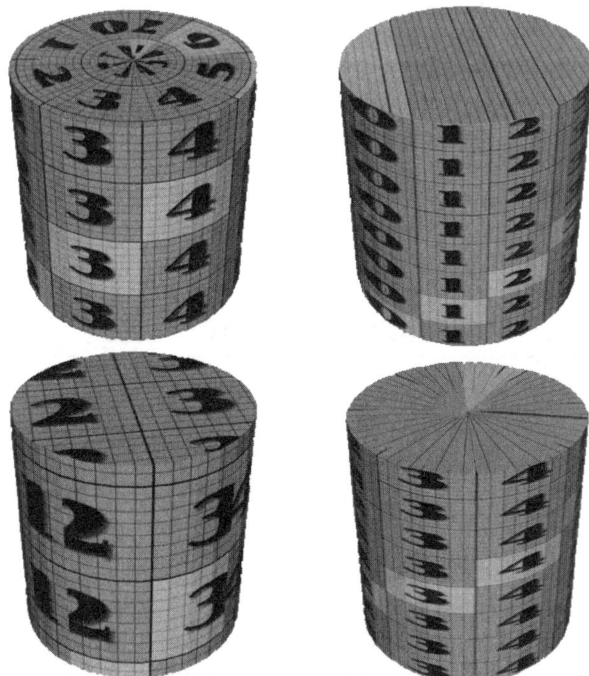

FIGURE 13.3 While cylindrical mapping (bottom right) is a logical choice for objects that are cylindrically shaped, spherical mapping (top left) also works very well.

Continuing with our cylinder examples, note that spherical mapping (top left in Figure 13.3) can also be used to successfully map a cylinder. The tops and bottoms of the cylinder will be mapped so that the texture meets in the center of the flat plane. Planar mapping (top right) will cause distortion at the sides and top, and box mapping (bottom left) will create unwanted seams.

With the basics out of the way, let's take a look at how you can actually apply this information. You'll use UV Mapper Professional (*http://www.uvmapper.com*), a demo of which is included in the Demos > UV Mapper folder on the CD-ROM that accompanies this book. Note that

ON THE CD

you won't be able to save your models with the demo version, so we've included a mapped version of the models on the CD-ROM to show you the final results.

USING UV MAPPER PROFESSIONAL

UV Mapper Professional, written by Steve Cox, is a utility that Poser enthusiasts use quite frequently to create UV maps and texture templates for their 3D models. UV Mapper Professional contains many features that are found in more advanced mapping utilities, yet the price is very reasonable. A free version, UV Mapper Classic, is also available. You can use the free version of UV Mapper Classic to create UV maps or templates, but you won't have the advanced selection modes or relaxing features that are available in the Pro version.

We'll start with something simple and basic: a skirt.

TUTORIAL 13.1 UV-MAPPING A SKIRT

Think about the main types of mapping that you have: spherical, planar, box, and cylindrical. (UV Mapper also creates *polar mapping*, but the needs for this type of mapping aren't as common as the others). Of these types of shapes, a skirt most closely resembles a cylinder.

To map a skirt with UV Mapper, follow these steps:

ON THE CD

1. Open UV Mapper Professional. Choose File > Open Model, and locate the Tutorials > Chap13 folder on the CD-ROM that accompanies this book. Choose skirt.obj and click Open.
2. UV Mapper displays the statistics of the object. Click OK to continue. A 3D version of the skirt appears in the perspective view on the right side of the screen. Initially, the left side is blank, indicating that the object does not have any UV information.
3. Choose Texture > Checker > Color. This puts a checkered pattern with numbers in the left Texture display. This helps you position objects so that seams match and also helps you determine if the texture map is facing in the right direction.
4. Since the skirt most resembles a cylinder in shape, choose Map > Cylindrical. The Cylindrical Mapping dialog shown in Figure 13.4 appears.
5. In the case of the skirt, we would like the UV mapping to map the skirt along the Y (up/down) axis, which is selected by default. Also note the Seam Rotation setting. When set at 0, the seam appears in the back of the garment, which is what you want. Accept the remaining default settings, and click OK.

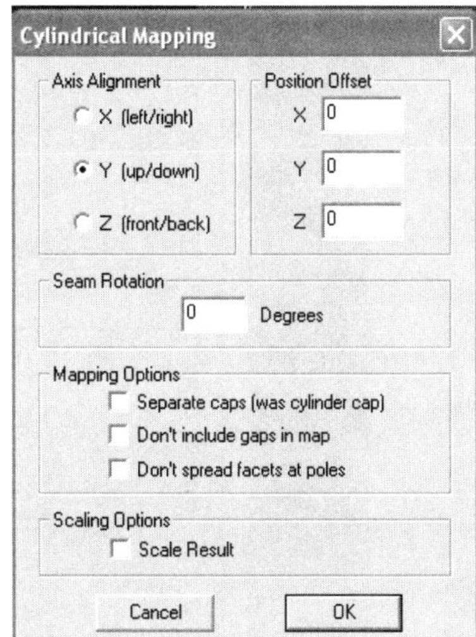

FIGURE 13.4 The Cylindrical Mapping dialog contains settings to help map objects that are cylindrical in shape.

6. Observe the left and right sides of the UV map. You may notice that the seam didn't break evenly along the same line of polygons. One way that you can fix this is to select polygons from one side, and move them to the other. You'll find it easier to perform this task if you turn the checkered texture off, so choose Texture > Clear. Answer YES when UV Mapper asks if you really want to clear the background.
7. Use the Magnifier tool and the Hand tool to move in closer to the left side of the texture area.
8. With the Selection tool, select the polygons that you want to move to the other side of the skirt. Figure 13.5 shows the polygons selected.
9. Pick the Hand tool and pan the Texture view down to see the remaining polygons if you couldn't get them all in the first round. Shift-click to add the additional polygons to the selection if necessary. You can also Alt-click to remove polygons from the selection.
10. Use the magnifier to zoom out until you can see the entire texture again. Or, use the View > Reset View command.
11. Press the Shift key while you use the right arrow key to move the selected polygons to the right side. When the polygons get close to where you want them, use the right or left arrow keys (without pressing the Shift key) to nudge them in place one pixel at a time. If necessary,

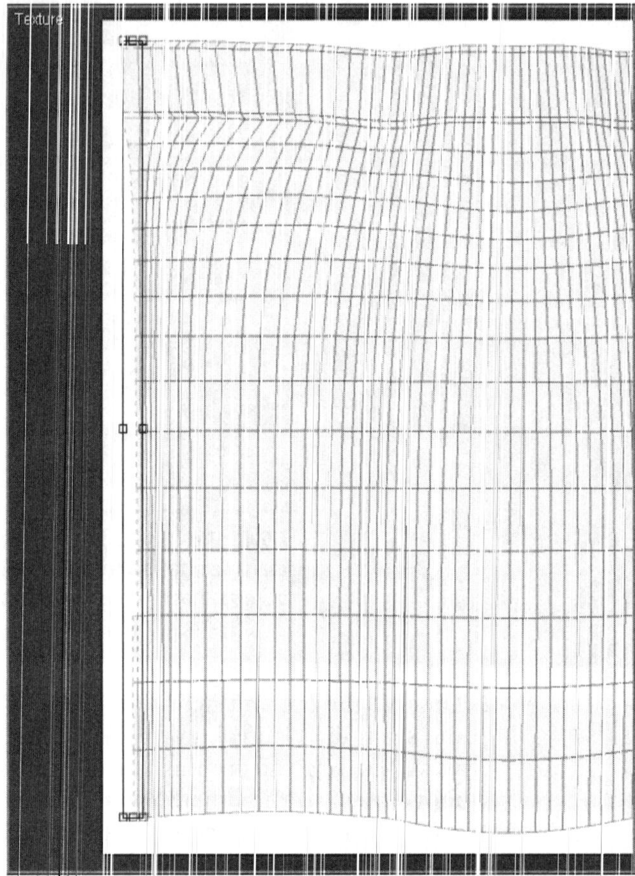

FIGURE 13.5 A portion of the polygons are selected. These polygons will move to the other side of the skirt.

zoom in closer with the Magnifier tool to position them immediately next to the existing polygons. Figure 13.6 shows proper placement.

12. To stitch the moved polygons back into the skirt, you need to switch to Vertex selection mode. To do so, choose Select > Select Method > By Vertex.
13. Zoom out until you see the entire right side of the skirt. Use the Rectangular Selection tool to draw a selection around the polygons on the right side, making sure that you enclose all of the polygons you moved plus some additional for good measure. The selected vertices turn red.

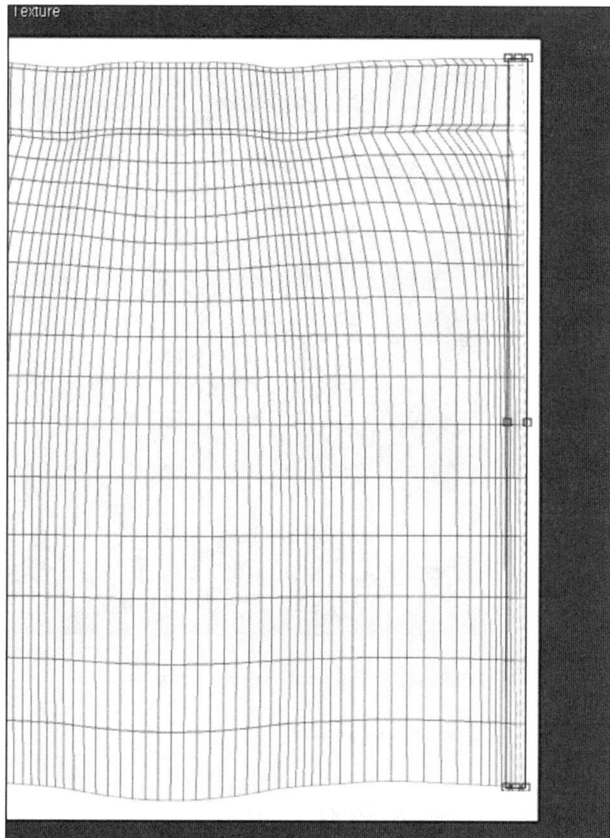

FIGURE 13.6 Place the polygons immediately adjacent to those on the other side.

14. To stitch them together, choose Tools > UVs > Stitch. When UV Mapper asks if you really want to stitch the vertices together, choose YES.
15. If desired, choose Texture > Checker > Color to view the final result before you save the new skirt. (Note that you cannot save with the demo version of UV Mapper Professional.)
16. If you have the full version of UV Mapper Professional, choose File > Save Model. Leave all options unchecked, and choose OK to save the model with its UV information. A mapped version of the skirt appears on the CD-ROM in Tutorials > Chapter 13 as skirt-mapped.obj. Figure 13.7 shows the final result of the UV maps.

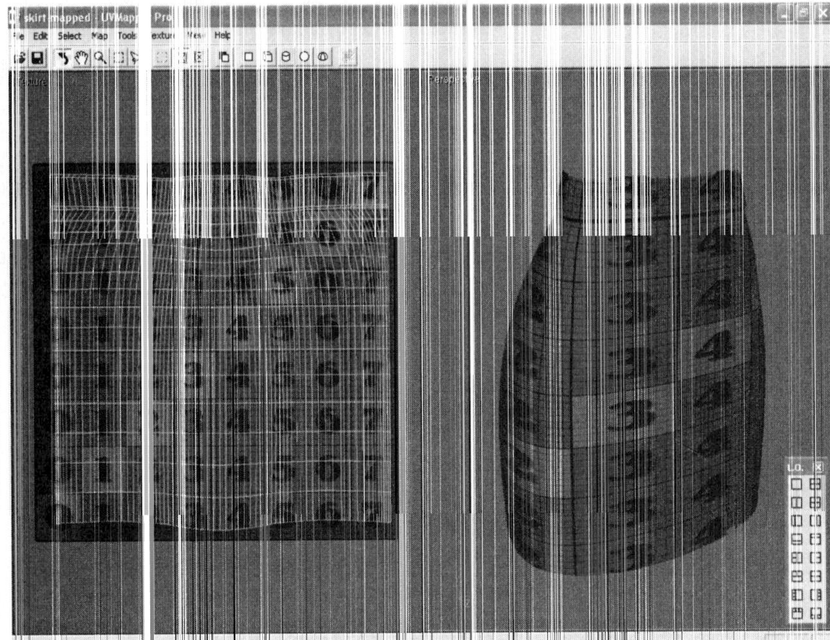

FIGURE 13.7 The final map for the skirt.

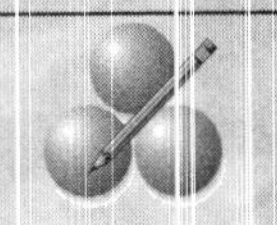

TUTORIAL 13.2 UV-MAPPING PANTS

Pants are a little more complicated to map than a skirt, but the process will teach you how to look at an object and break it into separate elements to map it properly.

When you look at a pair of pants, you basically see two separate cylinders that are joined together at the top, in the center. That is also the best way to approach the mapping. First, you divide it in half, with one cylinder in each half. Then you unfold each of the cylinders to flatten them. Finally, you stitch the two cylinders back together again.

To create UV maps for pants in UV Mapper Professional, follow these steps:

1. Open UV Mapper Professional. Choose File > Open Model, and locate the Tutorials > Chap13 folder on the CD-ROM that accompanies this book. Choose pants.obj and click Open.
2. UV Mapper displays the statistics of the object. Click OK to continue. A 3D version of the pants appears in the perspective view on the right side of the screen. Initially, the left side is blank, indicating that the object does not have any UV information.

3. Turn off the display of the background texture. It will help you see things more easily until you get to the final stage. To do so, choose Texture > Clear.
4. The best way to start with pants is to first map them in planar mode without separating the front and back. To do so, choose Map > Planar. The Planar Mapping dialog appears.
5. By default, UV Mapper Professional does planar mapping on the Z Axis, and By Orientation. These two options, together, split the clothing article between the front and back sides. We don't want to split the clothing right now, so choose Don't Split, as shown in Figure 13.8. Click OK to continue.

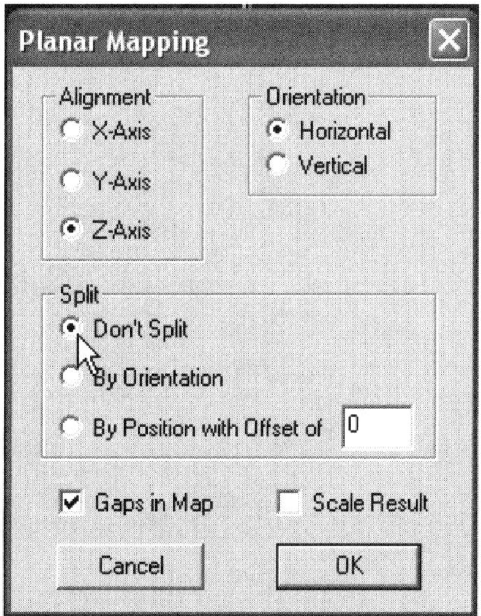

FIGURE 13.8 Don't split the pants when you begin to map them.

6. If you are continuing from the previous tutorial, you'll need to return to Facet selection mode. To do so, choose Select > Select Method > By Facet.
7. With the rectangular selection tool, select the entire left side of the pants to the center seam. Make sure that you select all of the polygons on the inside of the leg. The easiest way to do this is to start with the selection on the left side of the pants, and drag to the center until the selection box is exactly over the center line of the pants.
8. With the selection still active, choose Map > Cylindrical. The Cylindrical Mapping dialog appears. Accept the default for Y (up/down) Axis Alignment, and continue with the next step.

9. By default, cylindrical mapping places the seam toward the back when you are mapping to the Y axis. We want the seam to fall on the inside of the leg. To do this, enter "90 degrees" in the Seam Rotation field. Then click OK to exit the dialog. UV Mapper Professional maps the pants leg in a cylindrical fashion.
10. You'll notice that some of the facets in the bottom of the leg are flipped around the wrong way and create a tear in the leg. To fix that, use the Polygonal Selection tool to select the lower half of the pants, making sure that you start the selection above where the distortion begins. An example is shown in Figure 13.9.

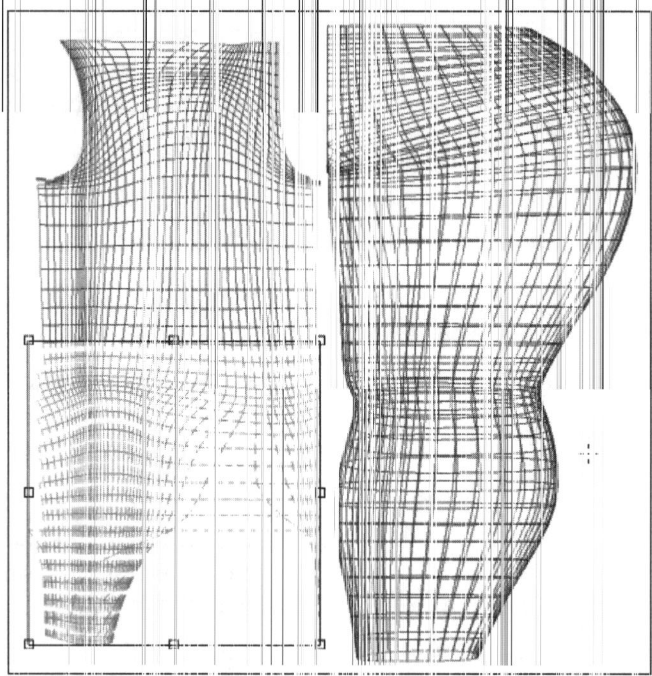

FIGURE 13.9 Select the lower portion of the pants to fix the distortions.

11. With the selection of the lower half of the pants leg in its original position, choose Map > Cylindrical again. The settings should remain from the previous time you used it. Click OK to exit the dialog.
12. Now, choose Vertex selection mode (Select > Select Method > By Vertex). Make a selection that includes the area where you broke the connection between the upper and lower portions of the pants, as

shown in Figure 13.10. Then stitch them together (Tools > UVs > Stitch). Select the other half and stitch them together as well.

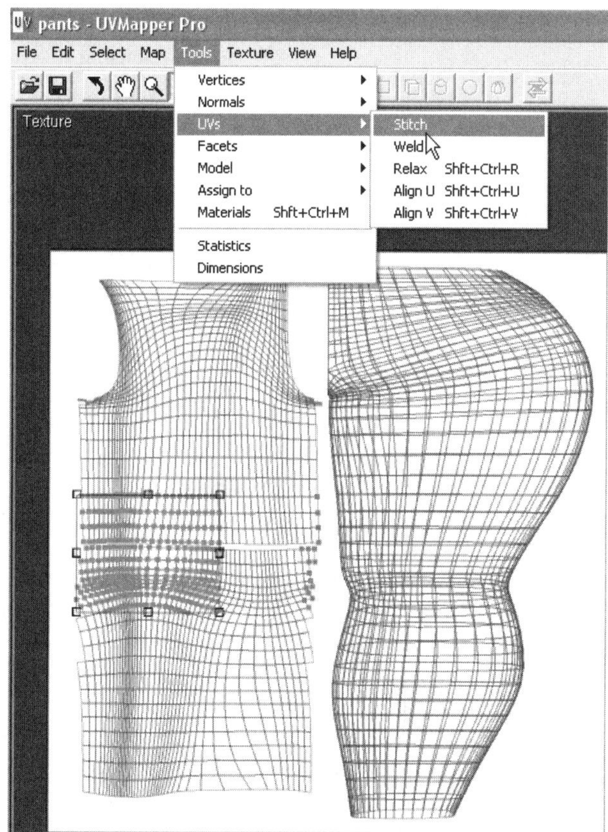

FIGURE 13.10 After remapping the lower portion, stitch the upper and lower leg back together, one half at a time.

If you select the entire width of the leg to stitch the vertices together, UV Mapper will stitch them together at the seam. This makes the UV map hard to read. Selecting half at a time prevents this from occurring.

13. Now, return to Facet selection mode (Select > Select Method > By Facet). Select the other leg, and choose Map > Cylindrical again. This time, enter "270 degrees" in the Seam Rotation field so that the seam appears on the inside of this leg. Then choose OK.
14. Remap and stitch the lower portion as you did in Steps 10 through 12. If the width of the lower section is different than that of the upper

section after you remap it, drag the selection from any side to resize them to match the upper section. Then stitch them together, one half at a time, in Vertex selection mode. The final result should look similar to Figure 13.11.

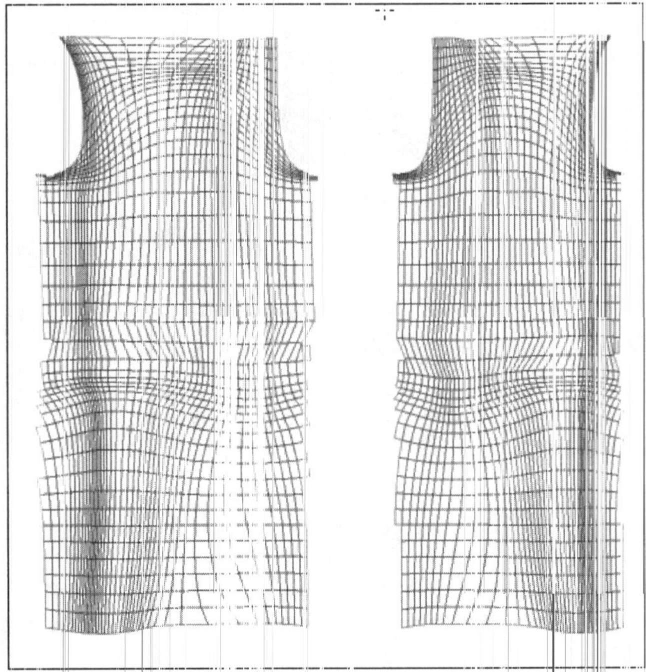

FIGURE 13.11 Both sides of the pants are mapped in cylindrical fashion.

15. The final problem that we have to tackle is cleaning up the seams so that the break falls along the same column of polygons. First, switch back to Facet selection mode (Select > Select Method > By Facet).
16. Let's add a little more space between the two sections of pants. Select the left half, and hold the Shift key while using the left arrow key once or twice to move the section toward the left edge of the work area.
17. Use the Polygon Selection tool to click just above the first two rows of polygons on the left side of the pants. As you work your way down, remain in the same column of polygons while you follow it down to the bottom of the pants. Then click outside of the selection to work your way back up to the top, as shown in Figure 13.12. Double-click the Polygon tool to end the selection.

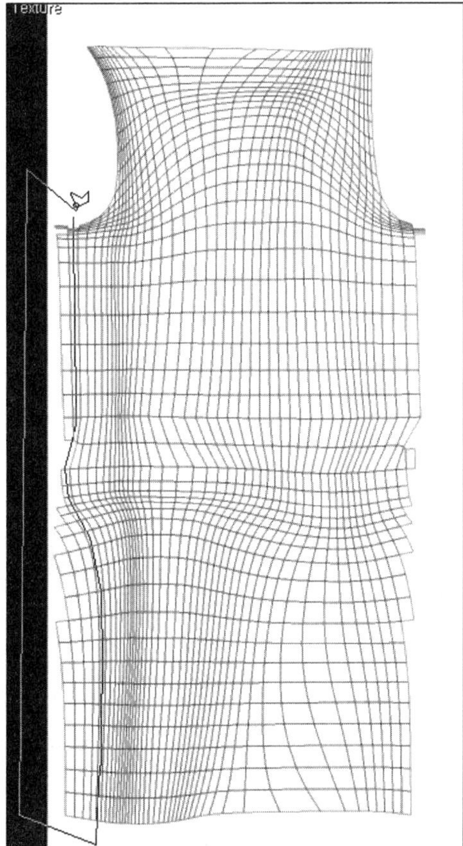

FIGURE 13.12 Select the polygons that you want to move to the other side of the pants leg.

18. Press the Shift key while you use the right arrow to move the selected polygons to the other side of the pants leg. When you get close to the target spot, release the Shift key and use only the arrow key to nudge the selection into place. Position them as close as you can without overlapping any of the polygons (note that some may not match up exactly, this is okay).
19. Switch to Vertex selection mode (Select > Select Method > By Vertex). Use the Selection tool to make a selection large enough to enclose the polygons you moved and the polygons you want to attach them to.
20. Choose Tools > UVs > Stitch. Answer YES to the confirmation dialog.

21. Repeat Steps 15 through 20 for the other leg, except that you will move polygons from the right side of the leg to the left side. When you are finished, both legs should look as shown in Figure 13.13.

If your legs are different sizes, select one of the legs with the Rectangular Selection tool, and drag the left or right side to change the width accordingly.

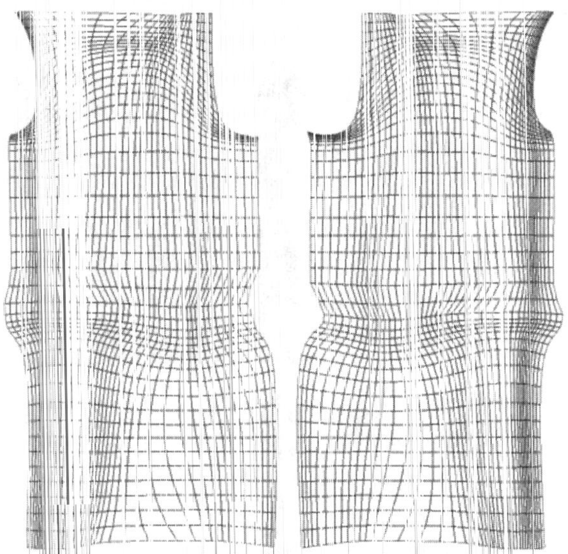

FIGURE 13.13 Both legs are now cleaned up and stitched.

22. Choose Texture > Checker > Color to check the final result in the mapping. A final version appears on the CD-ROM in Tutorials > Ch. 13 as "pants-mapped.obj" if you are unable to save your model with the demo version.

If desired, you can use UV Mapper Professional's Relax feature to even out the spacing between the polygons. To do so, first choose Edge selection mode (Select > Select Method > By Edge). Select both sections of pants, and the edge vertices should turn blue. Then choose Tools > UVs > Relax. Leave the settings at their defaults, and click the Apply button one or more times until you are satisfied with the results. Watch the checkerboard texture on the 3D Preview while you relax the vertices.

TUTORIAL 13.3 UV-MAPPING A SHIRT

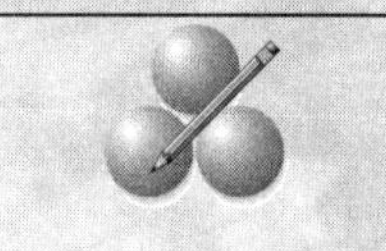

Shirts present a little bit of a challenge to those who are new to UV mapping, so it helps to know the right technique. Basically, the best way to UV-map a shirt is with a combination of planar and cylindrical mapping.

When you UV-map more complex objects, it makes the most sense to split the clothing object up into parts where seams would occur in a real garment. In other words, you should separate the sleeves from the torso of the shirt; and you should also separate the front from the back. This helps flatten the shirt more easily.

To UV-map a shirt in UV Mapper Professional, follow these steps:

ON THE CD

1. Open UV Mapper Professional. Choose File > Open Model, and locate the Tutorials > Chap13 folder on the CD-ROM that accompanies this book. Choose tshirt.obj and click Open.
2. UV Mapper displays the statistics of the object. Click OK to continue. A 3D version of the shirt appears in the perspective view on the right side of the screen. Initially, the left side is blank, indicating that the object does not have any UV information.
3. If necessary, remove the checkerboard background from the Texture view (Texture > Clear). Also verify that you are in Facet selection mode (Select > Select Method > By Facet).
4. To begin, we will planar-map the shirt so that we can remove the sleeves and map them separately. Choose Map > Planar. When the Planar Mapping dialog appears, choose Z-Axis (which divides the shirt into front and back), and By Orientation (which splits the sides, so that front appears on the left and back appears on the right). Then click OK to create the map.
5. Now use the rectangular selection tool to select the first row of polygons for each sleeve in both views, using Shift-click to add additional selections to the set. Your selection should look as shown in Figure 13.14.
6. Press the zero (0) key on your keyboard. This expands the selection by one row of polygons. Press nine additional times until you have selected all of the vertices in the sleeves.
7. Position the cursor inside the selection area, so that the selection tool changes into an arrow. Drag the sleeve polygons above the work area temporarily.
8. Now, select both sections of the shirt, and choose Map > Cylindrical. Accept the default of Y (up/down). All other options are not checked or set to zero. Click OK to map the shirt.
9. You can easily leave the shirt this way, but for one reason that will become obvious if you turn on the Color texture checker(Texture > Checker > Color). The polygons distort the mapping at the top of the shoulders. This is because they are too close together. However, it's a

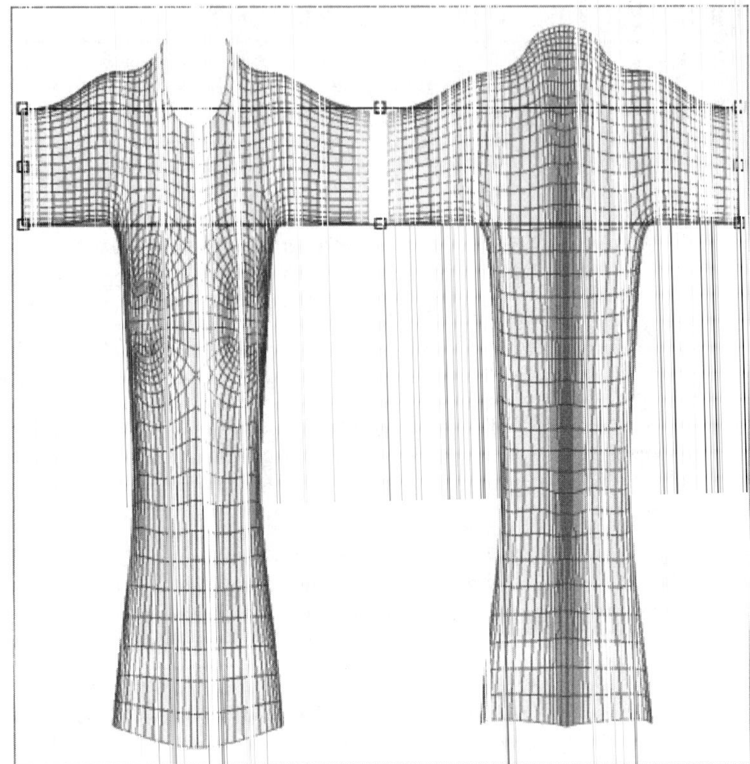

FIGURE 13.14 The first row of vertices is selected in all sleeves.

lot easier to select the front of the shirt while the shirt is in cylindrical mode. Use the Polygonal Selection tool to select the front portion of the shirt, dividing it along the center of each armhole. Figure 13.15 shows an example of the selection.

If necessary, you can also select polygons in the 3D-perspective view. Use the rectangular Selection tool, and Shift-click to add polygons to the existing selection. You only need to include a small portion of the polygon to add it to the selection. If you mistakenly add polygons to the selection that you do not want, Alt-click to remove them from the selection.

10. With the front of the shirt selected, choose Map > Planar. Choose Don't Split to prevent UV Mapper Professional from separating the side polygons into the back section of the shirt.

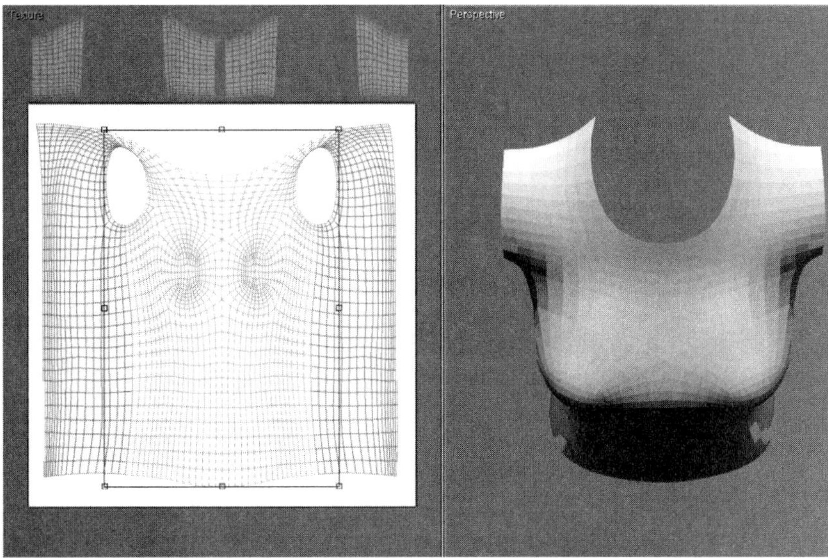

FIGURE 13.15 Select the front of the shirt, dividing the top and bottom of the armhole at the halfway point.

11. Press the slash (/) key on your number pad to halve the size of the front of the shirt, so that you have more room to work on the other two sections.
12. Select one of the back sections and choose Map > Planar. Accept the previous settings and choose OK. Divide it in half with the / key on the number pad. Then select the entire section, and choose Select > Rotate > Flip Horizontal so that the side with the sleeve opening faces the front sleeve opening.
13. Repeat Step 12 for the other back section.
14. Select one section at a time and move them in closer together if necessary. Space and size the three sections similar to those shown in Figure 13.16. You can also move the sleeves back on to the work area now.
15. Change to Vertex selection mode (Select > Select Method > By Vertex). Use the Rectangular Selection tool to enclose the vertices between the left side and the front of the shirt, starting from the underarm and continuing to the bottom. Then choose Tools > UVs > Stitch to join them.
16. Similarly, enclose the vertices between the right side and the front of the shirt. Then choose Tools > UVs > Stitch to join them. The result should look as shown in Figure 13.17.

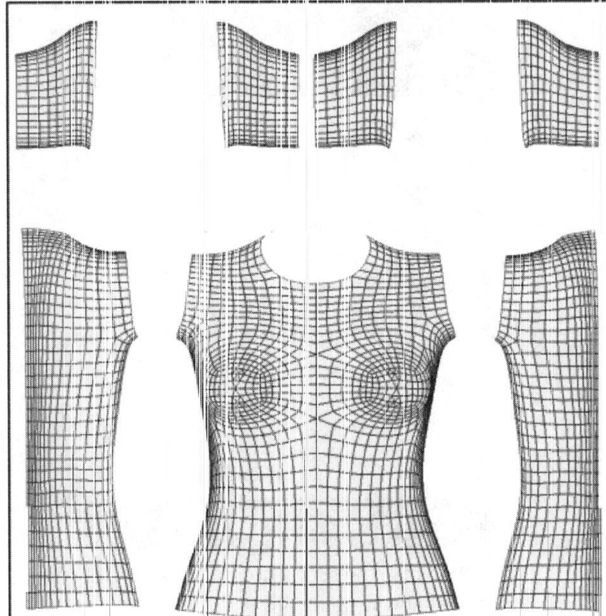

FIGURE 13.16 Scale and position the three sections of the shirt at the bottom of the UV map area.

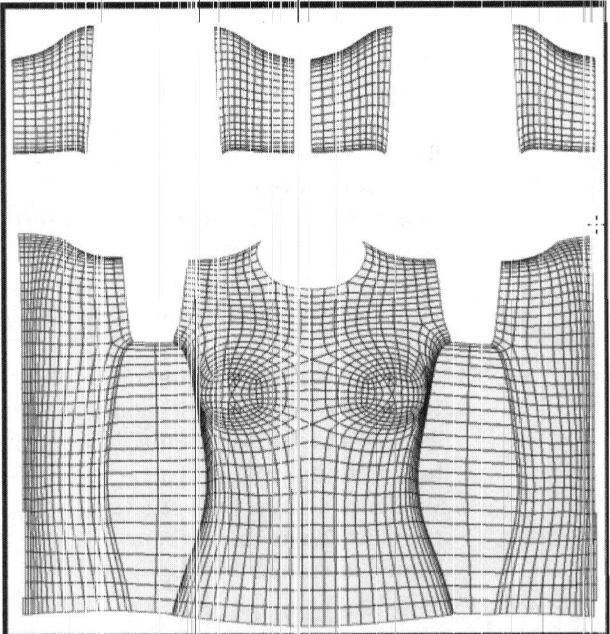

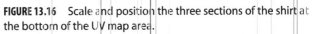

FIGURE 13.17 Stitch the front and sides together at the seams.

17. If you turn on the Color texture checker at this point (Texture > Checker > Color), you'll see that the sides look very distorted. This will result in stretching with any texture you apply to the shirt. UV Mapper Professional allows you to relax vertices to eliminate stretching. But first, we have to hide the parts that we don't want to relax. After you return to Facet selection mode (Select > Select Method > By Facet), select the sleeves. Then press the left square bracket ([ ) key to hide them.
18. Choose Edge selection mode (Select > Select Method > By Edge). Draw a selection around all three shirt sections. The outer vertices will turn blue, indicating that they are selected.
19. Choose Tools > UVs > Relax. When the Relax UVs dialog appears, accept the default choices. Click the Apply button one or more times, while watching the texture change in the perspective window. Choose OK to apply the changes when you are satisfied with the mapping on the sides of the shirt. Figure 13.18 shows the result.

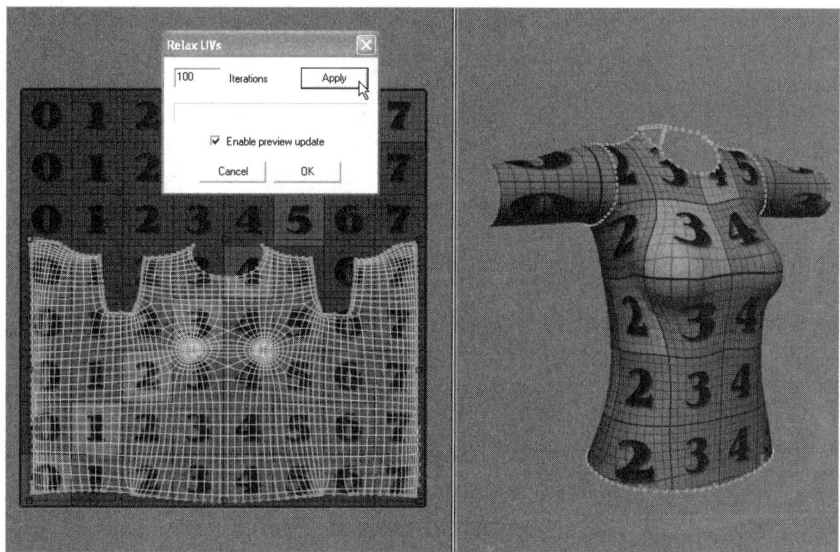

FIGURE 13.18 Relax the UV mapping until you are satisfied with the appearance of the sides of the shirt.

20. Return to Facet selection mode (Select > Select Method > By Facet). Press the right square bracket key ( ]) to unhide the sleeves. We need to join them at the top. First, select the two sleeves at the left of the screen (the front sleeves). Choose Select > Rotate > 180 degrees to rotate them so that they match up properly with the appropriate sleeve back. Then position the sleeve fronts above the sleeve backs.

21. Switch to Vertex selection mode (Select > Select Method > By Vertex) and draw a selection that encloses the vertices you want to join on the sleeves. Then choose Tools > UVs > Stitch to connect them. Figure 13.19 shows the result.

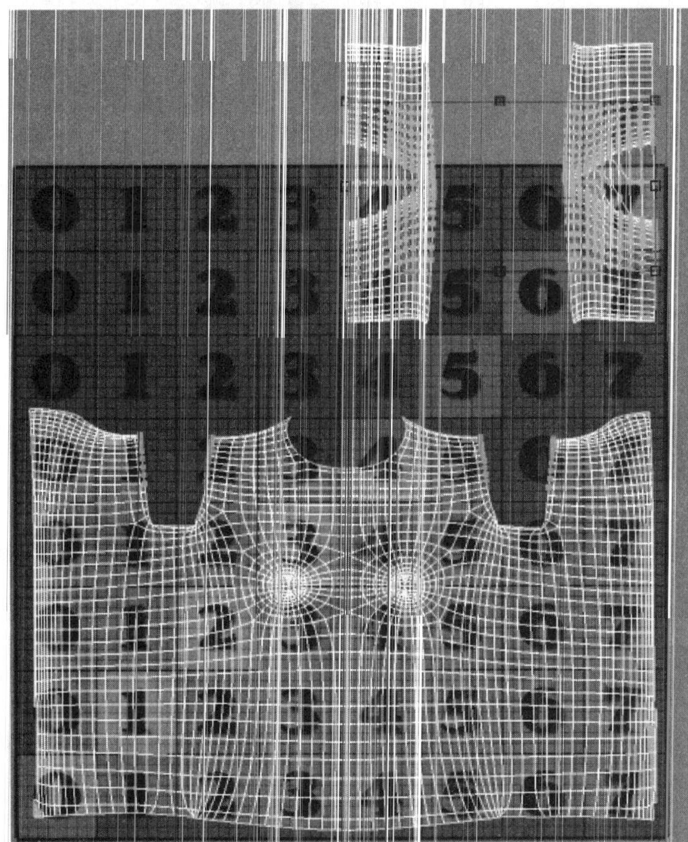

FIGURE 13.19 The sleeves are joined at the top.

22. The final step is to relax the sleeves and position them in their final place on the map. Make sure you hide the front of the shirt first to prevent it from relaxing further. First, return to Facet selection mode (Select > Select Method > By Facet). Select the front and back of the shirt and hide it with the [key.
23. Return to Edge selection mode (Select > Select Method > By Edge). Select both sleeves. Then use the Relax feature (Tools > UVs > Relax), clicking the Apply button one or more times until the top edges are blended better.

24. Press] to unhide the remainder of the shirt. Return to Facet selection mode, and then rotate and position the sleeves with the Select > Rotate command, and position them as shown in Figure 13.20.

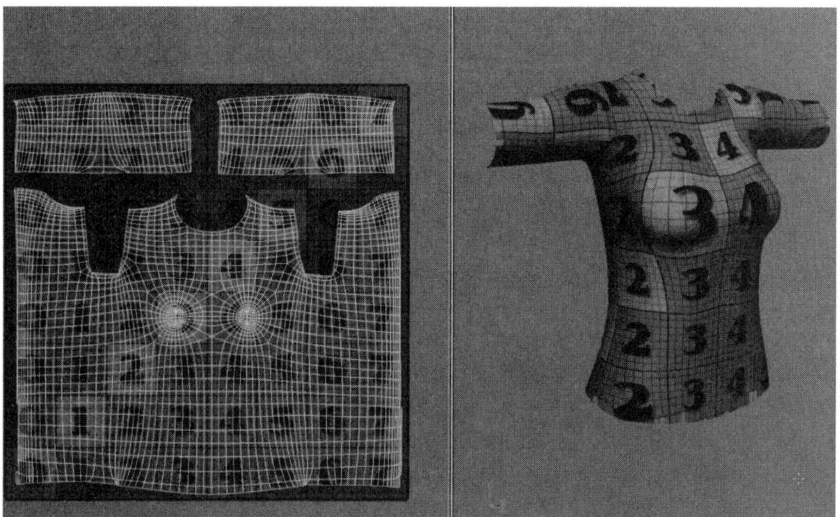

FIGURE 13.20 The finished shirt.

MAKING TEMPLATES

After you get your models UV-mapped and saved, it makes sense to make a *texture template* for it. You can use these texture templates as a guide to create textures for your models.

UV Mapper Professional colors the template based on the way it is displayed in the Texture preview. By default, the template is black and white (white background with black lines). You can also color the templates based on how they are assigned by Material, Group, or Region. For example, if your object is made of different materials, and you want to represent the materials with different colors in your template, choose Map > Color > By Material. You can also color the map by Group (such as the body part groups that you use in Poser), or by Region (for example, if you want to save the items on the head as one region, and the remainder of the body as another region). You'll learn more about assigning groups and materials in Chapter 14, "Assigning Groups and Materials."

It's fairly easy to save a template. After you save your model, just choose File > Save Template. The BMP Export Options dialog shown in Figure 13.21 appears.

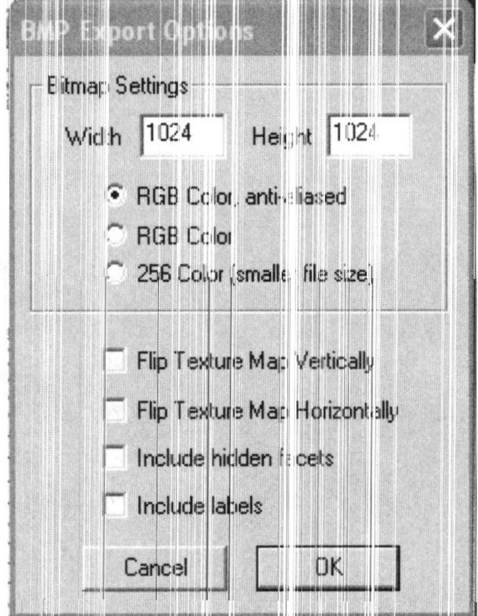

FIGURE 13.21 The options in the BMP Export Options dialog allow you to save a bitmap template of your UV map.

The options in the BMP Export dialog are as follows:

Width and Height: Enter the desired width and height for the template. While the dimensions do not have to be square, many programs (including Poser) use resources more efficiently when textures are 512, 1024, 2048, or 4096 pixels in width and height.

RGB Color, anti-aliased: Choose this option if you want your template to be recognized as a high-color or true-color image, with antialiased edges to smooth jagged edges on diagonal lines.

RGB Color: Choose this for full-color templates that are not antialiased.

256 Color: Choose this option to create a 256-color image that creates a smaller file size.

Even though you can create high-color or 256-color images for your templates, you'll find that the template only contains 16 colors. The color selections listed above determine how your image editor sees the template.

Flip Texture Map Vertically: Check this option to flip the texture vertically (up and down).

Flip Texture Map Horizontally: Check this option to flip the texture map horizontally (right to left).

Include Hidden Facets: When checked, also includes any facets that might be hidden from view by using the [key. This is handy when you need to create templates for models that require two or more texture maps.

Include Labels: If your texture map is colored by group, material, or region, you can include labels on the texture map that show the names of the groups, materials, or regions by their color.

After you make your selections, click OK to create the texture map. You can then open the map in an image editor, such as Photoshop, to paint a texture using the map as a guide.

CONCLUSION

UV mapping is a very important process in creating a good 3D model. When care is taken in UV mapping you can eliminate stretching and distortion that might occur in areas of a model. By breaking objects down into their basic shapes (spheres, planes, boxes, or cylinders) you can map complex objects with care and precision. In the next chapter, you will learn how to assign groups and materials to your objects to prepare them for importing into Poser.

CHAPTER

14

ASSIGNING GROUPS AND MATERIALS

In This Chapter

- About Group Names
- Decompressing an OBZ File
- Conclusion

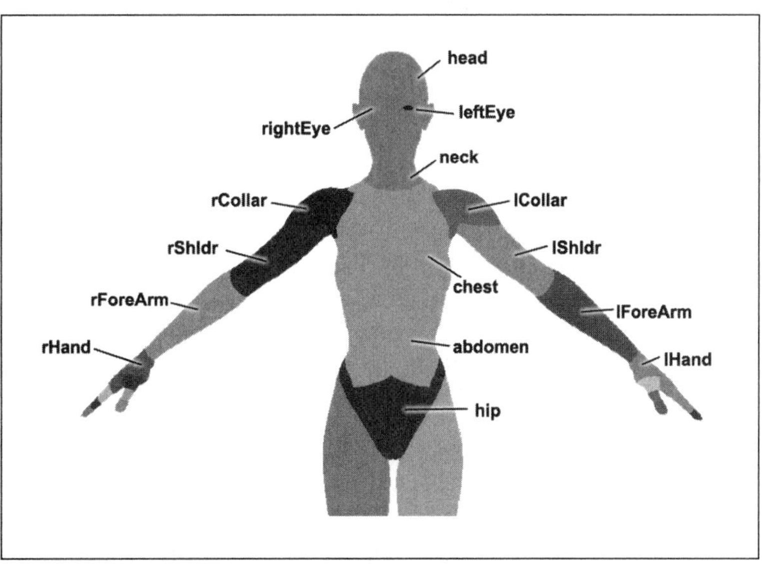

As you learned in the previous chapter, in order to make a model capable of having textures applied to it, you must create a UV map for the object. The UV map determines how the colors on a flat image are applied onto a three-dimensional model.

Once you create the UV map, you can assign one or more different materials to the model. For example, let's say you created a floor-length skirt for Jessi. You can select polygons from the waist to mini-skirt level and assign them to a material named "Mini." Select the polygons that start from the bottom of the Mini material and that fall to knee-length. Call the new material "Knee." Continuing on, you select polygons from knee level to midcalf length, and call the new material "Midi." Finally, take the last set of polygons from Midi to the floor and call the new material "Full." By dividing the skirt into several materials, you can make one or more layers invisible to vary the length of the skirt.

In addition, when you model clothing, you'll need to know ahead of time whether you want the clothing to be dynamic clothing (for the Cloth Room) or conforming clothing that poses automatically with your figure. If you decide to make conforming clothing, you will need to divide your clothing model into body part groups that coincide with the groups in your human figure. This chapter shows you how to use three different programs to assign groups and materials.

Most 3D-modeling programs allow you to assign materials and groups to 3D objects during the modeling process, and it is generally easiest to perform these tasks at that time. If you have obtained models that need groups or materials assigned or prefer to use other methods to accomplish these tasks, this chapter will introduce you to alternatives that you can use.

About Group Names

If you are creating dynamic clothing, you do not need to create predefined polygon groups. Instead, you use the Group Editor in the Cloth Room to assign vertices to one or more cloth groups. This process is explained in detail in Chapter 10 of the *Poser 6 Tutorial Manual.*

Conforming clothing, on the other hand, works much differently. In order for conforming clothing to conform to a human figure, you have to divide the clothing model into body part groups that coincide with those on the model that they cover. For example, if you are creating a shirt you'll probably need to create groups such as *chest, abdomen, lCollar, rCollar, lShldr,* and *rShldr* (the latter four being the required names for left and right collars and shoulders). The polygons in the clothing groups should be named the same and match the area of the corresponding polygons in the figure's groups as closely as possible.

The group names that you normally see for human figures in Poser 6 menus and lists have names such as *Left Forearm, Right Collar,* and *Left Shoulder*. However, there are also shorter *internal* group names that Poser references in its CR2 character library files. Internal group names can contain capital letters, but they must *always* begin with a small letter in order to work properly. You can see a group's internal name when you click a body part and view the associated properties in the Properties panel. For an example, you see James' Right Collar in Figure 14.1, where it has an internal name of *rCollar*.

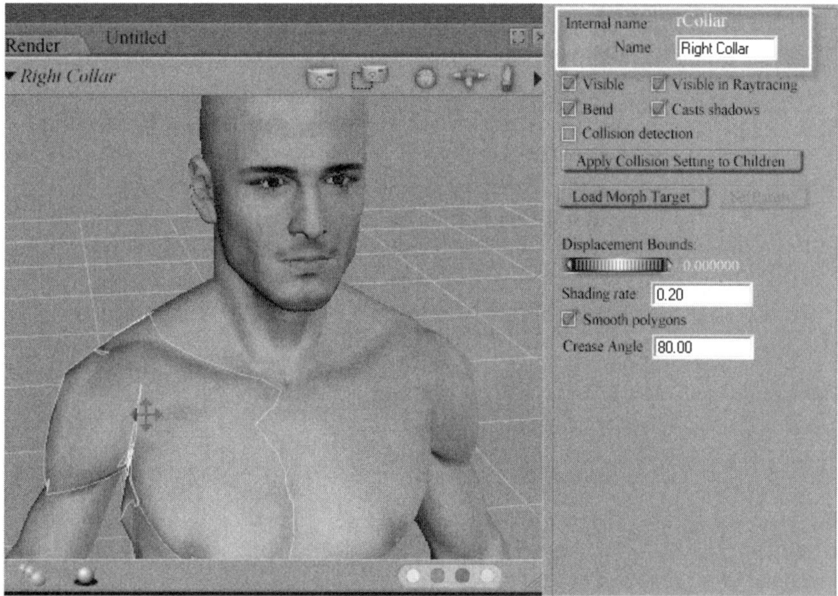

FIGURE 14.1 Each body part has an internal name that is referenced by Poser.

In order for conforming clothing to automatically pose the same as the figure that wears it, you have to create groups in the clothing that are named exactly the same as those in the figure. For the most part, all Poser figures use similar group names. There are minor exceptions, which will be mentioned when applicable.

It is important to understand how the polygons in a standard Poser figure are grouped. Just as the center of gravity of your own body is found at hip-level, the same is true of a Poser human figure. The hip is the central part of the figure and the point at which all of the hierarchical chains begin. The hip is the first *parent* in the hierarchy.

As you work your way from the hip to the feet, each subsequent level is a *child* of the body part that preceded it. For example, the hip is the parent of the thigh, which in turn is the parent of the shin, which is in turn the parent of the foot. Working your way backward up the chain, the left foot is a child of the left shin, which is in turn a child of the left thigh, which is in turn a child of the hip.

Figure 14.2 shows internal group names for Jessi. All Poser 6 figures use the same grouping that Jessi uses. Starting with the hierarchical chain that runs from the hip to the head and eyes, the internal group names are hip, abdomen, chest, neck, and head. The rightEye and leftEye parts are both children of the head. Other figures may have a second neck part, named "upperNeck," which falls between the neck and head. There are sometimes differences in the way that the chest and collar sections are grouped. In the Poser 6 figures, the chest contains the breasts. In other figures, you may see the breasts as part of the right and left collar sections.

The right and left collar and arm sections connect from the chest. Each arm has parts with similar internal names, except that the internal names for the right arm parts begin with a small 'r', and the left arm parts begin with a small 'l'. Starting from the chest and working downward, the right arm group names are rCollar, rShldr, rForeArm, and rHand. Left arm parts are named the same, with the exception of the 'l' prefix.

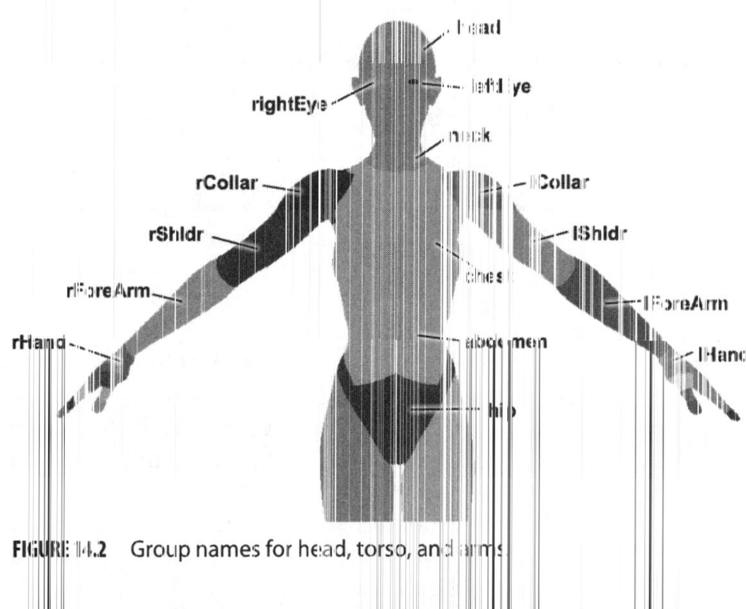

FIGURE 14.2 Group names for head, torso, and arms.

Finally, we reach the fingers, which are shown in Figure 14.3. Each hand branches out into five fingers, each of which is divided into three sections. The section closest to the base of the hand is number 1, the middle section number 2, and the last section (with the fingernail) is number 3. As for the names of the fingers, the right hand finger groups are named rThumb1, rThumb2, rThumb3, rIndex1, rIndex2, rIndex3, rMid1, rMid2, rMid3, rRing1, rRing2, rRing3, rPinky1, rPinky2, and rPinky3. The fingers on the left hand are named the same, with the exception that 'l' is the first letter instead of 'r'.

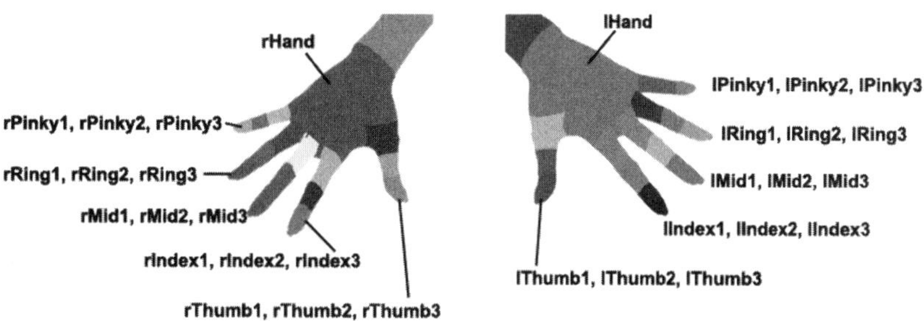

FIGURE 14.3 Left and right hand and finger group names.

The groups for the legs and feet of the Poser 6 figures are shown in Figure 14.4. Starting from the hip, the right leg is divided into rThigh, rShin, and rFoot. Other figures may also have a rButtock section that appears between the hip and the rThigh. Likewise, the parts on the left are similarly named, with the prefix being 'l' instead of 'r'.

Next, we come to the toes, where there are also differences between figures. The Poser 6 figures have articulated toes, meaning that each toe can be posed individually, just like the fingers in the hands. You will not find this feature in all Poser figures. When toes are not articulated, you will see groups in the right foot named rFoot and rToe; and groups in the left foot named lFoot and lToe. The toe sections move all five toes at the same time.

In the case of articulated toes, the rToe and lToe sections serve as a common first joint for all five toes—in other words, the rToe and lToe sections are equivalent to the ball of the human foot. From that point, each toe branches out into two joints apiece. For the right foot, these sections are named rBigToe1, rBigToe2, rIndexToe1, rIndexToe2, rMidToe1, rMidToe2, rRingToe1, rRingToe2, rPinkyToe1, and rPinkyToe2. As with the fingers, the toe closest to the common section is part number 1, and the part with the toenail is the highest numbered part (2, in this case). Left foot sections begin with an 'l' instead of 'r'.

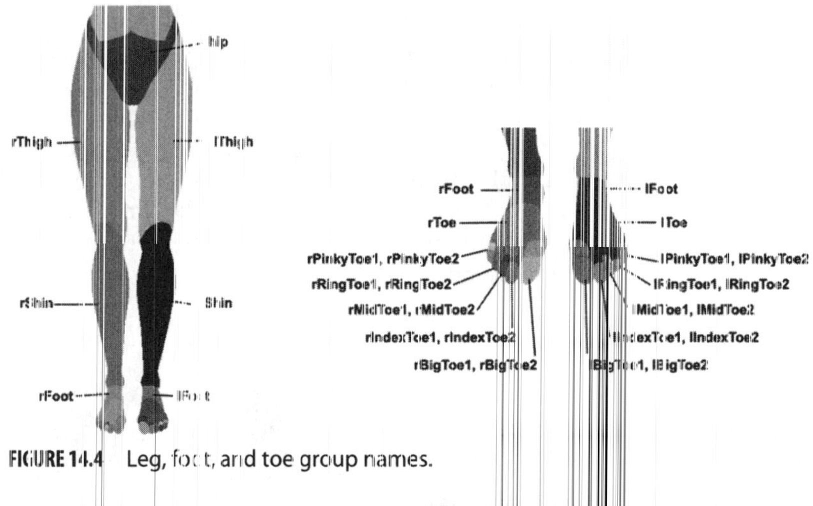

FIGURE 14.4 Leg, foot, and toe group names.

DECOMPRESSING AN OBZ FILE

In order to create groups in your clothing, it helps to view the model underneath your clothing at the same time. For example, if you know where the polygons for the *abdomen* fall on the human figure, you can select the polygons in your clothing that overlap that area and assign those polygons to the *abdomen* group in the clothing. This allows you to create the clothing groups more accurately. But because Poser 6 furnishes its figures in OBZ format (a compressed version of the OBJ file), you will need to decompress it before you import the model into any utility that imports OBJ files.

There are two ways to decompress an OBZ file into an OBJ file:

- Open the OBZ file in a utility that opens ZIP files, such as WinZip for the PC or its Mac equivalent. Then extract the OBJ file to a directory of your choice. Use this default model whenever you create or set up clothing or create morphs.
- Use the Python script furnished with Poser to decompress all compressed files in a specified folder. Choose Window > Python Scripts to open the Python Scripts window. From the Main menu, click the Utility Funcs button, and then the UnCompress Files button. A dialog prompts you to select the directory under which to decompress the files. Make sure you check the option to Uncompress geometry files (obj). Then click OK. Your OBJ file will be located in the same folder as the original OBZ file.

TUTORIAL 14.1 GROUPING WITH AUTO GROUP EDITOR

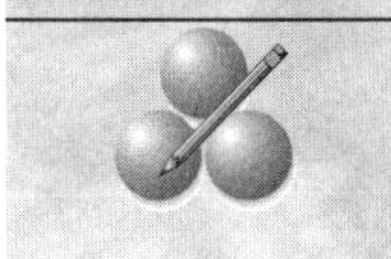

Auto Group Editor (written by markdc, and available for purchase at Renderosity) is a third-party utility that makes it much easier to add body part groups to your clothing models. The main reason for covering this utility first is because Auto Group Editor displays each body part group in a different color. This makes it very easy to determine where each group starts and ends, and helps you understand the process much more quickly.

Auto Group Editor allows you to import a human figure as a CR2 (Poser Figure Library character) or an OBJ (Wavefront 3D model) file. Each group on the original figure appears in a different color so that you can easily see where you need to create the corresponding groups on your clothing. When you import your clothing model, you can display it in wireframe mode while you use the colored groups of the underlying figure to create equivalent groups in the clothing.

A nice feature of Auto Group Editor is that it allows you to create symmetrical selections, and then assign the right and left sections individually. This extremely handy feature is not available in the other two methods that we discuss later in this chapter.

While Auto Group Editor does make it easy to create and assign polygons to groups for conforming clothing, it cannot assign materials. You will need to assign materials with another utility or in your modeling program.

To create clothing groups in Auto Group Editor, proceed as follows:

1. From Auto Group Editor, choose File > Load Source Figure. Use the Open dialog to locate the uncompressed OBJ file for your character. In this example, after uncompressing the OBZ file for Jessi, you can find the OBJ file in the same folder (Runtime: Libraries: Character: Jessi folder). Select the OBJ file, and click Open to import the figure.
2. Choose File > Load Clothing Object. Locate the clothing object that you want to assign groups to. For this example, we will use the T-shirt that was UV-mapped in Chapter 13. Locate the tshirt-mapped.obj file in the Tutorials > Chap13 folder on the CD-ROM that accompanies this book. Click Open to import the clothing object. Your project should look as shown in Figure 14.5.

3. Now we need to transfer some group names to the shirt. Notice that the bottom section of the Group Controls panel (in the left section of your screen) displays the name of all groups in the figure. Beneath the group list are several buttons. First, click the None button to deselect all of the group names in the figure. This will hide all of the figure groups.

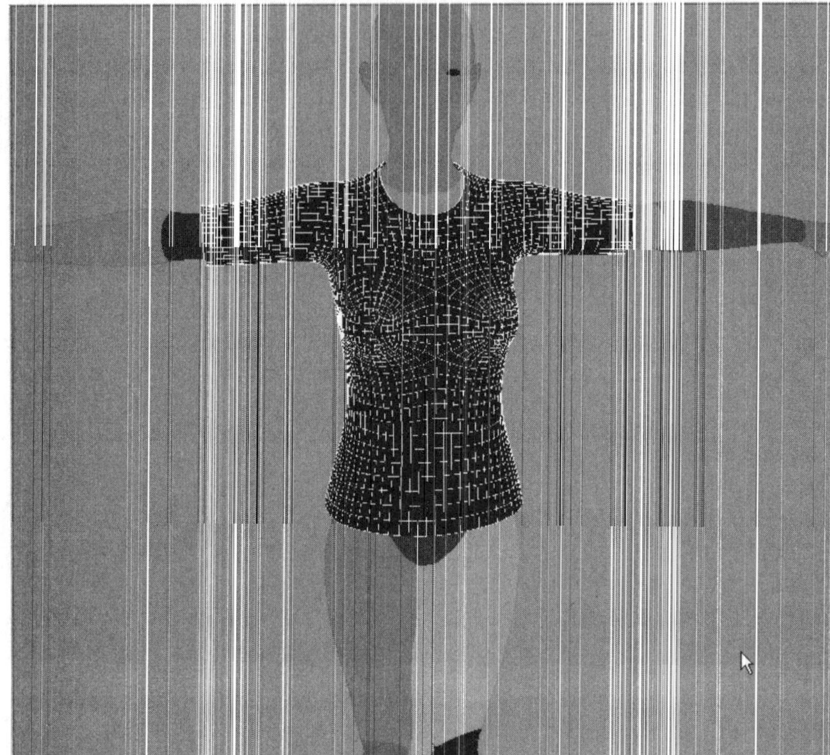

FIGURE 14.5 Import the geometry for the figure and for the clothing that you want to group.

4. Now, click the Upper button to select all of the groups in the upper torso and arms. In addition to those groups, check the neck and hip groups to add them to the selection.
5. To transfer the selected groups to the upper window, which will be the groups for the tshirt, click the Transfer Groups button at the bottom of the Group Controls panel. The group names should now appear in the top pane of the Group Controls panel.
6. It is easier to assign groups to your geometry when the clothing is in wireframe display mode. This allows you to view the groups in the original model. To display the clothing in wireframe, click the Transparent option beneath the upper section of the Group Controls window. Your project should now look as shown in Figure 14.6.
7. Groups are always symmetrical; that is, the right side and left side always contain the same number of polygons. To create symmetrical selections in Auto Group Editor, first click the Symmetrical Selection

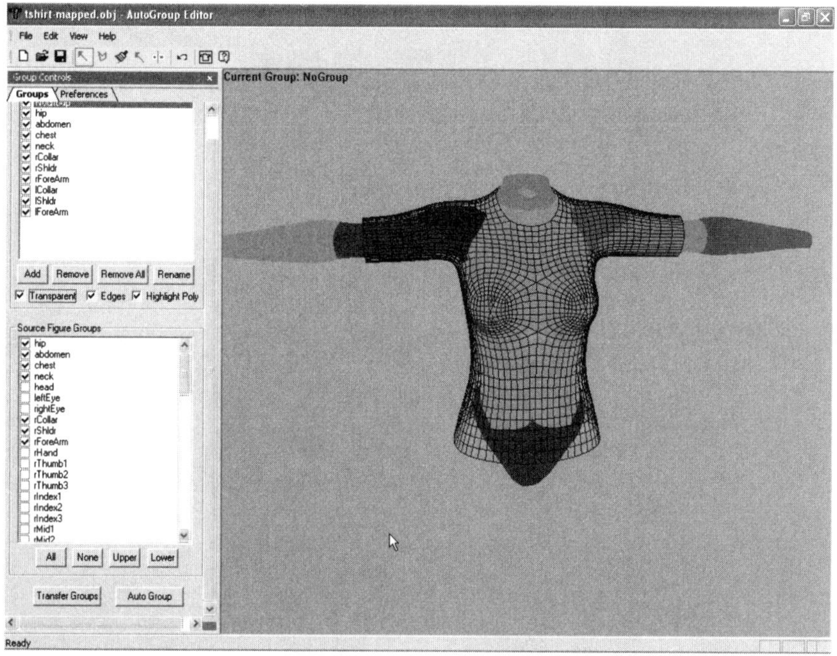

FIGURE 14.6 Transfer the appropriate group names from the figure to the clothing object.

icon. As you select polygons, Auto Group Editor automatically creates symmetrical selections if this option is activated.

Auto Group Editor makes use of a three-button mouse to perform some features. If you need to pan, move, or rotate the model while you are selecting polygons, use the following options:

- Select polygons with the left mouse button.
- Shift-click the left mouse button to deselect polygons.
- Click and drag the middle mouse button or wheel to rotate the view.
- Shift-click and drag the middle mouse button to pan the view up, down, right, or left.
- Ctrl-click and drag the middle mouse button to zoom in and out.

8. Select polygons in the chest group until your selection looks similar to that shown in Figure 14.7. Use the selection tools as follows:
   - The Normal Selection tool allows you to select all polygons in a rectangular area.

- The Polygon Selection tool allows you to select all polygons in an irregularly shaped area.
- The Paint Selection tool allows you to select polygons by "painting" over them.

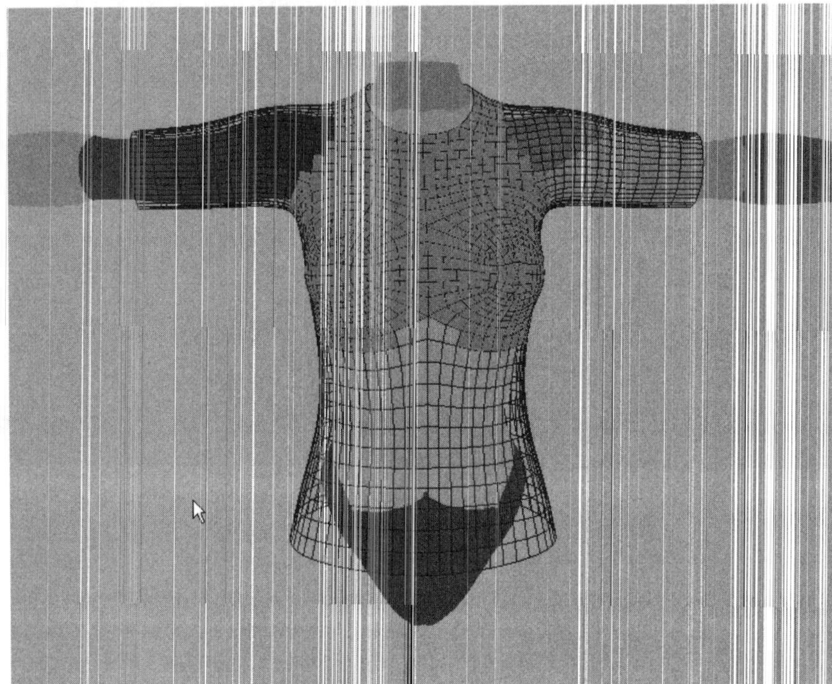

FIGURE 14.7 A symmetrical selection of polygons for the chest group is ready to be assigned.

9. With the selection made, verify that the chest is highlighted in the top section of the Group Controls panel. Then right-click over the selected polygons in the graphic view and choose Assign Left Select to Group. This assigns the left side of the selection to the chest group in the T-shirt. Right-click again, and choose Assign Right Select to Group.
10. Uncheck the chest group in the upper section of the Group Controls panel. This hides the polygons that you just assigned to the chest and protects them from being selected further.
11. Use the selection tools to select the polygons for the left or right collar. For Jessi, these are the polygons that separate the chest from the upper arm. As you select the polygons for one side, the polygons for the other side are automatically selected to create symmetrical groups.

12. To assign the right section of polygons to the right collar, verify that the rCollar group is selected in the top section of the Group Controls panel. Then, right-click over the selected polygons and choose Assign Right Select to Group. Uncheck the rCollar group in the upper section of the Group Controls panel.
13. In a similar manner, highlight the lCollar group in the Group Controls panel. Right-click over the remaining selection of polygons and choose Assign Left Select to Group. Uncheck the lCollar group in the upper section of the Group Controls panel.
14. Repeat Steps 12 and 13 to assign polygons for the right and left shoulder sections (named rShldr and lShldr).
15. Select polygons for the abdomen and assign right and left selections to the abdomen group.
16. All remaining polygons at the bottom of the T-shirt should be added to the *hip* group.
17. After you assign all polygons in the T-shirt to appropriate groups, you can save your model. Choose File > Save Clothing Object, as shown in Figure 14.8, to save over the previous version of the clothing, or choose File > Save Clothing Object As to save the grouped model to a location that you specify.

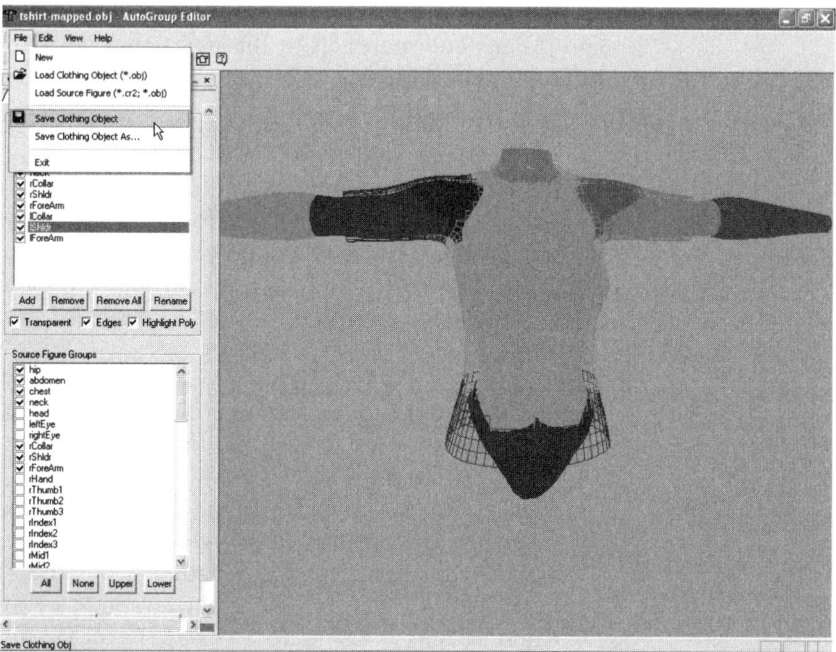

FIGURE 14.8 After you assign all polygons, use the Save Clothing Object or Save Clothing Object As command to save the grouped clothing object.

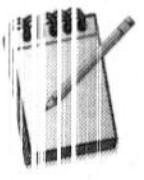

Though you can save OBJ files to the same folder in which your library files are located, you most often find OBJ geometry files in the Runtime > Geometries folders. A suitable location and filename for this T-shirt, for example, might be Runtime > Geometries > CustomFolder > Jessi > t-shirt.obj, where CustomFolder is an optional name for a folder that you assign to clothing objects that you create yourself.

TUTORIAL 14.2 GROUPS AND MATERIALS IN UV MAPPER PROFESSIONAL

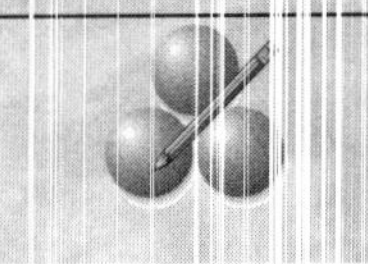

If you followed the tutorials in Chapter 13, you are already familiar with the UV mapping capabilities of UV Mapper Professional, a demo of which is in the Demos > UV Mapper folder on the CD-ROM that accompanies this book. In addition to UV mapping, this utility also allows you to assign groups and materials to a Wavefront OBJ file.

Unlike Auto Group Editor, you cannot use the human figure as a guide while you select polygons for your groups. Secondly, UV Mapper doesn't have an option to create symmetrical selections, so you have to keep track of the groups visually. The easiest way to do this is to hide faces as you assign them to groups. The following tutorial gives you some ideas for how you can overcome these situations.

For this tutorial, you will need UV Mapper Professional. You will assign groups and materials to the pants that you UV-mapped in Chapter 13. Follow these steps:

1. From UV Mapper Professional, choose File > Open Model. Locate the pants-mapped.obj file in the Tutorials > Chap13 folder on the CD-ROM that accompanies this book. Click Open to import the pants.
2. Use the Rectangular Selection tool to select the first row of each pants section. Make sure that all polygons in the top row are selected. Then press the zero (0) key on your keyboard to increase the selection by two rows. Your selection should look similar to that shown in Figure 14.9.
3. Choose Tools > Assign To > Group. When the Assign Selection Group dialog appears, enter abdomen and click OK. Answer Yes when UV Mapper Professional asks if you want to create the new group.
4. With the abdomen polygons still selected, choose Select > Display > Hide, or use the shortcut [to hide the selected polygons.
5. Select the bottom row of polygons on the left leg facing you (this is actually the right leg of the pants). Press the zero (0) key on your keyboard 14 more times to make a total of 15 rows selected.
6. Choose Tools > Assign To > Group. Enter rShin to assign these polygons to the right shin of the pants. Then hide the selected faces with the [keyboard shortcut or the Select > Display > Hide command.

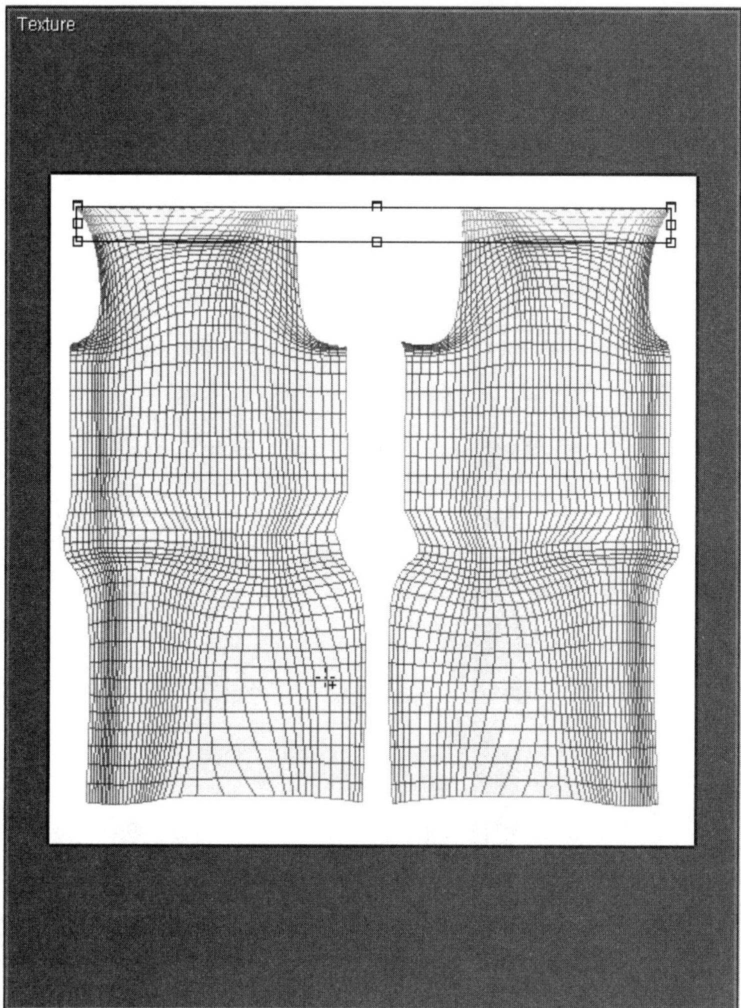

FIGURE 14.9 Assign the first three rows of the pants to the abdomen group.

7. Repeat Steps 5 and 6 for the same rows on the opposite leg. Assign these polygons to the *lShin* group and hide them from view.
8. If you look at the way Jessi's body is actually grouped, you'll see that the front of her shins are about three polygons higher than the back of the shins. To reproduce that in the pants, use the Polygon Selection Tool to select three rows of polygons on the leg on your right (the left leg of the pants), and extend the selection inward by 20 columns. Your selection should look similar to that shown in Figure 14.10. Use the Tools > Assign To > Group command to assign this selection to the lShin group

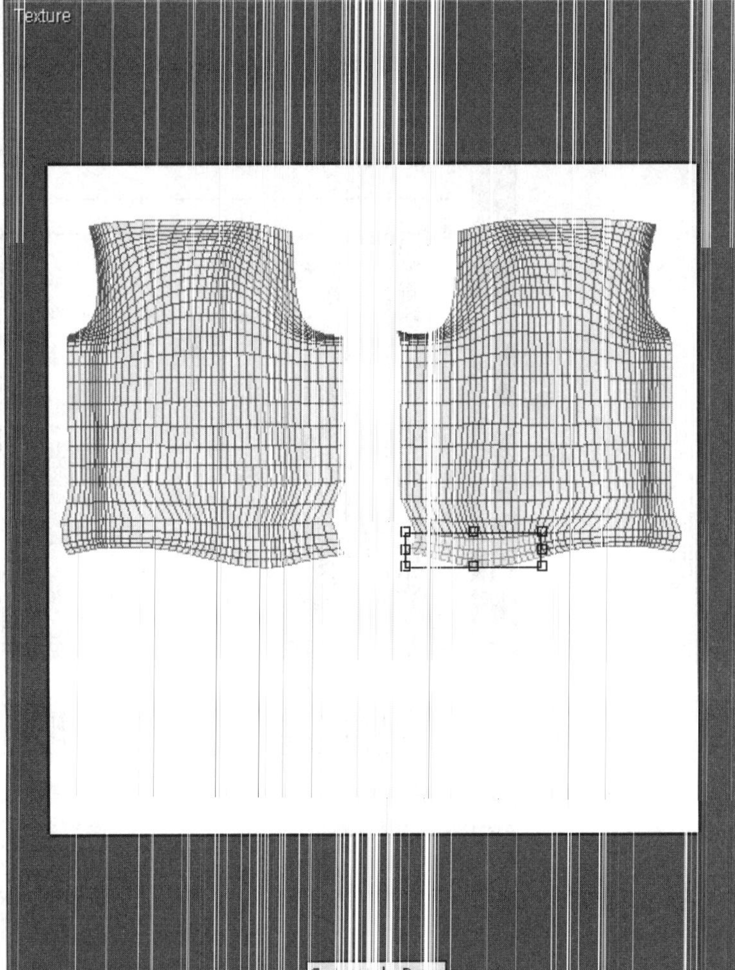

FIGURE 14.10 Select three rows and 20 columns of polygons to add to the shin groups.

9. Repeat Step 8 to assign three rows by 20 columns of polygons on the opposite leg to the rShin group.
10. Deselect all polygons (Select > Deselect), and then use the] shortcut or choose Select > Display > Show to unhide all of the previously hidden polygons.
11. Use the Rectangular Selection tool to select the top row of polygons on each side of the pants. Then extend the selection by pressing the zero (0) key 14 more times. The selection should look as shown in Figure 14.11.

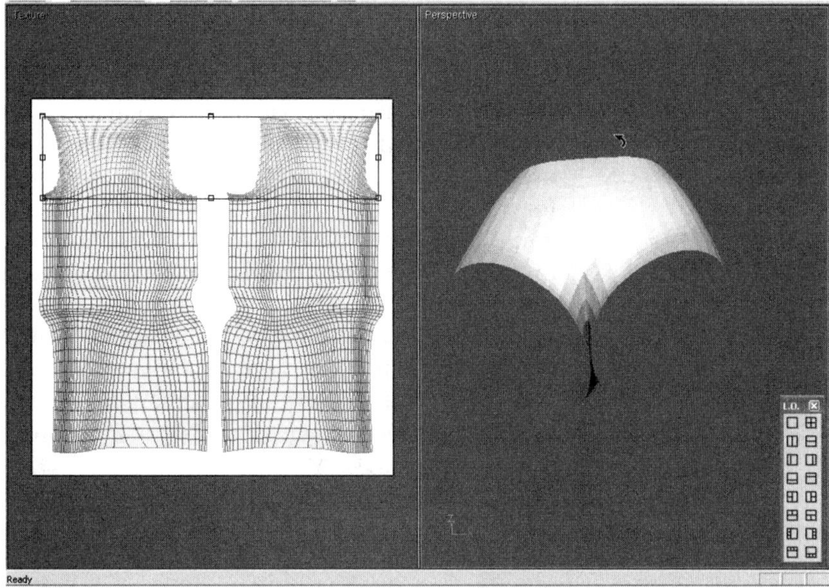

FIGURE 14.11 Make sure that the hip group includes polygons that separate the right and left legs.

12. Choose Select > Display > Hide Unselected. This hides the polygons in the remainder of the pants.
13. Now, choose Select > Select By > Group. When the Select By Group dialog appears, highlight abdomen and choose OK.
14. Hide the abdomen polygons with the Select > Display > Hide command, or by using the [shortcut.
15. Use the Rectangular Selection tool to select the polygons that remain in the Texture view. Then choose Tools > Assign To > Group. Assign these polygons to a new group named "hip."
16. With all polygons deselected, choose Select > Display > Show or use the] shortcut to unhide all faces. Now we need to unhide all of the polygons that have already been assigned.
17. Choose Select > Select By > Group. When the Select By Group dialog appears, highlight abdomen, hip, lShin, and rShin. Choose OK to select the polygons, then hide them with the [shortcut.
18. Use the Rectangular Selection tool to select the polygons on the left side of the texture view (the right side of the pants). Then choose Tools > Assign To > Group. Assign these polygons to a new group named rThigh.
19. Now, use the Rectangular Selection tool to select the polygons on the right side of the texture view (the left side of the pants). Then choose

Tools > Assign To > Group. Assign these polygons to a new group named lThigh. All of the polygons in the pants should now be assigned to groups.

20. It's actually a very similar process to assign materials in UV Mapper Professional. After you select the polygons you want to assign, you use the Tools > Assign To > Material command to create a material for the clothing. For purposes of this tutorial, we will assign all polygons to a material named Pants (material names can begin with capital letters, if desired, and do not have strict conventions like group names do). If you desire, you can optionally create more than one material zone in the pants. For example, you can select the upper portion of the pants and create a material named "Shorts"; and then add the remaining polygons to a material named *"Pants."*
21. With all groups and materials assigned, it's time to save the OBJ file. Choose File > Save Model. When the OBJ Export Option dialog appears, leave only one option checked: Don't Export Normals, as shown in Figure 14.12. This is extra information that Poser doesn't use, and it adds unnecessary file size to the object. Click OK to save the object to the folder that you will use as the final destination for your Poser clothing. For example, you can save the object to the Runtime > Geometries > *YourFolderName* > Jessi folder, and name the object pants.obj. Further information about file locations will be covered in Chapter 15, "From Modeler to Poser Library."

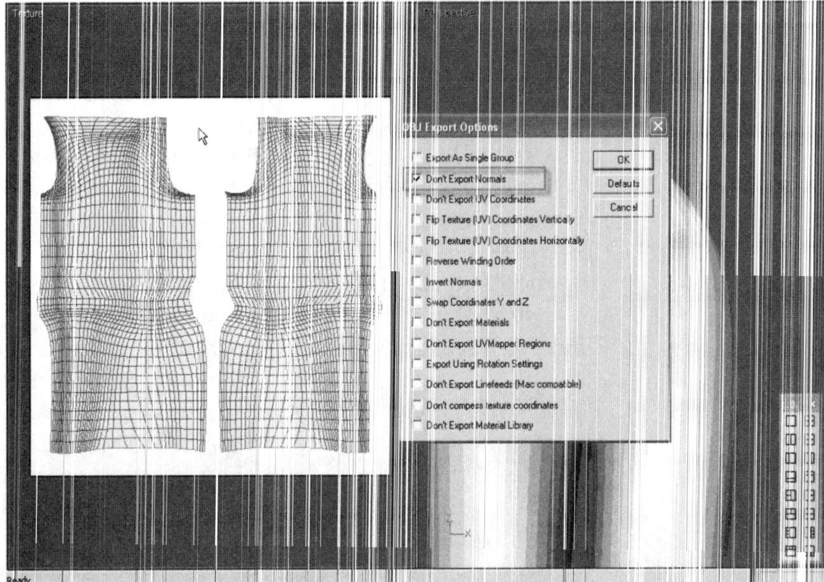

FIGURE 14.12 When you save the OBJ file, do not include Normals information.

TUTORIAL 14.3 USING POSER'S GROUP EDITOR

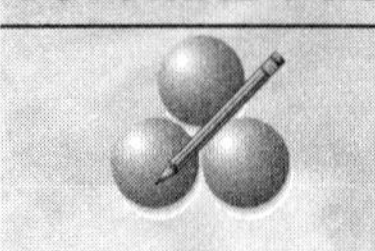

Poser's Group Editor serves a variety of purposes and operates in two modes—Polygon mode and Vertex mode. While in Polygon mode, the Group Editor allows you to select polygons in an object and assign them to a material or to body part groups for conforming clothing. Polygon mode also allows you to add polygons to hair growth groups in the Hair Room. Alternately, the Group Editor switches to vertex selection mode to enable you to assign selected vertices to cloth groups while you are in the Cloth Room.

When you use the Group Editor to assign groups and materials to an object, you work in Polygon mode, as shown in Figure 14.13.

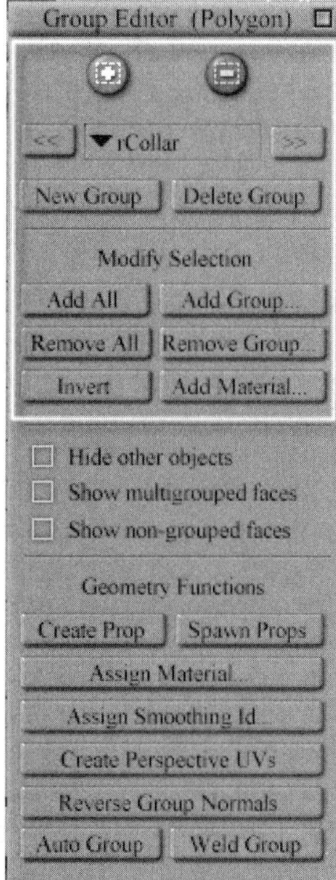

FIGURE 14.13 The Group Editor contains several buttons that help you assign groups and materials in an object.

When you select and assign polygons to groups, you will mainly use the following buttons:

- *To create a group in the clothing, click the New Group button. The New GroupName dialog prompts you to enter a name for the new group. Click OK to add the group. Use the Delete Group button to delete the currently selected group from your object.*
- *Previous and Next buttons allow you to move through the list of groups in your current object. Click the down arrow in between the Previous and Next buttons to select a group from the menu.*
- *When the Select button is enabled, you add polygons or vertices to the currently selected group. When the Deselect button is enabled, you remove polygons or vertices from the currently selected group.*
- *Several buttons help you add or remove polygons from the currently selected group. The Add All button adds all polygons in an object to the current group.*

The Group Editor also offers an Auto Group feature that you can use in conjunction with the Setup Room to add clothing groups. This method will be discussed in more detail in Chapter 15, "From Modeler to Poser Library."

To use Poser's Group Editor to assign groups and materials, follow these steps:

1. Starting with an empty scene in Poser, add Jessi or JessiHiRes from the Poser 6 > Figures > Jessi library. Turn Inverse Kinematics off, and zero the pose of the figure.
2. Choose File > Import > Wavefront OBJ. The Wavefront OBJ dialog appears.
3. Locate the OBJ file you want to open. In this case, choose skirt-mapped.OBJ (or the version of the skirt that you UV-mapped in Chapter 13).
4. The Prop Import Options dialog shown in Figure 14.14 appears. For this example, you don't need to check any of the options, because the geometry will import in the correct scale and in the correct location. These options will be discussed in more detail in Chapter 15, "From Modeler to Poser Library." After you uncheck the options, choose OK to continue. The skirt appears in the scene.
5. The skirt will consist of two groups: abdomen and hip. In order to select polygons for the abdomen of the skirt, you will have to do two things: display the skirt in wireframe mode and hide the abdomen of the human figure. To display the skirt in wireframe mode, make sure that skirt-mapped.obj is selected as the current actor. Then choose Display > Element Style > Wireframe. The skirt changes to wireframe display mode.

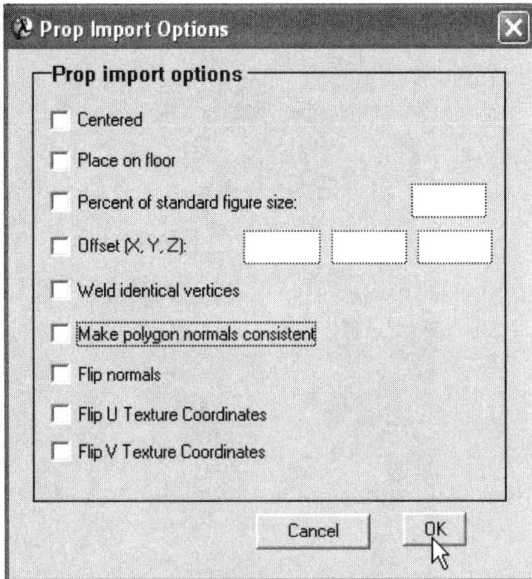

FIGURE 14.14 Uncheck all options in the Prop Import Options dialog.

6. To hide Jessi's abdomen, first click her abdomen to make it the current object. Then open the Properties panel. Uncheck the Visible option as shown in Figure 14.15. Now you'll be able to select the proper polygons on the dress to correspond with Jessi's abdomen.
7. From the Editing Tools, click the Grouping Tool icon to open the Group Editor.
8. The skirt has two groups that you will need to remove before you create the abdomen group. The groups are named *"Figure"* and *"1"*. Click the Delete Group button in the upper section of the Group Editor to delete each of these groups.
9. Now you'll create the new group for the abdomen. Click the New Group button in the upper section of the Group Editor. When the New GroupName dialog appears, enter abdomen (in lowercase letters) for the group name. Click OK to create the new group.
10. Select polygons in the skirt that overlap Jessi's hidden abdomen. Be sure to view the skirt from different camera angles to make sure that you include all polygons in the abdominal area. To select polygons, you can:
    - Left-click to select a single polygon to add to the current group, or Ctrl/Option+Left click to remove a single polygon.

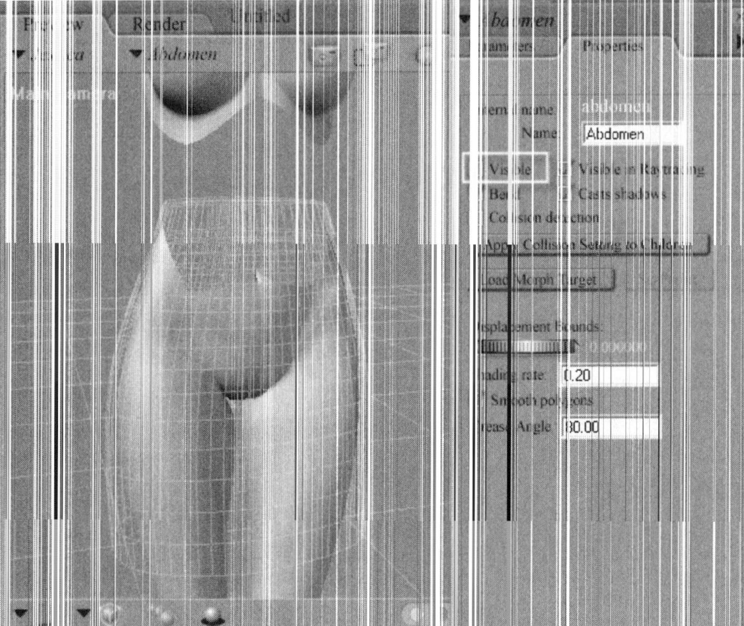

FIGURE 14.15 Hide the abdomen so that you can see where to select polygons for the skirt.

- Draw a rectangular selection area to select multiple polygons to add to the group, or press the Ctrl/Option key while you draw a rectangular selection area around the polygons you want to remove.

11. After you select the polygons that cover the abdomen, choose Display > Element Style > Use Figure Style to turn the skirt solid again. This displays the selected polygons in red so that you can see them more clearly. Add or remove polygons from the selection to make the abdomen symmetrical. Figure 14.16 shows an example of the faces that are selected for the abdomen.
12. The remaining polygons will be assigned to the hip. To begin this process, click the New Group button. When the New GroupName dialog appears, enter hip (in lowercase letters) for the group name. Click OK to create the new group.
13. Verify that the hip is selected as the current group. Then click the Add All button to add all of the skirt polygons to the hip group. All of the polygons in the skirt turn red.

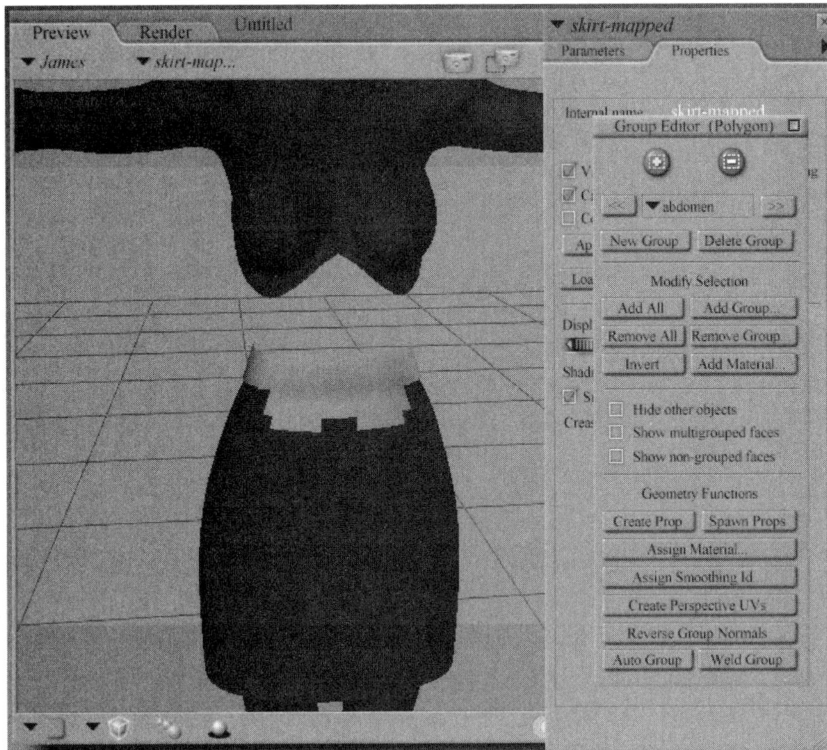

FIGURE 14.16 Switch from Wireframe display to Use Figure Style display to adjust the selection if necessary.

14. At this point, the polygons in the upper part of the skirt have been assigned to two groups: the abdomen and the hip. Polygons can only be assigned to one group, so you must remove the abdomen polygons from the hip group. To do so, click the Remove Group button in the Group Editor. Select abdomen from the drop-down list in the Remove Group dialog and choose OK to remove the abdomen polygons from the hip group. Your skirt should look similar to Figure 14.17.
15. The Group Editor also allows you to assign polygons to materials on a group-by-group basis. To assign the currently selected group (which should still be the hip section) to a material named *"Skirt"*, click the Assign Material button that appears in the Geometry Functions section in the bottom portion of the Group Editor. The Assign Material dialog opens.
16. Enter Skirt for a material name, and click OK.

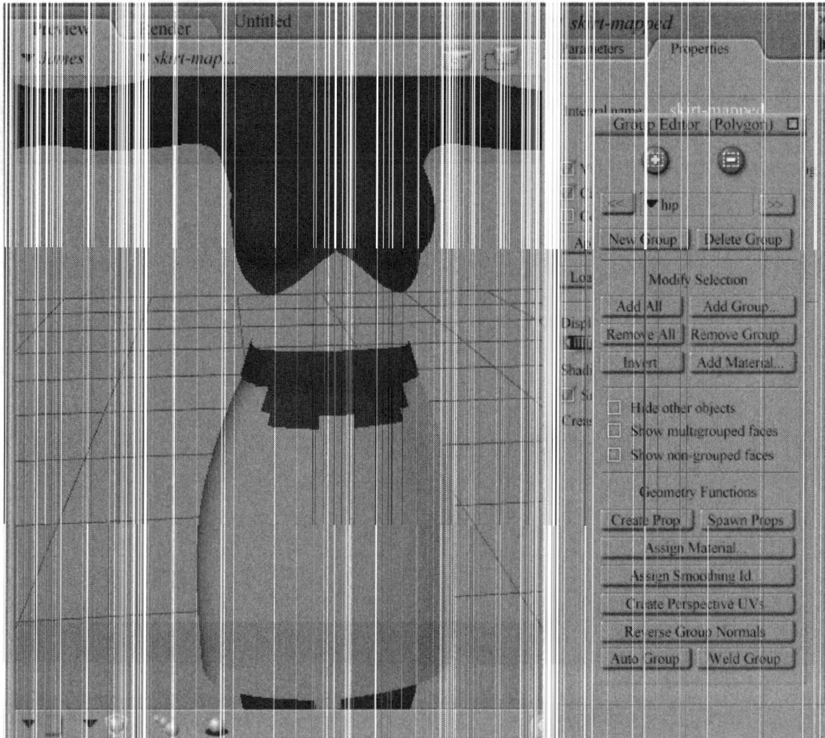

FIGURE 14.17 Select all polygons for the hip, and then remove the polygons that are assigned to the abdomen.

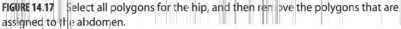

17. Return to the Group Editor, and select the abdomen group. Click the Assign Material button again. When the Assign Material dialog appears, click the Materials button and choose Skirt from the drop-down menu. Then click OK to assign the abdomen polygons to the Skirt material. Your groups and materials are now complete for the object.
18. Save the object, as described in the following tutorial. 

TUTORIAL 14.4 EXPORTING AN OBJ FILE FROM POSER

After you assign groups and materials in Poser, you'll need to save the OBJ file with its new information. The most logical place to save the file is in the final location that will be referenced in the Poser library file. Because most Poser users are accustomed to finding the original OBJ files in the Geometries folders, it is particularly important to locate the OBJ files in a folder beneath the Poser 6 > Runtime > Geometries folder if you intend to distribute your models.

To export an OBJ file from Poser, follow these steps:

1. From Poser 6, choose File > Export > Wavefront OBJ. The Export Range dialog appears.
2. Poser prompts you to select a range of frames for export. The only reason you choose Multi Frame Export is if you have morphed or animated the OBJ file, which is not true in this case. Keep the default selection (Single Frame) and choose OK to continue.
3. The Hierarchy Selection dialog appears. Initially, all objects are checked. To uncheck all items, click the UNIVERSE item that appears at the top of the list. After all items are unchecked, scroll to the bottom of the list and check the clothing object that you want to export, as shown in Figure 14.18.

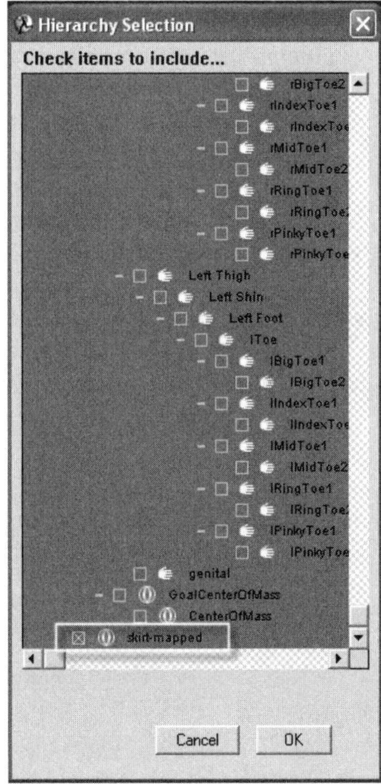

FIGURE 14.18 Deselect all objects in the Hierarchy Editor except for the clothing object.

4. Click OK to continue. The Export as Wavefront OBJ dialog appears. Create or navigate to the folder that will store your final object. For purposes of this tutorial, use a path called Poser 6 > Runtime > Geometries > PP6Projects, and name the object JessiSkirt.obj. Click Save to proceed.
5. The options shown in Figure 14.19 appear. Since you are exporting an object that will be used for conforming clothing, you need to check two options: Include Existing Groups in Polygon Groups, and As Morph Target (No World Transformations). Click OK to complete the exporting process.

When you export geometry from Poser, the options you select vary depending on the purpose of the object. For this example, check the options as follows:

- *Always leave Include Body Part Names in Polygon Groups, Use Exact Internal Names Except Spaces, and Include Figure Names in Polygon Groups unchecked. These options affect the names of the groups or can remove the grouping information from your model.*
- *Check the Include Existing Groups in Polygon Groups option when the OBJ contains groups for conforming hair or clothing. If left unchecked, the object will export with only one group. You do not need to check this option if you are exporting geometry for dynamic clothing or props because they typically do not contain more than one group.*
- *Check the Weld Body Part Seams option only if you are converting conforming clothing (which contains groups) into dynamic clothing (which should not contain groups). If you don't weld the groups at their seams, the dynamic clothing will split apart at the group seams during dynamic calculations.*
- *Check As Morph Target (No World Transformations) when it is important to reference the original position, scaling, and rotation of the geometry that you are exporting. This is particularly important when you are exporting an object for the purpose of creating morphs.*

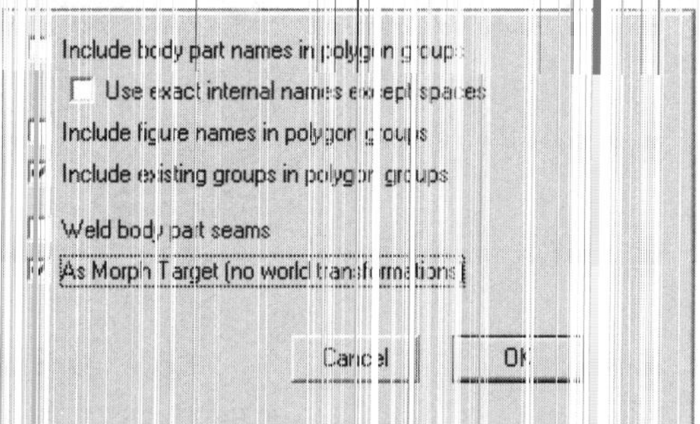

FIGURE 14.19 Make sure you include the existing groups and weld body part seams when you export the object from Poser.

After you save the OBJ file under its final name and location, it's always a good idea to perform a final check in UV Mapper Professional. Select each group, one at a time, and hide its faces to make sure that the group looks symmetrical and that it doesn't contain any stray faces or holes. Also, check the group list and the material list to make sure that there are no unwanted or erroneous groups and materials in the object, which can create confusion later on.

CONCLUSION

When an object contains multiple materials, you can use different textures or transparency settings on the different parts of the object. In order to make an object poseable, as in the case of conforming clothing, the object should contain groups that define the poseable parts of the object.

Unfortunately, you still aren't done with the process of creating Poser content. You still need to learn the proper way to add your model to the Poser libraries—and this process varies depending on the type of content you are creating. In the next chapter, you'll learn how you let Poser know the difference between props, smart props, dynamic clothing, and conforming clothing.

CHAPTER

15

FROM MODELER TO POSER LIBRARY

In This Chapter

- Importing OBJ Files
- Creating Conforming Clothing
- Cleaning Up the CR2
- Conclusion

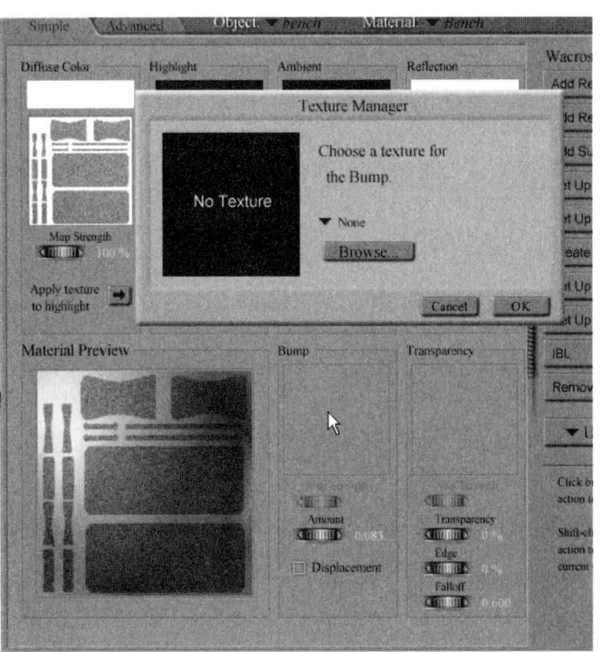

Objects modeled in a 3D program can serve many different purposes in Poser, and you'll hear these 3D objects referred to by many different content names. The objects that you model can be saved to the library as props, smart props, articulated props, dynamic clothing, conforming clothing, dynamic hair, conforming hair, and figures. The differences between these types of content are based upon the steps you complete before and during the time that you save them to the library.

In this chapter, you'll learn what distinguishes one type of content from another, how you prepare them for Poser, where to locate your content files, and how you save them to the library. This chapter will also address some of the edits that you must make to the files before you share them with others.

The procedures covered in this chapter are typical for creating objects that are compatible with Poser 6 only. If you want to create content that is compatible with previous versions of Poser, there are many other factors and procedures to consider. For example, Poser 4 uses proprietary file formats for bump maps and library thumbnails. Poser 5 and Poser 6 have the ability to use procedural shaders, dynamic clothing, and dynamic hair that cannot be used in earlier versions.

There are also supplementary files that users of older versions of Poser expect as a convenience, such as pose files that automatically apply material or morph changes to an object (MAT or MOR poses, respectively). Poser 6 provides solutions that help make it easier for users to share morphs or apply materials to their items.

Most of the issues that deal with creating content for older Poser versions are topics that go beyond the scope of this book. Further information about these procedures can be found at the various Poser community Web sites, forums, and tutorial archives.

In the last few chapters, you have covered quite a bit of ground, and it should be understood that with practice comes perfection. Though we've tried to show you the basics, we also understand that you will approach it with your own methods and innovations from this point on, as well as through learning from additional sources. Nevertheless, we have set the groundwork from modeling to UV mapping to group and material assignment, so that you now have the basic knowledge that you need to create content for Poser.

Here's a brief overview of what should be done before you complete the tasks covered in this chapter:

- Model your object in a 3D program. Most of the objects that are made for Poser are built with rectangular (four-sided) polygons and a minimal number of triangular (three-sided) polygons.
- Create UV maps for your geometry using your modeling program or a third-party utility such as UV Mapper Professional. This is a process that prepares your model so that it can accept textures. It also "flattens" your three-dimensional object onto a two-dimensional plane so that you can create realistic textures for your models using an image-editing program.
- Assign the polygons in your object to one or more materials using your modeling software, Poser's Group Editor, or a third-party utility.
- If you are creating an original poseable character, conforming clothing, conforming hair, or poseable props that require groups and bones, use Poser's Group Editor, UV Mapper Professional, Auto Group Editor, or any other similar method to create the necessary groups in your model. You'll learn later in this chapter how to associate those groups with bones that cause the object to become poseable.

After completing all of the preceding tasks, you can bring your content into Poser, apply the materials, and save your content to the library. The tutorials in this chapter will take you the rest of the way!

IMPORTING OBJ FILES

To bring your Wavefront OBJ file into Poser, choose the File > Import > Wavefront OBJ command. When you import geometry into Poser, you are presented with several import options. The import dialog box is shown in Figure 15.1. This dialog contains options that help you size and position your prop, as well as other options that can help resolve geometry problems.

The options in the Prop Import Options dialog serve the following purposes:

Centered: Places the object in the exact center of the scene (where the X coordinate is 0, the Y coordinate is 0, and the Z coordinate is 0). This is a good option to choose if you are not sure where the object will appear in the scene.

Place On Floor: Drops the lowest point of the object to ground level (where the Y coordinate is 0).

Percent Of Standard Figure Size: Poser uses scaling units that are very small in comparison to other 3D software programs. If you model content in another 3D software program that uses different scaling, your objects may import much larger than expected. When you check this option, your object will be sized in

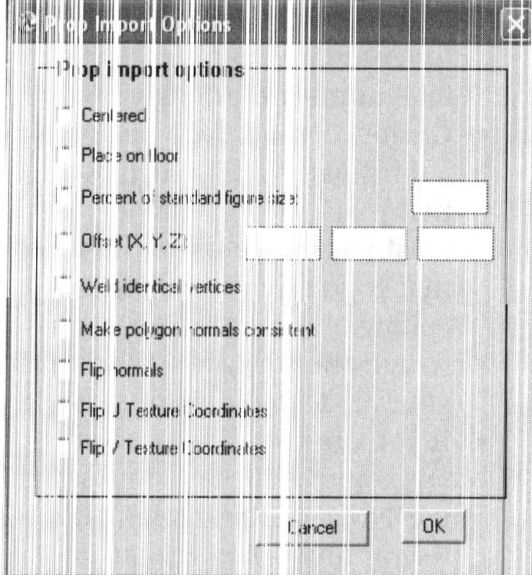

FIGURE 15.1 The Prop Import Options dialog presents options that help you size and position your prop when you import it.

relation to the standard height of a human figure. Enter a numerical value to rescale your object in relation to Poser's standard figure height (which is around six feet, give or take a few inches). Therefore, if you want your object to be approximately three feet high, check this option and enter a value of 50%.

In most cases, content that is created specifically for Poser is scaled correctly for use in Poser. On occasion, you'll find some wonderful content created in other 3D software. After you import the content into Poser, you quickly see that the content is substantially larger than the content you use in Poser. In fact, you may not be able to see it because it is too large, or it appears above or below the view of the camera.

One way to resolve this issue is to check the first three options in the Prop Import Options dialog so that your object appears in the center of the stage, on the floor, and approximately 100% of figure size. You can then use the Scale dials in the Parameters window to scale the model appropriately. After the object appears to be the correct size, choose Figure > Drop to Floor so that the object rests on the floor.

Next, export it from Poser, checking only the Include Groups in Polygon Groups option if your object has body part groups. Otherwise, you do not need to check any options.

When you reimport this new object into Poser it should appear in the center of the stage, at the correct scale, and on the floor just as you exported it. You can then complete the process of saving the object to the library.

Offset (X,Y,Z): Choose this option to offset your object from its default position or from the center position when used in conjunction with the **Center** option. Enter a positive or negative number (in Poser units) for the amount of offset from the zero coordinate for the X (left/right), Y (up/down) or Z (forward/backward) axis that you want to offset.

Weld Identical Vertices: Choose this option if your geometry is split apart into separate groups or contains many common vertices in the same location. This option welds the like vertices back together.

Objects that are made of right angles, such as boxes, may give better results if their common vertices are left unwelded. This is because Poser can smooth polygons at render time. If you weld the sides of a box together you may end up with a bloated balloon-like box if you try to smooth polygons. To prevent this from happening you will need to add a tiny row of polygons at each edge so that if polygon smoothing is selected, only the tiny polygons will be affected and the large portions of each side remain flat. When converting conforming clothing to dynamic clothing it is recommended that you select this option when you reimport the OBJ file.

Make Polygon Normals Consistent: 3D objects are made of faces that can be one-sided (where one side is visible and the other is invisible when facing the camera) or two-sided (where either side is visible when facing the camera). The direction of the "normals" defines which side of a one-sided face is visible and which is not. If your object appears with "holes" in it, the cause may be that some polygons face away from the camera. If you reimport the object with this option checked, it *may* alleviate the problem.

Flip Normals: Check this option if your object imports with all faces "inside out," so that the front of the object is invisible but the back of object is visible.

Reimport with Flip U Texture Coordinates if textures appear to be mirrored horizontally when you render. Reimport with Flip V Texture Coordinates if textures appear to be mirrored vertically when you render, as shown in Figure 15.2.

Prop Information at a Glance

Content Type:	Props
File Extensions:	PP2 (not compressed); PPZ (compressed)
Path to Geometry Files:	:Runtime :Geometries :(custom folder name)
Path to Texture Files:	:Runtime :Texture :(custom folder name)
Path to Library Files:	:Runtime :Libraries :Props :(custom folder name)

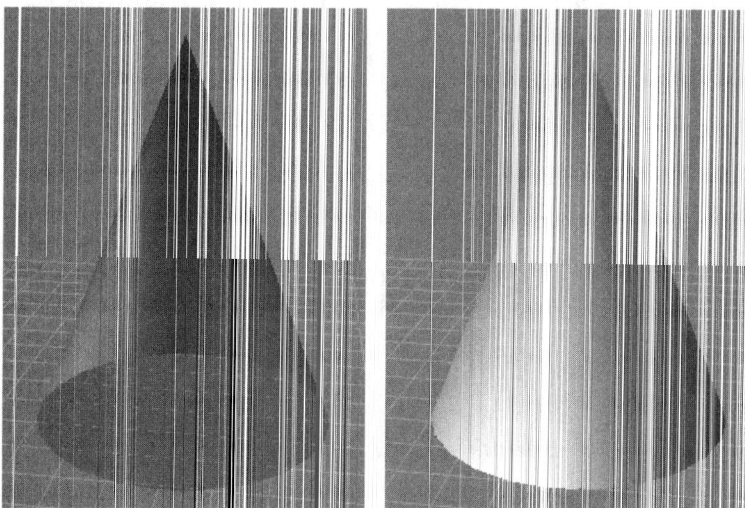

FIGURE 15.2 If an object appears "inside out" after you import it (left), reimport the object with the Flip Normals option checked (right).

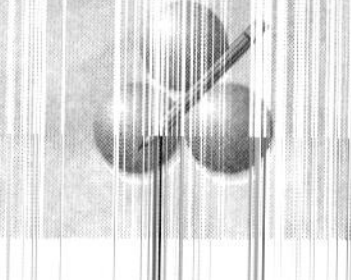

TUTORIAL 15.1 SAVING PROPS TO THE LIBRARY

Most people who become interested in creating Poser content start with props, because they are probably the easiest type of content to create. After you model your object and prepare it with UV maps and material assignments, you simply import the object into Poser, add morphs (if desired), and save the prop to the library.

In this tutorial, you'll import a garden bench into Poser, assign a stone texture map as the diffuse and bump channels for its material, and save the prop to the library. Follow these steps:

1. Locate the Poser 6 > Downloads > Runtime > Geometries folder on your hard drive. Beneath that folder, create a new subfolder named PracticalPoser6.

2. Locate the Tutorials > Chap13 folder on the CD-ROM that accompanies this book. Copy the bench.obj file into the Poser 6 > Downloads > Runtime > Geometries > PracticalPoser 6 folder that you created in Step 1.
3. Locate the Poser 6 > Downloads > Runtime > Textures folder on your hard drive. Beneath that folder, create a new subfolder named PracticalPoser6.

4. From the PracticalPoser6 > Tutorials > Chap15 folder, copy the bench.jpg texture map into the Poser 6 > Downloads > Runtime > Textures folder you created in Step 3.
5. From an empty Poser scene, choose File > Import > Wavefront OBJ. The Wavefront OBJ dialog appears.
6. Locate the bench.obj file that you saved in Step 2. Highlight the file and click Open. The Prop Import Options dialog shown in Figure 15.3 appears.

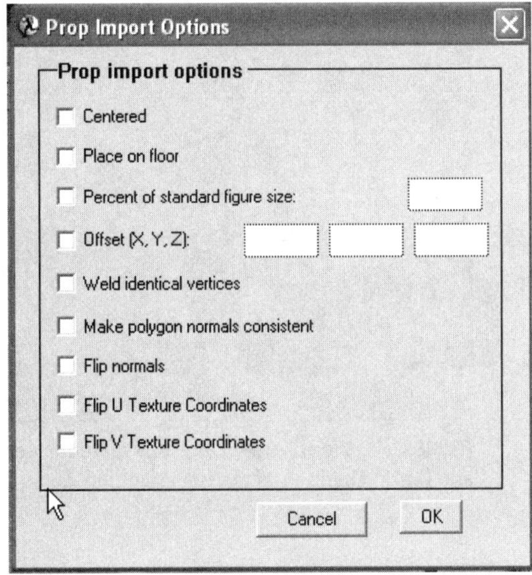

FIGURE 15.3 The Prop Import Options dialog appears when you import 3D content into Poser.

7. The bench is sized properly for Poser, and it will also load into the center of the scene by default. Because of this, you do not need to check any of the options in the Prop Import dialog. Click OK to continue. The bench should appear in the center of the scene.
8. Choose Display > Document Style > Texture Shaded. You won't see the bench change because it doesn't have a texture applied to it yet. To add one, click the Material tab to enter the material room.
9. If necessary, click the Simple tab to display the simple material editor shown in Figure 15.4.

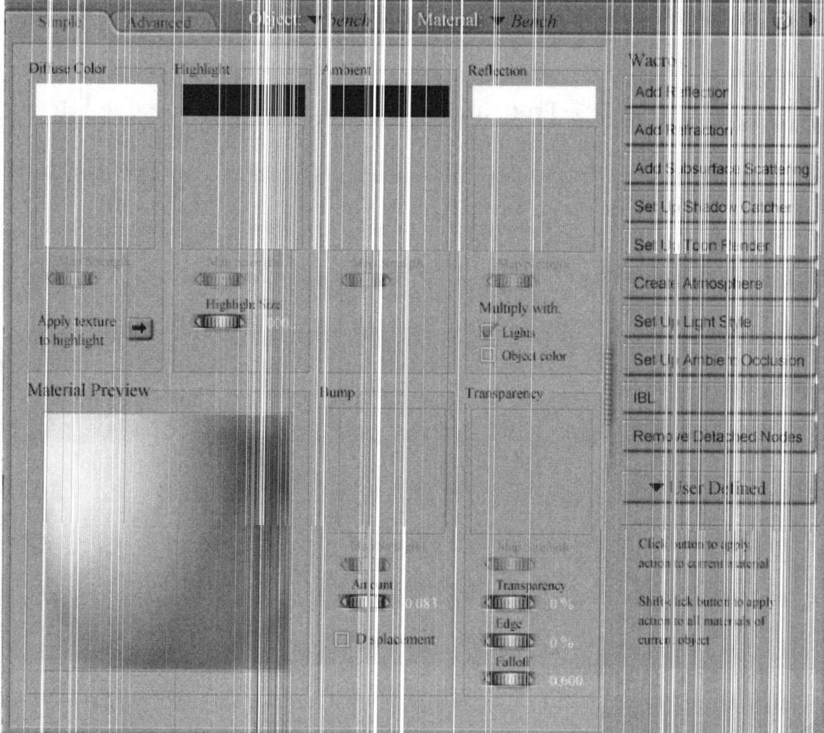

FIGURE 15.4 We will use the Simple material view to add a texture map to the diffuse and bump channels of the bench material.

10. The Diffuse Color settings are those that control the main color or texture of the object. To assign a bitmap texture, click the empty square that appears directly beneath the white Diffuse Color rectangle. The Texture Manager dialog shown in Figure 15.5 appears.
11. Click the Browse button to locate the bench.jpg texture that you saved in Step 4. After you return to the texture manager dialog, you'll see a preview of the texture in the preview window. Click OK to return to the Simple material editor. The bench in the preview window should update to show the texture applied to the bench.
12. We will use the same rock texture to add some "bumpiness" to the bench. To do so, click the square beneath the Bump heading in the Simple material view (the square beneath the cursor in Figure 15.6).
13. Click the Browse button to select the same texture (bench.jpg) for the bump map. After you return to the Texture Manger, click OK to assign the bump map.

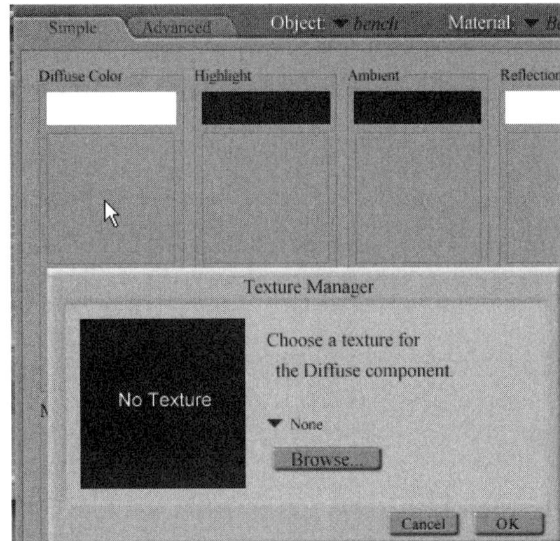

FIGURE 15.5 The Texture Manager dialog prompts you to browse for a texture for your object.

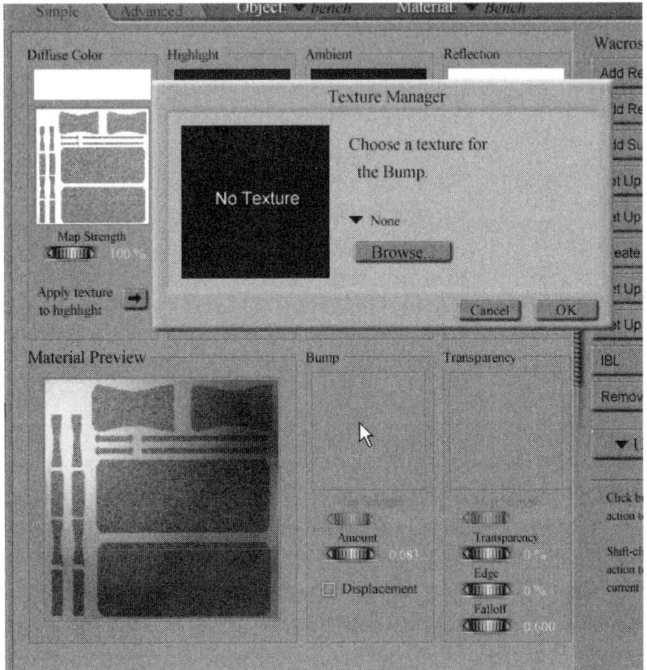

FIGURE 15.6 Click the Bump square to select the same texture for the bump map.

14. You might be able to tell from the Material Preview that the bump map is a little strong. To reduce the setting, click the numbers beside the Amount slider, and set the value to .02 as shown in Figure 15.7.

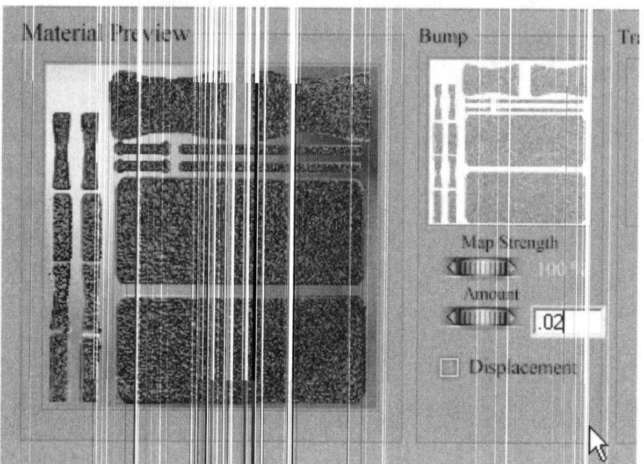

FIGURE 15.7 Reduce the Bump Map setting to .02.

15. If possible, do a test render of your bench to make sure that you are satisfied with the bump map setting. Increase or decrease the Amount slider until you are satisfied with the result.
16. Now you're ready to save the bench to the Prop library. Before doing so, verify that you have deselected the option in General Preferences to use compressed files. To disable this option, choose Edit > General Preferences. Click the Misc tab in the General Preferences dialog. Uncheck the Use File Compression option in the Save Files section as shown in Figure 15.8. The reason for this is because you will have to make some changes to the file after you save it, and compressed files are not directly editable.
17. Open the Poser library, and click the up arrow folders until you see the master folders for the Poser 6 and Downloads libraries. Double-click the Downloads folder to select it as the current library. Then choose the Props library as the current library.
18. We are going to create a new category for your new prop. To do so, click the down arrow at the top of the library window, and choose Add New Category from the menu, as shown in Figure 15.9.

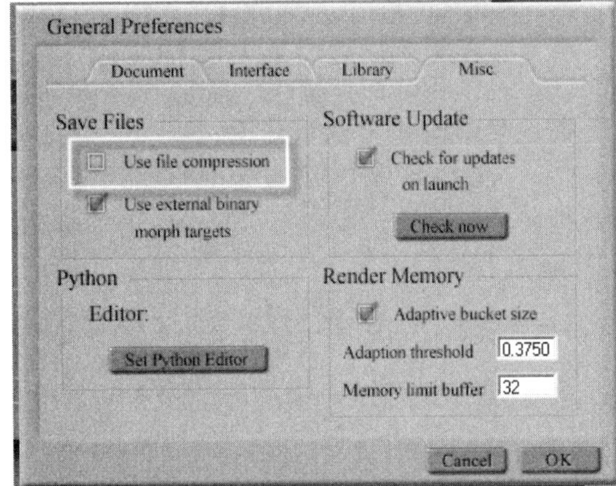

FIGURE 15.8 Disable the option to use file compression before you save your prop to the library.

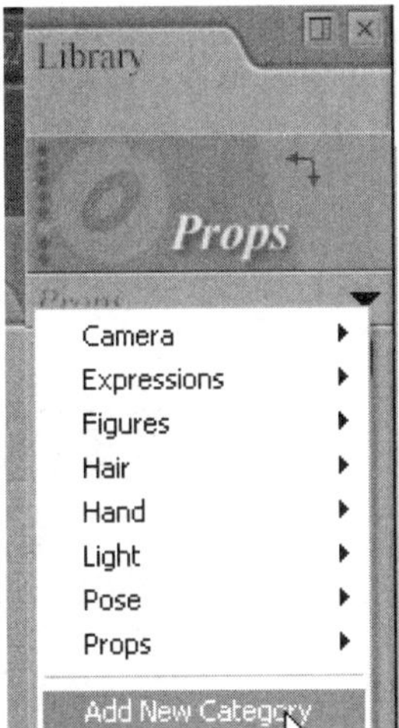

FIGURE 15.9 Click the Add New Category menu item to create a new library folder for your prop.

19. The Library Name dialog prompts you to enter a name for your new library. For purposes of this tutorial, enter "PracticalPoser6," and click OK to continue.
20. Scroll down if necessary to find the new PracticalPoser6 folder in your Props library. Double-click the folder to select it as the current library.

21. Now click the bench in the document window to select it as the current item. The Add to Library icon (with a plus sign) should appear at the bottom of the library window.
22. Click the Add to Library icon. The New Set dialog shown in Figure 15.10 appears. Enter "Bench" for the Set Name. Then click the Select Subset button.

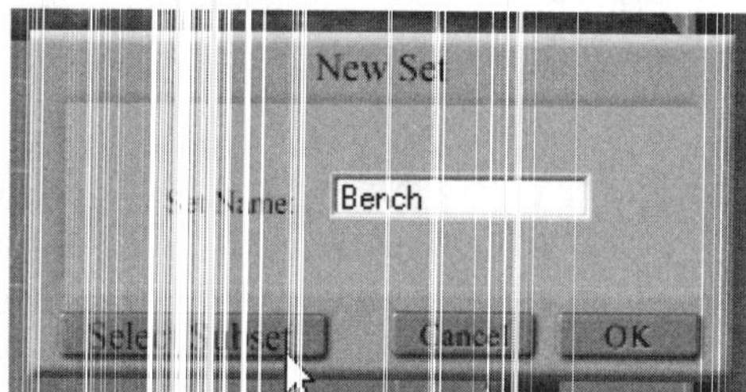

FIGURE 15.10 Enter a name for your prop and click the Select Subset button.

23. The Hierarchy Selection dialog prompts you to select the items that should be included with the prop. Check bench, as shown in Figure 15.11. Then click OK to continue.

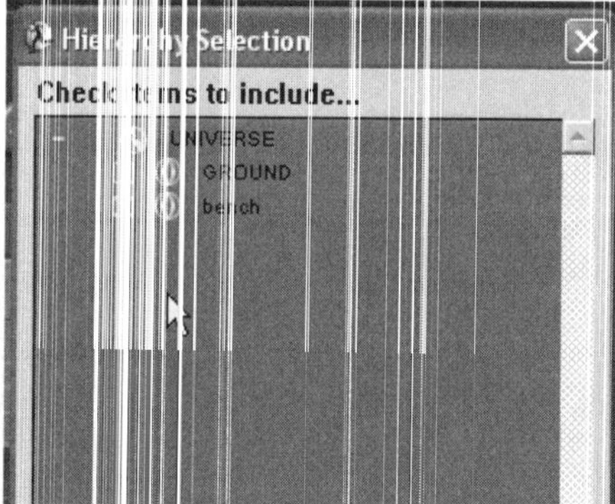

FIGURE 15.11 Select the bench in the scene to save it to the library.

24. Return to the New Set dialog and click OK. Your bench should now appear in the library.

You may notice that shadows appear in the thumbnail when you add your prop to the library. To prevent shadows in thumbnails, choose Display > Ground Shadows to turn off the shadow option. Then repeat Steps 21 through 25 to overwrite the previous version of your prop to remove the shadows from the thumbnail. When Poser asks if you want to replace the existing item, answer OK.

TUTORIAL 15.2 REMOVING EMBEDDED GEOMETRY FROM PROPS

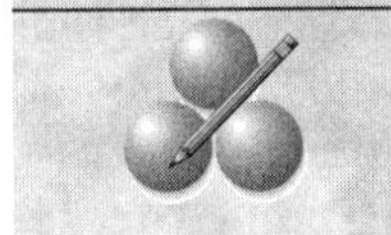

When you first save your prop to the library, Poser embeds the geometry information into the library file. This may seem to be advantageous, because it means you would only have to keep track of one library file, rather than a library file and a geometry file. However, if you embed the geometry in the prop file, you won't be able to alter it with morphs, make new UV maps, or regroup the object without destroying the prop file.

As a result, most content creators strip the geometry information out of the prop file and add some lines in the prop file that reference an external OBJ file in the Runtime > Geometries folder. What this means is that you will have to open the prop file in a text editor and make the changes manually. If you follow the procedures outlined below, the change should be relatively painless.

Hacking library files is not for the faint of heart. Always make a backup copy of the file you are editing before you make any changes. Keep the backup copy in a safe place in the event that you ever need the original file again!

To remove the embedded geometry from a prop file, and reference an external OBJ file, follow these steps:

1. Create a backup copy of your prop file. For this example, copy the bench.pp2 file that you created in the previous task, and save it as benchBAK.pp2.
2. Open bench.pp2 in a text editor that can save ASCII-compatible text files (such as Microsoft Word, WordPad, or an equivalent Mac program).
3. At the beginning of the prop file, you will notice several lines that appear similar to those shown in Figure 15.12. These lines are to remain untouched.

```
{
        version
        {
                number 6
        }
        prop bench
        {
```

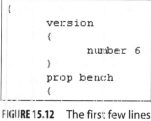

FIGURE 15.12 The first few lines of your prop file should remain untouched.

4. The custom geometry section begins with a line that reads *geomCustom*. Following that will be a few lines that tell the number of vertices for several different categories. Finally, there will be many lines that begin with the letters v, vt, and f. All of these lines should be removed. Figure 15.13 shows the beginning and the ending sections of the custom geometry. Make sure you also remove *only one* ending bracket that follows the lines that begin with *f*.

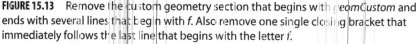

```
geomCustom
{
        numbVerts 1008
        numbTVerts 984
        numbTSets 4008
        numbElems 1002
        numbSets 4008
        v -0.396000 0.193000 0.100000
        v 0.396000 0.193000 0.100000
        v 0.396000 0.193000 -0.100000
        v -0.396000 0.193000 -0.100000
        v -0.396000 0.213000 0.100000
        v 0.396000 0.213000 0.100000
```

This section will include many lines that begin with the letters v, vt, and f, until you see the end of these lines as shown below ...

```
        f 1008/979 845/980 841/981 1006/977
        f 992/963 1004/972 1007/983 998/982
        f 1004/972 1003/970 1008/979 1007/983
        f 1003/970 840/984 845/980 1008/979
}
```

FIGURE 15.13 Remove the custom geometry section that begins with *geomCustom* and ends with several lines that begin with *f*. Also remove one single closing bracket that immediately follows the last line that begins with the letter *f*.

5. After you delete the custom geometry as outlined in Step 4, the lines that remain at the top of the prop file should look as shown in Figure 15.14. The dotted line in the figure shows where the custom geometry existed and where you need to add a couple of lines of code.

```
{
        version
        {
                number 6
        }
        prop bench
        {
........................................................
        }
        prop bench
        {
                name bench
                on
                bend 1
                dynamicsLock 1
                hidden 0
                addToMenu 1
                castsShadow 1
                includeInDepthCue 1
                useZBuffer 1
                parent UNIVERSE
                creaseAngle 80
                channels
                {
```

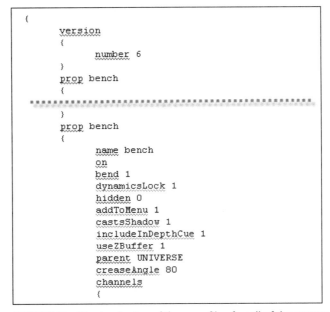

FIGURE 15.14 The beginning of the prop file after all of the custom geometry has been removed.

6. In the area designated by the dotted line in Figure 15.14, add the following lines of code, which provide a pointer to the location where you saved the OBJ geometry file. Once you add this code your altered prop file will look as shown in Figure 15.15.

```
storageOffset 0 0.3487 0
objFileGeom 0 0 :Runtime:Geometries:PracticalPoser6:
Chap16:bench.obj
```

7. Figure 15.15 also shows four lines that are highlighted with arrows. One of the lines contains the name of the object file (bench.obj). Make sure that the other three lines marked with the arrow name the prop the same as the object. For example, if your object is instead named "benchseat.obj", the other three lines should read "prop benchseat" or "name benchseat" in order for the external call to the object to work correctly.

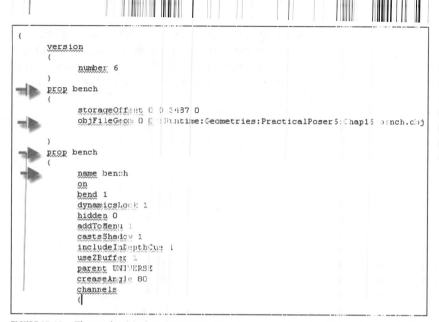

```
{
    version
    {
        number 6
    }
    prop bench
    {
        storageOffset 0 0.3487 0
        objFileGeom 0 0 :Runtime:Geometries:PracticalPoser5:Chap15:bench.obj

    }
    prop bench
    {
        name bench
        on
        bend 1
        dynamicsLock 1
        hidden 0
        addToMenu 1
        castsShadow 1
        includeInDepthCue 1
        useZBuffer 1
        parent UNIVERSE
        creaseAngle 80
        channels
        {
```

FIGURE 15.15 The embedded geometry section is now replaced with a reference to the external geometry file.

8. Save your edited prop file to the same location as previously saved, overwriting the version that contained the embedded geometry. The revision is now complete.

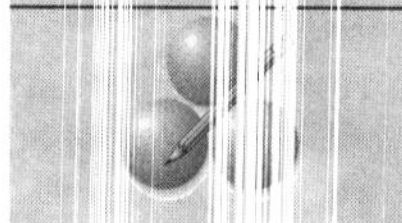

TUTORIAL 15.3 FIXING OBJ AND TEXTURE PATHS

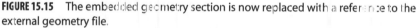

When you save any type of content to the Poser libraries, Poser sometimes creates absolute path references to the geometry and texture map files. Absolute paths give a complete reference to a file. For example, if you loaded a texture from an external runtime file on your D drive, you might see a texture reference like "D:\Runtime\Textures\Jess\Clothing\dress.jpg".

The path works fine on your computer, and it will also work fine if someone else creates exactly the same path on their own computer. But if someone else chooses to install his or her files to a different location, error messages will appear when he or she tries to load the product from the library. This is why you should always use *relative* paths to geometry and image files in the items that you save to the library. The path to the OBJ file or texture map must always begin with *:Runtime,* and use colons (:) rather than backslashes (\ ) as separators to maintain compatibility with Macintosh file structures.

To edit file paths, follow these steps:

1. Open your library file in a text editor that can save ASCII-compatible text files. Files that can include references to OBJ or image files can include items in your Figures, Props, and Hair libraries. Also make sure that you open an uncompressed version (CR2, PP2, or HR2) rather than a compressed version that cannot be edited (CRZ, PPZ, or HRZ).
2. Use the Search feature of your image editor to search for *OBJ* or *obj.* A reference to an OBJ file usually occurs only twice in a figure's CR2 file (see Figure 15.16), once in a prop's PP2 file (see Figure 15.17), and once in a hair set's HR2 file (see Figure 15.18). If your path contains forward or back slashes and does not start with Runtime as shown in these figures, edit the file paths to use the proper syntax as shown in these examples. Try to keep paths as brief as possible, and do not exceed 60 characters.

```
{
version
	{
	number 5
	}
figureResFile :Runtime:Geometries:ArtyMotion:PetiteChou:PetiteChouDress.obj
actor BODY:1
	{
```

Several sections that begin with the word actor appear between the two OBJ references.

```
actor skirt:1
	{
	storageOffset 0 0 0
	geomHandlerGeom 13 skirt
	}
	figureResFile
:Runtime:Geometries:ArtyMotion:PetiteChou:PetiteChouDress.obj
actor BODY:1
	{
```

FIGURE 15.16 A figure file (CR2) includes two references to external geometry that are separated by several *actor* sections. If the path is long, it may wrap around to two lines, which has the same effect as chopping the text at the place that the text wrapped to the new line.

```
{
version
	{
	number 4.01
	}
prop EgyptianThroneClassic
	{
	storageOffset 0 0.3487 0
	objFileGeom 0 0
:Runtime:Geometries:AntonsPeople:Treasures_Of_Egypt:EgyptianThroneClassic.obj
	}
```

FIGURE 15.17 A prop file (PP2) includes one reference to an external object.

```
{
version
	{
	number 4.0
	}
prop figureHair
	{
	storageOffset 0 0.34875 0
	objFileGeom 0 0 :Runtime:Geometries:3Dream:3DreamParadiseHair.obj
	}
```

FIGURE 15.18 A hair file (HR2) includes one reference to an external object.

3. In a similar manner, search for JPG or jpg in your library file. You'll see various types of references to JPG images in your library files that most often reference Diffuse, Bump, Displacement, or Specular maps. Figure 15.19 shows the correct syntax for an image map reference.

```
				}
			node "image_map" "Image_Map"
				{
				name "Image_Map"
				pos 473 23
				nodeInput "Image_Source"
					{
					name "Image_Source"
					value 29 29 29
					parmR NO_PARM
					parmG NO_PARM
					parmB NO_PARM
					node NO_NODE
					file
":Runtime:Textures:ArtyMotion:Jessi:Immortals:JessiImDressTop.jpg"
					}
```

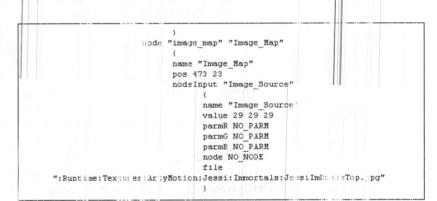

FIGURE 15.19 Image map references should also begin with *:Runtime*, and use colons rather than backslashes to denote the file path.

Verify that all paths to the images used as textures are correct, and use the correct syntax. Just as the paths to the OBJ files should be relative and not absolute, the same is true of the paths to image files. They should begin with *:Runtime*, and use colons instead of backslashes to trace the path hierarchy. Also, keep in mind that there may be multiple images used in an object, and there can also be more than one material reference to a single image. For complete results, do a search through the entire file for the JPG or jpg file extension, until your text editor informs you that it cannot find any additional instances of the extension. You should also do a search for any of the other image file types that Poser can use as an image map source. These file types include TIF, PSD, and BMP.

TUTORIAL 15.4 CREATING SMART PROPS

There is only one difference between a regular prop and a smart prop. When you add a regular prop to a scene, it doesn't automatically attach itself to anything. On the other hand, when you add a smart prop to a scene, it automatically finds and attaches itself to the appropriate figure or body part.

To explain this a little bit further, let's say you are creating a scene in which a man is kneeling on the floor, looking up at a woman who is sitting on a couch. She is looking down at her hand. You find a nice diamond ring in your Props library, and you add it to the scene. You quickly learn how difficult it is to move the ring into position on a figure that is already posed. When you try to grab the ring, you accidentally move other items in the scene. If you try to use the xTrans, yTrans, and zTrans dials in the Parameters window, it takes a lot of time to move the prop into place.

If you save the ring to your library as a smart prop, it automatically finds its way to the woman's left ring finger when you add it to the scene. To save the engagement ring to the library, select the ring, choose the body part that is supposed to be its parent (the body part to which the ring will attach itself), and then save the prop to the library. If the procedure is completed correctly, the ring will always attach itself to the figure's left ring finger whenever you add it to a scene, regardless of how that figure is posed.

Prop Information at a Glance

Content Type:	Smart Props
File Extensions:	PP2 (not compressed); PPZ (compressed)
Path to Geometry Files:	:Runtime :Geometries :(custom folder name)
Path to Texture Files:	:Runtime :Texture :(custom folder name)
Path to Library Files:	:Runtime :Libraries :Props :(custom folder name)

Before you save the smart prop to the library, use the Object > Change Figure Parent command to assign a parent to the prop.

1. Locate the ring.obj file in the Tutorials > Chap13 folder on the CD-ROM that accompanies this book.
2. Copy the ring.obj file to the Downloads > Runtime > Geometries > PracticalPoser6 folder that you created in Tutorial 15.1.
3. Locate the ring.jpg texture file in the Tutorials > Chap13 folder on the CD-ROM that accompanies this book.

4. Copy the ring.jpg image to the Downloads > Runtime > Textures > PracticalPoser6 folder that you created in Tutorial 15.1.
5. Create a new scene in Poser, and add Jessi to the scene. Turn off Inverse Kinematics, and use the Joint Editor to zero her pose as shown in Figure 15.20.

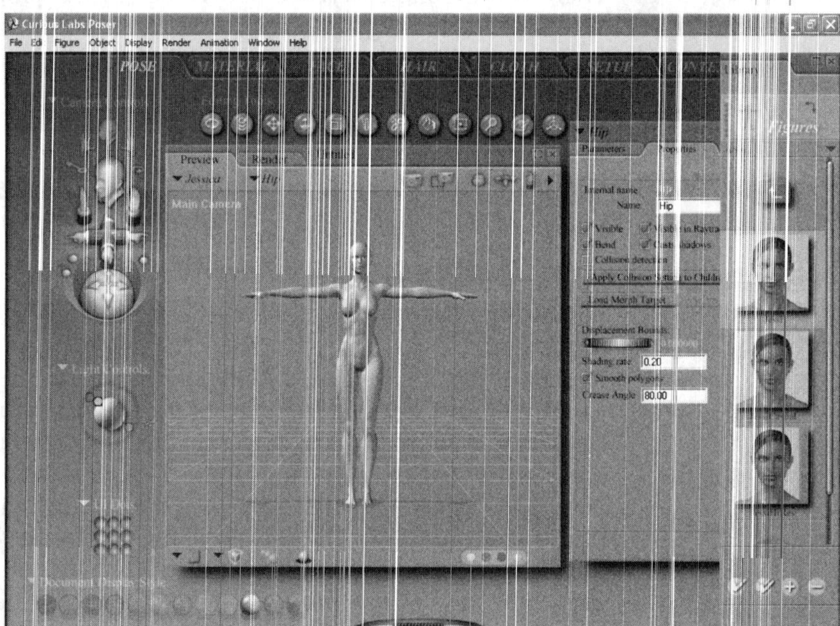

FIGURE 15.20 Add Jessi to an empty scene and zero her pose.

6. Choose File > Import > Wavefront OBJ. The Wavefront OBJ dialog appears.
7. Navigate to the Downloads > Runtime > Geometries > PracticalPoser6 folder, and highlight ring.obj. Click Open to continue. The Prop Import Options dialog appears.

8. To import the ring in the same position in which it was modeled, leave all options unchecked as shown in Figure 15.21. The ring should be positioned on Jessi's left ring finger when it appears in the scene. Click OK to continue.

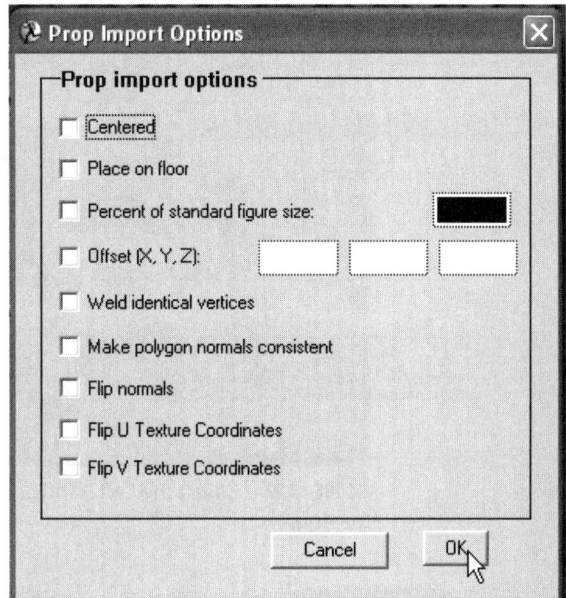

FIGURE 15.21 Leave all options in the Prop Import Options dialog unchecked.

9. Choose Display > Document Style > Texture Shaded, or click the Texture Shaded (last) icon in the Document Display Style controls. The textures appear on the figures in the scene.
10. Choose Display > Camera View > Left Hand Camera, or click the Left Hand Camera icon in the Camera Controls. This focuses your current view on the left hand, where you can see the ring. Adjust the camera as necessary to get a good view of the ring on the hand. This prepares the camera view for the image that you will see in the library thumbnail. Figure 15.22 shows an example.
11. Adjust the lighting as necessary to get a good view of the ring. In addition, you may want to turn the display of shadows off before you save your ring to the library. Choose Display > Ground Shadows to uncheck the option if necessary.

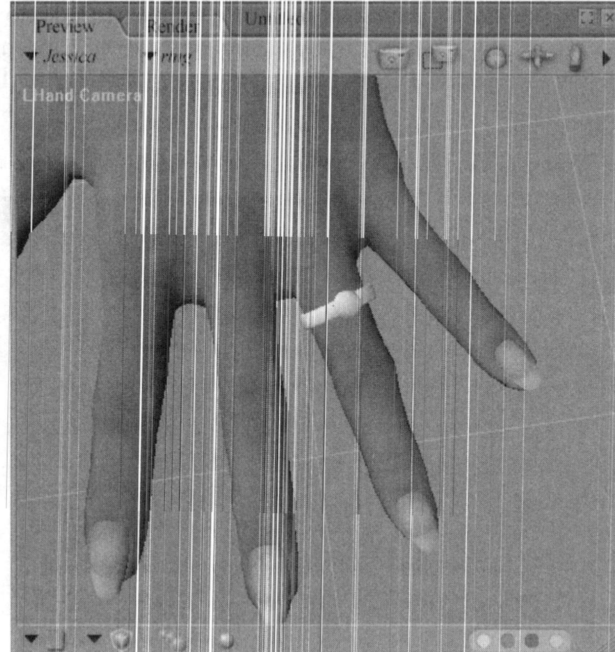

FIGURE 15.22 Adjust the Left Hand camera for a better view of the ring.

12. You might notice that the diamond on the ring does not appear to be faceted. This is due to the Smoothing feature of Poser, which softens rough edges on low-resolution geometry to make it appear as though it is higher in resolution. However, in cases when you want faceted geometry, you can adjust the Crease Angle setting in the Properties window. Any geometry that is below the setting will be smoothed. Any geometry that is above the crease angle setting will be faceted. For the ring, reduce the crease angle setting from 80 (the default) to 15 degrees, as shown in Figure 15.23. After you make this adjustment, you will see a faceted gemstone on the ring.
13. Click the Material tab to go to the Material room. Select the Simple view tab if necessary.
14. From the Object menu at the top of the Simple material view, select "ring" as the current object. The default material selection will be "Gem."
15. Click the square that appears underneath the Diffuse color rectangle. Locate the ring.jpg texture map in the Tutorials > Chap 15 folder, and select it for the texture for the gem. The gem displays the texture and now should look more like a diamond.

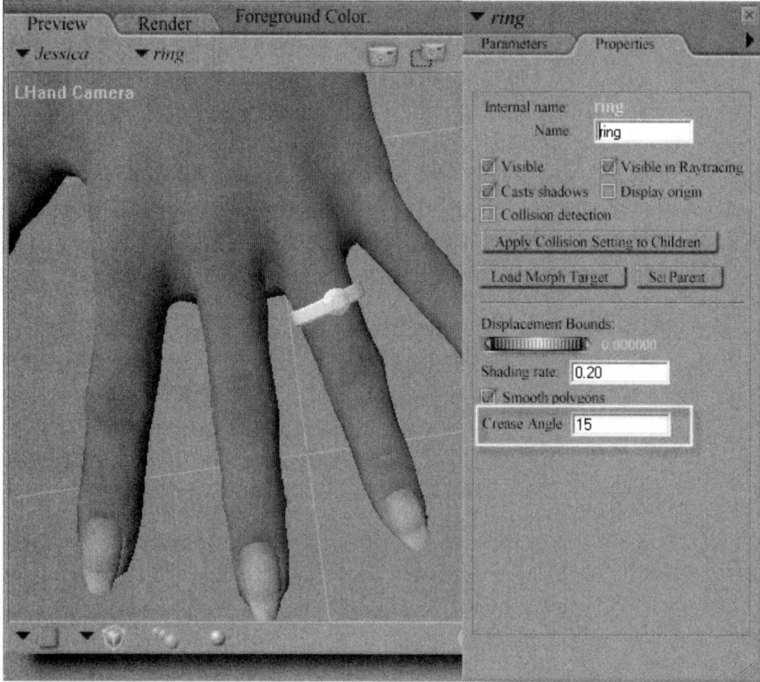

FIGURE 15.23 Reduce the Crease Angle setting in the Properties window so that the facets on the gemstone are not smoothed.

16. Select Ring from the Material drop-down menu, and again select the ring.jpg texture map. The ring turns silver.
17. Click the Add Reflection wacro in the Material Room to add a raytrace reflection to the ring band. Your material settings should now look as shown in Figure 15.24.
18. Click the Pose tab to return to the Pose Room. To attach the ring to Jessi's finger, select the ring by clicking on it or by choosing it from the Current Actor menu in the document window.
19. Click the Set Parent button in the Properties window. The Choose Parent window opens.
20. Scroll down the list and choose lRing1 as the parent for the ring, as shown in Figure 15.25. The ring should now be attached to Jessi's finger.
21. Locate the Downloads > Props > PracticalPoser6 library that you created in the previous tutorial. Verify that the ring is selected as the current object, and click the Add to Library icon at the bottom of the library window. The New Set dialog opens.

FIGURE 15.24 Click the Add Reflection macro to add a ray-trace reflection to the ring band.

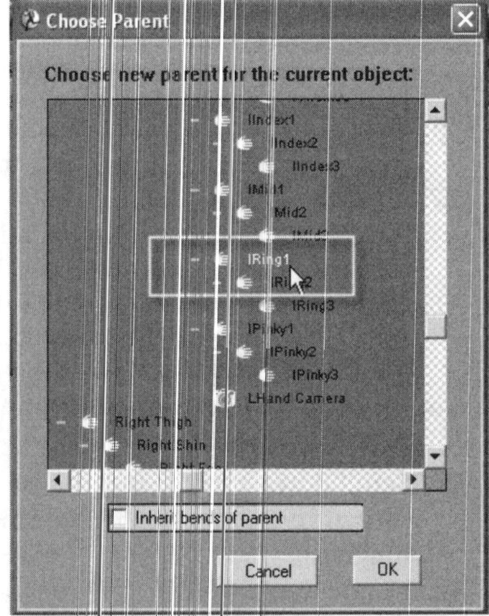

FIGURE 15.25 Choose the lRing1 body part as the parent for the ring.

22. Enter Diamond Ring as the name for the prop. *Do not* click the Select Subset button. Instead, click OK to continue.
23. The dialog shown in Figure 15.26 informs you that the prop has a parent (the left ring finger, in this case). It asks if you want to save the prop as a smart prop. Answer Yes to continue.

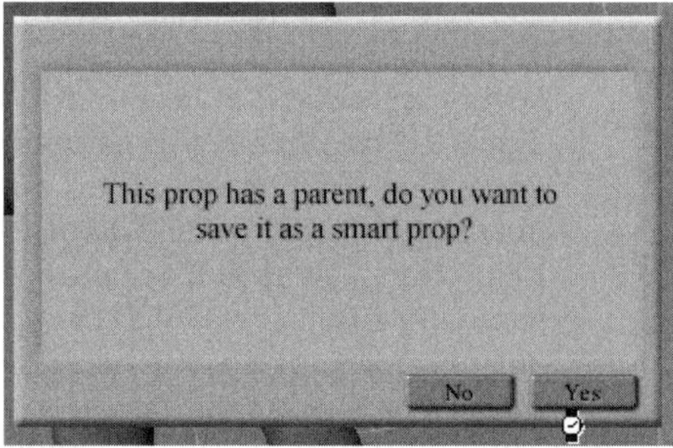

FIGURE 15.26 When a prop has a parent, Poser asks if you want to save it as a smart prop.

24. To test the figure, delete the existing ring from the left hand. Apply a pose to Jessi, and then add the engagement ring from the library. When you zoom in to the left hand with the Left Hand Camera, you should see the ring on her left hand.

CREATING CONFORMING CLOTHING

One of the most common questions asked by people who are new to Poser is, "How do I make my own clothing?" The good news is that we are going to show you where to begin. The bad news is that we can't address *everything* that is involved.

You're about to embark on a long, technical journey that will take time and a lot of practice to master. To put it succinctly, the hardest and most tedious part of creating conforming clothing is getting it to work. If you take it one step at a time, you'll eventually find it easier and easier to create your own clothing.

Before we get into the steps that add a grouped model into the Poser library as a poseable figure, we must stress one *very important* point. The steps that you are learning in this chapter are only the very beginning of a long road of learning. There are many intricacies and technicalities that you must overcome in order to make conforming clothing work well.

There are also many things that can go wrong, and it is hard to anticipate the difficulties that you will encounter along the way.

What we give you here is a starting point. For additional information beyond that which you will learn in this chapter, the following resources and solutions are recommended:

- A highly regarded member of the Poser community has prepared beginner-level tutorials that cover many features of Poser 4 and Poser 5. *Geep* (also known to the Poser community as *"Dr. Geep"*) has posted dozens and dozens of beginner-level tutorials that cover almost every aspect of Poser in an easy-natured and comical manner. In particular, you will probably want to seek out Geep's tutorials on the Group Editor, the Joint Editor, and Joint Parameters. The following thread at Renderosity gives links to most of the tutorials that Dr. Geep prepared as of January 2005: *http://www.renderosity.com/messages.ez?ForumID=12356&Form.ShowMessage=2063281.*
- *No question is a bad question.* Don't be afraid to post messages in the community forums such as Renderosity, Poser Pros, RuntimeDNA, and DAZ3D. Many of the experts there assist in any way they can. In fact, chances are good that many folks in the community have encountered the very same problems and you'll usually get an answer very quickly. Describe the problem that you're having. Provide screen shots if possible. And above all, don't be embarrassed to ask questions.

Making a CR2 File

You've already learned that you must divide a clothing object into body part groups before you make it a poseable figure. That isn't all that is necessary to make a figure poseable, however. Poser doesn't know where the joints are in that clothing, and how to bend, twist, and rotate the joints, without specific information—information that is contained in a CR2 library file.

A CR2 file (which is the extension for files saved in the Figures library) contains the information that turns your grouped clothing object into a piece of clothing that bends and moves. Basically, the CR2 tells Poser what body parts your clothing object has, where and how they bend, and what textures or materials each polygon in the object uses.

It's very difficult to create a CR2 for a totally original figure, such as a human character. Poser has the Group Editor to help you create groups, the Setup Room to help you create bones that move the groups, and the Joint Parameters window to help you specify how those joints move. However, when it comes to setting all of the parameters up for your model, it is a very tedious process.

When creating an original figure (such as a poseable human or animal), there are two methods that you can use. In the older method, you begin by creating a text file that lists each body part in a hierarchical list. Each body part is preceded by a number that lists the level in the hierarchy that they belong. At the end of each line is a three-letter designation (such as xyz), which defines the order in which the joints bend, twist, and rotate. You save this text file with a PHI extension. After this process is done, you use the File > Convert Hierarchy File command to convert the file to a Poser figure. The final step is to use the Joint Editor to configure joint parameters that define how the joints bend, move, and twist. This is without a doubt the most difficult and time-consuming process of figure creation, and it is typically used when creating a totally original figure rather than clothing for an already existing figure.

For a complete description of creating a PHI file and turning it into a CR2 character library file, refer to "Tutorial: Poser Figure Creation" on pages 343 through 355 of the Poser Tutorial Manual, furnished in PDF format with Poser 6.

In the new method, you can use the Setup Room instead of the PHI file to design your bone structure. Then you follow in the Joint Editor with configuring the joint parameters.

Because it's difficult to create joints from scratch, and because the clothing must bend almost identically with the original figure, most clothing modelers use the information from the original character when they create a CR2 for their clothing. That way, the clothing will bend and move exactly the same way that the original character does. It's much less tedious work. Reusing the information from the original figure is also the best option from a technical standpoint.

As you learned in the last chapter, you divide conforming clothing models into the same body part groups that are used in the human figure. That is the first step of the process. After you add groups to a clothing model, you have to tell Poser how those groups are connected. There are basically two ways to accomplish this:

- Use a copy of the original character's CR2 file as a donor to create a CR2 for your clothing, as described in Tutorial 15.6.
- Use the Setup Room to apply bones from the original figure to your clothing. This effectively accomplishes the same thing as editing the CR2 file in a text editor, but it gives you a visual indication of the bone structure and also allows you to add additional bones. This process is described in Tutorial 15.7.

It is common practice for clothing creators to derive their own CR2 files from information contained in the original figure's CR2 file. Though you can *technically* use the CR2 from clothing made by others, that data is copyrighted by the original creator. It would be illegal for you to use the data without permission from the creator or creators of the clothing. Their clothing items contain custom variations of joint parameters that they worked very hard to create. If you want to use their work for your own projects, contact the original developer and ask their permission first.

Removing Morphs from a CR2

When you use a donor CR2, or use the Setup Room to transfer bone and joint information to your own model, your clothing inherits the joint parameters from the donor object. That is exactly what you want to happen. What presents a bit of a problem, though, is that clothing *also* inherits the material and morph information from the donor object.

At first glance, you'll see the morph dials in the Parameters window, and you'll be delighted that the morph information appears in your clothing. However, when you try to adjust the morph dials you won't see anything happen. You see, in order for morphs to work, they must be copied between geometry objects that have exactly the same number of polygons, and the vertices that make up those polygons must be listed in exactly the same order. In other words, the geometry must be *identical* in its construction, and in the order in which the OBJ file lists all of the vertices in the geometry.

It is guaranteed that the geometry of the donor object is different than your clothing. As a result, the morph information from the original donor object does nothing but add extra and unnecessary overhead to your clothing object. It makes the file size much larger than it has to be, due to thousands of extra lines of text. So the best thing to do is remove the morph information *before* you use the donor file for one or more articles of clothing. There are a two ways that you can do this:

1. Open the Parameters window in Poser 6. Start with the head, and locate the morphs in the selected body part. Poser does not allow you to delete the dials in the Transform category, as they are necessary for posing and scaling the figure. Morphs usually appear beneath the category named Morphs. When you click the arrow at the right of a morph dial, choose Delete Morph from the menu that appears, as shown in Figure 15.27. After you delete all of the morphs, click the Add to Library icon at the bottom of your current Character library. Enter a new name for the figure, and use this figure as your donor CR2 whenever you create clothing for this character. For example, if you remove the morphs from Jessi, save the new version to the Figures library as *"JessiBlank."* Use this clean version as a source CR2 each time you create clothing for Jessi.

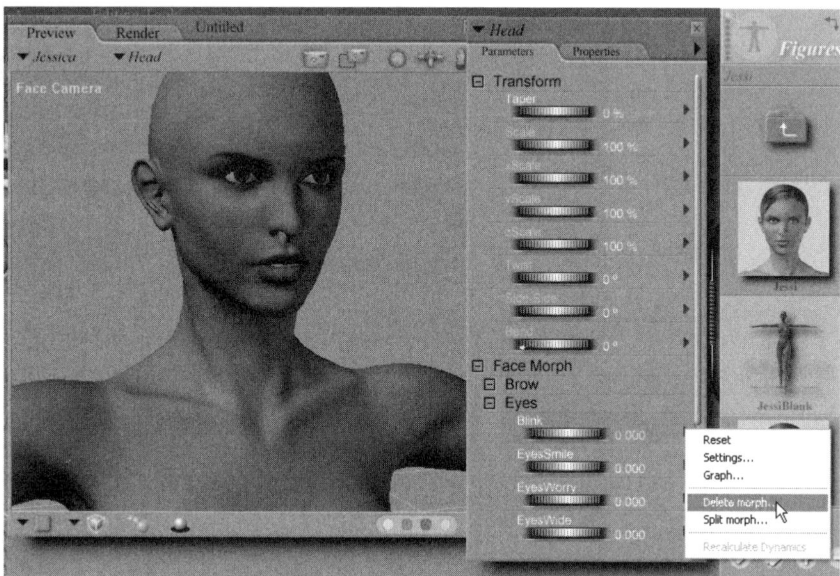

FIGURE 15.27 You can delete morphs from each body part using the Parameters window. Click the right arrow and choose Delete Morph from the menu that appears.

2. Open the figure's uncompressed CR2 (not the CRZ file) in Morph Manager 4.0, a free utility that you can download at *http://www.morphography.uk.vu/dlutility.html*. If a body part contains morphs, you will see a plus sign beside the body part. Expand the tree to reveal the morph names, which are preceded by the letter M as shown in Figure 15.28. *Do not remove the other joint parameters that are preceded with the letter 'C'*. To delete a morph, click the morph name and press the Delete key on your keyboard. Click OK when Morph Manager asks if you are sure you want to delete the morph. Complete this process until all morphs are removed, and then click the Save File button. Save the CR2 under a new filename, such as JessiBlank.

After you remove the morphs from your donor figure, be sure to save a copy to your Figures Library. Assign a different name so that you don't overwrite the original version that includes the morphs.

If you remove the morphs from Jessi.CR2 using the Remove Morph commands in the Parameters window, make sure that you have the Use File Compression option unchecked in the Misc tab of the General Preferences dialog before you save the unmorphed version to the library. This will save the file as an editable CR2 instead of a compressed CRZ file.

FIGURE 15.28 Morph Manager 4.0, a free utility that is widely used in the Poser community, allows you to delete morphs from your figures.

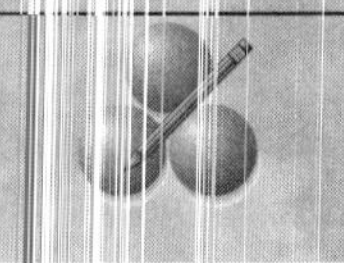

TUTORIAL 15.5 USING A DONOR CR2

As mentioned earlier in this chapter, it is common practice to use joint parameter information from a posable figure's CR2 file when you design clothing for that figure. Those who design original figures (such as Jessi, James, Victoria 3, Apollo Maximus, LaRoo, and so on) realize that it is common practice for clothing designers to use the joint information from the original character. *In most cases,* you usually don't have to ask permission. When in doubt, it won't hurt to ask the individual or company if it's OK to use the CR2 from a character when you create clothing for it.

On the other hand, it is an entirely different story when you use information from a similar piece of clothing that someone else has created for the same character. It is entirely possible that the clothing has custom joint parameters, morphs, or other configurations that are copyrighted by the original creator, and that you don't, by default, have the permission to duplicate. It's good, sound, professional practice to be respectful of the work of others from not only the moral perspective, but the legal one as well. If you don't have *written permission* to use joint parameters or morph information from clothing that has been created by others, *don't use it.* Use the information from the original character instead.

Figure and Character Information at a Glance

Content Type:	Characters, Conforming Clothing and Hair, Poseable Props
File Extensions:	CR2 (not compressed); CRZ (compressed)
Path to Geometry Files:	:Runtime :Geometries :(custom folder name)
Path to Texture Files:	:Runtime :Texture :(custom folder name)
Path to Library Files:	:Runtime :Libraries :Character :(custom folder name)

Your content can be placed beneath any Runtime folder that you choose, as long as you begin the file paths in your CR2 with :Runtime as shown above. Your custom folder can be named as you choose. Most content creators include their Artist name or the Product name within their folder names.

That being said, it is relatively easy to convert a figure's CR2 to a clothing CR2. Simply follow these steps:

1. Save the geometry and texture files in the locations shown in the note titled "Figure and Character Information at a Glance." You can locate the files in any Runtime folder, as long as the folders beneath the Runtime folder are as shown in the referenced note.
2. For purposes of this tutorial, you'll find three OBJ files in the Tutorials > Chap15 folder on the CD-ROM that accompanies this book. The files are named "JessiConfSkirt.obj," "JessiPants.obj," and "JessiTShirt.obj." Copy them to the Downloads > Runtime > Geometries > PracticalPoser6 folder.

3. If you have not already done so, remove the morphs from the Jessi.CR2 object (located in the Poser 6 > Runtime > Libraries > Character > Jessi folder), using the Remove Morph commands in the Parameters Window, or by using Morph Manager.
4. Save the unmorphed version as "JessiBlank.CR2". You can save it to the same folder as the original version as long as you assign a unique name. You might also want to make a copy of the Jessi.png thumbnail and save it as "JessiBlank.png" (the filename must be the same as the new CR2), so that the library item will have a thumbnail associated with it.

5. Open the JessiBlank.CR2 file in a text editor that can handle very large files (Microsoft Word, WordPad, or similar text editor capable of handling large files if necessary).

Some CR2 files can be hundreds, or even over a thousand pages long, especially when morphs are included. Windows users will find this far too large for Notepad, but WordPad is capable of handling larger CR2 files.

6. We'll work on the T-shirt in this tutorial. The T-shirt is located in the Poser 6 > Downloads > Runtime > Geometries > PracticalPoser6 folder, and the object name is JessiTShirt.obj. The paths in the CR2 should look as shown in Figure 15.29. *Notice that the edited path does not begin with the Downloads folder, and that it does begin with the Runtime folder.* This ensures that the path will work in any Runtime in which the files are placed. Edit the paths to the OBJ file so that it points to the object you want to make poseable, and remove the reference to the PMD file (the external binary morph file). Figure 15.29 shows both references in the CR2 file before and after they are edited.

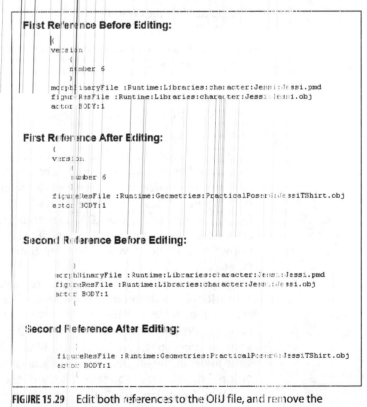

First Reference Before Editing:

```
{
version
	{
	number 6
	}
morphBinaryFile :Runtime:Libraries:character:Jessi:Jessi.pmd
figureResFile :Runtime:Libraries:character:Jessi:Jessi.obj
actor BODY:1
```

First Reference After Editing:

```
{
version
	{
	number 6
	}
figureResFile :Runtime:Geometries:PracticalPoser6:JessiTShirt.obj
actor BODY:1
```

Second Reference Before Editing:

```
	}
morphBinaryFile :Runtime:Libraries:character:Jessi:Jessi.pmd
figureResFile :Runtime:Libraries:character:Jessi:Jessi.obj
actor BODY:1
	{
```

Second Reference After Editing:

```
	}
figureResFile :Runtime:Geometries:PracticalPoser6:JessiTShirt.obj
actor BODY:1
	{
```

FIGURE 15.29 Edit both references to the OBJ file, and remove the references to the PMD file.

7. Save your edited CR2 in the Figures library in the same Runtime in which you saved your OBJ file. For example, we saved our OBJ files to the Downloads > Runtime > Geometries > PracticalPoser6 folder. You must also save the CR2 to the Downloads > Runtime library. Create a folder in your Downloads > Runtime > Libraries > Character folder named PracticalPoser6, and save the edited CR2 as JessiTShirt.CR2. Figure 15.30 shows the correct location for the Geometry OBJ and the Figures CR2.

Some text editors may enter a TXT extension after the filename when you save it. After you save your edited CR2, verify that the filename is JessiTShirt.CR2 and not JessiTShirt.CR2.TXT or JessiTShirt.TXT.

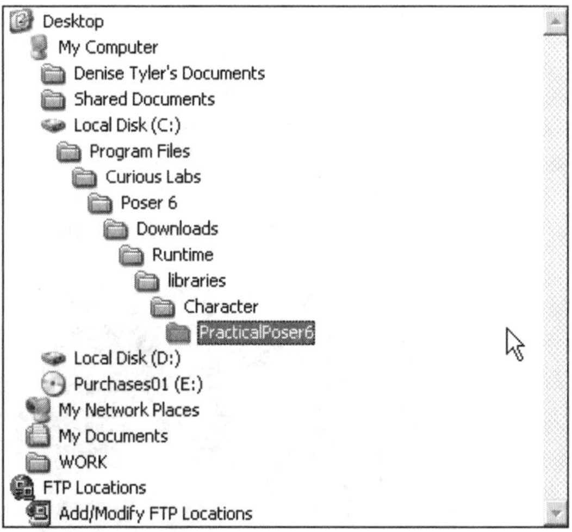

FIGURE 15.30 Make sure that you locate the Geometry file and the Figure library file in the same Runtime folder. In this case, both are located in the Downloads runtime library.

TUTORIAL 15.6 USING THE SETUP ROOM

The Setup Room is likely the most confusing room for most users. In actuality, it's not that difficult to use. For a thorough discussion of the areas in the Setup Room, refer to Chapter 30 in the Poser 6 Reference Manual, which covers the purposes for all controls in the Setup Room, along with the process required to set up joints and other information.

This tutorial will give you the basic steps involved to convert a grouped clothing model into conforming clothing using the Setup Room. After you complete this tutorial you should have the basic knowledge required to make your clothing poseable. However, you'll also need to remove some extraneous information from the CR2 file if you intend to share it with others.

One of three things can happen when you click the Setup tab to enter the Setup Room:

- If your scene is empty, or if you select an item that is not a figure or prop when you enter the Setup Room, Poser informs you that you must have a Prop or Figure selected in order to enter the Setup Room. Choose OK to close the dialog so that you can select the proper item.
- If you select a figure that is already grouped and boned (such as a poseable figure or conforming clothing), when you click the Setup tab you may receive a message that the figure contains morph targets, and that changing groups in the Setup Room could make morphs unusable. Choose OK to continue if you simply want to modify the bones or joints for the figure. When you enter the Setup Room, you'll see the figure in its default position. You'll also see the underlying bone structure that makes the figure poseable. An example is shown in Figure 15.31, where Jessi is shown in Outline display mode so that you can see the bones more easily.

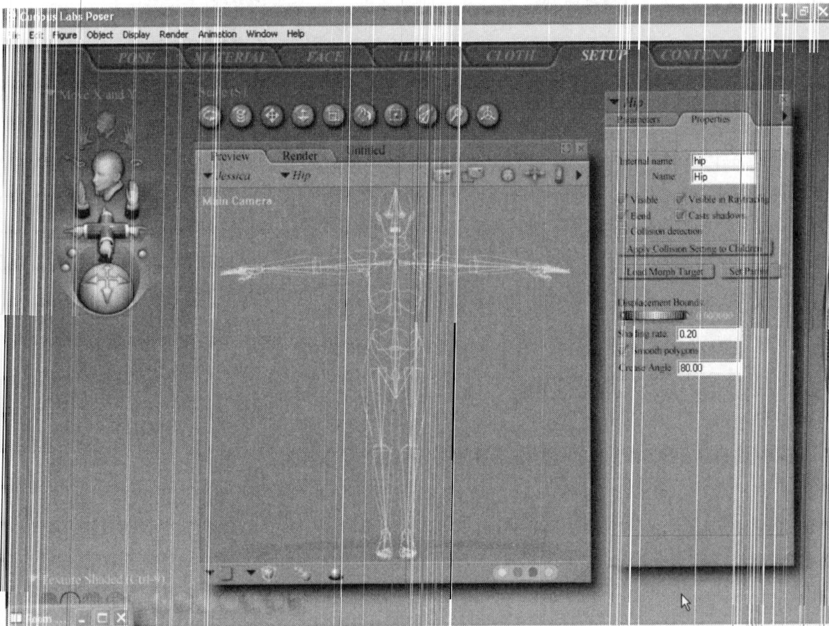

FIGURE 15.31 When you select a poseable figure and enter the Pose Room, you see the bone structure for the figure.

It is common practice to save geometry files to one of the Runtime: Geometries subfolders. If you use the Setup Room to make your geometry poseable, Poser 6 automatically saves an OBJ file in the same location as the CR2 file and references that location in the CR2. You will have to edit the CR2 if you want to point to an OBJ file in the Geometries folder.

- If you select a prop or an OBJ that you have recently imported into Poser, Poser informs you that your prop will be converted into a figure when you enter the Pose Room. The process to convert the figure is described in this tutorial.

In the tutorial that follows, we will apply the joint parameters from the JessiBlank.CR2 file that has had the morph information removed. We will apply the joint parameters to the JessiPants.obj file, which should be located in the Downloads > Runtime > Geometries > PracticalPoser6 folder.

To turn the JessiPants.obj file into conforming clothing using the Setup Room, follow these steps:

1. Use the File > Import > Wavefront OBJ command to import the JessiPants.obj file into an empty Poser scene. When the Prop Import Options dialog appears, do not check any options. The pants should appear in the center of the stage as shown in Figure 15.32.

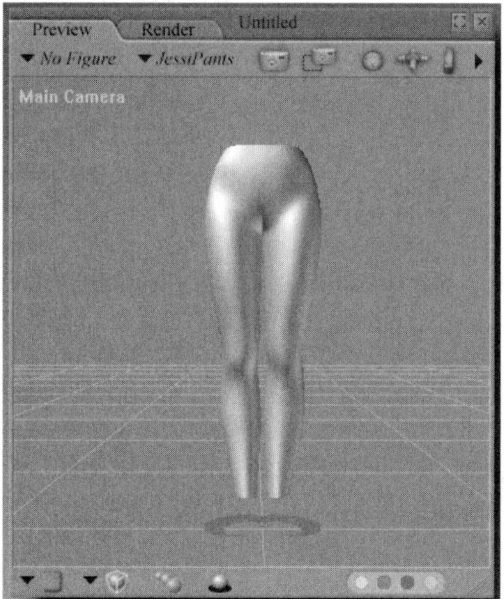

FIGURE 15.32 Import the JessiPants.obj file into an empty Poser scene.

2. With the pants selected as the current object, click the Setup tab to enter the Setup Room. Poser displays a message that your currently selected prop will be turned into a figure if you continue. Click OK to enter the Setup Room.
3. Open the Library window, and navigate to the Poser 6 > Figures > Jessi library (or, the library in which you saved your JessiBlank.CR2 file) as shown in Figure 15.33.

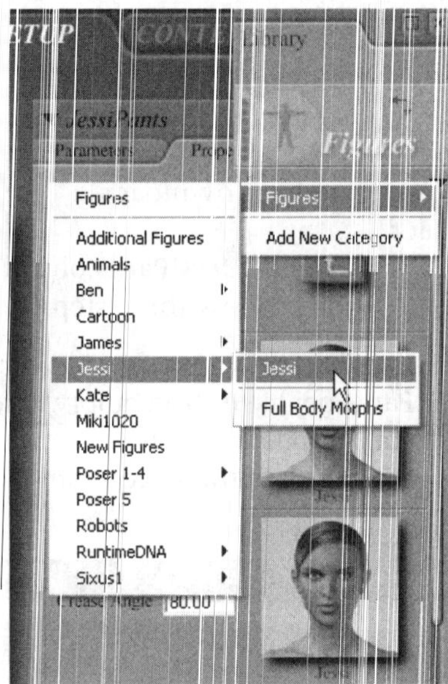

FIGURE 15.33 Navigate to the Poser 6 > Figures > Jessi library.

4. Double-click the JessiBlank CR2 library thumbnail. You will see bones appear on the figure as shown in Figure 15.34.
5. Return to the Pose Room. You'll notice that your pants are now poseable, except the legs are bent a little bit. You should zero the pose and then memorize that pose before you save the pants to the library. First, choose Window > Joint Editor to open the Joint Editor palette. Click any body part on the pants, and then click the Zero Figure button in the Joint Editor. The pants should go back to the default position.

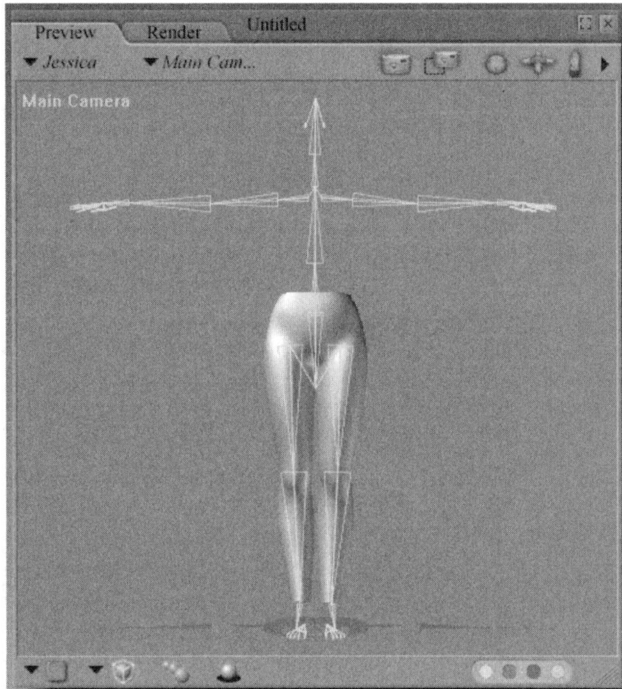

FIGURE 15.34 Apply the JessiBlank CR2 to the pants in the Setup Room. The bones appear on the figure.

6. To memorize the zero pose for the pants, choose Edit > Memorize > Figure. You won't notice any visible confirmation, but you can now save a preliminary copy of the pants to your library.
7. If you don't want shadows to appear in the library thumbnail, choose Display > Ground Shadows to uncheck the shadow option if necessary. Position the camera to display the scene as you want your library thumbnail to appear.
8. Backtrack to the top level of the Poser library, and then navigate to the Downloads > Figures > PracticalPoser6 library. Click the Add to Library icon located at the bottom of the library window, as shown in Figure 15.35. Your pants will appear in the library, and a miniaturized version of your document window will appear as the thumbnail.

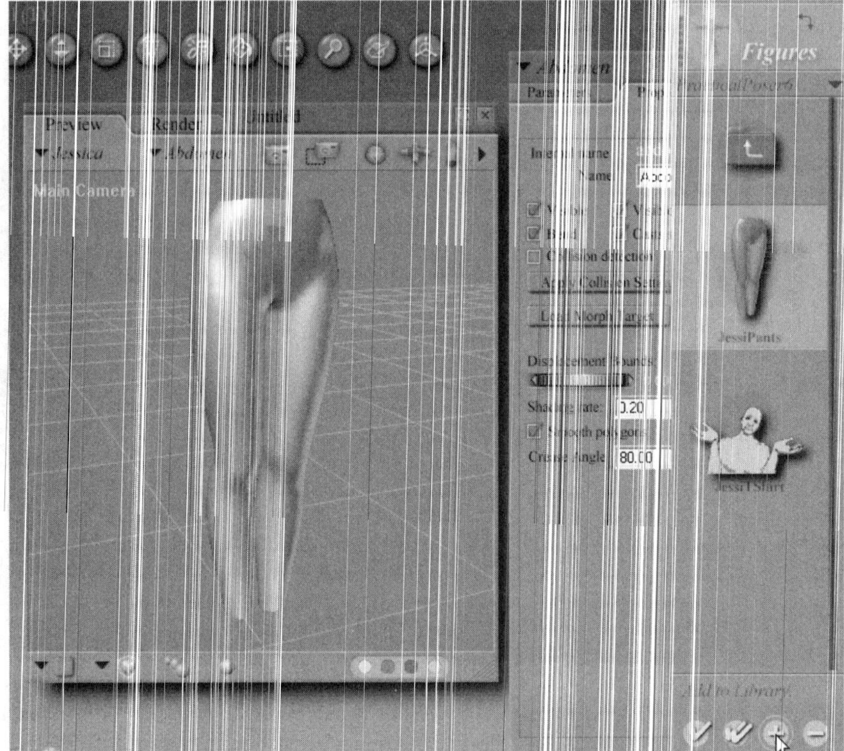

FIGURE 15.35 Click the Add to Library icon to add the parts to the library.

CLEANING UP THE CR2

Just because the clothing is now poseable, it does not necessarily mean that you are finished. There are some items that you will definitely have to clean up in the CR2 using either a text editor or a free CR2 editing program. Highly recommended is John Stalling's CR2 Editor, version 1.51, which displays the CR2 for JessiPants in Figure 15.36. You can download this file from *http://www.morphography.uk.vu/dlutility.html* (the same site that also provides Morph Manager 4.0, mentioned earlier in this chapter).

Common issues that you will have to clean up are the following:

- If the hip (on a male or female) and the chest (on a female) of your clothing disappear and display the hip and chest of the figure instead, your CR2 contains alternate geometry parts that must be removed.

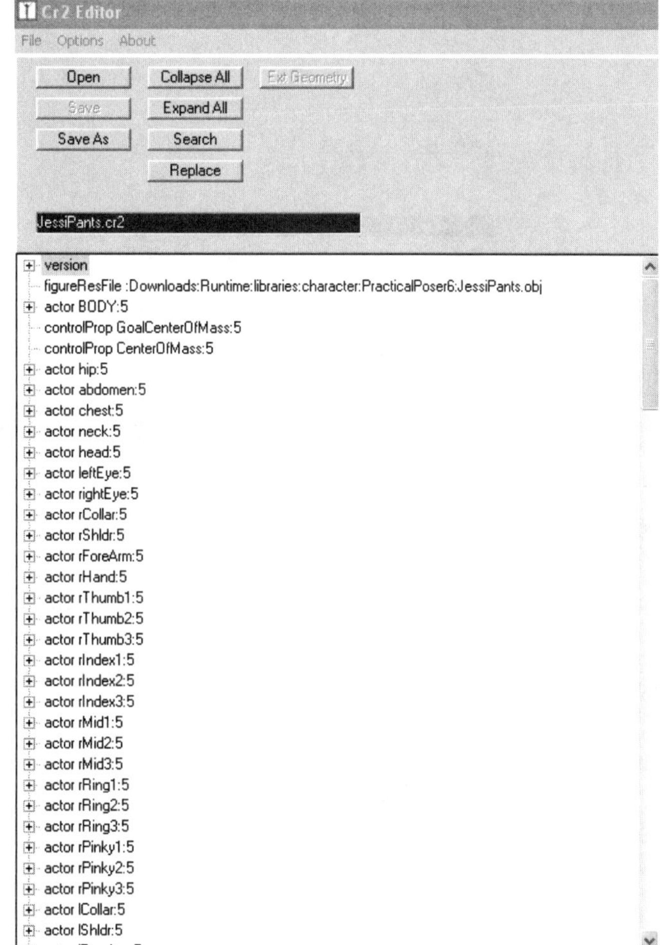

FIGURE 15.36 You will have to edit your CR2 in a text editor or a CR2 editing utility such as John Stalling's CR2 Editor.

Adult male and female Poser figures are often modeled with body parts that you can swap, depending on whether you want to show or hide the genitalia. There are lines in the CR2 that call other pieces of geometry when this is true. You have to remove those lines from the CR2. Use CR2 Editor to search for the string "alternateGeom". You will probably find one or two sections that reference it, and you'll have to remove it from the CR2. Figure 15.37 shows one such reference.

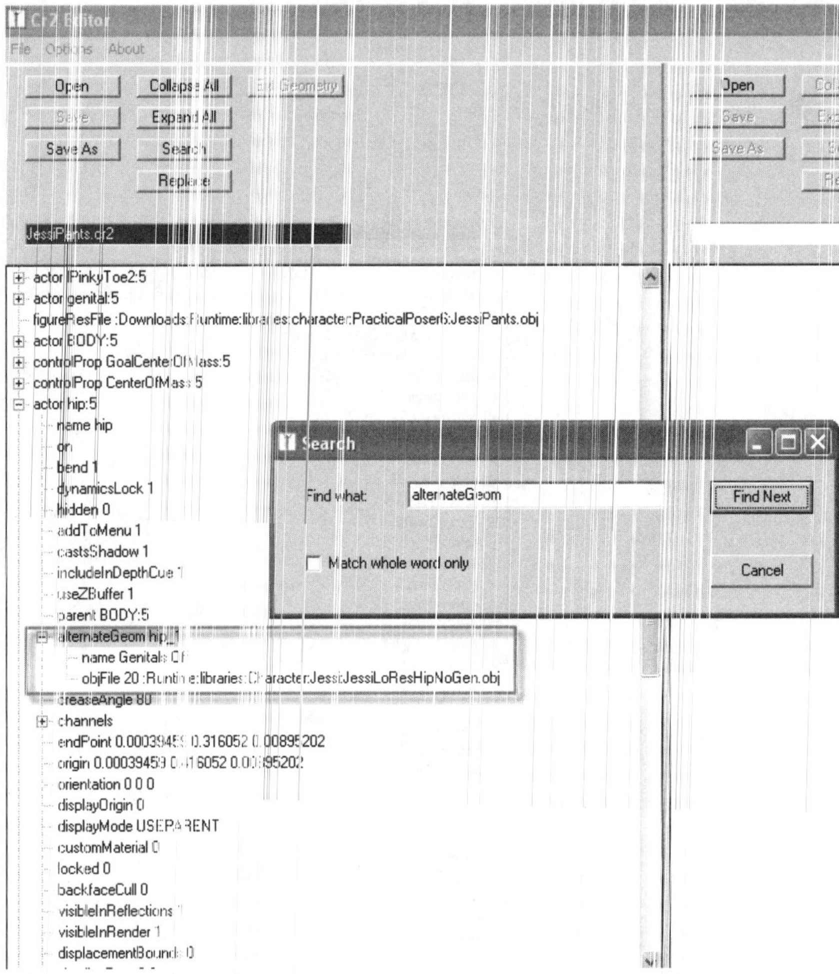

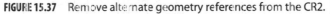

FIGURE 15.37 Remove alternate geometry references from the CR2.

- Each body part in the CR2 is followed by a colon (:) which is then followed by a number, depending on the number of figures that you opened in your scene before you created the figure. For example, you'll see lines that start with "actor hip:5" or "actor BODY:5". It is common practice to have this last number be the number 1, so you'll want to search and replace all instances of *:5* with *:1*.
- Remove extra body parts that aren't needed. The general rule of thumb is "Start with the hip, and work your way through all parts you need, *plus one*." So, for example, your pair of pants has abdomen, hip, left and right thigh, and left and right shin sections. You want to

keep all of those parts, plus chest (one higher than the abdomen) and the left and right feet (one lower than the left and right shins). Delete all other parts, because they aren't necessary and will add extra weight to your file.

- Remove extra materials that aren't needed. You'll find the materials listed toward the end of the CR2 file. Notice, in Figure 15.38, that the pants inherited all of the materials from the donor CR2. The only materials that are needed are the Pants material and the Preview material. All of the other materials (Body, BottomEyelashes, TeethTop, and so on through Toenails) can be deleted because they are not a part of the Pants geometry.

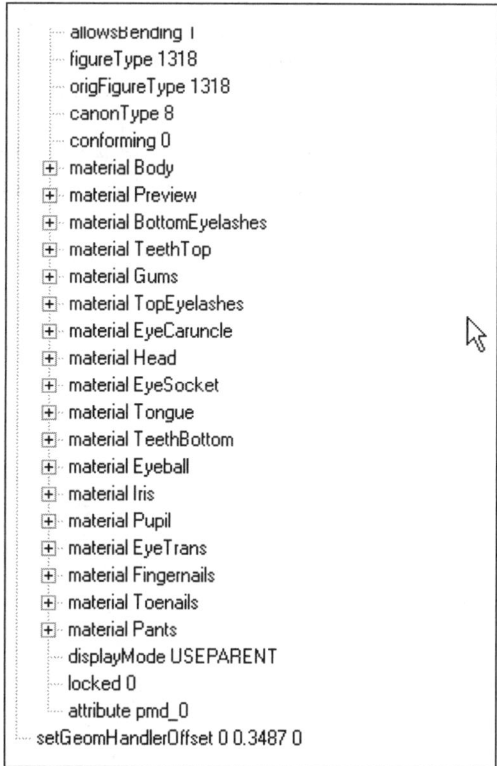

FIGURE 15.38 Remove extra material references from the CR2.

- And now for the not-so-good news—you may have to tweak the joint parameters. You might have faces that fly away when you pose the figure or parts that don't bend right when you conform the clothing to the figure. You may have to use the Joint Editor to tweak the joint parameters. Because there are so many different things that can happen with joint parameters, we advise that you seek out assistance from the experts in the Poser community. There are several forums online at Renderosity, DAZ3D, and PoserPros that are frequented by some of the best Poser content creators, who are more than happy to assist with questions and problems.

CONCLUSION

You've learned in this chapter, and in the previous few chapters, that it is a lot of work to model, UV-map, texture, group, and rig your Poser figures. However, in the long run, it is a very enjoyable and rewarding process. Along with learning something that is both artistic and technical, you are gaining the satisfaction of creating your own Poser content and enhancing your artwork with new skills and experience. The skills that you have learned in these last few chapters are only the beginning to a long road of learning and enjoyment, and we hope that we have inspired you to learn even more. Good luck with your Poser content creation efforts!

CHAPTER

16

RENDERING

In This Chapter

- Fundamentals
- Rendering Rules of Thumb
- File Resolution-DPI-Dimensions
- Poser 6 Rendering Environments
- Conclusion

Now that you know about textures, maps, and material shaders, it's time to dig into the Poser render system. In this chapter we'll explain basic concepts to help you understand and get the most out of your renders. We'll introduce you to the FireFly render engine, the heart of Poser 6. Though we'll concentrate on FireFly, we'll briefly introduce the other render options you have in Poser too. You will get information to help you:

- decide what settings to use, based on your needs---for speed or quality.
- work smarter and use your computer's resources wisely.
- make sense of the *resolution-DPI-file dimension* quagmire.

FUNDAMENTALS

Before you get into the specific parameters associated with the various render engines, let's review some of the general concepts that apply to rendering. While this isn't an exhaustive introduction, we'll touch upon key concepts to at least get you started.

We can't stress enough that your Poser 6 software comes with two invaluable manuals that go a long way toward helping even novice users understand and get the most out of Poser 6 specifically, and 3D projects in general. If you haven't at least skimmed both of these manuals, we strongly suggest you take a few moments to do.

Raytracing

The concept of raytracing is fairly straightforward; rays of light are traced from a light source as their path bounces or interacts with the various objects in the scene. When rays of light hit an object their properties change based on the material properties and shape of the object:

- Rays may get absorbed, which makes the object dark.
- Rays may bounce off of the surface of the object. When rays bounce, the color of the reflected light adjusts based on which frequencies of light get absorbed by the material. Reflected light also changes direction.
- When rays bounce off of smooth surfaces, they are reflected in basically the same direction, which creates hard, distinct specular highlights.
- When rays hit a surface that is slightly rough or has irregularities, the rays are reflected into different directions. This scatters the reflection and creates "fuzzy" or "soft" highlights. These reflected properties give the viewer clues to the properties of the surface.
- Rays may even split into several rays when they encounter materials that are translucent, refractive, or have subsurface scattering properties.

Rays eventually make their way into the camera "lens," at which point the color of each pixel is based on the aggregate color of the light rays that enter the lens *at that pixel*. The direction from which the renderer begins calculating the path of the ray doesn't change the concept of *how* raytracing works. That is, it may be that in actuality calculations start from a ray's ending location—which, for the purposes of this explanation, can be thought of as a pixel in the lens of the camera—and work back through the path of the ray to the point of its origin. Whichever way the calculations run doesn't change the underlying concept of tracing rays of light to create a *raytraced render*.

Raytraced reflections take longer to calculate. The following things are important to consider when you enable raytracing to calculate reflections:

- The number of lights you have in the scene will directly impact how long your raytracing will take. Each light increases render times significantly.
- Lights may also need to calculate Ray Traced Shadows in addition to all of the reflections.
- Other reflective surfaces will add to your render times. If your reflective surfaces interact with each other, you will additionally need to pay attention to the number of Raytrace Bounces you have configured. Allowing the rays to bounce more will give you more accurate results, but will take longer to render.
- Complex surfaces with properties that scatter light, such as skin and other subsurface scattering materials, will significantly increase your render times because each ray will generate several new rays when interacting with these types of materials. The effect in this case is exponential.
- Materials that have refractive properties will also increase your render times.

Raytraced Reflections versus Reflection Maps

It is important to understand the differences between reflections that are generated via raytracing and those that are generated via reflection mapping. (See Chapter 11, "Creating Your Own Image-Based Textures," and Chapter 9, "Assigning and Creating Materials," for additional information about Reflection Maps and other material properties.) Knowing which method you need to use for your particular project will help you set up your materials and render options efficiently. The rule of thumb is that if you need reflections that accurately represent the objects in your scene—for surfaces with mirrored finishes, for example—you will need to use raytracing.

However, if your surfaces are duller, exceedingly bumpy, or your mesh has intricate geometry, you can get away with using reflection mapping to give the impression of reflection. See Figure 16.1 for an example that compares raytraced reflections to reflection-mapped reflections. The figure on the left uses reflection mapping to simulate a reflective surface while the figure on the right uses raytraced reflections to actually reflect the surrounding elements. As a rule, reflection maps are a faster technique for creating the impression of a reflective surface.

FIGURE 16.1 A comparison of reflection maps (left) and raytraced reflections (right).

Refraction

This property describes the bending of light as it leaves one medium and enters another. For example, when you immerse a pencil into a glass of water and view the glass from the side it will look like the pencil is bending. Light passes from one medium (air) into the other (water), and changes velocity. As a result, the light changes direction. The amount of bending, which is nonlinear, depends upon the angle at which the light enters the medium. The amount of bending is also a function of the difference between the *refractive index* of each medium. (The refractive index is a measure of how much a material bends light.)

A diamond is a good example of a material with exceptional refraction properties. They are valuable as jewelry because they have a very high refractive index, which means that they really bend light. Because they don't bend all frequencies of light by the same amount, white light gets dispersed, or separated into rainbows, giving diamonds their beautiful colors. In Figure 16.2, you see an example of an object with refractive properties interacting with another object. The translucent material of the sphere has refractive properties, which are bending the light to cast a distorted "shadow image" of the checkered cone object. Calculating refraction will slow your rendering down, so use this property with caution.

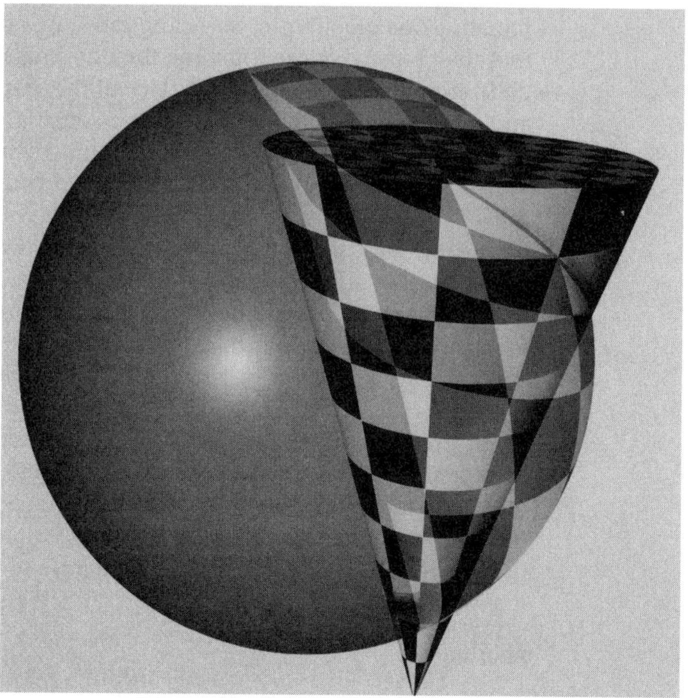

FIGURE 16.2 Refraction is a property that causes light to bend at the boundary of two different materials.

Subsurface Scattering

All materials, except metallic ones, have some type of surface translucence. Surface translucence allows light to penetrate the top-most surface layers and enter the material to some degree. When light enters a material some of it scatters just below the surface boundary causing both reflection and refraction within the material itself. Some light reflects back out of the surface layer. Additionally, some light that makes it into the material may get absorbed at various depths. This process is called *subsurface scattering*. Examples of naturally occurring subsurface scattering can be found in a number of very common substances. For example, look at a glass of milk under various light conditions and you'll notice that light penetrates into the milk by a surprising distance.

White grapes also exhibit very pronounced subsurface scattering effects. When you look at grapes in different lighting conditions, notice that the light actually gets transmitted *to* grapes through *other* grapes that are in contact. This makes the grapes appear as if they are illuminated from within, even if they aren't receiving any direct light from the light source. In fact, if you happen to have a laser pointer and some white grapes handy, try illuminating one grape from very close range in a darkened room. You will see that the grapes that are touching the illuminated grape will appear to be lit up from within. Beneath the surface of the grape skin, the material refracts and scatters light, such that what was once a very organized and focused beam of light is dispersed as the light bounces around within the grape.

Hold your own hand up to a light, and you'll see light through some of the areas between your fingers and between your thumb and fingers. Notice how the edges of your skin look. Examine your own face in the mirror under bright lights. Skin around your eyes and cheeks is particularly thin and delicate and you should be able to see hints of the veins underneath. Figure 16.3 shows a basic diagram that illustrates the concepts of subsurface scattering for a material such as human skin. There are several types of "ray-events" happening at each boundary layer and within each distinct type of layer. On the surface, light is reflected, scattered, and refracted. Once it enters the skin layer, it is again reflected, scattered, and refracted. What started off as one ray of light becomes many. This creates diffusion, or softening, of the light properties. In addition, light appears to be transmitted into areas that do not receive direct lighting of their own.

Aliasing

Aliasing is a term currently used in audio and graphics applications. In graphics applications, aliasing is more commonly known as "jaggies," which appear as rough, pixilated edges on an object that we *know* is supposed to be smooth. Jaggies can make the edges of your objects look like stair steps, when they are supposed to have a straight but diagonal line.

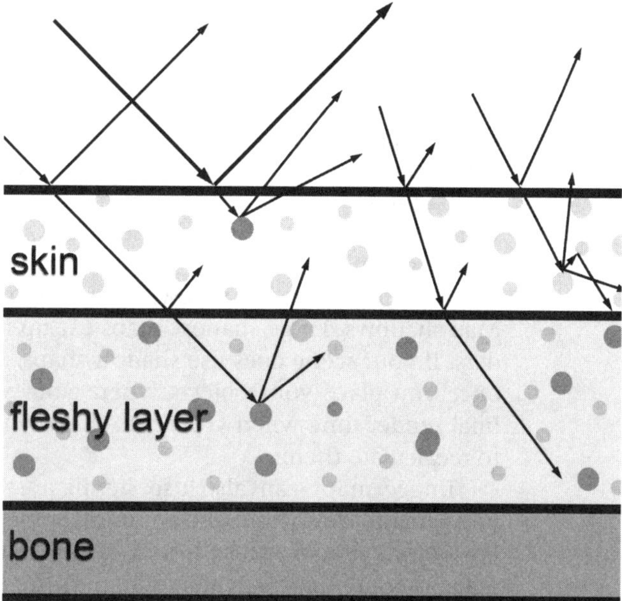

FIGURE 16.3 Subsurface scattering effects for skin-type materials.

Jaggies occur because the number of colors or resolution of the graphic is too low. As a result, you see large chunks or blocks of color where you would expect soft, smooth transitions to occur.

Most graphics software programs today provide a feature called *anti-aliasing*. This process fills in jagged edges with intermediate colors to reduce the stair-step effect and blend transitions smoothly. See Chapter 11, "Creating Your Own Textures," for an example of images that exhibit aliased effects. See Figure 16.4 for an example of what an aliased and an antialiased edge looks like.

FIGURE 16.4 The aliased edge on the left shows the distinct stepping effect of "jaggies." The edge on the right is antialiased to gradually smooth the transition between white and black.

RENDERING RULES OF THUMB

Lighting affects rendering speeds. Lights that cast shadows take longer to render than those that don't. Lights interact with materials; so if you are using complex materials that are transparent, reflective, scatter, or refract light, your renders will take longer. You can speed up renders by turning off shadows on lights that are not critical (usually all but one or two lights won't need shadows), or those that are not the primary shadow source for your scene.

Also, be aware that you will use more resources when you use Depth Map shadows. Large shadow maps eat up resources and slow down renders. If your scene does use shadow maps, you can choose to reuse them once you place your objects where you want them. You speed up the final render time when you reuse shadow maps, because you don't have to recalculate them.

Image maps can also use significant amounts of resources. Large image maps are a waste of computing power if you aren't doing close-ups. For objects that are close to the camera, such as full facial portraits, use maps that are approximately equal to the size of your final render. You can use smaller texture maps as objects get farther away.

Complex materials can also significantly increase your render times. Use less complex materials on objects that are farther away from your camera to help keep your render times as short as possible.

Apply the same philosophy to the objects in your scene as you do with image maps. Use low poly-count models for objects that are farther away from your camera. Many of the default Poser figures come with high and low poly-count versions. If you are doing scenes with crowds of figures, consider breaking up your render into two steps. First, create a background render that captures the crowd and other content that is far away from your camera. Take that render and use it as the background for your close-up object render. See the Tutorial in Chapter 5, "Mastering Lights and Shadows," to walk through the steps of casting shadows onto your background image.

Finally, the Auto Settings tab of the Render Palette is a very good place to start until you become familiar with render parameters and what they do. For example, when you are initially setting up a scene, use the Auto Settings slider to start at Draft quality. Then work your way up to Final quality as your scene nears completion. Auto Settings are an excellent resource that should work for most *normal* scenes.

A quick way to create some of the complex materials like those with reflection, refraction, subsurface scattering, shadow catchers, and image-based lighting is to use the Wacros in the Advanced Materials view. These Wacros give you an excellent place to start by connecting up all the required nodes for each type of material type. You may have to tweak the material to suit your particular circumstances but these Wacros are a great timesaving feature.

Render Preview and Render Compare

The Render Comparison feature allows you to compare two of your previously rendered images within the Preview window. Click the "stack of paper" icons on the bottom-left corner of the Render document window. This opens a list of your most recent renders. The Main Render, selected from the left list, is placed beside the Compare Render that you select from the right list. After you select a render from each list, you can use the Render Wipe slider at the bottom of the window to reveal the renders side-by-side. You can configure the number of renders held in the render cache in the Document tab of the Edit > General Preferences dialog.

Area Render

The Area Render feature allows you to select and render an area of your scene, and it is particularly useful when you make changes in your scene—especially changes in lighting. Instead of waiting for the entire screen to render again, you select a small portion of your screen for rendering. This allows you to see the effects of your changes more quickly.

Click the Area Render symbol at the top of the Preview window to enable the Area Render. Then, left-click and drag the mouse to select a rectangular area in the Preview window. Then release the left mouse button to render the selected area.

FILE RESOLUTION-DPI-DIMENSIONS

Often you will hear people referring to a file's resolution, or its DPI. Usually DPI means "dots per inch." DPI can also mean *pixels per inch* (PPI). It can be very confusing. Typically, when someone refers to file resolution, they will use the term DPI, but often, screen resolution is referred using the same acronym even though PPI is a more specific one.

File Resolution

When we say something has a resolution of 300 DPI, we mean that there are 300 pixels (dots) squeezed into one inch, or that each dot is 1/300 of an inch in size when it is displayed or printed. At 300 pixels per inch, you can pack a lot of image information into one square inch—those 90,000 individual pixels in that one little square inch make things look crisp and clear.

Now, let's compare that to an image that is 72 DPI, or has only 72 pixels per inch. In this case, there are only 5,184 pixels in one square inch. There is not even six percent of the detail in the 300-DPI image. The 72 DPI image has less detail in it so the image looks blocky and more blurry.

Another example to help you visualize and understand the concept of resolution is the rubber band example (you may want to actually go get a rubber band and follow along): Find yourself a big, fat rubber band, and cut it so you can lay it flat on your desk. Then, without stretching it, mark off one inch along its length. Now take a pen or marker and add evenly spaced dots from one end of the inch you marked off to the other. In our example, we managed to get 20 little dots marked onto our rubberband in the one inch we had marked off. The resolution of our rubberband is therefore 20 DPI, or 20 dots per inch.

Now, stretch the rubberband out to four times its original length, so that your rubber band is four inches long. The four-inch long rubberband still has twenty dots, and you should see your dots get far apart and blur. In this stretched state, each inch in the rubberband has only five dots per inch. You see the same dots, but they are spread out over four inches instead of just one.

If the dots were pixels, your image would have gone from sharp to blurry; in addition, each dot would be farther away from its neighbor. The resolution of the rubber band depends *entirely* on how much we've stretched it out. Image files work the same way. In both the stretched and relaxed rubberband examples, we had the exact same number of dots (20). When we pack those 20 dots into a smaller space, say one inch, our resulting image appears relatively sharp and when we spread those same dots out over four inches, our image looks fuzzy and blurry.

Figure 16.5 illustrates the concept of DPI. Each square of the check pattern represents a single pixel, or dot. In the top row, 40 squares exist per each inch of our illustration. In the middle, there are 20 squares in each inch; and in the bottom row, only 10 squares. At 40 DPI, the texture is fairly detailed and sharp. However, at 10 DPI, details get lost, the image gets blurry, and artifacts may be apparent.

Let's look at this from another angle. If we have an image that is 100 DPI and the image is 300 pixels in each dimension (length and width), it will be 3 inches wide and 3 inches tall. When we change the resolution of the file to 300 DPI, without resampling the number of total pixels, we still have 300 pixels total in our width and height, but the image is only 1 inch wide and 1 inch tall. At 300 DPI, the pixels are more tightly packed and the image *looks* sharper.

Most monitors have 72 tiny phosphorous, LCD, or plasma pixels in each linear inch of their surface. This means they are 72 DPI (Macs and some other types of displays can be 92 or even 120 DPI). Printers, on the

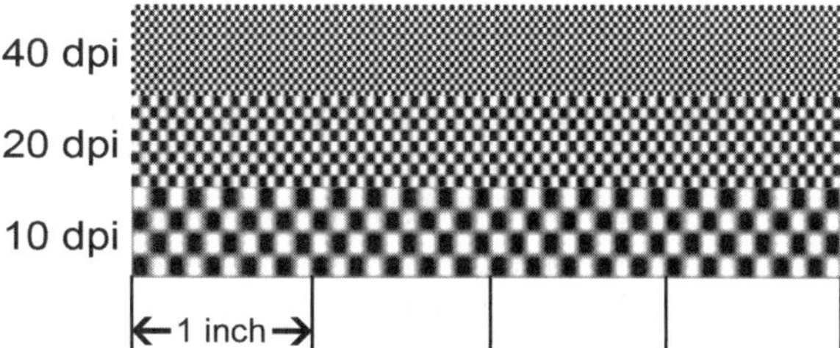

FIGURE 16.5 As the dots per inch decrease, there is less information in one inch.

other hand, are capable of outputting higher resolutions. The standard which has been adopted as a "typical printer resolution" is 300 DPI. Some printers can output several times that resolution and have sophisticated image processing algorithms, called RIPS (Raster Image Processors), that convert your image to the actual output resolution with minimal blurring or distortions. Other printers do a marvelous job with images that have less than 300 dots per inch of image data and some can create remarkably clear output from as little as 120 DPI! Check with your own printer specifications to find out what resolution you need to accommodate in your work for optimal output. If, for example, the printer tells you that you must provide your images at 300 DPI, and you want your printed image to be 8 inches by 10 inches, you must render an image that is 2400 by 3000 pixels at 300 DPI.

Resampling

Resampling an image is not always the same as resizing the image. When you resample an image, you change the number of pixels in the image. This can introduce unwanted artifacts. For example, if you have a 10 × 10-inch image that is 120 dots per inch, your image will be 1200 × 1200 pixels in dimension (120 DPI × 10 inches). If you resize that image to 5 inches in both dimensions without resampling, you still have the original 1200 × 1200 pixels but they are now 240 DPI. The image *appears* sharper when printed in a 5-inch square space verses a 10-inch square space, because more pixels are compressed into each inch. However, the total number of pixels has not changed.

Alternately, if you resample that same image to 5 inches in both dimensions, your DPI will remain at 120, which will result in the removal of pixels during the resampling process. The final image in this case will be only 600 pixels in either dimension since it remained at the original 120 DPI.

The danger with resampling an image is that you cannot undo the changes once you save your image. Also, if you start with a very low-resolution image it really isn't feasible to resample the image to create a quality, high-resolution image. This is because your software can only interpolate between adjacent pixels to create the additional pixels, which will result in blurry or aliased images. Figure 16.6 shows what resampling can do to an image.

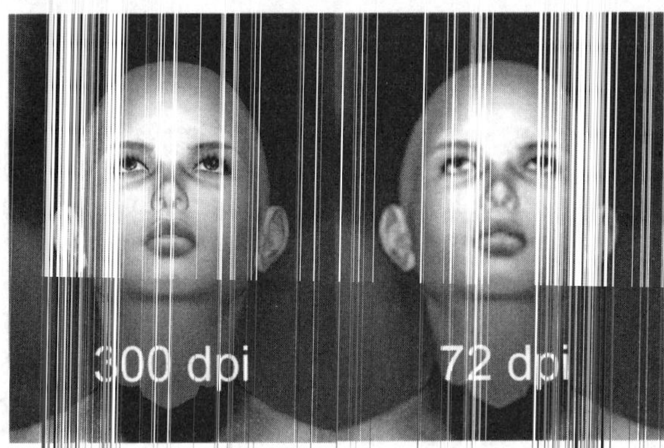

FIGURE 16.6 The image at left was rendered at 300 DPI. The image on the right shows what happens to that image when it is resampled down to only 72 DPI.

TUTORIAL 16.1 SETTING RENDER SETTINGS AND ASPECT RATIO

The aspect ratio of an image is simply the ratio of its width to its height. If an image is 11 inches wide by 14 inches tall, its aspect ratio is 1:1.27. (The 1.27 is derived by dividing the height by the width, which in our case is 14 divided by 11.)

Poser 6 makes it super easy to get the right dimensions and aspect ratio for your renders. You typically don't even have to do any calculations to set up renders for specific output dimensions. For example, let's say you need a 5 × 7-inch final image, and the printer requires 300 dots per inch of image to create optimal output. It is very easy to set this up in Poser:

1. Choose Render > Render Dimensions to open the Render Dimensions dialog shown in Figure 16.7.

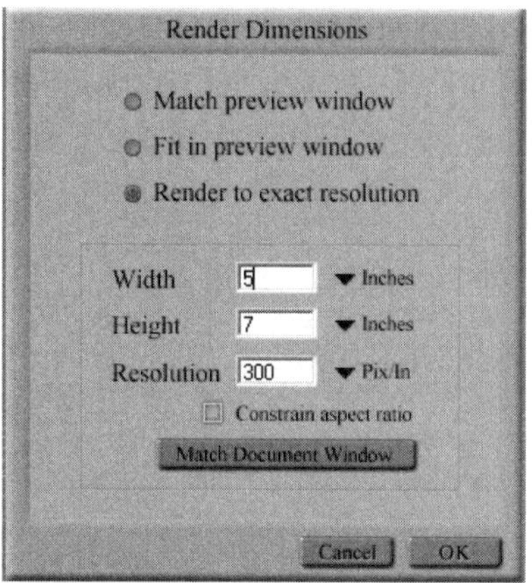

FIGURE 16.7 The Render Dimensions dialog allows you to specify the dimensions and DPI for your final renders.

2. Temporarily uncheck the Constrain Aspect Ratio option until you enter the final width, height, and resolution of the image.
3. Select "Render to exact resolution" from the upper section of the Render Dimensions dialog.
4. Enter "300" into the Resolution field, and select Pix/In from the units pull down. This sets the resolution at 300 DPI.
5. Now enter "5" into the Width field and select Inches from the units pull down.
6. Enter "7" into the Height field and select Inches from the units pull down. You will now have a render that is exactly 5 inches wide by 7 inches tall, which is 300 DPI.
7. Now, check the Constrain Aspect Ratio again. By doing so, you can change the Width or the Height value, and the other value will change automatically to keep the same relative proportions. Let's say that you have another frame which has the same aspect ratio as your 5 × 7-inch frame, but that is 8 inches wide instead of 5. As long as the Constrain Aspect Ratio option is selected, you can easily get a perfect fit by simply going back into your Render Dimensions dialog and changing the 5-inch Width entry to 8. Your height value will be calculated automatically for you when you change the width. Alternately, if you change the height value, the width will be recalculated to maintain the same aspect ratio.

Production Frame

The Display > Production Frame > Image Output size displays a production frame indicator inside your preview window. If your preview window's aspect ratio is not the same as your rendered output settings, you will see the Production Frame in your preview window to let you see what objects in your scene will appear in the render. The area that falls within the rendered area appears lighter than the area that will not be rendered. Figure 16.8 shows the Production Frame in our preview window. The aspect ratio of the Production Frame in this figure is different than that of the Preview Window. With this useful option you can see exactly what objects will appear in your render.

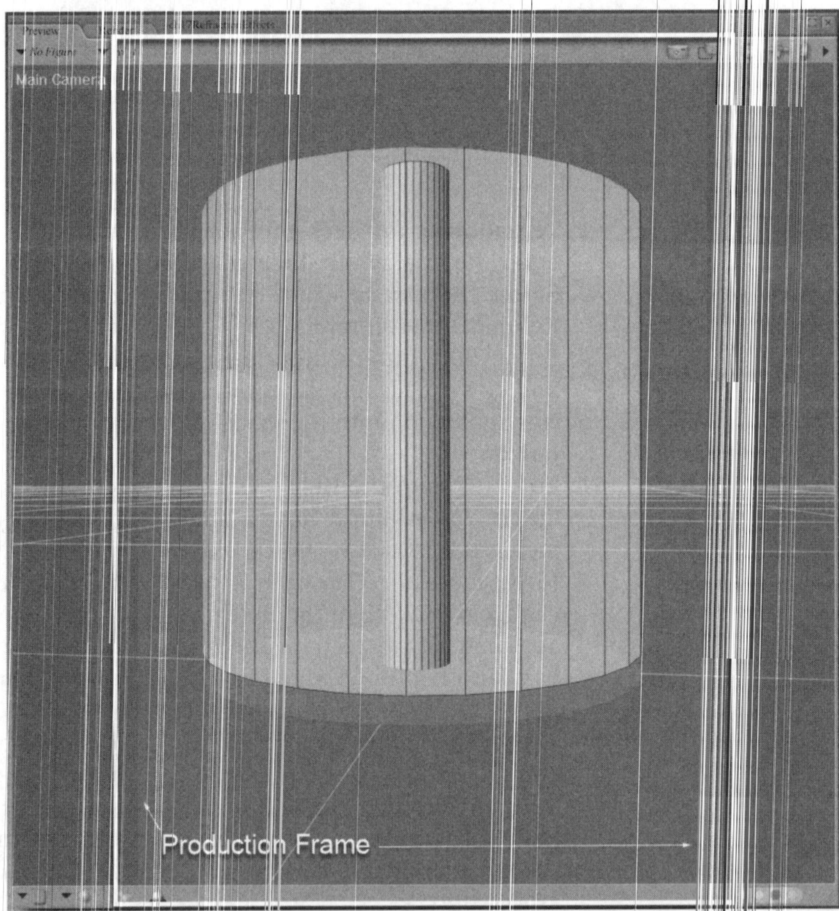

FIGURE 16.8 The Production Frame is indicated by the lighter gray rectangle (outlined in white) within the Preview Window.

There are several "standard" image aspect ratios such as 8×10 (1:1.25), 20×24 (1:1.24), and such. If you plan on creating prints of your work for framing, setting up your render in one of the popular aspect ratios will allow you to purchase pre-made mats and frames.

POSER 6 RENDERING ENVIRONMENTS

Poser 6 gives you four distinct engines you can use to render your output. You can choose from highly stylized rendered output, to cartoon-like renders, all the way to photorealistic renders, all without leaving Poser 6!

FireFly Renderer: Employs subdivision surface rendering of polygons, can smooth polygons at render time, calculate displacement maps, apply 3D-motion blur, utilize depth-of-field principles to create sophisticated camera lens effects, calculate raytraced materials with properties such as refraction, reflection, and subsurface scattering, and process complex procedural shader trees with many nodes.

Poser 4 Renderer: Before FireFly, Poser used this render engine. It's great for creating 3D figures that "look" like they've been rendered. The older renderer supports BUM files for bump-mapping but does not support procedural shaders.

Sketch Design Renderer: Simulates an assortment of artistic drawing and painting effects. It is a wonderful tool with the potential for some very creative results.

Preview Renderer: Excellent solution which allows you to render your preview window exactly as you see it. This means you can now have print-quality images using *any* of the display style options. The preview renderer is an excellent source for flat-shaded illustrations for things like instruction manuals and cartoon-style renders.

We're going to concentrate on helping you get the most out of the FireFly render engine because we simply don't have the space in this volume to thoroughly explore all the options available to you in Poser 6. This does not mean that the other render engines are not worth exploring. Quite the contrary, each of the other rendering engines really are wonderful tools and can offer an amazing variety of options for your work. We'll do our best to at least introduce them to you, and offer suggestions for further explorations on your own.

The FireFly Render Engine

What may not be obvious, given the surprisingly low price tag of Poser 6, is that the FireFly renderer is really a very sophisticated render engine. You'll probably be shocked to discover that FireFly uses technologically advanced concepts and techniques that can be traced to the ground-breaking image render concepts used by large animation studios developed to produce better and faster renders.

Poser's FireFly render engine has the added functionality of being able to also calculate raytraced material properties. This means you get the best of both worlds and don't have to take the performance hit associated with raytrace-only engines, which are notoriously resource intensive and slow. During rendering, FireFly breaks up the polygons into micropolygons. Then, if the material requires raytracing, it calculates the rays for the current render "bucket." (See the definition of Maximum Bucket Size in the Render Settings section later on in this chapter to get an idea of what a bucket is.) This is a wonderful solution that, while not perfect, gives FireFly unprecedented power at a fraction of the price of similarly capable render solutions.

One of the quirks that you should be aware of is that *reflections of objects are not smoothed*. This means that even though your objects are smoothed at render time, their reflections use the original polygon shape. In most cases, you can easily smooth out any sharp edges of your reflections in the postwork phase of your project.

Don't overlook the importance and benefit of reading the manual that came with Poser 6! The Poser 6 Reference Manual is really an outstanding resource. It has detailed explanations with excellent figures and examples to help explain some of the more difficult concepts. In particular, Chapter 37, "Using The FireFly Render Engine," is a great place to start for more information relating to what we're discussing in this chapter.

Render Settings Dialog

The Render Settings Dialog can be accessed from the menu by selecting Render > Render Settings, or from the preview window by using the Options menu > Render Settings pull-down menu. The Render Settings Dialog has two major tabs located along the top: the Render Settings and Movie Settings tabs. The Render Settings tab is where you select which render engine you wish to use. The Movie Settings tab configures your animation output. We'll start with the first tab in the Render Settings section, the FireFly tab.

Within the FireFly section are the Auto Settings and Manual Settings. We'll go over the Manual Settings because this is the area where each render parameter can be set individually. Once you understand the parameters in the Manual Settings you can apply that knowledge to determine which Auto Settings to use. These same parameters apply equally to both the Manual Settings and the Auto Settings section:

Cast Shadows: Enables the calculation of shadows. This is the default for the entire render. You can override this setting on a case-by-case basis for each individual object in your scene. However, you need to pay attention to this setting because if shadows are turned off *here*, they won't get calculated *anywhere*, regardless of individual object settings.

Texture Filtering: Applies to image-based maps. Texture Filtering helps soften the effect of *jaggies*, or aliasing, in an image. It also helps reduce moiré patterns. This does take computing power so use it only if your textures need help. Consider smoothing lower quality and resolution textures in your favorite graphics program instead of using this option. We suggest that you try both methods yourself, manually smooth textures in your graphics program first and then try Texture Filtering, to see which method you prefer. (Page 341 of the *Poser 6 Reference Manual* has an excellent figure showing the effects of the Texture Filter.)

Raytracing: Enables or disables raytracing. Some types of procedural shaders, like the refraction and reflection nodes, require that raytracing be enabled in order to work.

Raytrace Bounces: When raytracing is enabled this parameter sets the limit on how many bounces each ray of light is traced through. Higher values give more realistic reflections and refractions; however, they also eat up more of your CPU and take longer to render. You will find that materials that are transparent *and* reflective take longer to render, as will those with refraction and subsurface scattering. In cases where your reflections do not need to be photorealistic, reflection maps are a better choice for keeping render times shorter. (Page 342 of the *Poser 6 Reference Manual* has an excellent figure comparing a render with one raytrace bounce to a render with three raytrace bounces.)

Minimum Shading Rate: This value has to do with the micropolygon method of rendering a scene. It determines how small the micropolygons will be. A shading rate of 1, works out to mean that the polygons of the object will be broken down into small pieces that are the same size as a single pixel of your rendered image. The relationship between the Minimum Shading

Rate and the size ofthe micropolygons is fairly linear, which means that a Minimum Shading Rate of 6 would create micropolygons that are roughly 6 pixels large. Smaller numbers here will give crisper details; however, your rendering time will increase as well because the number of micropolygons is based on the total area, length times width, of your render.

You can adjust this value on each object of your scene separately. However, the value set with this parameter establishes the *smallest* micropolygon size any object will use. This means that you can set individual objects in your scene to have *larger* micropolygons to speed up renders on areas where details are not critical. (Page 343 of the *Poser 6 Reference Manual* has an excellent figure comparing a render with a high Minimum Shading Rate to that of a render with a low Minimum Shading Rate.)

Pixel Samples: This value is used to determine how many neighboring pixels are sampled during an antialiasing calculation. For each pixel that is being antialiased, the renderer samples a surrounding block of pixels and calculates the properties of the pixel based on the values of its neighbors. Things like color and brightness are considered. How many neighboring pixels are used in the calculation depends on the Pixel Samples parameter setting. Higher Pixel Samples values produce smoother images but take longer to render. A setting of 3 would create a 3 × 3 sampling grid for the pixel in the middle of the grid

Max Texture Size: This parameter controls a very convenient feature that allows you to use smaller versions of your image maps at runtime. The Maximum Texture Size option specifies the maximum size (in pixels) that FireFly will resample the image maps to. What this means for you is that you can load up high-resolution image maps—which normally would eat up resources and computing power—and have the renderer resample the image map to a smaller resolution on the fly. This smaller image file will be used for your renders, which would benefit by faster processing because fewer resources would be required to handle the image maps.

This is an excellent way to speed up renders while you are setting up your scene and don't need details. When you are done, you can reset the Max Texture Size so your image maps will render at their full resolution and in all their glorious detail for your final render. This saves you from having to use low-resolution and high-resolution versions of the same image map.

Reducing the image map size may blur your textures or otherwise degrade the way they look at render time so if you use this feature and find your textures blurring in a way you don't like, you may need to make this value larger.

Maximum Bucket Size: This is the area, measured in pixels, that is rendered at any single time. If you watch your image being rendered you will see that "chunks" of your image are processed at one time—these are the buckets. Larger bucket sizes use more of your system's resources. However, larger bucket sizes may also speed up your renders if you have the computing power to support them. Your system may run out of memory if your bucket size is too large for your system to handle. The good news is that Poser can *usually* detect when the current bucket size is using too much of your computer's resources. It will ignore your setting if it determines that you've got your bucket size set too high. The bad news is that Poser doesn't always detect this and your render may freeze, or slow down to the point of looking stalled. If this happens, try reducing the bucket size first.

Minimum Displacement Bounds: When you use Displacement maps (see Chapter 11, "Creating Your Own Image-Based Textures," for information about Displacement maps), you are telling FireFly to displace the surface of the object by the amount defined in the Displacement map, at the time of rendering. If your displacement is too large, it cannot be contained in the current render bucket, which means that it will go out of the bounds of the current calculation. When this happens your object will look like it has a black hole in it, or has black spots and polka dots sprinkled all over it. By default, FireFly is prepared to look above, below, and to each side of the actual geometry for any displacement that may need to occur. How far FireFly looks in each direction is the Displacement Bounds value. Setting this value too high will eat up resources quickly and will require much longer to render because this is a volumetric value (three dimensions, X, Y, and Z, need to be checked at every point). For simple materials, FireFly will do a fine job figuring out what displacement bounds your materials need to be safely contained in a single render bucket. However, if your material gets too complicated for the cursory check that FireFly does, you may find your materials "chopping off" if they have too much displacement. If this happens you will need a larger Minimum Displacement Bounds value or a smaller Displacement value on your material. (Page 344 of the *Poser 6 Reference Manual* has an excellent figure that illustrates the concept of Minimum Displacement Bounds.)

Acquire From Auto: Copies parameter settings from the Automatic Quality tab.

Render Over: Specifies the background to use when rendering. The Background Color, Black, and Background Picture options render objects in your scene over a color of your choice, black, or the background picture you have loaded, respectively. The Current Background Shader gives you the opportunity to specify a complex procedural shader as the background. The Shadow Only option renders only the shadows that are cast by the objects in your scene. This is a wonderful feature that allows you to combine the shadow-only render with a render that has no shadows enabled in a graphic program. The benefit here is that you can independently manipulate the shadows in your graphic program to get very fine control without sweating over minute material and lighting settings. When you choose to render shadows only, all other render settings are overridden.

Smooth Polygons: This is a wonderful feature that allows you to smooth the objects in your scene. The rendering engine uses polygon subdivision to smooth the polygon joints on objects. You can control the smoothing by specifying smoothing groups or by setting a crease angle threshold. The *Poser 6 Reference Manual* dedicates an entire chapter on this subject in Chapter 25, "Smooth Shading." You can override this global setting for each object in the object's Properties palette. (Page 346 of the *Poser 6 Reference Manual* has an excellent figure that shows the effects of Polygon Smoothing.)

Remove Backfacing Polygons: A great option that tells the FireFly renderer to ignore polygons that are on the backside of the object and not directly visible from the current camera position. This helps speed up your renders by telling FireFly to ignore polygons it cannot see. However, if you are raytracing reflective materials you need to make sure that the backs of your objects do not show up in any reflection, or you may get weird-looking reflections showing your objects with holes in them.

Use Displacement Maps: Enables Displacement mapping. When using displacement in your renders, set your Minimum displacement bounds if you see artifacts along the bucket boundaries in your renders.

Depth of Field: This parameter enables the FireFly renderer to calculate depth-of-field effects. The depth of field is set in Properties for the camera that is being used as the render view. (More information about depth of field can be found in Chapter 4, "Using Cameras.") Also, the tutorials section at the end of this chapter gives some advice on ways to easily use depth-of-field in your renders.

3D Motion Blur: A great way to give the impression of fast-moving objects is to blur them. This parameter enables blurring based on the rate of position change of an object from one animation frame to the next. Blurring is affected by shutter open and close times, with longer exposures (shutter open time) producing more pronounced blurring effects.

Toon Outline: This is a post-render operation that draws an outline around the objects in your scene. There are nine outline styles: Thin Pen, Thin Pencil, Thin Marker, Medium Pen, Medium Pencil, Medium Marker, Thick Pen, Thick Pencil, and Thick Marker. See the tutorials section at the end of this chapter to learn how to control what parts of your objects will be outlined as a single object. This is particularly useful if your figure has a separate head and body texture, with a seam that appears on the neck.

Post Filter Size: A post-render filter that smoothes, or antialiases, your render. The filter samples a group of pixels surrounding the current pixel and calculates a weighted average of the entire group to determine what that center pixel's characteristics are. Increasing the filter size increases the area used for group calculation, which in turn increases render times. Using too large a sample may cause undesirable blurring. The effect that this filter has is also dependant on the final size of your rendered output so you may need to change this as you change the size of your final output.

Post Filter Type: This defines the type of calculation the Post Filter uses to antialias your render. The types of post filters that FireFly supports are:

- **Box:** This gives each pixel in the sample equal weight.
- **Gaussian:** This filter varies the weight of a sample based on the distance from the center of the sample area. The Gaussian curve is sometimes called the "standard distribution curve" or the "Bell curve."
- **Sinc:** A Sinc filter applies a declining sine-wave weight to the samples based on the distance of the sample from the center. Imagine a rock falling into the water and the ripples in the surface that are created as a result. These ripples are the sine wave that will be produced—one large rise in the center with crests that decrease in amplitude the farther from the center you go.

More about this filter, along with a good diagram showing the characteristics of each of these filters can be found in Chapter 37 of the *Poser 6 Reference Manual,* "Using The FireFly Render Engine."

Saving Render Settings

You can save and later recall FireFly settings. To save a render setting, click on the Save Preset button. To restore your settings to the default settings, use the Restore Defaults button. Poser comes with several preset render settings that you can load by clicking the Load Preset option.

Poser 4 Render Engine

You may wish to use the Poser 4 render engine because you have content that uses BUM files (a proprietary bump map format used in Poser 4 or earlier versions) to get that classic "Poser Render" look for your final renders. It's definitely a computer-generated look and very recognizable. The Poser 4 render engine does not support displacement mapping, raytracing, 3D blurring, and a few of the new material shader node types. However, it is relatively fast and if you are looking for that classic "rendered" look, it's a great choice.

The settings are straightforward, and should already be familiar to you if you've read through the FireFly renderer section above. However, there are a few parameters that are worth pointing out because they are unique to the Poser 4 rendering engine:

BUM Format Bump Maps: The Poser 4 renderer allows you to continue using BUM files, usually provided with older Poser 4-compatible products; however, you can convert the BUM formatted file into something compatible with Poser 6. Then you can apply the converted image map to the Bump or Displacement channel of the material root node. See the tutorials section at the end of this chapter to find out how you can convert your old BUM files into a format you can use with procedural shaders and the FireFly render engine.

Ignore Advanced Shader Trees: Causes the Poser 4 renderer to ignore most shader nodes other than image maps.

The Ignore Advanced Shader Trees option, when enabled, will ignore the connections to the root node in the Material room.

Sketch Render Engine (Sketch Designer)

The Sketch Designer is a fascinating tool for anyone with an interest in creating uniquely styled images. It enables you to generate renders that look as if they were sketched by hand, with a pen, pencil, pastels, charcoal, watercolors, and even paints! The Sketch Designer works with both single-frame renders and animation renders.

You can bring up the abbreviated Sketch Designer render window from the Render Palette Sketch Tab by selecting Render > Render Settings from the menu and then accessing the Sketch Tab. This version of the Sketch Designer window has convenient shortcuts to the default render styles along with informative thumbnails to show what each default looks like. Figure 16.9 shows the abbreviated Sketch Designer render window with the thumbnails of the various default render styles.

FIGURE 16.9 The abbreviated interface of the Sketch Designer with thumbnails showing the default sketch render styles.

The Sketch Tab opens showing thumbnails of the default Sketch styles. Click on a thumbnail to load the preset associated with it and then click the Render Now button to render your image using those preset values. You can also access a list of standard presets and any custom presets you may have saved using the Sketch Designer using the Presets menu pull down. To render your sketch to the main render preview window, select Render > Sketch Style Render.

Alternatively, you can bring up the Sketch Designer (select Window > Sketch Designer from the menu). In this view, you will notice that it has its own preview window. You can resize the Sketch Designer window to allow you to see more of your scene in the preview window by clicking the resize corner at the lower right of the Sketch Designer window with your left mouse and dragging the window to your desired size. You can also pan, or move around, in your preview window at any time by clicking in the window with your left mouse and dragging the preview image. Dragging to the right will bring the left side of your preview into the window as if you were dragging a piece of paper. The Sketch Designer parameters allow you to control the characteristics of the rendered "sketch lines." Many of the parameters are set using sliders that increase the parameter value when you slide them to the right and decrease the parameter value when you move the slider to the left. The sketch preview updates each time you make a change to any parameter so you can instantly see the effect of the changes as you make them. Figure 16.10 shows what the Sketch Designer interface and its preview window look like.

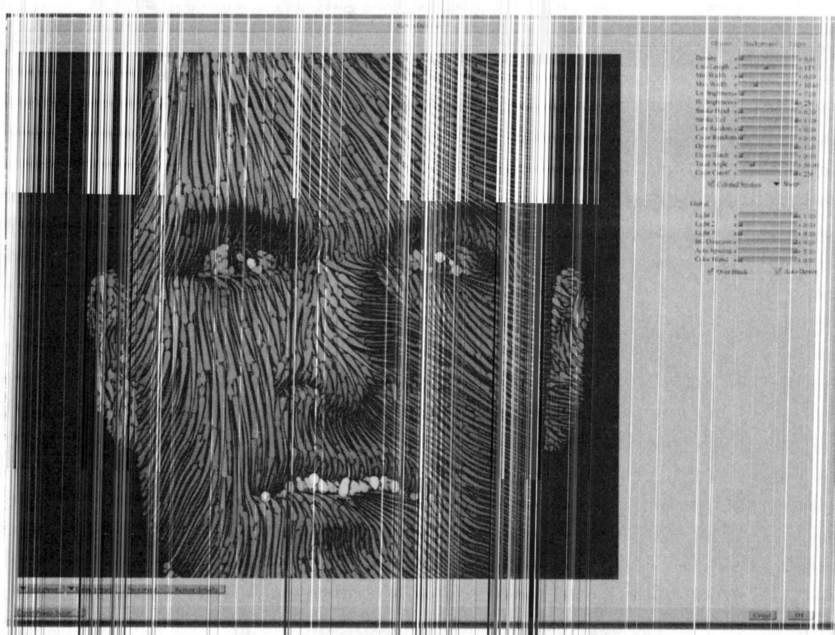

FIGURE 16.10 Sketch Designer Window with interactive preview.

Options and Parameters

Your scene is divided into three sections: Objects, Background, and Edges. Each section has its own sketch controls to allow you to customize how that section is rendered:

Objects: Determines the sketch style for all objects in your scene.

Background: Establish the sketch style for the background of your scene. Note that if you use any prop as a "background," such as a large plane or sphere, this is considered an object by the Sketch Designer.

Edges: Determine the sketch style for the edges, or the outline, of objects in your scene.

Density: Determines how closely packed your strokes will be in your render. Higher values increase the density of strokes and reduce the amount of space in between each stroke.

Line Length: Controls the length of each stroke.

Min Width: Defines the width of the edge of each stroke.

Max Width: Defines the width of the center of each stroke.

Lo Brightness: Defines the range of tones that will be used to render the strokes. Low values will render lines in the shadowed areas and darker parts of your scene.

Hi Brightness: Defines the upper range of tones that will be used to render the strokes. Refers to the brightness of source, which is the existing preview window view. Higher Hi Brightness values will pick up strokes with lighter value.

Stroke Head: Sets the amount that each stroke is tapered at its head. Lower values create even width strokes.

Stroke Tail: Sets the amount that each stroke is tapered at its tail. Lower values create even width strokes.

Line Random: Randomizes the orientation of rendered strokes. Higher numbers increase the randomness of the strokes.

Color Random: Randomizes the colors of rendered strokes. Higher numbers increase the randomness of the colors used.

Opacity: Sets the transparency of the rendered strokes. Higher values create more opaque strokes.

Cross Hatch: Determines the amount of cross-hatched strokes that will be rendered. Cross hatching creates strokes that are perpendicular to each other.

Total Angle: Defines the maximum angle that a stroke can change before it must end. High Angle values create longer lines, in general.

Color Cutoff: Limits the amount that a stroke's color can change.

Lights (1, 2, and 3): Sets the amount that each of the first three lights in your scene contribute to the direction of rendered strokes. This is an important setting that will determine the overall stroke direction for your rendered image.

BG Direction: Determines the orientation of the strokes that appear in the background.

Auto Spacing: When the Auto Density option is checked, Auto Spacing settings control the amount of space between rendered strokes.

Color Blend: Determines how much of the existing scene preview will be mixed, or blended, with the rendered sketch.

Over Black checkbox: When selected, this option creates a black background with white strokes, otherwise the background will be white and the strokes will be black.

Auto Density checkbox: Causes the Sketch renderer to ignore the Density slider settings and use an automatic density value that is based on the current scene

Colored Strokes checkbox: Sketches in color when checked, otherwise, the render will be in black and white.

Brushes pull-down menu: Several types of brushes are available from this pull-down menu. Brushes are affected by the Min Width and Max Width sliders.

Sketch Render Considerations

When using the Sketch Designer there are a few things to keep in mind: The sketch designer works with whatever is in your preview window. If you are viewing your scene in a particular Display Style, such as wireframe, the Sketch Designer will use the wireframe display as its basis. The process can be compared to finger painting where each stroke of the Sketch Designer is like dragging your finger across your image. You pick up the color of the image where you start your stroke and carry it along for a bit while blending the stroke with the underlying preview image as the stroke moves along. What this means is that your stroke will depend on not only the parameter settings of the Sketch Designer, but also the color of the image in your render preview window.

Also, when rendering with the Sketch Designer it is important to remember that stroke widths remain constant regardless of the resolution of your render. This mean that your strokes may appear fat while you view them in the preview window, but after rendering the final piece at several times your preview resolution your strokes will *appear* thinner.

Let's say that your current settings make your maximum stroke width 20 pixels wide. When viewing each stroke on a monitor set to a video resolution of 1024 × 768, 20 pixels is relatively large on your screen. That same 20-pixel stroke will be much smaller looking in a render that is 3000 × 3000 pixels in dimension. This makes it rather difficult to get exactly what you see in your preview if your final renders are in high resolution. However, with a bit of practice, you can get pretty good at gauging how the stroke proportions will look in your higher resolution render. Figure 16.11 shows an example of the type of render you can expect to achieve with the Sketch Designer with minimal effort.

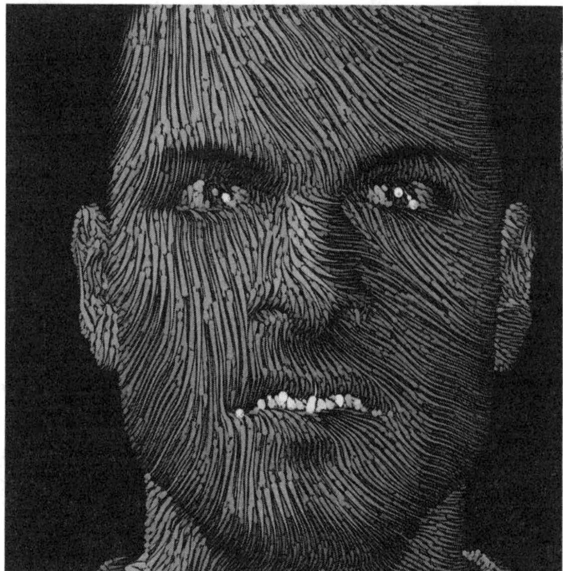

FIGURE 16.11 Sketch Designer render of James. The Sketch Designer offers unique and exciting options for creating highly stylized and artistic renders.

Preview Render Engine (OpenGL and SreeD)

This is where you customize the Scene Preview display in the Document window. You can configure how much transparency to display in your preview and which Style Options to use for your scene preview display. Style options include: Outline Width, which determines the width of the lines used in the Outline display style; Wireframe Line Width, which affects the width of the lines used in the Wireframe display style; and Cartoon Edge Line Width, which determines the width of the Toon Outline display option.

One of the really nice things about Poser 6 is that it renders print-quality output of your scene in whatever your current preview style is. You can create some interesting-looking images by using Wireframe, Flat Shaded, or even Lit Wireframe styles in your render. See the tutorials section at the end of this chapter to find out how you can quickly create flat-shaded illustrations to use in your next instructional project.

When rendering high-resolution images using the Preview rendering engine, things like wireframe widths remain constant, that is, they do not expand proportionately with the size of your render. So, what may appear rather large and chunky in your preview window may end up being very small and fine if you create a high-resolution version using the Preview renderer. For example, if you make your wireframe lines 5 pixels wide, when you view the scene on your computer these lines may appear fat and chunky. However, when you render that same preview out to high resolution, say 3000 × 3000 pixels, those 5-pixel wireframe lines will be very thin!

Rendering Animations

You can access the parameters specific to creating animations from the Movie Settings tab on the Render Options dialog. You can access the Movie Settings tab by selecting Animation > Make Movie from the menu bar or by selecting Render > Render Settings. Animation renders take much longer than single-image renders because each second of animation requires several renders—often as many as 30 if you plan on making a standard video. The following options are associated with animation renders:

Animation Options

Format: You can select the type of movie you wish to create from the Format pull-down menu. The available formats are: AVI, Image Files, and Flash. In general, the AVI option is the quickest method for rendering your movie for general-purpose applications. The Image Files option is used to create an image sequence, which is really just a series of single-frame renders created from your current animation. Just rendering a series of Image Files will not make an animation! To create an animation from the images created by the Image Sequence you will need to have the capability to combine the separate images into a movie using a movie editing program (like Adobe Premier). The Flash option is great for making animations used in Web applications and many of the parameters deal with file size reduction.

Renderer: This pull-down menu lets you select which render engine you wish to use to make your animation. You can use any of the Poser 6 render engines.

Antialias: You can choose to Antialias each frame of your rendered output to help smooth edges and transitions between objects. Antialiasing will take longer to render.

2D Motion Blur: 2D Motion Blur is a technique used to give the impression of very fast motion in an animation by blurring objects that change position quickly from frame to frame. 2D Motion Blur is available with the FireFly, Poser 4, and Preview render engines.

Resolution: The dimension of your animation, in pixels, as determined by its width and height.

Constrain Aspect Ratio: The Constrain Aspect Ratio option preserves the current aspect ratio of your animation when you make changes to the resolution. This is helpful if, for example, you wish to render a small version of your animation to preview before committing to a longer render at full production resolution. With Constrain Aspect Ratio enabled, you can change the width to a smaller value and Poser will automatically calculate what the height would be to maintain the same proportions. This is a very handy feature. Also, there is the Quick Scale Resolution pull-down menu, which lets you quickly set up renders that are Full Size, Half Size, and Quarter Size.

Time Span / Frame Rate settings: You can select the starting and ending frame of what portions of your animation that will get rendered. This allows you to render a subset of your current animation. Once you select the output range, you will need to decide if you want to render All frames that occur between your starting and ending frame. If you select All frames, your animation will render at the frame rate you have set up in your animation, as opposed to any value in the Frame rate field in the Movie Settings tab. If you wish to render your animation at a different frame rate than what you have defined as your default when originally setting up your animation, you can enter an alternate rate in the Frame rate field. Or, you can choose to render only Every Nth Frame, which will skip frames and render only every Nth one.

Output Format Options

Different output formats require different options. Depending on which you select you may need to set the following additional parameters:

Video Compression: Selects which *Codec* you wish to use to encode your animation. A Codec is basically a video encoder / decoder algorithm that uses a specific technique, calculation, or methodology to compress the video data and optimize colors. Some Codecs require a particular output aspect ratio to function properly. If you want to find out more about codecs, your favorite internet search engine is a great place to start.

Codec-specific options include things like:

Compression Quality: You can set compression quality to a value from 1 to 100. Lower numbers yield lower-quality animations that use less space and require less time to render, while higher quality compression produces larger files that take longer to render.

Data Rates: Data Rates can be configured. You can control the rate of data flow required to run your animation. Data rates are measured in KB per second

Keyframe frequency: Keyframe frequency specifies how many keyframes are added into the rendered animation. (These keyframes are not the same keyframes that you use when you are creating your animation. They are keyframes that the codec inserts to mark events within the animation.)

Overlap Colors: Creates a silhouette of each object using the color that appears most often in the scene and then places each subsequent color layer on top as needed. Alternately, deselecting this option causes each color to appear with no overlap, which may create discontinuous areas that appear broken in animated objects

Draw Outer Lines: Creates a border around each silhouette or object.

Draw Inner Lines: Outlines each color layer.

Line Width: Line width (in pixels) of the outlines.

Number of colors: Determines the number of colors that will be used in the rendered animation. Each additional color increases files sizes for animations. The maximum number of unique colors is 253.

Color Quantization: Color Quantization is the process of selecting or reducing colors in an image.

TUTORIAL 16.2 CONVERTING BUM FILES

Convert BUM files and use them in Poser 6. (We use Adobe Photoshop; however, this same process will probably work with other graphics editors as well.) All you have to do is:

1. Rename your BUM file to have a BMP file extension.
2. Open the BMP file in your image editor.
3. Convert the image to grayscale.
4. Resave your image as a TIF. (If you use JPG, be aware that it is a lossy file format and your image data will be slightly degraded.)
5. Your converted file should now be ready to use in Poser 6.

Some old BUM files may need a bit of tweaking using your paint program to soften some of the transitions between dark and light areas.

TUTORIAL 16.3 CONTROLLING OUTLINES

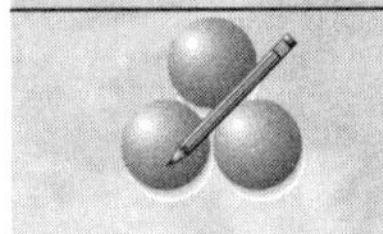

Controlling outlines when you use the Toon Outline option of the FireFly render engine is as easy as changing one value in the root material node! All you have to do is assign the same ToonID values to the material groups you wish to be outlined as a single group. For example, you can assign James' head material group the same ToonID value as his body material group to eliminate the line that would appear at the seam on his neck where the two material groups join together. See Figure 16.12 to see where the ToonID option is on the root node and a comparison of how the ToonID parameter value affects outlines. All you have to do is assign the same ToonID number to the material groups you want treated as a single outline group. The render in the middle uses the default ToonID settings for James. The render on the right assigns the head, body, and upper and lower eyelash material groups into the same ToonID value; all the material groups get treated as a single entity, which eliminates the line on James' neck and the annoying outline of his eyelashes.

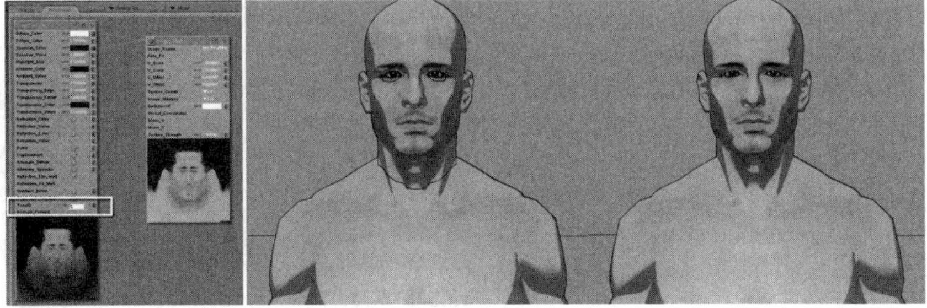

FIGURE 16.12 The ToonID property of the root node can be used to combine different material groups into a single "outline group."

TUTORIAL 16.4 QUICK TOON SHADED IMAGES

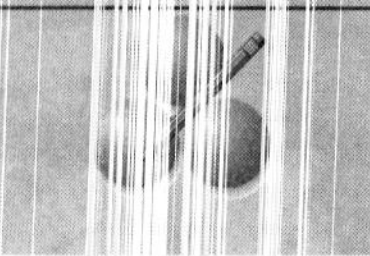

The Preview Renderer is a great way to create quick, flat-shaded illustrations. To render your scene in flat-shaded mode do the following:

1. Change your Display Style to Cartoon.
2. From the menu, select Display > Cartoon Tones > Three Tones.
3. Then go to the Render options palette and select the Preview Render tab.
4. If your computer will support OpenGL, select it; if not, you can use SreeD. Click Save Settings.
5. Switch to the Render Preview window by selecting the Render tab on the Preview window.
6. Make sure that Preview is the current Render engine. If not, select it from the Renderer pull-down menu list.
7. Render your image. Figure 16.13 shows an example of a flat-shaded render using three tones.

FIGURE 16.13 An example of a render created with the Preview renderer, which is suitable for comics and other instructional illustration. This example uses the three-tone option as the number of colors used.

TUTORIAL 16.5 USING DEPTH OF FIELD

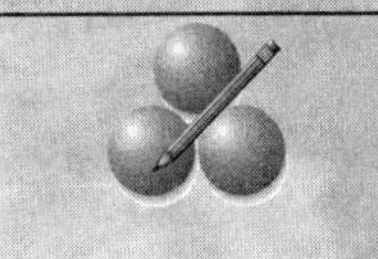

Depth of field effects can be achieved quite easily with the FireFly render engine. Special thanks to Stefan Werner, who was generous enough to not only write this fantastic script, but to allow it to be included with the base installation of Poser 6. Here's what you need to do:

1. Once you get your scene set up, select the object you wish to be in focus.
2. Go to your preferences dialog and make sure you are using feet as your default units (Edit > General Preferences > Interface).
3. Open the Python Scripts dialog (Window > Python Scripts).
4. While the object you wish to be in focus is the current object, locate and run the "Calc DoF Focal Distance" script. (The script is in the Render / IO category.)
5. After the script runs, you will see a popup window that has a number in it. This is the distance from your current camera to your currently selected object, in feet.
6. Copy the number into your Copy Buffer (in windows, it is Ctrl-C), or write it down.
7. Now open the Property palette for the current camera, and click on the Parameters tab.
8. Paste the number generated by the python script from your copy buffer (in windows, it is Ctrl-V) into the focus_Distance field, or enter it manually.
9. At this point, you'll need to decide how strong you want your depth of field effects. If you want more things to remain in focus, enter a larger value into the fStop field.
10. Now open the Render options palette (Render > Render Settings).
11. Then, in the Manual tab of the FireFly renderer, set the pixel samples to a high value, say around 10.
12. Enable Depth of field calculations by checking the Depth of field option box.
13. Save the render settings and render.

The camera's focal length, fStop, and focus_Distance all play a part in determining how much in front of and behind your focus_Distance will be in focus. Smaller fStop values will create a smaller area that is in focus. Figure 16.14 shows an example of a render that uses Depth of Field. In this example, we used the following settings: Focal: 38mm; Perspective: 38mm; focus_Distance: 5.133; fStop: 2.8.

FIGURE 16.14 Interesting results can be achieved using depth-of-field.

When you use the depth-of-field option, your renders will take much longer!

CONCLUSION

We thought it was important that you know about the power of the Poser rendering engines because we hope this knowledge will inspire you to try new things and go farther with your renders than you might have otherwise. The more you know and understand about *how* Poser's render engines work, the easier it will be for you to get the types of results you imagine. Being familiar with the capabilities of each renderer will also empower your choices when you create your materials to give you more options and control. Finally, knowing more about the renderers will enable you to quickly diagnose common render problems and fine-tune your render settings for optimal performance.

CHAPTER

17

POST WORK AND OTHER THINGS TO CONSIDER

In This Chapter

- What is Post Work?
- Solutions to Common Problems
- Conclusion

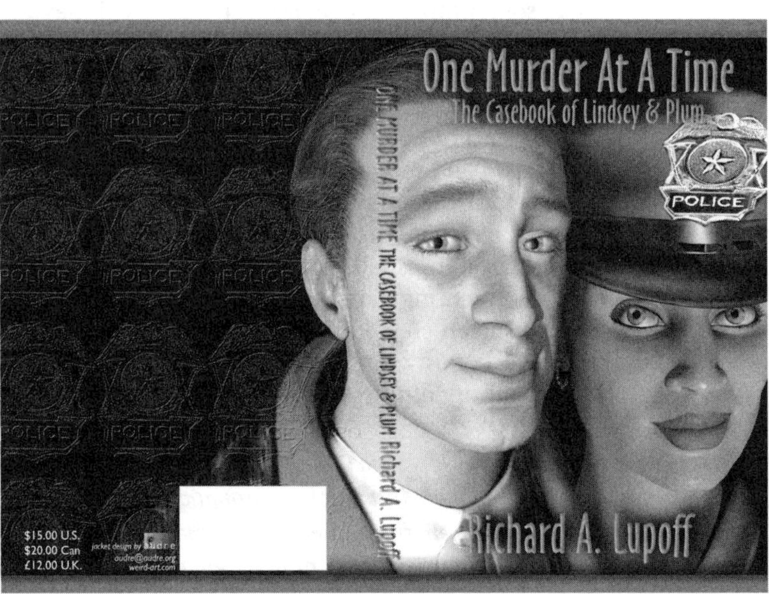

In this chapter we're not going to discuss Poser 6 software specifically. Instead, we'll introduce solutions to common problems, alternate approaches, and what happens after the render is done. We'll explain procedures for creating and finishing projects using a variety of methods. We'll identify cases where it is easier to do a spot of post work rather than spend the time and effort required to get the render just so. We'll point out instances when no amount of render magic will give the same bang for the buck that post can give (eyes, for example). We'll even talk about situations where post work is more than just a touch-up, and is a deliberate and major part of the process.

We'll be showcasing a real-life project or two that was actually done to satisfy a job requirement so you can see for yourself how the same procedures might apply to your own projects. You'll get acquainted with applications where Poser 6 is successfully used by professional and hobbyist illustrators and artists. After you finish this chapter, you'll be prepared to tackle your own post work projects, or gain the inspiration to try things with Poser 6 that you may not have considered before.

WHAT IS POST WORK?

While post work is not strictly part of "the software that is Poser 6," it is something that every Poser 6 user will have to deal with at one point or another; that is, unless they can afford to spend lots of time on each scene to insure that the render is absolutely perfect in every way. Post work is really part of the process of creating a finished piece of art. Judicial application of post work can make the difference between something that is good and something that is great.

In the most basic sense, post work is anything that happens to an image after you render it. Correcting the overall color or cast, fixing or accentuating shadows, enhancing eyes and specular highlights, adding or augmenting hair, or even reworking a render entirely to make it look like it's been created in a different medium—all of these are considered post work. Post work isn't just for minor touch-ups, either—it can also be the majority of the process by which the final image is created.

Post work is something that typically occurs only on single-image renders, where the final product is not an animation. This is because post-processing an animation requires enormous amounts of time and effort because one single second of animation typically has 30 unique renders! We'll concentrate on single-image renders, since the vast majority of post work applies to these types of projects.

There are purists in the computer graphics community who believe that the only good render is one that requires absolutely no post work. That is like saying that because you love knives and are an expert in their creation and use, the only way to eat your dinner is with your knife. Because you are a knife expert, you probably could successfully eat your dinner with your knife (and enjoy it), but for the act of getting your food from the plate to your mouth, we are suggesting that perhaps you should consider a fork, which is a better tool for that specific purpose. In short, avoid becoming dependant upon any single tool to the exclusion of all others.

Poser, or any piece of software for that matter, is simply a tool. It is easy to lose sight of that fact, especially when many people in the various graphics communities grow obsessively attached to their favorite application. This isn't necessarily a bad thing, unless they deny themselves the tools and techniques that can make their work better. In those cases, blind loyalty to their "favorite application" costs them more than they are probably aware of. It is admirable, even worthwhile, to become so familiar with your favorite software so that you can create amazing work without any other application. However, if you deliberately avoid the use of other tools, it may be costing you already. Unless you have an endless amount of time available to you, you should use whatever tools work for you, and consider post work as both a good thing and a smart thing to do.

Poser is an excellent tool that helps you use three-dimensional content to create amazing scenes with relative ease. We all know that it isn't practical to have one tool that does everything equally well. For example, Poser can't give you the control over individual pixels in an image like a good graphics editor can, because a graphics editor is created specifically to control individual pixels. Conversely, your graphics editor probably doesn't know what to make of three-dimensional data, so you would never consider setting up renders with it. Even if you tried to create the perfect Poser scene using perfect meshes, lighting, materials, and render configurations, the time and effort involved is something that most creative individuals cannot afford, especially if they are working on a tight schedule or limited budget.

SOLUTIONS TO COMMON PROBLEMS

As we present these examples, we will be talking at a relatively high level. Our goal isn't to give you the blow-by-blow of each tiny step; rather, we want to expose you to the concepts behind what is being done. Fortunately, the methods we explain here will be applicable using most graphics editing software available today. So, no matter which graphics editor you prefer you should be able to follow along. Where possible, we will try to explain which tools we select and even go as far as to describe what works for us in these various scenarios, but we'll leave it to you to translate specific tool names and application specific terms into your preferred graphics editor environment.

Post Work and Compositing to the Rescue

We're going to start off our example section with a real-life situation where Poser output was used in a professional application: a book cover. This example pulls together quite a few good lessons. Minimal post work on the eyes of your figure can make a huge difference. Post work can be used to create "content" in an otherwise three-dimensionally created image. Poser is an excellent tool when speed is of the essence. It is easier to break a project into multiple Poser renders to composite a final piece than to create the entire, more complex scene in one single render.

This book cover involved creating portraits of the two main characters from the book, *One Murder at a Time: The Casebook of Lindsey and Plum,* by Richard Lupoff. We chose this example because the cover was fairly well received by Lupoff fans and makes our point that Poser can come to the rescue in a professional environment if you are willing to work it into your creative process. Here's what one reviewer had to say about the book cover: ". . . the cover is truly wonderful. I think it shows off well Lindsey's slightly nebbishy qualities and Marvia's forthright cop nature."

Nebbish is a Yiddish word describing an inadequate, timid man who is submissive and weak, and unlucky solely because of his own pathetic nature. A nebbish is a man who is the epitome of a wimp.

This book was one of a long history of published works that featured these characters and had a devoted reader base. To up the ante, this was going to be the first time either character was illustrated. There was more than a little pressure to interpret and represent these beloved characters accurately. Additionally, there was little time or money available for lengthy or really in-depth studies so this had to be a very streamlined and quick process. In short, this project was the perfect application for using Poser.

During the character "discovery" stage, it is not uncommon to try and discard several entirely different concepts. Initially, it is uncertain what, if anything, the client will like. Because of the uncertainty in final image requirements, it doesn't make sense to spend money or props for these early "concept discovery" renders. In cases like this, judicious use of post work and compositing enables you to crank the project out as quickly and economically as possible.

"In visual effects postproduction, 'compositing' refers to creating complex images or moving images by combining images from different sources—such as real-world digital video, digitized film, synthetic 3D imagery, 2D animations, painted backdrops, digital still photographs, and text."—the http://en.wikipedia.org/wiki/Compositing Web site.

Creating the Female Character

Our first task was to create the female police officer character, known to fans as Marvia Plum. Since Plum is an African-American female, we decided to use DAZ's Victoria model and a dark-skinned image map that we previously purchased. We also happened to have a police hat prop, but not a police badge prop.

The author wanted us to use a real badge, if possible, that included some specific details to coincide with the description in the book. We'll talk about the trick we used to make ourselves a police badge a little bit later on in this chapter. For now, we're going to continue on with the process we used to create Plum's portrait.

We loaded, morphed, and posed the Victoria figure. Then we created a custom bump map to show imperfections on the skin of the figure's face. Since this character was a tough police officer, we wanted to have a strong sense of activity and competence. And we felt that showing minor scars and blemishes would help us give this impression of Plum. Once we had the figure basically configured, we added, posed, and then parented the police hat prop to her head. At this point we also added our police badge object (see below for explanation of how the badge was created). After that, we tweaked the lighting and created a baseline render. Things actually looked pretty good, so we were able to get client approval for the design for Plum at this point.

Once we knew this was the way the character would look, we came up with several alternative poses and lighting situations, keeping in mind that another figure will need to appear close to this one in the finished book cover. Three versions later, the client was happy with the raw output from Poser. The next phase, post work, could now begin.

Working with Layers

After the character was approved, the production-sized render was made. Figure 17.1 shows the raw Poser render of Marvia Plum. You can see that the skin has quite a bit of texture and imperfection as testament to a very active and sometimes harsh lifestyle. The character is posed with a direct gaze into the camera, coupled with the scars on the skin; this gives the impression of a direct and competent individual. The slight upturn of the lip helps to soften the effect while adding complexity and depth to the character.

Another version was created in which more prominent specular highlights were added to the skin. At this point, it was uncertain which version we were going to use, shiny or matte skin, but we felt that both were good candidates—or, at least there were portions of both renders that had features we liked.

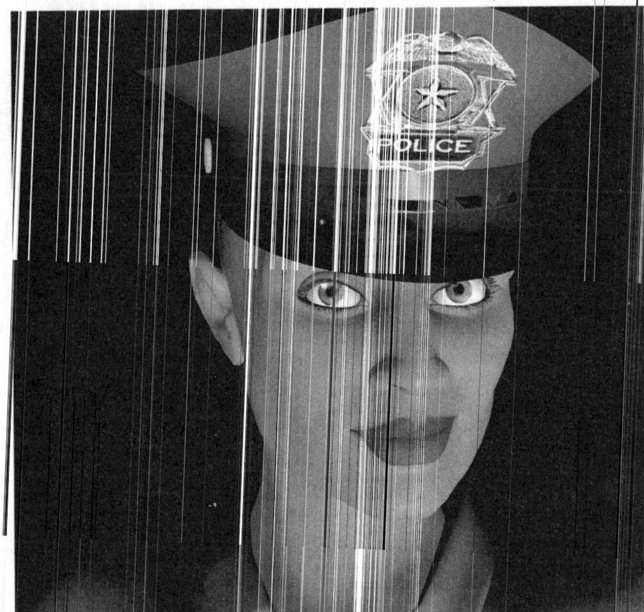

FIGURE 17.1 The first production render of the character Marvia Plum for use in the book cover project.

Because we could not immediately decide which version to use, we brought both renders into our graphics-editing program, Adobe Photoshop. We made the original render the background (bottom) layer and then added the version with stronger specular highlights as layer 1 because we were leaning toward using the version with stronger highlights. Once both renders were in the same image file, we corrected the color and gamma (brightness) of both layers. We were careful to apply exactly the same corrections to each layer.

Using layers is an excellent way to control post work. Placing each individual post-worked item or correction in its own layer, or series of related layers, allows you to control each independently. During the post-work process, the number of layers can become unmanageable. At some point, you may be required to combine layers to make room for additional layers.

In this project, we decided to combine several layers to make the file easier to manage. Figure 17.2 shows the layers that we ended up with. In this case, layer 1 is a combined result of several intermediate layers once we were satisfied with them. These intermediate layers were used to enhance the eyes, soften the edges of the skin, fix the eyelashes, and smooth out and darken the shadowing of the police hat.

Once layer 1 was safely combined, additional layers were added:

- Addition of more highlights.
- Creation of earrings.
- Enhancement of shadows.
- Creation of gold epaulette-like shirt adornments to give the overall impression that the character was wearing a uniform.

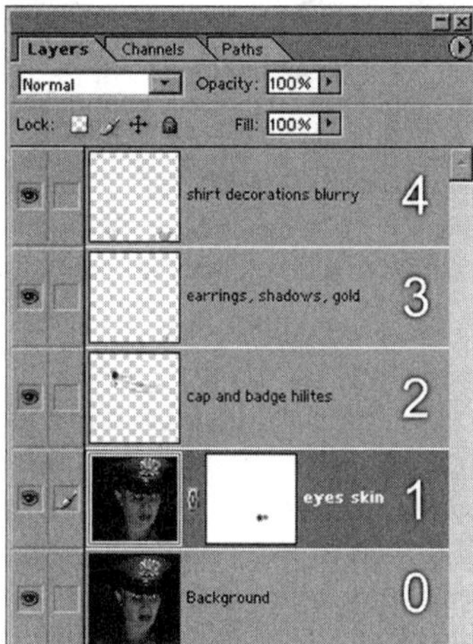

FIGURE 17.2 Layers were used to manage the post work process.

We finally decided that the lips of the render on layer 1 were too shiny, so we applied a transparency mask to them (the white square next to the layer 1 thumbnail in Figure 17.2), which made the lips from the layer below visible. Remember, the bottom layer contained the original, matte skin render with weaker specular highlights.

For the purposes of this book, it is difficult to show the transparent portions of the lips on layer 1, so we opted to show the layer over a black background. The right side of Figure 17.3, below, shows the dark area on the lips, which is the black of the background showing through. When layer 1 is applied over the top of layer 0, shown at left, the lips from the bottom layer are partially visible in those areas where the mask is dark. The layer is most transparent where the associated layer mask is darkest. The lips on the right in Figure 17.3 appear dark because they are partially transparent and are showing the black background used for this figure example. When layer 1 is actually "on top of" layer 0, the lips from layer 0 are partially visible through layer 1.

FIGURE 17.3 The original render is shown on the left, and first layer, after the first pass of post work is done, is shown on the right.

The remaining post work was done on several new layers and consisted of several specular highlights being applied to the badge on the police cap; the addition of a gold earring; and a hint of some kinky, light-brown hair added to the head just behind the ear. Figure 17.4 shows the contents of the new layer 2, on top of a black background to show exactly what is in the layer. The image on the right shows what layer 2 looks like as it is interacting with the layers below it.

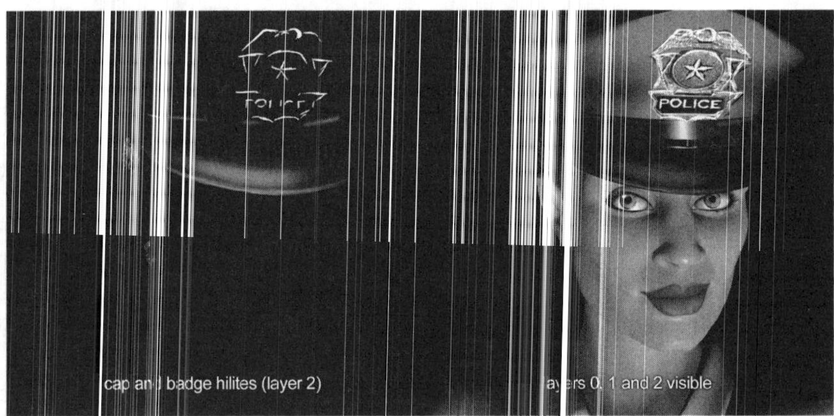

FIGURE 17.4 The image on the left shows the contents of layer 2 on top of a black background for clarity. The image on the right shows layer 2 as it interacts with the layers below it.

The post work looks rather rough when compared to the very controlled-looking effect of the original render. This is intentional and is meant to create a more hand-drawn final image. Also, remember we're working very fast at this point because this is only one part of the cover project, and much of the work still lies ahead.

Figure 17.5 shows layer 3 on the left, on top of a neutral gray background this time for clarity. The golden earring from the previous layer is reused and offset slightly to emphasize the earring a bit more. Shadows are applied to the badge to help make the badge look more dimensional. And the edges of shoulder epaulettes are quickly sketched in. In this case, the shadows on the badge, another copy of the earring from the layer below is slightly offset to give the earring more definition, and the first hints of something on the right shoulder appear.

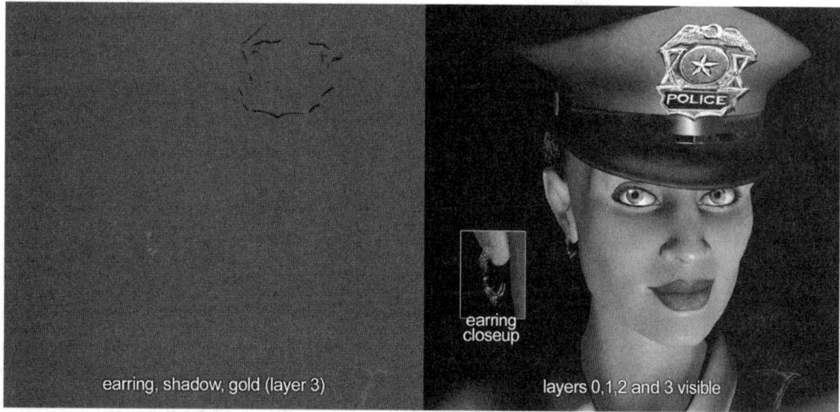

FIGURE 17.5 Layer 3, left, is shown on top of a neutral gray background for clarity. The image on the right shows what layer 3 looks like as it interacts with the layers underneath. In the center, is a close-up of the resulting earring.

The final post-work step is simply to give more definition to the shirt to turn it into a uniform. Most of the shoulders will probably be underneath text, so it's really not critical to get highly detailed or accurate in the shoulder areas. There is no sense wasting effort. However, even though we're not quite sure how this image will be used in the final cover, we do want to have enough in place to give us the ability to move the image around on if we need to. The final layer, layer 4, consists of a few golden smears intended to bolster the idea that there are epaulettes, "official doodads," attached to this character's uniform. The police hat is the key that sets the primary theme of this image and everything else just needs to support it.

One additional thing about layer 4 is that it is applied using a special layer property, hard light, which has the effect of making the layer interact nonlinearly with the layers below. Rather than just "sitting on top," like the other layers are doing, this layer affects everything based on its brightness—the brighter it is on the top layer, the more it interacts in that area with the layers below. This is a nice way to get very specular, glass-like effects using layers in Photoshop. On the left side of Figure 17.6., the vague golden smears on each shoulder are shown over a black background for clarity. The image on the right shows what the image looks like with layer 4 interacting with all the layers below.

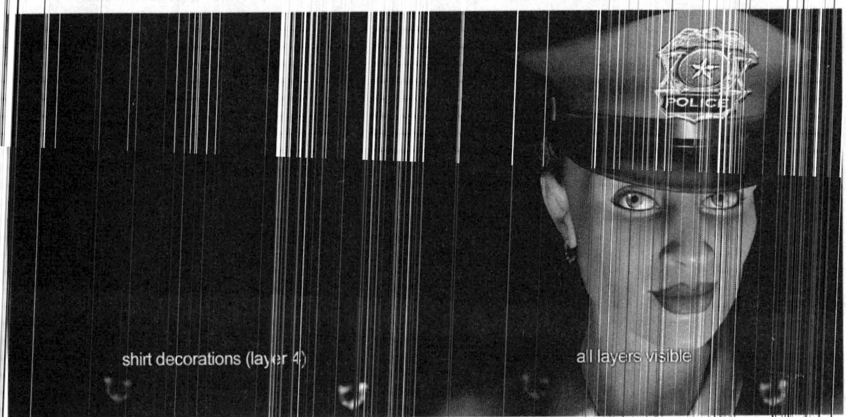

FIGURE 17.6 The image on the left shows layer 4, which contains hastily sketched epaulettes against a black background for clarity. The image on the right shows the image with all layers now visible and interacting with each other.

Eyes: Worth a Bit of Post Work

Now that you've seen the whole process, let's go back and take a closer look at the post work done on the eyes. Eyes do not glow! They are recessed into the head, which means they are heavily shadowed by the upper lid, lashes, and brow, and even get shadows from the lower lid and cheeks. There is a shadow that is cast onto the eyeball from the eyelashes and the structure of the upper eyelid. We use a very soft round brush with feathered edges to gently build up the shadow layer on the eyeball. The eye is a sphere so the edges will be darker than the forward-most parts. The size of the brush used to contour the eyeball should be large enough to leave soft areas of color rather than thin strokes that are visible.

The eyelid has depth. There is a definite shadow line directly underneath the lid (with respect to where your light is coming from, of course). We use a slightly darker color directly under the edge of the lid to create the lid shadow. We pick colors that already were in the eyeball to keep the same tones.

For this project we kept these eyes a bit brighter because printing on paper results in a loss of gamut. The more subtle details and color changes that you can see on your monitor won't always be visible when the image is transferred to paper. In this case, we wanted to make sure the eyes did stand out from under the brim of her police cap.

Skin and body tissue is translucent, so all the edges are soft. Even things like teeth are somewhat translucent so the very edge will have a slight blur. There are no sharp transitions or corners in a real-world flesh-and-blood creature. One of the things you can do to help your render is use the *finger paint* tool, or smudge tool as it is sometimes called, to gently rub all the sharp corners and to soften them up at the sharp transitions. Apply this smudge technique to all the sharp artifacts that may appear on the eyes and face, such as areas around the eyeball, lips, nose, eyebrows, and chin.

In this case, the post work done on the eyes is minimal and only took a few minutes. It's a great example of why you really should consider honing your post work skills. Figure 17.7 compares the straight Poser render, top, with the post-worked version, bottom. It really doesn't take much to soften the shadows and make the eyes appear more natural and compelling. (As a side note, we were having issues with the lashes at the time. Rather than mess around with the lash parameter dials, we just used our finger paint-tool—also called the smear tool in some applications—to extend the lashes. (We also added more random wispy lashes along the bottom to soften and naturalize.) It really does not take that much time or effort to create more natural-looking eyes, once you get a few under your belt. This example of post work only took a few minutes. Imagine what you can do if you really take the time!

FIGURE 17.7 The original render is shown at top. The post work is shown on the bottom.

Using Image Maps to Create an Insta-Prop

The next thing we want to show you is how we handled the police badge. This was pretty much an emergency situation since we couldn't find an acceptable mesh-based police badge prop at the time, and we really didn't want to invest any more resources into either looking for or making one. We did have a low-resolution photo of a real badge from the client, so we decided to use it: With the image we created a texture, bump, and transparency map. We applied these maps to a plane prop (a one-sided flat sheet object that can be found in the Props Library). We weren't too concerned about the low resolution because we were actually after more of a hand-drawn look and planned on post work anyway. At that point we were mostly trying to find something that would give the impression of a shiny police badge. Figure 17.8 shows the shield image maps along the top row and plane prop, as it ended up posed with the cap, along the bottom.

FIGURE 17.8 The police badge texture, bump, and transparency maps are shown along the top row; the plane prop, posed with the cap, is shown on the bottom.

Transparency Masks and Alpha Channels

One of the cool features of Poser is that if you don't use a background object of any type and save your render in a format that supports channels (such as TIF or PSD) you will get a nifty alpha channel in your image file that you can use to perfectly isolate (mask) your objects from the background. An alpha channel is used to define which pixels in the image have transparent properties, with the black areas of the alpha channel representing transparent areas and the white representing opaque areas. We used the alpha channel from the render file to create a mask to isolate our character from the background. This makes compositing a snap. Figure 17.9 shows the alpha channel created by Poser of our female police officer character. In Photoshop, the alpha channel can be accessed via the Channels Palette (Window > Channels). Alpha channels are a timesaving feature that let you quickly mask and isolate objects in your scene. The black areas of the alpha channel represent transparent areas of your image, the white represents opaque areas.

FIGURE 17.9 The alpha channel is created by Poser when you don't use any background objects.

The finished book cover includes two characters. The second character study was also created in Poser. The goal was to create a male "private detective" who is somewhat geeky, awkward, and not quite sure of himself. Those of you who have some experience with Poser figures will immediately recognize DAZ's Michael as the figure used to create the male detective character.

We're not going to go into the details for creating this second character since we applied the same process. After the second character was created, rendered, and post worked to our client's satisfaction, he was isolated from his background using the alpha channels supplied by Poser in the TIF file, and incorporated into the cover art file. The two "cut out" characters were then composited into the finished cover graphic.

The final layout of the characters ended up not showing Marvin's shoulder epaulettes. Even so, at the time we created the character study it was important to get as much of the image finished to a usable point without taking too much time. Figure 17.10 shows the cover layout with both Poser-based character renders in place.

FIGURE 17.10 Two separate Poser character renders, with post work, were incorporated into the finished cover design.

When doing "full-bleed" printed work, that is, work in which the art goes all the way to the edge of the paper, you must provide a larger image than the final cut-dimensions of your paper. Up to one-half of an inch may be lost around the edge of the image, depending on the cutting process and accuracy of the equipment used by the publisher. It's a good idea to always work larger than you need to give yourself the option to do full-bleed prints if you decide to do so later on.

Helping Poser Shadows

As a rule, Poser does a very good job with shadows. However, there are times when Poser shadows can use a bit of help; specifically, the areas in shadow that are created when two objects are close together. In the real world, there is usually some ambient property to the lighting, with additional radiosity, reflective, and subsurface scattering effects occurring in the materials as well. In the real world, shadows can be messy things that aren't uniform in all places, or even linear in their falloff. Most times it just isn't possible to get lighting just right or materials set up to accurately render these complex lighting conditions. Adding to this is the difficulty of posing the objects in your scenes. It's difficult to get all parts of your figures and objects positioned so that everything is level to the ground and at the right distance relative to everything else.

If you observe things around you, you will notice that typically the area directly behind/underneath an object, with respect to the strongest light source, will be slightly darker. This is especially true if the object receiving the shadow is really close to the object casting the shadow. Knowing how shadows really look will help you identify when your own shadows are in conflict with what you were trying to accomplish. Reproducing these types of details is what makes the difference between something that looks okay and something that looks dead-on.

Figure 17.11 shows how these tiny details can affect the perception of what is happening in the image. The image on the left is the straight Poser render. It does a pretty good job casting the shadow of James Casual's shoes onto the ground plane. However, because the toe of the shoe was not at its default position, they appear to be slightly elevated from the surface. In the left image, James looks as though he might be in motion or rocked back on the heels of his feet ever so slightly. The image on the right shows the same render with a very quick touch-up on the shadow immediately beneath the toes of his shoes. By adding this extra shadow directly underneath the shoe tips, we cannot completely "fix" the render to make his feet look firmly planted on the ground, but we go a long way toward helping his foot appear as if it is flatter to the floor. To completely fix the feet to the floor, with no room for doubt, we'd have to do a bit of work to move the actual toes of his boots down closer to the ground. But for a quick fix, thee little things can help your image overall.

Clearly, it all depends on what you were striving to tell your audience; in some cases, you may wish to leave the default shadows just as they are. The important thing here is that you pay attention to details such as these to insure that your entire scene conveys what you intend and there are no conflicting signals given to your audience. Other places where you might look for shadows that need help are clothing props, especially jewelry. Make sure that each item casts a shadow that is in tune with the overall message you are trying to present. By adding an extra shadow directly underneath, the toe looks like it is closer to the ground plane and the weight appears to be more evenly distributed along the entire foot.

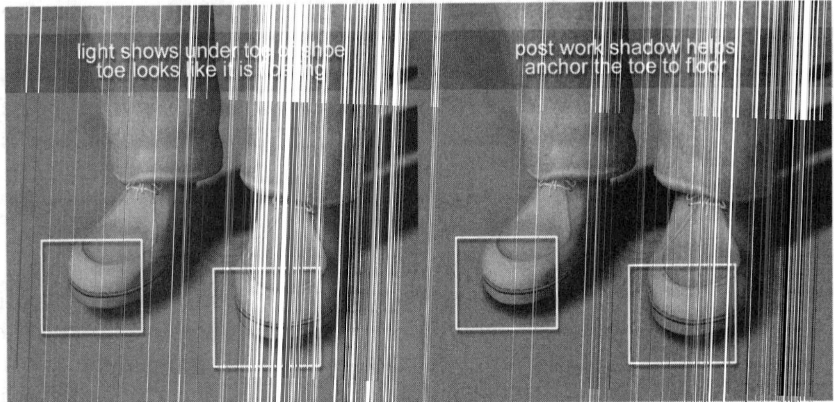

FIGURE 17.11 The toes of the shoes in the lefthand image appear to be slightly elevated from the surface. The image on the right shows the same render with a quick touch-up on the shadow immediately beneath the toe area of the shoes.

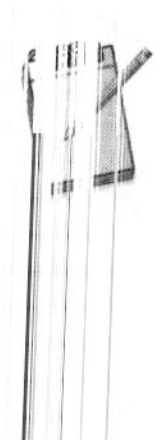

It only takes one single "untruth" to throw an entire image off balance. While it may seem like nit-picking all these little details like shadows on the eyes from the lashes and eyelids, anchoring shadows under the toes of your figure, smoothing the edges of the face and skin—they all add up. They reinforce each other to create an overall effect that helps your audience believe what you are trying to tell them. Just one single thing out of place or even one single thing that isn't conveyed with the same believability as everything else is enough to disrupt the illusion.

Poke-throughs

Every Poser user will have to deal with the dreaded "poke-throughs." Sometimes it's impossible to get everything morphed perfectly. Sometimes it seems that no matter what you try you end up with some portion of an object that interferes with portions of another object. Often when using displacement mapping this happens, or when you apply a full body morph to your figure and discover that the clothing you are currently using on the figure doesn't have exactly the same morphs. In cases such as this, post work is probably the least painful way to fix the problem. Figure 17.12 shows how JamesCasual's T-shirt problems have been fixed with post work. The image on the left is original render. The areas where shorts poke through the T-shirt are shown inside the white rectangles. The image on the right shows how judicious application of post work, in the form of the rubber stamp, sometimes called the clone tool, can save the day.

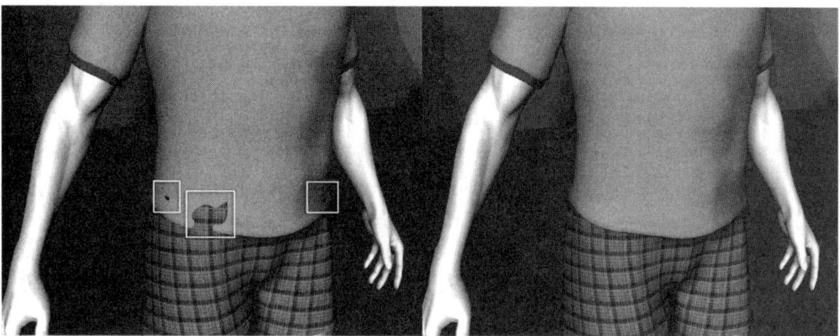

FIGURE 17.12 The poke-through is a common problem. The image on the left shows the shorts poking through the T-shirt. The image on the right shows what a minor amount of post work can achieve to save the render.

For this example, we specifically used only a mouse and our graphics application (Photoshop) to prove how effective and easy post work can be. In this instance, we had to deal with not only a texture on the T-shirt, but the shadow of the shirt on the shorts below. Even with the additional complexity of having to create and match an existing shadow line, this entire process only took us a few minutes—definitely less time than it would have taken to get the shorts and T-shirt objects to play nicely with each other using morph dials and magnets.

The first thing we did was create a duplicate of our image in a new layer. This is a good habit to get into, and it will save you much heartache if you do something stupid, like save your file when you weren't meaning to. We also make it a habit to lock our original layer to prevent any changes.

Then we used the magic wand tool to select as much of our T-shirt as possible. What we found is that portions of the shorts were being selected as well since the stripes in the shorts have similar colors to those in the T-shirt. We used the lasso tool, with the subtract option (hold the ALT key down while lassoing) to remove any unwanted portions from our active selection.

We copied the selected portion of the T-shirt on into a new layer. We wanted the working copy of the T-shirt on its own layer to allow us to add the shadow that the T-shirt casts onto the shorts more easily. By moving the T-shirt to its own layer we were able to add an intermediate layer, between the T-shirt layer above and the shorts layer below, where nothing but the shadow cast onto the shorts by the T-shirt could be created. Having the shadow on its own layer allowed us to manipulate it independently and modify it until we felt it was right, without having to worry about damaging either the T-shirt or the shorts.

We used the clone tool, also called the rubber stamp tool, to quickly fill in the areas that were missing as a result of the poke-through from the shorts. When using the clone tool, it helps use areas as close to the trouble spot as possible. This allows you to match the lighting easier. It also helps to use a soft round brush with slightly feathered edges. Feathered edges blend your strokes and prevent aliasing in portions where you are building the material. To prevent any unwanted pattern or texture repeats, change the source position often. The rhythm we work with is 3 to 1—for every three small dabs of our clone tool, we go back to reselect a new source position. This keeps from cloning too much of one area, which results in noticeable repeats in the "fixed" area. (Conversely, if you want repeats, do not change the source location of your clone tool.) We used an opacity value of 100% for our clone tool.

In our example, we also used the brighten highlights and darken shadows tools to match the brightness of our patch with the surrounding fabric. We used values around 5% to keep from making too drastic a change at each stroke. A common mistake is to apply strokes with too much pressure or change. You get more control if you do it in tiny, gradual steps.

After we got the fabric holes filled in with the clone tool, we created a new layer underneath the layer with the working T-shirt copy on it, above the layer with the shorts. We then used a soft brush set to a low opacity to brush in some dark shadows under the newly created section of the T-shirt. Figure 17.13 shows what the working T-shirt layer looks like, along with its shadow on the layer below. Both layers are shown over a white background so you can see where the shadow was brushed in.

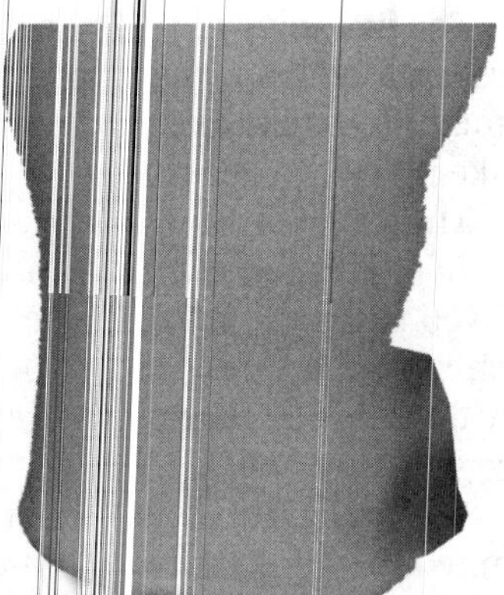

FIGURE 17.13 The repaired T-shirt and its shadow are in their own layers. Both layers are shown here over a white background to show the scope of the post work.

Masking Help with Poser's Preview Renderer

Sometimes it is very difficult to create a good mask of your object using any of the conventional graphic image-editor program tools, such as the magic wand or lasso tools. An alternate method of creating masks for post work utilizes Poser's Preview renderer. It is actually quite easy to do:

1. In Poser, select the object or element you wish to create a mask for. (You may want to save a copy of your Poser file before you do this.)
2. Set that item's display property to silhouette. Typically, a silhouette will work as a great source for masking right from the start. However, sometimes objects close to your silhouette are too similar in color and/or brightness. If this happens, you can add an infinite light and position it to point at your object to make it easy to distinguish from the other parts of your scene. Alternately, you can adjust the colors of other objects or even make them invisible if they interfere with your silhouette. Most times you won't have to do this, but even so, it only takes a few clicks to change the diffuse value in the root material node or uncheck the visible property.
3. Render the scene using the preview renderer. Make sure you render using the same camera, angle, and output resolution as your production render.
4. Now, open your Preview render image and add it to your production render as a new layer.
5. Use the magic wand to quickly select your item. Because it has been rendered in silhouette, it should be a one-click operation!

You now have a perfect selection mask to isolate the area you wish to work on. Figure 17.14 shows the Preview render we made of our T-shirt poke-through example. In this case, we also needed to make the shorts invisible. We adjusted James' skin tone to preserve his modesty, though, for the purpose of creating the mask of the T-shirt, this was not a necessity.

We Don't Need Clothing Meshes!

One of our favorite pastimes is creating fanciful and alien-looking characters. For these types of experimental projects the clothing that is available sometimes just isn't weird enough. Often, we don't the have time in between jobs to invest in trying to model our own clothing props. The good news is that there is a quick fix for people like us. We're going to share a technique that will allow you to expand your own renders without having to shell out the money for more props and accessories or even break out the modeling application to make your own new clothing.

The beauty of this technique is that anyone can do this. Use your texture map to simulate clothing on your figure. Once you render your image, all you need to do is accentuate and strengthen the illusion of the

FIGURE 17.14 The Preview renderer is an excellent resource for helping you create masks of objects or elements in your scene.

clothing you have created. You can even combine this technique with any of your "regular" renders to really expand the versatility of this process. That is, mix prop-based clothing with texture-simulated clothing.

Figure 17.15 shows a work in progress using this texture-mapping technique to create the intricate and exotic-looking clothing for this reclining female character. There are no clothing props or meshes in this picture. In fact, everything, with the exception of the figure model itself, is a primitive that comes free with Poser 6!

In this example render, only a very small portion of the image has been post worked, namely the area on her face, which makes up her mask. Eventually, all of the texture that appears on her body will be cleaned up where needed and enhanced with highlights and shadows to appear as if it is a separate layer of clothing on top of her skin.

With Poser 6's displacement mapping you can do remarkable things with just image maps. By applying the clothing right onto the texture map, you can create amazingly intricate designs without using any additional mesh objects. With displacement mapping you can go a long way toward creating just enough surface-level variation to cast shadows to make it actually look like there are multiple layers on the figure. Once you have rendered your scene you can use your graphics-editing program to enhance the highlights and shadows to create a really three-dimensional-looking end result.

Figure 17.16 shows the beginning of this process for making the head adornment appear three-dimensional. Because you are essentially following an existing pattern, you don't really need much skill, either. Just a bit of patience to stroke in the highlights and shadows, and perhaps a bit of the finger paint tool to blend other areas is really all that is required! Figure 17.16 shows that your starting render need not even be all that accurate.

FIGURE 17.15 This work in progress illustrates the technique of using texture mapping to create clothing and complex-looking props for very unique effects.

The idea is to create the basis for post work to happen—like a coloring book, where all you have to do is "color along the lines." The image on the left is the raw Poser render, the one on the right shows the first steps taken to lift the mask on her face away from the surface of her skin.

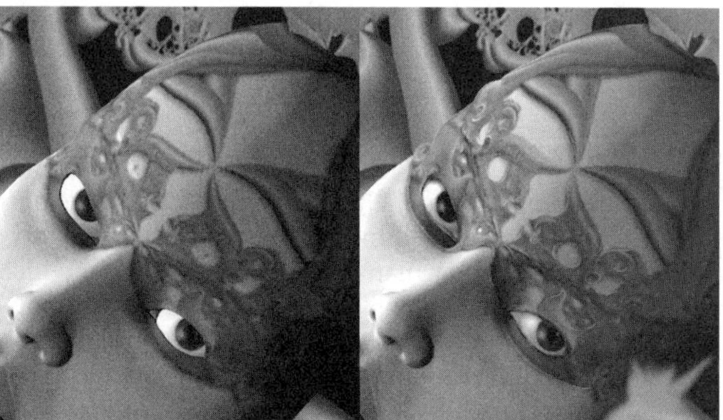

FIGURE 17.16 The image on the left is the raw Poser output. The image on the right shows the very first steps undertaken to lift the mask shape off from the surface of her skin.

To give you an idea of how the scene was put together, Figure 17.17 shows the scene using a lit wireframe display style so you can see the objects that were used: cloth planes, the ground plane, and two cylinders. Notice that her head piece was created using a simple flat, cloth plane object!

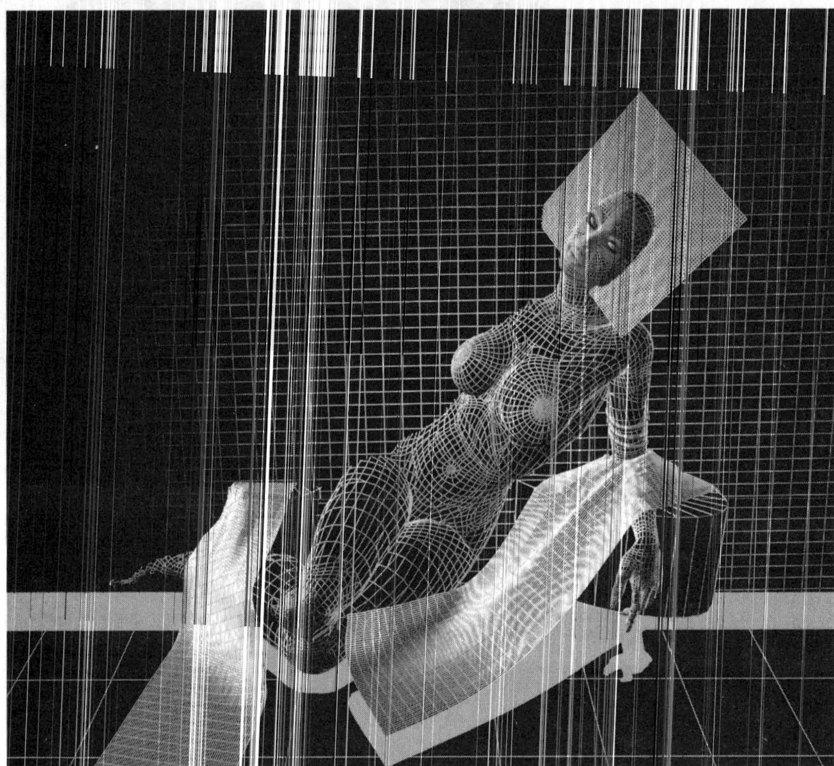

FIGURE 17.17 A lit wireframe view showing the position of the various objects used in the scene.

Texture maps based on the same design were applied to each object in the scene. The head and body texture of the figure also had the design incorporated into them. Figure 17.18 shows the texture maps. The Diffuse color map (1) is the basic design, which is repeated throughout the image. It is applied to the cylinders, ground plane, the head piece, and the draped cloth. The Displacement map (2), is a variation of the Diffuse color map image, with highlights and shadows accentuated to give more information to the Displacement channel to work with. The Transparency map (3) is also a derivation of the original Diffuse Color map image. It is basically the outline showing which areas are opaque (white areas). The figure uses a standard skin texture map (grayed out to protect the rights of the copyright holder, DAZ3D) with the chosen design applied on a separate layer of the texture map. Working in layers allows you to quickly replace the designs to create the Displacement map.

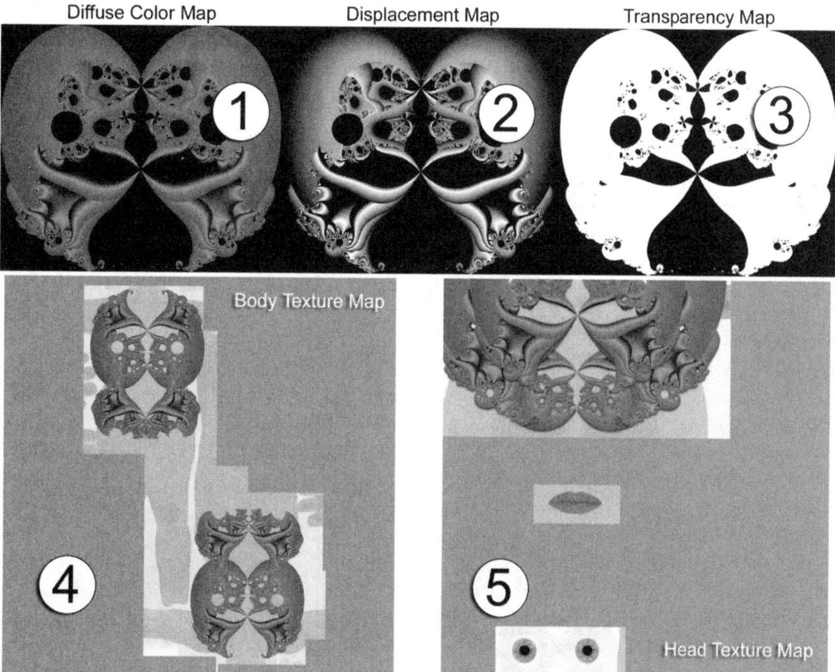

FIGURE 17.18 This image shows the various texture maps used to create the image. The Diffuse Color map (1), Displacement map (2), Transparency map (3), Body Texture map (4), and the Head Texture map (5).

Alpha Channels

One cost-saving feature of the Poser 6 render engines is that they automatically create an alpha channel for you if you leave the background behind your objects empty. This really helps when you use Poser to composite multiple renders. Our next example comes from another professional-level project that illustrates the various components of the human male anatomy.

In this case, the fantastic, medical-grade model from Zygote was used. By walking through each of the individual organs, and selectively making each one visible while the rest of them remain invisible, it was quick work to make a very complicated, multilayer transparent series of overlays.

Figure 17.19 shows three views of the composited, final piece. In the left-most image, the bottom layer showing the muscles of the figure was rendered as the only visible object in the Poser scene. The resulting TIF image came with an alpha channel that allowed the object to be masked and then quickly isolated from the background. Once isolated, the background was deleted so that objects behind, or underneath, the muscle layer could be seen. In this case, there is an outer skin layer that is below the muscle layer.

Alongside each body illustration you can see the associated Layers Palette from Photoshop, which allows each layer to be independently edited and made visible. The middle image shows the layer on top of the muscle layer, the skeleton, and its associated Layers Palette configuration. You can tell that the skeleton and the muscle layers are now visible because there is a little eyeball that shows to the left of the layer thumbnail. The image on the right shows what the finished illustration looks like with all the layers and organs visible.

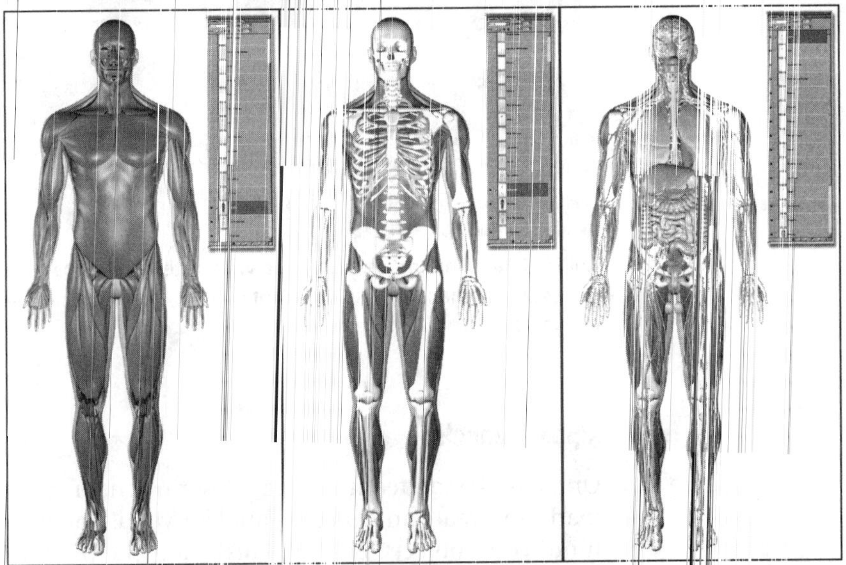

FIGURE 17.19 The Zygote male anatomy figure is a medical-grade model. By rending each organ by itself, Poser creates a handy alpha channel in the saved render file that can be used to quickly isolate the object and delete the unwanted background. A program that supports layers and alpha channels will allow you to "stack" successive organ renders to create a complex, layered illustration.

Figure 17.20 shows how to access the alpha channel in Photoshop. Just click on the Channel tab in the Layers Palette. You can see that where the alpha channel is white, the associated layer pixels are opaque. Black areas correspond with areas that are transparent. If the Channel tab is not visible on the Layers Palette, just go to the Window > Channels menu option to make it visible.

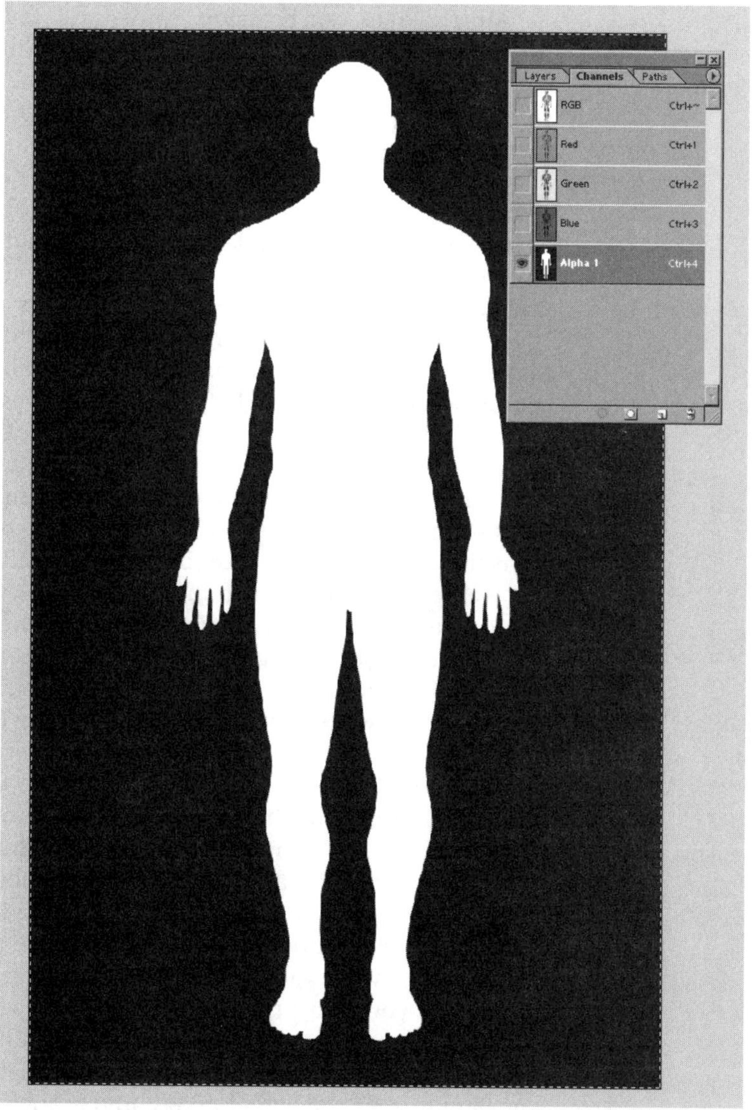

FIGURE 17.20 Poser creates alpha channels with renders. You can access them by saving your render in a file format that supports alpha channels. TIF and PSD file formats use alpha channels.

Quick Render Adjustments

Our last example will talk about making color and gamma adjustments to your finished render. One of the things to note is that your render will usually come out darker than it could be, especially if you use the default brown Poser lights. If you have plans to print your work, you should be aware that you will lose even more contrast when your work is printed and your image will look even muddier.

Most images can be safely color- and gamma-corrected using the Auto Levels command. You can access this through the Image > Adjustments > Auto Levels menu. In cases where you do not wish to have all of your colors equalized, say if you are doing a predominantly pastel piece, use the Auto Contrast command instead. The Auto Contrast will not affect the saturation of your colors, only the brightness. The good thing about using the Auto correct features of Photoshop is that Photoshop will never destroy any of your data. This means that it will not, by default, do anything to your image that will reduce the number of colors that appears in your image. It will just shift the colors around.

In cases where your image is too dark but there are already pixels that are totally black and some that are totally white, the Auto Level command probably won't help you much. This is because when Photoshop examines the dynamic range, your image already has a totally black and a totally white component. Photoshop cannot make value judgments so it cannot guess what gamma to use. (Gamma is the center brightness point of an image or device, or the value of the brightness that happens to be in the exact center of pixel brightness distribution curve). It assumes you wanted your pixels distributed exactly the way they currently are.

If your image data is predominantly in the dark half of your curve (which means your image is too dark) you can manually "push" those pixels up into the lighter portions of the curve by adjusting the gamma value. You access the gamma value through the Levels command (Image > Adjustments > Levels). This type of gamma correction is a linear process so the amount of correction that is applied to each series of levels is directly proportional to the amount of change of the center and the distance from the new center that the level is. Think of a rubber band. Tack both ends down and draw a line somewhere not in the middle. Then grab just that little area that has the mark and drag it over to the center point between the two tacked ends. One side of the rubber band will contract and the other will expand. Your data distribution will do the very same thing when you adjust the gamma.

If you want to have a nonlinear redistribution of your gamma, say, you want to push the dark pixels up into the lighter area of the curve, but you want to keep the lighter pixels pretty much at the levels that they are currently at, you use the Curves command. You access the Curves command via the Image > Adjustments > Curves menu.

It is important to realize that all of these commands will work on all of your channels. This means that you can independently adjust the Red channel, Green channel, and the Blue channel if you are working in RGB mode. Most people work in RGB mode because it is the native mode for many of the filters that come with the various graphics applications. However, you can also switch modes to gain different types of control over the data distribution of your image.

In cases where the image is either way too bright or way too dark you can do some amazingly good "fixing" by accessing the luminance component of your image and manipulating just the brightness data with the various Image > Adjustments tools. A quick way to get access to just the brightness data of your image is to change to the Lab color space. In Lab, you can select just the luminance channel and manipulate it either by adjusting the gamma or by doing more complex conversions using the Curves command. When you are done, remember to switch back to RGB mode so all your filters will function properly.

The Photoshop 7.0 help file defines the Lab color space as "a luminance or lightness component (L) and two chromatic components: the "a" component (from green to red) and the "b" component (from blue to yellow)."

Figure 17.21 compares a raw Poser render(left) with the render after it was corrected by converting it to Lab mode and then adjusting just the lightness component of the image (right). You can see that the image on the right is much more dynamic and "clearer" looking.

FIGURE 17.21 The image on the right was corrected by adjusting the brightness component while in Lab mode.

Figure 17.22 shows the image's channels while in Lab mode. As you can see, it is very easy to get access to the luminance component of your image because it appears in its own channel! Since you are just accessing the luminance, you don't have to worry about shifting colors no matter what you do with the Lightness channel. Sometimes, if you start off with an image that is way too dark, after you adjust the lightness to something relatively normal you will need to saturate the colors.

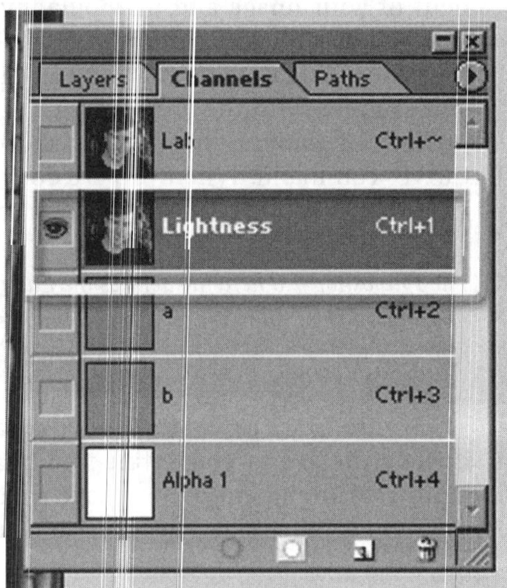

FIGURE 17.22 While in Lab mode, image luminance information is available in its own channel. This makes it really convenient to make luminance adjustments to your image without affecting any of the color data.

Be aware that when you switch modes to change the color space of your image, you may end up losing data! Each color space has its own way of defining color so there are differences to the number of colors that can be defined. If you switch to a color space with fewer colors than the one you are currently in, say going from RGB to CMYK, you will lose some colors forever, even if you switch back.

CONCLUSION

In this chapter we've introduced you to some professional applications where Poser was instrumental in getting the job done. In walking you though the steps used on the job, we've shown several processes and techniques that should be applicable to your own work, regardless of whether you use Poser for recreation or professional pursuits. You should have enough knowledge to start post working your renders to create more finished-looking pieces. Your characters will have more compelling eyes, and your scenes should be more cohesive now that you know some of the fine details that can throw them off. You also know several ways to create useful object masks and maybe you will do your next project using multiple renders. And, if you haven't gotten yourself a graphics-editing program capable of using layers yet, hopefully everything we've shown you will convince you to take the plunge.

Now that you've gotten a taste of some of the ways you can expand your repertoire of image creation and manipulation techniques, we hope that we've inspired you to experiment on your own to uncover even more ways to do things. From the examples we've presented it is clear that Poser is truly a professional tool capable of assisting in a variety of projects ranging from fine art to comic book illustration, hobby to professional. A tool, after all, is only as limited as the imagination of its user.

APPENDIX

A ABOUT THE CD-ROM

The CD-Rom included with Practical Poser 6 includes all of files necessary to complete the tutorials in the book. It also includes the images from the book and demos for you to use while working through the tutorials and exercises.

Denise and Audre wish to extend their humble gratitude and appreciation to those individuals and companies mentioned below, who have graciously and generously allowed us to share some exciting content with you on this CD-ROM. All of these individuals continue to demonstrate over and over that the Poser community is filled with passionate and generous individuals who come together to promote the phenomenon that is Poser.

CD FOLDERS

Content

Includes quality content from some of the leading content providers in the Poser community, including the following wonderful goodies for you to add to your Poser scenes:

Anton Kisiel, one of the premier Poser artists and a long-standing member of the various online Poser communities, presents **Apollo Maximus 2005 Compact**, a special version of his original, optimum Poser male figure. You can find additional accessories and clothing, as well as a support forum for Apollo Maximus, at *http://www.runtimedna.com*. Anton, thank you so much!

- **Audre**, co-author of *Practical Poser 6*, shares hundreds of seamless, tileable textures for you to enjoy and use in your projects.
- **DAZ Productions** (*http://www.daz3d.com*) shares PC and Macintosh-compatible versions of several Poser figures, including the DAZ Charger LE, Gorilla LE, EmotiGuy Base, Sea Dragon LE, and Victoria 1 Low Resolution female figure. Special thanks to Steve Kondris and Dan Farr for their generosity and contributions to this project.
- **E-Frontier** (*http://www.e-frontier.com*), makers of Poser 6 and Shade 8 have been a tremendous source of encouragement and content for this project. We thank them for their wonderful selection of poseable figures: the CP Crab, CP Dragonfly, CP Mantis, CP Parasarolophus, CP Scarab, CP Seahorse, CP TRex, CP Triceratops, PatchTheParrot Material Freebie, and Spot (the Toon Dog). Many thanks to Uli Klumpp, Steve Yatson, and Daryl Wise for these great gifts.
- **RDNA** (Runtime DNA, *http://www.runtimedna.com*) shares several sets of Poser 6 Materials for the Material Room. These fantastic materials add glitter, satin, sequins, suedes, leathers, gold, fantasy crystals, goth metals, irons, coppers, and rusty materials to your clothing and other Poser accessories. Thank you to my dear old friend Eric VanDycke for passing these along, and to Syyd Raven, Colm Jackson, and the rest of the crew at Runtime DNA for their never-ending support. Also, a gracious thank you to Linda White for the fantastic photograph, which came in very handy for the tutorial on image-based lighting and camera alignment!
- **Sixus 1**, (see *http://www.sixus1.com* for the main gateway to their various sites) has created a totally new toon figure especially for this book. Clearly two of the most generous folks in Poserdom, Les and Rebekah Garner didn't hesitate for a second to create something new and unique for our book. Meet Gunther . . . the Toon Werewolf! He's sure to be a popular little guy. Deepest thanks to you both!

Demos

- **E-Frontier** (*http://www.e-frontier.com*) provides a demo version of Poser 6 for Windows and Mac, along with an art gallery of Poser masterpieces. Additional folders contain artwork created with Shade, e-Frontier's flagship 3D modeling, rendering, and animation software.
- **The Forge** (*http://www.the-forge.ie*) the premier provider of solutions for the Poser animator fill a need quite generously with sample animation poses from their new PoseAmation 2 animated pose sets. Poses for battles, women, and eagles are provided. We also highly recommend that you check out the PoseAmation VT video tutorial on the Poser animation graph editor. Additional tutorials and anima-

tion poses are available at their Web site. Many kind words of gratitude to Chris DeRochie for these fantastic sets!

- **UV Mapper** (*http://www.uvmapper.com*) Perhaps the most widely used UV mapping program in the Poser community, Steve Cox has shared with us the free "classic" version of UV Mapper in both Windows and Mac format. But to fully appreciate the UV Mapping tutorials presented in this book, a demo version of UV Mapper Professional is also provided in both formats. Thank you, Steve, for sharing these files with us!

Images

All of the images from within the book and the color insert files. These files are set up by chapter.

Tutorials

All of the files necessary to complete the tutorials in the book including necessary Poser content, textures, and images. These files are all in common formats that can be read by most 3D applications, and they are set up in the applicable chapter folders.

System Requirements

Minimum system requirements are the same as those for the Poser 6 application, which are:

Windows

- Windows 2000 or XP
- 500 MHz Pentium class or compatible (700 MHz or faster recommended)
- 256 MB system RAM (512 MB or more recommended)
- 500 MB free hard drive space (2 GB recommended)
- 24-bit color display, 1024 × 768 resolution
- OpenGL-enabled graphics card or chipset recommended (recent NVIDIA GeForce or ATI Radeon preferred)
- Internet connection required for Content Paradise
- CD-ROM drive

Macintosh

- Mac OS X 10.2 or later
- 500 MHz G3 processor (700 MHz G4 or faster recommended)
- 256 MB system RAM (512 MB or more recommended)
- 500 MB free hard drive space (2 GB recommended)
- 24-bit color display, 1024 × 768 resolution
- OpenGL-enabled graphics card or chipset recommended (recent NVIDIA GeForce and ATI Radeon preferred)
- Internet connection required for Content Paradise
- CD-ROM drive

In addition, you will need Poser 6, with the latest service releases and the latest video drivers that are available for your video card.

INSTALLATION

To use this CD-ROM, you just need to make sure that your system matches at least the minimum system requirements. Each demo has its own installation instructions and you should contact the developer directly if you have any problems installing the demo. The images and tutorial files are in JPEG and OBJ file formats and should be usable with any 3D application.

APPENDIX

B

FREQUENTLY ASKED QUESTIONS

GENERAL INTERFACE QUESTIONS

Q: I set my General Preferences to customize my startup settings, but now my document window is stuck near the top of the screen when I open Poser. How do I get it back?

A: Go back to the General Preferences dialog (Edit > General Preferences) and reconfigure Poser to start up in factory state in both the Document and Interface tabs. Restart Poser again to get your Document window back. Then you can reconfigure your startup preferences again. If you previously saved a copy of your preferences, you can copy them back to the Poser 6 > Runtime > Prefs folder.

Q: You can change the background color of the Poser interface. Can you change the color of the fonts or the font that is used?

A: Neither the font or the font color can be changed at the present time.

Q: I have two monitors. If I put some items on the second monitor can I save my interface settings that way?

A: Yes, you can. For example, if the Document and Render windows are on your second monitor when you close Poser, they will open up in the same position when you next open Poser, providing that you selected the Launch To Previous State option of the General Preferences dialog.

BUILDING SCENES

Q: *What are the Editing Tools at the top of the screen used for?*

A: The editing tools, from left to right, are used as follows. To show or hide them, choose Window > Editing Tools. Note that the editing tools vary slightly from room to room.

- **Rotate:** Rotates a figure, body part, or prop.
- **Twist:** Twists a figure, body part, or prop. The same as using the Twist dial in the Parameters window.
- **Translate/Pull:** Moves a figure up, down, left, or right.
- **Translate In/Out:** Moves a figure forward or backward
- **Scale:** Increases or decreases the size of a figure or body part.
- **Taper:** Tapers a body part. Select the Taper tool, then drag over a body part to taper it. Drag left to increase the size of the outermost end of the chain, or drag right to decrease the size.
- **Chain Break:** The chain break tool allows you to prevent parts from moving when you pose other parts. For example, if you don't want the shoulders to move when you pose the forearm and hands, you can apply a chain break to the shoulders. Click the chain break tool to select it, then click the figure where you want to break the chain. Click the chain break icon again with the chain break tool to remove it.
- **Color:** Allows you to change the color of an item in your document window or the background color of the Poser interface. Click the Color tool, then click the object you want to change. A color palette then allows you to choose a color. Continue in this manner until you change the colors you want to change. Then click the Color tool again to turn it off.
- **Grouping Tool:** Allows you to create groups in your objects and assign polygons to them. The grouping tool is covered in Chapter 15, "Assigning Groups and Materials."
- **View Magnifier:** Allows you to zoom in to an area in the document window. Select the View Magnifier and then draw a rectangle around the area you want to view more closely.
- **Morphing Tool:** Allows you to visually adjust morph settings of a figure by sculpting changes.
- **Direct Manipulation:** Allows you to rotate, twist, or bend body parts using one tool. Three circles represent the axes that will be affected by the tool. Drag the yellow square along the axes that you want to change to rotate, twist, or bend the part.

Q: How about the Parameter dials? What do they do?

A: The Parameter dials can also help you pose a character, but they also contain several other dials that help you personalize your figures.

Q: What are Memory Dots used for?

A: There are actually three kinds of dots: UI Dots, Camera Dots, and Pose Dots. Click the down arrow near the label to choose between them. Choose Window > Memory Dots to show or hide the dots.

Memory dots allow you to store settings for poses, user interface, cameras so that you can go back to them later. For example, if you create a pose that you like, but want to experiment a little further in case you can make improvements, click one of the pose dots to store the pose in one of nine dots. When a dot contains information it will change color; a gray dot is empty. Experiment a bit, and then click the same dot again to return to the saved pose for more experimentation.

You can also store interface settings or camera positions in a similar manner. Pose and camera dots are saved until you begin a new project or close Poser. Interface dots are saved between projects, but you lose them when you close Poser.

Q: How are pose memory dots different from using the Edit > Memorize and Edit > Restore menu commands?

A: You can use the Pose Dots to memorize up to nine poses that are specific to your current scene. A good use for pose dots is to save incremental poses while you experiment on additional versions. This way you can experiment with slight changes to a pose as you perfect it and decide which version you like best.

The Edit > Memorize and Edit > Restore commands allow you to save *more* than just a pose. It also stores morph dial settings in addition to pose information. You can memorize and restore position, scale, morphs, parameters, materials, parent/child relationships, and so on for the entire scene (All), an entire figure, or an element (body part, prop, single camera, or single light).

Q: When I create a new scene, my figure appears all gray. How do I change that?

A: To change the way items are displayed you use the Display > Document Style, Display > Figure Style, or Display > Element Style commands. Alternatively, you can use the Document Style, Figure Style, or Element Style controls in your Poser interface.

The Document Display Style controls are shown in Figure B.1. If you do not see the controls on your screen, choose Window> Preview Styles to display them.

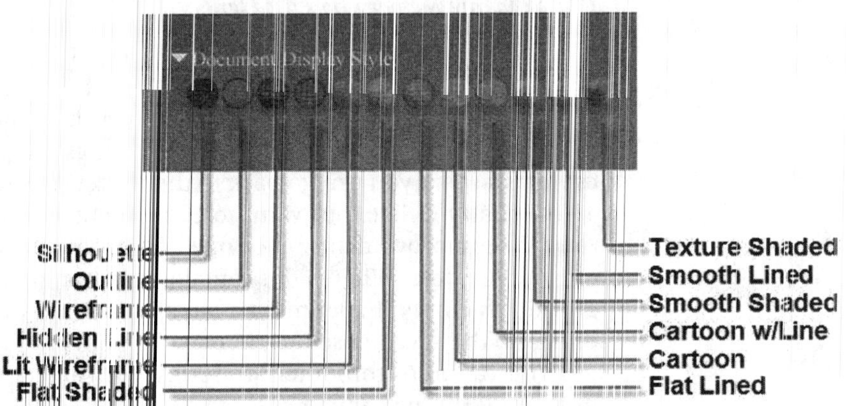

FIGURE B.1 You can choose a display style from the Display Style Controls.

You can actually display the contents of the entire document window, a single figure, or a part of a figure in one of 12 different styles, as follows:

To display everything in your document window in the same style, choose Display > Document Style, and then select the display mode you want to use.

To display one figure in your document window in a selected style, click the figure you want to change and choose *Display > Figure Style*. Then select the display mode you want to use. You can also choose "Use Document Style" to use the same display mode that you selected for the entire document.

To display part of a figure in a selected style, click the part you want to change. Then choose Display > Element Style and select the display mode you want to use. You can also choose "Use Figure Style" to use the same display mode as the figure that contains the selected part.

The various display modes are shown in Figure B.2.

Q: *When I add a second figure to the scene, it merges into the first one. How do I prevent that?*

A: You can move the character with the Translate tools. You might find it easier, though, to select the figure's body or hip, and use the xTrans, yTrans, or zTrans dials in the Parameters window to move the figure.

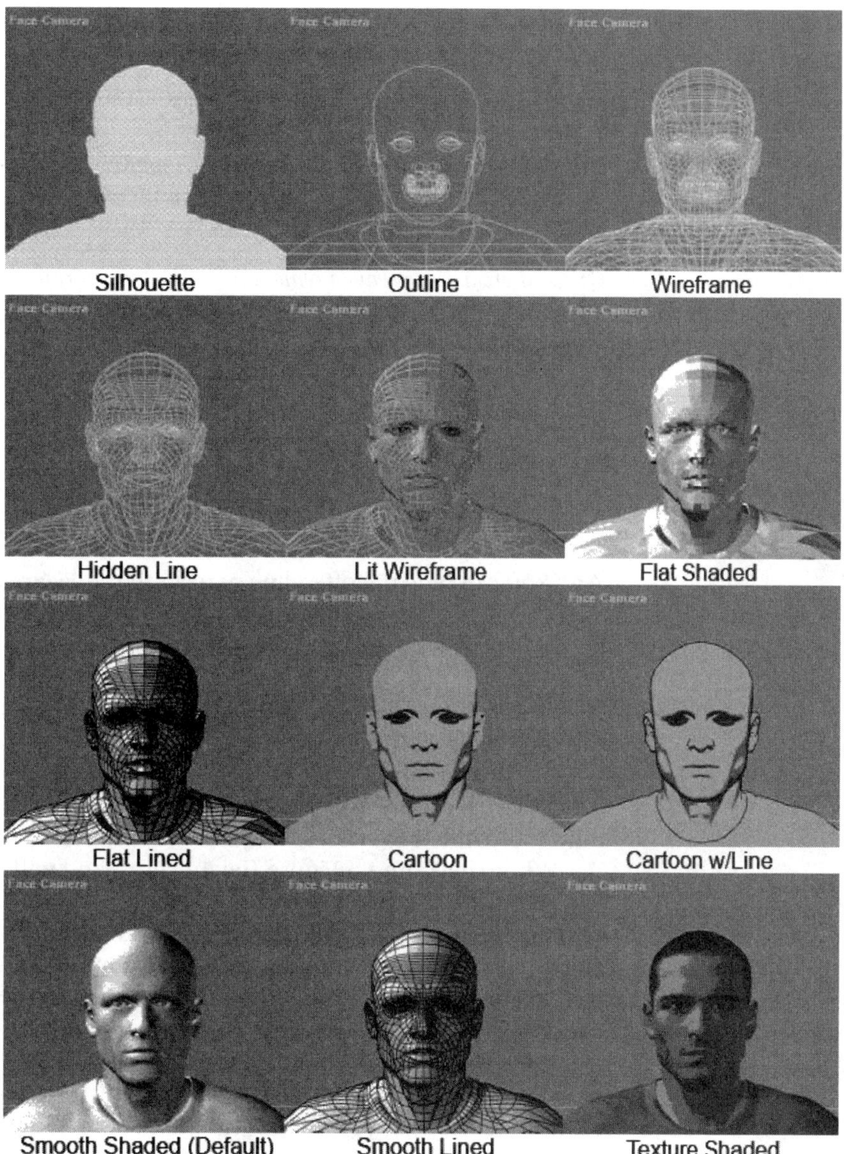

FIGURE B.2 Poser offers 12 different display style options.

Q: How do I remove a figure or prop from a scene?

A: Select the figure or object that you want to delete (either by clicking or by using the Select Figure menu in the Document Window), and press the Delete key.

Q: *I changed a lot of morph dials on my figure and I'm not happy with the results. Is there a quick way to remove all of the body morphs and start all over?*

A: If you don't want to lose your pose, save the pose to the library first. Then select the figure, and choose Edit > Restore > Figure. All morphs will be reset, and the figure returns to its default pose. After that, you can reapply the pose that you saved in the library.

Q: *Is there a quick way to remove all of the face morph settings and start all over?*

A: You can actually select any morphed part on a figure and return it to its default state. Click to select the face (or any other body part), and choose Edit > Restore > Element. The selected body part returns to its default state.

Q: *Some adult figures are anatomically correct. Sometimes it shows through the clothing. How do I fix that?*

A: You can hide the offending parts with the *Figure > Genitalia* command.

Q: *Can I make figures of different ages in Poser?*

A: The Figure > Figure Height command changes body proportions, but this method of altering a figure's proportions was created for earlier versions of Poser. Nowadays, it is more compatible with the older Poser 2 figures that come with Poser 6. Poser 2 didn't have the morphing capabilities that were introduced in later versions, and the figures weren't as detailed.

While the Figure > Figure Height command will work on more recent figures, you will probably find that the results it produces aren't quite as realistic as you would think. Because modern Poser figures are more detailed than earlier versions, applying this command to an adult figure will create a muscular toddler that isn't very realistic. Then you'd also have to adjust the clothing as well.

You can alter more modern Poser characters through the use of morphs. Recent Poser figures are often furnished with face and body morphs that allow you to create figures of any age or shape. You also have younger versions of Poser characters, such as Ben and Kate (the Poser 6 children), and the DAZ Young Teens, Preschool Kids, and baby.

Q: *Is there a way to copy one side of my figure's pose to the other side so that the left and right sides are symmetric?*

A: Yes, indeed there is! You can pose all or part of a figure the same as the other side, or even swap sides, with the options in the Figure > Symmetry command.

The options are as follows:

Left to Right: Applies the poses on the figure's left side to the right side to make the sides mirror each other.

Right to Left: Applies the poses on the figure's right side to the left side to make the sides mirror each other.

Swap Right and Left: Simultaneously applies the pose from the left side to the right, and from the right side to the left.

Left Arm to Right Arm: Applies the poses on the figure's left arm to the right arm to make the arms mirror each other.

Right Arm to Left Arm: Applies the poses on the figure's right arm to the left arm to make the arms mirror each other.

Swap Right and Left Arms: Simultaneously applies the pose from the left arm to the right, and from the right arm to the left.

Left Leg to Right Leg: Applies the poses on the figure's left leg to the right leg to make the legs mirror each other.

Right Leg to Left Leg: Applies the poses on the figure's right leg to the left leg to make the legs mirror each other.

Swap Right and Left Legs: Simultaneously applies the pose from the left leg to the right, and from the right leg to the left.

Straighten Torso: Straightens the torso as it relates to the position of the body.

Q: If I try to pose a body part with the editing tools, the pose gets way out of whack and the figure looks like a pretzel. How can I prevent that?

A: There are actually a couple of different commands in Poser that can help you with that:

Turn Limits On: The main figures that you use in Poser have limits on the joints. That is, there are predetermined settings that specify how far a joint is allowed to bend, move sideways, or twist. By default, Poser doesn't use these limits, and what happens is that joints very often get posed far beyond the limits that are humanly possible. However, when you enable the Figure > Use Limits option, Poser does not pose joints any farther than the set limits. This option helps you create poses that are more realistic.

Use Auto Balancing: The Auto Balance feature helps you achieve realistic poses. Basically, this feature adjusts poses to keep the figure as close as possible to the center of its weight distribution, which Poser calculates based on the shape of the body. Therefore, with Auto Balancing, a figure should automatically balance itself to respond to poses that are unnatural for a figure. To enable or disable auto balancing, choose the Figure > Auto Balance command. When there is a check beside the command, it is enabled.

Q: *When I load a figure from the library, its feet don't always line up with the default ground of my scene. How do I get my figure to drop to the default ground level of my scene?*

A: The Figure > Drop to Floor command drops your figure to ground level, which is at the 0 coordinate of the Y (up and down) axis.

However, sometimes you might have props or scenery in your document window that places "ground level" above or below the 0 coordinate. In that case, you will need to select the Hip or Body of your figure, and move the yTrans parameter dial up or down until your figure is placed correctly.

One of the most common mistakes made by new users of Poser is that figures hover over the ground. This is because in some cases, you need to make adjustments to the pose. The point closest to the ground makes contact with the ground when you use the Drop to Floor command. If, for example, the foot is bent, you may need to adjust the position of the feet so that they do not appear as though your figure is floating above the ground.

The best way to make these adjustments is to put your document display style to Outline mode (Display > Document Style > Outline) and to use one of the orthogonal cameras (Left, Right, Top, Bottom, Front, or Back) so that you are not viewing your scene at an angle while you fix the feet.

Q: *I have several objects in a scene. Sometimes when I want to pose or move a figure or object, I accidentally move another one by mistake. Is there any way to prevent that?*

There are several ways that you can control this. Once you get a figure or other item posed the way you like, you can prevent further changes using any of the following methods:

Hide the figure: You can hide the figure from view by using the *Figure > Hide Figure* command. Click the figure you want to hide, then choose the command. Continue in this manner until you hide all the figures that interfere with the parts you want to edit. To unhide all hidden figures, choose Figure > Show All Figures. You can also use the Hierarchy Editor (Window > Hierarchy Editor) to unhide selected figures. Simply click on the eye icon of a figure or part name to unhide it.

Lock the figure: Choose the figure that you want to protect. Then choose the Figure > Lock Figure command. This will lock the figure in place and prevent you from moving the figure or changing its pose.

Lock a body part or prop: If you want to prevent changes to a single body part or a prop, choose Object > Lock Actor. This will cause a body part to stay in place in relation to its parent. In other words, you can lock the position of a forearm in relation to the upper arm, but if you move the upper arm the forearm will move accordingly.

Lock the hands: Hands are the most time-consuming to pose, especially if you've posed them around an object. You can use the Figure > Lock Hand Parts command to lock a hand into position. This will prevent changes in hand and finger positions while you work with other areas in your Poser scene.

Use the Chain Break tool: The Chain Break tool, which displays a link on its icon, allows you to prevent movements of body parts below a specified level in the hierarchy. For example, if you want to pose the lower portions of an arm but leave the shoulder in place, you can put a chain break at the shoulder before you move the lower portions. In order for the Chain Break tool to work, you have to turn Inverse Kinematics off with the Figure > Use Inverse Kinematics command. Further information about the Chain Break tool can be found in the *Poser 6 Manual,* on page 143.

Q: *Can I raise or lower the level of the ground plane of my scene?*

A: No, you can only move the ground left, right, forward, or back. As an alternative, you can use the Square, Square Hi-Res, or One Sided Square props that are found in the Props > Primitives library. Scale the square prop to the desired size, and then adjust the yTrans setting to raise or lower the prop.

Q: *If I can't use Python scripts, how do I get a figure into its default pose?*

A: While it's not as quick as running the ZeroAll python script that is mentioned in Chapter 3, you can use the following procedure:

1. Click the figure you want to zero.
2. Choose Edit > Restore > Figure. This removes morphs and scaling from the figure, but may not return the figure to its proper default pose.
3. Choose Window > Joint Editor. The Joint Editor window opens.
4. If the Joint Editor informs you that no body part is selected, click any body part on the figure that you want to zero. Then click the Zero Figure button in the joint editor.
5. If the Parameters window is not open, choose Window > Parameters to open it.
6. Select the Hip body part for the character, and verify that the xTrans, yTrans, and zTrans values are all set to zero.
7. Select the Body part of the character, and verify that its xTrans, yTrans, and zTrans values are also set to zero.
8. For complete thoroughness, verify that each body part has Scale, and xScale, yScale, and zScale values set at 100%. If you have to change any values to get the scaling back to 100%, save the figure to the library so that you won't have to change them again the next time you have to zero the figure.

Q: Can I make a figure hold something (like a ball), so that when I move the hand, the ball moves with it?

A: Yes, you can. Using the ball as an example, here are the steps:

1. Use the Editing Tools or the x, y, and zTrans dials in the Parameters window to position the ball in your figure's hand.
2. Pose the fingers around the ball. You will probably get better results by using the dials in the Parameters window rather than trying to pose them with the editing tools.
3. Select the ball as the current figure.
4. Choose Object > Change Parent. Select the appropriate hand (right or left, depending on which hand is holding the ball) as the parent to the ball. Now whenever you move the hand, the ball follows. You can still move the ball, but its relation as a child to the hand will remain until you "unparent" it. To "unparent" the ball, select it, choose Object > Change Parent, and choose UNIVERSE (the first object in the hierarchy) as the parent.

CAMERAS

Q: How do I use the camera controls?

A: The camera controls allow you to select cameras for various purposes, or to move them so that you can get a better view of the items in your Poser document. Figure B.3 shows the camera controls:

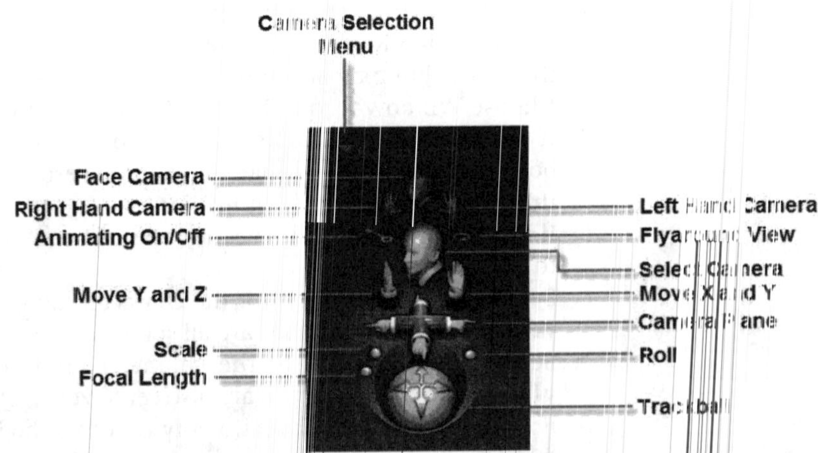

FIGURE B.3 Camera controls allow you to select and manipulate Poser's cameras.

The controls serve the following functions:

Camera Selection Menu: Click the Camera Selection menu to display a list of cameras to choose from.

Face Camera: The Face Camera is good to use when you are creating a face expression or using face morph dials to create a unique character. The camera remains fixed on the character's face, even as you zoom in, out, or rotate the camera view.

Right Hand and Left Hand Cameras: These cameras keep the designated hand in view, even while zooming in or out or rotating the camera. Their purpose is to keep the camera centered around the hand while you pose it—most especially while posing a hand to hold another object.

Animating On/Off: When you are posing body parts or props for the purposes of animation, you sometimes have a need to adjust cameras so that you can get a better view of things. However, each time you move a camera in a frame of an animation, it adds a "keyframe" that keeps track of the position change. As a result, you may accidentally add animation keyframes without intending to do so. One way to prevent this from happening is to turn camera animating off. To turn camera animation off, click the key icon to turn it red. Click it again to resume camera animation.

Flyaround View: Click this icon to get a 360-degree flyaround view of your scene. Click again to turn the flyaround view off.

Select Camera: Click to cycle through the various camera views. Starting from the Main camera, the icons appear in the order shown in Figure B.4.

The mouse displays a double-arrow cursor when you are able to select a camera. To advance forward in the list, click the icon at its right side, or drag the mouse to the right to advance quickly. To move backward in the list, click the left side of the icon or drag your mouse toward the left.

Move Y and Z: Your mouse cursor displays arrows when you position it over this control. Click and drag left or right to move the camera along the Z (forward/backward) plane. Drag up or down to move the camera along the Y (up/down) plane.

Move X and Y: Your mouse cursor displays arrows when you position it over this control. Click and drag left or right to move the camera along the X (left/right) plane. Click and drag up or down to move the camera along the Y (up/down) plane.

Camera Plane: Click and drag left or right to move the camera along the X (left/right) axis, or up or down to move the camera along the Z (forward or back) axis.

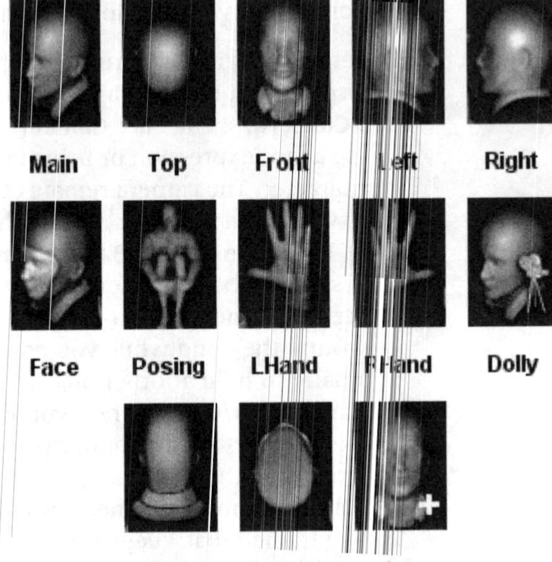

FIGURE B.4 Use the icons in the Select Camera area to select a camera view.

Scale: Click and drag left to increase the scale of the camera. This "zooms in" to the scene without affecting focal or perspective settings. Click and drag right to decrease the scale of the camera, which "zooms out" without affecting focal or perspective settings.

Roll: Click and drag toward the left to roll the camera clockwise. Click and drag toward the right to roll the camera counterclockwise.

Focal Length: Click and drag toward the left to decrease the camera's focal length; click and drag toward the right to increase the focal length.

Trackball: Click the trackball to give the current camera focus. You can move the trackball at any incremental angle to change the view. Drag the trackball up to look above a scene, down to look below a scene, and left or right to view the scene from either side.

Q: Can I make cameras always look at an object, even when I move the object?

A: If you want to make a camera follow an object, first select the camera. Then choose Object > Point At. When the hierarchy window comes up, choose the item or body part that you want the camera to follow.

You can also make objects follow the camera. For example, you can make eyes always look toward a camera as you position it. To do so, select the object (such as the left eye or right eye) and choose Object > Point at. Then choose the camera that you want the object to follow.

Note, however, that if you try to make the head follow a camera, the top of the head points to the camera rather than the front of the head.

LIGHTS AND SHADOWS

Q: How does a light probe work?

A: The purpose of a light probe is to simulate the lighting conditions in a photograph or movie. Imagine the light probe as an invisible hemisphere that surrounds your scene.

The area in the center of the light probe is the area of the hemisphere that is directly overhead at the highest part of the hemisphere. The outer edges of the light probe are the lowest parts of the hemisphere, which encircle the scene at floor height. The top of the light probe determines the lighting conditions at the back of your scene. The bottom of the light probe determines the lighting conditions at the front of your scene.

Q: Can I use an AVI or MOV file for an image-based light probe?

A: Yes, you can. One way to accomplish this is to set up your IBL light in the material room first, using the IBL wacro. During this process the wacro will prompt you to select an image. After this process is complete, your IBL light will be configured properly. All you have to do afterward is disconnect the Image Map node and replace it with a Movie node (New Node > 2D Textures > Movie).

Q: Can I make a light that looks something like a movie being projected onto a screen?

A: Yes, you can. After you create a spotlight, go to the material room, and change the color of the light to white. Then attach an Image Map node (New Node > 2D Textures > Image Map) or a Movie node (New Node > 2D Textures > Movie) to the Diffuse channel. Check the Auto Fit option in the Image Map node to fit the image in the spotlight.

FACE ROOM

Q: *If I apply the Face Room head to the figure so that the original head gets replaced, how do I get the old head back?*

A: The Edit > Restore > Element command won't work if you apply a face room head to your figure. To restore the original head, return to the Face Room. Click the Reset Face Room button that appears below the Face Sculpting area. Then click the Apply to Figure button in the Actions area. When you return to the Pose Room, the default head should appear on your figure.

Q: *I used the Face Room to create a face morph. But when I go back to the Pose Room and dial the Face Room morph to 1, the eyes look funny. What happened?*

A: When you use the Face Room to spawn morph targets for a face, it also spawns morph targets for the Left Eye and Right Eye. They also have to be set to 1 to restore the entire face to the shape you created in the Face Room.

Q: *Are there other programs available that work like the Face Room so that I can use them on other figures?*

A: The code used in the Face Room module was licensed by e-Frontier from Singular Inversions, the makers of FaceGen Modeler and FaceGen Customizer. You can learn more about these packages at *http://www.facegen.com*.

HAIR ROOM

Q: *When I save my hair projects to the library, you can't see the hair in the thumbnails. How do I get the hair to show up?*

A: The thumbnails in the Poser library are saved in PNG format and measure 91 by 91 pixels. Some people render a scene and save it as a PNG file with a transparent background. The transparent background is important in order for the thumbnail to display properly. After rendering, resize the PNG file to 91 by 91 pixels, and assign the same prefix as the library item. For example, if you have a hair file named Joni'sHair.HR2, name the PNG file Joni'sHair.PNG.

Q: How do I get rid of bald spots in dynamic hair?

A: "Bald spots" are less prominent if you use the proper lighting in conjunction with the "Opaque in Shadows" option in the hair material. Go to the Material Room and select one of the hair sections. Verify that the Opaque in Shadow option is checked in the hair material. If that does not resolve the problem, adjust the lighting so that some lighting comes from above the head so that shadows are generated. Finally, if you still see bald spots, you can increase the hair density a little bit at a time until the baldness is less obvious.

UV Mapping

Q: You've shown how to map skirts, pants, and shirts. What about dresses?

A: For the most part, you've learned the basic techniques for dresses already. Think of a dress as nothing more than a shirt and a skirt combined. If desired, you can then stitch the shirt and dress together at the waist, and relax it.

Q: What about organic models, such as humans or animals? How do you map those?

A: Break it down into pieces. For example, you can detach the head from the body and map it in cylindrical mode. The eyes, of course, are spherical. The teeth are arranged in the mouth in a shape of a 'C', which is basically half of a cylinder. The tongue can either be two planes (top and bottom), or cylindrical with a seam along the bottom of the tongue.

Now, what about the body? Take the hands and feet away from the remainder of the body for a moment. What basically remains is something similar to the shirt and pants that you learned how to map in this chapter! Go one step farther than the pants, though, and join the vertices in the center, near where the groin is. Then relax the two sides until the vertices that you joined are blended together.

As for the hands and feet, all you have to do is divide the hands in half as if you're slicing the top away from the bottom—one side of the hand shows the palm and underside of the fingers, while the other side of the hand shows the tops of the hands. Split the feet in half so that one view shows the top, and the other half shows the sole of the foot. Once you break it into individual sections like this, UV-mapping a human becomes predictable and methodical.

Q: *Sometimes after I relax things in UV Mapper there is still a little bit of distortion. Can I eliminate it entirely?*

A: It depends on the software you use and how skilled you are in using it. One thing that was not covered in this chapter was the Interactive Mapping mode in UV Mapper Professional. When you choose Interactive mode, you can move or rotate a spherical, planar, or cylindrical indicator to align the UV map more accurately with your models. The texture map updates in real time while you make the adjustments.

There are also additional UV-mapping programs that have more advanced mapping and relaxing features in addition to features that allow you to paint directly on the 3D models. However, they are also much more expensive than UV Mapper Professional. If you are interested in researching them further, go to *http://www.righthemisphere.com* for information about Deep Paint 3D and Deep UV; or *http://www.maxon.net* for information about Maxon Body Paint.

MATERIALS

Q: *What is a gather node?*

A: A gather node is a very powerful and complex procedural shader that allows you to create materials that actually accumulate light from their surroundings. This works well for simulating the reflected light interacting between two objects that are close to each other (think *"radiosity-effects"*), or even simulating a glowing object. The effect is perfect for creating a light-sabre or bio-luminescent sea creature.

In Figure B.5, you can see where the ground material has "gathered" the light from the bumpy-torus object. The material on the torus uses a high ambiance value to enable the gather node of the ground plane material to "collect" the light coming from the torus. In our example we did not use any lights, rather, we made the torus self-illuminating.

You will need to use the FireFly rendering engine to take advantage of the gather node. You will also need to make sure you have Raytracing enabled. Using the gather node will increase your rendering times significantly.

Q: *What is up with my Displacement? Why does it have black spots? Something very wrong happened here!*

A: When your Displacement Bounds are too small you may find that your materials develop black "specks", or even what appear to be large black "holes" in unexpected places. This happens because the Displacement on the material is too large to be contained within the current boundary.

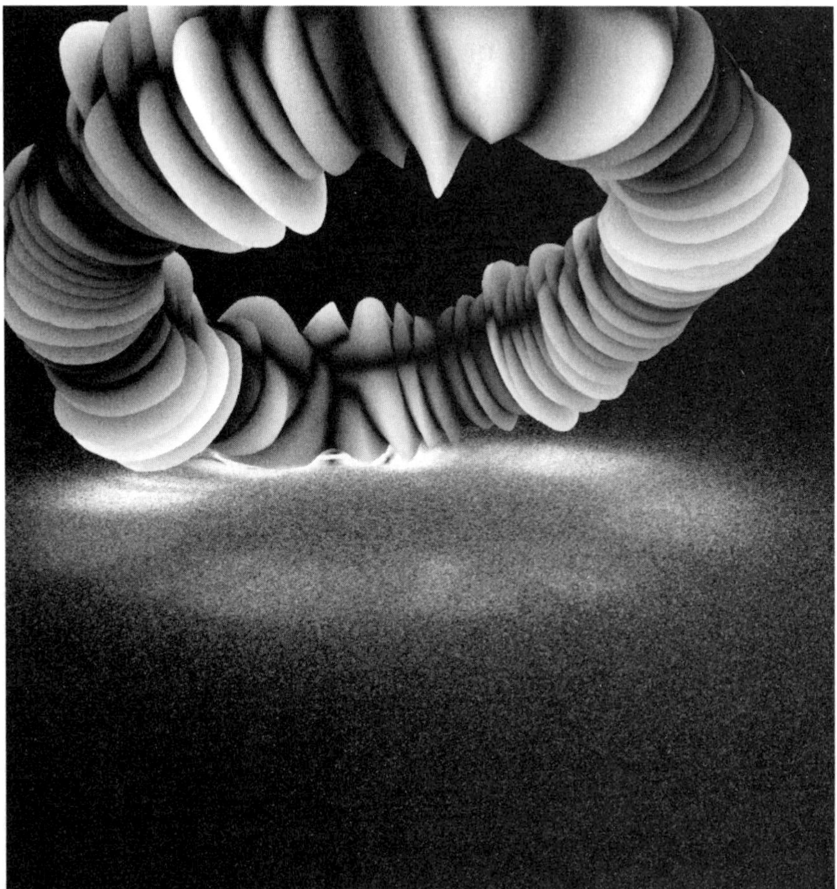

FIGURE B.5 The gather material node creates a material that collects and emits its own light.

Here's what happens: The render engine begins by assuming that every pixel in the image is black, or zero (R=0, G=0, B=0), until calculated otherwise by the interaction of light with the various material properties of objects visible at that pixel. When the Displacement calculation overflows the current Displacement Boundary, the tips of the Displaced mesh move outside the current render bucket. Once outside the current bucket, the color at that point remains unknown, or uncalculated, and therefore stays zero, its default value.

Whenever you use Displacement, make sure that you set the Min Displacement Bounds settings for the FireFly render engine. The Min Displacement Bounds should be large enough to handle the *largest* Displacement of all the materials in your current scene. Also, keep in mind that using Displacement in your materials will take longer to render. Setting the Min Displacement Bounds too high may have a negative impact on rendering performance. As a rule, set the Min Displacement Bounds to be roughly twice the largest displacement of any of your material.

Q: *Can I create water that actually looks like water?*

A: We found a really nice tutorial online that does a wonderful job explaining the aspects you should consider when creating a realistic water material. Stuart Runham's Water Tutorial can be found here: *http://www.stu-runham.co.uk/water.htm.*

Q: *I want to make a mirrored surface, what do I need to do?*

A: The quickest way to create a true reflective material is to use the Material Room wacro "Add Reflection." Once the reflection node has been added, you can tweak parameters to accommodate your lighting conditions

Remember to enable Raytracing, and pay attention to the number of ray bounces you have configured. More bounces will yield a more realistic mirror, but will also slow down the render considerably. Ray bounce setting as low as 2 may be sufficient to create a convincing mirror material.

Q: *What's the quickest way to create a Displacement map?*

A: If you are using a simple image-based texture, the quickest way to create a Displacement map is to tie the texture map that you use for your Diffuse channel into the Displacement channel as well.

If you want a bit more control, you can create a grayscale copy of the same map you are using for your Diffusion channel and use that instead. For the purposes of creating a Displacement map, you are only interested in the brightness component of the texture so the color data is extraneous. Once you have your grayscale image, you can edit it using your favorite image-editing program to maximize the range of brightness to give you the widest possible range of displacement at render time.

If you are using a procedural shader to drive the Diffusion channel of your root material node you can tie that node into the Displacement channel of the root node as well.

Don't forget that you can *always* include additional shader nodes to create more interesting and natural displacement effects, regardless of if you are using a procedural shader or image-based texture map to drive your Displacement channel. For example, you can add a Noise node to create some random bumps to bias the value of your existing Displacement output—essentially creating bumps within bumps.

The white values of your Displacement map or procedural shader will create a larger displacement than black areas, with absolute black areas not being displaced at all and absolute white areas being displaced the maximum amount.

Q: *Can I create glowing objects?*

A: YES! See the Gather Node answer on page 506.
Additionally, if you are not adverse to some post-work, there is a nice tutorial available online written by Jim Harnock, which shows how you can create a halo around your glowing objects. The tutorial can be found here: *http://www.students.yorku.ca/~harnock/tutorials/sabre.htm.*

Q: *How can I make fur without using Poser Hair?*

A: A quick technique to simulate the look of fur is to use Displacement at render time.

With Poser 6, all you need to do is add a Noise node and attach its output into the Displacement parameter's input on the root node. Once you have your Noise node attached, make sure you also set your Min Displacement Bounds and enable the use of Displacement Maps in the FireFly render engine's parameter palette.

Q: *What the heck is a "Node Mask" and why should I use one?*

A: A Node mask is simply a template that defines where, on your object, a certain node will have its effect. It's rather like using a stencil to control where paint goes on. Instead of paint, however, the Node Mask determines where a particular node will apply its effects to the object.

Once again, we'll point you to Jim Harnock's Web page to show you not only how you can create your own node masks, but also give you an idea of what you can do with them. The Jim's Node Mask tutorial can be found here: *http://www.students.yorku.ca/~harnock/tutorials/nodemask.htm.*

RENDERING

Q: *How can I speed up my renders?*

A: There are a few things you can do to help speed up your renders:
- Use smaller texture map images.
- Use low poly figures whenever possible.
- Use less complex procedural shaders and materials for objects that are not critical to your design.

- If you aren't using a true reflective material, try enabling the "Remove Back Facing Polygons" option.
- Decrease the Pixel Samples.
- Increase the Minimum Shading Rate.
- Don't use Texture Filtering.
- Use reflection maps rather than raytraced reflections.
- Disable Raytracing.
- Don't use Ambient Occlusion.
- Disable shadows on lights that are not the primary light sources for your scene.
- Reduce the complexity of as many textures in your scene that you can.
- Reuse texture and shadow maps whenever possible.
- Keep your hard drives de-fragmented.
- Don't run other applications.

Q: *FireFly looks like it has stopped rendering and/or stops responding while rendering.*

A: If you find that your Poser "goes out to lunch" when you try to render, you can do a few immediate things to help speed things up:

- Reduce shadow map sizes.
- Reduce the Render Bucket size.
- Reduce the number of Pixel Samples.
- Increase the Shading Rate.
- Disable shadows on non critical lights..

Q: *My objects have black holes where I don't expect them. Why?*

A: If you are using displacement, you may need to increase your Min Displacement Bounds. If you aren't using displacement, but have overlapping or closely positioned object surfaces, you may need to enable displacement on the material that is having problems to lift the surface of the object a bit. If you need to do this, remember to enable Displacement mapping in the Render Palette.

If you don't have overlapping object surfaces increasing the Shadow Min Bias on your light(s) might fix the problem.

If the holes are all facing away from the camera, you may have enabled the "Remove Backfacing Polygons" option.

Q: *Everything gets puffy when I render it! Help!*

A: If you have enabled "smooth polygons" in the object's properties, you may find that your object bloats at render time. This happens because the object's polygons are not specifically optimized for Poser or polygon smoothing algorithms. In order for an object to accommodate smoothing on selective polygon intersections, the object must be created with very small polygons right at the joints where smoothing is not desired.

The figure shown above illustrates why objects sometimes "bloat" when polygon smoothing is enabled. The top-left image represents two polygons that form a corner, polygon 1 (yellow) and polygon 2 (orange). The top-right image shows the surface that is created when polygons are smoothed. The bottom-left image shows an object that "looks" like it has the same corner; however, it is constructed with an additional, very small row, of polygons: 3 (blue) and 4 (green). The image on the bottom right shows the resulting smoothing that will occur.

You can see that in the two right side images that the corners will appear very different when the polygons are smoothed. This is because smoothing works relative to the scales of the affected polygons. Smaller polygons in the corners, or joints, will make the smoothed corner appear more crisp and less bloated.

In other cases, not all the joints on an object are actually "welded" together. This will keep the edges of the object crisp; however, unwelded edges may also affect how seamless and procedural textures appear. Welding or not welding edges of objects when they are created should be evaluated on a case-by-case basis depending on the type of object, the morphs that are typically applied to the object and the complexity and types of materials that object is usually mapped with.

Q: *What's the quickest way to set up a material that uses Refraction?*

A: The quickest way to set up a material that uses Refraction is to use the Wacro, "Add Refraction". This will create a new Refraction node, that plugs into the Refraction Color Channel of the root node. Make sure you set the Transparency, Transparency Edge, and Translucence_Value values and enable Raytracing. You'll have to use the FireFly rending engine, too.

Q: *Can Poser 6 load texture files larger than 4096 pixels?*

A: Yes! Unlike previous versions of Poser, Poser 6 now allows you to load image maps that are larger than 4096 pixels.

INDEX